HB 953.5 FER

D1760881

WITHDRAWN
FROM STOCK
QMUL LIBRARY

DATE DUE FOR RETURN

08 MAR 1999

The Fertility Transition in Latin America

international union for the scientific study of population

The International Union for the Scientific Study of Population Problems was set up in 1928, with Dr Raymond Pearl as President. At that time the Union's main purpose was to promote international scientific co-operation to study the various aspects of population problems, through national committees and through its members themselves. In 1947 the International Union for the Scientific Study of Population (IUSSP) was reconstituted into its present form.

It expanded its activities to:

- stimulate research on population
- develop interest in demographic matters among governments, national and international organizations, scientific bodies, and the general public
- foster relations between people involved in population studies
- disseminate scientific knowledge on population.

The principal ways through which the IUSSP currently achieves its aims are:

- organization of worldwide or regional conferences
- operations of Scientific Committees under the auspices of the Council
- organization of training courses
- publication of conference proceedings and committee reports.

Demography can be defined by its field of study and its analytical methods. Accordingly, it can be regarded as the scientific study of human populations primarily with respect to their size, their structure, and their development. For reasons which are related to the history of the discipline, the demographic method is essentially inductive: progress in knowledge results from the improvement of observation, the sophistication of measurement methods, and the search for regularities and stable factors leading to the formulation of explanatory models. In conclusion, the three objectives of demographic analysis are to describe, measure, and analyse.

International Studies in Demography is the outcome of an agreement concluded by the IUSSP and the Oxford University Press. The joint series reflects the broad range of the Union's activities; it is based on the seminars organized by the Union and important international meetings in the field of population and development. The Editorial Board of the series is comprised of:

John Cleland, UK   Henri Leridon, France
John Hobcraft, UK   Richard Smith, UK
Georges Tapinos, France

The Fertility Transition in Latin America

Editors

JOSÉ MIGUEL GUZMÁN
SUSHEELA SINGH
GERMÁN RODRÍGUEZ
EDITH A. PANTELIDES

CLARENDON PRESS • OXFORD
1996

Oxford University Press, Walton Street, Oxford OX2 6DP

Oxford New York
Athens Auckland Bangkok Bombay
Calcutta Cape Town Dar es Salaam Delhi
Florence Hong Kong Istanbul Karachi
Kuala Lumpur Madras Madrid Melbourne
Mexico City Nairobi Paris Singapore
Taipei Tokyo Toronto

and associated companies in
Berlin Ibadan

Oxford is a trade mark of Oxford University Press

Published in the United States
by Oxford University Press Inc., New York

© *IUSSP, 1996*

All rights reserved. No part of this publication may be reproduced, stored in a retrieval system, or transmitted, in any form or by any means, without the prior permission in writing of Oxford University Press. Within the UK, exceptions are allowed in respect of any fair dealing for the purpose of research or private study, or criticism or review, as permitted under the Copyright, Designs and Patents Act, 1988, or in the case of reprographic reproduction in accordance with the terms of the licences issued by the Copyright Licensing Agency. Enquiries concerning reproduction outside these terms and in other countries should be sent to the Rights Department, Oxford University Press, at the address above

British Library Cataloguing in Publication Data
Data available

Library of Congress Cataloguing in Publication Data
The fertility transition in Latin America / editors, José Miguel Guzmán . . . [et al.].
— (International studies in demography)
Includes bibliographical references.
1. Fertility, Human—Latin America. 2. Demographic transition—Latin America. 3. Fertility, Human—Latin America—Case studies. I. Guzmán, José Miguel. II. Series.
HB940.5.A3F47 1996 304.6'32'098—dc20 95–44762
ISBN 0–19–828951–0

1 3 5 7 9 10 8 6 4 2

Typeset by Alliance Phototypesetters
Printed in Great Britain
on acid-free paper by
Bookcraft (Bath) Ltd., Midsomer Norton. Nr. Bath

Contents

List of Contributors

Carlos E. Aramburú, Pathfinder International, Mexico

Lucille C. Atkin, Ford Foundation, Mexico

John Bongaarts, The Population Council, USA

Jorge H. Bravo, Centro Latinamericano de Demografía (CELADE), Chile

José Alberto Magno de Carvalho, CEDEPLAR–UFMG, Brazil

Sonia Catasús Cervera, Centro de Estudios Demográficos (CEDEM), Cuba

Juan Chackiel, CELADE, Chile

Delicia Ferrando, Pathfinder International, Peru

Carmen Elisa Flórez, Universidad de Los Andes, Colombia

Juan Carlos Alfonso Fraga, Instituto de Investigaciones Estadísticas (INSIE), Cuba

Tomás Frejka, UN Economic Commission for Europe, Switzerland

Jean-Pierre Guengant, UN Population Division, USA and Guadeloupe

José Miguel Guzmán (Editor and Contributor), UNFPA Country Support Team for Latin America and the Caribbean, and CELADE, Chile

Fátima Juárez, London School of Hygiene and Tropical Medicine, UK

Robert Lightbourne, Independent Consultant, USA

Silvia Llera, University of Pennsylvania, USA, and El Colegio de México, Mexico

Marta Mier y Terán, Instituto de Investigaciones Sociales, Mexico

Lorenzo Moreno, Mathematica, USA

Axel I. Mundigo, World Health Organization, Switzerland

Edith A. Pantelides (Editor and Contributor), Centro de Estudios de Población (CENEP), Argentina

Joseph E. Potter, University of Texas, Austin, USA

Elena Prada-Salas, Independent Consultant, Colombia

GERMÁN RODRÍGUEZ, Princeton University, USA

LAURA RODRÍGUEZ WONG, CEDEPLAR–UFMG, Brazil

LUIS ROSERO-BIXBY, Princeton University, USA, and Universidad Nacional de Costa Rica

SUSANA SCHKOLNIK, CELADE, Chile

SUSHEELA SINGH (Editor and Contributor), The Alan Guttmacher Institute, USA

ERICA TAUCHER, Instituto de Nutrición y Tecnología de los Alimentos, Universidad de Chile, Chile

HUGO TÓRREZ PINTO, Dirección de Políticas de Población, Ministerio de Desarrolló Sostenible, Bolivia

MARY BETH WEINBERGER, UN Population Division, USA

CHARLES F. WESTOFF, Princeton University, USA

MARÍA EUGENIA ZAVALA DE COSÍO, University of Paris X–Nanterre, France

List of Figures

List of Tables

Abbreviations

ASFR	Age-Specific Fertility Rate
CBR	Crude Birth Rate
CELADE	Centro Latinoamericano de Demografía/Latin American Demographic Centre
CEDES	Centro de Estudios de Estado y Sociedad
CENDES	Centre for Development Studies
DHS	Demographic and Health Survey
ECLAC	Economic Commission for Latin America and the Caribbean
FNUAP	Fondo de Naciones Unidas para Actividades en Materia de Población
GDP	Cross Domestic Product
GFR	General Fertility Rate
GNP	Gross National Product
GRR	Gross Reproduction Ratio
IFHIPAL	Investigation of Fertility using the Own Children Method for Latin America
IMR	Infant Mortality Rate
INE	Instituto Nacional de Estadísticas/National Institute of Statistics
IPPF	International Planned Parenthood Federation
IUSSP	International Union for the Scientific Study of Population
n.a.	not available
NDHS	National Demographic and Health Survey
NHHS	National Health and Housing Survey
NPHS	National Population and Housing Survey
PAHO	Pan American Health Organization
PNAD	Pesquisa Nacional Amostra de Domicilios/National Household Sample Survey
PROFAMILIA	Asociacíon Pro Bienestar de la Familia, Colombia

TFR	Total Fertility Rate
UNFPA	United Nations Fund for Population Activities
WFS	World Fertility Survey

Introduction: Social Change and Fertility Decline in Latin America

JOSÉ MIGUEL GUZMÁN

Introduction

Extensive social and economic changes have occurred in Latin America since the early 1960s. The level of childbearing and the pattern of reproduction were two important areas in which major transformations occurred. In turn, changes in these important demographic factors had strong repercussions on many other aspects of social life in the region. These changes did not follow any of the expected paths and they contradicted most predictions. Stated in general terms, the key aspect of these changes is that couples adopted new values and attitudes concerning childbearing and family size, which were reflected in changes in actual behaviour, resulting in a very different current pattern of reproduction as compared to that which had existed before 1960. Not only have the main demographic characteristics of the region changed in important ways, in the population as a whole, but in addition, the lives of individuals and families have changed.

From a natural or almost natural fertility pattern—which existed in most social classes in almost all countries—fertility changed increasingly and permanently towards a pattern of regulated fertility, in which those sectors that do not deliberately practise some control over their reproductive process or those who do not intend to reduce their family size by use of contraceptives or induced abortion, form an increasingly small proportion of the total. This new behaviour became a significant component of the everyday life of millions of people under apparently dissimilar conditions.

What is the real magnitude of this change and in what socio-cultural context does it appear? What are the causes of this phenomenon and what are its most important determinants? The chapters in this volume try to answer these questions. This introduction in particular reviews some of the broad social changes that occurred in the region before and during this stage of decline in fertility. It is expected that the chapters in this volume will serve as a general framework for more in-depth studies of fertility change.

The Fertility Decline: Some Relevant Facts

Before discussing social change in general, it seems useful to describe some unique features of the fertility transition in Latin America. These can be summarized as follows:

1. The moment at which fertility decline appears to have started in most of the countries in the region was in the first half of the 1960s. To a greater or lesser extent, countries have been integrated into this process of change that, as seen from the experience of the subsequent decades, became a sustained process of decreasing fertility based on radical change in the reproductive patterns of families. There has been a clear trend to the adoption of a more or less generalized behaviour of regulating fertility.

2. This change was made possible through increases in contraceptive use, which was the most important intermediate variable in explaining the change in the number of children per woman (see chapter 6). Fertility decline and increased use of contraception occurred at the same time as the development, diffusion, and distribution of modern contraceptive methods. While it is clear that induced abortion did play an important role in the fertility decline, the information available on this factor is very limited (see chapter 9).

3. Changes in nuptiality had a positive impact in some countries during the 1950s causing fertility to increase slightly. However, as has been shown (see chapter 7), changes in the components of nuptiality (age at first marriage, type of union, stability of the union, and permanent celibacy) did not seem to have a decisive influence on changes in fertility after 1960 in most countries.

4. Although fertility decline has become rather generalized, there are important differences among countries. In fact, an analysis of the Latin American experience regarding the fertility transition does not show a single pattern. Many differences appear when the specific experiences of individual countries are analysed (see chapter 1 on Latin American countries, and chapter 4 on the Caribbean countries). Argentina and Uruguay show the typical pattern found in European countries, where fertility started to decline around the end of the nineteenth and the beginning of the twentieth century (see chapter 5 for a comparison of the European fertility transition with that experienced in Latin America). Cuba is also peculiar, because fertility was already low at the end of the 1950s, then underwent an increase during the early 1960s to later descend rapidly to the present below-replacement level. By contrast, in the rest of Latin America, the total fertility rate at the beginning of the 1960s was more than 5 children per woman—and in some countries levels of 7 children per woman were reached—and only since that time did a clear process of fertility decline begin.

5. The process of change was also not homogeneous within countries. The heterogeneous social structure which is characteristic of Latin American societies also expressed itself in differing demographic behaviours. Whether one stratifies by demographic factors, place of residence, education, or social status, from the

beginning of the transition it seemed that a variety of reproductive patterns were in existence. The very process of change did not occur in the same manner (chapters 2 and 3 present details on change in the process of family formation, comparing countries and subgroups within countries). This fact may have lead some authors to mention the existence of several transitions within countries (see chapter 10).

6. Contrary to the experience of European countries, most countries in Latin America started their transition from a relatively high level of fertility. In some countries, such as Costa Rica, the Dominican Republic, and others, the national TFR was almost 7.5 children per woman. Moreover, in significant subgroups within these countries this measure was higher than eight children.

7. Before the transition to lower levels of fertility began, there were increases in fertility in at least five countries. For Costa Rica, Chile, and El Salvador, three of the countries which experienced a significant increase in the fifties, these increments appear to have been caused mainly by the marriage boom that took place in this period (see chapter 7).

Recent Changes in the Social and Economic Context of Latin America

A social structure characteristic of agrarian societies predominated in the majority of countries in the region up to the beginning of the post-war period. Some of the more important features were a high proportion of the population in rural areas, separation of the indigenous populations from sectors of the dominant society (in countries where the indigenous people were the majority), agriculture as the principal type of production, a low educational level and high rates of illiteracy (Rama 1984).

Beginning in the 1960s, Latin American countries underwent a remarkable transformation that encompassed different aspects of the social context. A recent study (ECLAC 1989) concludes that profound social changes have occurred which are expressed in greatly increased occupational, geographic, educational, and social mobility. This mobility is reflected in a decrease in the agricultural labour force, an increase in the proportion in non-manual work, and greater participation of women in the labour force. The urban population increased rapidly as a consequence of growing migration from the countryside and educational levels went up significantly. There was also a tremendous development in mass communications and in communication and transportation networks within and between countries.

The above-mentioned changes, according to the ECLAC study, occurred in the context of expansion of market modalities of production and consumption, remarkable increases in the qualification and productivity of the labour force and, at least until the beginning of the crisis of the 1980s, increases in per capita income, which, for Latin America as a whole, doubled between 1955 and 1980. In fact, during the 1960–75 period, GDP grew by an annual rate of over 5 per cent. This process, although not accompanied by an improvement in income distribution, nevertheless affected, in varying degrees, the lives of most people in almost all Latin American countries.

One of the most important results of this process was that a significant amount of occupational and social mobility occurred. In spite of the fact that many social groups would not see themselves benefiting directly from economic development (in fact, distribution of income did not improve noticeably), great expectations of social mobility were created. These expectations express themselves in the form of desire for access to certain goods and services which are increasingly considered to be necessities, and also in the search for a better standard of living. The rise in expectations may have affected groups who were not direct beneficiaries, such as persons with little or no education, non-salaried workers, etc. This phenomenon can be understood if it is considered that, within the modernization process, social aspects did not have an exact correspondence nor did they change directly as a consequence of economic conditions. In fact, it has been a complex and contradictory process in which the social was only partially related to the economic aspects of change. The role of the state, in social areas such as education and health, played a key role in the changes that occurred: improvements in these areas depended more on the 'style of development' than on economic growth itself.

The great improvements in education, for example, whose effects on fertility have been considered important in studies on the subject,[1] originated in the growing demands of capitalist development during the sixties, but did not follow its logic very closely. The results were, and continue to be, amazing. Changes in education have been truly spectacular. A recent study shows that, in almost all the countries examined, the level of education of the youngest female cohort (women aged 15–19 years) was twice as high as that of cohorts who were finishing their reproductive period (45–49 years); that is, the younger generation has been integrated *en masse* into the educational system and is attaining a much higher level of schooling (Weinberger *et al.* 1989).

A similar situation occurs with health and access to contraceptive methods. Strong expansion in these areas during the 1960s was not necessarily related to the economic strength of countries but had a relatively independent logic. Relatively, because it demanded none the less a minimum economic and service infrastructure. Family planning programmes are included in this category. These programmes were generally started in the mid-1960s by private groups, and then became officially regularized in many countries of the region (see chapter 10; Singh and Berrio 1989). Their development was not directly related to the

[1] Caldwell e.g. notes that education affects fertility through at least five mechanisms: (1) reduces the potential labour of the child in the home and outside; (2) increases the cost of child-rearing; (3) increases societal demands on the family to protect the social investment in the child as a future producer; (4) accelerates cultural change and creates new cultural phenomena; and (5) propagates Western middle-class values (Caldwell 1980: 228).

economic evolution of the country, since in most cases a high proportion of the funds to support these programmes depended on international aid.

Fertility Decline in the Context of Social Change

The study of fertility change includes three important aspects: characteristics of the high level of fertility in the pre-transition period; the moment at which change to a lower fertility pattern began; and the process of decline itself.

Let us analyse the first of these elements. It is well known that at the beginning of the fertility transition, all countries contained sectors in which some birth control was practised (see Guzmán 1991). Urban sectors (generally those who lived in large cities) and the highly educated had a lower level of fertility than the rest of the population. So at the national level, the differences among the countries corresponded not only to differences in patterns of marriage and breast-feeding but also fundamentally to the size of those sectors which practised birth control to some extent. This depended, of course, to a large extent on the socio-economic development of the country, in the sense that those countries with a high level of development had a bigger proportion of their population in the groups with a lower fertility. In fact, given these differences, it is not surprising that some countries such as Chile, and to some extent Brazil, had lower levels of fertility at the start of the transition than others.

On the other hand, there were also large social groups, mainly the rural population, in which fertility had always been high. Whenever one analyses the factors underlying the high fertility rationale, factors such as demand for child labour in the family, the low or non-existent demand for female labour outside the family, high child mortality, etc., it should be understood that high fertility was part of a reproductive logic consistent with the social characteristics of couples in the prevailing socio-economic structure.

However, the practices of the minority controlling their fertility apparently did not spread to other parts of society prior to the 1960s. It is argued here that the explanation of this phenomenon of diversity in reproductive behaviour may be found in the markedly élitist character of Latin American societies and the social, economic, and cultural marginalization of the great mass of the population, especially the peasantry. Instead, distinct social groups maintained their reproductive conduct in stagnant isolation,[2] because the social conditions which would have enabled the adoption of this conduct by a wider segment of the population did not exist. In this sense the lack of integration of the different social groups within

[2] This perspective of analysis is similar to that of Mundigo (see Ch. 10) who argues that there were two transitions in Latin America: one of the middle and upper classes with the highest educational levels which began before 1960 and later expanded to the rest of society, and another which was the result of the expansion of this conduct to the rest of society. Nevertheless, this author did not put emphasis on the apparent relatively stable differential between rural and urban fertility that is seen in some countries of Latin America.

one socio-productive structure resulted in this state of quasi-independence in the sphere of reproductive behaviour.

Since 1960, social changes have led to the general adoption of fertility control mainly by use of contraception, a pattern of behaviour that had been previously confined to limited sectors. Adoption of the new pattern of behaviour varied, usually as a function of level of development. During the 1960s and 1970s, the ideal of a smaller family took root among an increasing portion of the population, leading to the desire and later the practice of birth control.

This radical change in fertility behaviour resulted in major structural change, relative to the traditional situation. It is argued here that the social and economic changes that occurred in Latin America facilitated a major integration of social groups and the development of increasing expectations of achieving social mobility, within a process of 'generalized structural mobility' as ECLAC (1989) called it. This wider social and cultural integration did not necessarily result from economic integration through the labour-market but, as Paiva has pointed out, rather through generalization of the dependence of the family on consumption through the marketplace (Paiva 1984).

Because of social and economic change, and because of the survival of ever-larger numbers of children through the sustained decline in mortality, education became one of the fundamental means of achieving a better standard of living through access to the goods and services of a modern society. This was due to the increasing demand for a qualified labour force in the economy, and also to the pressure of a population that sees it as a way out. The education supply increases and education itself becomes the 'focus of social transformation' (ECLAC 1989).

It is the force with which these expectations were acquired and developed that explains the speed at which women or couples of low social status adopted new attitudes and values. Even if they did not have any role models in their own social class, they could observe the behaviour of the middle class, which served as a model for social mobility.

Migration to urban centres was another factor that fed the social transformation and lowered fertility. It is associated with education and it has been used as a complementary alternative in the search for better standards of living. One important effect of internal migration is that it can increase rural–urban integration, facilitating the transference to rural areas of urban ideas and mechanisms of fertility control. Moreover, migration may greatly weaken intra-family relations associated with high rural fertility, thereby diminishing the social costs associated with fertility control.

The third element in the study of fertility decline has to do with the process of change itself. This volume is largely focused on a detailed examination of this stage of fertility decline. It is believed that, at the national level, the continuation of the decline in fertility is determined by the speed at which the various social groups are integrated into the process. This process of social change is not linear, but rather an irregular one. The irregularities in the way in which the different groups join in fertility change depend not only on the appearance of innovative ideas, but also on the adoption of practices consistent with the new family ideal. Changes in fertility preferences, how far the preferences of women are implemented, and therefore the extent to which fertility is wanted, are discussed in chapters 12 and 13. The fact that some social groups controlled their fertility, even before the 1960s in many countries, suggests that an element of 'innovation' was already present in these societies.

One of the elements that needs to be considered in the adoption of an innovation is the process of social legitimization of the new behaviour. It is believed that one important reason for different patterns of change among social groups is variation in the costs of fertility regulation, as defined by Easterlin (1978). The cost of fertility regulation refers to public or private programmes of family planning. These programmes varied across countries in the time when they began, how they developed and how widespread was their network of services and their influence. Family planning programmes in Latin America contributed to an increase in the flow of information, to the promotion of the small family ideal, and these programmes also diminished the social and cultural cost of the adoption of birth control by helping in legitimizing it. Although it is true that programmes do not reach all women, they generally do reach a high proportion of those in need of services.

Social legitimization of the adoption of fertility control in Latin America differed from country to country and consequently also occurred in a different manner within the countries. What did seem true was that this process gained force when groups with the highest education, which were seen as a model of reference, became more important in the society. In other words, fertility values within the society changed at a faster rate when the highest educated group gained relative weight in the society.

Without doubt the secularization process which occurred in Latin America in the 1960s and the 1970s also contributed to this change. A decline in the strength of the Catholic Church, improvements in women's status in the areas of work and reproduction, progress towards increased equality between the sexes, and the massive expansion of the mass-media were all changes that contributed to fertility decline. These changes enhanced the value attached to having a small family, and at the same time provided an increased desire to engage in activities or to obtain certain goods and services which were to a certain extent incompatible with a high number of children. Chapter 11 discusses the role that change in ideas and attitudes (the diffusion hypothesis) played in the explanation of fertility decline.

Legitimization of family planning (understood as the promotion and supply of modern methods of contraception) was obstructed by several factors, chiefly the influence of powerful forces such as the Catholic Church and conservative political sectors (see Singh and Berrio 1989). These forces possibly slowed down change at the beginning of the fertility transition, partly by limiting the access of some social groups to information or contraceptives and partly by opposing the introduction of 'non-legitimate behaviour'. Chapter 10 looks at the historical background of family planning programmes in Latin America and the role they played in fertility decline, in some detail.

Despite opposing forces, however, access and availability of contraceptive services improved greatly from the 1960s to the 1990s. This was possible because of several factors, including the strength of the demand within the population for family planning services, the availability of international support for programmes, and the fact that governments were able to place family planning within the larger context of bettering the health of the mother and the child rather than focusing only on controlling the number of births.

Finally, it is important to note that the state also played a role, through policies that were not primarily aimed at reducing fertility, but which indirectly contributed to this end. The studies of González *et al.* (1978) of the cases of Brazil, Cuba, Chile, and Costa Rica, show the importance of the role of the state in these countries. Those countries which succeeded to some extent in redistributing income by managing government spending, were able to reduce differences between the social classes: declines in fertility were more rapid when those sectors which maintained high fertility were affected.

Fertility Decline in the Context of Economic Crisis

The economic stagnation experienced in Latin America during the 1980s had multiple effects in the social arena. The economic crisis not only resulted in stagnation in per capita income, but also in a declining standard of living and a slow-down in upward social mobility, compared to previous decades. Moreover, it also reduced the capacity of governments to respond to the demands of growing populations and, as Wolfe (1989) notes, produced a pessimistic view of the possibility that national policy could solve the crisis.

However, analyses of change in fertility showed that fertility continued to decline. (The case studies of individual countries presented in this volume provide some examples.) Economic development indicators such as per capita GDP had been related to fertility in the expected direction according to modernization theory. However, over time these relationships 'have shifted and become less steep over the last two to four decades' (chapter 11). It is argued here that if economic growth led to a decline in fertility at the start of the transition, it is also possible that a subsequent economic crisis may produce its own fertility decline (Carvalho *et al.* 1981).

While this seems to contradict the interpretations discussed above, it is possible that the effect of economic conditions on fertility behaviour once the fertility transition is underway may differ from what it was early in the transition. For example, social behaviours may still be influenced by the accumulated effect of economic growth and social change early in the fertility transition, and/or social behaviour may have gained a certain independence from economic factors later in the process of fertility transition. It is clear that there is need for exploring different mechanisms for explaining why and how fertility declined during the period after the crisis began.

As the demographic transition progresses, and fertility decline is maintained over a substantial period, it will begin to affect other demographic factors, such as the level of infant mortality (see chapter 16). Moreover, it will also influence and change how childbearing is valued and perceived in the society. For example, early childbearing (e.g. before age 20) may begin to be seen as a social problem, when an important societal goal is for a very high proportion of the population to achieve at least secondary education. In addition, a relatively small average family size will have implications for women's lives through changes in their activities (see chapter 18). This is a relatively undeveloped area of demographic research in the region, since it has only recently become relevant and assumed some importance. The chapters on the consequences of fertility decline included in this volume are therefore exploratory, and hopefully will stimulate more work in this area.

References

Caldwell, J. C. (1980), 'Mass Education as a Determinant of Fertility Decline', *Population and Development Review*, 6(2): 225–56.

Carvalho, J. A, Paiva, P. de T. A., and Sawyer, D. R. (1981), *The Recent Sharp Decline in Fertility in Brazil: Economic Boom, Social Inequality and Baby Bust* (Working Paper, No. 8, The Population Council; Latin American and Caribbean Regional Office).

Chahnazarian, A. (1991), *Hausse récente de la fécondité en Haiti: Un nouvel engouement pour la vie en union?* (Papers on Population, WP 91–03; Johns Hopkins Population Center, Baltimore, Maryland).

Easterlin, R. (1978), 'The Economics and Sociology of Fertility: A Synthesis', in Charles Tilly (ed.), *Historical Studies of Changing Fertility* (Princeton: Princeton University Press).

ECLAC (1989), *Transformación Ocupacional y Crisis Social en América Latina* (Santiago, Chile).

González, G. (1978), 'Estrategias de Desarrollo y Transición Demográfica: Los Casos de Brasil, Costa Rica, Chile y Cuba', CELADE, Santiago, Chile (Unpublished).

Guengant, J. P., and May, J. (1991), 'Quelle fécondité en Haiti?', ORSTOM, Pointe à Pitre, Guadeloupe (Unpublished).

Guzmán, J. M. (1991), 'The Onset of Fertility Decline in Latin America', Paper presented at the Seminar on Fertility Transitions in Sub-Saharan Africa, Harare, Zimbabwe.

Paiva, P. de T. A. (1984), *The Process of Proletarianization and Fertility Transition in Brazil* (Texto para Discussao No. 15; Belo Horizonte, Brazil).

Rama, G. (1984), 'La Evolución Social de América Latina (1950–1980): Transición y Cambio Estructural', Paper presented to the Seminar on Development Alternatives in Latin America, Bogotá, Colombia.

Singh S., and Berrio, D. (1989), 'Institutional Constraints on the Provision of Family Planning Services in Latin America', Paper presented to the Seminar on the Role of Family Planning Programmes as a Fertility Determinant, June, Tunis.

Weinberger, M. B., Lloyd, C., and Blank, A. K. (1989), 'Educación de la Mujer y Fecundidad: Un Decenio de Cambio en Cuatro Países Latinoamericanos', *Perspectivas Internacionales de Planificación Familiar* (Special Issue): 1–12.

Wolfe, M. (1989), 'Democratic Politics and Policy Formation in Latin America at the Beginning of the 1990's' (unpublished).

Part I

Overview of the Fertility Transition: A Comparative Perspective

1 Latin America: Overview of the Fertility Transition, 1950–1990

JUAN CHACKIEL and SUSANA SCHKOLNIK

Introduction

In the 1950s and early 1960s, Latin America had the world's highest rate of population growth, averaging 2.8 per cent a year. This rapid growth rate was due to sharp declines in mortality in various countries of the region, as fertility remained high and even increasing, in many countries. The TFR was approximately 6 children per woman, and was higher than 7 children per woman in several countries.

This situation led to rapid rates of population growth, which meant that fertility levels became a political issue. For that reason, there were innumerable studies of the relationship between population growth and economic development. Many such studies concluded that rapid growth was an obstacle to improved living standards. Within a relatively few years, family planning programmes expanded in both the private and the public sector, spreading knowledge of contraceptive methods and providing services to an ever-growing number of women. Today, these programmes tend to be more closely linked to the goals of improved maternal and child health and to the rights of the couple to have access to the means to plan the number of children they wish to have.

In the second half of the 1960s, the fertility transition began to occur in some countries, and gradually this process extended to almost the entire region. Within a period of only twenty years, overall fertility declined by 40 per cent, although this implies a reduction in the population growth rate of approximately 20 per cent, because of the very young age structure of the population and the continuing decline in mortality rates.

The process of fertility change has assumed very different forms both among and within different countries. In the period 1960–5, the TFR ranged from 2.9 to 7.5 children per woman, and the range was even wider in some sub-populations with widely differing living conditions.

One of the purposes of this chapter is to describe the way in which fertility has evolved since 1950 to the present day for the region as a whole. However, the more basic aim is to show the diversity that exists in patterns of change in the various countries. The report documents the status of the fertility transition for each country, as well as the way in which changes in overall and age-specific fertility have occurred. Differentials in fertility behaviour are also shown for sub-populations defined in terms of geographic, economic, and social characteristics, such as area of residence (degree of urbanization), the level of schooling reached by the mother or the head of the household, and the socio-occupational status of the household head.

Indicators and Data Sources

To examine the present situation and changes in fertility over time, we shall use the following indicators: the TFR; ASFRs; and the annual number of births, particularly among groups of women who are at highest health risk, that is, women under the age of 20, and those over the age of 34.

This study is based, among other sources, on estimates and projections prepared jointly by national agencies and by the Latin American Demographic Centre (CELADE), and currently in use (CELADE 1990). These estimates are based on data from population censuses and vital statistics, evaluated and processed using methods appropriate to each case. For this purpose, frequent use is made of indirect estimation methods, which use census and survey data. The use of information derived from these estimates, once they have been evaluated and corrected, is justifiable on the grounds that the vital statistics in most Latin American countries are seriously deficient, as a result both of omissions in the data and of a lack of consistency over time and among countries in the collection instruments used.

Many countries do not have recent fertility estimates, in which case we use the 'medium' variant of the population projections prepared by CELADE. Two other basic sources of information used in this study are the WFS and the DHS surveys, as well as special studies carried out within the framework of the project 'Investigation of Fertility using the Own Children Method in the Countries of Latin America' (IFHIPAL), carried out by CELADE, using data from the most recent population censuses. This information will be used in some cases to verify the figures derived from the population estimates and projections. In some countries, it will also permit the examination of differential trends in fertility by certain geographic and socio-economic variables.

Fertility Transition in Latin America

For the region as a whole, fertility declined substantially between 1950–5 and 1985–90, but the pace of decline varied considerably by country. Table 1.1 shows the TFRs for the region as a whole and by country. Latin America had the highest fertility in the world at the beginning of the period, with TFRs reaching an average of 6 children per woman in 1960–5. According to this indicator, which is the most commonly used to describe fertility change, the mean number of children per woman has now declined to 3.6, with an even lower level of 3 children per

Table 1.1. *Latin America: TFR, by quinquennia, by country, 1950–1990*

Country	quinquennia							
	1950 1955	1955 1960	1960 1965	1965 1970	1970 1975	1975 1980	1980 1985	1985 1990
Latin America	5.9	5.9	6.0	5.5	5.0	4.4	4.0	3.6
Argentina	3.2	3.1	3.1	3.1	3.2	3.4	3.2	3.0
Bolivia	6.8	6.7	6.6	6.6	6.5	6.4	6.3	6.1
Brazil	6.2	6.2	6.2	5.3	4.7	4.2	3.8	3.5
Colombia	6.8	6.8	6.8	6.3	4.7	4.1	3.5	3.1
Costa Rica	6.7	7.1	7.0	5.8	4.3	3.9	3.5	3.3
Cuba	4.1	3.7	4.7	4.3	3.5	2.1	1.9	1.8
Chile	5.1	5.3	5.3	4.4	3.6	2.9	2.8	2.7
Ecuador	6.9	6.9	6.9	6.7	6.1	5.4	4.8	4.3
El Salvador	6.5	6.8	6.9	6.6	6.1	5.7	5.2	4.9
Guatemala	7.1	6.9	6.9	6.6	6.5	6.4	6.1	5.8
Haiti	6.2	6.2	6.2	6.2	5.8	5.4	5.1	4.7
Honduras	7.1	7.2	7.4	7.4	7.4	6.6	6.2	5.6
Mexico	6.8	6.8	6.8	6.7	6.4	4.9	4.2	3.6
Nicaragua	7.3	7.3	7.3	7.1	6.7	6.3	5.9	5.5
Panama	5.7	5.9	5.9	5.6	4.9	4.1	3.5	3.1
Paraguay	6.8	6.8	6.8	6.4	5.7	5.1	4.8	4.6
Peru	6.9	6.9	6.9	6.6	6.0	5.4	5.0	4.5
Dominican Republic	7.4	7.4	7.3	6.7	5.6	4.7	4.2	3.8
Uruguay	2.7	2.8	2.9	2.8	3.0	2.9	2.6	2.4
Venezuela	6.5	6.5	6.5	5.9	5.0	4.5	4.1	3.8

Source: CELADE (1990).

woman expected by the end of the century, according to a median hypothesis of fertility decline over time.

Most countries in the region have begun to show unequivocal signs of having entered into a stage of fertility transition. The processes that this decline has unleashed will, in the future, create important changes in the future age structure of the populations of these countries. It is also noteworthy that in many cases, whatever a country's initial TFR level was, in the 1950s and 1960s, before the fertility decline began, there was an increase in this measure. This finding may be linked to improvements in the populations' living standards, which, even before reproductive patterns changed, made possible an increase in the number of children surviving, both on account of better health conditions among women and because of greater economic possibilities for sustaining child-rearing.

The estimated TFRs for the region generally coincide with estimates from the DHS programme (DHS 1989). There are, however, exceptions in the case of El Salvador and Guatemala, where the fertility estimates from the surveys are lower than those derived from population estimates used here. That there are so few discrepancies between the two types of estimate is due in part to the fact that the estimates and projections of some of the countries have recently been revised to reflect the results of these same surveys. At any rate, the forecasts of fertility behaviour have not changed as far as the intensity of the decline is concerned.

For descriptive purposes, fertility has been classified into four levels of the TFR: low, up to 3 children per woman; medium low, from 3.1 to 4.4; medium high, from 4.5 to 5.4; and high, 5.5 children or more. It should be mentioned, however, that these limits are arbitrary and the assignment of the countries to each group is somewhat flexible.

Table 1.2 shows that of the sixteen countries with high fertility in 1950–5, at present only four retain this characteristic (Bolivia, Guatemala, Honduras, and Nicaragua). Three others (El Salvador, Haiti, and Paraguay) have become medium high fertility countries, and the remaining countries (Brazil, Colombia, Costa Rica, Ecuador, Mexico, Panama, Peru, Dominican Republic, and Venezuela) currently have medium low fertility. The countries that now have low fertility levels showed more heterogeneous patterns of fertility in the past. Chile had high and medium high fertility, while Argentina and Uruguay had low and medium low levels. Fig. 1.1 shows the countries ranged in order of their current TFR.

Table 1.2. *Latin America: Countries by fertility levels in 1950–1955 and in 1985–1990*

Fertility level 1950–1955	Fertility Level 1985–1990			
	High	Medium high	Medium low	Low
High	Bolivia Guatemala Honduras Nicaragua	El Salvador Haiti Paraguay	Brazil, Colombia, Costa Rica, Dominican Rep., Ecuador, Mexico, Panama, Venezuela, Peru	
Medium High				Chile
Medium Low				Cuba
Low				Argentina Uruguay

Source: Table 1.1

Classification by Fertility Level

We have classified the countries of Latin America into various groups, according to their TFR in the five-year periods 1950–5 and 1985–90; that is, in terms of their initial fertility level and the speed of their decline in fertility. The groups may in turn be classified according to their fertility levels in 1985–90, as shown below.

Low Fertility: Transition Completed or Very Advanced (TFR < 3)

Group 1. Low fertility at the beginning of the period and at present. This group is made up of Argentina *and* Uruguay, where the fertility decline started long before the period under study, towards the end of the last century, and where the transition has been quite gradual throughout the century. It may be observed

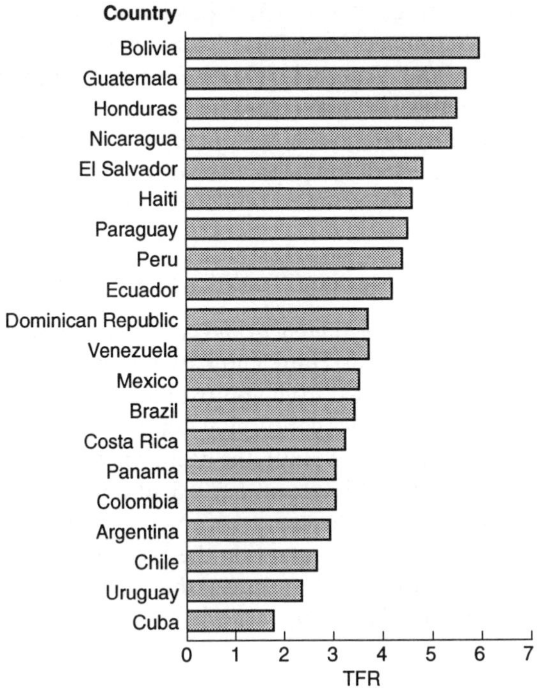

Fig. 1.1. ***Latin America: TFR by country 1985–1990***
Source: Table 1.1.

that the initial fertility in Argentina is a little higher than that indicated for this category. Moreover, there has been a slight increase between 1975–80 and 1985–90. None the less, given that this level is constant and that its evolution has been similar to that of Uruguay, albeit at a slightly lower level, it was felt that the two countries are examples of a particular type of change.

Group 2. Medium fertility at the beginning of the period and low at present. This group contains two countries that have experienced somewhat different types of change, although fertility has declined noticeably in both. In Cuba, the decline only began in the period 1970–5 from a level of medium low fertility. Although Cuba started from a higher fertility rate than countries in Group 1, its current fertility level is lower, in fact, the lowest in the entire region. This below replacement level fertility could lead to negative population growth in the future. On the other hand, Chile experienced a sharp decline in the fertility rate beginning in the period 1965–70. In contrast to Cuba, Chile started with a medium high rate of fertility and did not reach levels quite as low.

Medium Low Fertility: Advanced Transition (3 < TFR < 4.5)

Group 3. High fertility at the beginning of the period and medium low at present. This group of countries stands out because of its fertility decline from 6 or 7 children per woman during 1950–5 to 3 or 4 children per woman. This group is made up of Brazil, Colombia, Costa Rica, Ecuador, Mexico, Panama, Peru, the Dominican Republic, and Venezuela. Costa Rica underwent an even sharper decline in the period 1965–70 than the other countries in this group, starting from a very high fertility rate in the beginning of the period (6.7 children per woman). A high percentage of the population of Latin America is found in this group, as it includes three of the most populated countries.

Medium High Fertility: Intermediate Transition (4.5 < TFR < 5.5)

Group 4. High fertility at the beginning of the period and medium high at present. This group contains El Salvador, Haiti, and Paraguay where the average number of children per woman decreased from approximately 7 to less than 5, although the situations and official policies concerning family planning programmes vary by country. With the exception of Haiti, the decline in fertility in these countries began between the periods 1965–70 and 1970–5, although with varying rates of decline. In the case of Haiti, the trend became clear in the period 1975–80, although a recent survey calls into question the existing estimates for this country, suggesting the possibility of a rise in the fertility rate in recent years (Cayemittes and Chahnazarian 1989).

High Fertility: Initiating Transition (TFR > 5.5)

Group 5. High fertility at the beginning and at present. This group is made up of Bolivia, Guatemala, Honduras, and Nicaragua, countries which have shown smaller declines in fertility than the previous group. The decline also started later than for countries in Group 4. However, the data show a slight decline: in Bolivia, Guatemala, and Nicaragua, fertility began to decline after 1970–5. In Honduras, on the other hand, the decline was significant only after 1975–80. It is expected, however, that by 1995–2000 these countries will reach a level of fertility between 4.5 and 5.5 children per woman; that is, a medium high level.

In summary, Fig. 1.2 shows the different types or models of fertility change between 1950 and the year 2000. In addition to showing the distinct phases of the transition of the countries, it also shows that (independent of the level of fertility) increases in fertility occurred during the 1950s and 1960.

The Age Structure of Fertility in Latin America

Present Situation and Changes Between 1950–55 and 1985–90

Using the periods 1950–5 and 1985–90 as reference points, ASFRs are analysed by five-year age-groups within the women's reproductive years, from 15–49 years of age. Table 1.3 shows these rates for the twenty countries of Latin America,

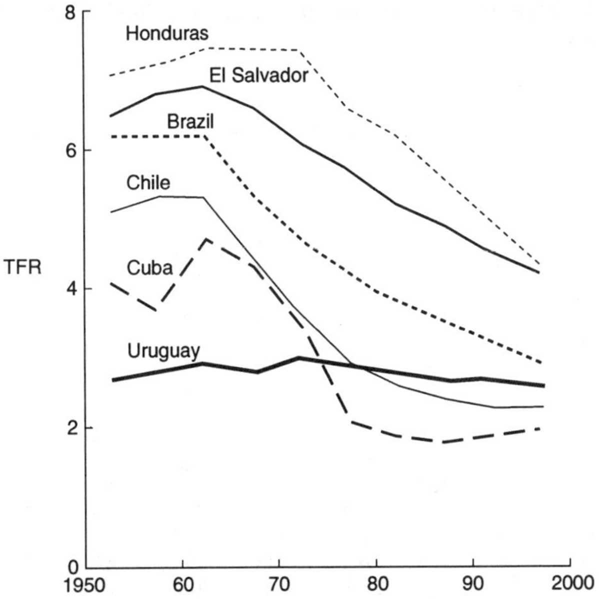

Fig. 1.2. ***Latin America: TFR, selected countries 1950–2000***
Source: Table 1.1.

demonstrating that the fertility declines have occurred fundamentally among women over 30 years old and those under 20. There is an association between the level and the structure of fertility rates. A decline in fertility levels is accompanied by a rejuvenation of its age structure. The ASFRs indicate that the contribution to total fertility by women between 20 and 29 years old has risen in all countries.

In general, ASFRs show three typical patterns: early peak, with a maximum between 20 and 24 years old; late peak, with a maximum between 25 and 29 years old; and dilated peak, with a maximum which extends from 20 to 29 years old, with similar rates of fertility in the 20–24-year-old age-group and that of the 25–29-year-old age-group.

In Fig. 1.3, the age-specific fertility patterns of selected countries are shown in relation to their TFR level in the period 1985–90. Over time, several countries have maintained the age structure of their fertility in terms of peak age. By peak age they are: Bolivia, Brazil, Haiti, Peru, and Paraguay (late); Guatemala and Uruguay (dilated); and Venezuela (early).

The remaining countries in which the fertility structure has changed over this thirty-five-year period are those that have shifted from a dilated to an early peak (Colombia, Costa Rica, Cuba, Nicaragua, Panama, and the Dominican Republic); those that went from a late to an early peak (Chile, El Salvador, and Honduras); and those which have moved from a late to a dilated peak (Argentina, Ecuador, and Mexico).

Factors that affect the changes in the ASFRs include the particular type of

Table 1.3. ***Latin America: fertility rates by age, by country 1950–1955 and 1985–1990 (per 1,000)***

Country	Years	Age-groups							
		15–19	20–24	25–29	30–34	35–39	40–44	45–49	TFR
Argentina	1950–5	62	160	172	128	76	26	7	3.2
	1985–90	71	158	162	115	63	20	4	3.0
Bolivia	1950–5	100	275	307	281	222	120	46	6.8
	1985–90	87	266	293	255	188	92	31	6.1
Brazil	1950–5	83	264	302	251	189	98	44	6.2
	1985–90	52	177	192	143	89	36	4	3.5
Colombia	1950–5	91	325	325	280	209	86	28	6.7
	1985–90	76	168	157	113	68	32	12	3.1
Costa Rica	1950–5	119	334	331	261	203	83	15	6.7
	1985–90	92	184	164	116	69	24	3	3.3
Cuba	1950–5	65	229	226	155	88	32	7	4.0
	1985–90	89	129	97	46	18	4	0	1.9
Chile	1950–5	84	224	255	212	148	77	20	5.1
	1985–90	67	158	147	99	53	18	2	2.7
Ecuador	1950–5	140	294	320	276	213	105	32	6.9
	1985–90	88	204	202	168	117	62	15	4.3
El Salvador	1950–5	142	314	332	263	162	64	15	6.5
	1985–90	128	271	237	168	108	50	10	4.9
Guatemala	1950–5	174	313	321	280	209	93	27	7.1
	1985–90	133	276	277	229	157	70	13	5.8
Haiti	1950–5	75	202	277	267	212	129	69	6.2
	1985–90	48	184	230	206	155	91	34	4.7
Honduras	1950–5	151	305	320	286	212	116	21	7.1
	1985–90	118	279	261	204	164	77	7	5.6
Mexico	1950–5	115	300	322	287	200	100	26	6.8
	1985–90	80	176	171	149	86	43	11	3.6
Nicaragua	1950–5	168	348	351	269	208	94	28	7.3
	1985–90	132	301	283	194	130	49	12	5.5
Panama	1950–5	145	283	278	208	136	63	23	5.7
	1985–90	91	185	159	105	62	22	5	3.1
Paraguay	1950–5	95	283	324	293	222	119	24	6.8
	1985–90	79	196	216	191	144	74	16	4.6
Peru	1950–5	130	283	317	278	205	113	45	6.9
	1985–90	75	215	234	183	133	48	9	4.5
Dominican Republic	1950–5	166	335	340	300	211	107	22	7.4
	1985–90	79	216	195	140	85	28	8	3.8
Uruguay	1950–5	60	150	148	104	60	20	4	2.7
	1985–90	61	135	133	91	49	15	1	2.4
Venezuela	1950–5	155	330	308	239	167	70	24	6.5
	1985–90	86	208	193	136	85	37	9	3.8

Source: CELADE (1988) and updated projections.

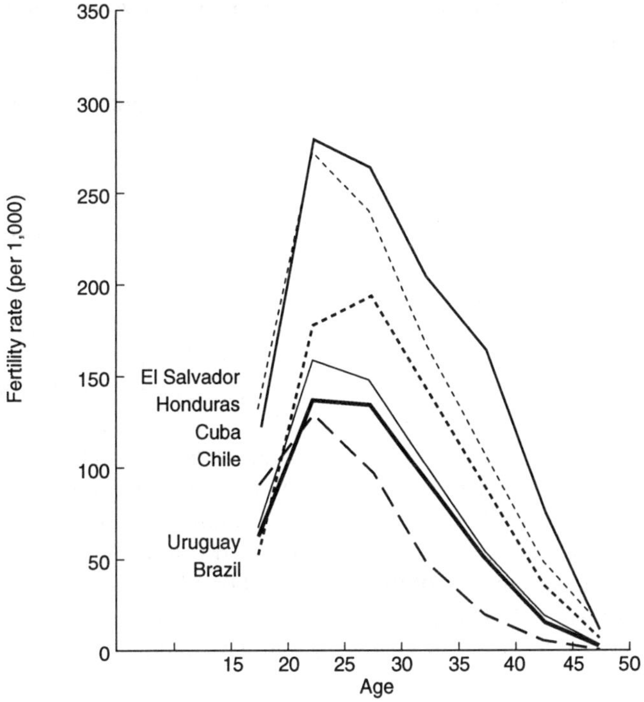

Fig. 1.3. ***Latin America: fertility rates by age, selected countries, 1985–1990***
Source: Table 1.3.

family formation characterized by childbearing during the early years of marriage as well as possibly the delay in first marriage, which affects the fertility rate of younger women.

Adolescent Fertility

The fertility of women under the age of 20, or adolescent fertility, is a matter of special interest due to the social consequences of this phenomenon and, above all, to its negative impact on the health of young mothers and their children; for these reasons, we shall examine this aspect in greater detail.

Countries and international organizations have recently become increasingly concerned about the high number of pregnancies and births among adolescents. Changing sexual attitudes and behaviour, greater exposure to sexually transmitted diseases, and an increase in age at first marriage, may lead to more frequent use of abortion to end unwanted pregnancies.

To establish a general overview of adolescent fertility, Table 1.4 presents the fertility rates of women aged 15 to 19 in Latin America. Since the data sources are population estimates and projections and given that these estimates did not have the specific objective of studying this aspect of fertility and are based on sources which only indicate the magnitude of this phenomenon, they can only approximate the true situation.

The range of variation in 1985–90 of the fertility rate for this age-group in Latin America is from 61 per 1,000 in Uruguay, a low-fertility country, to 133 per 1,000 in Guatemala, a country with high fertility. In general, the rates for the high- and medium-fertility countries are much higher than those for low-fertility countries. Among those with the highest rates, over 100 per 1,000, are Guatemala, Honduras, Nicaragua, and El Salvador. The lowest, approximately 60 per 1,000, are found in Argentina, Chile, and Uruguay.

Between 1950–5 and 1985–90, the majority of the countries' fertility rates declined steadily between the two periods, varying from a 10 per cent decrease in El Salvador to a 52 per cent decrease in the Dominican Republic. In contrast, Argentina, Cuba, and Uruguay, have experienced an increase in ASFR. In Cuba the rise has been evident since 1960, immediately after the revolution. But currently the rate has declined, tending to oscillate (Comité Estatal de Estadísticas 1987), contrary to what is indicated by the numbers in Table 1.4.

Nevertheless, these data do not reflect the magnitude of the current phenomenon with the desired degree of precision, nor do they allow the unequivocal identification of the direction of the most recent trends, for which no trustworthy figures are available (Wulf 1986).

Among the few countries in the region that have conducted studies of adolescent fertility, a case worth mentioning is that of Brazil. The fertility rate among adolescents in Brazil seems to have risen slightly between 1970 and the period 1981–6 (Henriques *et al.* 1989). For other countries, such as Panama and the Dominican Republic (Wulf 1986), data from surveys carried out in hospitals show an increase in the proportion of births to adolescent mothers, similar to Brazil. This trend still needs to be confirmed.

Comparative data for Peru indicate that although the national fertility rate of young women aged 15–19 years stayed practically constant over the past fifteen years, the fertility rate declined among urban adolescents while it rose among rural adolescents from 115 to 137 per 1,000 (Ferrando *et al.* 1989).

Even though the magnitude of adolescent fertility has not changed significantly in some countries, or the change has been less than that experienced by older women, other types of phenomenon may be occurring. Likely trends include an increase in the number of undesired pregnancies, a greater incidence of abortion, or, as has been observed in Chile, an increase in the proportion of women under 20 who have given birth before marriage (Wulf 1986).

Differentials in the Fertility Transition by Geographic Areas and Socio-economic Groups

National fertility rates obscure the internal heterogeneity, the result of the placement of different individuals and social groups within the society. Since these

Table 1.4. *Latin America: Fertility rate of the female population aged 15 to 19, by recent fertility level and country 1950–1955 and 1985–1990*

Recent fertility level and country	Fertility rate (per 1,000)				% Reduction
	1950–5	1975–80	1980–5	1985–90	1950–1955/ 1985–1990
Low fertility					
Argentina	62	79	77	71	–14.5
Uruguay	60	72	63	61	–1.7
Cuba	67	73	64	85	–36.9
Chile	84	73	69	67	20.2
Medium low fertility					
Brazil	83	64	58	52	37.3
Colombia	128	106	79	76	16.5
Costa Rica	119	110	98	92	22.7
Ecuador	140	107	95	88	37.1
Mexico	115	106	92	80	30.4
Panama	145	116	100	91	37.2
Peru	130	93	80	72	42.3
Dominican Republic	166	110	97	79	52.4
Venezuela	155	103	94	86	44.5
Medium high fertility					
El Salvador	142	144	134	128	9.9
Haiti	75	56	52	48	36.0
Paraguay	95	84	82	79	16.8
High fertility					
Bolivia	100	93	90	87	13.0
Guatemala	174	144	141	133	23.6
Honduras	151	145	136	118	21.9
Nicaragua	168	148	141	132	21.4

Source: CELADE (1988) and updated projections.

differentials are of crucial importance to understanding how the transition process occurs, heterogeneity within the countries will be examined through information collected from various sources.[1]

Information is available on fertility differentials according to several selected variables. These include the degree of urbanization, the years of education of the woman or of the household head, and their occupational status. Although the information obtained from the various studies is not strictly comparable since both the selection criteria for the data and the characteristics of the countries vary, they are valid for giving an overall picture of the differences mentioned above and of the changes in fertility in different groups. For greater comparability, the countries with similar data sources have been grouped together in Tables 1.5 and 1.6. Table 1.5 shows data for Chile, Cuba, Guatemala, Honduras, Panama, and Paraguay, from studies in CELADE's IFHIPAL programme. Table 1.6 contains data taken from fertility surveys for Colombia, Ecuador, El Salvador, Peru, and the Dominican Republic.

[1] This information comes from the studies carried out within the framework of the IFHIPAL project of CELADE, and from the DHS (Institute for Resource Development/Westinghouse).

Table 1.5. *Latin America: TFR by place of residence, years of schooling, and occupational strata obtained from estimates of the IFHIPAL programme*

Geographic and socio-economic variables	Chile		Cuba		Guatemala		Honduras[g]		Panama		Paraguay[g]	
	1970	1980	1967[b]	1977	1967[f]	1976	1969–70	1979–80	1967	1976	1969	1979
TOTAL	3.9	2.7	4.3	2.3	6.3	6.3	7.4	6.3	5.4	4.1	6.0	5.1
Place of residence												
Capital	3.1	2.4	3.2	1.7	4.3	3.9	4.5	3.8	4.2	2.8	3.1	2.7
Principal cities	3.2	2.5	3.6	2.1	4.9	4.5	—	—	4.9	3.2	4.4	3.9
Other urban	4.1	2.7	—	—	6.0	5.6	6.2	5.3	6.1	3.9	5.5	4.4
Rural	5.9	3.6	5.9	2.7	7.1	7.1	8.0	8.2	6.5	5.4	7.4	6.6
(Difference)	(2.8)	(1.2)	(2.7)	(1.0)	(2.8)	(3.2)	(3.5)	(4.4)	(2.3)	(2.6)	(4.3)	(3.9)
Years of schooling							8.0[h]	8.0[h]				
0–3	5.3	3.4	6.3	3.2	7.0	6.9	7.2	7.3	6.6	6.1	6.8	5.7
4–6	4.4	3.1	4.1	2.9	4.5	4.5	6.0	5.9	5.9	4.5	5.6	5.3
7–9	4.0	2.6	2.9	2.0	—	—	—	—	—	—	4.1	3.9
10[a]	3.0	2.3	2.5[c]	1.6[c]	—	—	—	—	—	—	3.2	3.1
7[a]	—	—	—	—	n.a	3.3	3.7	3.5	n.a	2.8	—	—
(Difference)	(2.3)	(1.1)	(3.8)	(1.6)	(n.a)	(3.6)	(4.3)	(4.5)	(n.a)	(3.3)	(3.6)	(2.6)
Occupation strata												
Low paid agr.	6.4	3.9	6.3	2.9	6.9	7.1	8.1	8.6	7.0	5.5	7.9	7.0
Low unpaid agr.	5.6	3.5	5.8	2.3	7.1	7.2	8.2	8.4	6.9	6.3	—	—
Low unpaid non-agr.	2.9	2.7	4.9[d]	2.1[d]	6.0	5.3	6.2	5.4	5.4	3.7	4.7	4.6
Low paid non-agr.	4.4	3.0	4.5[e]	2.0[e]	5.6	4.8	—	—	5.4	3.6	—	—
Middle	2.8	2.3	3.6	1.9	4.0	3.8	4.5	3.8	3.9	2.8	3.5	3.2
High	2.8	1.9	—	—	—	—	—	—	—	—	2.6	3.0
(Difference)	(3.6)	(2.0)	(2.7)	(1.0)	(2.9)	(3.3)	(3.6)	(4.8)	(3.1)	(2.7)	(5.3)	(4.0)

Sources: Chile and CELADE (1988), Cuba and CELADE (1981), Guatemala and CELADE (1984), CELADE (1986), Panama and CELADE (1984), and Paraguay and Censo and CELADE (1988).

a The difference between the highest and the lowest rate for each variable.
b Occupational strata for the year 1965.
c Refers to secondary and higher education.
d Includes state and private sector paid workers in goods- and service-producing occupations.
e Includes state and private sector paid workers in the service sector.
f Place of residence for the year 1969.
g Years of study of the household head.
h Refers to categories 0 years and 1–3 years respectively.

Table 1.6. *Latin America and the Caribbean: TFR by place of residence and level of schooling for countries with information available*

Geographic and socio-economic variables	Colombia		Ecuador	El Salvador	Peru	Dominican Republic		Trinidad and Tobago	
	1981–3	1984–6	1982	1980	1983	1980–2	1983–5	1981–3	1984–7
TOTAL	3.7	3.2	4.3	4.4	4.1	4.3	3.7	3.3	3.1
Place of residence				3.3[b]					
Urban	3.1	2.6	3.5	3.8[c]	3.1	3.5	3.1	3.0	3.0
Rural	5.1	4.8	5.5	5.9	6.3	5.9	4.8	3.6	3.1
(Difference)[a]	(2.0)	(2.2)	(2.0)	(2.6)	(3.2)	(2.4)	(1.7)	(0.6)	(0.1)
Level of schooling									
No education	5.6	5.1	6.4	6.0	6.6	6.5	5.3	—	—
Primary	4.5	3.9	5.2	—	5.0	5.1	4.3	4.2[e]	3.6[e]
1–3	—	—	—	5.2	—	—	—	—	—
4–6	—	—	—	3.9	—	—	—	3.9[f]	3.5[f]
7–9	—	—	—	3.5	—	—	—	2.9[g]	3.2[g]
Secondary	2.7	2.5	3.1	2.5[d]	3.1	2.8	2.9	2.3[h]	2.3[h]
Higher	1.6	1.4	2.3	—	1.9	2.2	2.1	—	—
(Difference)	(4.0)	(3.7)	(4.1)	(3.5)	(4.7)	(4.3)	(3.2)	(1.9)	(1.3)

Sources: CCRP and IRD (1988); CEPAR and IRD (1988); ADS (1987); INE and IRD (1988); CONAPO and (1987); and FPATT and IRD (1988).

[a] The difference between the highest and the lowest rate for the variable.
[b] Metropolitan Area.
[c] Other Urban.
[d] Secondary and Higher levels.
[e] Incomplete Primary.
[f] Completed Primary.
[g] Secondary I.
[h] Secondary II.

Differential Fertility by Area of Residence

Area of residence (urban–rural) is possibly one of the most studied variables in the analysis of fertility differentials. The information available has clearly indicated that the level of fertility is lower in more highly urbanized areas. Thus, as a general rule, urban women have fewer children than rural ones. This difference, however, can range from only 1 child per woman (Chile in 1980 and Cuba in 1977) up to nearly 4 (Honduras in 1979–80 and Paraguay in 1979). In general terms, the difference between urban and rural fertility is greater in those countries which are lagging in the transition process.

The rate of fertility decline for the countries in different phases of the transition process (Fig. 1.4) differs according to the women's area of residence (urban v. rural).

In Chile and Cuba, where the fertility rate decline has been more pronounced and which currently have low TFRs, the present trend shows differences in fertility rates narrowing between urban and rural areas although the decline began earlier in the urban areas. This may be due to the fact that the urban areas already have very low levels of fertility, but also because the rural areas have begun a more advanced phase of the transition. In Cuba, fertility in urban areas continuously declined and, by the end of the 1970s, had already reached the replacement level, whereas in Chile the TFR stabilized at values between 2.5 and 3.

At the other extreme are countries which still have high fertility rates (Fig. 1.4). In Honduras there has been a decline in fertility only in urban areas, while in rural areas fertility rates remain unchanged. At present, changes in fertility rates in Latin American countries with high fertility rates are due solely to changes in urban areas. In those areas which have reached somewhat lower levels of fertility, there has been a tendency toward stabilization at TFR levels which are relatively high.

Finally, in countries, such as Paraguay, whose fertility is still intermediate, there have been changes both in the urban and in the rural areas. In general, the changes in rural areas are smaller in these countries than in those that are already in an advanced stage of transition.

In summary, the transition process is more advanced in urban areas, but in countries in which urban areas have reached low levels of fertility, significant changes in rural areas may be expected in the near future.

Differential Fertility by Level of Education

The accumulated empirical evidence invariably shows a negative relationship between fertility and education. These relationships are at least as pronounced as those observed by area of residence. The more educated women clearly have much lower fertility than women with no schooling; their fertility can, in many cases, be as low as a third or a quarter that of the latter group.

In Chile and in Cuba, the decline in fertility has occurred primarily in the less educated groups. It is significant that the size of the decline diminishes as the years of schooling increase (Fig. 1.5). In Cuba, the fertility of women with university

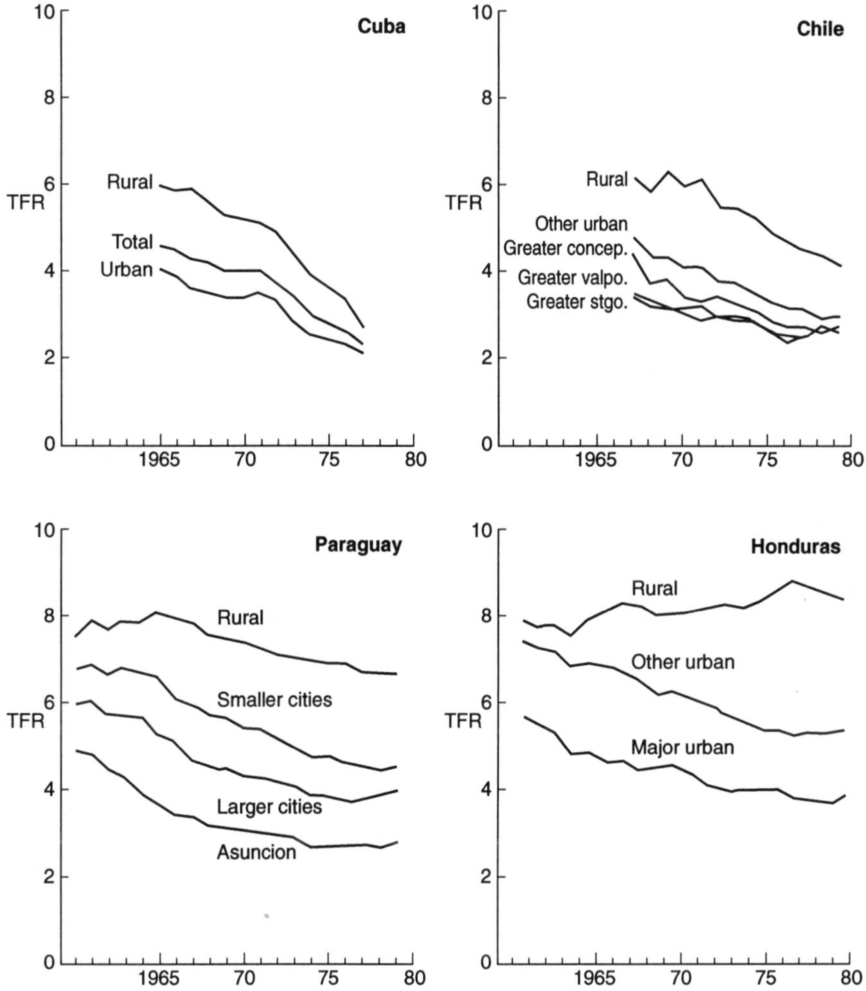

Fig. 1.4. ***Latin America: TFR by degree of urbanization, selected countries 1965–1980***

Source: Table 1.5.

education is considerably below the replacement level, while in Chile it seems to have stabilized at slightly higher levels. In Paraguay, fertility decline is observed in groups with less education, although the decline is not as pronounced.

In Honduras, a country which is just beginning its transition, the picture is different. The decline in fertility in this country is attributed to the experience of those that are more highly educated, while for illiterate women the fertility rate remains practically constant at a TFR of nearly 8 children per woman.

The data in Tables 1.5 and 1.6 and Fig. 1.5 reaffirm that fertility declined primarily in those populations that enjoy greater resources, or that are in more

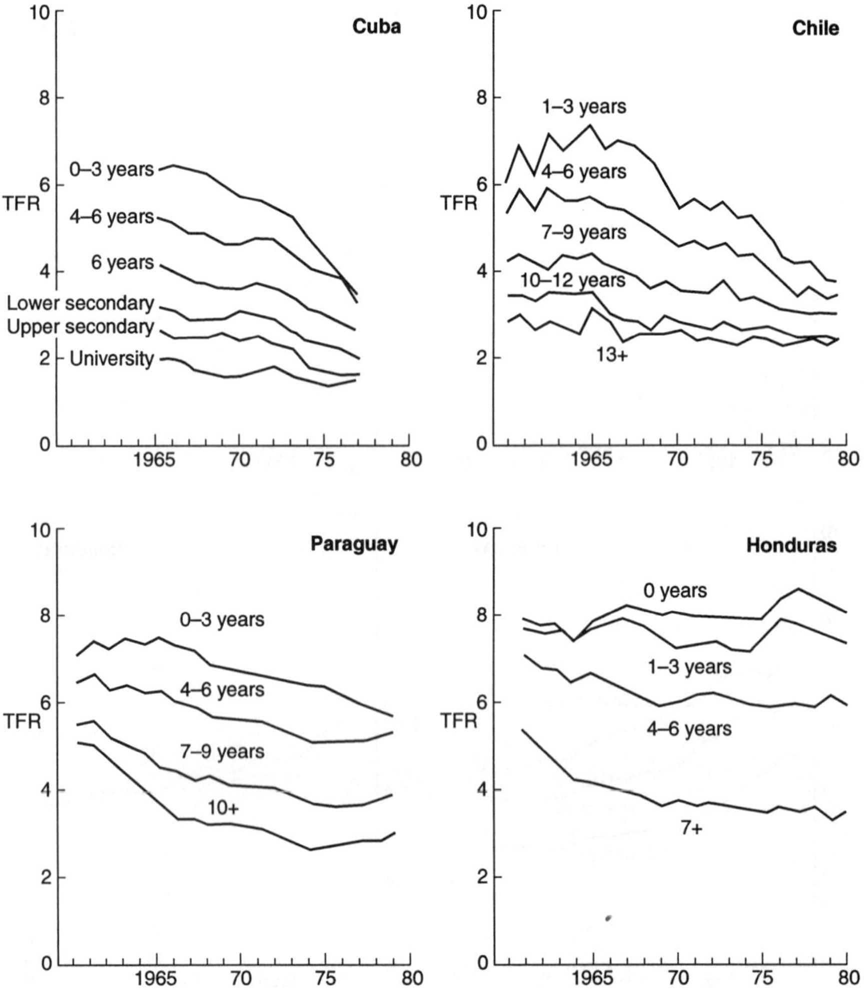

Fig. 1.5. ***Latin America: TFR by level of schooling, selected countries 1965–1980***
Source: Table 1.5.

advanced stages of modernization, generally among women in urban areas and with higher educational levels. Because of this, the countries that are more advanced in the transition show a greater relative fertility decline among the most disadvantaged groups of the society, given that the low levels of fertility already reached by the modern urban areas make it difficult for the declining trend to continue any further. Moreover, certain benefits of greater development are extended to the less advantaged groups.

It has been pointed out that in spite of the association between fertility and education, it is not necessarily education itself which affects fertility, but rather its relationship with other variables (UN 1987). While it may be true that education may have an indirect effect on fertility through the postponement of marriage and the age at which the first child is born, it follows that more educated women are also more exposed to a greater flow of information, tend to attach less value to high fertility, and have social and economic aspirations which are often incompatible with very large families.

Differential Fertility by Occupational Status

Among the differentials examined, occupational status is perhaps the most difficult to compare between countries, due to differences both in the productive structure and in the conceptualization of status in each country. Therefore, taking these differences into account, the focus is on comparison over time within each country, rather than between them.

In spite of these caveats, in all cases for which information is available, the highest fertility levels—whether *c.*1980 or 1970—correspond to agricultural workers, both independent small farmers and rural paid labourers. The groups which make up the lower level of urban occupations—labourers and craftsmen, self-employed workers, office workers, service workers, chauffeurs, etc.—have an intermediate level of fertility, whereas the middle (and in some cases upper middle) and upper occupational levels have the lowest number of children per woman. These last two levels, which are often considered together, primarily include employers in various occupations, professionals, administrators, managers, civil servants, technicians, etc.

Regarding the evolution of fertility among the different groups, there are differences between countries: in some countries the decline has affected all employment levels, although to a variable degree from one level to another. In others, fertility has only declined among the urban occupational level and has probably risen among agricultural workers. Of the countries presented as examples in the graphs, Cuba, Chile, and Paraguay are found in the first group, while Honduras is representative of the second; this is consistent with the data on area of residence (Fig. 1.6).

In the three variables analysed, the observed increases in fertility at the beginning of the period under study are attributed to the lower social classes, primarily in rural areas. In Chile, since a more complete data set is available, this phenomenon is more easily observable.

Relative Importance of the Socio-Economic Groups

In the analysis of the fertility differentials connected with fertility transitions, not only the magnitude of the differences and the observed trends are of interest; rather, it is of the utmost importance to consider the relative significance of the groups which have different reproductive behaviours.

For example, the information in Table 1.7 shows the proportion of women of fertile age by the number of completed years of education corresponding to the

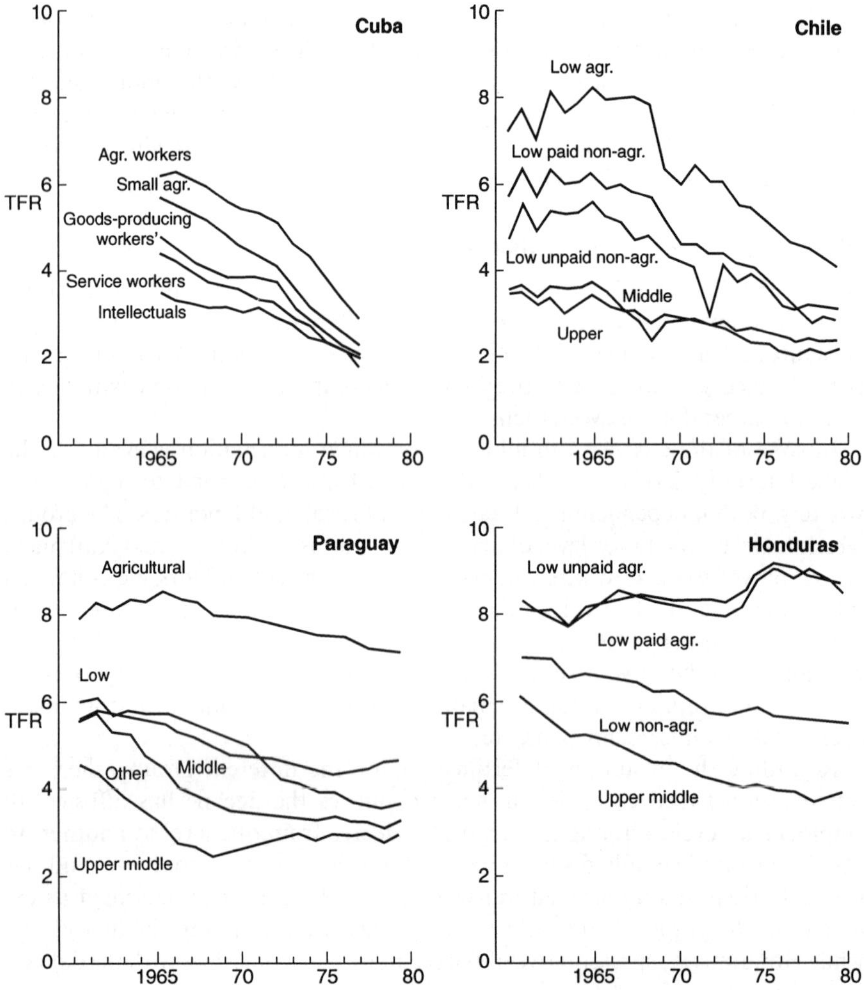

Fig. 1.6. ***Latin America: TFR by occupational group, selected countries 1965–1980***

Source: Table 1.5.

fertility levels in Table 1.5. In Latin America there are still countries in which the proportion of women exposed to greater risks during pregnancy and childbirth, as the result of high fertility and a low level of education, can be astonishingly large, as is the case in Guatemala, where 70 per cent fit this description. In countries like Honduras and Paraguay, the situation is also serious, with more than 45 per cent of women of fertile age characterized as illiterate or functionally illiterate (0–3 years of education) and who at the beginning of the 1980s exhibited fertility rates around 6 or 7 children. The majority of these women also live in rural or semi-rural areas, depending primarily on agricultural work.

Table 1.7. *Latin America: proportion of women, by completed years of schooling and female population under study for countries with information available*

No. of years of schooling and female population studied	Chile 1982	Cuba 1979	Guatemala 1981	Honduras 1983	Panama 1980	Paraguay 1982
Years of schooling						
0–3	11.0	15.5	70.4	47.3	16.6	45.0
4–6	26.1	37.8	16.8	23.0	34.5	35.0
7–9	24.0	43.4	—	—	—	8.0
10+[b]	33.3	3.3[b]	—	—	—	12.0
7+[a]	—	—	12.8	19.6	48.6	—
Unknown	5.6	—	—	0.1	0.3	—
Population studied	15–64	15–49	15–49	15–64	15–49	15–64

Source: IFHIPAL Project, CELADE.

[a] Secondary or higher education, 7 or more years.
[b] University education, 10 or more years.

The high proportion of women with low education levels who live in rural areas in the countries which are farthest behind in their transition, leads to the conclusion that a significant fertility decline in these sectors must occur if lower fertility levels are to be achieved for the whole country within a relatively short time. In any case, the impact which social mobility and the urbanization process has on the population's changing reproductive behaviour cannot be ignored. For the countries that are now advanced in the transition, both phenomena have occurred: fertility has declined in all sectors of the population, but these same countries also have a lower percentage of socially disadvantaged rural population.

The Effect of Fertility Changes on the Number of Births

The data on annual births in Table 1.8 show that, notwithstanding the fertility decline and due to the young age structure of the population, the number of births in Latin America has risen from approximately 7 million to 12 million between 1950–5 and 1985–90. These figures imply a considerable increase in the absolute numbers in the majority of the countries, although in certain periods the number of births appears to have declined.

Cuba, however, stands out as the only country where the decline in fertility has produced a stabilization and, perhaps, a reduction in the number of births. Another country where the rise in fertility has been slight is Uruguay due to its relatively low current fertility rate compared to many years ago combined with an older population and international emigration in recent decades.

In the remaining countries the increase ranges from approximately 50 to 100 per cent.

The fact that the decline in fertility is associated with a younger population has important consequences for the number of births contributed by each age-group of mothers. A displacement of fertility and corresponding births is observed

Table 1.8. *Latin America: Total births and proportion of births by age-group of women in selected quinquennia, by recent fertility level and country*

Recent fertility level and country	Total annual births (in 000s)			Proportion of births by age-group of women[a]					
				Central ages 20–34 years		High-risk ages 15–19 years		35 years and up	
	1950–5	1985–90	1995–2000	1950–5	1985–90	1950–5	1985–90	1950–5	1985–90
Low fertility									
Argentina	458	669	698	75.2	73.7	10.7	13.7	14.1	12.6
Uruguay	49	54	54	75.1	74.7	12.2	13.4	12.7	11.9
Cuba	182	181	181	76.2	70.0	10.4	26.0	13.4	4.0
Chile	239	301	309	70.5	76.6	10.5	13.6	19.0	9.8
Medium low fertility									
Brazil	2,589	4,086	4,121	71.7	77.9	9.3	9.1	19.0	13.0
Colombia	607	861	906	69.1	73.6	13.0	15.3	17.9	11.1
Costa Rica	45	80	82	72.9	74.2	12.4	16.3	14.7	9.5
Ecuador	166	328	360	67.2	70.8	14.5	14.6	18.3	14.6
Mexico	1,407	2,438	2,490	70.8	71.9	12.5	16.2	16.7	11.9
Panama	36	61	63	70.0	73.1	16.7	18.0	13.3	8.9
Dominican Republic	129	213	208	69.0	76.7	16.3	13.6	14.7	9.7
Venezuela	262	569	611	70.3	73.9	15.6	14.4	14.1	11.7
Medium high fertility									
El Salvador	100	182	221	72.2	69.2	15.0	20.3	12.8	10.5
Haiti	141	213	235	66.0	71.2	8.8	8.0	25.5	20.8
Paraguay	69	139	161	71.3	72.2	10.1	11.5	18.6	16.3
Peru	384	721	743	67.2	74.3	13.8	11.5	19.0	14.2
High fertility									
Bolivia	138	293	359	68.8	71.5	10.9	10.6	20.3	17.9
Guatemala	164	350	415	67.8	70.0	17.7	17.1	14.5	12.9
Honduras	78	189	217	67.9	70.2	15.4	16.4	16.7	13.4
Nicaragua	64	149	174	70.0	73.0	15.6	16.8	14.4	10.2

Source: CELADE (1988) and updated projections.

[a] This refers to the ratio of the births at the indicated ages to the total number of births in each country.

from extreme ages to central ages, which corresponds to fewer possible risks to mother and child.

Table 1.8 also shows the proportion of births by different age-groups of women, with the Latin American countries grouped according to their present fertility levels. For this purpose the ages have been classified into three groups: the youngest, aged 15 to 19, or adolescent fertility; women aged 20 to 34 years, which make up the central fertility ages; and those aged 35 and over, or of advanced age for fertility. The first and last groups are those at high risk of morbidity and mortality both for the mother and for the child, and for this reason their behaviour is observed separately.

As expected, the greatest contribution to total fertility in all cases comes from the central ages, between 20 and 34 years. Fertility ranged from between 66 and 76 per cent in 1950–5 to between 69 and 78 per cent in 1985–90, showing that generally there is a greater concentration of fertility in this age-group through time and declines in fertility. The exceptions are Argentina, Uruguay, Cuba, and El Salvador, where, in contrast, a reduction in the percentage of births to women of central ages is observed.

Despite this greater concentration of fertility in central ages, a relatively high proportion of births is attributed to the groups of women who have been classified as having high birth risk, those below age 20 and over age 34. The proportion of all births contributed by these women, which in 1950–5 varied between approximately 25 and 35 per cent, has declined but is still between 25 and 30 per cent in most countries.

Although this difference is not very striking, the higher the level of fertility, the higher the contribution made to total fertility or to total births by the women at the extremes of the range of reproductive ages. Procreation begins very early and lasts beyond first youth, which leads to the formation of larger families. The changes in social and economic factors which favour the decline of fertility affect the younger women since they postpone childbearing, and the older women because they stop bearing children sooner and may already have the number of children they wish.

The high-risk group of women is made up of two very different subgroups. When comparing each of the selected time periods, the contribution of women aged 35 and over was higher than that of the younger group in the majority of cases in 1950–5. The contrary is observed in 1985–90, since the relative contribution of women aged 35 and over to total fertility has diminished considerably with the decline in fertility, independently of the present fertility rate in each country.

Conclusions

The 1950s were characterized by high fertility rates in most Latin American countries. The TFR reached an average of 6 children per woman. Following a period in which there was actually a further rise in fertility in several countries, until the middle of the 1960s, a substantial decrease of the TFR began in the majority of the countries of the region, leading to a regional rate of 3.6 children by 1985–90.

This transition observed in Latin America varies greatly from one country to another. Considering present-day fertility, the countries could be classified into four groups as follows: (1) very advanced transition (TFR < 3): First Argentina and Uruguay (which previously had low rates) and then Cuba and Chile, which underwent sharp declines; (2) advanced transition (3 < TFR < 4.5): Brazil, Colombia, Costa Rica, Ecuador, Mexico, Panama, Peru, Dominican Republic, and Venezuela; (3) intermediate transition (4.5 < TFR < 5.5): El Salvador, Haiti, and Paraguay; (4) beginning transition (TFR > 5.5): Bolivia, Guatemala, Honduras, and Nicaragua.

The declines in fertility show up more clearly in the rates corresponding to women over 30 years of age and those under 20. There is some association between the level of fertility and the age structure of change. A decline in the TFR is accompanied by a rejuvenation of the age structure of the fertility rates. The data indicate that the contribution to total fertility of women 20–29 years of age has increased in all Latin American countries. Because of the associated social problems, the likely current trend of an increase in the level of adolescent fertility is especially worrisome. Even when fertility did not increase, there were other types of change, such as an increase in the number of unwanted pregnancies, a higher incidence of abortion, or an increase in the proportion of women under 20 who gave birth premaritally. However, solid information which would support the claim that this is a generalized process is still lacking.

A country's overall average fertility level often conceals considerable internal variation among subgroups of the population. For this reason, it is particularly interesting to examine behaviour within countries, because the nature and size of the internal differentials is crucial to an understanding of how the transition is proceeding. The fertility transition is much more advanced in urban areas, especially in the large cities, and particularly among the upper and middle classes. In the countries which are farthest along in the transition, there is a certain trend toward stabilization of the TFR in the upper middle and upper class groups, while the lower agricultural classes are beginning to participate in the process of change. Although the transition process is well advanced in urban areas, in the next few years, even greater changes can be anticipated in the rural areas of countries in which the urban sector has reached low fertility levels.

There is invariably an inverse relation between fertility and education, and the differentials are equal to or greater than those observed by place of residence. More educated women clearly have much lower fertility than those without education, in many cases as low as one-third or one-quarter the level.

Finally, the impact of the change in fertility on the evolution of the number of births is evaluated. In spite of the reduction in TFR, the number of births is generally still rising because of the large number of women of fertile age, which is the result of the high birth rates of the past. In any event, it is important to note that, of the total number of births, the proportion to women aged less than 20 and to women aged over 30, for whom the health risks of childbearing are higher than for 20–29-year-olds, is diminishing.

References

ADS (Asociación Demográfica Salvadoreña) (1987), *Encuesta Nacional de Salud Familiar FESAL-85* (San Salvador, El Salvador).

Cayemittes, M., and Chahnazarian, A. (1989), *Survie et santé de l'enfant en Haïti* (Port au Prince: Institut Haïtien de l'Enfance).

CCRP (Corporación Centro Regional de Población) Ministerio de Salud de Colombia, and IRD (1988), *Colombia: Tercera Encuesta Nacional de Prevalencia del Uso de Anticonceptivos y Primera de Demografia y Salud 1986* (Bogotá, Colombia).

CELADE (1986), *Fecundidad: Differenciales geográficos y socio-económicos de la fecundidad, 1960–1983. EDENH II y otras fuentes* (vol. 4, Series A, No. 1047/iv; San José, Costa Rica: Encuesta Demográfica Nacional de Honduras).

—— (1988), *Demographic Bulletin No. 41* (Year 21) (Santiago, Chile).

—— (1990), *Demographic Bulletin No. 45* (Year 23) (Santiago, Chile).

CEPAR (Centro de Estudios de Población y Paternidad Responsable), Instituto Nacional de Investigaciones Nutricionales y Médico Sociales, and IRD (1988), *Ecuador: Encuesta Demográfica y de Salud Familiar, 1987* (Quito, Ecuador).

Chile (Instituto Nacional de Estadísticas) and CELADE (1988), *La Transición de la Fecundidad en Chile: Un Análisis por Grupos Socioeconómicos y Areas geográficas 1950–1985* (Santiago, Chile).

Comité Estatal de Estadísticas (1987), *Anuario Demográfico de Cuba 1985* (Havana).

CONAPO (Consejo Nacional de Población y Familia) and IRD (1987), *República Dominicana: Encuesta Demográfica y de Salud, DHS-1986* (S. Domingo, Dominican Republic).

Cuba (Comité Estatal de Estadísticas) and CELADE (1981), *Cuba: El Descenso de la Fecundidad 1964–1978* (San José, Costa Rica).

DHS (1989), *Newsletter* (Winter).

Ferrando, D., Singh, S., and Wulf, D. (1989), *Adolescentes de Hoy, Padres del Mañana: Perú* (New York: Alan Guttmacher Institute).

FPATT (Family Planning Association of Trinidad and Tobago) and IRD (1988), *Trinidad and Tobago Demographic and Health Survey 1987* (Columbia, Md.).

Guatemala (Direccíon General de Estadística) and CELADE (1984), *Guatemala: Las Diferencias Socio-económicas de la Fecundidad, 1959–1980* (Series A, No. 1045; San José, Costa Rica).

Henriques, M. E., Silva, N., Singh, S., and Wulf, D. (1989), *Adolescentes de Hoje, Pais do Amanha: Brasil* (New York: Alan Guttmacher Institute).

INE (Instituto Nacional de Estadística) and IRD (1988), *Encuesta Demográfica y de Salud Familiar (ENDES 1986): Informe General* (Lima, Peru).

Panama (Ministerio de Planificación y Politíca Económica) and CELADE (1984), *Panamá: El Descenso de la Fecundidad según Variables Socio-económicas y Geográficas, 1965–1977* (Series A, No. 1046; San José, Costa Rica).

Paraguay (Dirección General de Estadística) and Censo and CELADE (1988), *Paraguay: Diferenciales Geográficos y Socioeconómicos de la Fecundidad, 1960–1979* (Asunción, Paraguay).

United Nations (1987), *Fertility Behaviour in the Context of Development: Evidence from the World Fertility Survey* (ST/ESA/SER. A. 100, New York).

Wulf, D. (1986), 'Embarazo y Alumbramiento en la Adolescencia en América Latina y el Caribe: una Conferencia Memorable', *Perspectivas Internacionales en Planificación Familiar* (Special Issue).

2 The Spacing and Limiting Components of the Fertility Transition in Latin America

GERMÁN RODRÍGUEZ

Introduction

In this chapter we present the results of an analysis of trends in marital fertility within categories of key socio-economic factors using data from six Latin American countries: Colombia, Dominican Republic, Ecuador, Mexico, Peru, and Trinidad and Tobago. These countries were selected for analysis because they have completed high quality surveys for two points in time, as part of the WFS and the DHS programmes. Our analysis of trends and differentials builds upon earlier work on all WFS countries by Rodríguez and Cleland (1987).

The focus of our analysis is on marital fertility—or more precisely, fertility following first union—rather than overall fertility. This choice reflects our view that an essential feature of the fertility transition is a change in childbearing within marriage, which in turn results from changes in spacing and limiting fertility behaviours. This is not to deny the fact that part of the observed decline in fertility in the region is due to rising ages at marriage, nor the fact that women in higher social strata tend to marry at later ages than women in lower strata. It turns out, however, that the effect of changes in age at marriage on fertility is relatively modest, compared to the magnitude of changes in marital fertility.

The socio-economic factors selected for analysis are three: type of place of residence, wife's education, and husband's occupation. These factors proved to be the three most important socio-economic determinants of marital fertility in our earlier analyses of WFS data, which considered in addition husband's education and husband's and wife's work status. The two work-status variables could not be included in the present study because they cannot be constructed from the information collected in the DHS. As regards husband's education, previous work has found that it adds rather little explanatory power to wife's education, so its introduction would be rather repetitious at this point.

Our main methodological tool is a model of the period marital fertility of individual women. The model has been extensively used with individual and aggregate WFS data (Rodríguez and Cleland 1987, 1988), and quite recently with aggregate DHS data (Moreno 1990). This chapter represents its first application to individual level DHS data. The model expresses fertility in terms of a spacing component, which is assumed to operate equally at all union durations, and a limiting component, which assumes greater importance with increasing duration of union. The model permits succinct description of both levels and patterns of marital fertility and yields parameters which may be interpreted in terms of underlying behavioural mechanisms such as breast-feeding and contraception.

The results of our analysis reveal the presence of remarkable regularities in the process of fertility transition in the six countries analysed, in spite of their diversity. In all social strata where fertility has started to decline the indices of spacing and limiting seem to have followed the same broad but well-defined paths over time, a feature which allows us to discern general patterns as well as highlight interesting exceptions. The general trends are consistent with a simple process of social diffusion, where the notion of fertility control not only trickles down from one stratum to the next, but once it has reached any stratum it appears to spread at a rate roughly proportional to the number of controllers.

Data and Methodology

In this section we comment briefly on our sources of data, definition of variables, choice of statistical model and selection of summary indicators. The general methodological strategy adopted in this study follows closely the approach developed in earlier work with Cleland, which should be consulted for further details (see Rodríguez and Cleland 1980, 1987, 1988; Cleland and Rodríguez 1988).

The Data

The data for this study come for the six countries in the Latin American region which have successfully completed fertility surveys as part of the WFS and the DHS programmes. The WFS surveys were conducted in the mid- to late 1970s, whereas the DHS surveys were done in the mid- to late 1980s, so we are able to study fertility change over a recent ten-year period. (The years in which the surveys were conducted are listed in Table 2.1.) The primary respondents in both types of surveys were women in the reproductive ages (usually between 15 and 49) selected irrespective of marital status.[1] Since we are interested in fertility following first union, we extracted the data for ever-married women only. The resulting sample sizes for the surveys considered here vary between 2,923 and 6,056 women.

Both the WFS and DHS programmes developed a standardized questionnaire which was used with minor changes in all participating countries. The WFS core questionnaire included complete birth and marriage histories, together with information on proximate determinants of fertility such as breast-feeding and contraception, and on socio-economic factors affecting fertility, such as place of

[1] The standard WFS survey was based on a sample of ever-married women, but all Latin American surveys are based on all-women samples.

Table 2.1. ***Latin America: National level estimates of age at union, indices of spacing and limiting, and equivalent Total Marital Fertility***

Country	Survey	Years	Age at union[a]	Indices		TMFR
				α	β	
Colombia	WFS	1976	19.8	30	34	5.5
	DHS	1986	20.2	39	48	3.9
Dominican Republic	WFS	1975	18.1	32	25	6.5
	DHS	1986	18.5	32	47	4.6
Ecuador	WFS	1979	19.5	34	22	6.1
	DHS	1987	19.8	35	38	4.8
Mexico	WFS	1977	19.2	26	21	7.1
	DHS	1986	19.7	34	40	4.9
Peru	WFS	1977	19.9	27	22	6.7
	DHS	1986	20.4	38	29	5.1
Trinidad and Tobago	WFS	1977	18.7	53	35	3.8
	DHS	1987	19.6	49	46	3.4

[a] Mean age at union of women first married in the twenty years before each survey.

residence, education, and employment. The DHS basic questionnaire covers essentially the same topics, but did not collect a complete marriage history; the information on marriage is limited to current marital status and date of first marriage. In addition, the DHS surveys used a different set of questions on husband's and wife's employment, which no longer permits distinguishing work for family, self, or others.

The dependent variable is defined for each woman who has ever been in a union, as the number of births in the five years preceding the interview which occurred after the date of first union. The decision to focus our attention on the five years preceding the interview (more precisely, the period from one to sixty months before the interview, excluding the month of interview itself) represents a compromise between our wish to have a sharp focus on fertility near the date of each survey and the need to keep variation due to sampling and response errors within reasonable bounds. The focus on births following first union rather than *within* a union avoids the need to classify each birth in relation to the dates of marriage formation and dissolution. This task could not be done with the DHS, which did not collect marriage histories, and even if it could be accomplished—as is the case for the WFS—would place excessive reliance on stated dates of births and marriages.

The explanatory variables include two demographic controls and three socio-economic factors. The demographic controls are age at and duration since first union, both of them measured in years as of the mid-point of the reference period for each individual woman. The difference between these two variables is age at marriage, which is thus implicitly taken into account in our modelling. The socio-economic factors are all treated as discrete or categorical variables, and include residence, wife's education, and husband's occupation.

The measurement of residence is somewhat problematic because no attempt was made in either survey programme to standardize the basic distinction between urban and rural communities. In both cases participating countries used their own classification, based on population size, the presence of amenities or some mixture of such criteria. Some comparability was imposed, however, by subdividing the urban sector into two components representing metropolitan and other urban areas, according to a set of objective rules developed by Lightbourne (1980). Under this scheme, national capital cities, the largest city in each country, and all cities with a population of one million or more, are included as metropolitan. In order to maintain comparability between the two surveys we applied these criteria as of the time of the earlier survey. For example in Colombia the metropolitan areas include Bogotá and Medellín, which met the criteria at the time of the WFS, but not Cali, which has now grown past the one million mark. An exception to this general rule is Mexico, where the metropolitan sector includes cities of half a million or more at the time of the respective survey. Details of the cities defined as metropolitan for each country may be found in Table 2.2.

Educational attainment was measured identically in the two survey programmes: a question on the highest educational level attained was followed by a question on the number of grades or years completed at that level. From this information one may derive the total number of years of schooling, which may then be used in grouped or ungrouped form in the analysis. To maintain consistency with our earlier work we have represented educational level using four categories based more closely on the level of schooling reached: none, incomplete primary, complete primary, and secondary or higher. We believe that this classification has greater substantive meaning than one based solely on years of schooling, because it captures critical educational transitions and seems to be more directly related to employment prospects and socio-economic status. This notion was tempered, however, by sample size considerations, which sometimes dictated a compromise. The number of years of primary schooling included in the complete primary category for each country is given in Table 2.3.

The current or most recent occupation of the current or last husband of the respondent was recorded in both the WFS and DHS using a standardized set of ten categories. In our earlier work we recoded this variable using four categories. The professional, technical, administrative, and clerical workers were collapsed to form a single professional and technical group. The more heterogeneous sales and services were combined in a single category, as were the skilled and unskilled manual workers. This left as a fourth category those engaged in agriculture, forestry, and fishing. Because of the standardized coding of occupation in both survey programmes, we had no practical problems of definition. We had, however, two problems regarding data availability. In Trinidad and Tobago, the question on occupation of most recent husband was asked only of currently married women. In Mexico the question was apparently asked of all women, but does not appear to have been coded in the standard recode file released for analysis. We therefore decided to omit these two countries from the analyses involving husband's occupation.

Table 2.2. *Latin America: distribution of exposure, estimates of age at union, indices of spacing and limiting, and equivalent Total Marital Fertility, by type of place of residence*

Country	Survey	Exposure			Age at union			Index α			Index β			TMFR		
		R	U	M	R	U	M	R	U	M	R	U	M	R	U	M
Colombia	WFS	36	47	17	19.1	19.9	20.9	22	33	25	20	44	62	7.7	4.6	3.8
	DHS	30	46	24	19.7	20.1	21.1	31	39	38	34	54	66	5.5	3.5	2.9
Dominican Republic	WFS	45	25	31	17.6	18.5	18.3	25	30	37	15	40	37	8.2	5.3	5.1
	DHS	36	34	29	17.8	18.7	19.0	29	33	28	36	54	61	5.8	4.1	3.8
Ecuador	WFS	52	23	24	19.3	19.3	20.1	30	31	37	14	30	51	7.3	5.8	3.9
	DHS	44	27	30	19.3	20.0	20.1	34	35	32	26	46	58	5.9	4.3	3.7
Mexico	WFS	42	31	27	18.4	19.4	20.2	21	29	24	15	22	38	8.4	6.6	5.7
	DHS	30	42	29	18.4	19.9	20.6	27	33	30	25	47	62	6.9	4.4	3.5
Peru	WFS	36	38	26	19.4	19.9	20.6	25	26	22	11	26	46	8.1	6.5	5.1
	DHS	36	35	29	19.3	20.7	21.3	34	32	38	9	47	55	7.3	4.3	3.4
Trinidad and Tobago	WFS	40	24	36	18.4	18.7	19.1	45	52	60	35	37	35	4.4	3.8	3.2
	DHS	54	5	42	19.6	19.1	19.7	44	48	56	49	43	43	3.6	3.7	3.1

Notes: Categories of residence: R = Rural, U = Urban, M = Metropolitan. Metropolitan areas are Bogotá and Medellín in Colombia; Santo Domingo in the Dominican Republic; Quito and Guayaquil in Ecuador; cities with over half a million inhabitants in Mexico; Lima in Peru; and Port of Spain in Trinidad and Tobago.

Table 2.3. *Latin America: Distribution of exposure, estimates of age at union, indices of spacing and limiting, and equivalent Total Marital Fertility, by women's educational level*

Country	Survey	Exposure				Age at union				Index α				Index β				TMFR			
		N	IP	CP	S+	N	IP	CP	S+	N	IP	CP	S+	N	IP	CP	S+	N	IP	CP	S+
Colombia	WFS	18	48	16	18	19.3	19.5	20.1	20.5	15	26	31	27	31	31	52	67	7.2	6.2	4.2	3.4
	DHS	10	41	17	32	18.9	19.9	20.2	20.8	11	37	25	35	44	42	67	69	6.3	4.5	3.5	2.9
Dominican	WFS	17	61	15	8	17.9	17.6	18.4	21.2	27	29	25	33	23	23	49	63	7.1	7.0	4.9	3.3
Republic	DHS	8	49	20	22	16.8	17.6	18.2	20.6	30	29	24	26	35	46	60	67	6.0	5.1	4.2	3.4
Ecuador	WFS	15	40	21	24	19.3	18.8	19.3	20.6	31	27	23	25	10	17	45	69	7.6	7.5	5.3	3.3
	DHS	11	31	25	33	19.5	19.2	19.3	20.6	37	26	32	26	17	34	48	67	6.3	6.0	4.5	3.4
Mexico	WFS	24	47	13	15	18.1	18.7	19.6	21.3	23	18	15	25	15	23	46	55	8.3	7.8	5.6	4.1
	DHS	17	34	24	25	18.5	18.9	20.2	20.6	32	21	23	25	23	40	63	70	6.5	6.0	3.9	3.3
Peru	WFS	33	29	17	22	19.6	19.0	19.8	21.4	27	19	17	14	10	26	45	61	7.8	7.3	5.6	4.3
	DHS	16	29	17	38	19.7	19.3	19.9	21.4	32	28	23	24	9	29	49	67	7.3	6.2	4.9	3.4
Trinidad and	WFS	4	37	28	31	17.3	18.1	18.5	19.5	19	39	45	61	42	41	43	40	6.1	4.6	4.0	2.9
Tobago	DHS	1	23	34	42	19.3	19.0	19.5	19.9	48	32	43	55	47	56	50	41	3.4	4.0	3.6	3.2

Notes: Categories of education: N = None, IP = Incomplete Primary, CP = Complete Primary, and S+ = Secondary or higher. The number of years classified as complete primary is 5 in Colombia, 6–8 in the Dominican Republic, 6 in Ecuador and Mexico, 5 in Peru, and 6–7 in Trinidad and Tobago.

The Statistical Model

The basic statistical model used in the analysis is a form of Poisson regression analysis which treats the number of births to each woman in the reference period as the dependent variable of interest. Let B_i denote the number of births for the i-th woman in the sample. We assume that B_i can be treated as a realization of a Poisson random variable with expected value equal to the product of exposure time E_i and a theoretical fertility rate $f(a_i, d_i, \mathbf{x}_i)$ which depends on the woman's characteristics, specifically on her age a_i, duration since first union d_i, and socio-economic attributes $\mathbf{x}_i$. Thus

$$E(B_i) = f(a_i, d_i, \mathbf{x}_i)\, E_i \tag{1}$$

To model fertility as a function of age and duration we adopt a formulation first proposed by Page (1977). In this model it is assumed that in the absence of deliberate parity-specific fertility limitation, marital fertility would follow a typical age pattern described by Henry (1961) and termed natural fertility.[2] In addition, the model assumes that deliberate parity-specific limitation of fertility causes a pattern of increasing departure from natural fertility as a function of duration since first marriage, which can be modelled as an exponential. Note that Coale (1971) proposed a closely related model, but assumed that fertility limitation was a function of age rather than duration of marriage. A similar notion, but with limiting behaviour depending explicitly on a schedule intended to represent the number of surviving children, may be found in Espenshade (1971).

In our work the marital fertility rate at any given age a_i and duration since first union d_i for someone with characteristics $\mathbf{x}_i$, will be modelled as

$$f(a_i, d_i, \mathbf{x}_i) = n(a_i)\, exp\{\alpha(\mathbf{x}_i) + \beta(\mathbf{x}_i)\, d_i\} \tag{2}$$

where $n(a_i)$ represents the age pattern of natural fertility, $\alpha(\mathbf{x}_i)$ is a parameter representing the level of natural fertility and $\beta(\mathbf{x}_i)$ is a parameter representing the degree of fertility limitation, or the extent to which marital fertility departs from natural fertility with increasing union duration. Note that both the spacing and limiting parameters are allowed to depend on individual level characteristics. This dependence may be expressed in quite general terms using a linear model, so that

$$\alpha(\mathbf{x}_i) = \mathbf{x}_i{}'\theta_\alpha \text{ and } \beta(\mathbf{x}_i) = \mathbf{x}_i{}'\theta_\beta \tag{3}$$

where θ_α and θ_β are vectors of regression coefficients. In this chapter we will consider only models involving the two demographic controls and one of the socio-economic factors at a time, so in effect we simply let the two parameters vary freely across categories of the explanatory variable of interest.

2 Henry used the term control to refer to departures from natural fertility caused by parity-specific behaviour, distinguishing it carefully from spacing practices which affect fertility at all birth orders. Most demographers, however, use the term control to refer to both spacing and limiting behaviours. In this chapter we will adhere to the latter usage.

Combining equations (1) to (3), we see that the birth counts B_i follow a log-linear Poisson regression model, with

$$log(E(B_i)) = log(E_i) + log(n(a_i)) + \mathbf{x}_i'\theta_\alpha + \mathbf{x}_i'\theta_\beta d_i \qquad (4)$$

The linear predictor includes an offset or known part equal to the log of exposure time plus the log of natural fertility, and a covariance-analysis type of model with main effects of the covariates, representing their effects on the spacing parameter, and interactions between duration and the covariates, representing the effects of individual characteristics on the control parameter. The resulting model belongs to the family of generalized linear models of Nelder and Wedderburn (1972), and therefore it can easily be fitted using the computer programme GLIM (Payne 1988). All calculations in this chapter, including maximum likelihood estimation of the parameters of the model and likelihood ratio tests of the significance of various effects, were performed using this package.

Fertility Indices

In presenting the results we have found it convenient to re-express the estimated values of the parameters α and β in terms of an index of spacing I_α and an index of fertility limitation I_β. The index of spacing is defined by re-expressing α as a per cent reduction from maximum possible natural fertility, which following Bongaarts (1982) is taken to be 15.3 births. Thus, a value of I_α of 0.20 means that the level of natural fertility is 20 per cent below the maximum; in the absence of fertility limitation this level would result in $0.8 \times 15.3 = 12.4$ births. Rodríguez and Cleland (1988) have shown that this index is affected by spacing factors, such as mean duration of breast-feeding and use of contraception for spacing purposes.

The index of fertility limitation I_β is defined as the per cent reduction in marital fertility after ten years of marriage, net of age. Thus, a value of I_β of 0.20 means that after ten years of marriage, deliberate parity-specific limiting behaviour has reduced fertility by 20 per cent relative to natural fertility at the age at which that union duration is attained. Rodríguez and Cleland (1988) show that this index is affected by contraceptive use for family limitation and induced abortion.

A final point concerning presentation of results: we have combined the estimated values of α and β (or equivalently the indices I_α and I_β) with a measure of mean age at union μ, to produce an estimate of total marital fertility. Previous work showed that we could get a very good fit to observed total marital fertility if we estimated μ using the mean age at marriage of women who started their first union in the twenty years preceding the survey. The constructed rate turns out to be extremely close to the conventional total marital fertility rate accumulated by marriage duration (see Rodríguez and Cleland 1988, and Moreno 1991).

The Fertility Transition

We start the presentation of our results with a brief overview of national level estimates, followed by a more detailed look at the fertility transition within social strata.

National Estimates

Table 2.1 shows the results of fitting our model to individual data from the six countries using only age and marriage duration as predictors, thus obtaining national level estimates of the spacing and limiting components of fertility. The same results are depicted graphically in Fig. 2.1.

Total marital fertility has declined in the recent past in all six countries. The magnitude of the decline ranges from a modest 0.4 births in Trinidad to 2.2 births per woman in Mexico. The cross-sectional mean age at first union has increased by a year in Trinidad and half a year elsewhere, but the changes are not large enough to have a perceptible impact on marital fertility.

Somewhat surprisingly, the index of spacing has increased in Mexico, Peru,

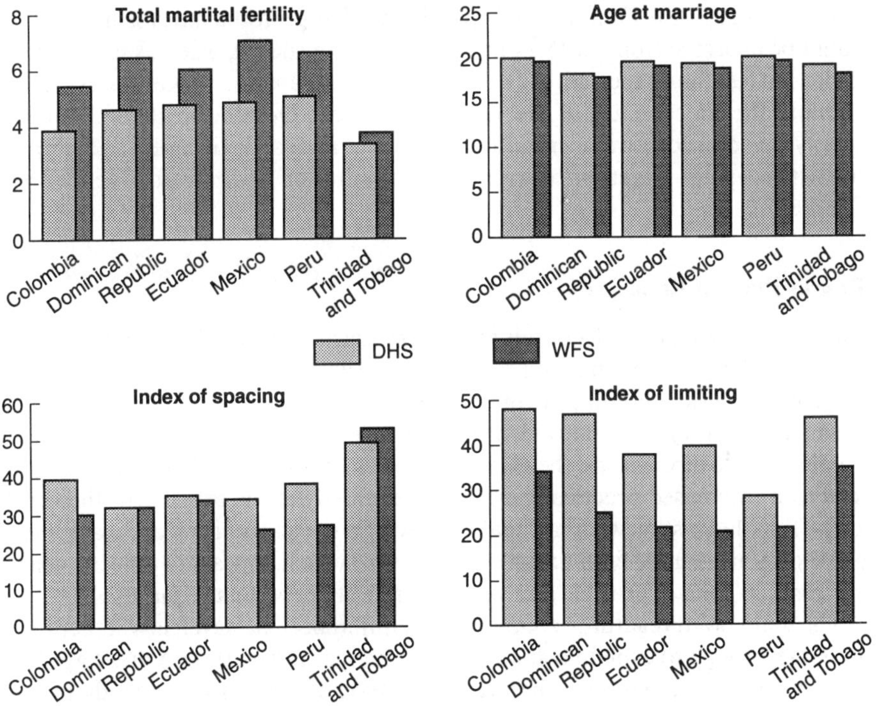

Fig. 2.1. *Latin America and the Caribbean: national level estimates of total marital fertility, age at marriage, and indices of spacing and limiting, selected countries*

Source: WFS 1975–8 and DHS, 1986–7.

and Colombia, reflecting a decline in levels of natural fertility. Part of the explanation may be found in the fact that the mean duration of breast-feeding appears to be increasing over time, Moreno and Singh (Chapter 6), but contraceptive use for spacing purposes probably plays a more important role. The very high level of the spacing parameter in Trinidad and Tobago stands out. We believe that the explanation may lie in the somewhat different nature of unions in Trinidad, where a high incidence of visiting relationships may result in reduced exposure to risk at all union durations.

The extent to which the fertility transition in Latin America is driven by an increased in parity-specific attempts to limit marital fertility is documented by the index of limiting, which has increased in all countries. The increase is quite striking in the Dominican Republic; the fertility of women ten years after their first union is nearly half the level of natural fertility. Next in the ranking of increases in limiting behaviour are Mexico and Ecuador, followed by Colombia and Trinidad. The smallest absolute increase in the limiting index is found in Peru, where the gain is only seven points.

The changes in limiting practices as captured by I_β match reasonably well increases in contraceptive use (see for example Chapter 6), with two exceptions worth noting. In the Dominican Republic the change in the index is more than would be expected from an 18-point increase in prevalence, whereas in Peru it is somewhat less than expected. We believe that the explanation in both cases can be found in the effectiveness of the methods used: the Dominican Republic relies heavily on contraceptive sterilization whereas in Peru a significant—and apparently increasing—fraction of women use rhythm or periodic abstinence (see Chapter 8).

Type of Place of Residence

Table 2.2. shows the results of our analysis of marital fertility by type of place of residence. The more interesting results concerning marital fertility and the indices of spacing and limiting are presented in Fig. 2.2. The first set of numbers following the country and survey identification in Table 2.2. gives the distribution of weighted exposure among the three categories of residence. The metropolitan sector has increased practically everywhere, mostly at the expense of the rural areas. Trinidad is somewhat unusual in showing a net gain of rural areas at the expense of non-metropolitan urban areas; a result which appears to reflect a genuine trend, in spite of possible lack of comparability between the surveys.[3]

The main point regarding compositional differences, however, is whether they are large enough to explain overall fertility change. To test this point we applied the distribution of exposure observed at the time of the DHS to the indices and

[3] The DHS report defines urban as Port of Spain; St George county; and the boroughs of San Fernando, Arima, and Pt. Fortin, and goes on to note that the urban percentage declined from 49 in the 1980 Census to 44 in the 1987 DHS (DHS and FPATT, 1987: 7). Regrettably, the WFS report does not define urban areas.

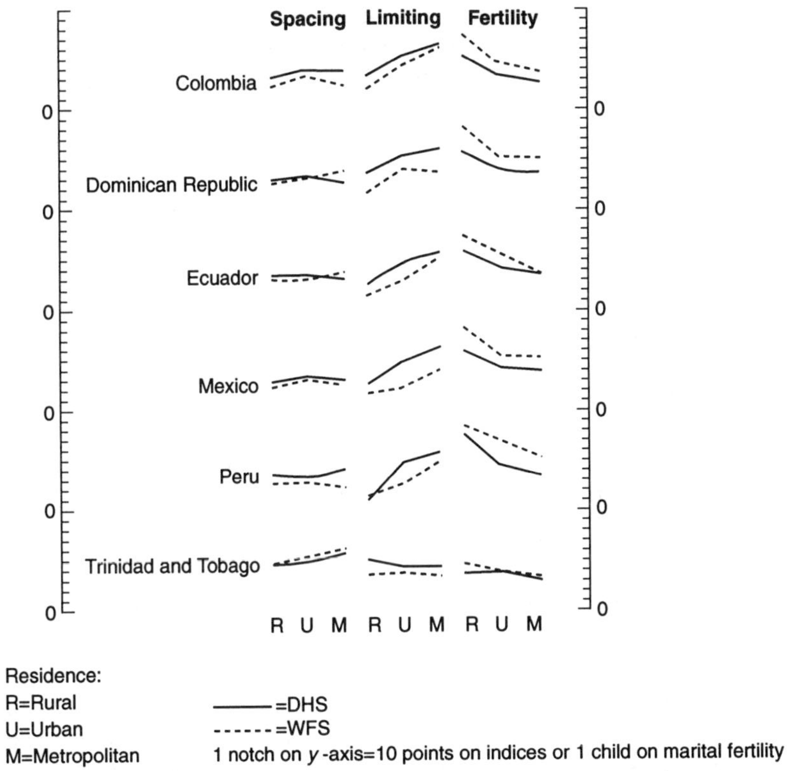

Fig. 2.2. ***Latin America and the Caribbean: indices of spacing and limiting and total marital fertility by type of place of residence***
Sources: WFS and DHS

rates observed at the time of the WFS. We found that compositional differences explain less than 15 per cent of the observed fertility decline, except in Trinidad where the trend away from urban areas would not explain a fertility decline at all. Clearly, the more interesting story lies in behavioural changes within the residence strata.

The remaining columns of Table 2.2 report cross-sectional mean ages at first union, estimates of the indices of spacing and limiting, and the implied total marital fertility rates. The first thing to notice is that marital fertility has declined over time for all strata in the six study populations. The largest decline is 2.5 births in rural Dominican Republic, the tiniest is one-tenth of a birth in urban Trinidad. In Mexico and Peru, which started from the highest levels of fertility, the decline has been more pronounced in the urban and metropolitan areas. As a result, these two countries have become more heterogeneous over time. In the other four countries, which are more advanced in their transitions, the largest declines occurred in rural areas. As a consequence, the urban–rural gap has been reduced and the countries are becoming more homogeneous. These results are consistent with a view of the fertility transition as a process which begins in the largest cities and gradually spreads to smaller towns and rural areas.

The changes just noted appear to be a direct consequence of trends in fertility limitation. The limiting index has increased over time in all strata except rural Peru. In Mexico and Peru the largest changes are found in the metropolitan or other urban areas. In all other countries the rural areas show significant—if not the largest—increases in fertility limitation. The one exception to this rule appears to be the Dominican Republic, where both Santo Domingo and the rural areas exhibit large increases. Changes in the spacing parameter are more modest in magnitude. Two different situations are apparent. The Dominican Republic and Trinidad, and to a lesser extent Ecuador, show little overall change and a hint of decreased spacing in the metropolitan sector. In contrast, Colombia and Peru, and to a lesser extent Mexico, show increased spacing in all strata, particularly the metropolitan areas. The latter result, however, is consistent with the notion that contraceptive use for spacing purposes may well increase as countries move along the process of transition.

Wife's Education

Table 2.3 presents the results by wife's education, classified into four strata: no education, incomplete and complete primary, and secondary or higher. Changes in marital fertility and its components are summarized in Fig. 2.3. All six study populations have experienced considerable gains in education in the recent past, with notable increases in the proportion who complete primary education or go on to secondary school. These compositional changes have undoubtedly contributed to lower the overall level of fertility, but once again the most significant changes have occurred within the educational strata.

Marital fertility has declined in practically all countries and educational groups with a few exceptions among some of the more highly educated, which had already achieved low levels of fertility at the time of the WFS. Typically the decline has been largest in the incomplete primary group, intermediate in the no education and complete primary, and lowest in the secondary or higher. These patterns are matched quite closely by changes in the limiting index, which has increased most for the incomplete primary group. The index of spacing shows no immediately apparent patterns, with some strata exhibiting modest increases and some moderate declines.

Husband's Occupation

The last factor to be considered here is husband's occupation, classified in four categories: agricultural, manual, sales and services, and professional and technical. As noted in the section on methodology, data problems have forced us to exclude Mexico and Trinidad and Tobago from this analysis. Results appear in Table 2.4 and Fig. 2.4. The changes over time in occupational distributions are not unrelated to the urbanization trends noted earlier: the agricultural sector has

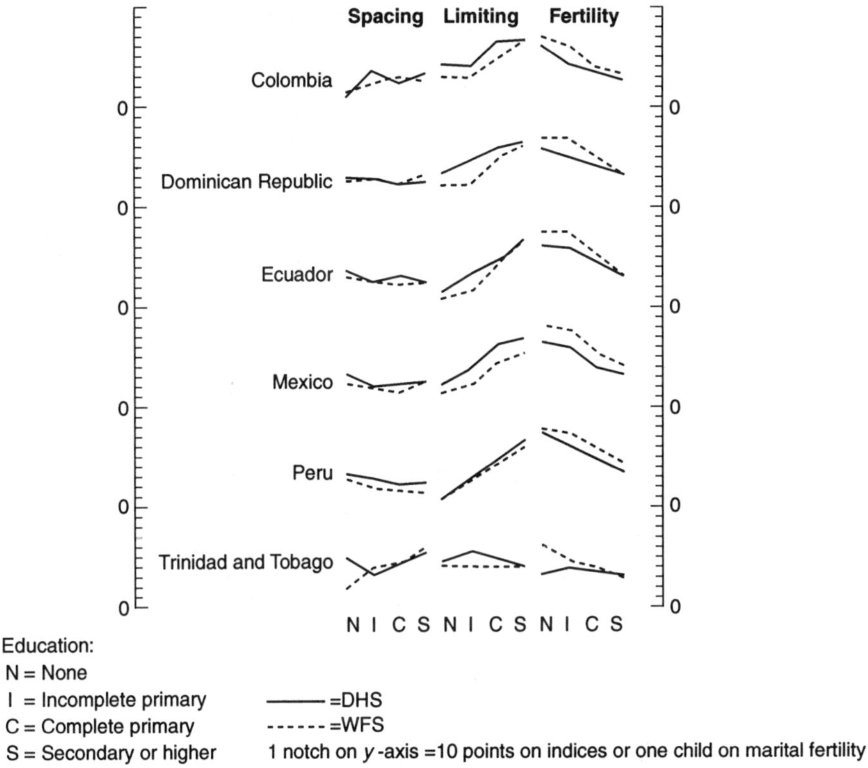

Fig. 2.3. ***Latin America and the Caribbean: indices of spacing and limiting and total marital fertility by wife's level of education, selected countries***
Sources: WFS and DHS

typically lost population; except in Ecuador where it may have increased slightly at the expense of manual workers. The large gain of white-collar occupations in the Dominican Republic is quite exceptional.

The figures in Table 2.4 tell a now familiar story. Total marital fertility has declined in the four occupational strata for the four study populations. In Colombia, the Dominican Republic, and Ecuador the reduction in fertility is largest for the agricultural sector and tends to become smaller as one moves up the occupational scale. As a result, the occupational strata in these three countries have become more homogeneous over time. In Peru the agricultural sector shows little change, but we find some evidence of declining fertility in all other occupational groups. The net result of this trend has been to make Peruvian society somewhat more heterogeneous than it was before. Again, the evidence is consistent with the notion that fertility decline is progressing from higher to lower strata.

The explanation for these changes lies mostly but not entirely in the limitation of fertility. Note first that the limiting index has increased nearly everywhere. In fact, in Colombia, the Dominican Republic, and Ecuador, the fertility decline

Table 2.4. Latin America: Distribution of exposure, estimates of age at union, indices of spacing and limiting, and equivalent Total Marital Fertility, by husband's occupation

Country	Survey	Exposure				Age at union				Index α				Index β				TMFR			
		A	M	S	P	A	M	S	P	A	M	S	P	A	M	S	P	A	M	S	P
Colombia	WFS	38	35	17	10	19.3	20.2	19.6	20.6	19	30	33	32	24	46	46	64	7.4	4.6	4.5	3.3
	DHS	29	38	21	12	19.7	20.3	20.1	21.2	34	33	38	45	32	58	60	65	5.4	3.7	3.3	2.6
Dominican	WFS	41	33	19	8	17.7	17.9	18.7	19.1	25	30	30	33	16	36	38	59	8.2	5.7	5.4	3.7
Republic	DHS	31	25	31	14	17.7	18.3	18.3	20.5	33	31	24	28	34	50	59	65	5.6	4.5	4.2	3.4
Ecuador	WFS	38	34	15	14	18.9	19.2	20.0	20.9	26	36	32	33	16	22	37	60	7.7	6.1	5.1	3.4
	DHS	40	28	15	17	19.4	19.4	19.5	21.2	35	33	28	36	30	39	48	60	5.5	5.0	4.7	3.3
Peru	WFS	41	29	15	16	19.4	19.5	20.2	21.6	25	23	28	18	13	28	33	56	7.9	6.7	5.7	4.5
	DHS	33	32	16	18	19.5	20.0	20.4	22.3	31	35	33	34	12	40	51	59	7.2	4.7	4.1	3.4

Notes: Categories of husband's occupation are: A = Agricultural; M = Manual (skilled and unskilled); S = Sales and Services; and P = Professional, Technical, and Clerical. Data on husband's occupation are not available for Mexico, and were collected only for women currently in union in Trinidad and Tobago.

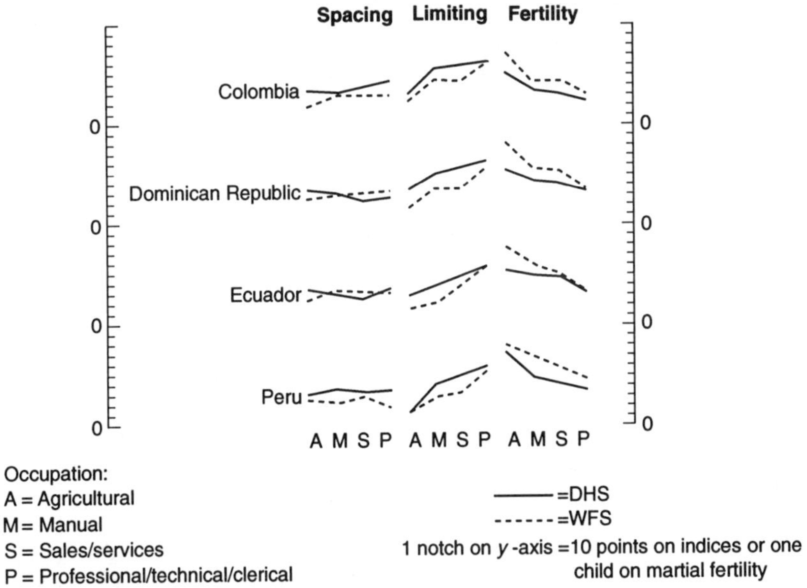

Fig. 2.4. ***Latin America: indices of spacing and limiting and total marital fertility by husband's occupation***
Sources: WFS and DHS

among manual workers is entirely due to increased limiting behaviour. The same is true for the decline among agricultural workers in the Dominican Republic, which is the largest decline of all fifty-eight strata considered in this study. In contrast, the fertility decline in the agricultural sector of Colombia has been aided by increases in spacing as well as limiting practices.

The Diffusion Within Strata

Examination of the results in Tables 2.2–4 suggests that the largest changes have generally occurred in the strata which started from low values of the spacing and limiting indices. To further explore this notion we plotted in Fig. 2.5 the percentage increase in each of the two indices and the percentage decrease in total marital fertility versus their baseline levels, for strata defined by each of the three socio-economic factors in turn.

The Spread of Spacing

The first row of plots in Fig. 2.5 shows the results for the index of spacing. These plots exclude Trinidad and Tobago, which had values of I_α substantially higher than all other study populations. The results by type of place of residence indicate that the strata starting from low levels of spacing experienced the largest proportionate increases, whereas those starting from very high levels actually had

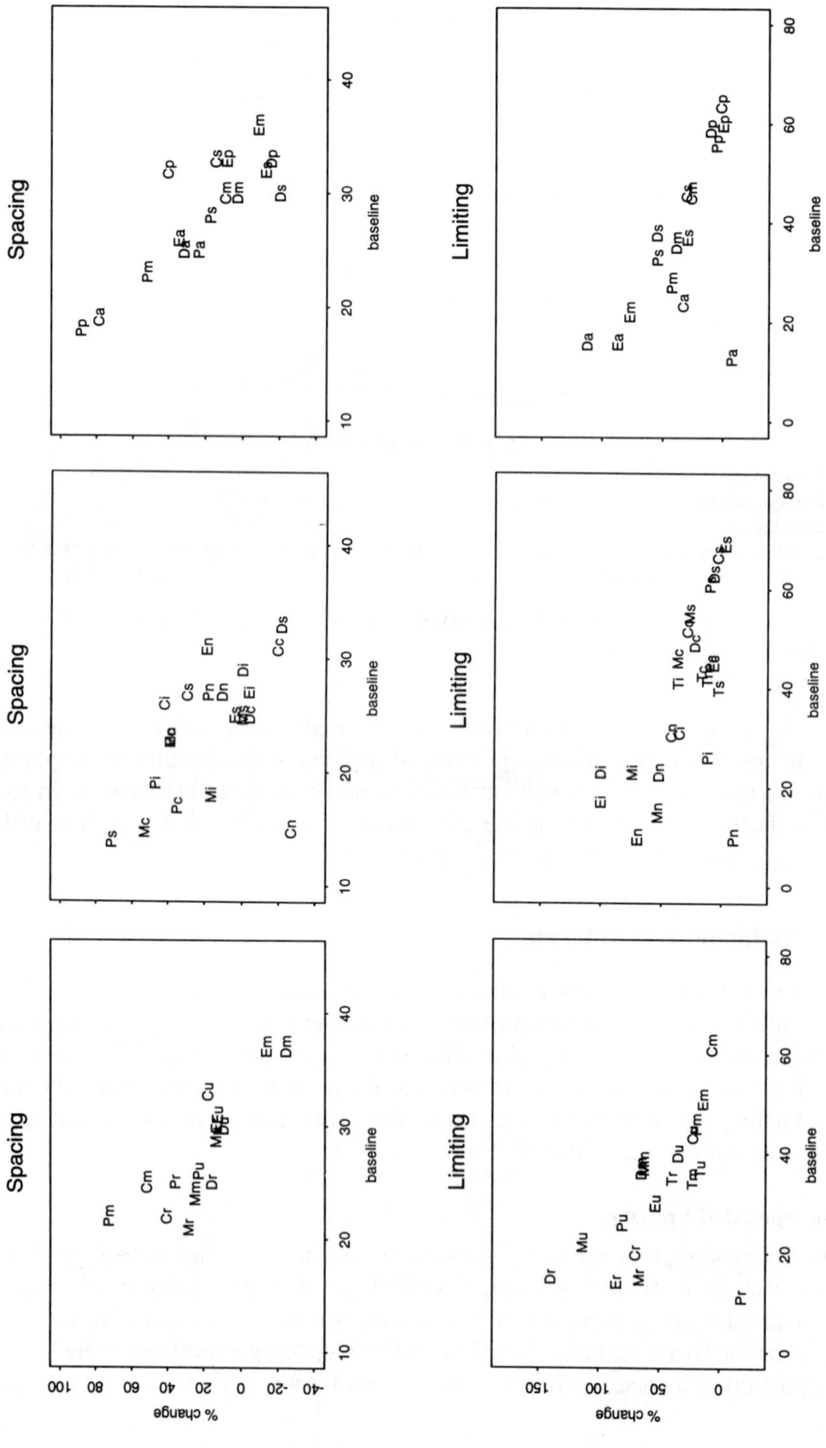
Spacing
Spacing
Spacing
Limiting
Limiting
Limiting
baseline
% change

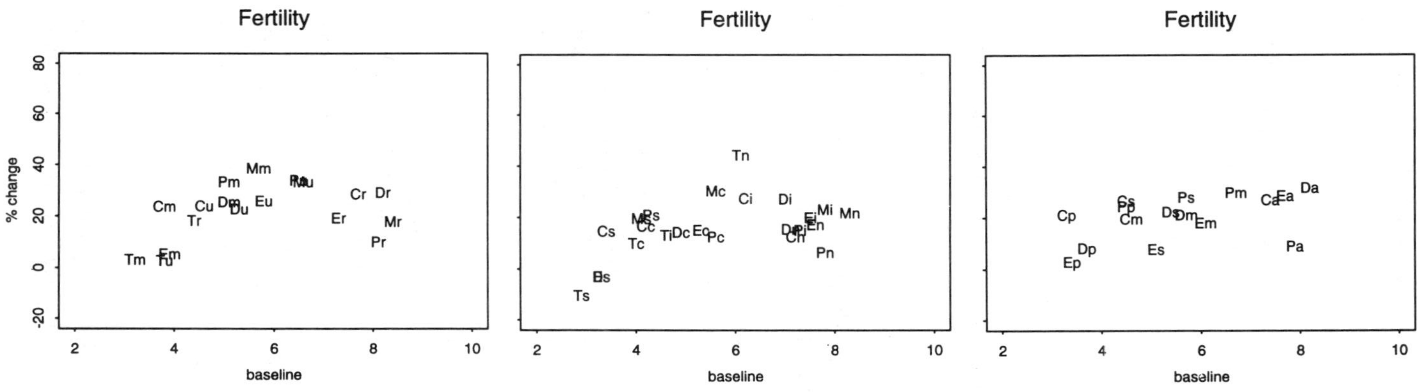

C= Colombia
D= Dominican Republic
E= Ecuador
M= Mexico
P= Peru
T= Trinidad and Tobago

r= rural
u= urban
m= metropolitan

n= none
i= incomplete primary
c= complete primary
s= secondary

a= agricultural
m= manual
s= sales/service
p= professional/technical

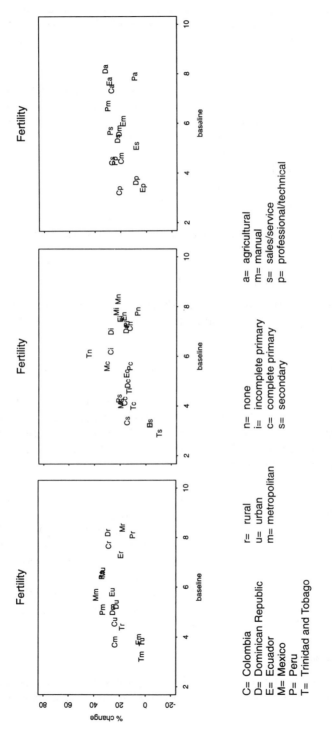

Fig. 2.5. ***Latin America and the Caribbean: % increase in spacing and limiting and % decrease in marital fertility versus baseline level, for social strata within countries***

decreases in the spacing index. The charts also serve as a device to identify interesting exceptions to the general trend. In terms of spacing we see that the metropolitan areas in Colombia and Peru (and to a lesser extent the other urban districts in Colombia) show larger increases in spacing than might be expected from their starting levels.

The results are broadly confirmed when we look at the breakdown by woman's educational level. The most glaring outlier here is the group of uneducated women in Colombia, who started from a value of only 15 and show a decrease instead of the expected increase. The incomplete primary stratum in Mexico is also somewhat unusual in showing no change. The remaining strata behave much closer to expectation, but the path of change in spacing practices seems broader for the educational strata than it did for the residence groups. In contrast, the breakdown by husband's occupation produces clustering along a narrower path. The only outlier of note is the professional and technical sector in Colombia, which shows a large increase from an already high baseline, which would have led us to expect no change.

The Spread of Limiting

The second row of plots in Fig. 2.5 shows the corresponding results for the limiting index and exhibits the same striking regularities. In general, the strata with the lower degrees of fertility limitation at the time of the WFS survey show the largest proportionate gains. Consider first the results by type of place of residence. The most glaring exception to the general rule is rural Peru, which shows essentially no change. A large outlier at the other extreme is rural Dominican Republic, which shows substantially larger gains than expected from its low initial level. This result supports earlier evidence that the family planning programme in the Dominican Republic may have been quite efficient in reaching rural areas (see DHS and CONAPOFA 1986). All the remaining strata, including metropolitan Colombia, which has now reached a limiting index of 65 per cent, appear to behave quite regularly.

Practically the same results are evident in terms of educational strata. The uneducated women in Peru show no signs of change, but practically all other groups conform broadly to expectation. The incomplete primary groups in Peru and the Dominican Republic provide an interesting example of strata that have deviated from expectation in opposite ways. The breakdown by husband's occupation produces again the expected pattern. Now it is the agricultural sectors in Peru and the Dominican Republic which provide the contrast of stationary conditions and very rapid change. Except for these two exceptions, relative change is seen again to decline linearly with the initial level.

Marital Fertility

The third row of plots in Fig. 2.5 shows proportionate changes in total marital fertility. Although the pattern for marital fertility is not as clear as it was for its two components, there is an indication of a curvilinear trend. The proportionate reduction in fertility is lowest for social strata starting from low levels of fertility, it increases to reach a peak at baseline levels of around six children and then declines again. In other words, it is groups in the middle of the transition which are experiencing the greatest relative change.

The breakdown by residence shows no distinct outliers. Note that rural Dominican Republic and metropolitan Colombia—which were highlighted earlier as showing outstanding increase in the limiting and spacing parameters, respectively—both show somewhat larger than expected declines in marital fertility. The results by education confirm the curvilinear trend noted above. The outlier at the top of the chart corresponds to a tiny group of uneducated women in Trinidad. Note the slight reduction in marital fertility among uneducated women in Peru, which is entirely due to increased spacing. The plot for occupational strata shows an interesting contrast between the agricultural sectors in Peru and in the Dominican Republic, which represent the extremes of very little and extremely rapid change from starting from rather high baseline levels.

The Diffusion Equation

Our examination of differentials in the spacing and limiting components of marital fertility has uncovered remarkable regularities in the process of transition. Although the path followed by the indices of spacing and limiting behaviour is wide enough to accommodate substantial inter-country differences, it is nevertheless quite well defined, suggesting the existence of a common explanation for the observed patterns of decline.

We believe that such an explanation may be broadly formulated in terms of a process of social diffusion, where fertility decline is seen as the result of the spread of new ideas and technologies. This notion has appeared often in the demographic literature, see for example the review by Retherford and Palmore (1983), the articles by Cleland (1985) and Watkins (1987) or the more recent discussion in Chapter 11. More specifically, we argue here that a very simple model of diffusion leads exactly to the type of regular patterns that we have encountered, provided the spacing and limiting indices can be interpreted roughly in terms of proportions of women spacing and limiting their fertility. That such an interpretation is reasonable at least for the limiting index is clearly demonstrated in Rodríguez and Cleland (1988).

Imagine classifying all members of a social stratum in two categories: those who have adopted the notion of fertility control and those who have not. Let $\gamma(t)$ represent the number of controllers. We assume with no loss of generality that all numbers are standardized to a stratum size of one, so the number of non-controllers is $1-\gamma(t)$. Consider now the rate of change of $\gamma(t)$ over time as measured by its derivative $\gamma'(t)$, the number of new adopters at time t. Let $\lambda(t)$ represent the adoption rate at time t. Applying this rate to the population at risk of adopting, which is $1-\gamma(t)$, should give the number of new adopters. Assume now that the rate of adoption is strictly proportional to the size of the group that has already adopted, say $\lambda(t) = \lambda\,\gamma(t)$. Then

$$\gamma'(t) = \lambda\,\gamma(t)\,[1 - \gamma(t)] \tag{5}$$

The fact that the rate of adoption is proportional to the number of adopters is consistent with a process of social diffusion. One way in which such a rate can be constructed is assuming that women within a stratum interact randomly with each other and end up adopting social change after they have met a sufficient number of times with innovators. The basic notion, however, is more general than that, implying that the process will acquire momentum as the number of adopters increases. This type of formulation is common in models of epidemic diseases. Dividing both sides of (5) by $\gamma(t)$ we find that

$$\gamma'(t)/\gamma(t) = \lambda - \lambda\gamma(t) \tag{6}$$

In words, in this model the proportionate increase in the number of adopters per unit of time is a linear function of the baseline level, with a negative slope. But this is exactly the type of result that we obtained repeatedly when we analysed the transition within strata defined by type of place of residence, wife's education and husband's occupation.

Thus, once the transition starts in a stratum it follows a self-sustaining course that seems guided by a basic diffusion process. This model does not account for the beginning of the transition in a stratum, although it seems natural to assume that change spreads to the lower strata once it has reached a critical mass in the upper strata. In all rigour, however, our analysis does not explain why the rural, agricultural, and uneducated strata in Peru have not started a transition to low fertility. It does indicate, however, that once the transition gets under way it will follow a broadly predictable course.

Finally, it should be noted that these explanations do not apply directly to the notion of low fertility, which throughout our analysis has exhibited more complicated patterns, but rather to the spread of ideas related to the two components of marital fertility: limiting and spacing.

References

Bongaarts, J. (1982), 'The Fertility-inhibiting Effects of the Intermediate Fertility Variables', *Studies in Family Planning*, **12**: 78–102.

Cleland, J. (1985), 'Marital Fertility Decline in Developing Countries: Theories and the Evidence', in J. Cleland and J. Hobcraft (eds.), *Reproductive Change in Developing Countries* (Oxford: Oxford University Press).

—— and Rodríguez, G. (1988), 'The Effect of Parental Education on Marital Fertility in Developing Countries', *Population Studies*, **42**: 419–42.

Coale, A. J. (1971), 'Age Patterns of Marriage', *Population Studies*, **25**: 193–214.

DHS and CONAPOFA (1986), *República Dominicana: Encuesta Demográfica y de Salud,*

DHS-86 (República Dominicana, Secretaria de Estado de Salud Pública y Asistencia Social, Consejo Nacional de Población y Familia; Institute for Resource Development/ Westinghouse).

—— FPATT (1987), *Trinidad and Tobago Demographic and Health Survey, 1987* (Family Planning Association of Trinidad and Tobago; Institute for Resource Development/ Westinghouse).

Espenshade, T. (1971), 'A New Method for Estimating the Level of Natural Fertility in Populations Practicing Birth Control', *Demography*, **8**: 525–36.

Henry, L. (1961), 'Some Data on Natural Fertility', *Eugenics Quarterly*, **8**: 81–91.

Lightbourne, R. E. (1980), *Urban–Rural Differentials in Fertility* (WFS, *Comparative Studies*, 10; Voorburg: International Statistical Institute).

Moreno, L. (1991), 'An Improved Model of the Impact of the Proximate Determinants on Fertility Change: Evidence from Latin America', *Population Studies*, **45**: 313–37.

Nelder, J. A. and Wedderburn, R. W. M. (1972), 'Generalized Linear Models', *Journal of the Royal Statistical Society, Series A*, **135**: 370–84.

Page, H. J. (1977), 'Patterns Underlying Fertility Schedules: A Decomposition by both Age and Marriage Duration', *Population Studies*, **31**: 85–106.

Payne, C.-D. (1988) (ed.), *The GLIM System: Release 3.77* (Oxford: Numerical Algorithms Group Ltd.).

Retherford, R. D., and Palmore, J. A. (1983), 'Diffusion Processes Affecting Fertility Regulation', in R. A. Bulatao and R. D. Lee (eds.), *Determinants of Fertility in Developing Countries* (New York: Academic Press).

Rodríguez, G., and Cleland, J. (1980), 'Socio-Economic Determinants of Marital Fertility in Twenty Countries: A Multivariate Analysis', *World Fertility Survey Conference, 1980, Record of Proceedings* (Voorburg: International Statistical Institute), ii. 337–403.

—— —— (1987), *Socio-Economic Differentials in Marital Fertility in Less Developed Countries: A Compendium of Results* (Informe Técnico, Departamento de Estadística, Facultad de Matemáticas, Universidad Católica de Chile).

—— —— (1988), 'Modelling Marital Fertility by Age and Duration: An Empirical Appraisal of the Page Model', *Population Studies*, **42**: 241–57.

Watkins, S. C. (1987), 'The Fertility Transition: Europe and the Third World Compared', *Sociological Forum*, **2**: 645–73.

3 The Process of Family Formation during the Fertility Transition

FÁTIMA JUÁREZ and SILVIA LLERA

Introduction

One of the challenges currently facing researchers is the need to identify and interpret the patterns underlying the reproductive strategies of families, especially those adopted during the fertility transition. If the family life cycle is viewed as a dynamic process that interacts with demographic aspects of the family, it may be studied in a number of stages. First, it is important to understand the type of transition that is occurring in Latin American fertility, and the particular characteristics of, and changes in, the family formation process in different countries of the region. Secondly, this knowledge of reproductive behaviour should be related to the intermediate mechanisms (proximate determinants of fertility, also known as intermediate variables), and their interaction with the process of social change should be analysed.

This chapter deals with the first of these stages, attempting to spell out similarities and dissimilarities in the fertility transition to small families that is occurring in a number of Latin American countries. In the first part of this research, the family building process is studied, taking into detailed account how couples move through the different reproductive stages of their lives: from marriage to first birth, from first to second birth, and so on. New demographic techniques and the data from fertility surveys now permit studies of this nature, using truncated birth histories as a starting-point. A description of the dynamics of the family formation process can be seen as a study of the family life cycle, whose various stages are the points at which the course of a woman's reproductive life, the family, and society all intersect.

In the last part of the analysis, the overall relationship between certain socio-demographic variables and family formation patterns is shown.

The results of the analysis are presented in the following order: a brief description of changes in general levels of fertility in Latin America is given in the first section; the next section contains details of variations in the family formation process over the past ten years among several countries of the region; then a general overview of family patterns in 1986–7 (inter-country analysis) is given; and finally, evidence is presented on certain variables that intervene in the process of change.

Methodology and Data Sources

Using data from the Latin American countries that took part in the World Fertility Survey, Juárez (1983 and 1987) described the changes that are taking place in the process of family formation in this region of the world. She proposed a methodology to calculate indices that are similar to the parity progression ratio (P_n). These probabilities, the indicators B_{60} and P_n, are specially treated to eliminate 'censoring' (truncation) biases and 'selectivity' biases.[1] Such biases stem directly from the birth histories which, for the incomplete cohorts, are interrupted by the date of the interview as they interact with the series of birth-intervals. Because calculation of the two indices, B_{60} and P_n, yields similar estimates of levels and trends of family formation, it is possible to use the two interchangeably.[2] For the purposes of this study, only the P_n indices were analysed. This measure corresponds to the proportion of women who are currently in the interval between event i and event $i + 1$. The estimates were adjusted ('truncation approach') to eliminate the biases that are produced by the retrospective birth histories of women who have not yet completed their reproductive lives.

The present study is based on information generated by both the WFS and the DHS for Colombia, the Dominican Republic, Peru, and Ecuador. In the case of Brazil,[3] information is only available from the DHS. The indicators calculated in the study provide an overview of the general process of family formation transition occurring in the past ten years, and of the specific course of change taken by each country.

The universe under study is restricted to women aged 20–49 years and ever in union. Women with pre-marital births are also excluded, not only because they represent a minority of the population, but mainly because they are a subgroup with special characteristics with respect to levels of fertility, probability of first marriage and socio-economic status. For Brazil, information is only included for women up to the age of 44, the maximum age in the sample frame of that country.

General Trends: TFR

Earlier studies have substantiated the fact that a fertility decline had already begun in Latin America by 1960. Some studies (Mauldin 1976, Ochoa 1981, and Juárez 1987) pointed out the changes in family size that had occurred in the region: several countries experienced declines in family size of between 20 and 40 per cent between 1965 and 1975 (Chile, Colombia, Costa Rica, Cuba, and the Dominican Republic, among others); some showed smaller declines of 10–20 per cent (Brazil, El Salvador, Venezuela); and in others, the reductions were even smaller (Bolivia).

1 For further details of the methodology, see Juárez (1983), and Brass and Juárez (1983).

2 Tests of this methodology are reported elsewhere (see Juárez 1983, 1987).

3 The only data available for Brazil at the time this research was carried out.

In the past, indicators such as the TFR had made it possible to identify changes in reproductive behaviour. By 1985, it was clear that all the countries of Latin America had entered into a phase of transition, including those that were lagging behind in the adoption of new reproductive patterns during the 1970s (see Table 1.1 and Fig. 1.2). In spite of the difficulty of discussing levels and trends of Latin American fertility as a single unit, since each country has its own special characteristics, the most general aspects of fertility will be referred to below.

Trends in the TFR of Latin America as a whole indicate that the 1960s were the starting-point of the demographic transition for many countries. The decline accelerated during the 1970s. There had been a slight rise in the TFR during the pre-transitional period (1957–62), but after 1965, there was a continuous decline. The slight rise has been confirmed in a number of countries, and has been explained as the effect of improvements in mortality associated with the medical and technological advances made in Latin America from the mid-1930s to the 1940s (Dyson and Murphy 1985; and Juárez, Quilodrán, and Zavala de Cosío 1989).

Not all countries followed the same rate of change, and the declines occurred at different times. Thus, we have the case of Argentina, with a relatively small family size since the beginning of the century, and an unchanged TFR of around three children per woman throughout the period 1950–85. Chile, which started from much higher levels in 1950 (more than 5 children per woman), was, by 1985, demonstrating even smaller families (2.8 children) than Argentina, with a fertility decline of 45 per cent during the period 1950–85. Honduras is another extreme case in which fertility remained constant and very high until 1975 (TFR of 7.1), showing some modification only in the past decade.

The fertility transitions of Costa Rica and Colombia, which began during the 1960s, have been fully documented. Table 1.1 shows clearly the similarity between Brazil and the early-transition countries. Although Ecuador and Peru could not be considered as having a late transition, as is the case with Honduras and other Central American countries, these two countries did adopt new reproductive models at a later date. On the other hand, Peru, which began its fertility decline at a much earlier date and at lower levels than Ecuador, now shows signs of little change in its most recent estimates (1985).[4] Finally, the case of the Dominican Republic is noteworthy, since the decline in fertility began in 1950, when levels were higher than those of Honduras, Ecuador, and Peru (a TFR of 7.4 children per woman). By 1985, the country showed levels close to those of Colombia.

This brief overview makes it clear that the pattern of decline has followed a somewhat different course in each country, reflecting different historical and socio-economic backgrounds. This finding underlines how important it is to analyse changes in family size in detail and separately for each country, while still seeking to uncover possible differences and similarities among them.

[4] There are certain differences between the levels and trends shown in Table 1.1 and those obtained from the DHS data, with the latter being slightly lower.

WFS Evidence of the Family Formation Process

Before presenting the changes in family formation that have occurred over the past ten years, we will summarize some of the most important findings from analyses of retrospective birth histories, based on published data (Juárez 1987) from the WFS.

The classification of countries by their current stage in the fertility transition would be a difficult task, in view of the fact that each country is at a different point along the continuum and, that each society has its own special characteristics. Nevertheless, in an attempt to systematically summarize the results of the parity progression ratios, the countries were grouped into three categories: (1) those in an early transitional phase (first stage); (2) those in an intermediate transitional stage (second stage); and (3) those at a stage of advanced transition (third stage).

Mexico, Peru, Ecuador, and the Dominican Republic are in the early stage of the transition. These countries are characterized by an absence of change in the first and second intervals (from union to first birth and from first to second birth), some indication of change in the third birth-interval, and a clear decline in the transition to the fourth birth. The cohorts began to experience these transformations in the interval from the third to the fourth birth as recently as the mid-1960s.

The countries in the second phase, Panama and Paraguay, represent the experience of earlier decline, and they have lower levels of fertility than the countries in the first phase. These populations show some reduction in the probability of transition from the second to the third birth, but this is clearer from the third to the fourth child.

Colombia, Costa Rica, and Venezuela fit into the last group. This third stage represents advanced fertility transition; societies characterized by a nearly complete fertility decline are found in this group. Their particular attributes are sharp decreases in the proportion of women of parity three or higher. However, what really distinguishes them from countries at the previous stage is the fact that women under the age of 30 are much more likely to have only one child.

Given this broad picture, one would expect to find few changes occurring in the subsequent decade (the 1980s) in those countries that were in the final phase of the transition, and substantial modifications taking place in the countries in the first and second phases.

Patterns of Change, Two Points in Time: Colombia, Dominican Republic, Peru, and Ecuador.

This section presents a comparison of two points in time, namely the mid-1970s (using data from the WFS) and the mid-1980s (using data from the DHS). Even though the analysis refers to changes that occurred between the two surveys, that is, over an approximately ten-year period, the indices reflect women's total reproductive experience, which, for the oldest women, would have started about 1940–5.

Considering marriage as the event that defines the beginning of the reproductive life cycle, and the first and last births as the events that set the boundaries for the expansion phase of the conjugal family, transformations in reproductive strategies can be seen as the basis of changes in the transition indices. As far as the initial event of the family formation process and its measurement (proportion of women entering union and age at marriage) are concerned, analysis of the mean age of single persons at the time of first marriage (SMAM[5]) suggests that there has been an increase in age at union, although behaviour varies among cohorts. With the exception of Ecuador, the proportion of women who had entered married life was slightly lower in 1986 (DHS data) than in 1977 (WFS data) (Weinberger, Lloyd, and Blanc 1989). Analysis of the indicator C_m[6] of Bongaarts's model leads to similar conclusions (Chapter 6).

Among the various family reproduction strategies—conceptualizing reproduction as a fundamental element of family and society—one would suppose that transition to the first child would remain relatively constant, whereas one would expect possible declines in transition to the second child, or longer intervals between first- and second-order births, and more pronounced changes at higher parities. Table 3.1 shows the evolution of family formation strategies illustrated by data from the WFS and the DHS.[7] Table 3.2 presents the indices of change for the two moments in time studied here: 1977, which corresponds to the WFS data, and 1986 in the case of the DHS. Finally, Table 3.3 shows, among all women in union (the universe under study), the proportion of women attaining each parity level.

First-Order Births

Reproduction continues to be the fundamental characteristic of the family: during both the 1970s and the 1980s, 95 per cent of all families complete the transition from union to the first child (Table 3.1 and Fig. 3.1). On the assumption that all couples want to have at least one child, it could be assumed that the small group of women who have no children at all suffer some kind of biological infertility.

Analysis of the indices of change (Table 3.2) at the two points in time (WFS and DHS) clearly reveals that the proportions of women having a first birth is slightly higher in the more recent period. This trend is found in every country and

5 'Singulate mean age of marriage', Manual X of the UN (1983), p. 23 in the English version and p. 24 in the Spanish version.

6 C_m refers to the index of non-entry into matrimony. This measures the impact of the reduction in fertility due to this factor

7 In Table 3.1, some of the P_n values show estimates greater than unity. This may be attributed to errors in locating events in time, possibly a residual effect of the reduction in the birth interval. These values are most noticeable in the interval between union and the first birth, because the estimates are very close to unity; they occur more frequently in the DHS data, because the values are higher than those of the WFS.

Table 3.1. *Latin America: Changes in family formation for various countries (Pn)*

Country/ age	WFS data							DHS data						
	Union–1st birth	1st–2nd birth	2nd–3rd birth	3rd–4th birth	4th–5th birth	5th–6th birth	6th–7th birth	Union–1st birth	1st–2nd birth	2nd–3rd birth	3rd–4th birth	4th–5th birth	5th–6th birth	6th–7th birth
Brazil														
20–24								1.0000*	0.8908					
25–29								0.9867	0.9117	0.6273	0.5707			
30–34								0.9656	0.9262	0.7207	0.6379	0.7235	0.6143	0.6895
35–39								0.9577	0.9345	0.7938	0.6849	0.7059	0.7135	0.7019
40–44								0.9479	0.9341	0.8314	0.7547	0.7813	0.7800	0.8051
Colombia														
20–24	0.9765	0.8420						0.9954	0.8273					
25–29	0.9598	0.8747	0.7955	0.7154				0.9724	0.8606	0.6676	0.6513			
30–34	0.9796	0.9399	0.9058	0.7919	0.7724	0.6863	0.8486	0.9670	0.9033	0.7738	0.6459	0.6353	0.5092	0.5988
35–39	0.9539	0.9362	0.9248	0.8571	0.8505	0.8377	0.8352	0.9681	0.9339	0.7937	0.6725	0.7699	0.7792	0.6791
40–44	0.9659	0.9498	0.9313	0.9098	0.8936	0.8772	0.8725	0.9707	0.9504	0.8775	0.8612	0.7845	0.7352	0.7118
45–49	0.9719	0.9646	0.9533	0.9301	0.8797	0.8718	0.8676	0.9844	0.9494	0.8933	0.8881	0.8529	0.8670	0.8295
Dominican Rep.														
20–24	0.9341	0.8527						0.9807	0.8398					
25–29	0.9638	0.9642	0.8232	0.8053				0.9658	0.8685	0.7543	0.6039			
30–34	0.9697	0.9680	0.8915	0.8884	0.9056	0.8056	0.7397	0.9640	0.8851	0.8480	0.6869	0.7010	0.6733	0.6081
35–39	0.9762	0.9804	0.9226	0.9464	0.8619	0.9249	0.8595	0.9557	0.9208	0.9042	0.7958	0.7889	0.7176	0.6278
40–44	0.9394	0.9493	0.9417	0.9282	0.8611	0.8845	0.7945	0.9602	0.9447	0.9205	0.8477	0.8381	0.8122	0.7909
45–49	0.9641	0.9302	0.9422	0.8936	0.8571	0.8819	0.8661	0.9780	0.9595	0.9460	0.9330	0.9202	0.8121	0.8932

Table 3.1. *(cont.)*

Country/ age	WFS data							DHS data						
	Union–1st birth	1st–2nd birth	2nd–3rd birth	3rd–4th birth	4th–5th birth	5th–6th birth	6th–7th birth	Union–1st birth	1st–2nd birth	2nd–3rd birth	3rd–4th birth	4th–5th birth	5th–6th birth	6th–7th birth
Peru														
20–24	1.0000*	0.9216						0.9953	0.7875					
25–29	0.9876	0.9731	0.9182	0.8602				1.0000*	0.8855	0.7588	0.7153			
30–34	0.9963	0.9322	0.9223	0.8683	0.8139	0.8047	0.8334	0.9956	0.9168	0.8271	0.7469	0.7513	0.8001	0.6475
35–39	0.9799	0.9499	0.9539	0.8939	0.8776	0.8589	0.8441	1.0000*	0.9377	0.9036	0.7890	0.7744	0.8426	0.8180
40–44	0.9728	0.9559	0.9599	0.8933	0.8698	0.8669	0.8385	0.9839	0.9564	0.9383	0.8476	0.8310	0.7917	0.7825
45–49	0.9688	0.9593	0.9276	0.9238	0.9093	0.8617	0.8237	0.9850	0.9818	0.9412	0.8947	0.8566	0.8197	0.7801
Ecuador														
20–24	1.0000*	0.8688						1.0000*	0.8077					
25–29	0.9629	0.8920	0.7790	0.7270				1.0000*	0.9044	0.7651	0.7654			
30–34	0.9652	0.9279	0.9007	0.8039	0.9232	0.8111	0.6812	1.0000*	0.9172	0.8074	0.7690	0.6186	0.7360	0.6640
35–39	0.9699	0.9688	0.9356	0.8758	0.8475	0.8103	0.7506	0.9895	0.9387	0.8770	0.8398	0.7196	0.7640	0.8383
40–44	0.9728	0.9775	0.9217	0.9217	0.9000	0.8460	0.8298	0.9846	0.9625	0.8799	0.8308	0.7659	0.8429	0.8247
45–49	0.9814	0.9649	0.9384	0.9045	0.8713	0.8750	0.8461	0.9622	0.9563	0.9087	0.8794	0.8571	0.8667	0.8308

Source: WFS and DHS

Note * = Values affected by residual errors.

Table 3.2. *Latin America: Indices of change in family formation at two moments in time*

Country/Age	Union–1st birth	1st–2nd birth	2nd–3rd birth	3rd–4th birth	4th–5th birth	5th–6th birth	6th–7th birth
Colombia							
20–24	0.02	–0.02					
25–29	0.01	–0.02	–0.16	–0.09			
30–34	–0.01	–0.04	–0.15	–0.18	–0.18	–0.26	–0.29
35–39	0.01	–0.00	–0.14	–0.22	–0.09	–0.07	–0.19
40–44	0.00	0.00	–0.06	–0.05	–0.12	–0.16	–0.18
45–49	0.01	–0.02	–0.06	–0.05	–0.03	–0.01	–0.04
Dominican Republic							
20–24	0.05	–0.02					
25–29	0.00	–0.10	–0.08	–0.25			
30–34	–0.01	–0.09	–0.05	–0.23	–0.23	–0.16	–0.18
35–39	–0.02	–0.06	–0.02	–0.16	–0.08	–0.22	–0.27
40–44	0.02	–0.00	–0.02	–0.09	–0.03	–0.08	–0.00
45–49	0.01	0.03	0.00	0.04	0.07	–0.08	0.03
Peru							
20–24	0.00	–0.15					
25–29	0.01	–0.09	–0.17	–0.17			
30–34	0.00	–0.02	–0.10	–0.14	–0.08	–0.01	–0.22
35–39	0.02	–0.01	–0.05	–0.12	–0.12	–0.02	–0.03
40–44	0.01	0.00	–0.02	–0.05	–0.04	–0.09	–0.07
45–49	0.02	0.02	0.01	–0.03	–0.06	–0.05	–0.05
Ecuador							
20–24	0.00	–0.07					
25–29	0.04	0.01	–0.02	0.05			
30–34	0.04	–0.01	–0.10	–0.04	–0.33	–0.09	–0.03
35–39	0.02	–0.03	–0.06	–0.04	–0.15	–0.06	0.12
40–44	0.01	–0.02	–0.05	–0.10	–0.15	–0.00	–0.01
45–49	–0.02	–0.01	–0.03	–0.03	–0.02	–0.01	–0.02

Source: DHS and WFS data

Note: The estimates presented here were obtained as the difference between unity and the quotient of the DHS values divided by the corresponding WFS values from Table 3.1.

among most of the cohorts. There are a number of possible explanations for this behaviour: an increase in pre-marital pregnancies that culminate in union,[8] which, consequently, are biasing the estimates; errors in the reporting of pregnancy histories for first child; a reduction in infertility; or a real change occurring in the process of family formation in Latin America.

An increase in pre-marital conceptions would not actually produce a biasing effect since the methodology used in the analysis controls for the selectivity effect of early fertility and for low age at marriage. On the other hand, the fact that a greater propensity to have a first child is found among the majority of age-groups, and in all countries (the quality of the data varies) eliminates the possibility of data error. Although it is not possible to completely rule out the fact that this phenomenon may be the result of a new pattern of fertility, a decline in biological

[8] Studies of adolescent fertility in Latin America have shown a strong association between pre-marital pregnancy and marriage (Singh and Wulf 1990).

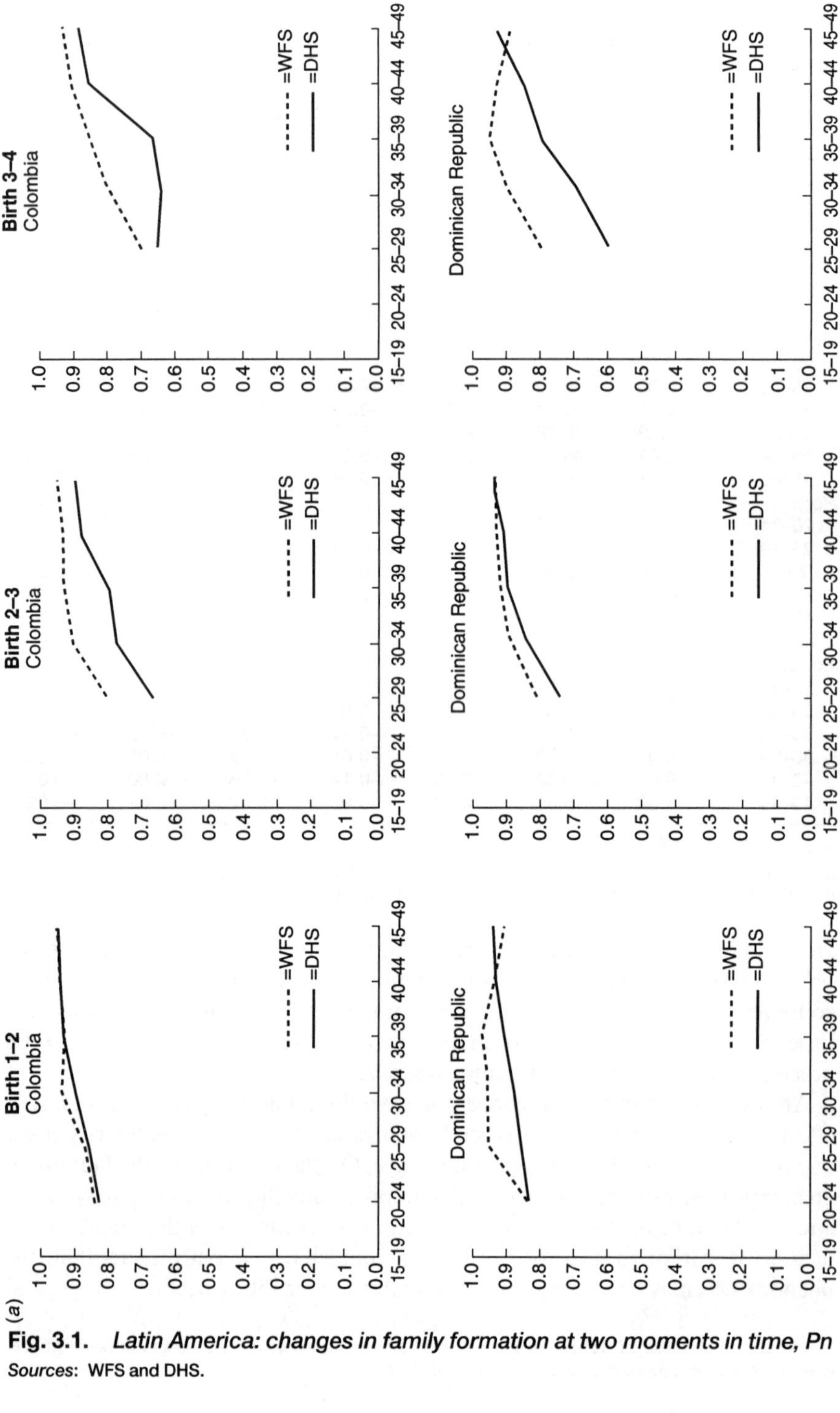

Fig. 3.1. ***Latin America: changes in family formation at two moments in time, Pn***

Sources: WFS and DHS.

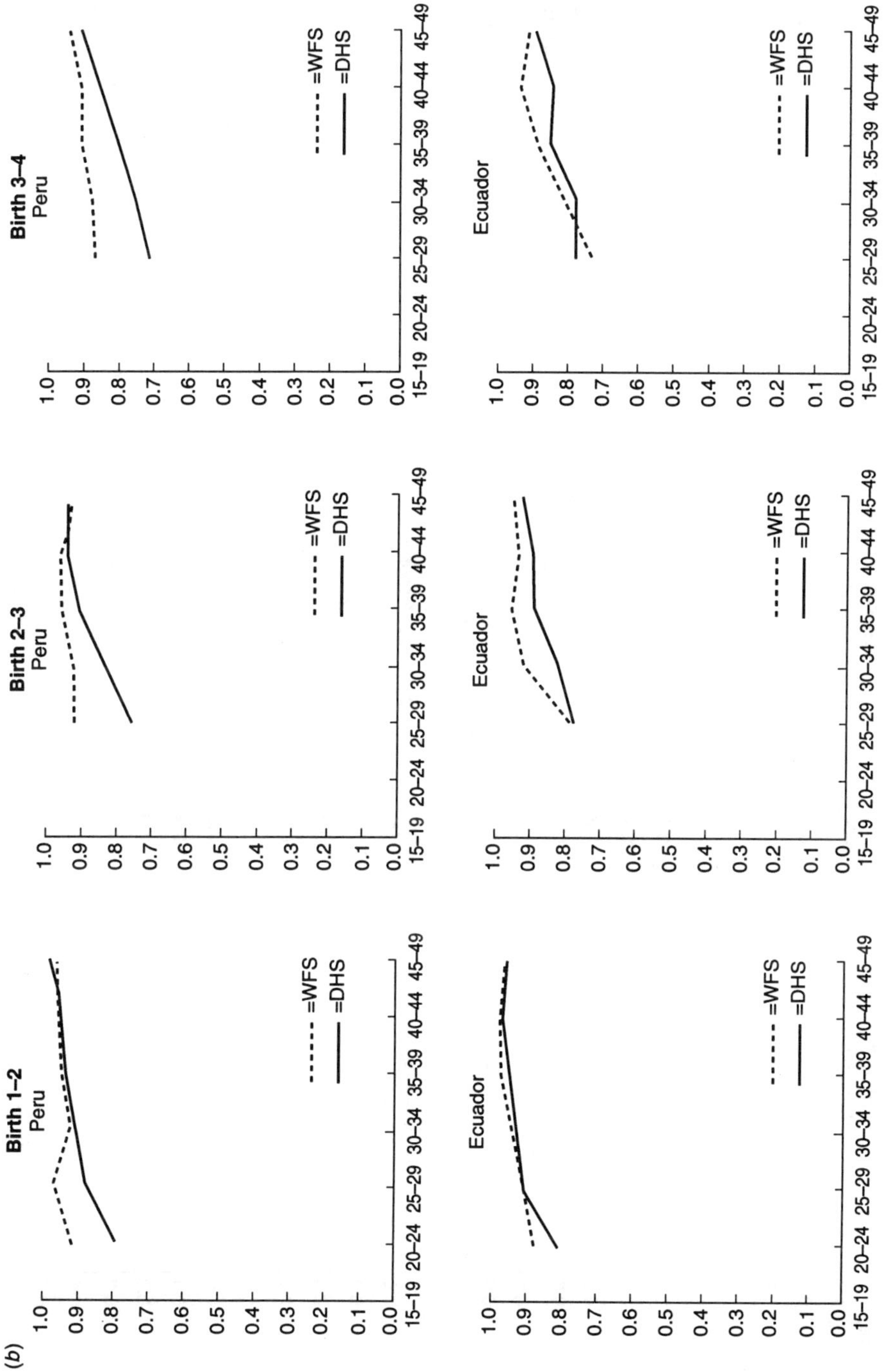
(b)
Birth 1–2
Peru
Ecuador
Birth 2–3
Peru
Ecuador
Birth 3–4
Peru
Ecuador
=WFS
=DHS
1.0
0.9
0.8
0.7
0.6
0.5
0.4
0.3
0.2
0.1
0.0
15–19 20–24 25–29 30–34 35–39 40–44 45–49

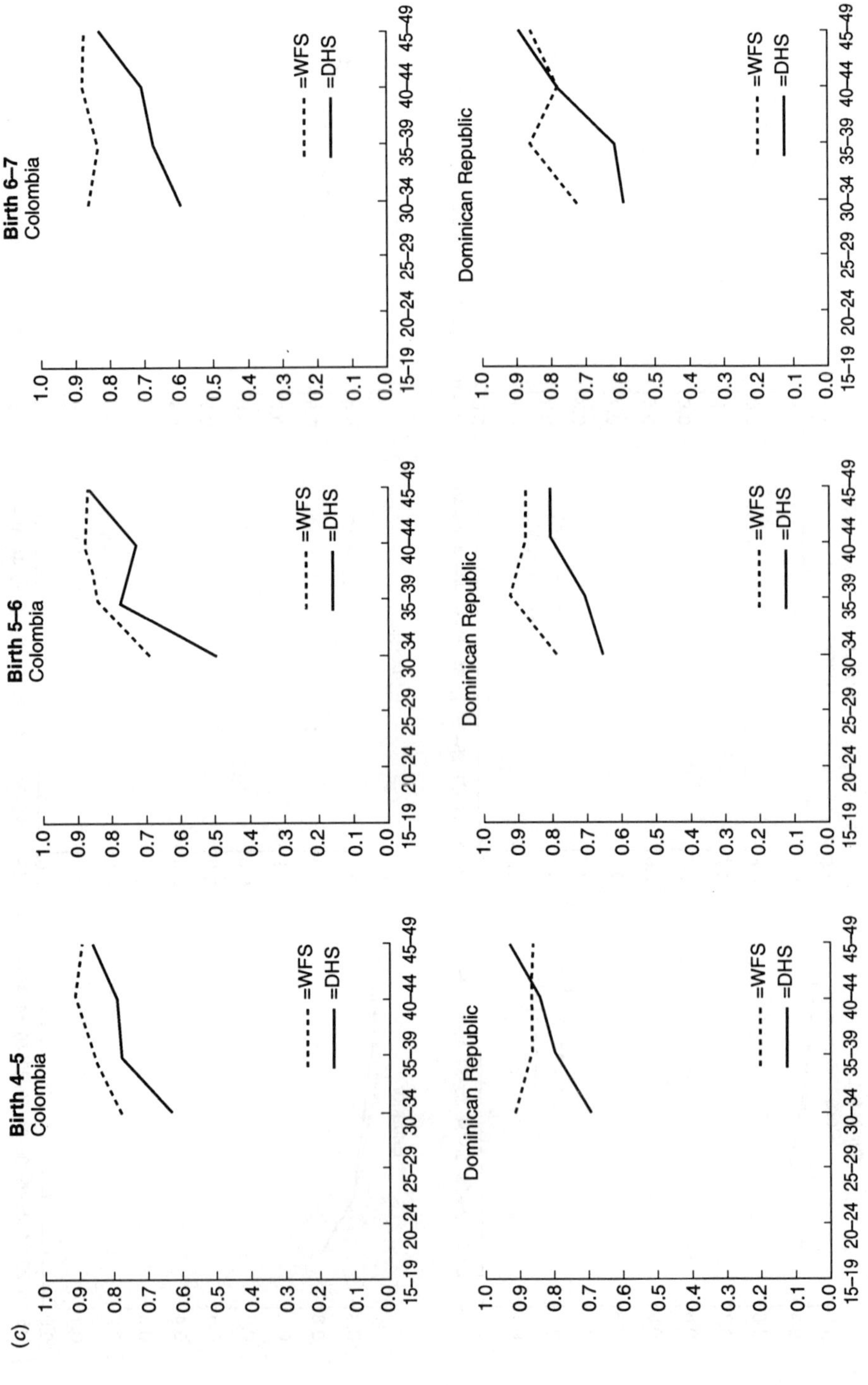
(c)
Birth 4–5
Colombia
Birth 5–6
Colombia
Birth 6–7
Colombia
Dominican Republic
Dominican Republic
Dominican Republic
=WFS
=DHS
1.0
0.9
0.8
0.7
0.6
0.5
0.4
0.3
0.2
0.1
0.0
15–19
20–24
25–29
30–34
35–39
40–44
45–49

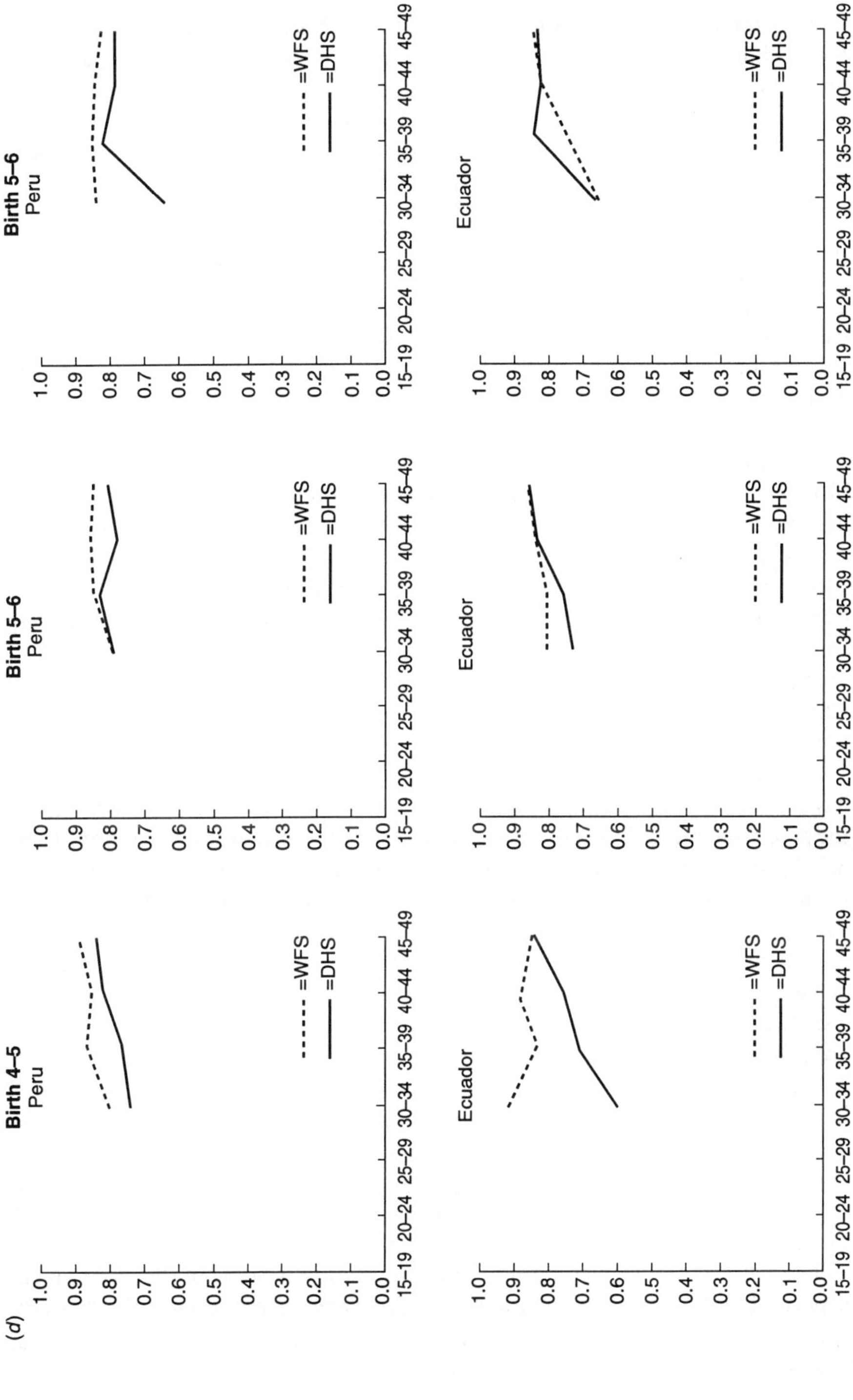
(d)
Birth 4–5
Peru
Ecuador
Birth 5–6
Peru
Ecuador
Birth 5–6
Peru
Ecuador
=WFS
=DHS
0.0
0.1
0.2
0.3
0.4
0.5
0.6
0.7
0.8
0.9
1.0
15–19 20–24 25–29 30–34 35–39 40–44 45–49

sterility remains a more plausible explanation. This hypothesis is reinforced by the finding that in the youngest cohorts, a higher proportion of women pass from union to the first birth. What is more, it is corroborated by the fact that the proportion of women who are still childless by the end of their reproductive lives drops in every country (with the exception of Ecuador for the group aged 40–44).[9] However, these findings deserve to be studied in greater depth.

Parities 2 to 7

Beginning with the second birth, parity progression ratios decline in all the countries studied. The range of variation among cohorts (and among countries) is very broad, reaching reductions of up to 25 per cent in the number of women who proceed from child i to child $i + 1$, but showing a relatively less marked change among the oldest cohorts (Table 3.1 and Fig. 3.1).

The indices of change and the graphs reveal that for all countries, and for every birth-interval, the proportion of women who continue to the next birth declines, in some countries reaching levels as low as 79 per cent for the young women in the second interval (from first to second birth).

Another general characteristic of the family formation pattern is that, at higher birth-order intervals, the fluctuations in P_n among countries and among cohorts within countries become more pronounced. Thus it can be seen that in the interval from the fourth to the fifth child, the values vary from 62 per cent to 92 per cent, while in the first interval, there is only a difference of 7 percentage points (from 93 per cent to 100 per cent).

Although the P_n appears to have high values (for example, 77 per cent of women having a fourth child proceed to parity 5), if we examine this statistic more closely, the percentage actually accounts for only 30 per cent of all women in union. Table 3.3 shows results expressed in these terms, that is, the parity levels achieved by women as a percentage of all women in union. These measures give a global picture of the state of fertility in the region. They demonstrate once again that in Latin America, nearly 90 per cent of families have a first child, slightly more than 50 per cent of the population in union reaches parity 3, and about 20 per cent have a sixth child. These last women, those with large families, who still have a significant impact on fertility estimates (Table 3.3), are more numerous in Peru (one out of every four families, or 25 per cent), and relatively less numerous in Brazil (one in every eight families, or 13 per cent). Finally, it can be concluded from the global indicators of achieved parity levels that there were significant reductions in cumulative fertility in all countries between the mid-1970s and the mid-1980s, and that the major indicator of this drop is a notable reduction in the fourth level of parity, that is, in the transition from marriage to the fourth birth.

The following section contains a brief description of some of the more salient aspects of the family formation transition taking place in each country in the study.

[9] The estimates for these findings were not included in the tables since it was considered that the study of this phenomenon was beyond the scope of this work.

Table 3.3. *Latin America: Cumulative parity of women ever in union (%)*

Country	Source	Total women in Union		Live–born children (%)						
		%	No.	1	2	3	4	5	6	7
Brazil	DHS	100	3,557	90.64	70.40	47.15	29.97	20.30	13.58	9.42
Colombia	WFS	100	2,979	91.37	77.44	61.43	47.50	37.16	28.43	22.36
	DHS	100	2,970	92.56	73.60	52.15	35.56	25.05	17.51	12.15
Dominican Republic	WFS	100	2,225	88.63	73.62	60.27	48.49	38.02	29.03	21.89
	DHS	100	5,057	89.32	71.23	54.16	38.20	28.57	19.56	14.08
Peru	WFS	100	4,950	94.55	81.19	66.42	52.16	40.89	31.58	23.88
	DHS	100	2,787	94.51	79.33	62.33	46.43	33.26	24.69	17.55
Ecuador	WFS	100	3,843	92.58	77.18	60.53	46.60	36.25	27.84	20.61
	DHS	100	2,909	92.47	75.32	55.93	40.05	27.02	19.28	13.41

Source: WFS and DHS data

Colombia

There have been extremely sharp changes in patterns of family formation in Colombia over the past ten years, both in transitions among the first two or three intervals and in transitions to high parities. Analysis of transitions to the third, fourth, and seventh birth orders illustrates most clearly the changes that have taken place. In the third interval, close to 15 per cent of women under the age of 40, having a second child, did not proceed to a third birth during the ten-year period (Table 3.1: DHS Data, Colombia); that is, about 1 out of every 7 women no longer went on to have a third child. The adoption of new reproductive norms is even more pronounced among younger women; hence, at present, only 67 per cent of women aged 25–29 have a third child. Another interesting variation is the extreme change shown by Colombian families in the transition from the third to the fourth birth, which dropped from 86 to 67 per cent (Table 3.1 comparing the WFS with the DHS data). Thus, during the decade in question one out of every five women aged 35–39 no longer went on to have a fourth child. There were also marked changes among large families. For the interval between the sixth and seventh birth, almost one-third of women aged 30–34 who would have had a seventh child in the past now no longer progress to that birth. These reductions are important, since they indicate changes at high parities. The fertility decline among high-parity families, even for women near the end of their reproductive years (a decline from 87 per cent in the WFS data, for progression from the sixth to the seventh birth for the cohort 40–44, to a level of 71 per cent in the DHS data in Table 3.1) was quite unexpected.

Dominican Republic

There have been significant changes over the past decade in patterns of family formation in the Dominican Republic, most noticeably in the fourth, sixth, and seventh birth-intervals. However, the declines in fertility have not been as great as those seen in Colombia. The exception is in the case of the fourth interval, where almost one-quarter of women under 35 who had a third birth did not progress to the next one. For example, 89 per cent of 30–34-year-olds progressed from the third to the fourth birth at the time of the WFS, but only 60 per cent did so at the time of the DHS (see Table 3.1). These changes in the parity progression ratio are quite substantial.

It is the youngest generations who tend to have the lowest P values: 75 per cent of women under the age of 30 with a second child go on to have a third, while in the past this percentage was over 82. If the current behaviour of women under 30 is compared with that of women aged 30–49 for the same birth-interval, the P_n values increase significantly: 85 per cent for women aged 30–34, 90 per cent for those aged 35–39, and in excess of 94 per cent for the oldest cohorts (Table 3.1: DHS data, Dominican Republic).

Peru

In this country, between 1977 and 1986, there were changes in all birth-intervals. The most pronounced changes are found in the third, fourth, and fifth birth-intervals. If the fourth interval is analysed in greater detail, it can be seen that ten years ago, 92 per cent of the oldest women (aged 45–49) went on to have a fourth child, whereas now the percentage is down to 89 per cent. The reductions in the proportion of women who reach this interval occur over the entire range of age-groups, with reductions of 5 per cent among women aged 40–44, 12 per cent among women 35–39, 14 per cent among those aged 30–34, and 17 per cent for the group aged 25–29 (Table 3.2). And again, the changes become systematically more pronounced at younger ages, which means that the most extreme cases correspond to the youngest women. These changes result in significantly modified parity progression ratios. Thus, the P_n values for women aged 25–29 going from the third to the fourth birth show very sharp declines, ranging from 86 per cent in the WFS to 71 per cent in the DHS (Table 3.1).

Ecuador

Examination of the changes in family formation patterns in Ecuador confirms that the most important transformations occurred from the third to the sixth birth. The most striking aspect is the marked changes occurring in the fifth interval, with indices of change as high as 33 per cent for women aged 30–34, and 15 per cent for women aged 35–44 (Table 3.2). In 1977, among women 30–34, there was an almost universal transition to the fifth birth, whereas now only 62 per cent in that age-group achieve this parity level (Table 3.1: Ecuador).

Of all the stages of family formation in the various countries, the fifth birth-interval in Ecuador shows the greatest reduction in parity progression ratios. In the seventh interval, the behaviour of certain cohorts is quite unexpected: higher fertility for the age-group 35–39 in the more recent period (data from the DHS) than ten years earlier (Table 3.1: data from WFS). Although this result requires further study, it is probably due to a reporting problem in the data, possibly in both the birth dates of the children and those of the mothers.

Summary

Although it is difficult to summarize both absolute values and rates of change in the phases of the reproductive cycle during the past decade, one can make the broad generalization that Colombia is the country in which the pattern of change is most pronounced. The Dominican Republic also reveals significant declines, although not in all birth-intervals. Peru and, finally, Ecuador, follow with relatively smaller changes. When the stages of the transition are compared among countries, it is remarkable that Colombia, which now finds itself in an advanced stage of transition (third phase, Juárez 1987), is the country registering the most extreme changes in the evolution of family formation patterns. At the same time, it is surprising that countries such as Peru—which in the mid-1970s were in the first phase of the transition—do not exhibit any distinctly rapid changes ten years later.

The Transition in 1986

Fig. 3.2*a* and *b* show family formation patterns at the time of the DHS surveys. For the reader's convenience, the curves for the countries involved have been separated into two parts. In the upper part, parity progression ratios are drawn for Brazil, Colombia, and the Dominican Republic, and in the lower part, for Peru and Ecuador. This division of the countries is based on the shape of the curves and on the levels of transition achieved up to the time of each survey.

In the countries that were in the third phase of the transition in the mid-1970s (Brazil and Colombia), and in those in the first phase (Dominican Republic, Peru, and Ecuador), declines in transition to the succeeding birth-interval occur ten years later in all cohorts. It should be pointed out once again that the measures that we are analysing (P_n) permit comparisons among consecutive cohorts even though these cohorts may not yet have completed their reproductive years.

Peru and Ecuador, countries that found themselves in the first phase of evolution in the adoption of new reproductive patterns at the time of the WFS, and which showed signs that women were practising fertility control at the third birth, now show changing family formation patterns in the transition to the second child. This is a characteristic that would have corresponded to the countries in the advanced phase of the transition in 1977 (WFS). In addition, it is interesting to note that for women under the age of 35, considering the interval between the second and third birth, the slope of the curves for Peru and Ecuador is equal to that of Colombia, Brazil, and the Dominican Republic.

Brazil presents family formation patterns that indicate a reduction in the number of children women bear. The estimates indicate, in a more or less systematic manner, parity progression ratios lower than Colombia's for the intervals from the third to the sixth. A particular characteristic of Brazilian society is the fact that successive cohorts of women have not modified the second interval. That is, there has been no change in this phase of the family life cycle, as is illustrated by a constant pace in the transition from the first to the second child, despite profound changes in the other intervals.

The Dominican Republic, which belonged in the first phase at the time of the WFS, shows changes more in accordance with the type of family building patterns found in countries in the advanced stage of transition. This finding suggests that the Dominican Republic changed its levels and patterns in a manner similar to those of Colombia and Brazil. The parity progression ratio curves are located slightly above those of Colombia, with the exception of the interval from the sixth to the seventh birth, where values are lower than those of Colombia and Brazil.

On the other hand, Ecuador, which at the time of the WFS was a little behind the remaining countries of the first phase (showing greater changes for younger women in the transition from the third to the fourth birth than those of the other countries), now shows P_n values below those of Peru in the progression to the third, fifth and sixth children. The progression to the fifth interval is strikingly lower. These changes, which have occurred at key intervals, are those that establish definitively the shift to small families. They place Ecuador on an accelerated path of transition, which, most probably, will lead to even more pronounced reductions in global fertility indicators (such as the TFR) than those seen in Peru.

In conclusion, it may be said that, in contrast to the behaviour patterns of ten years ago, all the countries studied here are showing changes at all birth-intervals. Parity progression ratios for Colombia, Brazil, and the Dominican Republic are declining, but to a lesser degree than those in Ecuador and Peru. In countries whose transition is more recent (Peru and Ecuador, represented in the graph by a straight line), the absence of change among older women after the sixth birth-interval suggests that some modification at these parities will be likely, and that as a result, there are bound to be reductions in completed family size in the coming years, particularly in Ecuador.

Discussion: The Fertility Transition and Socio-Demographic Factors

What can be said about the type of change that is occurring and its interrelationships with the intermediate and socio-economic variables? The answer to that question belongs to the second phase of the analysis, which will not be covered in the present chapter. However, a few reflections are in order.

In Latin America, the intermediate variable having the greatest influence on the decline of fertility has been contraception (Potter 1984; Pullum, Casterline, and Juárez 1985; and Chapter 6). On the other hand, a number of different socio-economic and other background determinants have been used to explain changes in fertility. Of these, women's educational level appears to be most closely associated (Rodríguez and Cleland 1984, Juárez 1989). The relationship between these two determinants of fertility transition (contraceptive use and women's education) and the P_n values is shown below (see Table 3.4 and Fig. 3.3).

The proportion of women who have ever used a contraceptive method follows the same country order as the phases of fertility transition described earlier: current use of a contraceptive method is higher in Brazil and Colombia than in Peru and Ecuador; similar results obtain for ever-use (Table 3.4). But neither this measure nor the proportion of women currently using a contraceptive method clearly reflects the different transition processes of each country. The Dominican Republic shows family formation patterns similar to those of Brazil and Colombia, while its contraceptive prevalence rates indicate levels closer to those of Peru. This behaviour may be due to the fact that the measure being used is a rough one. To obtain a more refined indicator, it would be necessary to know the women's

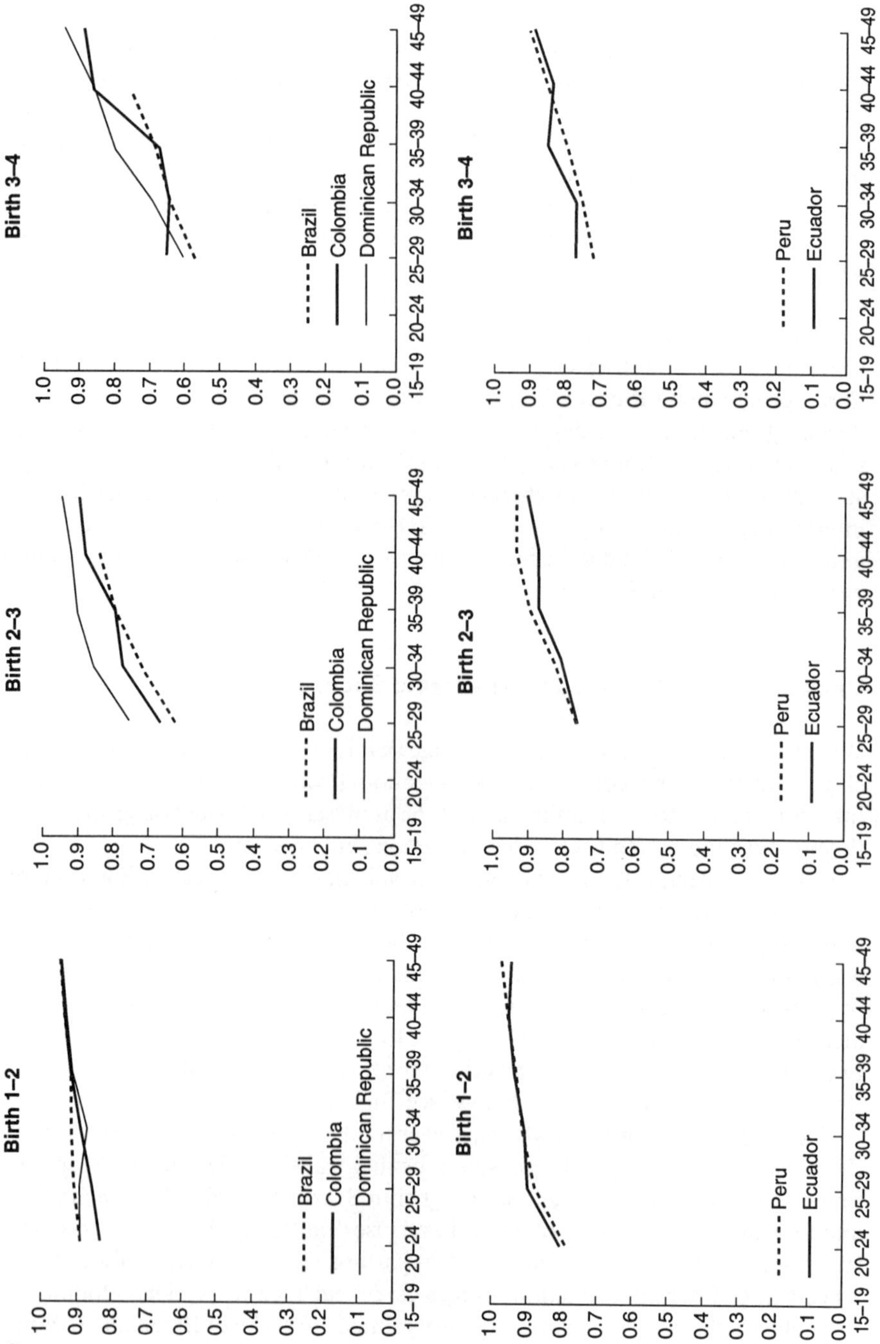

(*a*)

Fig. 3.2. *Latin America: patterns of fertility transition in the 1980s,* pn, *DHS*

Source: DHS.

(b)

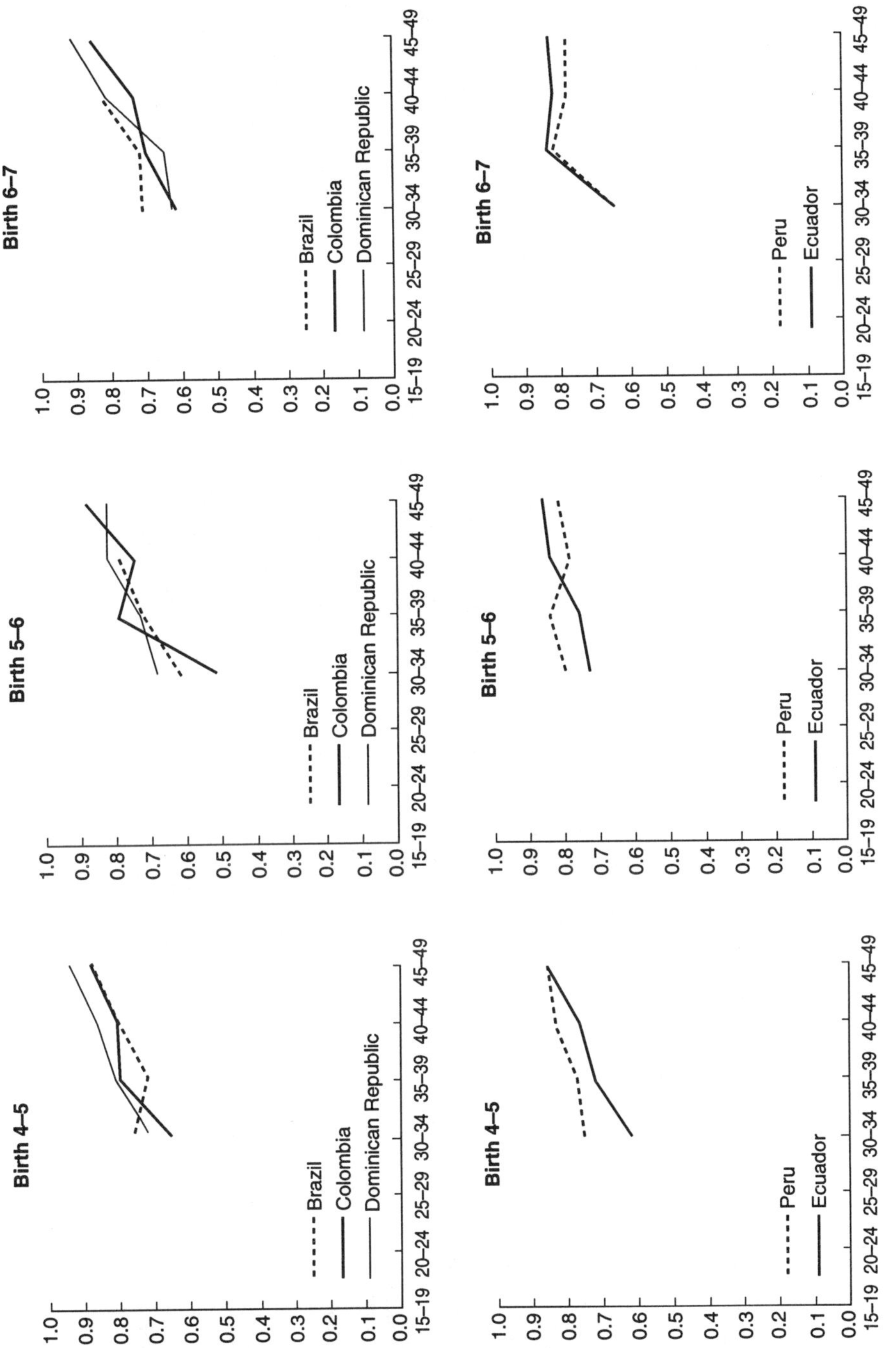
Birth 4–5
Birth 5–6
Birth 6–7
Brazil
Colombia
Dominican Republic
Peru
Ecuador
1.0
0.9
0.8
0.7
0.6
0.5
0.4
0.3
0.2
0.1
0.0
15–19 20–24 25–29 30–34 35–39 40–44 45–49

Table 3.4. *Latin America: some characteristics of women of reproductive age (who have had no premarital births), DHS.*

	Brazil			Colombia			Dominican Rep.			Peru			Ecuador		
	Age at first union			Age at first union			Age at first union			Age at first union			Age at first union		
	<20	20+	Total	<20	20+	Total	<20	20+	Total	<20	20+	Total	<20	20+	Total
Education (%)															
0–6 years	79.9	57.1	69.1	77.9	59.3	70.6	70.3	38.9	62.0	74.2	44.4	62.0	70.5	50.4	63.0
6+ years	20.1	42.9	30.9	22.1	40.7	29.4	29.7	61.1	38.0	25.8	55.6	38.0	29.5	49.6	37.0
Has used a method (%)															
No	15.0	12.4	13.7	18.8	18.2	18.6	31.3	25.7	29.9	39.1	29.1	35.0	38.4	36.8	37.8
Yes	85.0	87.6	86.3	81.2	81.8	81.4	68.7	74.3	70.1	60.9	70.9	65.0	61.6	63.2	62.2
Current user of a method (%)															
No	38.1	33.8	36.1	41.4	38.7	40.4	55.5	53.6	55.0	61.7	50.3	57.0	57.8	56.9	57.5
Yes	61.9	66.2	63.9	58.6	61.3	59.6	44.5	46.4	45.0	38.3	49.7	43.0	42.2	43.1	42.5
Parity when began using (%)															
0–2 children	55.5	71.4	63.0	39.6	53.8	45.2	28.8	46.6	33.5	23.1	41.9	30.7	22.2	35.7	27.2
3+	29.6	16.2	23.2	40.2	26.2	34.6	39.9	27.7	36.6	37.7	29.1	34.2	39.3	27.5	35.0
Non-user	15.0	12.4	13.7	20.2	20.0	20.2	31.3	25.7	29.9	39.2	29.1	35.1	38.4	36.8	37.8
TOTAL	52.5	47.5	100.0	60.4	39.6	100.0	73.5	26.5	100.0	59.1	40.9	100.0	62.9	37.1	100.0
	(1,867)	(1,689)	(3,557)	(1,794)	(1,175)	(2,969)	(3,714)	(1,341)	(5,055)	(1,648)	(1,139)	(2,787)	(1,830)	(1,079)	(2,909)
No. women ever in union			3,867			3,337			5,250			3,238			3,251
% women with premarital birth			8.0			11.0			3.7			13.9			10.5
TFR			(1983–6)[a] 3.5			(1984–6)[b] 3.2			(1983–5)[c] 3.7			(1983–6)[d] 4.2			(1984–7)[e] 4.2

Sources: [a] Arruda *et al*. (1987); [b] CCRP (1988); [c] SESPAS (1987); [d] Goldman *et al*. (1989); [e] CEPAR (1988). The remaining calculations were made by the authors.

Note: The figures in parentheses under Total relate to numbers of women surveyed.

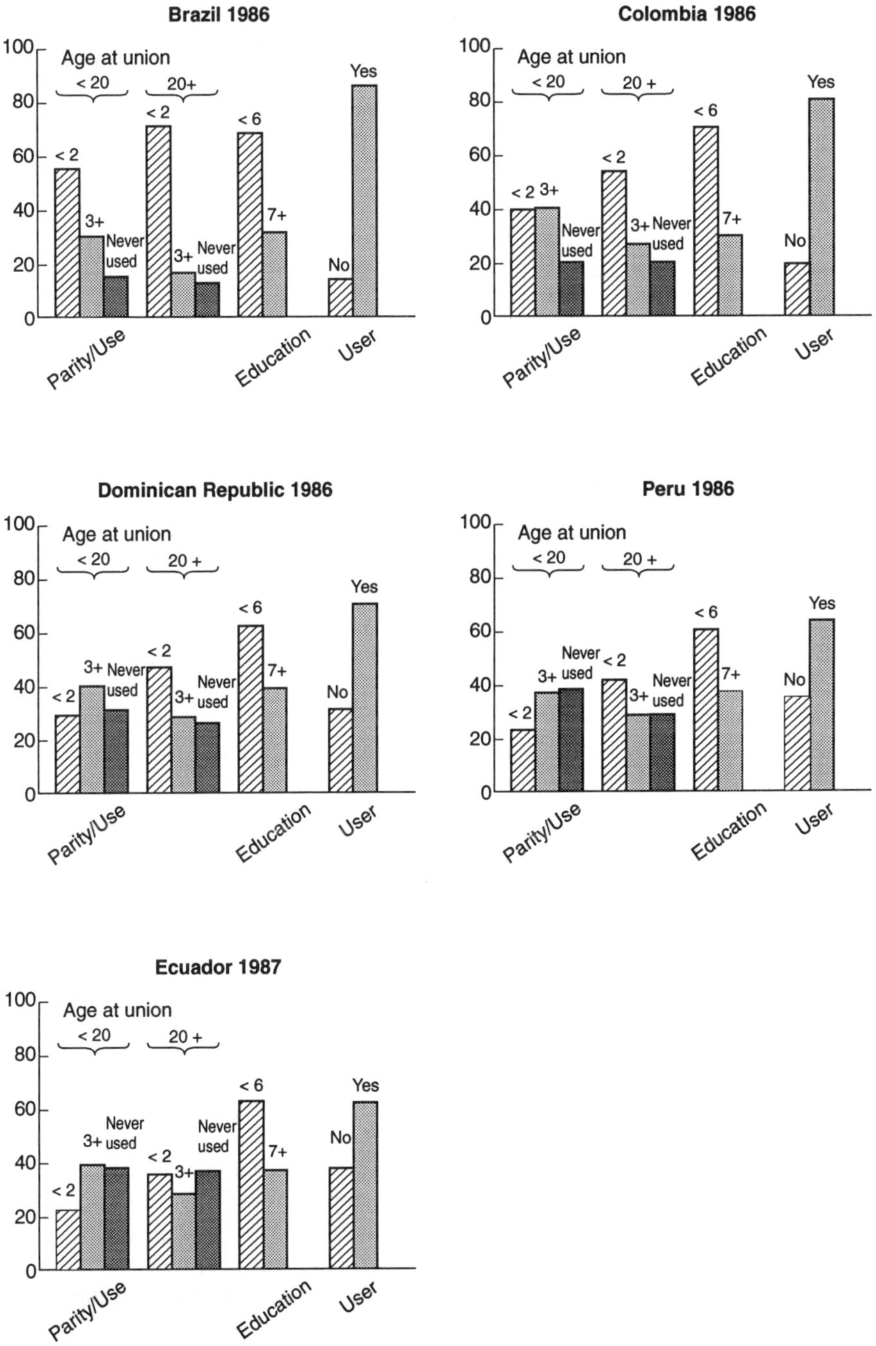

Fig. 3.3. ***Latin America: characteristics of women aged 15–49 (%), DHS***
Source: DHS.

contraceptive history. An approximation that makes it possible to separate out the pattern of contraceptive use as a factor in 'planning' or 'limitation' of the family can be obtained from the question asked in the DHS on parity at first use of contraception. By way of example, women using a method were separated into two groups: those who 'planned' their fertility, that is, who began to use contraception before the birth of their second child or at that parity; and those who adopted contraception as a form of 'limitation', at high parities. This distinction reflects the relationship between use and fertility for two specific types of women: women who used contraceptives from the beginning of the formation of their families, who are characterized by small families; and those who did so as a form of limitation when they already had a lot of children. This last group cannot truly be considered 'planners' in terms of the number and timing of their births. A third group of women, the residual group, would represent the female population that has never used any contraceptive method.

Another variable being introduced into this exercise is age at first union, since this marks entrance into the reproductive cycle and the duration of exposure to the risk of conception. Research (Ruzicka 1982) indicates that women who marry young are selective for high fertility. A larger proportion of women who entered union later (20 years or older) regulated the size of their families at the beginning of their married lives or at the time of their early births (parity 0–2); the percentages clearly follow trends in the fertility transition. Brazil is the country with the highest proportion of 'planning' families; 71 per cent of women practise contraception very early in the family formation process (by parity 0–2, see Table 3.4). Colombia follows with 54 per cent, the Dominican Republic with 47 per cent, Peru with 42 per cent, and Ecuador with 36 per cent. In contrast, the proportions that start to limit the number of children at high parities are lower, ranging from 16 per cent to 29 per cent. The proportion of women who started their first union at age 20 or older and who have never practised contraception is relatively low for the countries in the advanced stages of the transition—for example, 12 per cent in Brazil—but is as high as 37 per cent in Ecuador (Table 3.4).

If we examine the shape of the distribution of users (represented graphically as bars, or points connected by a line), Brazil has a curve with a very pronounced slope,[10] while the curve for the countries whose transition was more recent is smoother, until it practically becomes a straight line, not, however, changing direction. A totally different pattern is shown by women who married at an early age (before 20 years). In Brazil, the curve continues in all cases to move from higher to lower, that is, whether the woman spaces, limits or has never been a user. Colombia has equal proportions of 'planners' and 'limiters'. In the case of the Dominican Republic, the curve is distorted, and in Peru and Ecuador it is inverted. We conclude that this variable illustrates the gradual process of changing fertility as illustrated by the various family formation patterns found in each country.

[10] The steeper the slope, the greater will be the difference between the women who 'plan' and those who 'limit' their births.

In addition to the contraceptive measures analysed earlier, Fig. 3.3 (and Table 3.4) includes information on education, a socio-economic variable that is strongly related to the development process. It is to be expected that higher education for women means a larger decline in fertility. However, the estimates indicate that this is not the case. Brazil, where family size is small, is not the country with the highest educational levels. Similarly, Colombia has larger overall percentages of women with low education, larger than in both Peru and Ecuador, which are societies with larger family sizes and more recent signs of a fertility transition. The lack of a clear trend is repeated even if one considers levels of schooling among women who married while still very young and those who did so at a later age. From this we may conclude that there is no clear relationship between women's educational levels and the stage of transition in the life cycle, even when the estimates are disaggregated by age at union.

Comparing the Dominican Republic, where there have been sharp reductions in family size, with Peru, where fertility is still relatively high and the transition towards small families is less advanced, it is remarkable that educational levels and rates of contraceptive practice are very similar for both countries.

This brief examination illustrates the strong connection that exists between type of contraceptive use and the process of family formation, and the absence of a direct relationship with one of the major socio-economic variables (female education). This should help us recognize the importance of the separation that is occurring between the social and the intermediate determinants of reproductive behaviour. Some of these last factors appear to be becoming more and more independent of the first ones. To explore these aspects further would require an exhaustive analysis of each country, involving the socio-economic determinants in a more complex way, linking them to the family formation process.

Conclusions

This detailed analysis of patterns of fertility transition in Latin America, measured by means of the parity progression ratio (P_n), allows us to observe the behaviour of couples throughout the different reproductive phases of their lives. Latin America presents a wide range of fertility transitions, showing changes at all birth orders beginning with the second. These are profound transformations, which completely modify the family cycle and its internal momentum. In Colombia, Brazil, and the Dominican Republic, there are similar declines at every interval in the proportion of women who continue to the next birth. On the basis of this analysis, we can group the countries according to their stage of transition. Going from more to less advanced, they can be ranked in the following order: Brazil, Colombia, the Dominican Republic, Peru, and Ecuador. However, Ecuador, which began its transition more recently, is now showing signs of a more rapid transition than that of Peru.

This analysis of changes in family building over the past ten years demonstrates an unexpected pattern of behaviour in the initial phase of family formation: there has been an increase in the proportions of women who proceed from union to the first birth. This rise, found in every country, could be explained by a reduction in biological sterility. In the other phases of the life cycle, there have been changes at almost all birth-intervals, as couples adopt new norms of smaller family sizes. It is interesting that Colombia, a country that was already in a fairly advanced stage of the transition by 1977, is still the country showing the most rapid changes over time. This finding, and the way in which changes at each birth-interval are occurring, support the hypothesis that modifications in family formation will continue to be profound in Colombia, even at parities as low as the second child.

Contraceptive use and educational level are the intermediate variable and the social determinant to which most changes in fertility have generally been attributed. In this sense, our results indicate that patterns of contraception are indeed associated with the gradual changes taking place in each country's fertility transition. However, in the countries studied here, no clear association has been established between high educational levels and small family size. These findings allow one to speculate about the separation that is taking place between the social determinants of fertility and the intermediate variables. It appears that some of these variables, especially contraceptive use, are becoming increasingly independent of women's educational levels and their interrelationship with the internal dynamics of the family formation process. A deeper study of these trends would require a more detailed analysis of each country.

References

Arruda, J. M., Rutenberg, N., Morris, L., and Ferraz, E. A. (1987), *Pesquisa Nacional sobre Saude Materno-Infantil e Planejamento Familiar: PNSMIPF-Brasil, 1986* (Rio de Janeiro: Sociedade Civil Bem-Estar Familiar no Brasil (BEMFAM), Instituto para Desenvolvimento de Recursos (IRD)).

Brass, W., and Juárez, F. (1983), 'Censored Cohort Parity Progression Ratios from Birth Histories', *Asian and Pacific Census Forum*, 10/1: 5–13.

CCRP (1988), *Colombia, Encuesta de Prevalencia, Demografía y Salud 1986* (Columbia, Md.: Corporación Centro Regional de Población, Ministerio de Salud de Colombia and DHS, Institute for Resource Development, Macro Systems, Inc.).

CEPAR (1988), *Ecuador, Encuesta Demográfica y de Salud Familiar 1987* (Columbia, Md.: Centro de Estudios de Población y Paternidad Responsable, Instituto Nacional de Investigaciones Nutricionales y Médico Sociales and DHS, Institute for Resource Development, Macro Systems, Inc.).

Dyson, T., and Murphy, M. (1985), 'The Onset of Fertility Transition', *Population and Development Review*, 11/3: 399–440.

Goldman, N., Moreno, L., and Westoff, C. (1989), *Peru, Experimental Study: An Evaluation of Fertility and Child Health Information* (Columbia, Md.: Office of Population Research, Princeton University and Demographic and Health Surveys, Institute for Resource Development, Macro Systems, Inc.).

Juárez, F. (1983), 'Family Formation in Mexico: A Study based on Maternity Histories from a Retrospective Fertility Survey', Ph.D. thesis, University of London.

—— (1987), 'Probabilidades Censales de Agrandamiento de las Familias: Niveles y Tendencias de la Fecundidad en la América Latina', *Notas de Población*, 43: 9–24.

—— Quilodrán, J., and Zavala de Cosío, M. E. (1989), 'De una Fecundidad Natural a una Controlada: México 1950–1980', *Estudios Demográficos y Urbanos*, 4/1: 5–51.

—— (1989), 'Reproductive Behaviour and Social Sectors in Mexico', in *Social Sectors and Reproduction in Mexico* (New York: The Population Council).

Mauldin, W. P. (1976), 'Fertility Trends: 1950–1975', *Studies in Family Planning*, 7/9: 242–48.

Ochoa, L. H. (1981), 'Patterns of Fertility Decline in Latin America with Special Reference to Colombia', IUSSP, *International Population Conference* i, (Manila: IUSSP), 25–53.

Potter, J. (1984), 'Una Apreciación del Papel de las Variables Intermedias en el Descenso de la Fecundidad Latinoamericana', *Memorias del Congreso Latinoamericano de Población y Desarrollo, Mexico City, Nov. 8–10, 1983*, ii, (Mexico City: UNAM, El Colegio de México, and PISPAL).

Pullum, T., Casterline, J., and Juárez, F. (1985), 'Changes in Fertility and Contraception in Mexico, 1977–1982', *International Family Planning Perspectives*, 11/2: 40–7.

Rodríguez, G., and Cleland, J. (1984), 'Socio-Economic Determinants of Marital Fertility in Twenty Countries: A Multivariate Analysis', *World Fertility Survey Conference 1980: Record of Proceeding*, ii (London).

Ruzicka, L. T. (1982) (ed.), *Nuptiality and Fertility* (Liège: International Union for the Scientific Study of the Population).

SESPAS (1987), *República Dominicana, Encuesta Demográfica y de Salud, 1986* (Columbia, Md.: Consejo Nacional de Población y Familia, Secretaría de Estado de Salud Pública y Asistencia Social and DHS, Institute for Resource Development, Westinghouse).

Singh, S., and Wulf, D. (1990), *Adolescentes de Hoy, Padres de Mañana: Un perfil de las Américas* (New York: Alan Guttmacher Institute).

SS (1989), *México, Encuesta sobre Fecundidad y Salud 1987* (Columbia, Md.: Dirección General de Planificación Familiar, Secretaría de Salud and DHS, Institute for Resource Development, Macro Systems, Inc.).

United Nations (1983), *Indirect Techniques for Demographic Estimation* (Department of International Economic and Social Affairs, Population Studies No. 81, ST/ESA/SER.A/81; New York).

—— (1988), *World Population Prospects 1988* (Department of International Economic and Social Affairs, Population Studies No. 106, ST/ESA/SER.A/106; New York).

Weinberger, M. B., Lloyd, C., and Blanc, A. (1989), 'Women's Education and Fertility: a Decade of Change in Four Latin American Countries', *International Family Planning Perspectives*, 15/1: 4–14.

4 Demographic Transition in the Caribbean: An Attempt at Interpretation*

JEAN-PIERRE GUENGANT

Introduction

In the 1970s and 1980s, the thirty or so distinct geopolitical entities that make up the Caribbean region—defined here as the group of islands that constitute the West Indian archipelago plus the three Guianas (Guyana, Surinam, and French Guiana) and Belize—have in general undergone spectacular fertility declines. Fertility transition in the Caribbean does not, however, follow a single model. The latest known fertility levels range from 1.8–1.9 children per woman in five countries, to more than 5 children per woman in two countries. Furthermore, while the drop in fertility has been abrupt in some countries, it has been stretched over a long period in others. The following interpretation of these differing patterns of change is basically limited to an examination of the role of socio-economic factors. In the first place, the declines in fertility are briefly placed in their historical context, and in the context of the major transformations the countries of the region have undergone since the end of the Second World War. Secondly, an effort has been made to characterize the different types of transition. Finally, the importance of the following factors in the fertility decline is examined: the decline in infant mortality, the diffusion of contraception, the other proximate determinants of fertility, and economic and social change.

The Social and Economic Context

The Plantation Economy

In spite of their diversity in terms of surface area, population, and history, more or less all of the societies of the Caribbean have their origins in the plantation-based economic system imposed on them in the seventeenth and eighteenth centuries by the various European colonizing powers (Best 1968). Paradoxically, however, the elements that distinguish one country from another are also to be found in the gradual extension of the plantations throughout the region up until the nineteenth century. Thus, in a number of small islands, almost all available

* The author wishes to express his especial thanks to Alan B. Simmons of CERLAC, York University, Canada, for his comments and the assistance he provided.

land was occupied very early on by plantations, and the slave trade provided the basis of the population. The later development of plantations on other countries, in contrast, meant that up until the beginning of the twentieth century there was indentured immigration of Asiatic origin (to Guyana, Trinidad and Tobago, and Surinam in particular) or European immigration (to Cuba and the Dominican Republic), which accounts for the greater ethnic mix of those populations.

In this context, it is the availability of land, and/or the agricultural potential of the countries at the time of the abolition of slavery, that determined the possibilities for the establishment of peasant agriculture, leading in some cases to the emergence of 'peasant economies' (Beckford 1975), of which the extreme example is Haiti, where after independence in 1804, the former slaves developed a true counter-plantation economy.

The Caribbean: Geographic and Political Context

The geographical definition of the Caribbean includes all the islands of the archipelago of the Antilles, from the Bahamas to Trinidad and Tobago. Because of a common history and peopling, Bermuda, the three Guianas, and Belize are also often considered as part of the Caribbean. With this enlarged definition, the Caribbean comprises some thirty different geopolitical entities, in which five major groups can be distinguished.

First, the Greater Antilles group includes four countries, which in order of decreasing population size are: Cuba, Dominican Republic, Haiti, and Puerto Rico. These countries were colonized by Spain except for Haiti, which was the French colony of "Saint Domingue". Haiti and the Dominican Republic have been independent countries since 1804 and 1844 respectively, and Cuba since 1902. Puerto Rico fell under American control at the beginning of this century and is now "an associated state" within the United States. Puerto Ricans can freely move and settle in the mainland United States.

Next are the thirteen countries of an economic union called the CARICOM (the Caribbean Economic Market). These are all formerly British colonies which gained independence relatively recently, during the past thirty years, with the exception of Montserrat, which remains a British colony, but with substantial control over local affairs. These countries fall into several subgroups, three of which are used in this chapter for descriptive purposes:

- the four MDCs (more developed countries): Jamaica, Trinidad and Tobago, Guyana, and Barbados, so called because of their more diversified economies, as compared with the group of LDCs (Less Developed Countries). However, the name of this group does not correspond to present economic realities, in the sense that Guyana and Jamaica have lower per capita incomes than do the LDCs;
- the four countries (LDCs) called the Windward Islands: Dominica, Grenada, St Vincent and the Grenadines, and St Lucia;

- the three countries (also LDCs) called the Leeward Islands: Antigua and Barbuda, Montserrat, and St Kitts and Nevis.

The last two of the thirteen countries (the Bahamas and Belize) are combined with Bermuda and the US Virgin Islands, to form a group in this analysis. A few other dependent territories which are also part of the Caribbean are not treated in this analysis: Anguilla, British Virgin Islands, Cayman Islands, and Turks and Caicos, which are all still British colonies.

Finally, two more groups, defined on the basis of their colonial history, each made up of three countries, are used in the present analysis:

- Curaçao (a federal unit including Curaçao, Bonaire, Sint Maarten, and the two small islands of Saba and Saint Eustachius); Aruba (formerly part of Federation) both of which are part of the Netherlands Antilles); and Suriname (formerly Dutch Guiana);
- the three "French Overseas Departments" of Guadaloupe, Martinique, and French Guiana. These three countries have the lowest level of local power, even compared to other dependent territories.

The Fragility of the 'Peasant Option'

The adoption of the 'peasant option', as a strategy of resistance to work on the plantations and as a way in which former slaves might adapt to freedom, nevertheless ran into several problems: over and above the difficulty of access to land, there was a lack of capital and technical innovation, not to mention the limited size of the internal markets. This is why, at the household level, agricultural subsistence activities were often combined with cash crops and seasonal employment in the plantation sector; however, many also resorted to so-called intra-regional temporary migration.

Logically enough, the countries in which the development of peasant communities was limited—Barbados, the Leeward Islands (Antigua, Saint Kitts and Nevis, Montserrat), the Virgin Islands, the Bahamas—were heavily affected by intra-regional migration to Trinidad, Cuba, Panama, and the United States, from the 1880s to the 1920s, to such an extent that their populations decreased sharply (Guengant 1985). None the less, the countries in which large peasant communities had formed were also affected—Haiti, Jamaica, the Windward Islands (Grenada, Saint Vincent, Saint Lucia, Dominica)—thereby demonstrating the weakness of the peasant option towards the end of the nineteenth century.

Economic Diversification

Since the end of the Second World War, the increasingly grave crisis of the agricultural export sector has been associated with profound problems for the subsistence sector. In addition, the creation of relatively more stable and better-paid employment, in industry, construction, and especially services, has accelerated disaffection with agricultural work. Thus, at the beginning of the 1980s, in half the countries, no more than 15 per cent of the labour force were employed in the primary sector, and in seventeen of the twenty-five countries, more than half the labour force was employed in the tertiary sector (Table 4.1).

While the jobs created in the tertiary sector have generally benefited women more than men, they have nevertheless been singularly insufficient to meet the demand, which has led to the development of the informal sector and the persistence of very high unemployment rates. In most countries of the region, about 20 per cent of the labour force is unemployed, and the rates are generally higher for women than for men.

The relative importance of migration to these countries appears once again to be a good indicator of their changing economic structures. Thus, the countries which were the first to experience the highest rates of emigration—Puerto Rico, Jamaica, Barbados, and Montserrat in particular—are those which began their economic diversification in the 1950s, or which underwent an early decline in the agricultural sector (Simmons and Guengant 1987). On the other hand, the countries in which the proportion of the labour force employed in agriculture is still high (Haiti, the Dominican Republic, the Windward Islands, Guyana, Belize) underwent their greatest waves of emigration during the 1970s, reflecting the extent of the agricultural crisis in these countries.

As we shall see, awareness of this historical and structural context contributes to a better understanding of the diversity of the patterns of fertility decline in the Caribbean in recent years.

Transition or Transitions?

Mortality, Birth Rate, and Natural Growth

In the Caribbean, as in most of the Latin American countries, the increasing pace of mortality decline after the First World War was translated into a rapid drop in crude mortality rates, from 20–30 per 1,000 during the 1920s, to about 5–10 per 1,000 in the 1980s. The highly varying patterns of change in birth rates at the national level suggest, however, that several different types of transition distinguish each of the countries of the Caribbean from each other and from those of Latin America (Viel 1977).

In the first place, several countries in the region—Cuba, Jamaica, Dominica, and Barbados, for example—experienced declines in their crude birth rates between the two wars. In the case of Cuba, this development announced the beginning of a continuous fertility decline from then onward (Centro de Estudios Demográficos 1976). But that may also be the case in other countries, if only because of the consequences for fertility of the high rates of male emigration that were characteristic of most of the countries of the region during that period. Then, a new rise in fertility in the 1950s has been attributed to an increase in the frequency of unions and in their greater stability, and to a decrease in sterility (Harewood 1968).

Table 4.1. *The Caribbean: changes in the labour force by major sector of economic activity, from 1940–1950 to 1980, in various countries*

Country	Year of census or estimates											
	Primary sector[a]				Secondary sector				Tertiary sector			
	1940–50	1960	1970	1980	1940–50	1960	1970	1980	1940–50	1960	1970	1980
Cuba	42	(E)37	31	26	20	(E)24	26	27	37	(E)40	42	47
Dominican Republic	70	68	52	(E)46	12	12	14	(E)16	18	20	33	(E)39
Haiti	86	(E)80	80	68	6	(E)6	8	8	9	(E)14	12	24
Puerto Rico	39	24	8	3	23	29	32	24	38	46	59	73
Jamaica	48	40	34	(E)31	19	24	25	(E)16	32	36	41	(E)52
Trinidad and Tobago	30	23	22	16	28	30	26	33	42	47	52	51
Barbados	34	27	17	10	21	27	30	25	46	46	53	65
Guyana	51	41	35	30	19	25	21	19	30	34	45	51
Grenada	52	44	34	28	22	23	25	17	26	34	40	55
Saint Vincent	58	43	30	31	17	26	21	20	25	31	48	49
Saint Lucia	60	53	41	33	21	22	22	18	18	25	38	49
Dominica	43	52	40	37	28	23	18	21	29	25	42	42
Antigua	48	35	12	(E)5	18	26	24	(E)20	34	39	64	(E)75
Saint Kitts and Nevis	59	48	35	29	14	20	22	27	28	32	42	44
Montserrat	66	49	21	10	15	20	39	26	19	31	40	63
Belize	46	42	(E)39	37	16	24	(E)21	16	38	34	(E)40	47
Bahamas	27	16	8	6	25	24	22	16	48	60	70	77
Bermuda	7	(E)4	2	1	27	(E)24	21	13	66	(E)72	77	86
US virgin Islands	21	6	1	1	19	22	25	17	60	72	73	81
Curaçao	(E)8	4	(E)2	1	(E)50	41	(E)34	24	(E)42	55	(E)65	75
Aruba	(E)5	1	(E)1	0	(E)70	64	(E)30	19	(E)25	35	(E)69	81
Surinam	(E)35	(E)30	(E)25	(E)20	(E)25	(E)22	(E)21	(E)20	(E)40	(E)48	(E)54	(E)60
Guadeloupe	50	49	22	15	26	22	23	20	25	29	55	65
Martinique	48	40	18	11	22	22	19	17	30	38	63	72
French Guiana	(E)50	33	18	15	(E)18	21	22	20	(E)32	46	60	65

Sources: For the estimates: United Nations, Economic Commission for Latin America and the Caribbean (1989). The different censuses utilized in the preparation of this table were carried out at various dates. The data used and the corresponding years are as follows: Cuba: censuses of 1953, 1970, 1981, and estimates for 1960; Dominican Republic: censuses of 1950, 1960, 1970, and estimates for 1980; Haiti: censuses of 1950, 1971, 1982, and estimates for 1960; Puerto Rico and US Virgin Islands: censuses of 1950, 1960, 1970, 1980; Jamaica: censuses of 1943, 1960, 1970 and estimates for 1980; other CARICOM countries, Trinidad and Tobago, and Belize: censuses of 1946, 1960, 1970, and 1980/2 (Grenada's last census was held in 1982, and Dominica's in 1981. Since Antigua did not conduct a census in 1980, the data for 1980 are estimated); Bahamas: censuses of 1953, 1963, 1970, 1980; Curaçao and Aruba: censuses of 1961 and 1981, and estimates for 1950 and 1970; Surinam: United Nations estimates from 1950 to 1980; Guadeloupe, Martinique, and French Guiana: censuses of 1954 (estimates for French Guiana for 1954), 1961, 1974, 1982.

Note: (E) = an estimate when no census or complete data was available.

[a] The primary sector includes agriculture, hunting, forestry, and fishing, as well as the extractive industries. Some of the estimates used include the extractive industries in the secondary sector. However, in view of the marginal number of persons employed in this sector, the comparability of the data is not seriously affected.

However, not all the countries in the region, to say the least, fit this picture of pronounced and brief transition which is characteristic of developing countries (Chesnais 1986). In Cuba, for example, the rise in the birth rate after Castro's revolution is a special phenomenon. In Haiti, fertility, and therefore the birth rate, seem to have risen during the 1980s (Cayemittes and Chahnazarian 1989; Guengant 1990). Finally, in several countries, including Barbados and the Bahamas as well as Antigua, Montserrat, and Bermuda, birth rates have barely exceeded 35 per 1,000, and the increase in the birth rate during the 1950s was very modest, even insignificant (Guengant 1985). In these countries, the transition appears to have been rather gradual, since the maximum natural growth rates have been of the order of 2 per cent per annum, as contrasted with 3.5 per cent in the Windward Islands. However, while in the case of Barbados we may speak of a gradual and brief transition, in the case of the Bahamas we have rather a case of a gradual and long transition, since the population growth rate has remained at around 2 per cent since the end of the Second World War.

Changing Total Fertility Rates

This diversity of types of transition is made even clearer if one considers changes in the observed (or estimated) TFRs since 1950 in the various countries of the region (Fig. 4.1). In the first place, the initial levels cover a twofold range, going from 4 to 8 children per woman. Some countries have seen sharp increases. In the Windward Islands and Saint Kitts and Nevis, for example, the fertility indicators rose from 4–5 children per woman to more than 7 in the 1960s. In contrast, these indices varied little in such diverse countries as Puerto Rico, Trinidad and Tobago, Barbados, the Bahamas, and Guadeloupe. Finally, while the fertility decline in most of the countries started during the 1960s, in certain cases it began as early as the end of the 1950s, or the beginning of the 1960s—Grenada, Montserrat, Saint Kitts and Nevis, Aruba, Curaçao—while in others, it only really became established around the beginning of the 1970s: Dominica, Antigua, US Virgin Islands. Haiti, on the other hand, by the mid-1980s seemed to be still going through the stage of rising fertility experienced by a number of countries in the region in the 1950s (Guengant 1990).

On the basis of these observations, it is possible to develop a rough typology of the various demographic transitions found in the Caribbean. These are described in terms of fertility levels in the 1950s or 1960s, the most recent fertility levels, and the speed of the decline (Fig. 4.1, Table 4.2).

In the first place, among the eleven countries whose maximum level of fertility was only moderately high—around 5 children per woman—eight now show fertility measures close to or even below the replacement threshold. The remaining three countries, the Bahamas, US Virgin Islands, and French Guiana, are the countries that experienced very high levels of immigration from neighbouring countries with higher fertility levels. A common factor among these countries is the limited development of their peasant agriculture, in many of them the tertiary

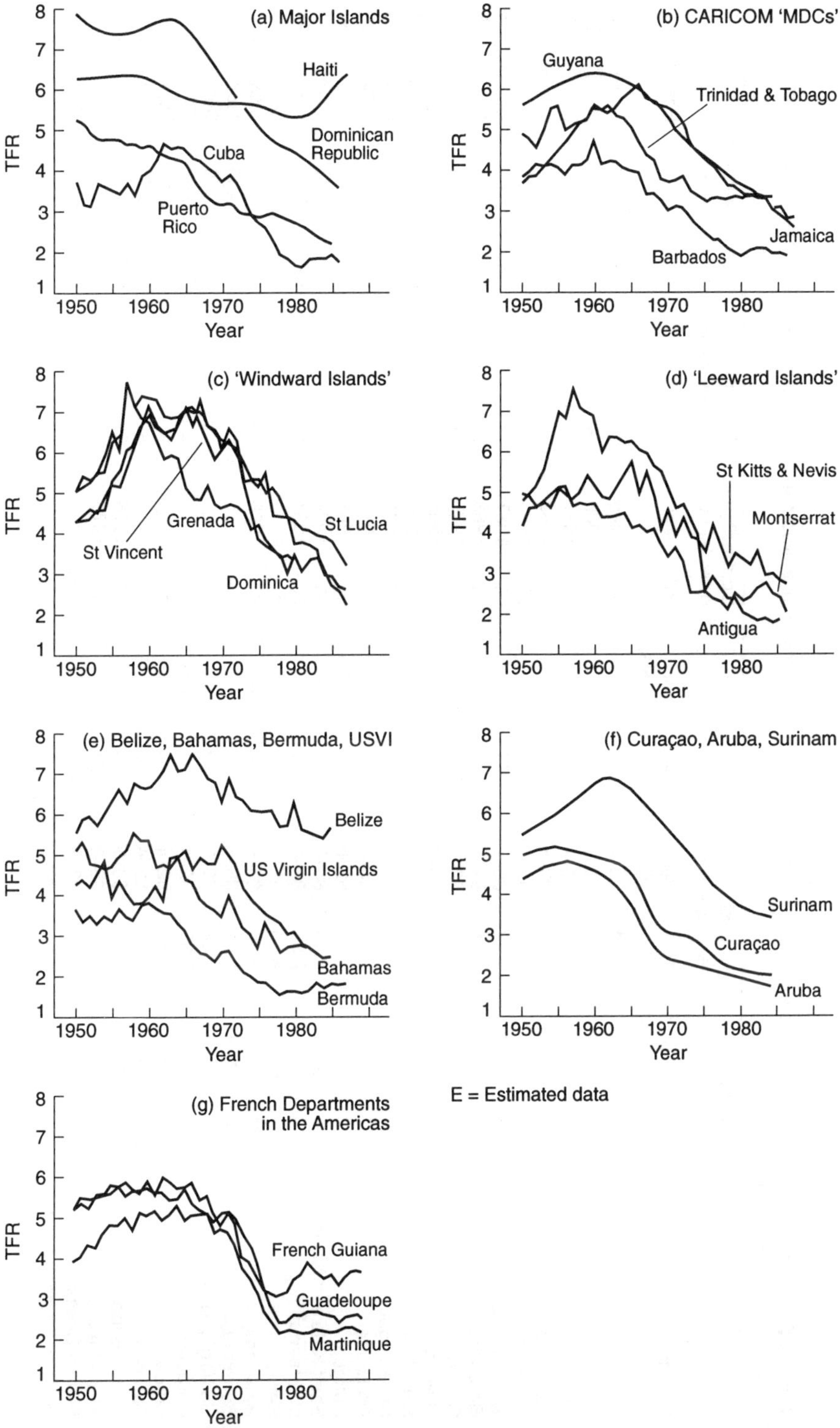

Fig. 4.1. *The Caribbean: changes in the TFR since 1950, selected countries*

Table 4.2. *The Caribbean: TFR, fertility rates among women 15–19 years of age, and rates of contraceptive prevalence,[a] according to latest available data*

Country	Maximum fertility level		Recent fertility level		Fertility rate, ages 15–19		Contraceptive prevalence[a]		Country Abbreviation	Classification of countries by			
	TFR	Year (1900s)	TFR	Year (1900s)	Rate	Year (1900s)	%	Year		TFR		Rate, 15–19	
Cuba	4.60	62–4	1.82	84–6	88	84–6	68	1980	Cuba	Aru.	1.80	Guad.	34
Dominican Republic	7.74	50–2	3.68	84–6	98	84–6	50	1986	DR	Ber.	1.81	Mart.	35
Haiti	6.34	56–8	6.18	85–7	87	85–7	7	1987	Haiti	Cuba	1.82	Ber.	36
Puerto Rico	5.09	50–2	2.27	83–5	68	83–5	70	1982	PR	Ant.	1.86	Aru.	48
Jamaica	5.97	65–7	2.72	85–7	114	85–7	52	1983	Jam	Bar.	1.91	Cur.	57
Trinidad and Tobago	5.55	60–2	2.92	85–7	94	85–7	53	1987	T&T	Cur.	2.06	Bar.	64
Barbados	4.36	60–2	1.91	84–6	64	84–6	55	1988	Bar	Mart.	2.24	Ant.	68
Guyana	6.38	60–2	3.35	82–4	103	78–80	31	1975	Guy	PR	2.27	PR	68
Grenada	7.21	57–9	3.39	78–80	115	78–80	31	1985	Gre	Mont.	2.33	Bah.	70
Saint Vincent	7.33	57–9	2.73	85–7	111	85–7	58	1988	SV	Bah.	2.48	Haiti	87
Saint Lucia	7.01	65–7	3.48	85–7	117	85–7	47	1988	SL	Dom.	2.49	Cuba	88
Dominica	7.01	65–7	2.49	85–7	95	85–7	50	1987	Dom	Guad.	2.54	USVI	90
Antigua	4.98	55–7	1.86	83–5	68	83–5	53	1988	Ant	Jam.	2.72	T&T	94
Saint Kitts and Nevis	7.24	57–9	2.85	84–6	104	84–6	41	1984	SKN	SV	2.73	Dom.	95
Montserrat	5.46	63–5	2.33	84–6	105	84–6	53	1984	Mont	SKN	2.85	DR	98
Belize	7.21	65–7	5.49	83–5	150	83–5	n.a.		Bel	USVI	2.88	Guy.	103
Bahamas	4.74	63–5	2.48	83–5	70	83–5	62	1988	Bah	T&T	2.92	SKN	104
Bermuda	3.73	59–61	1.81	85–7	36	85–7	n.a.		Ber	Guy.	3.35	Mont.	105
US Virgin Islands	5.39	58–60	2.88	80–2	90	80–2	n.a.		USVI	Gre.	3.39	Sur.	106
Curaçao	5.18	53–5	2.06	82–4	57	78–80	n.a.		Cur	SL	3.48	SV	111
Aruba	4.82	55–7	1.80	82–4	48	78–80	n.a.		Aru	Sur.	3.50	Jam.	114
Surinam	6.87	61–3	3.50	82–4	106	78–80	n.a.		Sur	F. Gui.	3.65	F. Gui.	114
Guadeloupe	5.80	62–4	2.54	88–9	34	88–9	44	1976	Guad	DR	3.68	Gre.	115
Martinique	5.71	56–8	2.24	88–9	35	88–9	51	1976	Mart	Bel.	5.49	SL	117
French Guiana	5.09	59–61	3.65	88–9	114	88–9	n.a.		F.Gui	Haiti	6.18	Bel.	150

Sources: UN (1989); CFPA (1989).

Notes: The TFR and the rates among 15–19-year-olds were calculated, for most countries, from registered births; and the number of women of reproductive age was, estimated from the results of the general population censuses conducted in the different countries of the region during the 1970s and 1980s. For Guyana and Surinam, the indices and rates were estimated on the basis of the 1980–4 estimates made by the UN. For Curaçao and Aruba, the indices and rates were estimated on the basis of the most probable trends in fertility.

[a] The contraceptive prevalence rate represents the percentage of women aged 15–49 (in some cases women aged 15 to 44) in union who were using some contraceptive method at the time of the survey.

sector of the economy grew rapidly after the end of the Second World War, and several of them had already had reductions in their birth rates between the two wars.

Furthermore, among the fourteen countries that had high fertility levels—that is six or more children per woman—eleven now have fertility rates between 2.5 and 3.5 children per woman. In this group, only Martinique has low fertility, 2.2 children per woman, typical of the preceding group, and two countries, Haiti and Belize, retain high levels of fertility. In almost all these countries, there was extensive development of peasant agriculture during the nineteenth century.

If the present differences in fertility levels among the countries of the region are thus largely a function of the previous levels, the rates of fertility decline are none the less far from equal from one country to another. Hence in a number of anglophone countries, and independently of initial levels, the present levels seem to be the result of a more or less regular decline, often spread over more than twenty years (Jamaica, Barbados, Saint Vincent, Saint Lucia, Saint Kitts and Nevis, Antigua). In the case of the non-anglophone countries, on the other hand, the present levels often appear to be the result of a sudden change (Martinique, Guadeloupe, Aruba, Curaçao, Cuba, but also the Dominican Republic). Any explanation of these differing rates of change derives from cultural and political factors, and from the history of the diffusion of contraception in the countries in question, all of which are factors that are not easy to untangle.

It is, therefore, very difficult to reduce the present fertility differences among the countries to a simple difference in the stage of the transition between those countries that had moderate maximum fertility levels, and those with very high levels. It is true that fertility seems to have stabilized in several countries (Cuba, Barbados, Antigua, Bermuda, Aruba) below the replacement threshold—as in European countries—and it is not out of the question that more countries may join this group before the end of the century. Nevertheless, the recent stability of the fertility indices around 3 children per woman in Trinidad and Tobago, and around 3.5 children in French Guiana, 2.5 children in Guadeloupe, and 2.2 children in Martinique, suggest caution in hypothesizing about the future.

The fertility levels of adolescents, however, remain high in most of the countries (Table 4.2), and the decline in these rates which is under way in some countries may influence future TFRs in a downward direction. None the less, the more or less complete control over their completed family size towards which the women of the Caribbean are heading also implies control over the reproductive timetable. In these conditions, changes in timing might soon play an increasingly important role in future variations in the TFRs, and should then become the object of increasing attention on the part of researchers.

The Determinants of Fertility Decline

The Decline in Infant Mortality

Among the many factors that account for fertility decline, the necessity of a prior decline in mortality, in particular of infant mortality, is frequently mentioned

(Chesnais 1986). In this respect it should be noted that in most of the countries of the region, infant mortality rates have been relatively low since the early 1950s. The data and some estimates indicate, in fact, that during the period 1950–4, two-thirds of the countries already had infant mortality rates below 100 per 1,000, and that it was during the 1960s that infant mortality fell below 100 per 1,000, in every country except Haiti and the Dominican Republic.

The beginning of fertility decline during the 1950s and 1960s—that is, before the diffusion of modern contraceptive methods, and in the context of the economic and social conditions then prevalent in the Caribbean—thus coincided with the stage at which infant mortality rates dropped below 100 per 1,000.

This statement lends some credibility to the hypothesis of the need for a prior decline in infant mortality as a condition for fertility decline. It also suggests that the decline in infant mortality before the Second World War, and its subsequent continuation, leading to infant mortality rates of no more than 30 per 1,000 for the period 1975–9, in two-thirds of the countries, have contributed to a change in modes of reproduction in the region. It is interesting to note, in this regard, that the eight countries in which infant mortality was lowest during the 1950s—Bermuda, US Virgin Islands, Cuba, Martinique, Puerto Rico, Aruba, Curaçao, Guadeloupe—include six of the eight countries in which the most recent total fertility rates are known to be near or below replacement level (Table 4.2).

Contraception and the Other Proximate Determinants

Bongaarts's work has made clear the importance of the proximate determinants of fertility in historical demographic regimes, and the major role played by the diffusion of contraception in recent fertility transitions (Bongaarts 1982).

In the Caribbean, the instability of unions and the importance of unions without cohabitation—called 'visiting unions' in the anglophone countries, *ami* in the French Antilles, *rinmin, fiancé, vivavek* in Haiti—have had an important inhibiting effect on fertility in the past. Because of the economic contribution of children to household income in peasant economies, fertility control through frequency and type of union must have been weaker in practice in the countries with a large peasantry than in the others. The reduction in the birth rate between the two wars in the countries with a smaller peasant population—which were also more affected by the essentially male emigration of the period—and their lower fertility rates at the beginning of the 1950s, in fact lend some credence to this hypothesis.

For the present period, the low fertility levels are above all the result of the spread of contraceptive practice, as is confirmed by Bongaarts's indices calculated on the basis of the results of surveys carried out at ten-year intervals in three different countries: the Dominican Republic (a case of rapid decline), Haiti (a unique case of recent increase) and Trinidad and Tobago (a case of stagnation), and the results of surveys conducted in Jamaica in 1976 and in Barbados in 1981 (Table 4.3).

Table 4.3. *The Caribbean: the proximate determinants of fertility, according to various surveys*

Indicators		Average fertility (Sources and periods, by country)							
		Dominican Republic		Haiti		Trinidad and Tobago		Jamaica	Barbados
		DFS-75 1970–4	DHS-86 1981–6	HFS-77 1976–7	EMM-US 1985–7	WFS-77 1974–5	DHS-87 1982–7	WFS-76 1971–5	CPS-81 1980–1
1. Basic indicators									
TFR (observed)	TFRo	5.85	3.82	5.95	6.4	3.19	3.15	4.32	2.16
% of women 15–49 in union	%m	n.a.	n.a.	57.9	72.2	63.1	68.7	83	72.2
% of "unstable" unions among all unions	%uu	n.a.	n.a.	25.6	17.3	14.9	20.8	20.5	51.8
Union fertility index[a]	UFI	9.74	6.82	11.31	9.25	5.24	5.59	7.99	3.91
Rate of contraceptive use in % among women in union	u*100	32	49.6	14.4	7.4	53.9	52.7	40	51.2
Prevalence modern and scientific methods	um*100	26.9	46.7	5.6	5.4	47.9	44.4	8.5	49.1
Overall effectiveness of methods	c	0.898	0.949	0.794	0.888	0.825	0.841	0.84	0.905
Induced abortion rate for women in union	AR	0	0	0	0	(E)0.7	(E)1	0	1.8
Mean duration of breast-feeding	MDB	8	9.4	11.3	(E)17	8	6	7	(E)8
Mean duration of post-partum infertility[b]	i	4.8	5.5	6.7	11	4.8	3.8	4.2	4.8
2. Bongaarts's indices									
Marriage index: Cm = TFR/UFI	Cm	0.601	0.559	0.526	0.691	0.609	0.563	0.541	0.552
Contraception index: Cc = 1 – 1.08*c*u	Cc	0.69	0.492	0.877	0.929	0.52	0.521	0.637	0.5
Abortion index: Ca = TFR/ TFR + 0.4*(1 + u)	Ca	1	1	1	1	0.881	0.837	1	0.664
Post-partum infertility index: Ci = 20/18.5 + i	Ci	0.86	0.833	0.794	0.679	0.86	0.897	0.879	0.86
Total natural fertility (assumed)	NFa	15.3	15.3	15.3	15.3	15.3	15.3	15.3	15.3
TFR(E)	TFRe	5.45	3.5	5.61	6.67	3.67	3.38	4.63	2.41
Difference TFRe – TFRo	TFR diff.	–0.4	–0.31	–0.35	0.28	0.48	0.23	0.31	0.25
Difference in %: (TFRe–TFRo)*100/TFRo	%TFR diff.	–6.8	–8.25	–5.8	4.32	14.99	7.34	7.26	11.81

3. Decomposition of Fertility									
TFR (E)	TFRe	5.45	3.5	5.61	6.67	3.67	3.38	4.63	2.41
Union fertility index	UFI	9.08	6.26	10.65	9.65	6.02	6	8.57	4.37
Natural fertility without abortion	NFU – a	13.16	12.74	12.15	10.39	11.59	11.5	13.45	8.74
Natural fertility of unions	NFU	13.16	12.74	12.15	10.39	11.59	11.5	13.45	8.74
Total natural fertility (assumed)	NFa	15.3	15.3	15.3	15.3	15.3	15.3	15.3	15.3
TFR (observed)	TFRo	5.85	3.82	5.95	6.4	3.19	3.15	4.32	2.16
Union fertility index	UFI	9.74	6.82	11.31	9.25	5.24	5.59	7.99	3.91
National fertility without abortion	NFU – a	14.12	13.88	12.9	9.96	10.08	10.71	12.54	7.82
Natural fertility of unions	NFU	14.12	13.88	12.9	9.96	10.08	10.71	12.54	7.82
Total natural fertility (calculated)	NFc	16.42	16.67	16.24	14.67	13.31	14.25	14.26	13.68
Difference NFc – NFa	NF Diff.	1.12	1.37	0.94	–0.63	–1.99	–1.05	–1.04	–1.62
	%NF Diff.	7.3	8.99	6.16	–4.14	–13.03	–6.84	–6.77	–10.56

Note: (E) = estimate

[a] Unions without cohabitation (visiting unions) are counted as 1/2.

[b] The mean duration of post-partum infertility is estimated from the mean duration of breast-feeding by the formula: 1.753 exp(0.1396*MDB – 0.001872*MDB^2).

The indices of contraception found in the most recent surveys in fact appear to be low in all cases except that of Haiti: on the order of 0.5, reflecting the major impact of contraception on the present fertility levels of these countries. In spite of variable average lengths of breast-feeding, on the other hand, the indices of post-partum infertility are now all in excess of 0.8, except, again, in Haiti in 1987. Frequency and type of union, however, continue to have a greater inhibiting effect on fertility. The importance of unions not involving cohabitation, in particular, which are conventionally counted as representing half of all stable unions, is reflected in low indices of nuptiality: on the whole, between 0.5 and 0.6, near the values of the contraceptive indices, confirming the major role that unions continue to play with respect to fertility levels. Thus, the low level of fertility in Barbados seems to be largely attributable to the importance of unions that do not involve cohabitation, about half of all unions. At the other extreme, it is the rise in the frequency and stability of unions that in large measure explains the increase in the total fertility rate observed in Haiti between the surveys of 1977 and 1987 (Guengant 1990).

Finally, the role of abortion in the recent fertility declines should not be overlooked. In fact, to arrive at reasonable overall results for Trinidad and Tobago and for Barbados, it was necessary to assume high, though not implausible, rates of induced abortion. It is well known, in fact, that the number of legal abortions in Cuba is roughly equal to the number of births. In Guadeloupe, where abortion has been legal since 1975, the number of abortions at the end of the 1970s was estimated to be 40 per cent of the number of live births (Guengant 1982). Finally, the legalization of abortion in Barbados in 1983 was specifically aimed at reducing the risks associated with the practice of (illegal) abortions, the number of which were judged to be too high.

That being said, it is indeed the rapid diffusion of contraception that explains the breadth of the observed fertility declines. The fertility levels of the 1960s probably correspond, in fact, in most of the countries, to contraceptive prevalence rates not exceeding 10 per cent of women in union. The results of the most recent surveys and the latest known levels of fertility suggest, on the other hand, that by the mid-1980s, the percentages of women in union who were using a contraceptive method were between 50 and 70, except in Belize, and Haiti, where it was 7 per cent (Table 4.2).

This rapid diffusion is largely the result of the campaigns to promote contraception and responsible parenthood, undertaken in the early 1960s by the family planning associations which were members of the IPPF (International Planned Parenthood Federation), and the various delivery programmes put into effect which, very soon, integrated family planning services into the public health structure, in maternal and child health centres, and in hospitals. The participation of the private sector (general practitioners and pharmacies), which today plays an important role in several countries, is only of quite recent origin.

In this context, and in the face of less vigorous opposition—particularly religious—than in Latin America, the use of the so-called traditional methods remained relatively low. In fact, the indices of method effectiveness calculated from the most recent surveys are of the order of at least 90 per cent—except in Trinidad and Tobago—and this index reaches 95 per cent in the Dominican Republic, where sterilization is the most widely used method.

The entry into and the spread of fertility decline do not, then, always correspond with the beginning of family planning activities and/or the size of these programmes. Thus, in Barbados, family planning activities began as early as the mid-1950s with government support. None the less Barbados never had very high fertility levels, and it is the importance of unstable unions and the probably high level of induced abortion that explain in large measure that country's presently low fertility level. In Trinidad and Tobago, the first family planning clinic was opened in 1959, and in 1967 the government adopted a national family planning programme and set up a National Population Council (United Nations 1978). However, in the last ten to fifteen years, fertility has remained around three children per woman, and the rate of contraceptive prevalence has stagnated at about 50 per cent of women in union. Similarly, Haiti, with substantial external resources, started a national family planning programme in 1973, but its results seem modest to say the least. Between 1977 and 1987, the use of modern methods has remained at about 5 per cent of women in union.

Social Change

It does in fact appear that a number of socio-economic conditions favourable to declines in fertility were present in most of the countries during the 1960s, and that it is within this underlying context that the rapid diffusion of contraception occurred. In order to test this hypothesis, the possible relationships between certain socio-economic indicators and the TFRs observed around the years 1960, 1970, and 1980 have been studied (Fig. 4.2.) Interestingly, it is the link between fertility levels and the percentage of the population engaged in agriculture—both sexes together—which seems strongest. In 1970 and in 1980 in particular the observed coefficients are quite strong, with R^2 in excess of 0.60 ($P < 0.001$). The relation to the percentage of the population working in the tertiary sector—again for both sexes—is equally important, since, for 1970 and 1980 again, the observed R^2 values are around 0.50 ($P < 0.001$). In contrast, the relationships between fertility level and GDP per capita, on the one hand, and the female employment rate, on the other, calculated for 1980, appear to be relatively weaker, although they are still statistically significant ($P < 0.01$).

Next, a multiple regression model was constructed using four independent variables: the per centage of persons engaged in agriculture around 1980, the percentage of persons engaged in the tertiary sector at the same date, female employment rates, and a variable that characterizes the economies as peasant-based or not. This model explains 71 per cent of the variance of the TFRs around 1980 ($P < 0.001$), but by far the strongest factor is the percentage of the labour force in agriculture, followed by the peasant character of the economy.

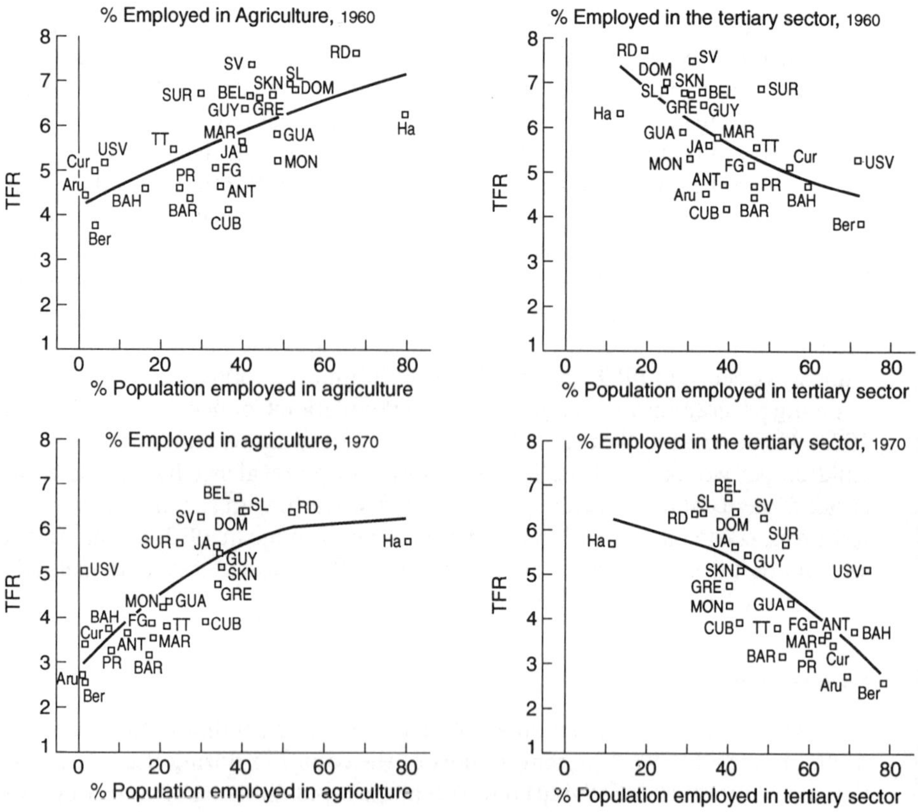

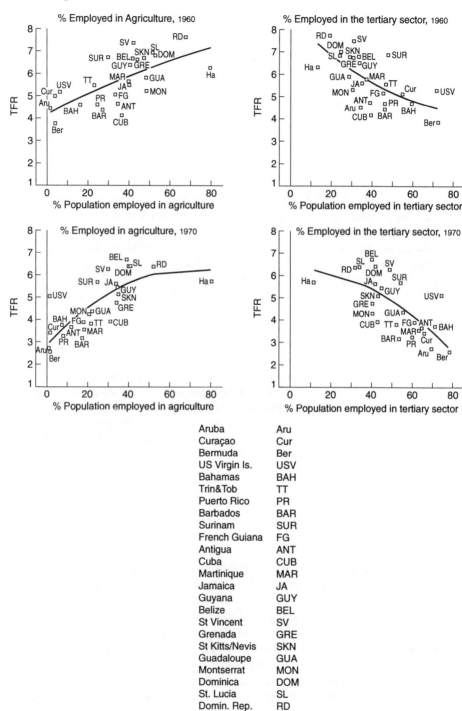

Aruba	Aru
Curaçao	Cur
Bermuda	Ber
US Virgin Is.	USV
Bahamas	BAH
Trin&Tob	TT
Puerto Rico	PR
Barbados	BAR
Surinam	SUR
French Guiana	FG
Antigua	ANT
Cuba	CUB
Martinique	MAR
Jamaica	JA
Guyana	GUY
Belize	BEL
St Vincent	SV
Grenada	GRE
St Kitts/Nevis	SKN
Guadaloupe	GUA
Montserrat	MON
Dominica	DOM
St. Lucia	SL
Domin. Rep.	RD
Haiti	Ha

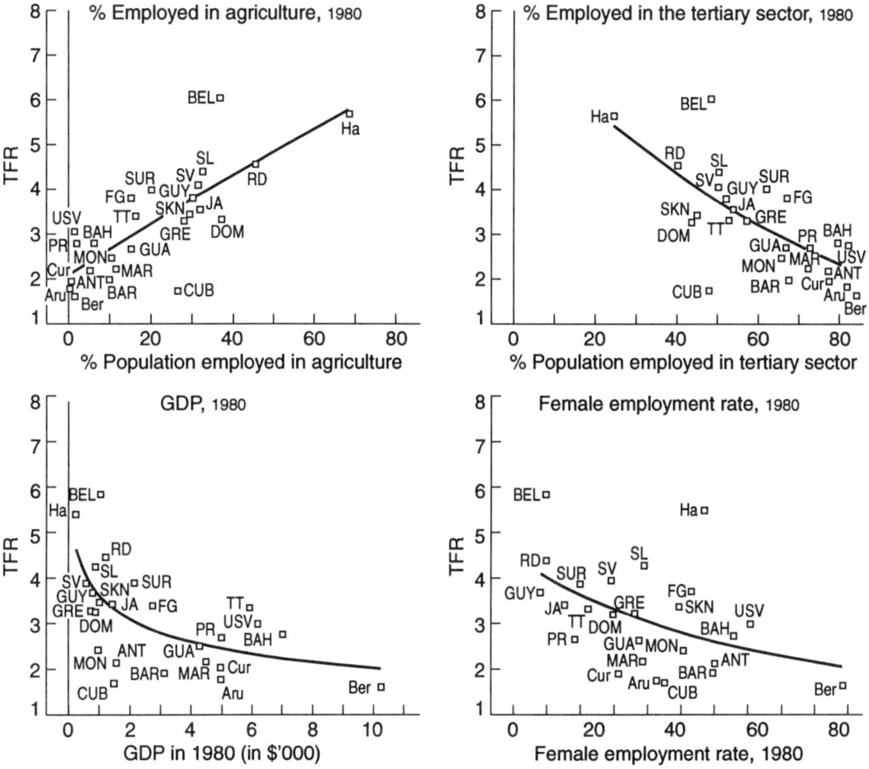

Fig. 4.2. ***The Caribbean: changes in the TFR as a function of several economic variables, various countries, 1960, 1970, 1980***

In spite of the limitations of this model, its results, and the quite strong correlations among the independent variables, strongly suggest the following interpretation of the recent fertility declines in the region. In the first place, the fertility declines in the Caribbean appear to be linked, as was also observed in a number of European and Third World countries (McGreevey 1985), to declines in agriculture and to the societal changes accompanying that decline. In the Caribbean, there has not really been a transition from rural societies to industrialized and/or urbanized societies. The transition has frequently been made directly to societies in which the tertiary sector dominates, and urbanization has been largely transnational, as rural migrants have become urbanized in the industrialized metropolises of North America and Europe. In the past forty years, in fact, nearly six million people from the Caribbean left their country of origin, and in practically every country these movements are more important than the rural–urban migrations within each country (Guengant and Simmons 1988).

These changes, which have been of varying importance from one country to another, have not necessarily been associated with a pronounced increase in living standards. They do none the less call into question the earlier explanations, which, especially in countries with a large peasant population, favoured high fertility (Gauvreau *et al.* 1986). The combination of various factors such as the deepening of the crisis in the agricultural sector—especially subsistence agriculture—declining infant mortality, the spread of primary schooling, but also new values introduced by returning or visiting emigrants, all would have led to the emergence of a new reproductive timetable, rejecting the idea of large families in favour of smaller ones. These factors would, to some degree, have come to maturity in most of the countries of the region during the 1960s, probably leading to a drop in fertility, first among the more favoured social sectors, then fairly quickly among the remaining social classes, as has been demonstrated in the case of Guadeloupe (Poirier 1989).

All in all, recent societal changes in the region, linked as much to social progress (reductions in mortality and extension of schooling) as to crisis situations (the non-viability of subsistence agriculture, high unemployment rates and massive under-employment), would have opened the way to an even more rapid diffusion of contraception to the extent that socio-economic conditions lent themselves to such diffusion and to the extent that the family planning programmes in the countries concerned were well organized.

Conclusions

This attempt to interpret the various types of demographic transition occurring in the Caribbean stresses the impact of economic and social factors on the initiation, the speed, and the breadth of fertility decline. The various types of transition seem, in particular, to have been conditioned largely by the existence of larger or smaller peasant populations, and by the degree of their marginalization since the end of the Second World War.

The economic system of plantations and the existence of peasant masses (campesinos, minifundistas) living on the fringe of this system are also to be found in several Latin American countries. However, comparisons between the Caribbean and Latin America should be made cautiously. In fact, with the exception of Haiti, Latin American countries have been independent for much longer than those of the Caribbean. They are also larger, generally less homogeneous, and it is not always clear that they can easily be studied as national entities. As far as fertility is concerned, before the First World War, no country of the Caribbean experienced the kind of fertility decline found in Argentina and Uruguay. On the other hand, the declines in fertility that began in the late 1950s in several countries of the English-speaking Caribbean have no equivalent in Latin America.

In spite of these differences, in Latin America, as in the Caribbean, the decline in infant mortality preceded the decline in fertility, and in both cases the latter is the result of the diffusion of contraception, as well as of a probably non-negligible use of abortion in many countries. Furthermore, the observed declines in fertility occurred in the context of rapid social change, characterized, among other factors, by advances in the schooling of children, the growth of urbanization, easier access to the mass media, etc. However, the mechanisms by which these patterns of social change have contributed to an increase in the rate of fertility decline are still largely unknown.

The profound economic and social crises that have occurred in a number of Latin American and Caribbean countries over the last fifteen years actually highlight the weaknesses of the long-accepted hypothesis of the adoption by 'imitation' of the small-family model, in a context of 'modernization'. However, the alternative hypothesis, according to which the decline in fertility is an adaptive response to the increasing difficulties of survival faced by the people of Latin America and the Caribbean, still has to be verified empirically.

References

Beckford, G. (ed.) (1975), *Caribbean Economy: Dependence and Backwardness* (University of the West Indies, Mona, Kingston, Jamaica).

Best, L. (1968), 'Outlines of a Model of Pure Plantation Economy', *Social and Economic Studies*, 17/3 (Sept.): 283–326.

Bongaarts, J. (1982), 'The Fertility-Inhibiting Effects of the Intermediate Fertility Variables', *Studies in Family Planning*, 13/6–7 (June–July 1982): 179–89.

Caribbean Family Planning Affiliation (CFPA) (1989), *Results of 1987–1988 Contraceptive Prevalence Surveys* (Antigua).

Cayemittes, M., and Chahnazarian, A. (1989), *Survie et santé de l'enfant en Haïti* (Port au Prince: Institut Haïtien de l'Enfance).

Centro de Estudios Demográficos (1976), 'La Población de Cuba', *Editorial de Ciencias Sociales* (Instituto Cubano del Libro / CICRED Series, 1974 World Population Year, Havana).

Chesnais, J. C. (1986), *La Transition démographique* (Presses Universitaires de France/INED, Collections Travaux et Documents, No. 113; Paris).

Gauvreau, D., Gregory, J., Kempeneers, M., and Piché, V. (1986), *Démographie et sous-développment dans le Tiers Monde* (Centre for Developing-Area Studies, No. 21; McGill University, Montreal).

Guengant, J. P. (1990), *Haïti* (*Monographs on Population Policy* series, Department of International Economic and Social Affairs, Population Policy Document, No. 25; United Nations, New York).

—— (1985), 'Evolutions démographiques et politiques de population dans la Caraïbe', Doctoral thesis in economics of development, Université de Droit et de Sciences Économiques de Clermont-Ferrand.

—— (1982), *Demographic Trends in Guadeloupe* (Caribbean Family Planning Affiliation, *Occasional Papers*, 1 (Aug.); St John's, Antigua).

—— and Simmons, A. (1988), 'Les Migrations caraïbéennes, pour une lecture historico-structurelle', Paper presented at the Journées Démographiques de l'ORSTOM on Migration, Changements Sociaux et Développement, Paris, 20–2 Sept. 1988.

Harewood, J. (1968), 'Recent Population Trends and Family Planning Activity in the Caribbean Area', *Demography*, 5/2: 874–93.
McGreevey, W. (1985), *Economic Aspects of Historical Demographic Change* (World Bank Staff Working Papers, Population and Development Series, Washington).
Poirier, J. (1989), 'Structure sociale, modes d'organisation familiale et fécondité: Une analyse des déterminants de la baisse de la fécondité en Guadeloupe (1954–1982)', Doctoral thesis, Department of Demography, University of Montreal.
Simmons, A., and Guengant, J. P. (1987), 'Population Flight, The Origins of the Caribbean Diaspora, 1950–80', Workshop on Caribbean Migration and the Black Diaspora, Institute of Commonwealth Studies, University of London, 17–19 June 1987.
United Nations (1978), *National Experience in the Formulation and Implementation of Population Policy: Trinidad and Tobago* (Department of International Economic and Social Affairs, United Nations, New York).
—— (1989), *Levels and Trends of Contraceptive Use, Assessed in 1988* (UN Population Studies, 110; New York).
—— Economic Commission for Latin America and the Caribbean (1989), *Statistical Yearbook 1988.*
Viel, B. (1977), 'Crecimiento de la Población de Europa y Las Américas', *Portada de Elena Mogollón Publicaciones* (Bogotá, Colombia).

5 The Demographic Transition in Latin America and Europe

MARÍA EUGENIA ZAVALA DE COSÍO

The foundations of the theory of demographic transition have recently been discussed in the light of changing fertility in the developing countries, and the universal applicability of this theory has been called into question, particularly in the case of Africa (Blake 1985; Tabutin 1985; Locoh 1986). A study by Jean-Claude Chesnais, based on a masterly reconstruction of world-wide demographic and economic time series, attempts to reaffirm the validity of the demographic transition theory for the countries of the developing world (Chesnais 1986*b*). Chesnais emphasizes propositions derived from the original formulation of the theory (Landry 1934; Notestein 1945 and 1953): 'Hence, apart from differences in context or rhythm, the demographic transition in the poor countries in reality follows the same fundamental mechanisms as in Europe' (Chesnais 1986*b*). None the less, Chesnais admits certain deficiencies in the theory, such as the underestimation of the roles of mortality and international migration, its excessive focus on natality, and the absence of an explanatory framework for demographic change: 'In spite of its robustness, the original transition theory only provides a relatively imprecise and rather inexplicit framework for the overall functional mechanism and for the structural causes of the observed demographic mutations' (Chesnais 1986*b*).

In point of fact, thinking on this issue has happened at two different levels: the one analyses the fundamental mechanisms of demographic change during the transition process; the other identifies the socio-economic and cultural variables that explain the process of change. Unfortunately, these two aspects have not been very clearly separated, either in defence or criticism of the theory.

Models of Demographic Transition

The definition of population dynamics or regimes is the first important contribution of the theory of demographic transition. The empirical scheme is the shift from a traditional regime of high mortality and fertility to a modern one of reduced mortality and fertility. The richness of the theory lies in its considerable broadening of the concept of demographic regulation, in which the dynamics of a population do not depend only on mortality and fertility, but also incorporate other parameters. The different variables interact among themselves, leading to complex systems of demographic reproduction that combine mortality, nuptiality, migration, and fertility. These systems exist in every type of society, but their characteristics vary considerably in different historical and geographic contexts.

Knowledge of demographic dynamics in Europe is based on studies of local and regional demographic micro-systems, between 1750 and 1940. Following the breakthrough established by the innovative work of Louis Henry, the results of the Princeton project on the demographic transition in 19th century Europe were published (Coale and Cotts 1986), as well as recent studies of Canada (Charbonneau *et al.* 1987), Geneva (Perrenoud 1985), Spain (Reher and Iriso-Napal 1989) and Catalonia (Cabre 1989). The demographic transitions described in these studies show a great variety of responses to the economic, social, and cultural changes occurring in the nineteenth century and at the beginning of the twentieth century.

From the lessons of the past may be drawn implications for the populations of the less developed countries (Knodel and van de Walle 1979), but this should be done prudently, bearing in mind the key role played by ideological forces in society (Lesthaeghe 1980). For this reason, when dealing with societies outside Europe, we must take new concepts into account. For example, in West Africa, demographic regulation depends on family systems very different from European ones, which explains some of the strong resistance to the introduction of family planning. In these societies, the fertility transition must necessarily be preceded by structural changes (Locoh 1988).

The results of the WFS have made available greater knowledge about the intermediate variables associated with fertility, which act directly on childbearing (Davis and Blake 1956; Bongaarts 1978): age at first union, breast-feeding, abortion, sexual abstinence, and contraception. The importance of these variables depends on the particular context of each population. As Locoh wrote: 'Every society exercises controls over its fertility. The transition should be seen as the evolution of the forms of control' (Locoh 1986).

This leads us to consider the second contribution, probably the more stimulating one, of the theory of demographic transition: an analytic framework for the relationships between changes in the demographic variables and economic, social, and cultural changes. The interactions should be understood as being reciprocal, that is, variations result both from the influence of economic and social change on demographic reproduction, and from the influence of the demographic variables on economic and social conditions.

Various explanatory models of the demographic transition have been constructed that included indirect cultural factors, such as, for example, the influence of religion (Lesthaeghe and Wilson 1982), the notion of authority (Le Bras and Todd 1981), the value of children (Aries 1980) and the status of women (Boserup 1985). However, it is impossible to define a single model of demographic transition, since the conditions in which it is produced vary, both at different periods and locations, and in the particular context of the norms and beliefs of each society. From this point of view, it is very useful to conduct comparative studies of demographic change, comparing past situations with the processes occurring in the contemporary developing world. For example, a comparison of Europe between 1800 and 1930 with Latin America between 1900 and 1970 reveals quite different demographic dynamics. However, there are also very significant similarities between the European and Latin American demographic transitions, despite the differences in time and place.

In the first part of this study, we present what we shall call the 'European model of demographic transition', based on the demographic parameters emphasized by Chesnais (1986*a*). In the second part, the fertility transitions of Latin America and Europe are compared. In this comparison we attempt to go beyond individual differences to the identification of some of the general mechanisms that mark the appearance of new reproductive norms in non-Malthusian societies.

The European Model of Demographic Transition

Chesnais defines three principal postulates of the theory of demographic transition, which, in his view, are universally applicable (Chesnais 1986*a*), in spite of the strong regional variations brought to light in the Princeton study (Coale and Cotts 1986). The three paradigms are as follows:

- the precedence of mortality decline;
- the model of reproductive transition in two phases (limitation of marriages, then limitation of births);
- and the influence of the beginning of modern economic growth (according to Kuznets) on the start of the long-term fertility decline (Chesnais 1986*b*).

In this schema may be found the two levels of analysis of the theory of demographic transition mentioned earlier: the first two postulates refer to demographic dynamics, and the third, to the explanatory framework.

The Precedence of Mortality Decline

In every case that has been analysed, a drop in mortality precedes changes in fertility. The exceptions cited in the literature, such as cases in France, Belgium, and Germany (Coale 1973; Knodel and van de Walle 1979) are probably false exceptions, resulting from omissions in the data series or variations in the quality of the data series (Chesnais 1986*a*: 334–40). What clearly does vary a great deal is the level of mortality. It is more or less high at the beginning of the transition, and the pace of change is more or less rapid. These are the characteristics that confirm the particular structure of each of the cases of demographic transition.

In the absence of changes in reproductive patterns, mortality decline tends to increase the number of descendants of each generation, because individuals are more likely to survive to reproductive age, and because unions are not dissolved so frequently by the death of one of the partners. In addition, improved sanitation directly increases levels of fertility, as sterility vanishes and as a result of conditions more favourable to the satisfactory development of pregnancy.

A decline in mortality is thus a key and endogenous variable to the model of demographic transition: without changes in other determinants, the immediate result is a rise in fertility. Therefore, a decline in mortality encourages attitudes favourable to reproductive control, which, in specific situations, lead to the voluntary limitation of births. However, there may be other more traditional solutions, such as 'Malthusian preventive control', which consists of delaying and postponing marriage, or migration as a way of controlling population replacement.

There are many indications that fertility actually rose at the beginning of the European demographic transition. In England, total fertility went from five children per woman between 1750 and 1775 to more than six between 1805 and 1825 (Wrigley and Schofield 1981). Fertility levels increased in a number of German towns between 1860 and 1890, in the Flemish provinces of Belgium between 1856 and 1890, in fourteen administrative units of Italy between 1861 and 1911, and in fifteen Spanish regions between 1887 and 1910 (Lesthaeghe 1980: 547–8 n. 26).

In France, on the other hand, as early as 1750 reductions in mortality were quickly accompanied by changes in the patterns of nuptiality and marital fertility (Blayo 1975). Some French departments registered increases between 1856 and 1890, due to a reversal of the system of late marriage (earlier ages at marriage are observed), that is, a change of a short-term nature (Le Bras 1989). The disequilibrium caused by a drop in mortality underlies all modern fertility transitions. This explains the very late transition in Spain, after 1918 (Reher and Iriso-Napal 1989), at a time when mortality began to drop increasingly rapidly: Spanish infant mortality was still 214 deaths per 1,000 live births in 1900!

The effect of mortality on the population replacement has been calculated, in France, using conditions of mortality, nuptiality and fertility for women born in 1750 who did not limit their births. With 8.7 births per marriage, the net number amounted to only 2.0 live-born children per woman, or barely the level required for population replacement (Leridon 1987). The high mortality of these women from birth onwards, late marriage, and the high proportion who remained single or were widowed, seriously limited the reproductive capacity of the 1750 cohort.

In the totally different context of a contemporary generation that has just completed its reproductive cycle (women born in 1950), with low mortality, early marriage, and only small proportions widowed or remaining single, 'maximum' fertility could reach 12.3 children per marriage and 8.7 live-born children per woman, if there were no birth control. With that level of reproduction, each generation would quadruple in size in under thirty years (Leridon 1987).

These results for the end of the nineteenth century show the impressive impact of reductions in mortality on fertility. They also herald the inevitable appearance of birth limitation among European couples. In most cases, marital fertility began to decline after 1870: before 1900 in northern and western Europe, between 1900 and 1920 in eastern and southern Europe. In France, marital fertility changed much earlier, from the middle of the eighteenth century. In the face of the steady decline in mortality that began in the seventeenth century, France did not resort to a solution that involved massive levels of emigration, as did the rest of the countries of northern and southern Europe. The French demographic transition is distinguished by the early appearance of birth limitation within marriage as part of the regulation of population growth.

In the rest of Europe, during the pre-transitional phase, the traditional systems of reproduction were regulated above all by the control of nuptiality. Only during a second phase was control of marital fertility achieved, when limitations on marriage had already become an insufficient demographic solution or had exceeded the socially acceptable limits.

The Two-Phase Model of Reproductive Transition (Limitation of Marriage, followed by Limitation of Births)

The second postulate defined by Chesnais, that of a two-phase transition of reproductive patterns, considers the control of nuptiality as a first stage, in which the proportion of a cohort that enters matrimony is limited, and age at marriage is delayed. In northern and western Europe, nuptiality was already at a secular low, with clear trends toward deferred marriage and high proportions remaining single. However, starting in the eighteenth century, when the demographic situation began to change, until the time when couples began to limit their births, all the countries of northern and western Europe registered increases in the proportions remaining unmarried for life.

Around 1870, 10–20 per cent of women in western Europe were still single (Table 5.1), and the differences in this measure between the countries of emigration, with lower nuptiality (Sweden, Norway, Ireland, Portugal) and the countries

Table 5.1. *Europe: demographic indicators, 1870 and 1930*

Country	Age at first marriage	% single at age 50	Completed Family Size		Relative Decline 1870–1930(%)
			c.1870	c.1930	
Denmark	27.1	11.6	4.40	2.25	48.9
Finland	25.5	14.4	4.80	2.43	49.4
Norway	27.2	17.0	4.50	2.01	55.3
Sweden	27.5	17.6	4.38	1.84	58.0
England	25.2	12.4	4.88	1.81	62.9
Scotland	26.0	18.7	6.10	n.a.	n.a.
Ireland	26.4	18.5	5.80	3.20	44.8
Belgium	27.7	17.5	4.50	2.01	55.3
France	24.7	13.1	3.38	1.98	41.4
Netherlands	27.5	13.7	5.06	2.81	44.5
Germany	25.8	10.5	5.30	2.08	60.8
Austria	25.1	15.1	5.06	n.a.	n.a.
Switzerland	27.5	18.4	4.02	1.98	50.7
Spain	24.6	10.6	5.00	2.53[a]	49.4
Italy	24.0	11.7	5.10	2.25[b]	55.4
Portugal	26.0	22.0	5.10	n.a.	n.a.

Source: Festy 1979.

[a] 1948
[b] 1956

of immigration with high nuptiality (Australia, the United States) are well known (Festy 1979: 21). Accordingly, mean ages at first marriage in excess of 27 years are observed among women in the Scandinavian countries (Denmark, Norway, Sweden), in the Netherlands, in Belgium, and in Switzerland. In the remaining countries of Western and Southern Europe, women married between the ages of 24 and 26 (Table 5.1). Only in Eastern Europe was marriage much earlier, between the ages of 20 and 22.

As a general rule, when nuptiality was high, it was also early, and when it was lower it was also later. Also, when nuptiality was early, legitimate fertility was low, and when nuptiality was late, marital fertility was high, so that the final number of offspring was fairly low in all cases (Festy 1979: 45–8).

During the early years of the demographic transition, at the end of the nineteenth century, average fertility reached 4 or 5 children per woman (Table 5.1). Towards the first third of the twentieth century, as birth control techniques became more widespread, levels of 2 children per woman were reached. The reduction in total fertility ranged from 40 to 63 per cent between the years 1870 and 1930 (Table 5.1).

After a recovery, which led the generations born during the 1930s to have the largest families of the century, there was a general reduction in levels of fertility, starting in 1964, and this has been called 'the second contraceptive revolution' (Leridon 1987). At that time, the use of modern contraceptive methods became widespread throughout Europe, with the appearance of the hormonal pill and the intra-uterine device (IUD), and with the adoption, in many European countries, of legislation legalizing abortion. The practice of birth control became widespread among women of all social classes. Fig. 5.1 shows the converging trend in fertility found in every European country except those of Eastern Europe.

The Influence of Modern Economic Growth

Another basic postulate of Chesnais's model is that it emphasizes the connection between economic growth and the fertility transition, bearing in mind that economic growth, in the broad sense used by Kuznets, includes economic progress, political change, and social development (Chesnais 1986*a*). However, this postulate in Chesnais's model cannot be dealt with at the same level as the two previous ones, since it has explanatory value. Therefore, it is not comparable to the two first postulates, which refer precisely to the demographic dynamics that are now to be explained. For example, the principle that a reduction in mortality must precede a decline in fertility has already been enunciated. It is obvious that changes in mortality are themselves due to socio-economic and cultural change. Among the three principles defined by Chesnais, the last moves the analysis to a different level.

A key factor in the fertility transitions of Europe is the influence of change at the individual level: in schooling, urbanization, economic activity, family strategies, new cultural and religious values, individualism, and changes in the value of children, etc. (Lesthaeghe 1983). These changes are related to the formation of

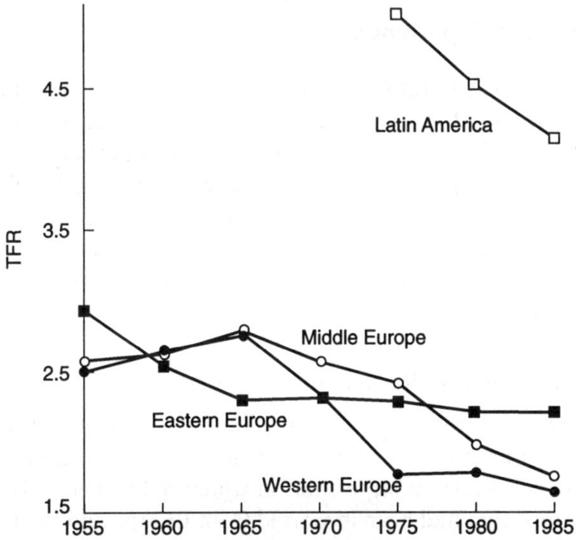

Fig. 5.1. ***Europe and Latin America:TFRs 1955–1985***

modern states, equality among citizens, secularization and the loss of religious observance (Le Bras 1989; Lesthaeghe and Wilson 1982), the development of social infrastructures (schools, hospitals) and communications networks (canals, highways, railways), and substantial increases in agricultural and industrial productivity (Chesnais 1986*a*).

However, one of the most interesting theoretical contributions relates demographic change to cultural change, independently of the socio-economic context. This has been explained as follows: 'Neighboring areas with similar socio-economic conditions but distinct cultures entered the transition period at different times, while areas with differing levels of socio-economic development but similar cultures entered the transition at the same time' (Knodel and van de Walle 1979: 235). There is insufficient space in the present work to present the arguments about the respective influence of economic, social, and cultural factors in determining demographic change (Chesnais 1986*a*). As further advances are made in the case studies of regional population dynamics in Europe, it becomes increasingly clear that there is no simple and general model to explain the process of demographic transition (Coale and Cotts 1986; Reher and Iriso-Napal 1989). What is more, current socio-economic conditions in Latin America are so radically different from the conditions prevailing in Europe in the eighteenth and nineteenth centuries, that the interpretive schemes constructed on the basis of historical experience become of very little use for explanatory purposes.

Therefore, with the limited aim of comparing changes in population patterns during the demographic transitions of Europe and of Latin America, we analyse only the first two postulates of Chesnais's model: the precedence of the decline in mortality, and a two-phase reproductive transition.

The Latin American Experience

This section analyses the Latin American demographic transition and compares it to the European model. We shall refer to the Latin American countries as a whole, but, even though Argentina and Uruguay are not excluded from the analysis, they are treated separately from the other countries. In Argentina and Uruguay, the demographic transition began towards the end of the nineteenth century, seventy years earlier than in the remaining countries. This phenomenon can be explained by the fact that large numbers of European immigrants came into the country in that period.

The Precedence of Mortality Reduction

The demographic transition began in Latin America at the end of the nineteenth century with declining mortality. There is evidence of very large reductions in mortality occurring in certain large cities in which public health benefited from medical innovations that had been imported from Europe and the United States. For example, in the city of Havana, the 1905–7 life expectancy of 39.1 years was on a par with European levels of that period (Díaz-Briquets 1981). Nevertheless, the overall 1890 life expectancy of 26 years for Latin America (Arriaga 1970) is similar to that of France in 1750. Very rapid reductions in mortality began about 1930, and a life expectancy of 66 years was reached in 1987.

The sharp drop in mortality in Latin America had a dual impact on the birth-rate: on one hand, as the population became younger, the proportion of women of childbearing age declined; on the other, the pattern of fertility shifted to older women, as couples survived longer. These structural changes had a negative impact on natality. Table 5.2 shows, for the period 1950–60, the effects on the birth rate of changes in population structure and changes in fertility. If fertility levels had not altered, birth-rates would have been reduced by 1 to 6 points per 1,000 population, as a result of the rejuvenation of the population. Such reductions did not occur, however, because levels of fertility rose between 1.5 and 4.5 points per 1,000 (Table 5.2). Fertility rates increased at younger ages as a result of shorter birth intervals, and at older ages, because of the higher survival rate of spouses.

Table 5.2. ***Latin America: variations in birth rates due to structural effects, 1950–1960 (per 1,000)***

Country	Change in Birth Rate	Effects of structures			Fertility
		Total	Population	Fertility	
Brazil	+0.9	−2.5	−2.4	−0.08	+3.4
Costa Rica	−2.4	−3.9	−3.5	−0.4	+1.5
Panama	−0.02	−1.72	+0.01	−1.7	+1.7
Mexico	−1.8	−6.3	−4.7	−1.8	+4.5
Venezuela	+1.0	−3.5	−2.9	−0.6	+4.5

Sources: Data on populations by age-groups and sex and ASFRs in 1950 and 1960: CELADE and national sources.

The examples of Chile and Costa Rica are presented in Figs. 5.2 and 5.3. Between 1950 and 1960, women aged 35–39 years registered the greatest proportional rise in age-specific fertility: 27 per cent in Chile, and 20 per cent in Costa Rica, compared with a 14 per cent increase in the TFRs of both countries. Women aged 25–29 in both countries had the highest ASFRs. The rise in ASFRs is reflected in high-level total fertility rates until the early 1960s (Figs. 5.2 and 5.3).

The rise in fertility in Latin America occurred for the same reasons as it did in Europe: a reduction in sterility caused by infection and a decline in widowhood. However, the impact was greater, since mortality declined much more rapidly than it had done in Europe, and because much more advanced medical means of combating infection, sterility, and intra-uterine mortality were available in 1950 than in the nineteenth century. The reduction in sterility is perfectly illustrated by the case of Mexico: the proportion of women who still had no children after five years of union, which was 15 per cent for the 1927–31 birth cohort, fell to 5 per cent for the 1947–51 cohort. In addition, the proportion of women in union without any child after the age of 35 dropped from 4 per cent to 2 per cent between the 1927–31 and 1947–51 cohorts (Zavala de Cosío 1988).

According to the Mexican life tables, the proportion of women who were widowed declined by 54 per cent between 1920–30 and 1960–70 and, with the same completed family size, the net reproduction ratio rose by 88 per cent, from 1.48 to 2.79, solely from the effect of that drop in mortality.

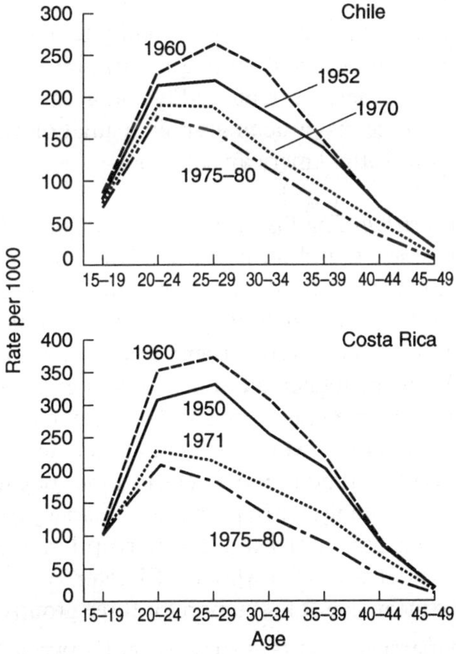

Fig. 5.2. ***Chile and Costa Rica: fertility rate by five-year age groups***

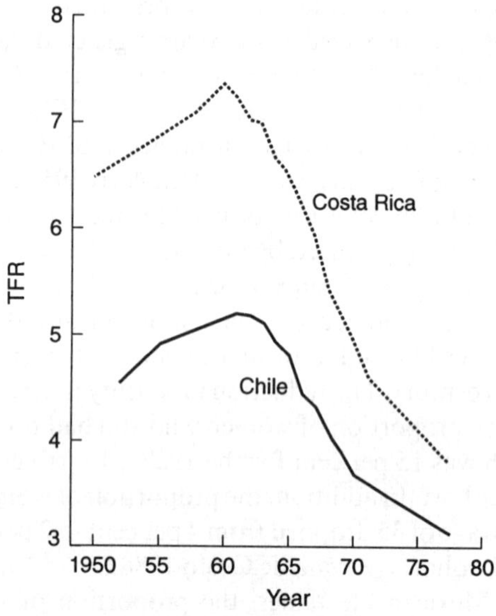

Fig. 5.3. *Chile and Costa Rica: TFRs 1950–1980*

The Fertility Transition

In Latin America, in the face of the rise in fertility starting in the middle of the twentieth century, there was no control of nuptiality to limit the size of families similar to the one that had occurred among the traditional European populations. Rather, there was an increase in nuptiality and in earlier unions. The use of marriage limitation as a means of demographic regulation was never a socially acceptable pattern in the Latin American context.

The Prelude to the Transition: The Rise in Both Nuptiality and Fertility up until the 1960s A CELADE study found an increase in the proportions of women in union at the ages of 20–24 and 40–44, and higher and earlier nuptiality (Camisa 1971). These data might appear fragile evidence, since the quality of the censuses has always been doubtful, but several recent studies using other sources have confirmed the trend toward higher nuptiality (Chapter 7). Between 1950 and 1960 in Latin America, the median proportion of women in union rose from 58 to 63 per cent. The proportion of women who never married dropped from a median value of 19 per cent in 1950 to 9 per cent in 1980. Beginning in the 1950s, legal marriage increased notably, while permanent celibacy declined, along with the proportion of consensual unions and the interruption of unions (because of the reduction in the incidence of widowhood) (Chapter 7).

Table 5.3 shows the mean age at first union for three groups of countries:

- countries in which marriage occurs at an early age (between 20 and 21): Colombia, Costa Rica, Ecuador, Mexico, Panama, Paraguay, Peru, and Venezuela;

Table 5.3. *Latin America: demographic indicators, 1960 and 1985*

Country	Age at first marriage	%Single at age 50	TFRs 1960	TFRs 1985	Relative Decline 1960–1985(%)
Bolivia	n.a.	n.a.	6.63	6.30	5.0
Colombia	21.3	11	6.72	3.60	46.4
Ecuador	20.7	4	7.00	5.00	28.6
Peru	21.7	12	6.85	5.20	24.1
Venezuela	20.2*	9	6.70	4.10	38.8
Brazil	23.0*	n.a.	6.15	4.00	35.0
Paraguay	21.7*	7	6.62	4.90	26.0
Chile	23.5	4	4.98	2.60	47.8
Argentina	23.1	13	3.09	3.40	–10.0
Uruguay	22.8	13	2.90	2.80	3.4
Costa Rica	21.3	4	6.95	3.50	49.6
Cuba	19.4*	n.a.	4.67	1.80	61.5
Panama	20.4*	16	5.92	3.50	40.9
El Salvador	18.9	16	6.85	5.60	18.2
Guatemala	18.8	5	6.85	6.10	10.9
Honduras	17.9	17	7.35	6.50	11.6
Nicaragua	n.a.	3	7.33	5.90	19.5
Haiti	22.4	n.a.	6.15	5.50	10.6
Mexico	20.3	8	6.75	4.70	30.4
Dominican Republic	19.2	14	7.32	4.10	44.0

Source: United Nations 1985; Camisa 1971; CELADE 1983.

Note: * = in 1970

- countries where marriage occurs at a later age (between 22 and 23 years, on average): Argentina, Brazil, Chile, and Uruguay;
- and countries where the age at first union is very early (between 18 and 19 years): some of the countries of Central America (El Salvador, Guatemala, Honduras), and two Caribbean countries (Cuba and the Dominican Republic).

The table indicates that, parallel to the European 'marriage boom' of 1950–60 (Hajnal 1953), there was also a Latin American marriage boom. Accelerated urbanization, rapid rates of economic growth, the large supply of employment opportunities in the industrial and tertiary sectors, and migration to metropolitan centres, all led to changes in matrimonial practices that were in direct contrast to Western practices. The mean age at first union declined, and between 87 and 97 per cent of women eventually married, even in the countries of the Southern Cone (Table 5.3). Thus, the pre-transitional level of fertility, which was higher in Latin America than in Europe, can be explained by two factors:

1. higher and more universal nuptiality;
2. and a rise in fertility, between 1940 and 1960, immediately following a rapid reduction in mortality levels.

At the threshold of the demographic transition, completed family sizes of between 6 and 7.5 children per woman were much higher than those found in the European case: 4–5 children per woman (Tables 5.1 and 5.3). In 1960, during the period of maximum fertility, only four countries had total fertility rates below 6 children per woman: Chile (4.98) and Cuba (4.67), two countries in which fertility had risen between 1950 and 1960; and Argentina (3.09) and Uruguay (2.90), two countries that were already at the end of their fertility transition (Table 5.3).

Marital Fertility Despite the observed differences in general fertility, levels of marital fertility during the pre-transitional period were broadly similar in Latin America and in Europe, although improved health conditions in the middle of the twentieth century led to slightly higher marital fertility in the Latin American countries, in the absence of voluntary limitation of births. For example, completed family sizes were quite similar among French women married in 1670–79 and rural Mexican women born in 1920–4: 8.3 children in France and 8.8 children in Mexico among women who had entered union by the age of 15–19 years; and 7.1 children in France and 7.0 in Mexico among women who entered union at age 20–24. The persistence of 'natural' fertility in the 1960s and the progressive abandonment of breast-feeding explain the extremely high levels of marital fertility seen in rural areas of Latin America (between 8 and 10 children per woman).

The reduction in marital fertility in Latin America was due, right from the beginning, to the use of contraception, as has been demonstrated by several studies of the intermediate variables, using Bongaarts's methodology. In the majority of countries, TFRs declined by between 10 and 61 per cent between 1960 and 1985, except in Uruguay and Bolivia (Table 5.3). In general, there is a positive association between the speed of fertility change and the contraceptive methods used, especially when the method is sterilization (practised by 50 per cent of all users in Panama, the Dominican Republic, and El Salvador).

The fertility transition started in the urban areas and among more educated women. In addition, it appeared first among women who formed their unions after the age of 20, since a delay in first union, which was limited only to a small sector of society, signalled profound changes in attitude. Among these privileged social groups, the fertility transition resulted from the same determinants as in Europe, factors that can broadly be described as modern attitudes to reproduction. This explains why fertility levels in metropolitan areas of Latin America are reaching levels of fewer than 2.5 children per woman (in Colombia, Cuba, Chile, Mexico, Panama, and Paraguay). On the other hand, in rural areas, fertility has remained at about 5 or 6 children per woman, and is still associated with very early nuptiality (Chapter 1).

Two Models of the Demographic Transition

On the basis of a detailed analysis of the completed family sizes of fifty cohorts of Mexican women born between 1917 and 1947, we concluded in another study that two models of demographic transition have co-existed in Latin American societies (Zavala de Cosío 1988). The first model reflects profound changes in reproductive patterns, resulting from modifications in family structure, in the degree of urbanization, in education, the labour-market, and the status of women. Then new reproductive patterns appeared, in which births were limited through the use of modern contraceptive methods (the pill), probably abortion, and even traditional methods if religious and social pressure was strongly opposed to the modern ones. This model of the transition is very similar to that of 'the societies which invented modernization' (Ryder 1983) and coincided, from 1964 onwards, with the 'second contraceptive revolution' of the developed countries (Leridon 1987). Additionally, it was spread by a diffusion process, as has been shown cartographically in Ecuador (Delaunay 1989).

The second transition model has been observed in the poorest sectors of society, 'in which modernization has imposed itself to a certain degree' (Ryder 1983). Fertility began to decline with the implementation of public or private family planning programmes, even though the decline was not due to fundamental improvements in living standards. The main factor in the decline in this case is the existence of an abundant supply of modern contraceptive methods, within reach of the poorest sectors of society. In general, women have principally resorted to sterilization after the birth of many children. This type of transition is very different from the European case in both its modalities and its determinants. It is found in rural populations and among the disadvantaged urban sectors of Latin America. In the sectors of society that have benefited little from development, traditional reproductive patterns have been maintained: high and early nuptiality and short birth intervals. Fertility has declined among these groups in the past decade because women know about contraceptive methods and use them when they feel that their families are large enough, but levels have remained relatively high (5–6 children per woman). The decline in fertility does not reflect improvements in living conditions. Quite the reverse, declines in economic conditions clearly lead to a decline in fertility, since having many children poses serious economic problems for poor families (Boserup 1985; Chapter 21).

The effects of this type of incomplete transition are necessarily limited, but they do explain the still high levels of fertility to be found in rural areas. The process of demographic transition in Latin America demonstrates that different forms of fertility reduction coexist among the various classes of society, and these are translated into different rhythms of incorporation into the process of change.

Before fertility can be reduced to any significant extent, sooner or later improvements in living conditions must be achieved. The same is true of mortality rates, which, despite modern health services, have not dropped beyond a certain level. The example of El Salvador shows that widespread resort to sterilization (52 per cent of users of medical methods depended on this technique) is not equivalent to low fertility (the total fertility rate was 5.6 children per woman in 1985).

It is also apparent from this analysis that the form taken by the transition process depends largely on the historical and cultural context. In Europe, nuptiality was at a secular low even before birth control appeared. In Latin America, nuptiality and fertility rose first, and birth control came afterwards. However, whatever the context, the disequilibrium provoked by the decline in mortality is always at the origin of the transition process, and the disequilibrium occurs some time before marital fertility finally declines.

References

Arriaga, E. (1970), *Mortality Decline and its Demographic Effects in Latin America* (Berkeley and Los Angeles: University of California).

Aries, P. (1980), 'Two Successive Motivations for the Declining Birth Rate in the West', *Population and Development Review*, **6**: 645–50.

Blake, J. (1985), 'The Fertility Transition: Continuity or Discontinuity with the Past?', in IUSSP, *International Population Congress 1985* (Liège: IUSSP), iv. 393–405.

Blayo, Y. (1975), 'Le Mouvement naturel de la population française de 1740 à 1860', *Population* (special issue), 15–64.

Bongaarts, J. (1978), 'A Framework for Analyzing the Proximate Determinants of Fertility', *Population and Development Review*, **4**: 105–32.

Boserup, E. (1985), 'Economic and Demographic Interrelationships in Sub-Saharan Africa', *Population and Development Review*, **11**: 383–98.

Cabre, A. (1989), *La Población de Cataluña* (Barcelona: Centro de Estudios Demográficos).

Camisa, Z. (1971), *La Nupcialidad Femenina en América Latina durante el Período Intercensal 1950–1960* (San José, Costa Rica: CELADE).

CELADE (1983), *Boletín Demográfica*, XVI: 32 (Santiago).

Charbonneau, H. *et al.* (1987), *Naissance d'une population: Les Français établis au Canada au* XVII *siècle* (Paris: PUF/INED).

Chesnais, J. C. (1986*a*), *La Transition démographique, étapes, formes, implications économiques* (Paris: PUF/INED).

—— (1986*b*) 'La Théorie originelle de la transition démographique: validité et limites du modèle', in *Les Changements ou les transitions démographiques dans le monde contemporain en développement* (Paris: ORSTOM), 7–23.

Coale, A. J. (1973), 'The Demographic Transition', IUSSP, *International Population Conference 1973*, i. (Liège: IUSSP), 53–72.

—— and Cotts, S. (1986), *The Decline of Fertility in Europe* (Princeton: Office of Population Research).

Davis, K., and Blake, J. (1956), 'Social Structure and Fertility: An Analytic Framework', *Economic Development and Cultural Change*, 4: 211–35.

Delaunay, D. (1989), *Géographie de la transition démographique en Equateur* (Paris: ORSTOM).

Díaz-Briquets, S. (1981), 'Determinants of Mortality Transition in Developing Countries before and after the Second World War: Some Evidence from Cuba', *Population Studies*, **35**: 399–411.

ENFES (1986), *Encuesta Nacional de Fecundidad y Salud* (Mexico: Secretaría de Salud, Dirección General de Planificación Familiar).

Festy, P. (1979), *La Fécondité des pays occidentaux de 1870 à 1970* (Paris: PUF/INED).

Hajnal, J. (1953), 'The Marriage Boom', *Population Index*, **19**: 80–101.

Knodel, J., and van de Walle, E. (1979), 'Lessons from the Past: Policy Implications of Historical Fertility Studies', *Population and Development Review*, **5**: 217–45.

Landry, A. (1934), *La Révolution démographique: Études et essais sur les problèmes de population* (Paris: Sirey).

Le Bras, H. (1989), 'Echelle temporelle et Echelle spatiale des variations de Fécondité: La France au XIX siècle', Seminar on Dynamics and Reconstitution of Past Populations INED.

—— and Todd, E. (1981), *L'Invention de la France* (Paris: Pluriel).

Leridon, H. (1987), *La Seconde Révolution contraceptive* (Paris: PUF/INED).

Lesthaeghe, R. (1980), 'On the Social Control of Human Reproduction', *Population and Development Review*, **6**: 527–48.

—— and Wilson, C. (1982), 'Les Modes de production, la laïcisation et le rythme de la baisse de la fécondité en Europe de l'Ouest de 1870 à 1930', *Population*, **37**: 623–45.

—— (1983), 'A Century of Demographic and Cultural Change in Western Europe', *Population and Development Review*, **9**: 411–35.

Locoh, T. (1986), 'Transitions de la fécondité et changements sociaux dans le Tiers Monde', in *Les Changements ou les transitions démographiques dans le monde contemporain en développement* (Paris: ORSTOM), 205–33.

—— (1988), *La Fécondité en Afrique Noire: Un progrès rapide des connaissances mais un avenir encore difficile à discerner* (Paris: CEPED).

Notestein, F. W. (1945), 'Population, the Long View', in E. Schultz (ed.), *Food for the World* (Chicago: University Press), 36–57.

—— (1953), 'The Economics of Population and Food Supplies', *International Conference of Agricultural Economists* (London), 13–31.

Perrenoud, A. (1985), 'La Transition démographique et ses conséquences sur le renouvellement d'une population urbaine', in P. Bairoch and A. M. Piuz (eds.), *Des économies traditionnelles aux sociétés industrielles* (Geneva: Droz), 81–117.

Reher, D. S., and Iriso-Napal, P. L. (1989), 'Marital Fertility and its Determinants in Rural and Urban Spain, 1887–1930', *Population Studies*, **43**: 405–27.

Ryder, N. (1983), 'Fertility and Family Structure', *Proceedings of the Expert Group on Fertility and Family* (New Delhi: ONU), 279–319.

Tabutin, D. (1985), 'Les Limites de la théorie classique de la transition démographique pour l'Occident du XIX siècle et le Tiers Monde actuel', IUSSP, *International Population Congress, 1985* (Liège: IUSSP), iv. 357–71.

United Nations (1985), *World Population Trends, Population and Development Interrelations and Population Policies* (1983 Monitoring Report), i.

Wrigley, E. A. and Schofield, R. S. (1981), *The Population History of England 1541–1871: A Reconstruction* (London: E. Arnold).

Zavala de Cosío, M. E. (1988), *Changements de fécondité au Mexique et politiques de population* (Paris: Université de Paris V), 2 vols.

—— (1989), *Historia e Populaçao: Estudos sobre a América Latina* (São Paulo: ABEP, IUSSP, CELADE).

Part II

Proximate Determinants of Fertility Change

6 Fertility Decline and Changes in Proximate Determinants in the Latin American and Caribbean Regions*

LORENZO MORENO and SUSHEELA SINGH

Introduction

The transition in fertility, while varying in degree across countries in Latin America and the Caribbean, is being achieved by changes in the proximate determinants, through which any other social change must operate. Categorization of these determinants began with a model developed by Davis and Blake (1956), where the aim was to identify all factors that intervened between the norms and social structure of a society and its level of fertility (hence the term intervening or proximate variables). This scheme identified three groups of factors: those related to exposure to the risk of pregnancy, to conception, and to gestation. Subsequently, researchers found that an important variable—post-partum infecundity—was not taken into account in this early model. Later developments expanded the list to include this factor, and narrowed the full set of eleven factors to focus only on those which were both major determinants of the level of fertility and, at the same time, varied across population groups: marriage, contraception, post-partum infecundity, and abortion. Most analyses of the proximate determinants, including this one, consider only three factors: marriage, contraception, and post-partum infecundity; abortion is usually omitted because of the lack of information on the subject.

While each of the determinants have played a role in fertility change in Latin America, it is also clear, at the simplest level, that increases in contraceptive use have accounted for the greatest part of the decline in fertility in Latin America. By comparison, marriage patterns and breast-feeding duration have changed little in absolute terms. However, these three factors are interrelated, and their relative contribution to the level of fertility and fertility change may vary depending upon the absolute level of fertility itself. The aim of this chapter is to examine the changes in the relative contribution of the three main proximate determinants as fertility declined in Latin America.

* The authors are grateful to Germán Rodríguez for his useful comments on the structure and content of an earlier version of this chapter. John Bongaarts provided useful criticisms on the application of his model. José Miguel Guzmán and other participants to the Buenos Aires seminar provided valuable suggestions. The computer assistance of Ozer Babakol is gratefully acknowledged.

There are now several quantitative approaches to measuring the contribution of proximate determinants to fertility decline. Gaslonde and Bocaz (1970) utilized a one-year table that obtained detailed monthly information to describe the role of some of the proximate determinants. The model proposed by Bongaarts (1978, 1982) has simple data requirements, has been widely used, and has been shown to be robust. A more recent model proposed by Hobcraft and Little (1984) requires more complex data, that will enable the allocation of each month of a (five-year) period before a survey to one of several possible exposure statuses. Both models produce summary indices which should be comparable across countries, across subgroups, and across periods of time, to describe the relative importance of each of the three principal proximate determinants. These models have been evaluated and problems have been found (Menken 1984; Reinis 1992). A model developed by Moreno (1991) proposes to take into account some of these problems, and provides estimates of the contribution of the proximate determinants to fertility.

In this chapter we first look at the pattern of change by absolute measures of the three proximate determinants. Secondly, we present results from the most widely applied model, that of Bongaarts, comparing the pattern of changes in indices from an earlier period of higher fertility with a later period of lower fertility, for a number of countries. Inconsistencies that arise from the comparison of changes in the actual measures of the determinants and changes in the indices are discussed. We then compare results from the Bongaarts model with those from the model developed by Moreno.

Data Availability

Estimates of the proximate determinants are generally obtained only from survey data. Some countries in Latin America have not had any fertility or contraceptive prevalence surveys and, for most purposes of comparison across time, at least two surveys are needed for a country. At the time of this analysis, there are ten countries in the latter situation: Colombia, Costa Rica, Dominican Republic, Ecuador, Haiti, Honduras, Jamaica, Mexico, Peru, and Trinidad and Tobago. In almost all of these ten cases, the survey for the earlier point in time (mid-1970s) is from the WFS series;[1] however, the source varies for the second point in time (the mid–late 1980s): for six of the countries the second survey is from the DHS programme, and in four the surveys are done by the country in association with other organizations (Costa Rica, Haiti, Honduras, and Jamaica). The source and year of surveys are shown in Table 6.1

In addition, surveys are available for one point in time for a few other countries: DHS surveys were done in the 1980s in Bolivia, Brazil, El Salvador, and Guatemala, and WFS surveys were done in the mid-1970s for Guyana, Panama,

[1] Honduras is the exception.

Paraguay, and Venezuela. For other countries shown in Table 6.1, no national fertility survey data are available; however, a few data items are presented, based on CELADE estimates, but measures of proximate determinants are unavailable for either the earlier or later period for Argentina, Chile, Cuba, Nicaragua, and Uruguay.

Extensive analyses applying the Bongaarts model have been carried out on the WFS data for all countries, including the Latin American and Caribbean region (Casterline *et al.* 1984; United Nations 1987).

Methodology and Issues of Comparability

The formulae for calculating the Bongaarts indices may be found in Bongaarts (1978). It is important to remember the interpretation of these indices: the smaller an index is, the greater is its importance in determining the level of fertility. In general, the age-specific application of the model is used here, however in a few instances this was not possible, and these cases are indicated in the tables. In most instances, fertility estimates were based on a five-year period before a survey; again, some exceptions occur when survey from the Contraceptive Prevalence Surveys (CPS) programme are used, and fertility data are for the year before the survey. The age-group covered by the surveys varied somewhat, although in most cases women aged 15 to 49 were included.

Given differences in the detail in which data were collected between the two main series of surveys (i.e. WFS and DHS), as well as the need to use data from secondary sources for surveys which are neither WFS nor DHS, the indices of the proximate determinants of fertility presented here are calculated with differing degrees of exactness. Nevertheless, every effort is made to use for comparison across the two points in time those measures which are the lowest common denominator, but which are at least most comparable. This may mean not calculating an index as exactly as the data in one or the other series may allow. In this chapter, we present the different ways of measuring a given index, but point out which ones are more closely comparable and, hence, which are therefore best for studying change.

Two versions of the C_m index are presented for each of the six countries which have both a WFS and DHS survey. Because the WFS surveys collected a full marriage history it was possible to calculate the proportion of time spent within unions in the five years before the survey, as well as marital fertility rates based on births occurring within union. This was not possible with the DHS surveys, which, although they obtained a full birth history, only asked the date of the first marriage and the current marital status. The two versions of C_m presented in this chapter are: (1) a current status index, using the proportions of women in a union at the time of the survey and ASFRs; (2) a 'within union' measure. In the case of the WFS surveys, the latter measure uses the proportion of time spent in union during the five years before the survey, and marital fertility rates that are based on births that occurred during the period within union,[2] and for the DHS surveys, on the proportions currently in union and ever-married 'marital' fertility rates that exclude pre-marital births.

In the case of C_i, two versions of the index are presented for the DHS surveys. DHS surveys collected the duration of amenorrhoea and abstinence after the birth of each child, and can therefore provide a more exact measure of the index of post-partum infecundity. In the case of WFS surveys, only the duration of breast-feeding was asked and, therefore, the index must be estimated by the indirect method, i.e. relating breast-feeding to the likely duration of post-partum infecundity. Two measures are presented for the DHS surveys; one is the more exactly measured version, and the second is comparable to that from the WFS surveys. The WFS and DHS C_i measures are slightly different, however. In the case of the WFS estimates, breast-feeding duration was calculated for three large age-groups, 15–24, 25–34, and 35–49, and the index was calculated age-specifically. In the case of the DHS estimates, one overall mean duration of breast-feeding, for all age-groups of women, was used in calculating the index. We decided to maintain the WFS estimates in order to be consistent with other published data. We did calculate C_i from WFS data based on one overall mean duration of breast-feeding, and found that the C_i were the same in five cases (Costa Rica, Dominican Republic, Jamaica, Mexico, and Venezuela), one point lower in five more cases (Colombia, Ecuador, Guyana, Peru, and Trinidad and Tobago), and two points different in three cases (Haiti and Paraguay (lower) and Panama (higher). Indices based on both sets of surveys utilize the prevalence–incidence method to calculate the duration of breast-feeding and post-partum infecundity.

In the case of the C_c index, the measure was calculated in as similar a manner as possible for the WFS and DHS surveys. Exceptions are the use of a country's own observed proportions fecund for the C_c index for DHS surveys, as compared with an average of proportions fecund observed in twenty-eight surveys, for WFS-based indices. In both instances, self-reported fecundity status is used. The assumption of effectiveness of contraceptive methods was the same for sterilization, the pill, IUD, and rhythm; however, while WFS-based C_c indices were calculated assuming that all other methods had a use-effectiveness of 0.70, DHS-based estimates assume that other modern methods (i.e. condom, diaphragm, and vaginal methods) had an effectiveness of 0.80, and all other methods averaged 0.35. DHS-based C_c indices do not count users who are actually amenorrheic or abstaining, while WFS-based C_c indices do not count users who are breast-feeding a child aged 6 months or less.

Indices which are calculated for surveys other than these two sets are indicated on the tables. Calculations based on published data required making some assumptions. We used the percentage fecund and the effectiveness rates applied in the WFS set of analyses for these few cases. When breast-feeding duration was

[2] These are the indices published in UN (1987).

available only for all women, or for two large age-groups, we assumed that the average held for all the relevant age-groups.

Absolute Measures of the Proximate Determinants: Patterns of Change

Substantial fertility declines occurred in several countries, in most cases a reduction of between 1 and 1.5 children in the TFR, between the early 1970s and the early 1980s. In two cases, the Dominican Republic and Mexico, the decline was larger, i.e. about two children (see Table 6.1).

Some changes also occurred in the three proximate determinants seen in countries with data available for two periods. A very large decline (3.5 years) in the Singulate Mean Age at Marriage (SMAM) was found for Haiti, which may be partly due to differences between surveys in the way unions were reported and recorded. Increases in SMAM of about one year were found in Colombia and the Dominican Republic; all other countries for which data are available show very little change in the age at marriage: less than half a year (Costa Rica, Ecuador, Jamaica, Mexico, Peru, and Trinidad and Tobago). The SMAM is based on proportions never-married, and the index of marriage calculated in the Bongaarts model is more closely related to proportions currently married. Therefore, we also looked at a second measure of change in marriage: the I_m index (Coale and Trussell 1974). This index is a weighted average of the proportion currently married by age-group, the weights being a standard schedule of marital fertility rates. This second measure (presented in the last column of Table 6.2) shows the greatest change for Haiti, a decline in the impact of marriage. However, the only country in which the I_m index shows a noticeable increase in strength is Dominican Republic, where the index declined from 0.630 to 0.585. Ecuador, whose SMAM did not change much between 1979 and 1986, shows a weakening effect of marriage, as measured by the I_m index, i.e. from 0.614 to 0.649. All other countries had very little change during the recent period.

Increases in the duration of breast-feeding of between 2.0 and 3.9 months were found in a few countries: Ecuador, Haiti, Honduras, Jamaica, Peru, and Trinidad and Tobago, while increases in other countries were somewhat smaller: Colombia, Costa Rica, Dominican Republic, and Mexico (see Table 6.1). However, increases in contraceptive prevalence, or the percentage of currently married women using contraception (also in Table 6.1), was substantial in most countries: over 20 percentage points in Colombia, El Salvador, and Mexico; between 15 and 19 points in Dominican Republic, Guatemala, Jamaica, and Peru; and 9–14 points in Ecuador, Honduras, and Paraguay. Only in Costa Rica and Trinidad and Tobago was there almost no change in the percentage using, and only in Haiti was a large decline recorded. The decline in Haiti may be related more to changes in how inefficient method use was recorded, rather than being a true decline.

Table 6.1. *Latin America and the Caribbean: comparison of measures of fertility and its proximate determinants for 1970s and 1980s*

Country	Earlier period						Later period					
	Year and source	TFR		Contra-ceptive preval-ence (%)[m]	SMAM	BF-MTHS	Year and source	TFR		Contra-ceptive preval-ence (%)[m]	SMAM	BF-MTHS
		Total	Within union or marriage					Total	Within union or marriage			
Argentina	1970–5(E)	3.14	n.a.	n.a.	n.a.	n.a.	1985–90 (E)	2.96		39[a]	n.a.	n.a.
Bolivia	1970–5(E)	6.50	n.a.	n.a.	n.a.	n.a.	1986 (DHS)	5.06		30	22.2	16.1
Brazil	1970–5(E)	4.70	n.a.	n.a.	n.a.	n.a.	1986 (DHS)[b]	3.55		65	22.3	9.3
Chile	1970–5(E)	3.63	n.a.	n.a.	n.a.	n.a.	1985–90 (E)	2.73		n.a.	n.a.	n.a.
Colombia	1976 (WFS)	4.70	(4.27)	43	22.1	9.2	1986 (DHS)	3.34	3.12	65	23.2	10.7
Costa Rica	1976 (WFS)[c]	3.84[d]	(3.17)	64	22.7	5.0	1981 (other)	3.69[e]		65	22.1	6.1
Cuba	1970–5 (E)	3.48	n.a.	53[f]	n.a.	n.a.	1985–90	1.98		n.a.	n.a.	n.a.
Dominican Rep.	1975 (WFS)	5.71	(5.39)	32	20.5	8.6	1986 (DHS)	3.81	3.77	50	21.4	9.8
Ecuador	1979 (WFS)	5.32	(4.98)	34	22.1	12.3	1987 (DHS)	4.33	4.21	44	21.9	14.4
El Salvador	1975 (other)	6.01	n.a.	19	n.a.	n.a.	1985 (DHS)	4.40		47	20.1	14.7
Guatemala	1970–5 (E)	6.45	n.a.	4[g]	n.a.	n.a.	1987 (DHS)[b]	5.60		23	20.6	20.6
Guyana	1975 (WFS)	4.92	(4.75)	31	20.0	7.2	1985–90	2.7		n.a.	n.a.	n.a.
Haiti	1977 (WFS)	5.50	(5.15)	19[i]	21.8	15.5	1987 (other)	6.33		7	18.3	17.5
Honduras	1981 (other)[a]	6.40[e]	n.a.	27	n.a.	15.2	1987 (other)	5.60		41	n.a.	17.3
Jamaica	1976 (WFS)	5.00	(4.52)	38	19.2	8.6	1989 (other)	2.90		55	18.0	12.5
Mexico	1976 (WFS)	6.18	(5.93)	30	21.7	9.0	1987 (DHS)	4.00	4.00	53	22.1	10.5
Nicaragua	1970–5 (E)	6.71	n.a.	9[j]	n.a.	n.a.	1985–90 (E)	5.50		27[a]	n.a.	n.a.
Panama	1976 (WFS)[c]	4.44[d]	(3.84)	54	21.2	7.4	1985–90 (E)	3.14		61[b,k]	n.a.	n.a.
Paraguay	1979 (WFS)	4.96	(4.56)	36	22.1	11.4	1985–90 (E)	4.58[l]		45[b]	n.a.	n.a.
Peru	1977 (WFS)	5.57	(5.35)	31	23.2	13.1	1986 (DHS)	4.36	4.30	46	23.7	16.8
Trinidad and Tobago	1977 (WFS)	3.38	(3.18)	52	20.9	6.8	1987 (DHS)	3.10	3.10	53	20.8	9.9
Uruguay	1970–5 (E)	2.99	n.a.	n.a.	n.a.	n.a.	1985–90 (E)	2.61		n.a.	n.a.	n.a.
Venezuela	1977 (WFS)[b]	4.59[d]	(4.36)	49[b]	21.8	7.4	1985–90 (E)	3.77		n.a.	n.a.	n.a.

Sources: CELADE (1988); WFS data: TFR for all births, contraceptive use, and SMAM in UN 1987; TFR for within union births—Casterline *et al*. 1984; breast-feeding means—Ferry and Smith 1983, and Balkaran and Ferry 1984. DHS data: unpublished tabulations and country reports. Costa Rica, 1981: Rosero–Bixby 1981, and Sosa (1984). El Salvador, 1985: El Salvador 1987. Haiti, 1989: Cayemittes and Chahnazarian (1989). Honduras: Bailey *et al.* (1988). Jamaica, 1989: McFarlane and Warren (1989)

Note: (E) = Estimate from CELADE, *Boletín demográfico*, 41: other = other survey; SMAM = Singulate Mean Age at Marriage; BF-MTHS = Average duration of breast-feeding, in months, prevalence-incidence method

a IPPF/WHR (1988). Honduras = 1981; Argentine data = 1988 (E).
b 15–44-year-olds.
c 20–49-year-olds.
d fertility rate was adjusted to include the missing age-group.
e Rate is for 1979–80.
f 1972.
g 1974.
h United Nations, World Population Chart, 1988.
i Married women 15–50.
j 1977.
k 1984.
l 1987.
m This is the %age of currently married women using contraception.

Table 6.2. *Latin America and the Caribbean: age-specific proportions currently married and* Im *indices*

Country and year	Age-group							Index *Im*[a]
	15–19	20–24	25–29	30–34	35–39	40–44	45–49	
Colombia 1976	0.127	0.501	0.702	0.787	0.737	0.746	0.674	0.577
Colombia 1986	0.120	0.460	0.670	0.740	0.770	0.710	0.740	0.555
Costa Rica 1976	0.132	0.507	0.680	0.781	0.766	0.782	0.721	0.581
Costa Rica 1981	0.150	0.540	0.720	0.790	0.800	0.780	0.740	0.605
Dominican Rep. 1975	0.204	0.593	0.748	0.804	0.844	0.721	0.691	0.636
Dominican Rep. 1986	0.170	0.490	0.680	0.780	0.780	0.760	0.740	0.585
Ecuador 1979	0.162	0.510	0.747	0.802	0.831	0.780	0.788	0.614
Ecuador 1986	0.170	0.550	0.800	0.850	0.840	0.840	0.800	0.649
Haiti 1977	0.143	0.492	0.740	0.836	0.797	0.811	0.736	0.608
Haiti 1987	0.442	0.759	0.840	0.848	0.836	0.750	0.689	0.742
Honduras 1981	0.237	0.547	0.762	0.845	0.802	0.801	0.000	0.635
Honduras 1987	0.217	0.595	0.745	0.812	0.790	0.769	0.000	0.628
Jamaica 1976	0.244	0.744	0.794	0.843	0.825	0.822	0.726	0.696
Jamaica 1989	0.438	0.794	0.865	0.847	0.808	0.776	0.714	0.751
Mexico 1976	0.178	0.604	0.801	0.840	0.838	0.812	0.773	0.657
Mexico 1987	0.180	0.550	0.760	0.820	0.810	0.820	0.800	0.631
Peru 1977	0.124	0.466	0.705	0.820	0.829	0.834	0.786	0.596
Peru 1986	0.120	0.440	0.690	0.820	0.850	0.830	0.830	0.591
Trinidad and Tobago 1977	0.183	0.609	0.825	0.886	0.867	0.843	0.818	0.679
Trinidad and Tobago 1987	0.200	0.600	0.840	0.860	0.880	0.840	0.840	0.680
Standard ASFRs, *n(a)* (per 000)	411	460	431	395	322	167	24	

Source: for natural fertility schedule, *n(a)*: Coale and Trussell 1974

[a] This index is the weighted average of the proportions married in each age group, with weights equal to the natural fertility schedule, *n(a)*.

Estimates of Bongaarts's Indices: Patterns of Change

The three indices are presented for as many countries as possible in Table 6.3, for both time periods when available, and for one time period for those countries with only one survey. The most comparable measures are shown for all countries, and this is especially important for those countries with data for two points in time: for the six countries with WFS and DHS data, this involved special calculations for C_m and C_i. For three other countries with two surveys (i.e. Costa Rica, Haiti, and Jamaica), one survey was of the WFS type and the second was either of the CPS type or a fertility survey from which only secondary data were available to us. In these three cases, the C_m index for the WFS survey and for the recent survey are both current status measures; the C_i indices for both points in time are based on breast-feeding only. Honduras is the only country with two surveys but since neither was part of the WFS or DHS programme the indices were obtained from a secondary source (see Table 6.1), are current status measures, and are comparable.

The C_m for three countries (i.e. Brazil, El Salvador, and Guatemala) is calculated with a slightly different definition than that for other countries with DHS

Table 6.3. ***Latin America and the Caribbean: comparison of Bongaarts's indices for earlier and later periods***

Country	*Cm*		*Cc*		*Ci*[a]	
	Earlier	Later	Earlier	Later	Earlier	Later
Bolivia	n.a.	n.a.	n.a.	n.a.	n.a.	n.a.
Brazil	n.a.	0.58	n.a.	0.43	n.a.	0.84
Colombia	0.58	0.53	0.63	0.44	0.85	0.81
Costa Rica	0.58	0.61	0.43	0.35	0.91	0.90
Dominican Rep.	0.64	0.56	0.70	0.49	0.85	0.83
Ecuador	0.61	0.63	0.71	0.59	0.78	0.73
El Salvador	n.a.	0.65	n.a.	0.53	n.a.	0.72
Guatemala	n.a.	0.69	n.a.	0.81	n.a.	0.61
Guyana	0.70	n.a.	0.72	n.a.	0.89	n.a.
Haiti	0.61	0.74	0.86	0.93	0.73	0.67
Honduras	0.76	0.78	0.74	0.61	0.71	0.67
Jamaica	0.75	0.79	0.64	0.49	0.85	0.77
Mexico	0.67	0.62	0.73	0.52	0.84	0.81
Panama	0.64	n.a.	0.51	n.a.	0.85	n.a.
Paraguay	0.60	n.a.	0.71	n.a.	0.81	n.a.
Peru	0.58	0.57	0.76	0.63	0.77	0.68
Trinidad and Tobago	0.66	0.66	0.57	0.52	0.89	0.82
Venezuela	0.58	n.a.	0.58	n.a.	0.87	n.a.

Sources: see Table 6.1

Notes: *Cm* = index of marriage. *Cc* = index of contraception *Ci* = index of post-partum infecundability. See Table 6.1 for years.

[a] The *Ci* for countries in the early period with WFS surveys are done age-specifically, to maintain comparability with other published estimates. *Ci*s for the DHS surveys are calculated with a single mean duration of breast-feeding for all births. WFS-based *Ci* are 1 point lower if they were calculated based on an overall mean duration of breast-feeding in Colombia, Ecuador, Guyana, Peru, and Trinidad and Tobago they differ by 2 points in Haiti, Panama and Paraguay, and they are the same in Costa Rica, Dominican Republic, Jamaica, Mexico, and Venezuela.

survey data, i.e. excluding pre-marital births. However, since use of these two definitions for C_m made no difference for the six countries in which a current status definition was used (see Table 6.4, cols. 3 and 4), it is highly unlikely that the values for these three countries would change if recalculated with a current status definition.

The index of marriage (C_m) varied in importance as a determinant of fertility levels in the region, from moderate to strong, both in the mid-1970s and in the mid–late 1980s. By the 1980s, it was strongest in Brazil, Colombia, Dominican Republic, and Peru (indices ranging from 0.53 to 0.58). It was weaker in Haiti, Honduras, and Jamaica (indices ranging from 0.74 to 0.78). The (geometric) mean C_m in the mid-1970s was 0.637 and in the mid–late 1980s was 0.642.

For most countries in the region with data for two points in time, there was little change in the strength of this factor: in Jamaica, Peru, and Trinidad and Tobago, there was practically no change, and small declines in strength apparently occurred in Haiti, but this was probably due to differences in how data were collected on unions (see Table 6.3). Overall, these changes are more or less consistent with small changes in the SMAM and I_m indices. The C_m index increased in strength by a moderate amount in Colombia, Dominican Republic and Mexico. In all three cases, these changes correspond to changes in the I_m index (although these are smaller in absolute size) and in the SMAM.

Results for the index of contraception are presented in Table 6.3. The (geometric) mean C_c was 0.654 in the mid-1970s, and it rose greatly in strength by the mid-1980s, to 0.547. The index of contraception decreased in Haiti, as may be expected, given the decline in percentage using. Small increases in C_c were found in Trinidad and Tobago (5 points) and Costa Rica (8 points), and larger increases in other countries: 12–13 points in Ecuador, Honduras, and Peru; 15 points in Jamaica; and 19–21 points in Colombia, Dominican Republic, and Mexico. Most of these changes in the index are congruent with changes in contraceptive use. Two exceptions are Costa Rica, where there was a small decline in the percentage using, and Trinidad and Tobago, where there was almost no change. Nevertheless, an increase in the effectiveness of methods used could account for some increases in the index.

In general, post-partum infecundity remains the least important of the three measured proximate determinants, but it has increased overall in strength for the six countries with comparable measures from the WFS and DHS (see Table 6.4). The C_i index was 0.830 in the 1970s, strengthening to 0.780 in the mid-1980s. The index of post-partum infecundity (C_i) showed small increases in strength (3 or fewer points) in Dominican Republic and Mexico; moderate increases in Colombia, Costa Rica, Ecuador, Haiti, and Honduras (4 to 6 points); and slightly larger increases in Jamaica, Peru, and Trinidad and Tobago (7 to 9 points). There is a high correlation between the duration of breast-feeding and the C_i index across the 27 points of observation. In addition, the changes in the C_i index for the ten countries with two observations parallel changes in the duration of breast-feeding closely, except in two cases. For instance, in Mexico and in the Dominican

Table 6.4. *Latin America and the Caribbean: alternative constructions of* Cm *and* Ci *Bongaarts's indices for the countries with data from both WFS and DHS*

Country	*Cm*				*Ci*		
	WFS current status	WFS within union	DHS current status	DHS within union	WFS breast-feeding only	DHS breast-feeding only[a]	DHS amenorrhoea and absti nence
	(1)	(2)	(3)	(4)	(5)	(6)	(7)
Colombia	0.577	0.602	0.533	0.531	0.846	0.806	0.834
Dominican Rep.	0.641	0.689	0.559	0.558	0.852	0.825	0.802
Ecuador	0.613	0.656	0.634	0.634	0.782	0.731	0.710
Mexico	0.667	0.684	0.618	0.618	0.842	0.810	0.800
Peru	0.584	0.629	0.570	0.570	0.769	0.683	0.697
Trinidad and Tobago	0.662	0.702	0.662	0.663	0.887	0.823	0.887

Source: WFS and DHS data.

[a] This estimate uses the overall breast-feeding mean. The median values for $p(a)$ and $q(a)$ in the equation for converting breast-feeding duration to duration of post-partum infecundity are 20.00 and 18.5 months respectively. See Casterline *et al*. (1984).

Republic, the duration of breast-feeding rose slightly (0.8–0.9 months); in Colombia, Ecuador and Honduras, the increase in duration of breast-feeding is moderate (1.3 to 1.7 months); and in Jamaica, Peru, and Trinidad and Tobago, the increase is larger (2.4 to 3.8 months). The two exceptions to this pattern of congruency are Costa Rica and Haiti, which experienced no increase in mean breast-feeding duration, but whose C_i measures show moderate increases in strength.

Alternative measures of C_m and C_i are presented in Table 6.4. It is clear from these estimates that it is very important to use the same or very similar definitions of the indices in applying the model to study change. The within union definition of C_m (based on time spent within union in the five years before interview, and on the fertility rates based on births occurring within periods spent in union)[3] is notably different from that based on proportions currently in union at interview and age-specific fertility rates. In the countries studied here, this difference is of 2 to 4 points. The two versions of C_i based on DHS data, the more exact measure based on reported durations of amenorrhoea and abstinence, or that of amenorrhoea alone, differ from that based on breast-feeding duration. In three countries, the indirect estimate produces a slightly stronger C_i, and in one case, a slightly weaker C_i. In the cases of Colombia and, especially, Trinidad and Tobago, the effect of using breast-feeding only is to produce a much stronger C_i—this is apparently due to an actual difference in reported amenorrhoea from that which would be estimated indirectly. Since the effect of breast-feeding on post-partum infecundity varies depending on the intensity and frequency of suckling, this is a plausible explanation for the difference in the data.

The observed TFRs are shown for the earlier and later time-periods in Table 6.5, as well as the level of fertility predicted by the model for the later period. This predicted TFR is obtained by taking the Total Fecundity Rate implied for each country, given the actual TFR and the three indices in the earlier period, and applying the indices for the later period to it. Table 6.5 also shows the percentage change between the observed TFRs and between the observed TFR for the earlier period and the estimated rate for the later period. Notice that the reported changes in TFRs refer to different time periods, and direct comparisons of these changes across countries should not be made.[4] Differences between the observed change and the estimated change is under 8 per cent in six of the ten cases for which data are available. In the cases of Colombia and Peru, the differences are slightly larger (about 10 per cent), and in the cases of Costa Rica and Jamaica, the difference is about 15 per cent. While a positive difference suggests that the model is not capturing all of the effect of the proximate determinants, a negative difference suggest that the model is over-explaining the impact of the three measured determinants.

Results from Bongaarts's model may also be decomposed to give an approximate idea of the relative contributions of the proximate determinants to change in

[3] This definition was used in the cross-national analyses of WFS data.

[4] The comparison of annual rates of change across countries is the correct approach.

Table 6.5. *Latin America and the Caribbean: differences between observed and estimated fertility change based on the Bongaarts model*

Country	TFR					
	Observed			Estimated		Difference in % change[c]
	Early[a]	Later	% change	Later[b]	% change	
	(1)	(2)	(3)	(4)	(5)	(6)
Colombia	4.70	3.34	–28.9	2.86	–39.1	–10.2
Costa Rica	3.84	3.69	–3.9	3.25	–15.4	–11.5
Dominican Rep.	5.71	3.81	–33.3	3.40	–40.5	–7.2
Ecuador	5.32	4.33	–18.6	4.28	–19.5	–0.9
Haiti	5.50	6.33	15.1	6.62	20.4	5.3
Honduras	6.40	5.60	–12.5	5.11	–20.2	–7.7
Jamaica	5.00	2.90	–42.0	3.65	–27.0	15.0
Mexico	6.18	4.00	–35.3	3.94	–36.2	–1.0
Peru	5.57	4.60	–17.4	4.04	–27.5	–10.1
Trinidad and Tobago	3.38	3.10	–8.3	2.87	–15.1	–6.8

[a] These include all births, to maintain comparability with the TFR for the later survey.
[b] The TFR is estimated based on the Total Fecundity Rate derived from the TFR and the *Cm*, *Cc*, and *Ci* indices estimated for the early survey.
[c] Estimated change minus observed change (col. 5 minus col. 3)

the level of fertility. These results are presented in Table 6.6. The situation varies from country to country, but it is clear that contraception is the primary factor explaining fertility decline in the six countries shown here, followed equally by changes in breast-feeding and changes in marriage. The relative contributions of these three factors add up to more than 100 per cent of the change that occurred, implying that a rise in fecundity occurred during this period.

Table 6.6. *Latin America and the Caribbean: % decomposition of the change in the TFR between the WFS and DHS, for the six countries with data from both surveys*

Country	Factors responsible					
	Total	Marriage	Contra-ception	Post-partum insus-ceptibility	Other proximate deter-minants[a]	Inter-action[b]
		(1)	(2)	(3)	(4)	(5)
Colombia	100	26.4	107.0	16.3	–58.6	8.9
Dominican Rep.	100	38.4	88.8	9.5	–36.6	–0.1
Ecuador	100	–18.4	90.2	35.0	–6.3	–0.5
Mexico	100	20.9	81.1	10.8	–4.4	–8.4
Peru	100	11.0	75.0	51.5	–36.2	–1.3
Trinidad and Tobago	100	0.0	101.8	87.1	–96.0	7.1

Sources: WFS and DHS data

[a] Natural fecundability, spontaneous intra-uterine mortality, and permanent sterility.
[b] 'A complex function of the proportional fertility changes due to the different proximate determinants' (Bongaarts and Potter 1983: 107).

An Alternative Approach to Estimating the Impact of the Proximate Determinants

An alternative approach to estimating the contribution of the proximate determinants to the level of fertility and to fertility change has been proposed and is fully described elsewhere (Moreno 1991). This model is derived from the work of Rodríguez and Cleland (1988), who formulated Page's (1977) model of marital fertility in the framework of generalized linear models; and of Coale (1971) and Coale and Trussell (1974), who modelled age-specific fertility schedules based on the (age) structures of marital fertility and proportions ever married. The new model is also based on the assumption common in all these models that, in the absence of deliberate birth control, marital fertility follows a typical age-pattern termed 'natural' fertility (Henry 1961). In addition, it is assumed that fertility control causes a distinctive pattern of increasing departure from natural fertility, as a function of period elapsed since first marriage. The estimates of the parameters of the generalized linear model of marital fertility proposed by Rodríguez and Cleland serve, in turn, to link the degree of fertility control to direct measures of its proximate determinants. Finally, it is assumed in the new model that fertility rates for all women can be generated by combining the fertility experience of women since first marriage, and the reproductive behaviour of women before this event.

Fertility Rates

The first assumption of the model is based on Coale's (1967) conceptualization of fertility at any age *a* as the sum of two components: the fertility of women within (first) union by age, $f_m(a)$, weighted by the proportion ever-married at that age, $g(a)$, and the fertility of women preceding the first union, $f_{pm}(a)$, similarly weighted by the proportion never-married at each age, $[1 - g(a)]$,

$$f(a) = g(a)\, f_m(a) + [1 - g(a)\,]\, f_{pm}(a). \tag{1}$$

Although summing the expression in (1) across all possible ages should yield an estimate of total fertility, the sum of these rates produces meaningless measurement of total marital fertility since it misrepresents the rate of childbearing by duration since first union.

One solution would be to re-express the age-specific fertility of women in terms of the duration of marriage in Equation (1), and then to estimate the total fertility of ever-married women by summing over all durations of marriage.[5] This solution requires that marital fertility rates be available by age and duration of marriage, $f_m(a,d)$.

[5] This concept of a (synthetic) total marital fertility index was first used by Westoff and Ryder (1977).

Marital Fertility

The modelling of marital fertility by age and duration since first marriage by Rodríguez and Cleland (1988) resulted in the construction of a model in which the logarithm of the ratio of marital fertility at a given age and duration to natural fertility at that age is a linear function of time elapsed since first marriage,

$$log[f_m(a,d)/n(a)] = \alpha + \beta d \quad (2)$$

where $n(a)$ is the age pattern of natural fertility, α is a parameter which represents the level of natural fertility, and β the extent to which marital fertility departs from natural fertility as a function of increasing duration of marriage.

This specification has considerable advantages for modelling fertility rates in terms of proximate determinants. First, it could be re-expressed as a class of generalized linear models, i.e. statistical models which permit expression of counts of events as a linear combination of factors or predictors and an error term, for which maximum likelihood estimates of the parameters, estimated standard errors and a likelihood-ratio goodness-of-fit χ^2-statistic are available. This formulation implies that well-known statistical criteria could be used to assess the magnitude of error implicit in the modelling of fertility. Secondly, it offers a simple and tractable approximation to the estimation of marital fertility by age as a function of duration of marriage, from which total fertility can be calculated by summation (integration) across all durations. The third, and most attractive feature, is the possibility of representing the parameters α and β as a function of proximate determinants of fertility. For instance, Rodríguez and Cleland have interpreted these parameters as spacing and limiting components respectively, and devised indices I_α (or α-Index), of the level of natural fertility, and I_β (or β-Index) of deviation from the age pattern of natural fertility due to spacing or limiting practices among ever-married women in the population under consideration. The interpretation of these indices as measurements of the spacing and limiting components of marital fertility is precisely what made Rodríguez and Cleland's model attractive for linking the proximate determinants of fertility to the marital fertility of a population, then to be used in Equation (1). Indeed, the new model proposes to predict fertility rates by using a linear regression of the α-Index and β-Index on measures of the proximate determinants of fertility.

Pre-Marital Fertility

The other term in Equation (1), $f_{pm}(a)$, refers to the fertility of women before their first union, or pre-marital fertility. This component is frequently regarded as negligible, and there is little evidence of how fertility before marriage varies by age or by time elapsed since first intercourse. In the exploratory stages of the proposed model, it was found that, in Latin America at least, pre-marital fertility could well account for between 10 and 15 per cent of total fertility in populations with WFS and DHS surveys. In addition, the sum of pre-marital fertility rates seemed to be a function of the number of years elapsed between the average age at menarche and first marriage, with a rate of childbearing probably determined mainly by the frequency of sexual intercourse. The limited data available show that contraceptive use in these populations was negligible before first union and, therefore, fertility could be regarded as uncontrolled at these ages (Singh and Wulf 1990). In order to be consistent with the model proposed for marital fertility, the same expression for estimating total marital fertility was adopted for estimating pre-marital fertility, assuming that $\beta = 0$ (hence, independent of length of exposure), and $\alpha = 1.3539$ (representing a level of natural fertility that is 20 per cent of the maximum total natural fertility).[6] This formulation implies that pre-marital fertility varies by age according to the natural schedule, which is an assumption difficult to test.[7] However, for purposes of fitting fertility rates, the approximation works very well.

Proportions Married

The third component in Equation (1), the proportions ever married at each age, $g(a)$, has been successfully modelled by Coale (1971) and Coale and McNeil (1972) in terms of three parameters, which were later re-expressed by Rodríguez and Trussell (1980) as the mean age at (first) marriage, its standard deviation, and the ultimate proportion of women who enter a (first) union. In the exploratory stages of the model proposed here, the use of the fitted proportions married (employing Coale's nuptiality model) resulted in substantial loss of goodness of fit of total fertility. For this reason, the observed proportions married at each age are used as the weighing factors in Equation (1).

Total Fertility

In summary, the model proposes to measure total fertility as a combination of pre-marital and marital fertility rates, where the latter can be interpreted in terms of a spacing component and a limiting component

$$TFR = 0.25 \int_{\gamma}^{\mu} [1 - g(a)] n(a) da + \int_{\mu}^{50} g(y)\, n(y)\, exp\{\alpha + \beta(y - \mu)\} dy. \quad (3)$$

In turn, the proximate determinants of fertility will be linked to the overall fertility rate through the modelling of the indices α and β.

Finally, expressing total fertility in terms of marriage, spacing, and limiting factors permits the decomposition of changes of rates across time. Well-known statistical techniques are available for this purpose (Kim and Strobino 1984; Nathanson and Kim 1989). Moreover, it is possible to decompose the spacing component to identify an effect that is approximately the same as post-partum

[6] This value was determined empirically from WFS data in Latin America and the Caribbean by taking the ratio of the observed total pre-marital fertility to the cumulated rates of the natural fertility schedule, $n(a)$, between the age at menarche, γ, and the mean age at marriage, μ. The natural fertility schedule is taken from Coale and Trussell (1974). Total marital fertility (TMF) derived from the Coale–Trussell schedule is 11.85 children per woman.

[7] For instance, pre-marital fertility is virtually negligible in China, India, and Muslim countries. Hence, the level of maximum total natural fertility, α, would be close to zero in these societies.

infecundity.[8] In this chapter we present some summary results from this new model to enable comparison with the Bongaarts estimates of the contributions of the proximate determinants.

Table 6.7 compares the relative contribution to change in fertility of the three main proximate determinants, as estimated by the Bongaarts model, and as estimated by the newly proposed model. The results presented are based on the main effect of each factor, i.e. the change in the TFR due to the observed change

Table 6.7. ***Latin America and the Caribbean: comparison between Bongaarts and New Model on the total and % contribution to the predicted change in the TFR between the WFS and the DHS due to marriage, contraceptive use, and post-partum insusceptibility, main effects models***

Country and model	Change in TFR	Marriage	Post-partum insusceptibility	Contraception	Interactions
Colombia					
Bongaarts	–1.36	–0.36 (26.4)	–0.22 (16.3)	–1.45 (107.0)	0.68 (–49.7)
Moreno	–1.36	–0.28 (20.6)	–0.08 (5.9)	–1.14 (83.8)	0.14 (–10.3)
Dominican Republic					
Bongaarts	–1.90	–0.73 (38.4)	–0.18 (9.5)	–1.69 (88.8)	0.70 (–36.7)
Moreno	–1.44	–0.41 (27.7)	–0.07 (4.9)	–1.06 (73.6)	0.10 (–6.2)
Ecuador					
Bongaarts	–0.99	–0.18 (–18.4)	–0.35 (35.0)	–0.89 (90.2)	0.07 (–6.8)
Moreno	–0.71	0.20 (–28.2)	–0.11 (15.5)	–0.82 (115.5)	0.02 (–2.8)
Mexico					
Bongaarts	–2.17	–0.45 (20.9)	–0.23 (10.8)	–1.76 (81.1)	0.27 (–12.8)
Moreno	–1.62	–0.14 (8.6)	–0.08 (4.9)	–1.56 (96.3)	0.16 (–9.8)
Peru					
Bongaarts	–1.21	–0.13 (11.0)	–0.62 (51.5)	–0.91 (75.0)	0.45 (–37.5)
Moreno	–1.37	0.15 (–11.0)	–0.24 (17.5)	–1.39 (101.5)	0.11 (–8.0)
Trinidad and Tobago					
Bongaarts	–0.28	0.00 (0.0)	–0.24 (87.1)	–0.29 (101.8)	0.25 (–88.9)
Moreno	0.32	0.15 (46.9)	–0.31 (–96.9)	0.47 (146.9)	0.01 (3.1)

Sources: WFS and DHS data.

Notes: Figures in parentheses refer to % changes. For the Bongaarts model, results are based on current status *Cms* and on *Cis* based on breast-feeding. The interactions column combines 'Other proximate determinants' and the 'Interaction' factors (cf. Table 6.6, col. 4 and 5).

[8] Based on a model of the spacing component (α-Index), where this index is modelled as a function of the proportion of women using contraception for spacing, at parity 4, the effectiveness of all use, and the mean duration of breast-feeding, in months.

in a given factor, holding the other two constant. Both sets of estimates ignore errors in measurement of the underlying variables. This comparison was only possible for the six countries which have both WFS and DHS data.

In Table 6.7 we present the total and percentage contribution to the change in TFR attributable to marriage, contraception, and post-partum infecundity, as accounted for by the Bongaarts and new models.[9]

Results seem to confirm the assertions by Reinis (1992) that the effect of marriage seems to be overstated by the former model. With the exception of Ecuador, while Bongaarts's procedure always predicts a decline in fertility due to the delay of marriage, the new model suggests increases in fertility due to this factor in Ecuador, Peru, and Trinidad and Tobago. The impact of contraceptive use is lower according to Bongaarts's model, as with the new model, in Ecuador, Mexico, and Peru, indicating that the new model captures the changes in fertility attributable to use not only for limiting, but also for spacing purposes in these countries. Finally, the predicted impact of post-partum infecundability is at least twice as high in all countries according to Bongaarts's approach as with the model proposed here.

Discussion

Results from Bongaarts's Model

The results of the model proposed by Bongaarts presented above suggest that increases in contraceptive use largely account for the substantial declines in fertility that have occurred from the 1970s to the 1980s in Latin America. By comparison, change in the duration of breast-feeding and in the patterns of marriage accounted for relatively less of the change in fertility. In three out of the six cases studied here, marriage made a larger contribution than breast-feeding and in the other three breast-feeding was more important (Table 6.6).

In interpreting results from the Bongaarts model it is important to bear in mind that each index measures the effect of a proximate determinant on fertility, assuming that other determinants included in the model stay constant. This can lead to some difficulties in interpretation since changes in one index may actually cause changes in another index. For example, if the age at marriage rises, it may be accompanied by increased contraceptive use among single women, who, according to Bongaarts's model, are not exposed to the risk of pregnancy. Alternatively, if the age at marriage rose and the proportion of single women in sexual relationship did not increase, the level of use among married women would have to rise if the contraceptive index were to remain unchanged.

[9] For the new model, the figures presented correspond to the total and % contribution to the predicted change in total fertility between the WFS and the DHS due to changes in the proximate determinants rather than to the observed change in fertility. This might be a limitation of the new model, since the decomposition proposed can only be conducted on the predicted change in total fertility which is subject to non-negligible sources of error.

The results presented above also highlight the importance of the fact that, in analyses of fertility change, the indices from different sources, e.g. surveys, should be comparable. It does make a significant difference if the definition for constructing the indices varies from survey to survey. Such variation may come about because of data limitations or because it is not possible to calculate the indices directly from the data tapes and published estimates are used. From our experience in the analyses presented above, we recommend the utilization of the most comparable set of indices when comparing changes between two points in time, even though this may mean giving up more exact measures that are available for one or other survey.

Results from the Alternative Model

The new model yields estimates of the contribution of each of the marriage, spacing and limiting components of the change in TFRs.[10] However, as discussed elsewhere (Moreno 1991), the estimates for the spacing and limiting factors cannot be directly compared with Bongaarts's indices, nor do they represent multiplicative effects. Only the effect of marriage is directly comparable with the effect of a change in the C_m index. The reason is that the spacing component (the α-Index) is correlated with the use of contraception. For this reason, a 'pure' effect attributable to post-partum infecundity needs to be calculated.[11]

The alternative model shows that the bulk of the change in fertility rates is due to the increase in contraceptive use (Table 6.7). In all countries, this factor accounts for at least 70 per cent of the changes in rates and, in some instances, e.g. Ecuador and Peru, the sole change in contraceptive use for control and spacing would have contributed to a decrease in fertility larger than the observed changes in the rates. Post-partum insusceptibility contributed only marginally to lowering fertility in all countries except Trinidad and Tobago. Finally, changes in the age at marriage and the proportions ever-married contribute to a reduction in fertility in Colombia, Dominican Republic, and Mexico, and the model suggests increases in fertility due to this factor in Ecuador, Peru, and Trinidad and Tobago.

[10] This decomposition is measured as the sum of a main effect, i.e. the difference in TFRs due to the observed change in the corresponding factors, holding the other two constant; and the sum of a linear combination of four interactions or higher order terms. In the case of this model—a three-factors model—there are three second-order interactions and one third-order interaction. The former are calculated as the differences in TFRs due to the change in two of the components at a time, holding the third factor constant, whereas the latter is calculated as the difference in fertility rates when the three components are changed simultaneously.

[11] The predicted effect of the spacing factor was decomposed into its sub-components: breast-feeding duration, contraceptive use for spacing, and use-effectiveness. The contribution of the latter two should be added to that of contraceptive use for limiting purposes—the β-Index; this new estimate would be more comparable to that produced by Bongaarts's model. In turn, the effect attributable to breast-feeding could be more correctly compared with the contribution of the C_i index. To simplify the calculations, this decomposition was done only for the main effect of the spacing component. The overall consequence of concentrating on the main effect of a specific factor, e.g. spacing, will be to overestimate (in absolute and percentage terms) its contribution to the change in fertility by an amount which depends on the magnitude of the interactions.

Comparison of the Results from the Two Models

The results presented above suggest that Bongaarts's model estimates a higher impact of marriage than the new approach. While the results from the former model show that change in marriage caused an increase in fertility only in one country, the new model suggests increases in fertility due to this factor in three countries: Ecuador, Peru, and Trinidad and Tobago. In these countries, the age at marriage either declined or remained virtually unchanged. The impact of contraceptive use is lower according to Bongaarts's model as compared with the new approach in Ecuador, Mexico, and Peru, suggesting that the latter model captures the changes in fertility attributable to use not only for limiting (i.e. the limiting component), but also for spacing purposes in these countries. Finally, in all countries, the predicted impact of post-partum infecundability is at least twice as high according to Bongaarts's approach as with the model proposed here. In summary, both models agree that the bulk of the decline in fertility between the mid-1970s and mid-1980s in Latin America and the Caribbean should be attributed to an increase in the proportion of women who used contraception for purposes of limiting the number of children they have, or for spacing their births. However, in regard to the other two determinants (marriage and post-partum insusceptibility), we feel that the results of the new model better describe their contribution to fertility change.

For both approaches, results should be regarded cautiously, because these models attempt to explain the impact of the proximate determinants on the change in period fertility rates and not in cohort fertility rates. It is likely that the relative importance of the three factors measured here would be somewhat different if their contribution to change in cohort fertility could be estimated. A further limitation on the results of both models for the Latin American and Caribbean regions is the omission of the contribution of induced abortion to fertility decline. Indirect estimates of the level of abortion in three countries studied here (Brazil, Colombia, and Peru) show that this factor is an important one, and it is likely that abortion may also be significant in other Latin American and Caribbean countries (Singh and Wulf 1991).

The most important lesson from this analysis is that, given the intricacies of human reproduction, the models proposed to assess the importance of the most relevant inhibitory factors on the potential fertility of populations generate results which are to be regarded only as crude approximations to the real effects.

References

Bailey, P. *et al.* (1988), 'Changes in the Proximate Determinants of Fertility in Honduras: 1981–1987', paper presented at Annual Meeting of the American Public Health Association, Boston, Nov. 1988.

Balkaran, S., and Ferry, B. (1984), 'Socioeconomic Differentials in Breastfeeding' unpublished.

Bongaarts, J. (1978), 'A Framework for Analyzing the Proximate Determinants of Fertility', *Population and Development Review*, **4**: 105–29.

—— (1982), 'The Fertility-Inhibiting Effects of the Intermediate Fertility Variables', *Studies in Family Planning*, **13**: 179–89.

—— and Potter, R. G. (1983), *Fertility, Biology and Behavior* (New York: Wiley).

Casterline, J. B. *et al.* (1984), *The Proximate Determinants of Fertility* (WFS Comparative Studies, No. **39**; Voorburg: International Statistical Institute).

Cayemittes, M., and Chahnazarian, *Survie et santé de l'enfant en Haïti* (Port au Prince: Institut Haïtien de l'Enfance).

CELADE (1988), *Demographic Bulletin*, No. 41 (Year 21) (Santiago, Chile).

Coale, A. J. (1967), 'Factors Associated with the Development of Low Fertility: An Historic Summary', *World Population Conference, Belgrade 1965, Proceedings*, ii. 1–8 (New York: United Nations).

—— (1971), 'Age Patterns of Marriage', *Population Studies*, **25**: 193–214.

—— and McNeil, D. R. (1972), 'The Distribution by Age at First Marriage in a Female Cohort', *Journal of the American Statistical Association*, **67**: 743–9.

—— and Trussell, T. J. (1974), 'Model Fertility Schedules: Variations in the Age Structure of Childbearing in Human Populations', *Population Index*, **40**: 185–258.

Davis, K., and Blake, J. (1956), 'Social Structure and Fertility: An Analytic Framework', *Economic Development and Cultural Change*, **4**: 211–35.

El Salvador (1987), *Encuesta Nacional de Salud Familiar, FESAL-85* (Asociación Demográfica Salvadoreña and IRD/Westinghouse).

Ferry, B., and Smith, D. (1983), *Breastfeeding Differentials* (WFS Comparative Studies, No. **23**; Voorburg: International Statistical Institute).

Gaslonde, S., and Bocaz, A. (1970), *Método para Medir Variaciones en el Nivel de Fecundidad* (CELADE, Serie **A**, No. **118**; Santiago).

Henry, L. (1961), 'Some Data on Natural Fertility', *Eugenics Quarterly*, **8**: 81–91.

Hobcraft, J., and Little, R. J. A. (1984), 'Fertility Exposure Analysis: A New Method for Assessing the Contribution of Proximate Determinants of Fertility Differentials', *Population Studies*, **38**: 21–45.

International Planned Parenthood Federation, Western Hemisphere Region (IPPF/WHR) (1988) *Country Fact Sheets* (New York).

Kim, J., and Strobino, D. M. (1984), 'Decomposition of the Difference between Two Rates with Hierarchical Factors', *Demography* **21**: 361–72.

McFarlane, C., and Warren, C. (1989), '1989 Jamaica Contraceptive Prevalence Survey: Draft of Final Report', prepared for National Family Planning Board of Jamaica.

Menken, J. (1984), 'Estimating Proximate Determinants: A Discussion of Three Methods Proposed by Bongaarts, Hobcraft and Little, and Gaslonde and Carrasco', paper presented at the Seminar on Integrating Proximate Determinants into the Analysis of Fertility Levels and Trends (London: IUSSP and WFS).

Moreno, L. (1991), 'An Alternative Model of the Impact of the Proximate Determinants on Fertility Change: Evidence from Latin America', *Population Studies*, **45**: 313–37.

Nathanson, C., and Kim, Y. J. (1989), 'Components of Change in Adolescent Fertility 1971–1979', *Demography*, **26**: 85–98.

Page, H. (1977), 'Patterns Underlying Fertility Schedules: A Decomposition by Both Age and Marriage Duration', *Population Studies*, **30**: 85–106.

Reinis, K. I. (1992), 'The Impact of the Proximate Determinants of Fertility: Evaluating the Bongaarts and Hobcraft–Little Methods of Estimation', *Population Studies*, 46: 309–26.

Rodríguez, G., and Cleland, J. (1988), 'Modelling Marital Fertility by Age and Duration: An Empirical Appraisal of the Page Model', *Population Studies*, **42**: 241–57.

—— and Trussell, T. J. (1980), *Maximum Likelihood Estimation of the Parameters of Coale's Nuptiality Schedule from Survey Data* (WFS Technical Bulletin, **7**; Voorburg: International Statistical Institute).

Rosero-Bixby, L. (1981), *Fecundidad y anticoncepción en Costa Rica 1981* (San José).

Singh, S., and Wulf, D. (1990), *Today's Adolescents, Tomorrow's Parents: A Portrait of the Americas* (New York: Alan Guttmacher Institute).

—— —— (1991), 'Estimating Abortion Levels in Brazil, Colombia and Peru, using Hospital Admissions and Fertility Survey Data', *International Family Planning Perspectives*, **17**: 8–13.

Sosa, D. (1984), 'Costa Rica: Los componentes intermedios de le fecundidad, 1981', in Asociación Demográfica Costarricenses, *Mortalidad y fecundidad en Costa Rica* (San José).

United Nations (1987), *Fertility Behavior in the Context of Development: Evidence from the World Fertility Survey* (Population Studies Series, No. **100**; New York: United Nations).

Westoff, C. F., and Ryder, N. B. (1977), *The Contraceptive Revolution* (Princeton: Princeton University Press).

7 Nuptiality Trends and Fertility Transition in Latin America*

LUIS ROSERO-BIXBY

Introduction

The purpose of this chapter is to determine the role played by nuptiality changes in the fertility transition in Latin America. As other contributions to this book show, most Latin American countries have reduced substantially their fertility since 1960 approximately. In this chapter we examine the extent to which changes in marriage patterns explain this generalized fertility decline.

Fertility transition in Europe occurred without the help of nuptiality changes, or even in spite of a marriage boom (Hajnal 1956; Watkins 1981; Dyson and Murphy 1985). Late age at marriage and widespread spinsterhood had brought about moderate levels of fertility long before the European transition, in what Coale has called a 'first' transition (Coale 1973). In developing countries, in contrast, prevalent patterns of almost universal and precocious marriage have suggested that important fertility decline can occur because of nuptiality changes. Several studies have, indeed, showed meaningful effects of marriage changes, particularly in East Asia. For example, Mauldin and Berelson (1978) found that delayed marriages account for 35–40 per cent of birth rate reductions in ten developing countries with major fertility declines. Cho and Retherford (1974) also estimated an important contribution of nuptiality to birth rate declines in seven Asian populations between 1960 and 1970, which range from 23 per cent in Taiwan to 102 per cent in the Philippines.

The literature on nuptiality and its effect on fertility in developing countries has been dominated by observations from Asia and tropical Africa, however. Nuptiality and family patterns in Latin America are intermediate between those in Western Europe and those in Asia or Africa (Merrick 1986; De Vos 1987). The female mean age at marriage is 22 years and the proportion of never married women by age 50 is 13 per cent in Latin America as a whole, figures that contrast with, for example, 19 years and 2 per cent respectively in South Asia (United Nations 1988: table 5). Regional trends in Latin American nuptiality and their impact on fertility have not been well documented.

A distinctive characteristic of most Latin American countries is the high

* This chapter was supported in part by a grant from the Population Reference Bureau Inc., Option's Fellows programme.

proportion of consensual unions (Camisa 1978; Quilodrán 1985). Over 50 per cent of couples are in consensual unions in several Central American and Caribbean countries. About half of these couples eventually legalize their union, which has suggested that de facto unions might be serving a function as trial marriages (Goldman and Pebley 1981). Instability is high in many consensual unions though, especially in early months of the union (Rosero-Bixby 1978). This high instability results in two other typical Latin American patterns: (1) considerable proportions of households headed by women, and (2) high circulation of formerly-married adults who, together with young unmarried adults, join other households (De Vos 1987). These lateral family extensions aside, a nuclear family structure clearly dominates in the region (Merrick 1986).

In studying the impact of nuptiality on fertility it is important to distinguish direct from indirect effects (Caldwell *et al.* 1980; Smith 1983). Direct, or exposure-time, effects are those conceptualized by Davis and Blake (1956) in their framework of intermediate fertility variables as affecting exposure to intercourse, namely: (1) age of entry into sexual unions, (2) permanent celibacy, and (3) reproductive periods spent after or between unions. Indirect effects include those mediated through other intermediate variables, such as frequency of intercourse, infecundity, and contraception. An example of indirect effects is the 'catching-up' behaviour of late marriages. Another example is the probable formation of role definitions antithetical to high fertility in a period of adolescent or adult status before marriage. Indirect effects are thus changes in marital fertility caused by nuptiality. Estimating these indirect effects is a rather complicated exercise, beyond the scope of this chapter. Most of the analyses here assume that indirect effects of nuptiality on fertility were negligible, i.e. that marital fertility is essentially independent of nuptiality patterns. In populations with little or no birth control—hence in the early stages of fertility transition—the exposure-time effect overshadows indirect effects, if any. The direct effect, however, becomes irrelevant when fertility control is widespread (Smith 1983).

Although this chapter does not address the vast topic of the determinants of nuptiality, some considerations about the causes of nuptiality change are necessary to put in perspective the analysis of its effect on fertility.

In his 'multi-phasic demographic response' theory, Davis (1963) postulates a sort of social strategy to cope with demographic strains brought about by mortality declines. One of these responses is celibacy and late marriage; another is birth control. Nuptiality, in this view, is thus complementary to fertility rather than an intermediate fertility determinant. The Davis perspective is in line with Malthus's 'preventive checks' and it is supported by European history, where populations indeed used marriage restraints to regulate their growth. If this 'nuptiality value' operated in Latin America, one should see declines in nuptiality preceding the fertility transition, especially in the post-war years, as a consequence of the mortality decline that swept the region in those years.

Another viewpoint is that essentially the same set of factors produce marriage delay and fertility control, as part of a broader movement of social change and modernization. Increased education, urbanization, expanded labour-markets, and the improved status of women are some of the postulated common determinants of both variables. Widespread socio-economic differentials in nuptiality support this viewpoint. For example, WFS data show that the proportion married is systematically and substantially higher in rural settings and among women with no or low education (Casterline *et al.* 1984). If this viewpoint holds, nuptiality should decrease (later marriages and higher celibacy) contemporarily with fertility transition, and the impact of the former on the later would be hard to sort out.

In a third perspective, cultural factors, including family systems and ideational shifts, are the paramount determinants of nuptiality change (and of fertility change too) (Caldwell *et al.* 1980). Nuptiality and fertility could be influenced by an entirely different set of factors and nuptiality changes could go in any direction during the fertility transition.

Data and Methods

This analysis, which covers the period from 1950 to the early 1980s, is based on nuptiality data for the age-specific distribution of women by marital status in four rounds of population censuses (one per decade) conducted in the region in these years. Nuptiality data from censuses conducted prior to 1980 were taken from the United Nations Demographic Yearbook (1958, 1968, 1976, and 1982). Census data for the 1980s come from national publications.

The study includes sixteen of the twenty Latin American countries. Bolivia, Haiti, Honduras, and Nicaragua were excluded because at least three census observations were not available. These four countries account for 5 per cent of the population in the region in 1980. Since El Salvador did not take a census in the 1980s, some estimates for this country are based on the 1985 DHS.

Fertility surveys conducted in the 1970s and 1980s complemented the census information on nuptiality. When possible, two surveys (the earliest available in the 1970s and the latest available for the 1980s) were considered for each country in the data base. Survey estimates served mainly to validate census data. Table 7.1 shows the source and year of the information on nuptiality used in each country.

Since data on differential fertility by type of union are scarce, this chapter does not address the issue of the impact of changes in the type of union (if any) on the fertility transition. Consensual unions are included in the present analysis, but they are treated equivalently as legal marriages. Unless stated otherwise, the terms marriage and married couple will be used to mean both legal and consensual marriages.

Information on fertility originates from CELADE (1988). Estimates for the first quinquennium of each decade (updated by 1988) were used. For brevity these are referred to as 1950, 1960, 1970, and 1980. Census data on nuptiality are also referred to as if they correspond to these years, even though several censuses were taken a few years later.

An index analogous to Coale's index of marriage, I_m, was used to summarize

Table 7.1. Latin America: nuptiality data sources

Country	Population censuses				Surveys	
	1950s	1960s	1970s	1980s	1970s	1980s
Argentina	—	1960	1970	1980	—	—
Brazil	[a]	1960	1970	1980	—	DHS-86
Chile	1952	1960	1970	1982	—	—
Colombia	1951	1964	1973	1985	WFS-76	DHS-86
Costa Rica	1950	1963	1973	1984	WFS-76	CDC-86
Cuba	1953	—	1970	1981	NAT-79	—
Dominican Rep.	—	1960	1970	1981	WFS-75	DHS-86
Ecuador	1950	1962	1974	1982	WFS-79	DHS-87
El Salvador	1950	1961	1971	—	—	DHS-85
Guatemala	1950	1964	1973	1981	—	DHS-87
Mexico	—	1960	1970	1980	WFS-77	DHS-87
Panama	1950	1960	1970	1980	WFS-75	CDC-84
Paraguay	1950	1962	1972	1982	WFS-79	DHS-87
Peru	—	1961	1972	1981	WFS-78	DHS-87
Uruguay	—	1963	1975	1985	—	—
Venezuela	1950	1961	1971	1981	WFS-77	—

Notes: CDC = Collaboration with the Centers for Disease Control; NAT = National survey.
[a] The 1950 census did not ask for consensual unions.

nuptiality levels (Coale 1967). This indicator, henceforth called the in-union index, describes a weighted average of the age-specific proportions of women in legal or consensual union, with weights that give more importance to the peak reproductive ages. The weights are the proportion of children that a cohort with fertility as that of the Hutterites would have in each age-group. Because of the weights, observed changes in the index already give some idea of the impact of nuptiality patterns on fertility. The age-specific proportions of Hutterites' fertility used as weights are (Coale 1967: 209):

Ages	15–19	20–24	25–29	30–34	35–39	40–44	Total
Factors	0.124	0.227	0.207	0.184	0.167	0.091	1.000

Four additional indicators were computed to describe the following components of nuptiality:

1. A consensual union index, computed as a weighted average of age-specific proportions of couples in consensual unions, using Coale's weights. This index shows the importance of consensual unions, relative to both consensual and legal unions. Once again, since the peak reproductive ages receive larger weights, the index shows the importance of consensual unions for reproductive purposes.

2. The proportion of teenagers (age-group 15–19) ever in union. By measuring the frequency of precocious marriages, this proportion is an alternative indicator of the age of entry into sexual unions.

3. The proportion of never married women in the age-group 40–44, as a measure of permanent celibacy. Although this proportion refers to women who have never been in either a legal or a consensual marriage, it is likely that some censuses classify women separated from a consensual marriage as 'never married'.

4. A marital disruption index, computed as a weighted average of age-specific proportions of women who are widowed, separated or divorced, using Coale's weights. This index gives an idea of the loss of reproductive time due to marital disruption, assuming that fertility among these women is null.

It is worth noting that several censuses (especially the oldest ones) did not ask for the marital status 'separated'. The indicators of permanent celibacy and marital disruption were not computed for these censuses.

The technique of decomposition of fertility changes into marriage pattern and marital fertility components (Cho and Retherford 1974) was used to estimate the direct, or exposure-time, effect of nuptiality changes on fertility transition. The following equation estimates the percentage change in the TFR, C_m, between times 0 and 1, attributable to changes in age-specific proportions of women in union (see formula's derivation in Appendix 7.1):

$$C_m = 100 \frac{\sum_i \left(\frac{f_{i0}}{m_{i0}} + \frac{f_{i1}}{m_{i1}}\right) \Delta m_i}{2 \sum_i \Delta f_i}, \qquad (1)$$

where the second subscripts refer to times 0 and 1, f_i is the ASFR in age-group i, m_i is the age-specific proportion of women in union; and the operator Δ indicates change over time, so $\Delta m_i = m_{i1} - m_{i0}$.

This relation assumes that births occur in unions exclusively. An estimate based on surveys in rural areas of four Latin American countries indicates that the proportion of births occurring not in a legal or consensual union averages 3 per cent across all age-groups (Rosero 1978: table 31). This relation also assumes that marital fertility is independent of nuptiality patterns, i.e. that there are no indirect effects of nuptiality on fertility. This assumption seems appropriate only before or during the early stages of the fertility transition. Results obtained with this relation can be larger than 100 per cent and negative. A larger-than-100-per-cent nuptiality contribution means that nuptiality changes explain all the observed fertility change and more. A negative result indicates that nuptiality changes offset the observed fertility decline by C_m per cent. The formula, applied to the age-group 15–19 alone, served also to estimate the impact of nuptiality on fertility among teenagers.

Results

Table 7.2 presents the in-union index and its four components. Figs. 7.1 and 7.2 help to analyse the substantial amount of information in this table.

The comparison of survey and 1980s census estimates gives insights about the validity of census information (Fig. 7.1). Both estimates are, in general, consistent. In particular, there is a striking consistency between surveys and census estimates in Guatemala, Mexico, Brazil, Peru, and Paraguay. The largest discrepancies

Table 7.2. *Latin America: indices of proportion in-union, consensual union, teenagers in union, celibacy, and marital disruption*

Country	Population censuses				Surveys	
	1950s	1960s	1970s	1980s	1970s	1980s
In-union index per 000						
Argentina	n.a.	616	616	633	n.a.	n.a.
Brazil	n.a.	644	621	644	n.a.	645
Chile	552	572	586	580	n.a.	n.a.
Colombia	555	604	593	582	611	591
Costa Rica	581	626	623	611	616	640
Cuba	646	n.a.	715	676	694	n.a.
Dominican Republic	n.a.	690	671	607	647	618
Ecuador	631	671	658	658	639	686
El Salvador	585	608	643	n.a.	n.a.	673
Guatemala	695	724	721	716	n.a.	712
Mexico	n.a.	690	690	682	679	668
Panama	646	647	655	693	652	752
Paraguay	518	582	593	629	615	638
Peru	n.a.	642	659	637	630	629
Uruguay	n.a.	617	625	612	n.a.	n.a.
Venezuela	567	627	615	600	633	n.a.
Consensual union index per 000						
Argentina	n.a.	100	131	159	n.a.	n.a.
Brazil	n.a.	70	80	138	n.a.	173
Chile	77	67	53	79	n.a.	n.a.
Colombia	221	202	215	349	297	399
Costa Rica	165	153	178	208	208	246
Cuba	422	n.a.	375	399	335	n.a.
Dominican Republic	n.a.	577	542	610	641	654
Ecuador	273	263	289	309	316	353
El Salvador	555	501	549	n.a.	n.a.	592
Guatemala	708	597	548	465	n.a.	412
Mexico	n.a.	173	169	153	151	172
Panama	603	506	583	598	n.a.	587
Paraguay	356	282	269	247	263	281
Peru	n.a.	293	321	310	283	376
Uruguay	n.a.	85	102	150	n.a.	n.a.
Venezuela	448	403	337	339	n.a.	n.a.
Teenagers in union per 000						
Argentina	n.a.	98	108	122	n.a.	n.a.
Brazil	n.a.	148	126	168	n.a.	148
Chile	89	95	92	92	n.a.	n.a.
Colombia	163	158	135	152	150	142
Costa Rica	149	163	151	155	153	202
Cuba	205	n.a.	296	288	244	n.a.
Dominican Republic	n.a.	249	222	211	274	220
Ecuador	176	196	195	189	184	193
El Salvador	195	206	204	n.a.	n.a.	300
Guatemala	317	290	284	279	n.a.	262
Mexico	n.a.	187	212	206	192	199
Panama	244	213	266	207	199	292
Paraguay	128	122	117	144	165	165
Peru	n.a.	161	170	145	140	130
Uruguay	n.a.	98	124	113	n.a.	n.a.
Venezuela	213	214	161	189	202	n.a.

Permanent celibacy per 000						
Argentina	n.a	139	116	104	n.a	n.a.
Brazil	n.a	96	97	88	n.a	46
Chile	156	151	134	135	n.a	n.a
Colombia	224	185	159	123	86	74
Costa Rica	187	163	142	140	109	74
Cuba	*	n.a	*	34	46	n.a
Dominican Republic	n.a	165	166	82	20	23
Ecuador	*	*	115	106	89	48
El Salvador	*	*	*	n.a	n.a	28
Guatemala	*	*	*	64	n.a	28
Mexico	n.a	*	73	74	122	140
Panama	*	*	66	79	51	22
Paraguay	*	*	*	*	80	131
Peru	n.a	145	106	91	51	31
Uruguay	n.a	122	108	98	n.a	n.a
Venezuela	*	*	*	138	28	n.a
Marital disruption index per 000						
Argentina	n.a.	22	39	44	n.a.	n.a.
Brazil	n.a.	71	68	64	n.a.	99
Chile	59	54	54	61	n.a.	n.a.
Colombia	80	58	62	103	127	132
Costa Rica	68	55	49	67	100	124
Cuba	*	n.a.	*	171	135	n.a.
Dominican Republic	n.a.	34	34	150	214	209
Ecuador	*	*	66	64	108	82
El Salvador	*	*	*	n.a.	n.a.	178
Guatemala	*	*	*	73	n.a.	104
Mexico	n.a.	*	64	65	69	66
Panama	*	*	145	54	143	88
Paraguay	*	*	*	*	116	29
Peru	n.a.	37	49	58	96	97
Uruguay	n.a.	32	64	80	n.a.	n.a.
Venezuela	*	*	*	105	160	n.a.

Note: * = The census did not ask for the category 'separated'.

occur in Panama, but these seem to be due to the time-lag between surveys and census, coupled to a genuine increase in the index. The comparison in Venezuela, the Dominican Republic, Cuba, and, perhaps, Costa Rica and Colombia, suggests that census data might slightly underestimate the proportion in union.

The in-union index ranges between about 600 and 700 per thousand women (Fig. 7.2). Although this index is not strictly comparable to Coale's I_m index, it is noteworthy that in Asian and African populations I_m ranges between 750 and 900, whereas in West Europe just before the fertility transition it ranges between 350 and 500 (Coale 1973). Nuptiality patterns in Latin America are thus intermediate when compared to the extremes presented by Coale. The range observed in 1980 is similar to that in 1960 and 1970. The ranking of countries is stable too, except for Panama and the Dominican Republic. Guatemala, Mexico, Ecuador, and Cuba consistently rank at the top, and Colombia and Chile at the bottom of the classification by this index. Panama presents a considerable increase and the Dominican Republic a substantial decrease in this proportion over time.

The Tukey box plots in Fig. 7.2 show a rather stable distribution of countries

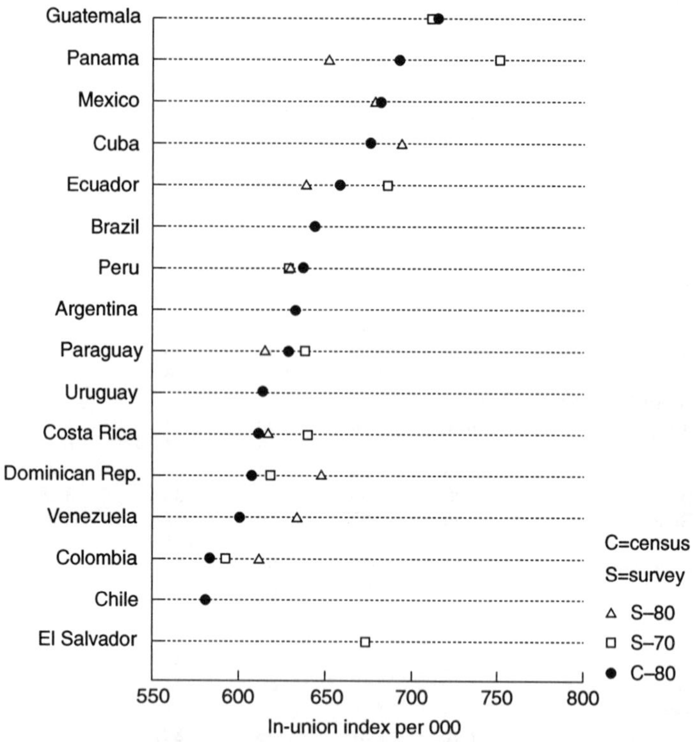

Fig. 7.1. *Latin America: in-union index, 1980 censuses and surveys*

by the in-union index, except in the 1950s. The regional median of the proportion in union increased from 58 per cent in 1950 to 63 per cent in 1960, and it remained around this level across censuses and surveys of the 1970s and 1980s. The second part of Fig. 7.2 shows that an increase in this proportion occurred in practically all Latin American countries in the 1950s. In contrast, in the 1960s, 1970s, and between surveys, the number of countries with rising proportions in union counterbalanced the number with declining proportions.

How were these trends influenced by the components of nuptiality mentioned before? The most clear regional trend was a decline in the proportion of permanent celibacy from a median of 19 per cent in 1950 to 9 per cent in 1980. This was in part compensated, since 1960, with an increasing marital disruption index, whose median value changed from 4.6 per cent in 1960 to 6.7 per cent in 1980. The regional median proportion of consensual unions increased from 28 per cent in 1960 to 32 per cent in 1980, whereas the median proportion of teenagers in union remained stable at around 17 per cent (medians computed from Table 7.2).

The distributions of changes in the four nuptiality indicators, depicted in Fig. 7.3, show that in the 1950s all of the countries reduced the proportion of consensual unions, permanent celibacy, and marital disruption, whereas no dominant

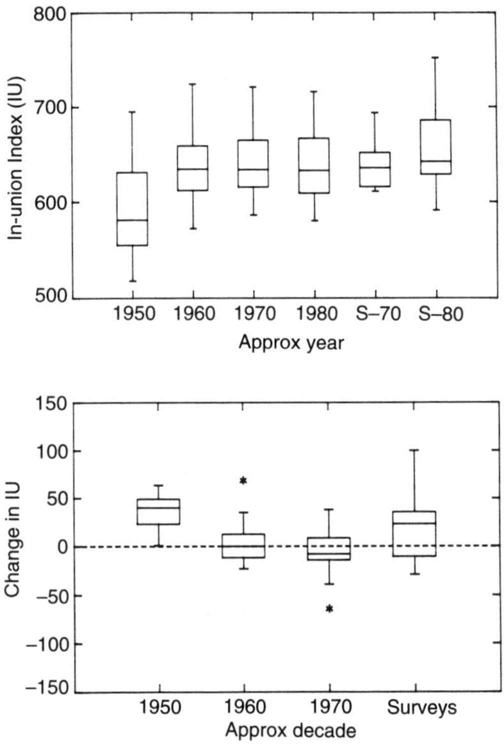

Fig. 7.2. ***Latin America: Level and change in the in-union index***

Note: In the Tukey box plots, the box indicates the range from the 25th to the 75th percentile, the central line in the box is the 50th percentile, and the lines outside the box continue until the 90th and 100th percentile; values beyond these percentiles are graphed individually

trend occurred in teenage unions. In other words, the nuptiality surge of the 1950s took place not because of an earlier age at union, but because of an increased prevalence of legal marriages. The dramatic increase in life expectancy in the region between 1945 and 1965 (Merrick 1986) probably contributed to the observed decline in marital disruption in the 1950s, by reducing the proportion of widows.

Fig. 7.3 also demonstrates that an upward trend in consensual unions is under way in Latin America. Since 1960, the number of countries where consensual unions are increasing outweighs the number where they are decreasing. In particular, all countries with two fertility surveys have seen an increase in this proportion between the surveys. A predictable effect of this pattern is a growth in the proportion of illegitimate births. For example, according to the United Nations Demographic Yearbooks, between 1960 and 1980, the proportion of out-of-legal-marriage births has increased from 16 per cent to 28 per cent in Chile, from 23 per cent to 35 per cent in Costa Rica, and from 24 per cent to 31 per cent in Argentina.

A striking finding in Fig. 7.3 is the lack of any systematic trend in the age at marriage, as measured by the proportion of teenagers in union. There are, of

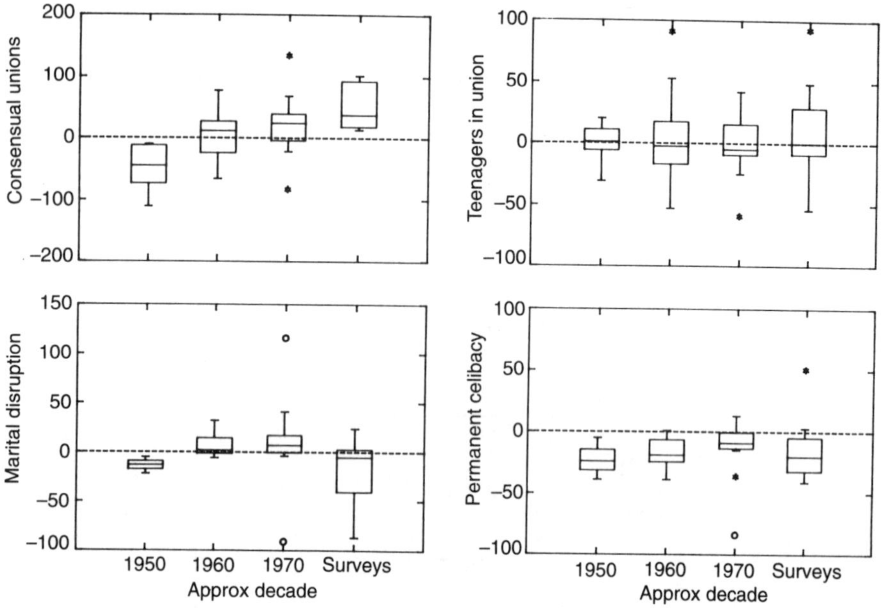

Fig. 7.3. ***Latin America: changes per decade in the four components of nuptiality***

course, countries where this proportion has declined by as much as 5 percentage points, but there are also countries where it has increased by almost 10 percentage points.

The data presented thus far suggest that regional patterns of change in nuptiality hardly could contribute to the fertility transition in Latin America. To verify this, country fertility trends are linked to nuptiality changes.

According to estimates from CELADE (1988), the median TFR of the sixteen countries under study fell from about 6.5 children in 1950 and 1960 to less than 4 children in 1980. In three-fourths of the countries the TFR slightly increased or did not change in the 1950s. In all of the countries, except Argentina and Uruguay, the TFR declined in the 1960s, in some by more than 2 children. In the 1970s, the TFR declined again almost everywhere. In each decade, the median TFR reduction was about 1 child.

How do these TFR figures correlate with the in-union index analysed previously? The scatterplot in Fig. 7.4 shows minimal correlation among them. The Gaussian Bivariate Ellipsoids, which enclose approximately half of the observations and whose shape and orientation give an idea of covariation, move horizontally from 1950 to 1960, indicating an increase in nuptiality and no change in TFR, and they move down in 1970 and 1980, which indicates a constant nuptiality index and a declining TFR. The horizontal orientation of the 1950 ellipsoid and the almost circular shape of the other three ellipsoids also indicate a lack of association.

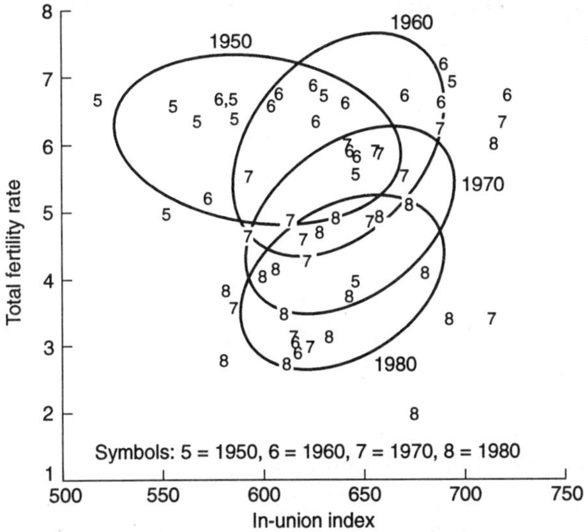

Fig. 7.4. ***Latin America: TFR and in-union index 1950–1980***

For TFR changes larger than 0.10, Table 7.3 presents the estimates of the impact of nuptiality on fertility, computed with the method of decomposition described before. In the 1950s, from the five countries with meaningful changes, the TFR increments in El Salvador, Chile, and especially Costa Rica appear to have been caused mainly by a marriage boom. The small TFR decline in Guatemala

Table 7.3. ***Latin America: TFR and the % change explained by changes in the proportions in union***

Country	TFR[a]				Change explained (%)		
	1950	1960	1970	1980	1950s	1960s	1970s
Argentina	3.12	3.06	3.12	3.13	n.a.	*	*
Brazil	5.93	5.93	4.61	3.78	–	20	–29
Chile	5.00	5.21	3.59	2.79	93	–6	5
Colombia	6.58	6.58	4.67	3.84	*	10	9
Costa Rica	6.65	6.87	4.29	3.48	236	3	6
Cuba	3.97	4.63	3.44	1.97	n.a.	n.a.	13
Dominican Republic	7.29	7.21	5.56	4.16	n.a.	15	43
Ecuador	6.74	6.74	5.92	4.91	*	18	2
El Salvador	6.38	6.76	6.03	5.15	71	–43	–39
Guatemala	6.95	6.74	6.36	6.05	–96	14	20
Mexico	6.62	6.62	6.25	4.12	n.a.	–2	4
Panama	5.57	5.83	4.89	3.43	–35	–11	–8
Paraguay	6.68	6.68	5.55	4.74	*	–6	–45
Peru	6.63	6.63	5.90	4.93	n.a.	–22	27
Uruguay	2.71	2.88	2.98	2.74	n.a.	*	43
Venezuela	6.34	6.34	4.89	4.05	*	25	5

Note: * = absolute change in the TFR lower than 0.10.

[a] TFR was computed for ages 15 to 44.

and the small increase in Panama are in part so small because nuptiality counterbalanced larger changes that took place in marital fertility (note the negative sign in the percentage of change explained).

With regard to the fertility transition from 1960 to 1980, Table 7.3 suggests the following clusters of countries:

1. The sharpest TFR declines (about 2 children in a decade) were only modestly (10 per cent or less) fuelled by nuptiality. This is the case for Costa Rica and Colombia in the 1960s and Mexico in the 1970s. In Cuba—the other case of dramatic decline—there is no nuptiality data for 1960, but comparing the 1953 and 1970 censuses (Table 7.2) one concludes that a post-revolution boom of marriages took place in the 1960s, which probably prevented fertility from declining even faster. The waning of that boom seems responsible for some of the TFR decline in the 1970s.

2. Nuptiality has made meaningful contributions to somewhat important fertility reductions in the Dominican Republic and Venezuela. In the Dominican Republic, in particular, the TFR fell from 7.2 to 4.2 children and marriage patterns contributed to this decline by an estimated 15 per cent in the 1960s and 43 per cent in the 1970s.

3. Nuptiality has contributed moderately (less than 20 per cent) to mild TFR declines in Ecuador and Guatemala.

4. Oscillating marriage trends resulted in swings in the TFR effects in Brazil, Peru and Chile. The case of Brazil is the most prominent. A fifth of the TFR reduction from 5.9 to 4.6 in the 1960s appears caused by nuptiality, but a marriage boom seems to have impeded a TFR decline 29 per cent larger in the 1970s, which has been a major cause of a deceleration in the Brazilian fertility transition.

5. Nuptiality has persistently retarded the fertility decline in El Salvador, Paraguay, and Panama. Particularly in El Salvador, the somewhat modest TFR decline in the 1960s and 1970s would have been about 40 per cent larger if increases in the proportion of women in union had not occurred.

Even though nuptiality did not substantially contribute to the regional reduction of the TFR according to these results, it is possible that marriage patterns have concentrated their influence on a limited range of ages. This limited effect seems particularly plausible with regard to teenage fertility. To examine this hypothesis, Table 7.4 presents estimates of the effect of the proportion of teenagers in union on fertility rates in the age-group 15–19. A clear regional pattern emerges from the estimates for the 1960s: in five countries almost all of the decline (79 per cent or more) originated in reductions of teenage unions; and in another three countries, about one third of the decline is explained by this factor. For the 1970s, however, a huge variability inhibits drawing any regional pattern in the relationship between nuptiality and fertility among Latin American teenagers.

Table 7.4. Latin America: teenage fertility and the % change explained by the changes in the proportion in union

Country	ASFR 15–19				Change explained (%)		
	1950	1960	1970	1980	1950s	1960s	1970s
Argentina	62	61	68	77	n.a.	80	99
Brazil	83	83	68	58	n.a.	79	−184
Chile	84	85	84	69	*	*	0
Colombia	91	91	76	66	*	87	−57
Costa Rica	119	115	106	98	*	80	−27
Cuba	65	120	138	68	n.a.	n.a.	21
Dominican Republic	166	164	117	97	n.a.	34	102
Ecuador	140	140	121	98	*	33	13
El Salvador	142	165	151	134	23	−11	−143
Guatemala	174	161	143	141	125	20	*
Mexico	115	115	110	92	n.a.	*	20
Panama	145	145	133	100	*	−101	48
Paraguay	95	95	88	82	*	86	−324
Peru	130	130	86	85	n.a.	−11	*
Uruguay	60	63	65	63	n.a.	*	*
Venezuela	155	155	116	94	*	98	−39

Note: * = Absolute change in the teenage fertility rate lower than 5.

Conclusions

This chapter examined the role of marriage patterns in the fertility transition in Latin America. The evidence from census data refutes the expectation that, in the region as a whole, the role of nuptiality has been meaningful. There are, of course, a few countries where nuptiality has been an important factor for TFR decline, as in the case of the Dominican Republic. There are also countries, such as El Salvador, where increases in marriage prevented important TFR declines. But the most compelling evidence comes from the cases of rapid fertility decline, i.e. from Costa Rica, Colombia, Cuba, and Mexico, where nuptiality made only modest, if any, contributions.

The former conclusion has to be qualified when one speaks about teenage fertility. Changes in the proportion of teenagers in union in the 1960s caused, indeed, important reductions in teenage fertility in eight Latin American countries.

Prior to the onset of fertility transition, a clear regional increase in the proportion married took place, some of it probably caused by a reduction in widowhood. This trend translated in TFR increases of some significance in three countries. Dyson and Murphy (1985) have used some of this evidence to document their 'ski jump effect', which, they suggest, might trigger fertility transition.

The lack of identifiable regional upward trends in the age at marriage is a striking result of this analysis. This result is in accord with findings from the WFS that explicitly pointed out that 'in the Americas there is only a modest trend towards later marriage' (WFS 1984: 14). Contrasting with this stability, celibacy clearly has diminished and, starting in 1960, marital disruption has slightly increased in the region.

The findings of diminishing celibacy and no trend toward later marriage are against the expectation that demographic strains might produce 'preventive checks' in marriage patterns. The increasingly rapid demographic growth in the post-war years did not produce the multiphasic response in nuptiality postulated by Davis. These results are also contrary to the hypothesis that modernization brings about, more or less mechanically, delays in age at marriage in developing countries. Moreover, they suggest that nuptiality and fertility are influenced by quite different sets of factors.

Given that Latin America has undergone an important process of urbanization and modernization, the pattern of a more or less constant age at marriage suggests that the entry into unions depends more on cultural factors than on socio-economic change. This is somewhat puzzling given the wide socio-economic differentials in marriage patterns documented by the WFS and other studies in Latin America and elsewhere (Casterline *et al.* 1984). The combination of these differentials with a modernization process should produce an upward trend in age at marriage. The lack of such a trend in Latin America might indicate that the socio-economic differentials do not denote a causal relationship. It also suggests that within some socio-economic strata, age at marriage might have declined.

A final finding that should be pointed out is the upward trend in the prevalence of consensual unions. Since the relationship between type of union and fertility is complex and poorly understood (Merrick 1986), the demographic effect of this rise is hard to disentangle. What does seem clear is that a surge in illegitimate births is probably under way in Latin America.

Appendix 7.1: Formulae for Decomposing Fertility Changes

Assuming no out-of-union births, the following relation links fertility rates (f) with marital fertility rates (g) and the proportion in union (m):

$$f = m\,g \qquad (1)$$

which results in the following first-order difference equation for changes from time 0 to 1:

$$\Delta f = g_0\,\Delta m + m_0\,\Delta g + \Delta m\,\Delta g \qquad (2)$$

where the operator Δ represents changes over time

$$\Delta f = f_1 - f_2;\ \Delta m = m_1 - m_0;\ \Delta g = g_1 - g_0. \qquad (3)$$

The three terms at the right hand side of equation (2) decompose fertility change into that resulting from nuptiality change alone, marital fertility change alone, and the joint contribution of both factors, respectively. The third term in the equation—the joint effect—is usually small and it can be ignored without meaningful loss of precision. Under the assumption that the joint effect distributes evenly between the two sources of change, the following approximate relations estimate the proportional contributions of nuptiality (*Cm*) and marital fertility (*Cg*):

$$Cm = [g_0\,\Delta m + (\Delta m\,\Delta g/2)]\,/\,\Delta f \tag{4}$$

and

$$Cg = [m_0\,\Delta g + (\Delta m\,\Delta g/2)]\,/\,\Delta f \tag{5}$$

where

$$Cm + Cg = 1. \tag{6}$$

Substituting in equation (4) $g = f/m$ and reordering:

$$C_m = 100\,\frac{(\frac{f_0}{m_0} + \frac{f_1}{m_1})\,\Delta m}{2\Delta f}. \tag{7}$$

This relation is good for estimating the contribution of Δm in specific age-groups i. In order to break up changes in the TFR, which is the sum of the age-specific f_i, formula (8) becomes:

$$C_m = 100\,\frac{\sum_i (\frac{f_{i0}}{m_{i0}} + \frac{f_{i1}}{m_{i1}})\,\Delta m_i}{2\sum_i \Delta f_i}, \tag{7}$$

where the subscript i represents age-groups and the subscripts 0 and 1 represent time.

References

Caldwell, J. C., McDonald, P. F., and Ruzicka, L. (1980), 'Inter-Relationships between Nuptiality and Fertility: The Evidence from the World Fertility Survey', paper presented at WFS Conference, London.

Camisa, Z. (1978), 'La Nupcialidad de las Mujeres Solteras en América Latina', *Notas de Población*, **18**: 9–76.

Casterline, J. B., Singh, S., Cleland, J., and Ashurst, H. (1984), *The Proximate Determinants of Fertility* (WFS Comparative Studies, No. 39; Voorburg: International Statistical Institute).

CELADE (1988), *Demographic Bulletin*, **41** (Santiago, Chile).

Cho, L. J., and Retherford, R. D. (1974), 'Comparative Analysis of Recent Fertility Trends in East Asia', in IUSSP, *International Population Conference 1973* (Liège: IUSSP), ii, 163–81.

Coale, A. J. (1967), 'Factors Associated with the Development of Low Fertility: An Historic Summary', in UN, *Proceedings of the World Population Conference, 1965*, ii (New York: UN), 205–9.

Coale, A. J. (1973), 'The Demographic Transition', in IUSSP, *International Population Conference 1973*, i (Liège: IUSSP), 53–72.

Davis, K. (1963), 'The Theory of Change and Response in Modern Demographic History', *Population Index*, **29**: 345–66.

—— and Blake, J. (1956), 'Social Structure and Fertility: An Analytic Framework', *Economic Development and Cultural Change*, **4**: 211–35.

De Vos, S. (1987), 'Latin American Household in Comparative Perspective', *Population Studies*, **41**: 501–17.

Dyson, T., and Murphy, M. (1985), 'The Onset of the Fertility Transition', *Population and Development Review*, **11**: 399–440.

Goldman, N., and Pebley, A. R. (1981), 'Legalization of Consensual Unions in Latin America', *Social Biology*, **28**: 49–61.

Hajnal, J. (1956), 'The Marriage Boom', in J. J. Spengler and O. D. Duncan (eds.), *Demographic Analysis* (Glencoe, Ill.: The Free Press), 220–40.

Mauldin, P., and Berelson, B. (1978), 'Conditions of Fertility Decline in Developing Countries, 1965–1975', *Studies in Family Planning*, **9**: 90–147.

Merrick, T. W. (1986), 'Population Pressures in Latin America', *Population Bulletin*, **41**.

Quilodrán, J. (1985), 'Modalités de la Formation et Evolution des Unions en Amérique Latine', in IUSSP, *International Population Conference, 1985*, i (Liège: IUSSP), 269–81.

Rosero-Bixby, L. (1978), *Nupcialidad y Fecundidad en Cuatro Zonas Rurales de América Latina* (Series C, No. 1008; San José, Costa Rica: CELADE).

Smith, P. S. (1983), 'Age at Marriage and Proportion Marrying: Levels and Trends, Fertility Impact, and Determinants', in R. A. Bulatao and R. D. Lee (eds.), *Determinants of Fertility in Developing Countries*, ii (New York: Academic Press), 473–571.

United Nations (1988), *First Marriage: Patterns and Determinants* (ST/ESA/SER.R/76; New York: UN).

Watkins, S. C. (1981), 'Regional Patterns of Nuptiality in Europe, 1870–1960', *Population Studies*, **35**: 199–215.

WFS (1984), *World Fertility Survey Major Findings and Implications*, (Voorburg: International Statistical Institute).

8 Changes in the Mix of Contraceptive Methods during Fertility Decline: Latin America and the Caribbean

MARY BETH WEINBERGER

Growing use of contraception is, without question, the main proximate force underlying the fertility transition in Latin America (Chapter 6; Potter 1983). The transformation in contraceptive practice has depended on supporting changes in public attitudes, policy, and service provision, as well as innovations in the contraceptive methods themselves (see Chapter 10). This chapter however, is limited to a summary of the actual changes in contraceptive practice, as revealed through fertility surveys.

The discussion begins with an overview of contraceptive practice in Latin America as compared with other major regions. After a brief look at trends in the overall level of contraceptive use in Latin American and Caribbean countries, this chapter examines changes over time in the use of specific contraceptive methods. Finally, for six countries, trends in the use of female sterilization are examined in more detail, drawing on DHS data.

Current Contraceptive Use in Latin America and Other Regions

Table 8.1 shows estimated average contraceptive prevalence and average method mix for the world and major regions, based on recent data. The overall level of contraceptive prevalence in Latin America, including the Caribbean, is estimated to be 56 per cent of couples with the wife in the reproductive ages.[1] This is above the level for the world as a whole, and is much higher than the averages for South Asia and Africa. It is, though, still substantially lower than in most developed countries, where the average is around 70 per cent, or in East Asia (primarily China).[2] In the large majority of Latin American and Caribbean countries and areas, contraceptive prevalence is between 30 and 60 per cent of couples (Table 8.2), although the values range from only 7 per cent in Haiti to around 70 per cent in Costa Rica and Puerto Rico.

[1] In the Latin American surveys, consensual unions are included with legal marriages in the data reported here. In Guyana and in English- and French-speaking Caribbean countries, visiting unions are also included. 'Marriage' as used here includes these informal unions.

[2] Table 8.1 is based on data available up to May 1988. Data for new surveys, incorporated in other tables shown here, do not appreciably change the regional average figures for Latin America, or the population-weighted average date to which the figures apply.

Table 8.1. *Prevalence of specific contraceptive methods for selected regions*

Region	Method											
	All	Modern[a]	Sterilization		Pill	Inject-able	IUD	Condom	Vaginal barrier methods	Rhythm	With-drawal	Other
			Female	Male								
	(1)	(2)	(3)	(4)	(5)	(6)	(7)	(8)	(9)	(10)	(11)	(12)
(A) Percentage of married women of reproductive age												
Less developed regions	46	40	15	5	6	1	11	3	0.4	2	1	1
Latin America	**56**	**46**	**20**	**1**	**16**	1	**5**	**2**	**1**	**5**	**3**	**1**
Africa	14	11	1	—	5	1	2	0.5	0.2	1	1	2
Asia and Oceania	50	45	17	7	4	1	13	3	0.4	2	1	1
East Asia	74	73	27	9	5	—	29	3	0.5		1	
South Asia and Oceania	34	27	10	6	4	2	2	3	0.4	3	2	2
More developed regions	70	46	7	3	14	—	6	13	2	9	14	2
Asia (Japan)	64	59	8	2	1	—	4	45		5		
Europe												
Eastern	70	25	0.4	—	9	—	5	8	2	19	24	2
Northern	80	76	11	11	22	—	11	19	3	1	3	1
Southern	67	30	2	—	13	—	3	10	2	6	29	2
Western	78	56	7	2	30	—	10	6	1	6	15	1
North America	69	63	19	11	13	—	5	10	6	3	1	1
World	51	42	13	5	7	1	10	5	1	4	4	1

(B) Percentage of contraceptive users												
Less developed regions	100	89	33	12	12	2	24	6	1	5	3	3
Latin America	**100**	**83**	**36**	**1**	**29**	**2**	**9**	**3**	**1**	**9**	**6**	**2**
Africa	100	75	9	—	38	9	14	3	1	6	5	15
Asia and Oceania	100	91	34	14	9	2	26	6	1	4	3	2
East Asia	100	98	37	12	6	—	39	4	1		2	
South Asia and Oceania	100	79	29	17	12	4	7	9	1	8	7	6
More developed regions	100	65	10	5	20	—	8	19	3	13	20	2
Asia (Japan)	100	92	13	3	2	—	5	69		8		
Europe												
Eastern	100	36	1	—	13	—	7	12	2	27	34	3
Northern	100	95	14	13	28	—	13	23	4	1	3	1
Southern	100	45	2	—	19	—	5	15	3	9	44	2
Western	100	78	10	3	41	—	15	8	1	7	13	2
North America	100	92	28	16	19	—	7	14	9	4	2	1
World	100	81	26	10	15	1	19	10	2	7	8	2

Source: United Nations (1989).

Note: Based on recent survey data. The average date of these surveys, weighted by the estimated number of married women of reproductive age, is late in 1983. The average date ranges from mid-1982 for more developed regions to mid-1986 for Latin America. The prevalence estimates reflect 'medium' assumptions about contraceptive use in countries with no data, comprising approximately 13 per cent of the population of developing and 28 per cent of that of developed regions (see United Nations 1989: annex I).

[a] Includes methods in columns (3)–(9).

Table 8.2. *Latin America and the Caribbean: % currently using contraception among couples with the woman of reproductive age, latest available data*

Percentage using any method				
<15	15–29	30–44	45–59	60+
Haiti (1987)	Guatemala (1987) Nicaragua (1981)	Antigua (1981) Bolivia (1989) Grenada (1985) Guadeloupe (1976) Guyana (1975) Honduras (1987) St Kitts and Nevis (1984) St Lucia (1981) St Vincent (1981)	Barbados (1980/81) Dominica (1981) Dominican Republic (1986) Ecuador (1989) El Salvador (1988) Jamaica (1988) Martinique (1976) Mexico (1987) Montserrat (1984) Panama (1987) Paraguay (1984) Peru (1986) Trinidad and Tobago (1987) Venezuela (1977)	Brazil (1986) Colombia (1986) Costa Rica (1986) Puerto Rico (1982)

Source: Table 8. A1

Latin America as a region has a notably high prevalence of female sterilization (estimated at 20 per cent of couples with the woman of reproductive age) and of the oral pill (16 per cent). These two methods together make up around two-thirds of total contraceptive practice in Latin America. Of the regions shown in Table 8.1, only East Asia has a higher level of use of female sterilization, and only Northern and Western Europe surpass Latin America in level of use of the pill. Compared to other developing (but not developed) regions, Latin America also has a higher-than-average level of reliance on periodic abstinence or rhythm; 5 per cent of couples are using some form of periodic abstinence as their main contraceptive method. An additional 5 per cent of couples use an intra-uterine device (IUD).[3]

In contrast to the high level of use of female sterilization, the practice of male sterilization is uncommon in Latin America (around 1 per cent of contraceptive use). Although several other regions also have a low prevalence of male sterilization, Latin America is the only region where a low level of vasectomy use coexists with heavy reliance on female sterilization.

Each of the other methods shown—including injectables, condom, vaginal barrier methods, withdrawal, and others—is used by at most 3 per cent of Latin American couples and together these methods, plus vasectomy, account for only about 15 per cent of contraceptive practice.

[3] This is well below the average of 10% of couples using the IUD for the world as a whole. However, that average is heavily influenced by the high level of IUD use in China. For all countries other than China, the estimated average level of IUD use is only 4% of couples.

The Table 8.A1 shows the prevalence of various contraceptive methods for Latin American and Caribbean countries and areas, for various dates, and Fig. 8.1 summarizes the prevalence of specific methods at the most recent available date. The countries listed in Tables 8.2 and 8.A1 include roughly 85 per cent of the region's population, with Argentina, Chile, Cuba, and Uruguay accounting for most of the remaining population. The latter countries have lower fertility than the regional average and almost certainly have above-average levels of contraceptive practice. But, since comparable survey data are lacking for these countries, they are omitted from this review.

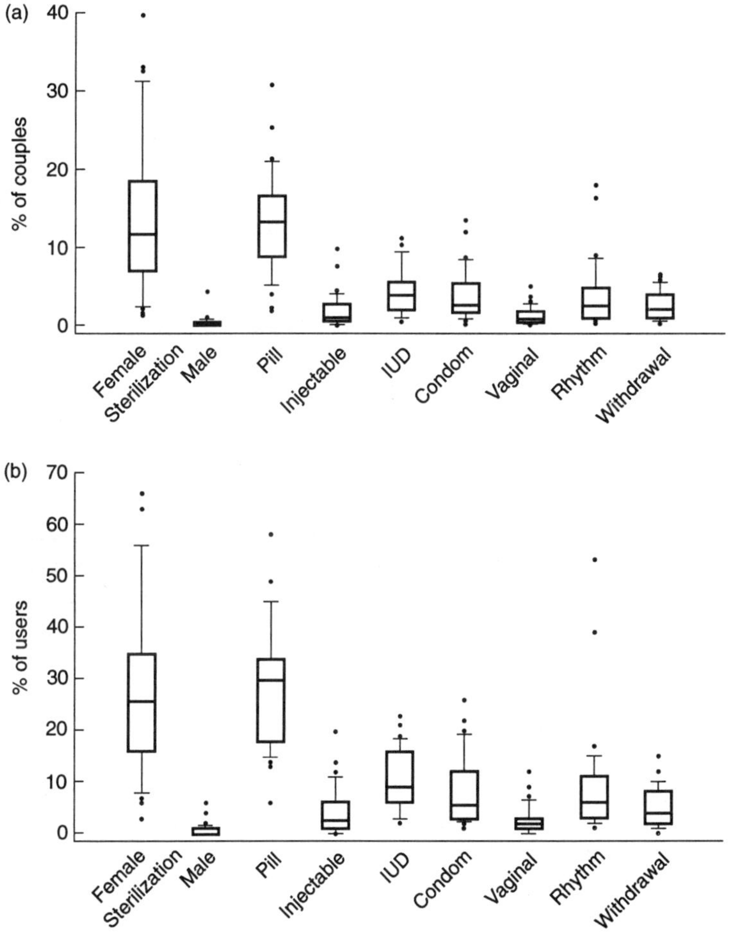

Fig. 8.1. ***Latin America and the Caribbean: distribution of countries by prevalence of specific contraceptive methods among couples with the woman of reproductive age, and among contraceptive users***

a % of couples using each method
b % of contraceptive users employing each method

Source: Table 8.A1; see note to Fig. 7.2.

The method mix varies considerably between Latin American countries, as is also true in other regions. However, in most cases female sterilization and the pill each account for at least 15 per cent of use at the most recent date (Fig. 8.1). The exceptions include several countries where sterilization is relatively little practised but where the pill accounts for at least one-quarter of total use—Grenada, Montserrat, Paraguay, and St Kitts and Nevis—as well as Bolivia and Peru where, unusually for Latin America, rhythm and other 'non-supply' or traditional methods account for most of current practice. The pill also accounts for under 15 per cent of the total in Puerto Rico, where sterilization is the main method.

There are several countries where use of female sterilization or the pill reaches remarkably high levels. Over one-fourth of reproductive-aged married women in Brazil are sterilized, as are approximately one-third of such women in the Dominican Republic, El Salvador, and Panama. In Puerto Rico 40 per cent are sterilized. Use of female sterilization is probably higher in Puerto Rico than anywhere else in the world, although for male and female sterilization combined, similar or even higher levels are found in a few countries outside Latin America.[4] Prevalence of pill use ranges from 20 to 31 per cent in Brazil, Costa Rica, Jamaica, Montserrat, St Kitts and Nevis, and St Lucia.

Current levels of use of particular methods are discussed in more detail below.

Trends in Contraceptive Prevalence

In most Latin American countries the earliest national-level surveys inquiring about contraceptive practice occurred after 1970, at a time when the level of contraceptive use was already moderate. Fig. 8.2 shows trends in the overall level of use among couples with the woman of reproductive age, based on surveys with national (or near-national) coverage. Most of the countries show a rise in the level of contraceptive use up to the most recent available date.[5] Thus, the dominant impression is of a rapid and continuing spread of contraceptive practice.

However, in a few countries where it is possible to observe trends after contraceptive prevalence surpassed 50 per cent, growth in prevalence has stalled at a level somewhat below that seen in most developed countries, and with fertility still above replacement level, in the range of approximately 2.5 to 4 children per woman. This is in contrast to the continued rise in contraceptive prevalence (to 70–7 per cent), and the continued decline in fertility to the replacement level or below, in a few Asian populations: Hong Kong, Singapore, and Republic of Korea.[6]

[4] A 1988 survey in the Republic of Korea showed that in 48% of reproductive aged couples, either the husband or the wife was sterilized. In Canada in 1982, the proportion was 44%.

[5] In some cases the prevalence levels shown in Fig. 8.1 differ from those given in Table 8.A1, reflecting adjustments to the base population or specific methods included, in order to improve comparability between surveys. Table 8.A1 shows the full range of methods, women's ages, and geographical coverage that was available for each survey from published tabulations.

[6] Fertility has also fallen below replacement level in Cuba, for which information about contraceptive prevalence is not available. The ready availability of legal abortion in Cuba has clearly

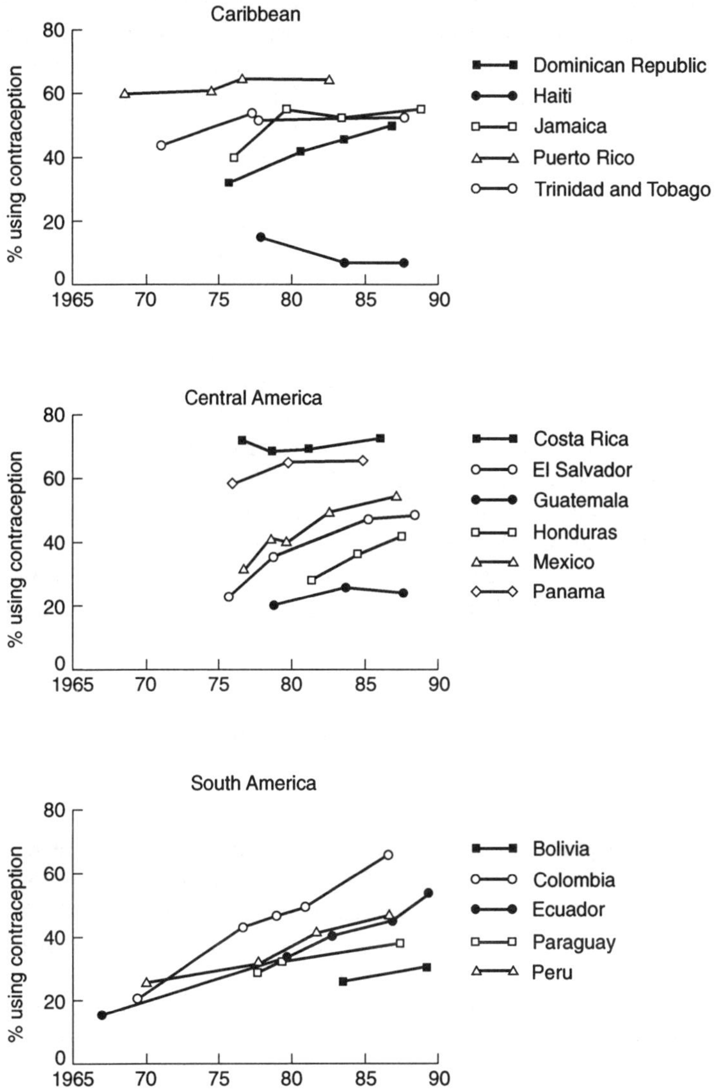

Fig. 8.2. ***Latin America and the Caribbean: trends in contraceptive prevalence***
Source: Table 8.A1 and files of the UN Population Division.

In Jamaica and Trinidad and Tobago between 50 and 55 per cent of couples were practising contraception in the late 1980s; the levels are only marginally higher than in the mid- or late 1970s. Despite this, in Jamaica the level of fertility has apparently continued to decline, from a TFR of roughly 4.5 children per woman in the mid-1970s to 2.9 in the late 1980s;[7] in Trinidad and Tobago the TFR declined modestly, from 3.4 children per woman in the mid-1970s to 3.0–3.1 for the mid-1980s.[8] In Costa Rica and Puerto Rico, the level of contraceptive use was already in the range of 60–70 per cent at the time of the earliest national survey, and has increased only slightly since. In Panama use has also levelled off below 65 per cent of couples. In these cases the TFR has not declined appreciably in recent years. Though in Puerto Rico the TFR, at approximately 2.4, is not far above replacement level, in Costa Rica and Panama it remained in the range of 3–4 children per woman for the period spanned by the surveys.

Apart from these instances of stabilization of contraceptive use at moderately high levels, there are a few cases of an apparent slowdown or cessation of growth at lower levels, as in Guatemala between 1983 and 1987. However, in El Salvador the situation is unclear, because the surveys do not have the same geographic coverage. In Haiti, although there is no question that the level of use is far lower than anywhere else in the region, the impression of decline after 1977 may be an artefact of differing completeness of measurement of the use of traditional methods (Cayemittes and Chahnazarian 1989).

Trends in Use of Specific Contraceptive Methods

Early Surveys

The extent of change in the types of contraception employed can be seen by comparing recent survey data with a 1963–4 set of surveys in seven Latin American metropolitan areas.[9] By the early 1960s, contraceptive prevalence had already reached moderate to high levels in these metropolitan areas, with between 31 per cent (in Mexico City) and 69 per cent (in Buenos Aires) currently using contraception, among couples with the woman aged 20–39 (Table 8.3). Except in Panama City, where sterilization was already well established as the most popular

contributed to the fertility decline there. Abortion has also been an important factor in the low-fertility Asian countries mentioned.

[7] Estimated from WFS data for years 1973–75 and from 1989 Jamaican Contraceptive Prevalence Survey for years 1986–88 (McFarlane *et al.* 1989).

[8] As estimated from either vital registration or survey data (Heath *et al.* 1988).

[9] Note that direct comparison between the early surveys and later ones is complicated by differences in sample coverage and coding practices employed in available tabulations. For most of the surveys in Table 8.3, couples using more than one method in combination or alternation are shown under each method. Published tabulations of more recent surveys, as well as those for the USA and Puerto Rico in Table 8.3, usually show the principal or most effective method only. In addition, for the USA in 1955, it is not possible to separate sterilizations done solely for health reasons from those done at least partly from contraceptive motives.

Table 8.3. *Percentage of women in a union using various types of contraception, surveys conducted 1963–1971*

	Age range	Any method	Steril-ization	Pill	IUD	Condom	Vaginal barrier	Rhythm	With-drawal	Douche	Other
(A) Percentage of women in a union											
Metropolitan areas, 1963–4											
Buenos Aires	20–39	69.2	0.0	1.1	–[a]	31.0	4.4	14.8	31.6	9.7	0.6
Bogotá	20–39	31.6	1.0	2.1	–[a]	5.3	3.9	11.6	11.5	6.4	0.9
Caracas	20–39	53.1	6.5	0.3	–[a]	21.1	3.5	11.6	16.0	16.0	0.4
Mexico City	20–39	31.0	1.7	3.2	–[a]	3.8	2.6	8.6	3.4	6.9	0.8
Panama City	20–39	46.9	23.3	2.2	–[a]	6.8	3.8	5.8	4.0	9.7	0.0
Rio de Janeiro	20–39	45.6	6.7	3.1	–[a]	5.2	5.8	12.2	3.4	11.6	2.8
San José	20–39	55.2	6.3	1.2	–[a]	21.1	3.1	12.0	15.8	9.7	0.8
Rural areas, 1969–70											
Colombia	20–39	14.4	0.7	2.5	1.2	0.6	0.9	3.9	4.9	1.5	0.2
Costa Rica	20–39	26.1	3.5	9.8	3.0	1.7	0.1	4.8	3.9	1.5	0.7
Mexico	20–39	6.0	0.9	1.6	0.1	0.3	0.5	1.6	1.1	0.5	0.3
Peru	20–39	7.2	0.3	0.9	0.2	0.4	0.1	3.4	1.0	1.9	0.0
Puerto Rico, 1968	15–49[b]	60.0	35.5	11.3	1.6	2.1	0.3	1.7	4.4	3.2	
Trinidad and Tobago, 1970/1	15–44	43.6	2.1	17.1	3.0	9.8	4.5	2.4	4.3	0.7	1.8
United States											
1955 (Whites)	18–39[c]	58.8	9.3[d]	—	—	15.9	12.1	11.0		10.4	
1965	15–44[c]	63.2	7.9	15.1	0.8	13.9	8.3	6.8	3.6	3.2	3.7

Table 8.3. *(cont.)*

	Age range	Any method	Steril-ization	Pill	IUD	Condom	Vaginal barrier	Rhythm	With-drawal	Douche	Other
(B) Percentage of users											
Metropolitan areas, 1963–4											
Buenos Aires	20–39	100	0	2	–[a]	45	6	21	46	14	1
Bogotá	20–39	100	3	7	–[a]	17	12	37	37	20	3
Caracas	20–39	100	12	1	–[a]	40	7	22	30	30	1
Mexico City	20–39	100	6	10	–[a]	12	9	28	11	22	3
Panama City	20–39	100	50	5	–[a]	14	8	12	9	21	0
Rio de Janeiro	20–39	100	15	7	–[a]	12	13	27	8	25	6
San José	20–39	100	11	2	–[a]	38	6	22	29	18	2
Rural areas, 1969–70											
Colombia	20–39	100	5	18	9	5	6	27	34	10	1
Costa Rica	20–39	100	13	38	11	7	0	18	15	6	3
Mexico	20–39	100	14	26	1	5	8	26	18	8	6
Peru	20–39	100	4	12	2	6	1	47	13	26	0
Puerto Rico, 1968	15–49[b]	100	59	19	3	4	1	3	7	5	
Trinidad and Tobago, 1970/1	15–44	100	5	39	7	22	10	6	10	2	4
United States											
1955 (Whites)	18–39[c]	100	16[d]	—	—	27	21	19		18	
1965	15–44[c]	100	13	24	1	22	13	11	6	5	6

Sources: United Nations (1979 and 1989); Goldscheider and Mosher (1988).

Notes: Except in Puerto Rico and United States (1965), women using a combination of methods are shown under each; thus, figures for specific methods do not add up to the total level of contraceptive use.

[a] Combined with vaginal barrier methods.
[b] Women ever in a union.
[c] Women in legal unions.
[d] Includes sterilization for non-contraceptive reasons.

method, contraceptive users in 1963–4 relied mainly on rhythm, withdrawal, condoms, and contraceptive douches. The pill had only recently become available, and was used by 1–3 per cent of couples; IUDs were either unavailable, or were used too infrequently to be reflected separately in the survey coding. Vaginal barrier methods were not popular, being employed by only 3–6 per cent of the women.

A second series of surveys, fielded in 1969–70, covered rural areas in four Latin American countries, including three (Colombia, Costa Rica, and Mexico) that had participated in the metropolitan survey programme (Table 8.3). The overall level of use was much lower than in the metropolitan areas surveyed earlier, but the method mix shows signs of modernization. In rural areas of Costa Rica, the overall level of contraceptive use was half that seen earlier in San José, but 10 per cent of the rural women were using the pill, compared to 1 per cent of the metropolitan women. The pill accounted for 12–38 per cent of total use in the rural areas, as opposed to 1–10 per cent in the metropolitan areas surveyed earlier. The IUD had also begun to appear in the rural areas. The prevalence of other methods (among women) was much lower than in the metropolitan areas, but considered as a percentage of total use, the relatively ineffective and traditional methods—rhythm, withdrawal, douche—were nearly as important as in the metropolitan areas in 1963–4. Condoms, though, were employed by a lower proportion of users in the rural areas (5–7 per cent) than in the metropolitan areas (11–45 per cent).

The high levels of use of withdrawal in several of the metropolitan areas suggests a lingering influence of practices brought by immigrants from Europe. Extensive indigenous practice of withdrawal has been seen in only a few developing countries, while in Europe withdrawal was widely employed before modern methods became available, and it remained the single most common contraceptive method in many countries of Eastern, Western, and Southern Europe at least through the 1970s (see United Nations 1989). In contrast to most of Europe, in several of the Latin American metropolitan areas the rhythm method had by the early 1960s become more commonly used than withdrawal. This is one of several points of similarity between contraceptive practices in Latin America and North America.

Table 8.3 also includes statistics for several other early surveys in the Americas: the United States in 1955 and 1965, Puerto Rico in 1968, and Trinidad and Tobago in 1970/1. All the latter areas had moderate to high levels of contraceptive use, with sterilization already firmly established as the dominant method in Puerto Rico and with the pill a major method (except, of course, in the USA in 1955).

In 1955, contraceptive practice in the United States, as in several of the Latin American metropolitan areas, involved heavy reliance on condoms and the rhythm method, as well as appreciable levels of use of withdrawal and contraceptive douching. Sterilization was also practised, though it was much less common than it has since become, and it included a non-negligible level of male sterilization (not shown). The USA also had a heavier reliance on vaginal barrier methods—diaphragm, foam, etc.—than did the Latin American populations (a difference that persists today), and by 1965 the contraceptive pill was already employed by 15 per cent of US couples.

Recent Surveys

Starting in the mid-1970s, nationally representative fertility and contraceptive prevalence surveys were conducted in a much larger number of Latin American countries. Table 8.4 shows changes in method use between two dates for sixteen Latin American and Caribbean countries and areas.[10] The two surveys are separated by between approximately six to fourteen years, with the earlier dates ranging from 1968 to 1981, and the more recent from 1982 to 1989.[11]

The rapid rise in the overall level of contraceptive use in many of these populations has already been noted. Between the dates shown in Table 8.4, contraceptive prevalence rose at an average pace of 2 percentage points per year or more in five of the sixteen countries (El Salvador, Honduras, Mexico, Colombia, and Ecuador), by 1.0 to 1.9 points per year in three (Dominican Republic, Jamaica, and Peru), and by 0.5–0.9 points in three. Of the countries with initially low prevalence, two—Haiti and Guatemala—showed little or no increase in use levels, and three populations with moderately high levels of use at the earlier date—Puerto Rico, Trinidad and Tobago, and Costa Rica—showed little change in overall use levels.

Whether overall contraceptive prevalence rose or not, the mix of methods usually showed appreciable change. The most striking feature is the rise in use of female sterilization. At the beginning of the period in Table 8.4, female sterilization accounted for an average (median value) of 21 per cent of contraceptive practice (ranging from 1 to 57 per cent); at the end the median value was 30 per cent (range 11 to 66 per cent). In six of the sixteen populations, female sterilization (or sterilization of both sexes, when not separately reported) grew in prevalence by over 1 per cent of couples annually, with a total increase over the period in percentage of couples relying on female sterilization of 21–2 percentage points in the Dominican Republic and El Salvador, and of 10–16 points in Mexico, Panama, Colombia, and Ecuador. In most of the other populations female sterilization also rose in prevalence, the only exception being Costa Rica, where, after 1976, regulatory and legal changes restricted the availability of sterilization by requiring that sterilization be justified by medical indications, not just contraceptive wishes of the woman or the couple (Hollerbach 1989).

Even though use of sterilization is rising nearly everywhere, there are some Latin American countries where prevalence of sterilization remains low (Fig. 8.1

[10] The statistics sometimes differ from those shown in Table 8.A1 for the same date, because of adjustments needed to improve comparison over time.

[11] Where there were more than two surveys with tabulations showing full detail about contraceptive methods, the most recent survey and the one closest to ten years earlier were chosen.

Table 8.4. *Latin America and the Caribbean: contraceptive prevalence at two times, and change in prevalence by contraceptive method*

Country	Year	Age range	Any method	Clinic or supply		Non-supply method	Clinic and supply methods							Non-supply methods		
				Total	Temporary methods		Sterilization		Pill	Injectable	IUD	Condom	Vaginal barrier	Rhythm[a]	Withdrawal	Other or not stated
							Female	Male								
Caribbean																
Dominican Republic	1975	15–49	31.7	26.0	14.0	5.7	11.9	0.1	7.9	0.2	2.8	1.5	1.6	1.2	3.7	0.9
	1986	15–49	50.0	46.7	13.7	3.3	32.9	0.1	8.8	0.3[b]	3.0	1.4	0.2	1.4	1.5	0.4
Difference	11.3		18.3	20.7	−0.3	−2.4	21.0	0.0	0.9	0.1	0.2	−0.1	−1.4	0.2	−2.2	−0.5
Annual change			1.6	1.8	0.0	−0.2	1.9	0.0	0.1	0.0	0.0	0.0	−0.1	0.0	−0.2	0.0
Haiti	1977	15–50	14.9[c]	5.4	5.1	9.5	0.2	0.1	3.5	0.0	0.4	1.1	0.1	4.8	4.7	0.0
	1987	15–49	6.1[c]	4.8	3.5	1.3	1.3	—	2.2	0.7	0.4	0.2	0.0	0.9	0.3	0.0
Difference	9.8		−8.8	−0.6	−1.6	−8.2	1.1	−0.1	−1.3	0.7	0.0	−0.9	−0.1	−3.9	−4.4	0.0
Annual change			−0.9	−0.1	−0.2	−0.8	0.1	0.0	−0.1	0.1	0.0	−0.1	0.0	−0.4	−0.5	0.0
Jamaica	1975/6	15–49	38.3	36.2	28.1	2.1	8.1	0.0	11.8	6.2	3.5[d]	6.6	—[e]	0.3	1.4	0.4
	1988	15–49	54.6	50.9	37.3	3.7	13.6	0.1	19.5	7.6	1.9[d]	8.6	—[e]	1.1	2.4	0.0
Difference	12.8		16.3	14.7	9.2	1.6	5.5	0.1	7.7	1.4	−1.6	2.0	—	0.7	1.0	−0.4
Annual change			1.3	1.1	0.7	0.1	0.4	0.0	0.6	0.1	−0.1	0.2	—	0.1	0.1	0.0
Puerto Rico	1968	15–49[f]	60.0	50.5	15.0	9.5[d]	34.1[g]	1.4	11.3	—	1.6	2.1	—[h]	1.7	7.9	
	1982	15–49[f]	64.1	57.6	15.0	6.5[d]	38.6	4.0	7.7	—	3.6	3.7	—[h]	4.4	2.2	
Difference	14.0		4.1	7.1	0.0	−3.0	4.5	2.6	−3.6	—	2.0	1.6	—	2.7	−5.7	
Annual change			0.3	0.5	0.0	−0.2	0.3	0.2	−0.3	—	0.1	0.1	—	0.2	−0.4	
Trinidad and Tobago	1977	15–49	51.6	45.7	41.2	5.9	4.3	0.2	18.0	1.0	2.2	15.0	5.0	2.3	2.8	0.8
	1987	15–49	52.7	44.4	36.0	8.3	8.2	0.2	14.0	0.8	4.4	11.8	5.0	2.6	5.3	0.3
Difference	10.0		1.1	−1.3	−5.2	2.4	3.9	0.0	−4.0	−0.2	2.2	−3.2	0.0	0.3	2.5	−0.5
Annual change			0.1	−0.1	−0.5	0.2	0.4	0.0	−0.4	0.0	0.2	−0.3	0.0	0.0	0.3	−0.1
Central America																
Costa Rica	1976	20–44	70.1	59.0	43.1	11.1	14.9[g]	1.0	25.0	1.7	5.5	9.1	1.8	5.6	4.8	0.7
	1986	20–44	70.8	59.5	44.1	11.3	14.8[g]	0.6	20.2	1.1	8.4	13.7	0.7	8.1	3.1	0.1
Difference	9.6		0.7	0.5	1.0	0.2	−0.1	−0.4	−4.8	−0.6	2.9	4.6	−1.1	2.5	−1.7	−0.6
Annual change			0.1	0.1	0.1	0.0	0.0	0.0	−0.5	−0.1	0.3	0.5	−0.1	0.3	−0.2	−0.1
El Salvador	1975	15–44[f]	19.3	18.0	9.4	1.3	8.6		6.5	0.4	2.0	0.5	—[h]	1.0		0.3
	1988	15–44	47.1	43.1	12.9	4.0	30.2		7.6	0.9	2.0	2.4	—[h]	3.4		0.4
Difference	12.9		27.8	25.1	3.5	2.7	21.6		1.1	0.5	0.0	1.9	—	2.4		0.1

Table 8.4. *(cont.)*

Country	Year	Age range	Any method	Clinic or supply: Total	Clinic or supply: Temporary methods	Non-supply method	Clinic and supply methods: Sterilization: Female	Sterilization: Male	Pill	Injectable	IUD	Condom	Vaginal barrier	Non-supply methods: Rhythm[a]	Withdrawal	Other or not stated
Annual change			2.2	1.9	0.3	0.2	1.7		0.1	0.0	0.0	0.1	—		0.2	0.0
Guatemala	1978	15–44	19.2	14.6	7.9	4.6	6.7	—[h]	5.7	—[h]	1.4	0.8	—[h]	2.7	1.9	
	1987	15–44	23.2	17.3	6.9	5.9	10.4	—[h]	3.9	—[h]	1.8	1.2	—[h]	2.8	3.1	
Difference	9.0		4.0	2.7	−1.0	1.3	3.7	—	−1.8	—	0.4	0.4	—	0.1	1.2	
Annual change			0.4	0.3	−0.1	0.1	0.4	—	−0.2	—	0.0	0.0	—	0.0	0.1	
Honduras	1981	15–49	26.9	23.5	15.3	3.4	8.1	0.1	11.7	0.3	2.4	0.3	0.6	1.6	1.6	0.0
	1987	15–44	40.6	32.9	20.1	7.7	12.6	0.2	13.4	0.3	4.3	1.8	0.3	3.5	3.9	0.2
Difference	6.3		13.7	9.4	4.8	4.3	4.5	0.1	1.7	0.0	1.9	1.5	−0.3	1.9	2.3	0.2
Annual change			2.2	1.5	0.8	0.7	0.7	0.0	0.3	0.0	0.3	0.2	0.0	0.3	0.4	0.0
Mexico	1976	15–49	30.3	23.3	20.4	7.0	2.7	0.2	10.8	1.7	5.7	0.8	1.4		7.1	
	1987	15–49	52.7	44.6	25.2	8.1	18.6	0.8	9.7	2.8	10.2	1.9	0.6		8.1	
Difference	10.6		22.4	21.3	4.8	1.1	15.9	0.6	−1.1	1.1	4.5	1.1	−0.8		1.0	
Annual change			2.1	2.0	0.5	0.1	1.5	0.1	−0.1	0.1	0.4	0.1	−0.1		0.1	
Panama	1976	20–44	57.0	51.6	27.7	5.4	23.9		18.7	—[i]	4.0	1.3	3.7[j]	2.5	2.9	0.0
	1984	20–44	63.6	60.0	22.6	3.6	37.4		12.5	—[i]	6.2	1.7	2.2[j]	2.2	1.4	0.0
Difference	8.8		6.6	8.4	−5.1	−1.8	13.5		−6.2	—	2.2	0.4	−1.5	−0.3	−1.5	0.0
Annual change			0.7	1.0	−0.6	−0.2	1.5		−0.7	—	0.2	0.0	−0.2	0.0	−0.2	0.0
South America																
Bolivia	1983	15–44	26.0	12.0	9.0	14.0	3.0	0.0	3.0	1.0	4.0	0.0	1.0	14.0	1.0	0.0
	1989	15–49	30.3	12.2	7.8	18.1	4.4	0.0	1.9	0.7	4.8	0.3	0.1	16.1	1.0	0.9
Difference	5.8		4.3	0.2	−1.2	4.1	1.4	0.0	−1.1	−0.3	0.8	0.3	−0.9	2.1	0.0	0.9
Annual change			0.7	0.0	−0.2	0.7	0.2	0.0	−0.2	−0.1	0.1	0.1	−0.2	0.4	0.0	0.2
Colombia	1976	15–49	42.5	30.4	26.2	12.1	4.0	0.2	13.3	0.4	8.5	1.7	2.3	5.1	4.7	2.2
	1986	15–49	64.8	52.5	33.8	12.3	18.3	0.4	16.4	2.4	11.0	1.7	2.3	5.7	5.7	0.9
Difference	10.3		22.3	22.1	7.6	0.2	14.3	0.2	3.1	2.0	2.5	0.0	0.0	0.6	1.0	−1.3
Annual change			2.2	2.1	0.7	0.0	1.4	0.0	0.3	0.2	0.2	0.0	0.0	0.1	0.1	−0.1
Ecuador	1979	15–49	33.6	25.7	17.7	7.9	7.8	0.2	9.5	0.8	4.8	1.0	1.6	4.8	2.3	0.8
	1989	15–49	52.9	41.5	23.0	11.3	18.3	0.2	8.6	0.7	11.9	1.3	0.8	8.8	2.5	0.0
Difference	9.8		19.3	15.8	5.3	3.4	10.5	0.0	−0.9	−0.1	7.1	0.3	−0.8	4.0	0.2	−0.8

Annual change			2.0	1.6	0.5	0.3	1.1	0.0	–0.1	0.0	0.7	0.0	–0.1	0.4	0.0	–0.1
Paraguay	1977	15–44	28.6[c]	23.3	20.1	5.3	3.2		11.8	0.9	4.0	2.6	0.8	1.9	3.3	0.0
	1987	15–44	37.6[c]	29.0	25.0	8.6	4.0		13.5	3.6	5.1	2.3	0.5	5.7	2.9	0.0
Difference	10.0		9.0	5.7	4.9	3.3	0.8		1.7	2.7	1.1	–0.3	–0.3	3.8	–0.4	0.0
Annual change			0.9	0.6	0.5	0.3	0.1		0.2	0.3	0.1	0.0	0.0	0.4	0.0	0.0
Peru	1977	15–49	31.4	11.0	8.2	20.4	2.8	0.0	4.1	1.0	1.3	1.0	0.8	10.9	3.3	6.0
	1986	15–49	45.8	23.0	16.9	22.8	6.1	0.0	6.5	1.3	7.4	0.7	1.0	17.7	3.6	1.5
Difference	9.1		14.4	12.0	8.7	2.4	3.3	0.0	2.4	0.3	6.1	–0.3	0.2	6.8	0.3	–4.5
Annual change			1.6	1.3	1.0	0.3	0.4	0.0	0.3	0.0	0.7	0.0	0.0	0.7	0.0	–0.5

Sources: Data and source references for most surveys are given in United Nations (1989). Other sources: ADS and USCDC (1989), Bolivia INE (1990), Cayemittes and Chahnazarian (1989), CEPAR *et. al.* (1990), CEPEP and USCDC (1988), Costa Rica Demographic Association and USCDC (1987), DGPF and IRD (1989), Heath *et. al.* (1988), HMPH *et. al.* (1989), INCAP and IRD (1989), McFarlane and Warren (1989), PMOH and USCDC (1986).

a Mainly calendar rhythm; also includes newer methods of periodic abstinence.
b Including 0.2 per cent using implants.
c Excluding douche, abstinence, and folk methods.
d Including vaginal barrier methods.
e Combined with IUD.
f Ever-married women.
g Including some cases of sterilization for non-contraceptive reasons.
h Combined with 'other'
i Combined with vaginal barrier methods.
j Includes injectables.

and Table 8.A1). At the most recent date, fewer than 5 per cent of couples were using female sterilization in six (20 per cent) of the thirty countries and areas with at least one survey. Even in these cases this may be due more to poor availability of contraceptive sterilization than to a lack of interest on the part of women.[12]

Puerto Rico has the highest level of reliance on male sterilization (4.4 per cent of couples) and also provides the only instance in Table 8.4 where prevalence of this method grew by more than 1 percentage point over the period shown. Most Latin American and Caribbean countries show negligible use of this method and little sign of an increase. In Mexico there was a small increase (from 0.2 to 0.8 per cent of couples).

Methods other than female sterilization show less consistent trends from country to country. Pill use grew in prevalence by at least 1 per cent of couples in six of the sixteen populations in Table 8.4, with the largest increases occurring in Jamaica (7.7 percentage points) and Colombia (3.1 points). In nine populations pill prevalence declined by at least 1 percentage point; the largest declines were in Panama (6.2 points), Costa Rica (4.8), Trinidad and Tobago (4.0), and Puerto Rico (3.6). In some cases these declines accompanied larger increases in female sterilization (e.g. Panama, Puerto Rico), but in Trinidad and Tobago, the increase in sterilization use was no greater than the decline in pill use, and in Costa Rica reliance on sterilization did not increase at all. For the sixteen countries, the median percentage of total contraceptive use contributed by oral contraceptives declined from 31 per cent, at the earlier time in Table 8.4, to 19 per cent at the more recent date.

In contrast to pill use, reliance on IUDs has been increasing in most Latin American countries. In ten of the sixteen countries, IUD prevalence increased by 1 per cent of couples or more, with the largest increases being observed in Ecuador (7.1 percentage points), Peru (6.1 points), and Mexico (4.5 points). IUD use decreased by 1 or more per cent of couples only in Jamaica (1.9 points).[13] IUDs are currently used by 10–12 per cent of couples in four countries—Colombia, Ecuador, Mexico, and Montserrat—and are used by 5–9 per cent in eight others (Table 8.A1).

Injectables are employed by under 5 per cent of couples, except in Jamaica and Dominica (7.6 and 9.8 per cent respectively). However, increases in injectable use by 1 per cent of couples or more occurred in five countries in Table 8.4, and only in Costa Rica was there a decline of more than 0.5 per cent of couples.

Condoms are used by over 5 per cent of couples in about one-quarter of the countries in Table 8.A1; Costa Rica and Trinidad and Tobago are the only countries where prevalence of condom use exceeds 10 per cent of couples at the most recent date. The prevalence of condom use changed little in most of the countries

[12] Around 1982, sterilization was judged not to be readily accessible to a majority of the population of many Latin American and Caribbean countries, including Bolivia, Chile, Costa Rica, Ecuador, Guyana, Haiti, Honduras, Nicaragua, Paraguay, Peru, and Venezuela (Lapham and Mauldin 1984; Singh and Berrio 1989; United Nations 1989).

[13] For Jamaica, the available statistics for the most recent survey combined IUDs with vaginal barrier methods; it is not clear how much of the decrease in this category is due to a decline in IUD use.

with information about trends, but in five countries this method grew in prevalence by at least 1 percentage point, with the largest increase, 4.6 points, occurring in Costa Rica. Condom prevalence decreased by more than 0.5 per cent of couples only in Trinidad and Tobago, where the decline amounted to 3.2 per cent of couples.

Vaginal barrier methods—including diaphragms; cervical caps; and spermicidal foams, tablets, and jellies—are used by as many as 5 per cent of couples only in Trinidad and Tobago. Five countries experienced declines of more than 1 percentage point in prevalence of these methods' use between the dates shown in Table 8.4; none experienced an increase in their use of as much as 0.5 per cent of couples. However, because methods in this group are often used in combination with other methods (particularly spermicides with the condom), the total number of women using vaginal barrier methods is likely to be higher than indicated in the figures presented here.

Levels of use, as well as trends, are more difficult to assess for methods such as rhythm and withdrawal that require no supplies or clinical services. Measured levels of use of these methods are known to be sensitive to seemingly minor differences in questions asked, and sometimes vary over time in implausible ways. In Haiti, for instance, the apparent decline in contraceptive prevalence after 1977 may be an artefact of more complete detection, at the earlier date, of use of rhythm, withdrawal, and other traditional methods.

Use of rhythm (including newer methods of periodic abstinence) appears to be increasing more often than not. Apart from Haiti, there are no instances of an appreciable decline[14] in use of rhythm in Table 8.4. In seven countries the prevalence of rhythm grew by 1 per cent of couples or more, with the largest increases recorded in Peru (6.8 percentage points), Ecuador (4.1), and Paraguay (3.8 points). Bolivia and Peru have by far the highest levels of use of rhythm: 16–17 per cent of couples. In seven other countries between 5 and 9 per cent of couples rely on this method.

In four of the countries with trend data, use of withdrawal increased by 1 per cent of couples or more, and in four it decreased by at least that amount. Withdrawal was used as the main method by 5–6 per cent of couples in six of the thirty populations, and by under 5 per cent in the rest.

Table 8.4 also shows changes in prevalence for groups of methods. The group of clinic and supply methods grew in prevalence in almost all the countries (exceptions are Haiti and Trinidad and Tobago). As the discussion above makes clear, female sterilization often contributed most of this increase. Taken together, the temporary clinical and supply methods (orals, injectables, IUDs, condoms, and vaginal barrier methods) increased in prevalence by 1 or more percentage point in nine of the countries in Table 8.4 and declined in prevalence by that amount in five cases. As a percentage of total contraceptive practice, the latter methods accounted for a median of 51 per cent of the total at the earlier and 46

[14] More than 0.5% of couples.

per cent at the more recent date. The category of less effective 'non-supply' methods more often than not shows a modest increase in overall prevalence, though the share of total use that is attributable to these methods has not, in general, grown. At both times in Table 8.4, these methods accounted for an average (median) of 18 per cent of total use.

Can Levels of Sterilization Go Much Higher?

Since sterilization is, for all practical purposes, a permanent method, the percentage sterilized increases as a cohort grows older. At present, though, the highest percentages sterilized are usually found among women in their thirties rather than at the oldest reproductive ages. This is a consequence of the recent increase in rates of adoption of sterilization, coupled with the fact that most sterilizations are obtained by women between the ages of 25 and 40, ages at which many women already have all the children they want and need contraceptive protection for many years. In the countries where the overall prevalence of sterilization exceeds 20 per cent of couples, over 40 per cent of currently married women aged 35–39 have been sterilized: 42 per cent in Brazil, 48 per cent in El Salvador, 57 per cent in the Dominican Republic, 63 per cent in Panama and 60 per cent in Puerto Rico (ADS and USCDC 1989; Arruda *et al.* 1987; PMOH and USCDC 1986; RDCNPF and IRD 1987; Warren *et al.* 1986).[15]

High as the current prevalence of sterilization is in these countries, there is little sign that growth in use of sterilization is levelling off. Several studies have calculated synthetic-cohort estimates based on age-specific or marriage-duration specific rates of sterilization in the several years preceding recent surveys. In most cases these studies have found that, if recent sterilization rates were to persist, the percentages of women who would eventually be sterilized substantially exceed the levels of sterilization currently observed in any age or marriage-duration group. In Panama and Puerto Rico nearly 80 per cent of women would eventually be sterilized, if recent rates of sterilization adoption persisted (Ross *et al.* 1987; Warren *et al.* 1986). This sort of comparison, applied to surveys conducted from the mid-1970s to mid-1980s, also suggested that sterilization prevalence could rise substantially in Brazil, Colombia, the Dominican Republic, Ecuador, and Guatemala, with more modest increases being indicated in Guyana and Jamaica (Ross *et al.* 1987; Rutenberg and Ferraz 1988). However, in the latter countries the eventual levels of sterilization implied by recent adoption rates are well below the levels implied for Panama and Puerto Rico. Costa Rica, as noted earlier, is an exception to the general pattern of increasing levels of sterilization; rates of sterilization adoption were higher in the early 1970s than since, and prevalence of sterilization has declined since 1981 (see Table 8.A1).

[15] These figures are for the most recent dates shown in Table 8.A1. Percentages sterilized among all women aged 35–39 are somewhat lower; for instance 38% in Brazil and 52% in the Dominican Republic.

Fig. 8.3 shows synthetic-cohort estimates of cumulative percentages sterilized, for single years preceding 1986–7 surveys in six Latin American and Caribbean countries, based on dates of sterilization reported in the surveys.[16] Also shown are percentages of all women currently sterilized at ages over 30. These countries, though chosen solely on the basis of availability of DHS data tapes, give a good representation of the varying degrees of reliance on sterilization within Latin America today. They include Peru, where only 6 per cent of married women of reproductive age are sterilized, as well as the Dominican Republic (33 per cent) and Brazil (27 per cent). All six countries show some evidence of increased levels of sterilization over time, as judged from the trend in annual synthetic-cohort rates in Fig. 8.3 and from sterilization prevalence measured in successive surveys (Tables 8.4 and 8.A1). The amount of increase ranges from quite small—prevalence among married women in Peru grew from 2 per cent in 1969/70 to 6 per cent in 1986—to very large: in the Dominican Republic, prevalence of female sterilization was 12 per cent of couples in 1975 and 33 per cent in 1986.

Except in Peru, the synthetic-cohort rates of sterilization for the several years preceding the surveys indicate a substantially higher prevalence of sterilization than is currently observed in any five-year age-group of women. If recent age-specific rates of sterilization were to persist, only about 10–15 per cent of women in Peru would be sterilized by the end of the reproductive years, as compared to 20–30 per cent in Trinidad and Tobago, nearly 40 per cent in Ecuador, 40–50 per cent in Colombia, 60 or 65 per cent in Brazil, and around 80 per cent in the Dominican Republic.

It is an open question whether as many as 80 per cent of actual cohorts of women will ever choose sterilization. Where sterilization has only recently become readily available, a pent-up demand may have contributed to high synthetic-cohort rates over the recent past, and the period rates may subside once this demand has been satisfied. Yet, as noted earlier, around 60 per cent of couples in their late thirties or early forties have already been sterilized in a few populations, and these levels may be reached in an increasing number of countries in the coming years.

The synthetic-cohort sterilization rates for several countries show marked annual fluctuations within the fifteen-year period shown. In general, annual family planning acceptance rates often vary in response to such factors as changes in programme organization or in laws, regulations, or incentives regarding provision of particular methods, and favourable or unfavourable publicity about

[16] These are actually annual sterilization rates, which—if there were an unusually high concentration of sterilizations in a single year—could assume values greater than 1 sterilization per woman, when summed over the reproductive ages; this does not occur in these data, though. These rates are not strictly comparable to synthetic measures of proportions sterilized presented by Westoff *et al.* (1979), Ross *et al.* (1987), and others. The synthetic-cohort rates shown here are based on 'cohort-period' rates (as defined in Goldman and Hobcraft 1982) for single years of age and single years before the surveys. Rates for each year before the survey were summed to the ages indicated, including 0.5 of the single-year rate for women whose age in completed years was, at the end of the year in question, equal to the final age of summation (45, 40, 35, or 30 years). The estimates shown are for female sterilization only and pertain to all women, regardless of marital status.

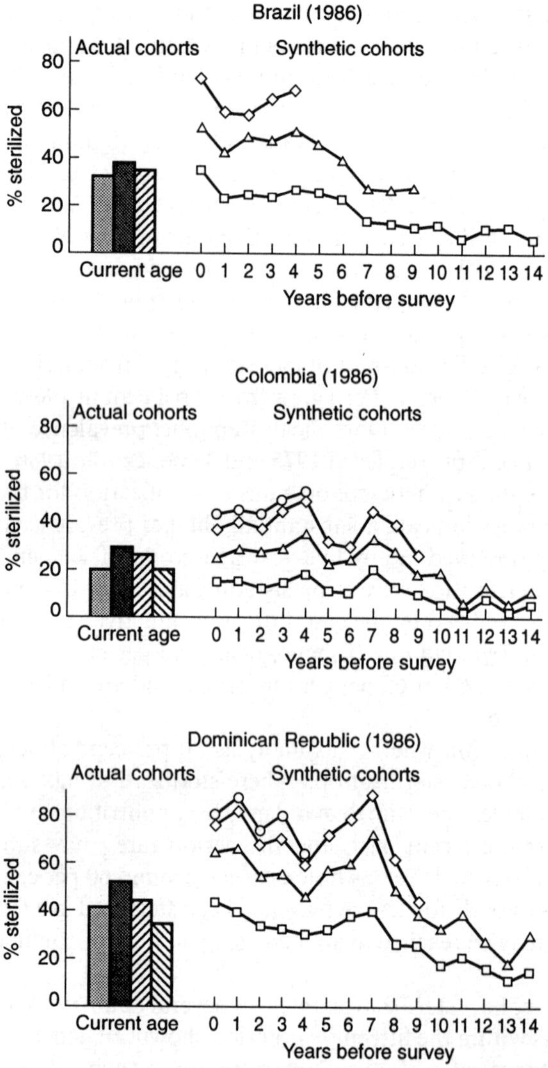

method safety. In Colombia the number of sterilizations performed by PROFAMILIA, the largest sterilization provider, shows fluctuations that approximately correspond to those seen in Fig. 8.3 during years 0–7 before the survey. Judging by PROFAMILIA's service statistics, the declining sterilization rates evident in Fig. 8.3, in the few years immediately before the survey, represented merely a temporary slowdown; during 1986 and 1987, the number of sterilizations provided by PROFAMILIA rose to levels exceeding those of any of the earlier years (Ross *et al.* 1988; see also Hollerbach 1989). In the Dominican Republic, programme records also show a temporary drop in number of sterilizations corresponding approximately to the dip evident in Fig. 8.3 (Ross *et al.* 1988). Thus,

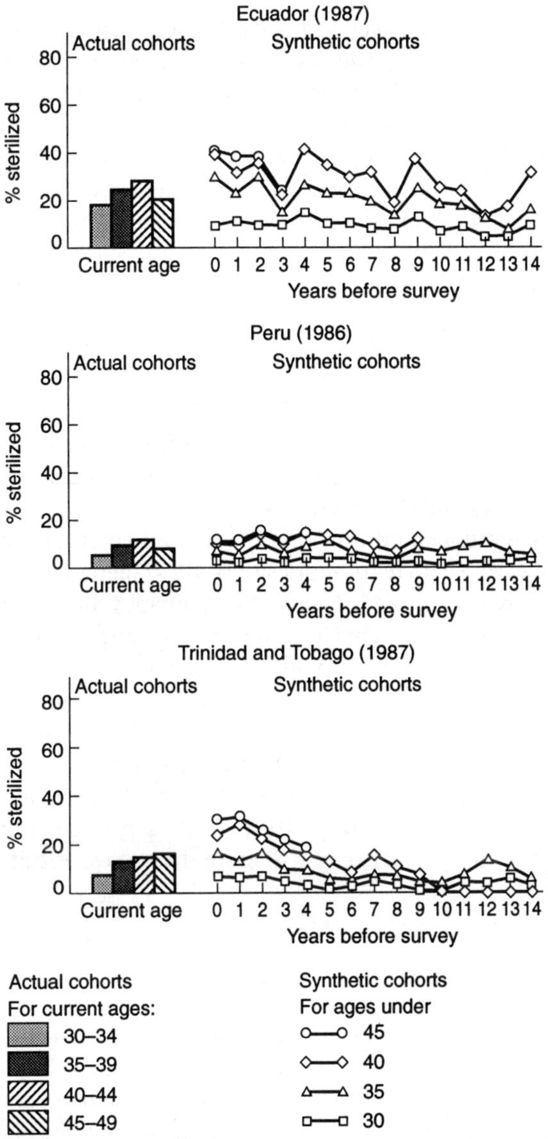

Fig. 8.3. ***Latin America and the Caribbean: % of women sterilized by age, and synthetic-cohort estimates based on sterilization rates for single years before 1986–1987***

marked changes in annual rates visible in Fig. 8.3 probably reflect genuine changes in the recent past. However, the rates calculated from these retrospective data deserve to be checked more thoroughly for consistency with similar data from earlier surveys and programme records.

The evident willingness of such large numbers of women to choose an irreversible method of contraception is itself a commentary on women's judgement of the drawbacks of the available temporary methods; though it should also be borne in mind that the full range of methods is frequently not readily available. In the case of modern methods such as the pill and IUD, concerns about method safety are mentioned repeatedly, in interviews, as a major reason for non-use among women who are at risk of unintended pregnancy. Side effects, or fears about them, are also among the major reasons for discontinuing use of the more effective methods. The data gathered in most fertility surveys contain little or no information about the type and severity of side effects experienced, or perhaps merely feared. Separate investigations are needed in order to judge whether women's concerns are medically well founded, and whether provision of more complete and more accurate information would increase the use of the effective reversible methods. Many women may have received medical advice against using certain methods; pill use by older women is often discouraged, for instance. In the United States in 1982, over one-third of former pill users said a doctor had told them to stop (Mosher and Bachrach 1988).

While barrier methods and non-supply methods (periodic abstinence, withdrawal) typically arouse no fears about safety, these methods are less convenient to use and are more likely to fail. Accidental pregnancy during contraceptive use becomes more common, in relative terms, as the proportion of contraceptive users rises. In Latin America today an appreciable proportion of births result from contraceptive failure. For example, in the two years preceding the 1986–7 surveys in Brazil, Ecuador, and Peru, 15, 10, and 18 per cent respectively of all births were conceived while the couple was using contraception (Bongaarts and Rodríguez 1991; Rutenberg and Blanc 1991); in Colombia, the Dominican Republic, and Trinidad and Tobago 10, 16 and 22 per cent respectively of the most recent births during the five years before the surveys resulted from contraceptive failure.[17]

Summary and Conclusions

The overall level of contraceptive prevalence in Latin America—estimated at 56 per cent of couples with the woman of reproductive age—is higher than in other developing regions, with the exception of East Asia. In most countries in Latin America and the Caribbean, contraceptive prevalence is in the range of 30–60 per cent at the most recent date, with most of the more populous countries having values in the range of 45–65 per cent.

Where trends can be assessed, the overall level of contraceptive practice is usually increasing, and in many cases is increasing rapidly. Countries with annual increases in prevalence of 2 or more per cent of couples per year (between the dates shown in Table 8.4) include Colombia, Ecuador, El Salvador, Honduras, and Mexico. Several others have increases that are only slightly less rapid. Indeed,

[17] Based on unpublished tabulations from DHS data tapes.

among countries with trend data, in nearly all cases where prevalence was below 50 per cent of couples, subsequent surveys show some growth in use (Haiti and Guatemala are exceptions).[18]

In general, changes in the method mix in Latin American countries have tended to favour increased effectiveness of contraceptive practice. This review makes it clear, though, that in recent years this is mainly a matter of increasing reliance on female sterilization. The introduction and rapid adoption of the oral pill was the most striking trend during an earlier (and less well-documented) period, from the early 1960s to the mid-1970s when, in many countries, use of the pill reached a peak. It is an open question whether, if there had not been improvements in sterilization techniques and sterilization availability, the population would have turned instead to even greater use of the pill and other effective modern methods. In Costa Rica, where access to contraceptive sterilization has been curtailed in recent years and sterilization prevalence has begun to decline, the method mix has on balance shifted toward methods with higher failure rates; although use of the highly effective IUD increased, pill use has declined, and reliance on condoms and periodic abstinence (combined) grew from 21 to 31 per cent of total use between 1976 and 1986 (see Table 8.4).

Female sterilization has been increasing in prevalence in most countries. This method is currently used by over one-fourth of all married women of reproductive age, in at least five Latin American and Caribbean countries; in certain age-groups, the percentage sterilized is as high as 60 per cent. Although current levels of sterilization are unprecedented, it should be noted that a few of these populations already relied heavily on sterilization by the mid-1960s if not before (Panama, Puerto Rico). Male sterilization remains very uncommon in most of Latin America.

Trends for methods other than sterilization are less consistent. Pill use has been rising in some countries, but in others reliance on this method has declined in recent years. Methods whose prevalence is rising in many countries include the condom, IUD, injectables and rhythm (periodic abstinence). Nevertheless, in a majority of Latin American countries, each of the latter methods is employed by under 5 per cent of couples, while the pill is used by 10 per cent or more of couples, in two-thirds of the countries with data available.

Together, female sterilization and the pill account for approximately two-thirds of all contraceptive practice in Latin America and the Caribbean. In 10 of the 16 countries and areas with trend data reviewed here, female sterilization accounted for over half of the increase in the general level of contraceptive practice (Table 8.4).[19] In five cases, the increase in sterilization use exceeded the overall rise in contraceptive prevalence; that is, the use of reversible contraceptives declined. Use of female sterilization has been increasing in most Latin American countries, and, if recent rates of sterilization acceptance persist, sterilization prevalence will continue to rise, even in countries where the level is already high.

[18] See Rosenhouse (1989) for a critical discussion of service delivery in Guatemala.

[19] This includes Haiti, where prevalence of sterilization grew even though the overall level of contraceptive use did not (see Table 8.4).

Appendix 8.1

Table 8A1. *Latin America and the Caribbean: %age currently using specific contraceptive methods, for couples with the woman of reproductive age*

Country	Year	Age range	% of women											% of women			% of users			
			Any method	Sterilization		Pill	Injec-table	IUD	Condom	Vaginal barrier methods	Rhythm	With-drawal	Other not stated	Ster. (F+M)	Reversible		Total	Ster. (F+M)	Reversible	
				Female	Male										Clinic, supply	Non-supply			Clinic, supply	Non-supply
														(2–3)	(4–8)	(9–11)		(2–3)	(4–8)	(9–11)
			(1)	(2)	(3)	(4)	(5)	(6)	(7)	(8)	(9)	(10)	(11)	(12)	(13)	(14)	(15)	(16)	(17)	(18)
Caribbean																				
Antigua	1981	15–44	38.9	8.7		16.1	4.5	4.6	1.9	1.3	1.0	0.6	0.2	8.7	28.4	1.8	100	22	73	5
Barbados	1980/1	15–49	46.5	14.4	0.2	15.8	2.2	4.0	5.4	2.6		1.9		14.6	30.0	1.9	100	31	65	4
Dominica	1981	15–44	49.0	14.7		16.5	9.8	2.0	3.6	0.6	1.0	0.7	0.0	14.7	32.5	1.7	100	30	66	3
Dominican Republic	1975	15–49	31.7	11.9	0.1	7.9	0.2	2.8	1.5	1.6	1.2	3.7	0.9	12.0	14.0	5.8	100	38	44	18
	1980	15–49	42.0	21.0	—	9.0			5.0			6.0		21.0	14.0	6.0	100	50	33	14
	1983	15–49	45.8	27.4	0.1	8.6	0.0	3.8	1.5	0.3	1.1	2.5	0.5	27.5	14.2	4.1	100	60	31	9
	1986	15–49	50.0	32.9	0.1	8.8	0.3[a]	3.0	1.4	0.2	1.4	1.5	0.4	33.0	13.7	3.3	100	66	27	7
Grenada	1985	15–44	31.0	2.2	—	7.8	2.9	2.6	8.0	3.8	0.6	2.9	0.0	2.2	25.1	3.5	100	7	81	11
Guadeloupe	1976	15–44	43.6	11.5	—	9.7	—	3.4	5.7	0.2	4.9	6.5	1.7	11.5	19.0	13.1	100	26	44	30
Haiti	1977	15–50	18.9	0.2	0.1	3.5	—	0.4	1.1	0.1	4.8	4.7	4.0	0.3	5.1	13.5	100	2	27	71
	1983	15–49	6.9[b]	0.7	0.1	2.2	0.2	0.2	0.5	0.0	1.4	1.6	—	0.8	3.1	3.0	100	12	45	43
	1987	15–49	6.7	1.3	—	2.2	0.7	0.4	0.2	0.0	0.9	0.3	0.6	1.3	3.5	1.8	100	19	53	27
Jamaica	1975/6	15–49	38.3	8.1	0.0	11.8	6.2	2.0	6.6	1.5	0.3	1.4	0.4	8.1	28.1	2.1	100	21	73	5
	1979	15–44	54.9[b]	9.8	0.0	23.8	11.4	2.0	6.5	0.7	0.2	0.5	—	9.8	44.4	0.7	100	18	81	1
	1983	15–49	51.4[b]	10.9	0.0	19.3	7.6	2.0	7.6	1.0	1.1	1.9	—	10.9	37.5	3.0	100	21	73	6
	1988	15–49	54.6	13.6	0.1	19.5	7.6	1.5	8.6	0.4	1.1	2.4	0.0	13.7	37.6	3.5	100	25	69	6
Martinique	1976	15–44	51.3	11.7	—	17.3	—	2.6	4.6	1.7	4.7	6.2	2.6	11.7	26.2	13.5	100	23	51	26
Montserrat	1984	15–44	52.6	1.6		30.6	3.2	11.0	3.4	2.4	0.3		0.0	1.6	50.6	0.3	100	3	96	1
Puerto Rico	1947/8	15–49[c]	—	6.6		—	—	—	—	—	—	—	—	6.6	—	—	—	—	—	—
	1953/4	20–49[c]	—	16.5		—	—	—	—	—	—	—	—	16.5	—	—	—	—	—	—
	1965	20–49[c]	—	31.9		—	—	—	—	—	—	—	—	31.9	—	—	—	—	—	—
	1968	15–49[c]	60.0	34.1[d]	1.4	11.3	—	1.6	2.1	0.3	1.7	4.4	3.2	35.5	15.3	9.3	100	59	26	16
	1974	15–49[c]	61.1	28.5		20.0	—	3.6	2.9		6.1			28.5	26.5	6.1	100	47	43	10

1976	15–49[c]	64.6	35.4	2.8	12.7	—	3.4			10.3				38.2	16.1	10.3[e]	100	59	25	16[e]
	1982[f]	15–49[c]	64.1	38.6	4.0	7.7	—	3.6	3.7	—[g]	4.4	2.2		42.6	15.0	6.6	100	66	23	10
	1982[f]	15–44	70.4	39.7	4.4	9.3	—	4.1	4.6	—[g]	5.5	2.8		44.1	18.0	8.3	100	63	26	12
St Kitts and Nevis	1984	15–44	40.6	2.6		19.7	2.3	3.8	5.6	3.0	3.6		0.0	2.6	34.4	3.6	100	6	85	9
St Lucia	1981	15–44	42.7	10.8		21.1	2.3	1.0	3.9	1.1	0.8	1.5	0.2	10.8	29.4	2.5	100	25	69	6
St Vincent	1981	15–44	41.5	11.8		13.0	2.7	2.3	8.3	1.4	0.9	0.6	0.4	11.8	27.7	1.9	100	28	67	5
Trinidad and	1970/1	15–44	43.6[h]	2.0	0.1	17.1	—	3.0	9.8	4.5	2.4	4.3	2.5	2.1	34.4	7.1[i]	100	5	79	16[i]
Tobago	1977	15–49	51.6	4.3	0.2	18.0	1.0	2.2	15.0	5.0	2.3	2.8	0.8	4.5	41.2	5.9	100	9	80	11
	1987	15–49	52.7	8.2	0.2	14.0	0.8	4.4	11.8	5.0	2.6	5.3	0.3	8.4	36.0	8.2	100	16	68	16
Central America																				
Costa Rica	1976	20–49	64.4	12.3	1.0	22.5	2.0	5.2	8.8	1.7	5.1	4.6	1.2	13.3	40.2	10.9	100	21	62	17
	1978	15–49	63.8	14.0[d]	0.8	23.3	2.0	4.8	8.7	1.3	4.9	3.5	0.5	14.8	40.1	8.9	100	23	63	14
	1981	15–49	65.2	17.3[d]	0.5	20.6	2.2	5.7	8.4	1.2	6.2	2.8	0.3	17.8	38.1	9.3	100	27	58	14
	1986	15–44	69.5	13.9	0.5	20.7	1.0	8.0	13.4	0.7	8.1	3.1	0.1	14.4	43.8	11.3	100	21	63	16
El Salvador	1975	15–44[c]	19.3	8.6		6.5	0.4	2.0	0.5	—	1.0		0.3	8.6	9.4	1.3	100	45	49	7
	1978	15–44	34.4	17.8	0.2	8.7	0.4	3.3	1.5	0.4	1.7	0.3	0.0	18.0	14.3	2.0	100	52	42	6
	1985	15–44	48.4[j]	31.8	0.7	7.2	0.8	3.5	1.3	0.2	2.1	0.8	0.1	32.5	13.0	3.0	100	67	27	6
	1988	15–44	47.1	29.6	0.6	7.6	0.9	2.0	2.4	0.4	2.4	1.0	0.0	30.2	13.3	3.4	100	64	28	7
Guatemala	1978	15–44	18.1[b, k]	5.9	0.4	5.4	1.1	1.3	0.7	0.4	2.6	0.3	—	6.3	8.9	2.9	100	35	49	16
	1983	15–44	25.0[b]	10.2	0.9	4.7	0.0	2.6	1.2	1.0	3.4	1.0	—	11.1	9.5	4.4	100	44	38	18
	1987	15–44	23.2	10.4	0.9	3.9	0.5	1.8	1.2	0.4	2.8	1.2	0.1	11.3	7.8	4.1	100	49	34	18
Honduras	1981	15–49	26.9	8.1	0.1	11.7	0.3	2.4	0.3	0.6	1.6	1.6	0.0	8.2	15.3	3.2	100	30	57	12
	1984	15–44	34.9	12.1	0.2	12.7	0.3	3.8	0.9	0.4	2.9	1.7	0.0	12.3	18.1	4.6	100	35	52	13
	1987	15–44	40.6	12.6	0.2	13.4	0.3	4.3	1.8	0.3	3.5	3.9	0.2	12.8	20.1	7.6	100	32	50	19
Mexico	1976	15–49	30.3	2.7	0.2	10.8	1.7	5.7	0.8	1.4	3.1	3.6	0.4	2.9	20.4	7.1	100	10	67	23
	1978	15–49	40.0	7.0	0.2	13.8	2.8	6.5	1.0	1.5	3.0	3.3	1.0	7.2	25.6	7.3	100	18	64	18
	1979	15–49	38.9	9.2		13.1	2.6	6.1	0.9	1.1		5.9		9.2	23.8	5.9	100	24	61	15
	1982	15–49	47.7	13.4	0.3	14.2	5.1	6.6	0.9	1.0	3.8	0.4	1.9	13.7	27.8	6.1	100	29	58	13
	1987	15–49	52.7	18.6	0.8	9.7	2.8	10.2	1.9	0.6		8.1		19.4	25.2	8.1	100	37	48	15
Nicaragua	1981	15–49	27.0	7.1	0.1	10.5	1.4	2.3	0.8	0.6	1.0	0.4	3.0	7.2	15.6	4.4	100	27	58	16
Panama	1976	20–49	54.1	21.2	0.4	17.2	0.7	3.7	1.2	1.8	2.6	3.0	2.5	21.6	24.6	8.1	100	40	45	15
	1979	15–44	60.6[b]	29.7[d]		19.0	—[l]	3.7	1.7	2.2[m]	2.9	1.4	0.0	29.7	26.6	4.3	100	49	44	7
	1984	15–44	58.2[b, n]	32.4[d]	0.4	11.8	0.8	6.0	1.6	1.2	2.3	1.4	0.3	32.8	21.4	4.0	100	56	37	7
South America																				
Bolivia	1983	15–44	26.0	3.0	0.0	3.0	1.0	4.0	0.0	1.0	14.0	1.0	0.0	3.0	9.0	15.0	100	12	35	58
	1989	15–49	30.3	4.4	0.0	1.9	0.7	4.8	0.3	0.1	16.1	1.0	0.9	4.4	7.8	18.0	100	15	26	59
Brazil	1986	15–44	65.8	26.9	0.8	25.2	0.6	1.0	1.7	0.5	4.3	5.0	0.0	27.7	29.0	9.3	100	42	44	14
Colombia	1969	15–49	20.5	1.4		4.8	—	2.7			11.5			1.4	7.5	11.5[e]	100	7	37	66[e]

Table 8A1. (*cont.*)

Country	Year	Age range	% of women: Any method (1)	Sterilization: Female (2)	Sterilization: Male (3)	Pill (4)	Injec-table (5)	IUD (6)	Condom (7)	Vaginal barrier methods (8)	Rhythm (9)	With-drawal (10)	Other not stated (11)	% of women: Ster. (F+M) (2–3) (12)	Reversible: Clinic, supply (4–8) (13)	Reversible: Non-supply (9–11) (14)	% of users: Total (15)	Ster. (F+M) (2–3) (16)	Reversible: Clinc, supply (4–8) (17)	Reversible: Non-supply (9–11) (18)
	1976	15–49	42.5	4.0	0.2	13.3	0.4	8.5	1.7	2.3	5.1	4.7	2.2	4.2	26.2	12.0	100	10	62	28
	1978	15–49	46.1	7.5	—	17.2	⌟	7.7	1.4	3.5[m]	4.0	—	4.7	7.5	29.8	8.7	100	16	65	19
	1980	15–49	48.5	10.7	0.2	17.4	⌟	8.1	4.6[m]		4.9	—	2.7	10.9	30.1	7.6	100	22	62	16
	1986	15–49	64.8	18.3	0.4	16.4	2.4	11.0	1.7	2.3	5.7	5.7	0.9	18.7	33.8	12.3	100	29	52	19
Ecuador	1979	15–49	33.6	7.8	0.2	9.5	0.8	4.8	1.0	1.6	4.8	2.3	0.8	8.0	17.7	7.9	100	24	53	24
	1982	15–49	39.9	12.4	0.0	10.3	0.7	6.4	1.1	2.0	4.8	1.5	0.7	12.4	20.5	7.0	100	31	51	18
	1987	15–49	44.3	15.0	0.0	8.5	0.7	9.8	0.6	1.2	6.1	2.1	0.3	15.0	20.8	8.5	100	34	47	19
	1989	15–49	52.9	18.3	0.2	8.6	0.4	11.9	1.3	0.8	8.8	2.5	0.0	18.5	23.0	11.3	100	35	43	21
Guyana	1975	15–49	31.4	8.5	0.1	9.0	0.3	5.6	2.9	1.9	1.0	1.1	1.0	8.6	19.7	3.1	100	27	63	10
Paraguay	1977	15–44	28.6[b]	3.2		11.8	0.9	4.0	2.6	0.8	1.9	3.3	—	3.2	20.1	5.2	100	11	70	18
	1979	15–49	36.4	2.1	0.1	11.9	1.7	5.4	1.5	0.8	4.2	2.4	6.3	2.2	21.3	12.9	100	6	59	35
	1987	15–44	44.8	4.0	0.0	13.5	3.6	5.1	2.3	0.5	5.7	2.9	7.2	4.0	25.0	15.8	100	9	56	35
Peru	1969/70	15–49	26.0	2.0	—	3.0	—	1.0	3.0	1.0	7.0	4.0	5.0	2.0	8.0	16.0	100	8	31	62
	1977/8	15–49	31.4	2.8	0.0	4.1	1.0	1.3	1.0	0.8	10.9	3.3	6.0	2.8	8.2	20.2	100	9	26	64
	1981	15–49	41.0	4.0	0.0	5.0	2.0	4.0	1.0	1.0	17.0	4.0	3.0	4.0	13.0	2.0	100	10	32	59
	1986	15–49	45.8	6.1	0.0	6.5	1.3	7.4	0.7	1.0	17.7	3.6	1.5	6.1	16.9	22.8	100	13	37	50
Venezuela	1977	15–44	49.3	7.6	0.1	15.3	0.2	8.6	4.8	1.1	4.0	4.7	2.8	7.7	30.0	11.5	100	16	61	23

Sources: See Table 8.4.

Note: Due to rounding, figures for individual methods may not add to the total.

a *Including 0.2 per cent using NORPLANT.*
b *Excluding abstinence, douche and folk methods.*
c *Ever-married women.*
d *Including some cases of sterilization for non-contraceptive reasons.*
e *Including condom and vaginal barrier methods.*
f *Figures for a single date are from the same survey, shown for more than one base population.*
g *Combined with 'other methods'.*
h *Figures do not add to the total because women using a combination of methods are shown under each.*
i *Calculated assuming that clinic and supply methods are not used in combination with other such methods.*
j *Prevalence is 46.3 per cent when data are weighted to compensate for areas that were not covered in 1985.*
k *For the same geographical areas as covered in the 1983 survey: 19.2 per cent using in 1978.*
l *Combined with vaginal barrier methods.*
m *Includes injectables.*
n *For the same geographical areas as covered in 1976 and 1979: 60.5 per cent using in 1984.*

References

Asociación Demográfica Salvadoreña, and United States Centers for Disease Control (1989), *Family Health Survey, El Salvador 1988—Final English Language Report* (Atlanta, Ga.: US, CDS).

Arruda, J., Rutenberg, N., Morris, L., and Ferraz, E. A. (1987), *Pesquisa Nacional Sobre Saúde Materno-Infantil e Planejamento Familiar, Brasil—1986* (Rio de Janeiro: Sociedade Civil Bem-Estar Familiar no Brasil).

Bolivia, Instituto Nacional de Estadística (1990), *Encuesta Nacional de Demografía y Salud 1989* (La Paz: INE).

Bongaarts, J., and Rodríguez, G. (1991), 'A New Method for Estimating Contraceptive Failure Rates', in United Nations, *Measuring the Dynamics of Contraceptive Use* (New York: United Nations).

Cayemittes, M., and Chahnazarian, A. (1989), *Survie et santé de l'enfant en Haïti* (Port au Prince: Institut Haïtien de l'Enfance, Ministère de la Santé Publique et de la Population).

Centro de Estudios de Población y Paternidad Responsable, Ministerio de Salud Pública, and United States Centers for Disease Control (1990), *Ecuador Encuesta Demográfica y de Salud Materna e Infantil, ENDEMAIN-89* (Quito: CEPAR).

Centro Paraguayo de Estudios de Población, and United States Centers for Disease Control (1988), *Family Planning Survey, Paraguay 1987: Final English Language Report* (Atlanta, Ga.: USCDC).

Costa Rica Demographic Association, and US Centers for Disease Control (1987), *The Costa Rica Fertility and Health Survey, 1986* (Atlanta, Ga.: USCDC).

Dirección General de Planificación Familiar, and Institute for Resource Development/Macro Systems (1989), *México Encuesta Nacional sobre Fecundidad y Salud 1987* (Mexico City: DGPF).

Goldman, N., and Hobcraft, J. (1982), *Birth Histories* (WFS Comparative Studies, No. **17**, Voorburg: International Statistical Institute).

Goldscheider, C., and Mosher, W. D. (1988), 'Religious Affiliation and Contraceptive Usage: Changing American Patterns 1955–1982', *Studies in Family Planning*, **19**: 48–57.

Heath, K., Da Costa-Martinez, D., and Sheon, A. R. (1988), *Trinidad and Tobago Demographic and Health Survey 1987* (Port-of-Spain: Family Planning Association of Trinidad and Tobago).

Honduran Ministry of Public Health, Association for Family Planning in Honduras, Family Health International, and Management Sciences for Health (1989), *Epidemiology and Family Health Survey—Honduras, 1987* (Research Triangle Park, NC).

Hollerbach, P. (1989), 'The Impact of National Policies on the Acceptance of Sterilization in Colombia and Costa Rica', *Studies in Family Planning*, **20**: 308–24.

Instituto de Nutrición de Centro América y Panamá, and Institute for Resource Development/Macro Systems (1989), *Guatemala Encuesta Nacional de Salud Materno Infantil 1987* (Guatemala City: INCAP).

Lapham, R. J., and Mauldin, W. P. (1984), 'Family Planning Program Effort and Birthrate Decline in Developing Countries', *International Family Planning Perspectives*, **10**: 109–18.

McFarlane, C., and Warren, C. (1989), *1989 Jamaica Contraceptive Prevalence Survey: Final Report* (Kingston: National Family Planning Board).

Mosher, W. D., and Bachrach, C. A. (1988), *Contraceptive Use, United States, 1982* (Data from the National Survey of Family Growth, Series 23, No. 12; Hyattsville, Md.: US National Center for Health Statistics).

Panama Ministry of Health, and United States Centers for Disease Control (1986), *Maternal-Child Health/Family Planning Survey, Panama 1984: Final English Language Report* (Atlanta, Ga.: USCDC).

Potter, J. E. (1983), 'Una Apreciación del Papel de las Variables Intermedias en el Descenso de la Fecundidad Latinoamericana, in *Memorias del Congreso Latinoamericano de Población y Desarrollo*, ii (Mexico City: El Colegio de México), 1061–81.

República Dominicana, Consejo Nacional de Población y Familia, and Institute for Resource Development, Westinghouse (1987), *República Dominicana Encuesta Demográfica y de Salud: DHI-1986* (Santo Domingo: RDCNPF).

Rosenhouse, S. (1989), 'Weak Demand or Inappropriate Supply: Program Efforts in Indigenous Guatemala', paper presented at the IUSSP/Population Council/Rockefeller Foundation/Arab League seminar on the Role of Family Planning Programmes as a Fertility Determinant, Tunis, June.

Ross, J. A., Wardlaw, R. M., Huber, D. H., and Hong, S. (1987), 'Cohort Trends in Sterilization: Some International Comparisons', *International Family Planning Perspectives*, **13**: 52–60.

——Rich, M., Molzan, J. P., and Pensak, M. (1988), *Family Planning and Child Survival: 100 Developing Countries* (New York: Columbia University).

Rutenberg, N., and Blanc, A. (1991), 'The Analytic Potential of DHS Data on Coital Frequency and Its Implications for the Estimation of Failure Rates', in United Nations, *Measuring the Dynamics of Contraceptive Use* (New York: United Nations).

——and Ferraz, E. A. (1988), 'Female Sterilization and its Demographic Impact in Brazil', *International Family Planning Perspectives*, **14**: 61–8.

Singh, S., and Berrio, D. (1989), 'Institutional Constraints on the Provision of Family Planning Services in Latin America', paper presented at the IUSSP/Population Council/Rockefeller Foundation/Arab League seminar on the Role of Family Planning Programmes as a Fertility Determinant, Tunis, June.

United Nations (1979), *Factors Affecting the Use and Non-use of Contraception: Findings from a Comparative Analysis of Selected KAP Surveys* (Sales No. E.79.XIII.6; New York: UN).

—— (1989), *Levels and Trends of Contraceptive Use as Assessed in 1988* (Sales No. E.89.XIII.4; New York: UN).

Warren, C. W., Westoff, C. F., Herold, J. M., Rochat, R. W., and Smith, J. C. (1986), 'Contraceptive Sterilization in Puerto Rico', *Demography*, **23**: 351–65.

Westoff, C. F., McCarthy, J. M., Goldman, N., and Mascarin, F. (1979), *Illustrative Analysis: Contraceptive Sterilization and Births Averted in Panama* (WFS Scientific Reports, No. **4**, Voorburg: International Statistical Institute).

9 The Role of Induced Abortion in the Fertility Transition of Latin America

TOMÁS FREJKA and LUCILLE C. ATKIN

Introduction

In every society of the contemporary world there is a demand for induced abortions. The extent of this demand depends on many interdependent factors (Frejka *et al.* 1989), which are determined by the stage of the transition from natural to controlled fertility of the respective society. The main determinants of this demand are the developing motivation for a smaller number of children per woman/couple, and the availability, access to, and utilization of contraceptives.

In traditional societies couples practise a minimum of deliberate fertility control through contraception and induced abortion. In these societies the average number of live births per couple tends to be around 7. With modernization a desire to limit the number of births appears and progressively permeates the respective society. As part of this process, marriage patterns and breast-feeding practices tend to change and the desire for a smaller number of births materializes, mainly by practising either contraception and/or induced abortion (Tietze and Bongaarts 1975).

If a wide choice of contraceptive methods is available; if there is easy access to them; and if couples know how to, and want to use them, then the numbers of induced abortions will be relatively small. If, however, the above conditions are not present, the numbers of induced abortions will tend to be relatively large. The nature of the legal restrictions to induced abortion, the prevailing moral attitudes and cultural values, as well as the political milieu, may modify the relationship of contraception to the practice of induced abortion.

Tietze and Bongaarts (1976) hypothesize that there are essentially two extreme alternative trends in the utilization of induced abortion in the transition from high to low fertility. The incidence of induced abortion will be relatively small if historically widespread contraceptive use precedes abortion. Conversely, the incidence of induced abortion will be quite large, if extensive use of induced abortion precedes the widespread use of contraception. Requena (1966) suggested that the latter pattern appears to be typical for Latin America.

In this chapter we will present and discuss data and information on the incidence of induced abortion in Latin America. These will be briefly compared to data from other parts of the world. In order to be able to estimate the relative contribution of induced abortion to fertility control in Latin America, we will use model calculations to approximate the actual situation. Finally, we will discuss the causes of the high incidence of induced abortion in Latin America.

The Incidence of Induced Abortion in Latin America

Induced abortion has been practised by the indigenous population for centuries, and included the use of medicinal herbs. The Venezuelan bishop in 1551 reported to the King of Spain on the practice of induced abortion by the indigenous population who did not wish their children to become slaves (Machado 1979). Recent anthropological studies provide ample evidence of the widespread use of induced abortion in contemporary Latin American populations (Machado 1979; Weisner 1982; Pick de Weiss and David 1989).

There are two countries in Latin America with reasonably reliable data on induced abortions: Cuba and Chile. For almost three decades Cuba has experienced liberal induced abortion legislation and practice. Induced abortions have been available on request in government hospitals since the mid-1960s for up to ten weeks of gestation; later abortions require official approval (Hollerbach 1980). Since 1986 menstrual regulation (MR), i.e. vacuum aspiration of the uterus up to and including the fourth week after the first missed period without proof that conception has actually occurred, is also available. The numbers and rates of legal induced abortions increased rapidly during the late 1960s until they reached a peak in 1974 of almost 70 per 1,000 women of childbearing age. This implies a total abortion rate of about 2.1, i.e. an average of over 2 abortions per woman of childbearing age. During the following eight years (1974–82) the level of induced legal abortions declined by over 30 per cent, probably due to an increased and more effective use of contraception. By 1986, however, the incidence of induced abortions (including MRs) was again at the level of about 2 abortions per woman of childbearing age. As of the late 1980s there are almost as many induced abortions as there are live births (SOCUDEF 1989).

The legal situation in Chile is the opposite to Cuba: induced abortion legislation is very restrictive. However, reasonably comprehensive and reliable information is available, because of a very good statistical system of the health sector, and due to the many surveys conducted on induced abortions, particularly in the 1960s. It has been documented that induced abortions were fairly common practice in the 1930s and their incidence increased from then on into the 1960s. The rate of hospitalization for abortion complications in 1965 was 29.8 per 1,000 women of childbearing age (Liskin 1980). Surveys conducted in the early 1960s indicated that there were at least 2 induced abortions per every hospitalized one. This would imply a reasonable, probably low, estimate of the total abortion rate in the mid-1960s of about 2.7 induced abortions per woman. The reason why this might be a low estimate is that contrary to the evidence of the surveys, there were probably more than 2 additional induced abortions per each hospitalized abortion. As a consequence of increasing contraceptive use, due mainly to a family planning programme introduced by the government National Health Service in Chile in the 1960s, the rates of abortion hospitalization declined significantly. By the mid-1980s rates of abortion hospitalization declined to about a quarter of the level of the 1960s. However, the ratio of induced abortions to hospitalized ones was believed to have increased, because of the accumulated experience of induced abortion providers and their use of modern methods, so that the decline in the number of induced abortions must have been much slower. A study conducted by the Ministry of Health in 1976 provides an estimate of 130,000 induced abortions (Anon. 1978). This estimate corresponds to a rate of about 70 induced abortions per 1,000 women of fertile age, or a total abortion rate of around 2 abortions per woman.

From the other Latin American countries we have data mainly from population and hospital-based surveys. Interestingly enough, more data are available for the 1960s than for the 1970s, and even less for the 1980s. Although, the comparability and reliability of these data are questionable (also because often the distinction between induced and spontaneous abortions is blurred), they do provide evidence of the widespread use of induced abortion in Latin America. The population based surveys provide estimates from a number of countries, from Mexico to Argentina, that significant proportions of women, between 20 and 46 per cent, report having had an abortion. Between 6 and 48 per cent of women report that their pregnancies terminated in abortions. The hospital studies provide data on the proportions of admissions due to abortions (from 8 to over 90 per cent); on the proportion of women of fertile age hospitalized due to abortion (from 7 to 43 per cent); and on the proportion of maternal deaths due to abortions (from 8 to over 50 per cent).

A number of other surveys, especially an international comparative study conducted by CELADE, provide evidence of a significant incidence of induced abortion in Latin American cities during the 1960s (Gaslonde 1976). The women surveyed on average experienced close to one life-time induced abortion.

Some of the assembled information permits the calculation of estimates of total abortion rates, the average number of life-time induced abortions per woman, for several Latin American countries of the 1960s to the 1980s. These range from around 1.0 to 4.1. With the exception of Cuba and Chile, these estimates are not very reliable, but they do indicate an order of magnitude (Table 9.1). Similarly, IPPF estimated that about five million illegal abortions per year occurred in the region in the early 1970s, corresponding to an abortion rate of about 65 per 1,000 women aged 15–44, or a total abortion rate of 2.0 (Tietze and Henshaw 1986).

In terms of the fertility transition in Latin America, the documented incidence of induced abortion fits into the following scenario. Up until the 1960s, fertility had started to decline in only a few Latin American countries, principally in Argentina and Uruguay. Throughout the rest of the region, fertility was high. On average, women were having more than 6 live births, which indicates that the

Table 9.1. *Latin America: Estimates of total abortion rates, 1960s–1980s*

Country	1960s	1970s	1980s
Cuba	0.5–0.8	1.2–2.1	1.4–2.0 (legal)
	1.3–1.6	1.8–2.6	n.a. (all)
Chile	2.7	2.0	
Brazil		0.5–1.5	
Colombia		1.2–1.5	
Dominican Republic		1.3	
Mexico		1.5	
Peru		1.3	
Venezuela	1.1–4.1		

Sources: *Cuba*: Hollerbach and Díaz-Briquets 1983; SOCUDEF 1989; *Brazil*—Merrick, 1983; *Other Countries*—authors' calculations based on Liskin 1980; anony. 1978; Acosta *et al.*, 1976; Paiewonsky 1988; Machado 1979.

Note: Data do not necessary refer to whole decade.

prevalence of contraceptive use and the incidence of induced abortion were both low. Since the 1960s, fertility declined rapidly, differentially by country. At the same time there was a substantial and rapid increase in contraceptive prevalence (Mauldin and Segal 1988). Also, the evidence documented above indicates a formidable incidence of induced abortion in virtually all countries of the region. It is important to point out that during the 1960s contraceptive prevalence was low and the incidence of induced abortion was already high. This corresponds to the hypothesized pattern of fertility regulation wherein extensive use of induced abortion precedes contraception and the incidence of induced abortion is high. A consensus exists that the incidence of induced abortion in the region in the 1980s remains elevated, although the actual level in most countries is unknown.

A Comparison of the Incidence of Induced Abortion in Latin America with Other Parts of the World

The overall high level of incidence of induced abortions in Latin America is confirmed by comparing existing estimates with those from other parts of the world. According to a 1976 survey of IPPF affiliates in sixty developing countries (Rochat *et al.* 1980), the incidence of induced abortions in the late 1970s was higher in Latin America than in any other IPPF region of the developing countries (Table 9.2). In terms of the ratio of induced abortions per 1,000 births, the level of induced abortions in Latin America was 30 per cent higher than in the Indian Ocean region, more than 80 per cent above the other Asian countries, and almost four times higher than in Africa and the Middle East.

Further, the above estimates (particularly of Table 9.1) suggest that the incidence of induced abortion in Latin America is similar to some East Asian countries, such as the Republic of Korea and the People's Republic of China, as well as

Table 9.2. ***Regional estimates of level of induced abortions in IPPF regions*[a]**

Region	Estimated births (per 000)	Induced abortions (per 000)	No. of abortions (per 000 births)	% illegal abortions[b]
Africa				
West	5,421	116	21.4	100
East	5,117	456	89.0	100
Middle East and				
North Africa	5,714	537	94.0	95
Indian Ocean	29,901	7,568	253.1	99
E. and SE Asia				
and Oceania	20,064	1,778	176.7	96
Caribbean	389	66	169.7	80
Latin America	9,814	3,192	325.2	100
TOTAL	66,420	13,713	206.5	99

Source: IPPF Unmet Needs Survey, 1977; Rochat *et al.* 1980.

[a] Excludes Europe, USA, Canada, Australia, New Zealand, Japan, South Korea, Hong Kong, Singapore, countries with fewer than 1 million population, and countries lacking IPPF affiliates.

[b] Median value for these countries in 1977.

similar to most East European countries (Frejka 1985). The East Asian and the East European rates were among the highest in the world.

Demographic Analysis of Data

Ideally, for the purpose at hand, one would want to execute analyses of the relative impact of the main fertility inhibiting proximate determinants for individual countries or for the whole region. While reasonably reliable input data are available to conduct such analyses for the impact of marriage, breast-feeding, and contraceptive use patterns (Bongaarts 1982; Chapter 6), these analyses have not included induced abortion, mainly due to the unavailability of data. We shall attempt to fill that gap in the present analysis by using the evidence provided above, in conjunction with model calculations comparing the relative impact of contraception and induced abortion on fertility regulation.

The analyses presented in Bongaarts (1982) and Moreno and Singh (Chapter 6) permit calculations that demonstrate that in Latin America between 25 and 40 per cent of fertility control is due to non-exposure to the risk of pregnancy. The proportion of fertility control brought about by amenorrhea through intensive breast-feeding varies significantly by country. In Costa Rica in 1976 it was under 10 per cent, whereas in Haiti it has been between 40 and 50 per cent in recent years, clearly a consequence of average short periods of breast-feeding in the former and long periods in the latter. The remainder of fertility control is achieved through contraception and induced abortion. In countries which are further along the path towards controlled fertility, 60 per cent or more of overall fertility control is achieved by these two means. In this section we shall estimate the relative importance of the fertility inhibiting effect of induced abortion compared to

Table 9.3. *Latin America: Likely impact of induced abortions on fertility regulation, late 1980s*

Measure	Alternatives			
	1	2	3	4
1. Observed live births (millions)	12.4	12.4	12.4	12.4
2. Potential live births (millions) assuming *no* fertility control	21.3	22.3	23.4	24.4
3. Total births averted by fertility control (line 2 minus line 1)	9.1	10.1	11.2	12.2
(a) Births averted by contraception	8.8	8.8	8.8	8.8
(b) Births averted by induced abortion (line 3 minus line 3*a*)	0.3	1.3	2.4	3.4
4. Induced abortions (millions)	0.5	2.4	4.4	6.2
5. Induced abortions per 100 live births	4	19	35	50
6. Induced abortions per 1,000 women 15–49	5	23	41	58
7. Total abortion rate (lifetime abortions per woman)	0.2	0.8	1.4	2.0

Source: Dorothy Nortman, calculations specifically requested for this purpose. For details see App. 9.1.

contraception by the help of alternative calculations prepared by Dorothy Nortman (Table 9.3).

In line 1 of Table 9.3 we have the actual annual number of live births, 12.4 million. In line 2, different plausible assumptions about natural fertility (general fertility rates ranging from 200 to 230 births per 1,000 women 15–49 years of age) are used to generate hypothesized numbers of live births assuming no birth control. Line 3 gives the total number of births averted by direct methods of fertility control. These are disaggregated into line 3*a*, births averted by contraception: 8.8 million in all alternatives; and line 3*b* (a residual), births averted by induced abortion, which is the difference between lines 3 and 3*a*, and which range from 0.3 to 3.4 million. Estimates of the total number of induced abortions in Latin America are then between 0.5 and 6.2 million induced abortions per year in the late 1980s (line 4). The births averted by induced abortion can be compared to the births averted by contraception. If one assumes the lowest alternative of 0.5 million induced abortions per year, less than 6 per cent of the total number of births averted are due to induced abortion. In the highest alternative, almost 28 per cent of the total number of births averted in Latin America are due to induced abortion.

The real situation could indeed be around or between the two extreme calculations. In line 5 of Table 9.3, ratios of induced abortions per live births are listed. The estimates in Table 9.2 for the 1970s indicate that the situation in Latin America could be close to alternative 3. In line 7, we have corresponding total abortion rates. The estimates of total abortion rates for various countries in Table 9.1 indicate that the calculations of alternatives 3 and 4 are quite plausible. A realistic estimate for the 1980s appears to be that about one quarter of the total number of births averted are averted by induced abortions. Thus, a quarter of deliberate fertility control in Latin America is being achieved by induced abortions.

Causes of High Incidence of Induced Abortion in Latin America

Why do so many women resort to induced abortion in spite of the fact that modern contraceptive methods are generally available, and in spite of the legal restrictions in most of the region and of the risks involved? What are the principal factors which contribute to the apparently high incidence of induced abortion throughout Latin America?

It is quite clear that women/couples throughout Latin America are motivated to have relatively small families. Data from the WFS show that in the 1970s mean desired family size in Latin America was among the lowest in the developing countries, averaging 4.2 with a low of 3.5 in Haiti and a high of 5.1 in Paraguay. Over half of the women interviewed desired from 2 to 4 children. Percentages of currently married women who wanted no more children ranged from 32 to 63. Over half of the women with three children in all Latin American countries, except Paraguay, wanted no more children (UN 1987).

Given that the motivation exists to limit family size, induced abortions will be relatively frequent if modern contraceptive methods are not readily available and easily accessible to the population. This is the situation throughout Latin America where important problems persist in terms of both availability and accessibility. Historically, any tradition of contraceptive use in Latin America was very weak. Modern contraceptives began to be introduced in the 1960s. Their use has greatly increased over the past two decades throughout the region and by the mid-1980s about 55 per cent of married women of reproductive age practised contraception (Mauldin and Segal 1988). Only in Bolivia, Guatemala, and Haiti are the proportions of women practising contraception far lower, 26 per cent (1983), 23 per cent (1987), and 7 per cent (1983) respectively. However, problems of availability exist: supplies may be continually or intermittently inadequate to meet the demand and method alternatives may be highly restricted. While some governments have assumed active leadership in provision of family planning services, others have been ambivalent, openly pro-natalist at times, or silent on the issue. In some countries, for instance in Colombia and in Brazil, the pharmaceutical industry, pharmacies, private physicians, and non-governmental organizations have been quite successful in providing family planning services. Reliance on the private sector can mean that poorer women will be at a disadvantage. The frequent lack of alternative methods means that many women will be compelled to use inappropriate ones which will more likely lead to discontinuation, discomfort, and ineffectiveness.

In addition to limited availability, unequal access to existing methods among subgroups within the population is a serious problem throughout the region. Too often the women most at risk of unwanted pregnancy are the ones whose needs are not being met by existing services: adolescents, single women, and the poor. Given the societal denial of adolescent sexuality and censure imposed on women against sexual relations for pleasure, adolescents and the single woman are often ignored or denied access to family planning services and made to feel rejected or at best uncomfortable in whatever services are open to them. The expense of maintaining effective contraceptive use, especially when provided through the private sector, may be an insurmountable obstacle in light of the instability and extremely low levels of income found among many poor women throughout the region.

Considering the fact that historically women's health and family planning services in Latin America were instituted as means to achieve fewer and healthier babies rather than as services designed to improve the health, well-being, and social status of women *per se* (Faúndes *et al.* 1989), it is not surprising to find that many services neglect the broader aspects of women's health and ignore qualitative elements of service delivery which are essential for insuring patient satisfaction and more effective contraception. Many aspects of services tend to block the development of trust and mutual respect between women and service providers and to inhibit the possibility of offering the educational experience that many women need in order to understand and accept modern contraceptive methods. Furthermore, the process may be relatively complex, entailing various visits to the health centre or doctor, which ends up eliminating women who are not persistent. The women who survive the system are those who have greater conviction and desire, more time available, better acceptance of the codes implied by the health system and better ability to understand how each activity is related to the final goal (Balán and Ramos 1989).

Another obstacle to effective prevention of unwanted pregnancies in the region is deficient knowledge concerning reproduction and contraception. Although information on modern contraceptive methods has certainly improved, evidence suggests that there are still important sectors of women who possess surprisingly inadequate information concerning the basic facts of human reproduction and, more specifically, about contraceptives (Balán and Ramos 1989; Weisner 1982 and 1989; Pick de Weiss *et al.* 1988). Fears and prejudice, as well as shame concerning sexual relations in general, compound such ignorance, creating additional and powerful obstacles to effective contraceptive use.

The presence of inaccurate ideas concerning menstruation and reproduction will impede proper assimilation of modern contraceptive methods. Women with such erroneous beliefs, confronted with modern family planning services will often feel confused and insecure, unable to understand the new concepts to which they are being exposed and unable to develop a coherent strategy of behaviour (Balán and Ramos 1989). Furthermore, attempts to avoid pregnancy, while well-intentioned, will frequently be unsuccessful.

Fears and fantasies, widely supported by informal social networks women have with other women, exist concerning various health hazards associated with contraceptive use. These revolve around dangers for one's own health, including cancer, diabetes, and sterility, as well as for the product of future pregnancies, such as physical malformations or mental deficiencies (Balán and Ramos 1989; Weisner 1989; Pick de Weiss *et al.* 1988; Atkin and Givaudan 1989).

In addition to erroneous beliefs and fears about adverse health repercussions, there are various culturally, socially, and emotionally determined costs, with immediate and powerful perceived consequences, which exist in relation to contraceptive use that prevent some women from using them effectively. Particularly, within cultures that are predominantly Catholic, in which machismo exists, and in which female sexuality is generally repressed or denied, and motherhood held as a central cultural value for women, the costs of using contraception may be very high, especially for single and for young women, but even for married women. Using contraception means acknowledging intercourse both to oneself and to significant others. Obtaining contraceptives means planning intercourse. This goes against traditional female passivity, suggesting to the woman and perhaps to her partner that 'she is looking for sex' and is 'sexually available'. For some couples, using contraceptive methods, particularly barrier methods, is perceived as interruptive of natural spontaneity. Furthermore, the Catholic Church's prohibition of contraception and sexual relations without procreation, makes the use of contraception a double sin for many women. For women who do not participate in sexual relations willingly but rather as a marital obligation, the supposed advantage of greater sexual pleasure due to less concern about getting pregnant may become an added deterrent to contraceptive use.

Male domination makes contraception even more costly for some women. Opposition from husbands who want to show their machismo or prevent infidelity by keeping their wife pregnant may place the woman in danger if she does anything to avoid pregnancy. In many circumstances a woman must unconditionally accept sexual intercourse with her partner to avoid humiliation, beating, or other forms of punishment. Barriers within couple communication may make it unfeasible to discuss the topic or for the woman to even suggest preventive measures.

The immediate costs of contraception are weighed against the anticipated benefits of pregnancy (Luker 1975). Clearly, however, for many women who seek induced abortions these imagined benefits do not become reality once the pregnancy has occurred. What is important though is that women initially believe they are feasible and act accordingly.

In other cases, some women may actually risk unwanted pregnancy thinking that abortion is available as a back-up measure with few risks and some potential 'advantages': it is a single event (if performed safely); it is coitus-independent; it does not require knowledge or consent of the male partner; it provides immediate evidence of success rather than continuous uncertainty; it is based on the certainty of existing pregnancy rather than on an estimate of an unknown probability; it is the only feasible method to avert a birth that is unwanted due to changed circumstances *ex post facto*; and finally, for women with infrequent and/or unanticipated intercourse abortion may be cheaper and/or less threatening to the woman (Campbell n.d.).

It becomes apparent then that for many women, the process of deciding to use modern contraception and of carrying out effective preventive behaviours is a far more difficult process than it initially appears. The relative costs and benefits of contraceptives must be weighed against the costs and benefits of a pregnancy as well as of the perceived availability and risks associated with obtaining an induced abortion in case of an unwanted pregnancy. All this takes place in a situation in which many women perceive the probability of becoming pregnant as an unknown factor in the equation: all too often women think that it is quite unlikely that they will actually become pregnant at all. Of course, once pregnancy does occur, the cost accounting is radically reassessed in light of the new event.

Many women do try to use modern contraception but fail. Indeed a large proportion of women who seek induced abortion have previously used contraceptive methods. They tend to have used less effective methods, to have changed methods more frequently, to have used them more inconsistently (Llovet and Ramos 1988), and to refer to having previously suffered negative side effects from contraceptives, user discomfort, and method failure (Toro and Wilches 1986).

Bongaarts and Rodríguez (1989) have analysed contraceptive failure rates, and their data for six Latin American countries show annual levels of between 6.4 (Costa Rica) and 16.4 per cent (Peru). Cumulatively, over several years such contraceptive failure rates imply large numbers of unwanted pregnancies. Thus, if couples really wish to achieve their desired family size, the option of backing up contraception with induced abortion is going to be continually utilized.

Given all these obstacles to effective contraceptive use, and despite high levels of use, it is not surprising to find that a relatively large proportion of pregnancies are unwanted or not fully desired. Data on pregnancies which were originally unwanted probably underestimate the incidence since they do not include women who may have aborted early on. Nevertheless, they do give us an idea that unwanted pregnancies are quite frequent. Based on data from various regional surveys in the 1980s, Morris (1988) reports that the percentage of unwanted pregnancies ranges from a low of 4.3 in Paraguay to a high of 26.5 in El Salvador. Mistimed pregnancies are also relatively frequent, ranging from 4.9 per cent in Guatemala to 34.7 per cent in the Dominican Republic.

Confronted with unwanted pregnancies, many women undergo a process of adaptation and resignation, carrying their pregnancies to term. However, many others resort to desperate and sometimes bizarre behaviours in order to abort, often placing their lives and well-being in great danger. Considering the many obstacles that still exist between women's motivation to limit their family size and their ability to obtain and effectively use contraception, the high incidence of induced abortion throughout the region is quite understandable and signals the need for coordinated actions to improve family planning services throughout the region.

The interaction of the modernization trends and of the availability and access to contraceptives will continue to affect the demand for induced abortions in the future. As modernization and the transition to controlled fertility progress, by definition, the demand for contraception and induced abortion will increase. At the same time, however, depending on the availability, access to, and utilization of contraception, the demand for induced abortion may decline, be stable, or increase.

The impact of induced abortion on the fertility transition in Latin America will continue to be significant. Recent historical experience suggests that even with a continued increase in contraceptive prevalence, the incidence of induced abortion in Latin America will remain high, at least through the 1990s, even if its legislation continues to be restrictive. Such a situation implies serious reproductive health, and economic as well as social, problems for a large number of women and their families. These problems ought to be taken into account and dealt with by appropriate public and private institutions.

Appendix 9.1: Methods and Background Data Used to Estimate Reasonable Range of Induced Abortion Numbers, Rates and Impact in Latin America

The basic demographic data are females 15–49 (106.3 million) and observed live births (12.4 million [line 1])[1] for 1985–90 (UN 1988 and 1989*a*). Potential live births, assuming natural fertility, were calculated for alternatives 1 to 4 by multiplying females 15–49 (106.3 million) by hypothetical GFRs, of 200, 210, 220, and 230 births per 1,000 females 15–49 [line 2]. The total number of births averted by birth control [line 3] is the difference between line 2 and line 1. To estimate births averted by contraception [line 3*a*], one first has to calculate the GFR that would result if no contraception were used. The formula is the following: observed GFR/[1 – eU/f] (Bongaarts and Potter 1983). The respective data are: observed GFR = 117; e, the use effectiveness index, = 0.84, which is based on method mix; $U = 0.75 \times 0.59$, based on 59 per cent contraceptive prevalence rate among married women (UN 1989*b*) and an assumed 75 per cent of females 15–49 in union; f, the proportion of fecund among women in union, = 0.9; the result of the calculation, i.e. GFR assuming no contraception, is 199; and the number of births assuming no contraception is 21.1 million; minus the actual number of births, 12.4 million, equals the number of births averted by contraception, 8.8 million [line 3*a*]. The number of births averted by induced abortion [line 3*b*] is then the difference between line 3 and line 3*a*. The actual number of induced abortions [line 4] is estimated with the following formula: line 3b/0.4[1 + eU] (Bongaarts and Potter 1983), which takes into account that more than one abortion is needed to avert one birth, and equals 0.5487; concepts e and U are described and their values are given above. Line 5 = line 4/line 1 × 100. Line 6 = line 4/females 15–49 × 1000. The total abortion rate [line 7] is estimated by multiplying line 6 by 0.035 (number of years in the childbearing period divided by 1,000).

References

Acosta, M., Botton-Burla, F., Dominguez, L., Molina, I., Novelo, A., and Nunez, K. (1976), *Abortion in Mexico* (Mexico City: Fondo de Cultura Económica).

Anon. (1978), 'Falling Mortality in Chile', *People*, 5/2.

Atkin, L. C. and Givaudan, M. (1989), 'Perfil Psicosocial de la Adolescente Embarazada Mexicana', in S. Karchmer (ed.), *Temas Selectos en Reproducción Humana* (Mexico City), 123–33.

[1] Line nos. refer to Table 9.3.

Balán, J., and Ramos, S. (1989), 'La Medicalización del Comportamiento Reproductivo: Un Estudio Exploratorio Sobre la Demanda de Anticonceptivos en los Sectores Populares', *Documentos CEDES*, 29.

Bongaarts, J. (1982), 'The Fertility-inhibiting Effects of the Intermediate Fertility Variables', *Studies in Family Planning*, 13: 179–89.

—— and Potter, R. G. (1983), *Fertility, Biology, and Behaviour* (New York: Academic Press).

—— and Rodríguez, G. (1989), *A New Method for Estimating Contraceptive Failure Rates* (Population Council Working Papers, 6; Population Council, New York).

Campbell, E. (n.d.), *International Inventory of Information on Induced Abortion* (New York: Columbia University).

Faúndes. A., Hardy, E., Pinotti, J. A. (1989), 'Commentary on Women's Reproductive Health: Means or End?', *International Journal of Gynecology & Obstetrics*, 3 (suppl.): 115–18.

Frejka, T. (1985), 'Induced Abortion and Fertility', *Family Planning Perspectives*, 17/5: 230–7.

—— Atkin, L. C., Toro, O. L., Paxman, J. (1989), 'Research Programme for the Prevention of Induced Abortion' (Working Paper, No. 23, Mexico City: the Population Council).

Gaslonde, S. (1976), 'Abortion Research in Latin America', *Studies in Family Planning*, 7: 211–17.

Hollerbach, P. E. (1980), 'Recent Trends in Fertility, Abortion and Contraception in Cuba', *International Family Planning Perspectives*, 6: 97–106.

—— and Díaz-Briquets S. (1983), *Fertility Determinants in Cuba* (Center for Policy Studies Working Paper, 102; New York: Population Council).

Liskin, L. S. (1980), *Pregnancy Termination: Complications of Abortion in Developing Countries* (*Population Reports*, Series F-7, VIII, 4; Baltimore: Johns Hopkins University).

Llovet, J., and Ramos, S. (1988), 'La Práctica del Aborto en las Mujeres de Sectores Populares de Buenos Aires', *Documento CEDES*, 4 (Buenos Aires: CEDES).

Luker, K. (1975), *Taking Chances: Abortion and the Decision Not to Contracept* (Berkeley and Los Angeles: University of California Press).

Machado, G. (1979), *En Defensa del Aborto en Venezuela* (Caracas: Editorial Ateneo).

Mauldin, W. P., and Segal, S. J. (1988), 'Prevalence of Contraceptive Use: Trends and Issues', *Studies in Family Planning*, 19: 335–53.

Merrick, T. (1983), *The Effect of Piped Water on Early Childhood Mortality in Urban Brazil, 1970–1976* (Working Paper, No. 594; Washington: The World Bank).

Morris, L. (1988), 'Young Adults in Latin America and the Caribbean: Their Sexual Experience and Contraceptive Use', *International Family Planning Perspectives*, 14: 153–8.

Paiewonsky, D. (1988), *El Aborto en la República Dominicana* (Santo Domingo: CIPAF).

Pick de Weiss, S., Atkin L.-C., and Karchmer, S.-K. (1988), '¿Existen Diferencias entre Adolescentes Embarazadas y la Población en General?' in L. C. Atkin, M. Arcelus, A. Fernández-Macgregor, and K. Tolbert (eds.), *La Psicología en el Ambito Perinatal* (Mexico: INPER).

—— and David, H. P. (1989), 'Illegal Abortion in Mexico: Provider and Client Perceptions', *Transnational Family Research Institute*.

Requena, M. (1966), 'Condiciones Determinantes del Aborto Inducido', *Revista Médica de Chile*, **94**: 714.

Rochat, R. W., Kramer, D., Senanayake, P., and Howell, C. (1980), 'Induced Abortion and Health Problems in Developing Countries', *The Lancet*, 30/2: 484.

SOCUDEF (Sociedad Científica Cubana para el Desarrollo de la Familia) (1989), 'Evaluación de la Fecundidad en Cuba' (unpublished).

Tietze, C., and Bongaarts, J. (1975), 'Fertility Rates and Abortion Rates: Simulations of Family Limitation', *Studies in Family Planning*, 6: 114–20.

—— —— (1976), 'The Demographic Effect of Induced Abortion', *Obstetrical and Gynecological Survey*, 31/10: 699–709.

—— and Henshaw, S. (1986), *Induced Abortion: A World Review* (New York: Alan Guttmacher Institute).

Toro, O. L., and Wilches, I. (1986), 'Placer Sexual y Anticoncepción', in O. Giraldo and M. C. Santamaría, Sociedad Colombiana de Sexología y Depto. de Psicología (eds.) *Sexualidad y Planificación Familiar* (Bogotá. UNIANDES).

United Nations (1987), 'Fertility Behavior in the Context of Development', *Population Studies*, 100.

—— (1988), *World Demographic Estimates and Projections, 1950–2025*, (New York: UN).

—— (1989*a*), 'World Population Prospects', *Population Studies*, 106.

—— (1989*b*), 'Levels and Trends of Contraceptive Use as Assessed in 1988', *Population Studies*, 110.

Vargas-Trujillo, E., and Atkin, L. C. (1988), 'Grupos Educativos con Metodología Participativa para Adolescentes Embarazadas', *La Psicología Social en México*, ii (Mexico City), 343–9.

Weisner, M. (1982), *Aborto Inducido, Estudio Antropológico en Mujeres Urbanas de Bajo Nivel Socioeconómico* (Santiago: University of Chile).

—— (1989), *Reproductive Behavior and Induced Abortion in Chilean Popular Women: an Anthropological Perspective* (Santiago: University of Chile).

10 The Role of Family Planning Programmes in the Fertility Transition of Latin America

AXEL I. MUNDIGO

Onset of the Fertility Transition

In the twenty-year period following the end of the Second World War, Latin America experienced slow but important improvements in mortality due to the expansion of public-sector health programmes and services whose objective was to eradicate endemic diseases. During this period fertility remained high or even increased in some countries as a result of improved health conditions. By the 1960s Latin American demographers began producing estimates and charting trends for the future population growth. Regional and national research centres began to study the influences of demographic factors on development. In the United States, Coale and Hoover (1958) published a study showing the negative results of high fertility for economic development in developing countries arguing that investments made to sustain rapidly expanding populations impeded needed investment in vital sectors of the economy. Their conclusions, based on data for India and Mexico, and the debate that followed were important in creating a climate favourable to international assistance for population programmes, and influenced the policies of the United States government. As reliable new information became available documenting the magnitude of population growth, the effects of rapidly doubling populations, and the implications of younger age structures, more vocal arguments for controlling demographic growth emerged and by the end of the 1960s population had become a 'crisis' of global dimensions.

In Latin America, during the 1950s and 1960s, governments for the most part believed that 'to govern is to populate' (*gobernar es poblar*) and initially expanding populations were seen as a resource for the future growth of the national economies. The main ideological position among government leaders was pronatalist. Population growth was considered the essential ingredient to accelerate production, generate demand, and increase the labour pool necessary for industrial development. In some cases a larger population was viewed as essential for national security. Few public leaders were concerned about the fact that productivity has more to do with the capacity and training of the workers than with their absolute numbers. For others, as long as the rate of population growth remained below that of the GNP, there was no reason to be concerned.

The mainstream populationist philosophies are reflected in statements made by leaders or intellectuals of the time. For example, the well-known Mexican economist and government official Gilberto Loyo (1963) expressed the view that: 'demographic pressures create social and political forces which tend to accelerate progress and to show, with greater clarity, the characteristics and the gravity of [economic] problems. Without these demographic pressures . . . the progressive evolution of this world would be slower and I doubt that it would be less burdensome.' These views have become popular again in some sectors and have found a strong spokesman in the writings of the economist Julian Simon (1981: 345–6) in the United States who argues that:

> There is no physical or economic reason why human resourcefulness and enterprise cannot forever continue to respond to impending shortages and existing problems with new expedients that, after an adjustment period, leave us better off than before the problem arose. Adding more people will cause us more such problems, but at the same time there will be more people to solve these problems and leave us with the bonus of lower costs and less scarcity in the long run.

It should be noted though that Gilberto Loyo was not opposed to family planning. In another article, he remarks that (1974: 198): 'the application of family planning measures, based on a couple's right to determine the dimensions of its family . . . would permit in the 1980's most of the Latin American countries with high birth rates to register significant decreases'.

Against this background, this chapter explores the various factors—individual, political, international—that triggered the onset of the fertility transition in Latin America and particularly the role played by family planning programmes. This mix of factors includes important demographic, social, and economic pressures that acted on families to reduce family size. It is important to stress that not all groups within a particular society were exposed to the same pressures or had access to fertility regulation or methods at the same time. This produced a multiphasic demographic transition.

Latin America: A Multi-phasic Transition

The fertility transition in Latin America has not followed a smooth trend, nor has it been a generalized phenomenon involving all social groups simultaneously. Instead, it has unfolded in a stepwise sequence. An earlier or initial phase, restricted to the better off groups in these societies and more reduced in terms of overall demographic impact, was important in setting new reproductive behaviour norms. As subsequent or advanced phases began, other groups started to lower their reproductive values, which eventually reached the entire social fabric. These later transitional phases are more complex and were triggered by modernization and newer economic conditions that brought about the collapse of the traditional rationale for larger families.

This argument builds on Caldwell's (1982: 338) transition theory based on the direction in which family wealth is invested and the rationality of economic decisions: when families begin to invest in their children, thus reversing the 'wealth flow' of peasant societies where the young support the old, 'most couples will continue to have children but they will manage to do so by receiving all parental pleasure they desire from a smaller and more concentrated source . . . They will have a [smaller] number in the full knowledge that having children is not economic.' In Latin America, especially in the post-war period, middle-class families began to place increasing emphasis on the long-term education of their children, with the expectation that the next generations would improve both their economic and occupational status, thus ensuring the betterment of the family's future in the society. The families who pioneered fertility behaviour changes were those whose economic status would have been severely eroded had they not realized that unlimited reproduction was economically disadvantageous to them individually and, consequently, to their social group. Their motivation to lower family size was buttressed by the rising costs of the commodity that ensured their longer-term status: education. Schooling itself made children more costly as both the direct and indirect costs increased; and, as children demanded more and more from their parents, the reproductive behaviour of middle-class families changed. Lower fertility values emerged and were sustained by the fear of inflation which threatened economic gains made during the post-war years by the middle-classes. Inflation also meant increased educational costs, not to mention housing, food, clothing, and other expenses directly related to the preservation of family lifestyles.

In Latin America, evidence of these early fertility behaviour changes at the individual level initially came from epidemiological studies that pointed at the high incidence of induced abortion and the costs of attending to growing numbers of abortion complications in public hospitals in Chile (Armijo and Monreal 1965). These studies also showed that 'middle-class women had more abortions than the dependants of workers', illustrating the commitment of the middle-class to controlling family size even when faced with an unwanted pregnancy. The lower fertility of these groups was also shown by the early CELADE surveys (1963–4) of Latin American cities. Miró and Rath (1965: 50) noted in their report of surveys in Panama City, Rio de Janeiro, and San José that the data for these cities 'show unequivocally the inverse correlation which exists between the level of education and fertility'. In Rio de Janeiro, to take just one case, the women with secondary education had on average 1.4 children, while those with three years of primary education or less had 3 or more children, on average. In Panama and San José, the differences were even more striking. The authors noted that level of education gives a more exact measure of socio-economic status than other measures, such as occupation of husband, but that regardless of the index used, the findings consistently showed that fertility was lower among the more affluent families in these cities.

Evidence of changing values, based on a study of males in Brazil and Mexico conducted in 1960, provides another indication of changing attitudes towards family size among aspiring middle-class workers (Kahl 1967). The study was based on a sample of 627 men in Brazil and 740 in Mexico (residents of Rio de Janeiro and Mexico City, but with different urban and rural backgrounds, and occupational status). The family-size ideals of these men were surprisingly small, on average, for the time: 2.6 children among Brazilians and 3.9 among Mexicans. The desire for slightly larger families in Mexico was consistent for all occupational categories. In Brazil the mean ideal family size was quite consistent among all occupational groups but in Mexico men in manual occupations had slightly higher family-size ideals than those in professional or administrative positions; the study attributes a 'middle-class' status as the determining factor in family-size aspirations in Mexico, and metropolitan residence to the Brazilian case. The study predicts that 'metropolitanization' would ultimately account for the decline of fertility in Brazil, while in Mexico it would occur more naturally among 'middle-class' sectors lowering family size in order to maintain that status.

The next identifiable phase of the fertility transition in Latin America begins for most countries in the mid-1960s or around 1970, when new patterns of reproductive behaviour become more generalized throughout the population. Middle-class fertility norms now spread out and are adopted by lower socio-economic groups while different motivations to reduce family size propel these changes. The transformation of many economies to consumer-oriented markets, the arrival of mass media communications, the universal desire to own a television set, even among the poorest sectors of the population, all contribute to the generalization of new behaviour patterns, including reproductive ones. While middle-class families originally acted to protect their future position in the society, other social groups began to reduce fertility in order to meet a set of financial obligations imposed by a new mass-market economy. A broad-based debate on the 'survival strategies' that families adopt when faced with economic crises suggests a variety of individual or household-level adaptations, including reproductive ones (Jelin and Feijoo 1980; Schmink 1984).

Unquestionably, women during the 1960s were having 'excess fertility' and an unmet demand for family planning did exist at all levels. Miró and Rath (1965: 60–1) concluded that 'the number of children regarded as ideal by the women interviewed [in three Latin American cities] is quite different from the number of children they actually bear' and 'that the general attitude of women toward family planning is favourable, but apparently the use of contraceptives is still rather ineffective, either because they are not seriously and persistently employed or because inappropriate methods are used'. Requena (1965) had also concluded from his 1962 Quinta Normal Study in Santiago, Chile, that among a representative sample of this essentially middle-class neighbourhood, only 18.5 per cent of women used a contraceptive method and that these methods were mostly of low efficacy: condoms, diaphragms, rhythm, and withdrawal. When abortion was added to the use of methods, prevalence rose to 46 per cent, confirming not only a high incidence of abortion but a high motivation to reduce family size. Requena noted that among the more educated women contraception was more prevalent while the less educated poorer women tended to resort to abortion, suggesting that education was not only important in taking steps to reduce fertility but also in determining the means adopted to regulate reproduction.

The earlier family planning programmes began to appear first in large urban centre's and later branched out to provincial cities in response to the growing demand for contraception. These programmes, as well as much of the pioneer research in this field, were initiated by medical leaders or groups of physicians, mostly gynaecologists, concerned with the health consequences of practices such as induced abortion. Their efforts were small in scale, and originally served the unmet need for family planning of urban middle-class groups. It is difficult to argue here that family planning programmes were responsible for the onset of the demographic transition in Latin America. Rather, they seem to have been the mediating instruments that contributed to already ongoing behavioural changes and were legitimized by the existing demand for such services. As fertility declines accelerated and fertility behaviour changed throughout the entire social structure, family planning programmes began to assume a more important role, broadening their outreach through commercial distribution and other innovative schemes. As the fertility transition advanced, their role shifted to respond to the growing demand from the urban and later the rural poor where the unmet need for services was greatest. In Latin America, pharmacies, as we shall see later, also play an important role in meeting the demand for contraception.

Programme Origins

The origins of family planning programmes in Latin America date, in most cases, to the 1960s. As mentioned earlier, they were largely private in nature. Initial efforts to provide public-sector family planning services responded to somewhat similar sets of circumstances. The various stages in the development of these programmes was noted by Taucher (1979: 204): (1) the better-off groups, utilizing private services, begin the use of contraceptive methods; (2) with increased public debate about the 'population crisis' and the resurgence of neo-Malthusian theories, private medical groups, with international funding assistance, organize small-scale family planning activities for lower income sectors; (3) as research on abortion shows that there is an unmet need for family planning, national health authorities begin to press for incorporation of family planning in national public health systems, to be included as part of maternal and child health services; and some governments incorporate family planning into maternal and child health programmes, others leave family planning to operate vertically within the health system, and others continue to rely on growing private-sector programmes for the delivery of family planning services (Brazil and Colombia are notable examples of this policy).

The following dates (Soto 1976) mark the beginning of organized (private or public) family planning services in Latin America:

1959 Mexico
1961 Uruguay
1963 Chile, Honduras, Venezuela
1965 Colombia, Guatemala, Dominican Republic
1966 Argentina, Brazil, Costa Rica, Ecuador, El Salvador, Haiti, Panama, Paraguay
1967 Bolivia, Peru
1968 Nicaragua

Except in Nicaragua, these programmes were initially developed with the assistance of the IPPF but as the decade of the 1970s brought additional funding to family planning, namely from the United Nations Fund for Population Activities (UNFPA), governments gradually incorporated these programmes into existing maternal and child care services (García and Carvajal 1979: 220–4). For example, in Colombia PROFAMILIA started offering services in 1965 but by 1970 the government began including family planning in its maternal and child health services.

Table 10.1 shows the level of contraceptive-use prevalence in the mid-1970s for Central American countries. With the exception of Costa Rica, where prevalence was 16 per cent, the others' was very low. However, by the late 1980s, most had achieved rates three to four times higher. Early users of these programmes were beginning to adopt social norms already widely accepted among higher socio-economic groups and their use of modern contraception was initially to limit family size. Their average age in most cases was 26 or 27 years yet as some programmes expanded, the average age of new users tended to decline to 25 or 24, as in Costa Rica. Similarly, as programmes grew and family planning became more acceptable as a social norm, a shift occurred as increasingly women used family planning to space their pregnancies. Most of these early users relied on the pill and about 10–15 per cent on the IUD. With the exception of El Salvador, acceptance of sterilization in Central America was negligible (García and Carvajal 1979).

Table 10.1. *Central America: new users and active users, and prevalence rate, c.1974–1975*

Country	Year	New users	Active users	Prevalence rate
Costa Rica	1974	25,827	68,888	16.0
El Salvador	1974	15,367	76,836	8.4
Guatemala	1974	22,182	29,609	2.5
Honduras	1974	8,520	10,201	7.4
Nicaragua	1974	9,384	47,705	9.5
Panama	1976	11,408	40,105	11.1

Source: Garcia and Carvajal 1979: 222–3.

A New Political Climate

During the 1960s, the data quality and breadth of population analyses in Latin America improved notably, especially as a result of the efforts by the then new CELADE in Santiago, Chile. CELADE began to publish official statistics and well-constructed demographic estimates showing that indeed birth rates in Latin America were extremely high. For example Bolivia, Colombia, Costa Rica, the Dominican Republic, Ecuador, El Salvador, Guatemala, Haiti, Honduras, Mexico, Nicaragua, and Venezuela, all had crude birth rates of 44 births per 1,000 or higher. Record birth rates exhibited by Nicaragua and Honduras were 50 and 52 per 1,000 respectively (Taucher 1979: A-2).

Latin American governments were at first slow in reacting to the implications of the new demographic reality depicted by CELADE and by studies undertaken by national research institutions. The first population forum—and historically a policy setting landmark—was the 1967 Caracas Conference entitled 'Reunión sobre políticas de población en relación al desarrollo en América Latina'. It probably remains, even today, as the most important region-wide debate on population, both in terms of its influence on subsequent government positions and also in legitimizing family planning as a public-sector responsibility. This conference was sponsored by the Organization of American States (OAS) and was the result of a long-term internal debate on population. In fact, in 1964 the Secretary-General of the OAS called an informal meeting to discuss the relationship between population and development. Up to that time, the consensus of many government representatives to OAS meetings was reflected in statements such as 'population increase, in general, was a positive factor in economic development' (OAS Venezuelan representative, quoted in Stycos 1968). Most OAS references to population issues had been vague, generally suggesting that governments formulate policies according to national needs, or calling for increased research and greater involvement by international technical agencies. The next step came in 1966 when the OAS, the Pan American Health Organization (PAHO), the Population Council, and the Aspen Institute for Humanistic Studies, held informal discussions on the possibility of organizing a major technical meeting under OAS auspices to debate population issues affecting Latin America. A decision was made to go ahead with the planning of a conference to discuss population policy objectives and to formulate strategies to implement these within the context of development programmes. A preparatory meeting held in Washington in February 1967, reached final agreement on the technical content and conference programme.

The Caracas Population Conference, which took place from 11 to 16 September 1967, was sponsored by the OAS, in collaboration with PAHO, the Population Council, and the Aspen Institute. It's host was the government of Venezuela. To facilitate an open exchange of views all participants were invited in a technical rather than in an official capacity (Unión Panamericana 1967: 1–7). Despite its significance, the conference was not opened by the highest OAS official, nor by the President of Venezuela, indicating how politically sensitive the population issue still was at the time. Instead, the inaugural session included the Under Secretary for Economic and Social Affairs of the OAS, the Deputy Director of PAHO, and the Minister of the Interior of Venezuela. The meeting was presided by an academic personality, Dr Luis Lander, Director of the CENDES, of the Universidad Central de Venezuela, and its main rapporteur was Victor Urquidi, President of El Colegio de México. This ensured that the meeting would be conducted within a technical framework yet allowed for open political discussion.

The conference resulted in a 'Declaration' and a set of 'Recommendations', both of which include important points that subsequently influenced policy positions, especially on the future role of family planning programmes in the region. Of particular interest are items 6, 7, and 15 of the Declaration. Item 15 is an important landmark statement because it recognizes that fertility reduction can be affected by programmes specifically designed to make family planning more accessible to the population and because it recognizes, implicitly, the role of the state in family planning policy and in programmes in this area. The Recommendations of the conference contributed to setting the future course of family planning programmes in the region. It should be noted that family planning references in these Recommendations are under the subheading of Health, which reflects the medical nature of early interventions and programmes. Among the key recommendations should be listed items 1–2, 5, 24–6, and 28–30. These recommendations, of extreme significance in the history of Latin American population policy, set the correct political tone and provide an acceptable argument for nations to make decisions concerning demographic growth and the role of family planning programmes. They emphasize the integration of population and development, as well as the integration of family planning and maternal and child health services; they present a rationale for contraception as a means to eliminate unnecessary induced abortions performed under unsafe conditions; and stress the importance of the study and evaluation of population and family planning issues.

Soon after the Caracas conference, countries began to change long held pronatalist positions and acted to adopt public policies in this field, most significantly Mexico. It is important to note that Victor Urquidi, the rapporteur of the conference, later played an instrumental role in the drafting of Mexico's Population Policy. Several personalities attending the conference were to play important roles in their own countries, either in the formulation of population policies, or in the development of family planning programmes.

The Influence of the Medical Profession

The role of the medical profession in changing political attitudes and in developing the pioneer family planning services that eventually became the building blocks for larger programmes in Latin America deserves due recognition. The first studies documenting the unmet demand for fertility-regulation services were conducted by medical or public health researchers. Research groups addressing family planning issues were organized in medical or public health schools in Chile, Colombia, Brazil, Mexico, and elsewhere, under a variety of names and acronyms, e.g. ASCOFAME, the Colombian Association of Medical Schools. Similarly major family planning programmes, such as PROFAMILIA in Colombia, BEMFAM in Brazil, and the wide-ranging service programmes in Mexico, were initiated and directed by leading medical personalities.

A significant contribution of medical researchers that opened the way to family planning was the effort made to document the incidence of induced abortion in Latin America. Abortion studies played a key role in influencing the climate of opinion in favour of family planning and of public policy relating to population and health in Latin America. The pioneer work of Armijo and Monreal, and of Requena in Chile, in the early 1960s, was instrumental in starting a new wave of health-based arguments and justifications for the provision of family planning (Armijo and Monreal 1965; Requena 1965). These researchers conducted what have become the classic studies of abortion in Latin America. They were joined later by others not only in Chile but in other countries, arriving at similar conclusions: basically, that women who want to stop having children will go to any extreme to do so, even at the risk of their own lives. Furthermore, they showed that unsafe abortions are a heavy economic burden for national health systems, as maternity hospitals have no other options but to provide services to women who arrive with complications from incomplete abortions. The Chilean research provided a powerful argument for considering family planning within public health policy. At the time the Chilean Committee of Family Protection was created in 1964, only two hospital departments provided contraceptive advice as part of routine gynaecological services in Santiago (Delgado-García 1966).

Armijo and Monreal (1965) documented a steady increase in the number of admissions due to clandestine incomplete abortions, reaching a total of 57,368 cases in 1960. They also noted that over a span of twenty years of observation of hospital statistics, the number of hospital deliveries had increased 1.8 times while the number of cases admitted due to abortion complications had increased 4.4 times, or a rise from 84 abortion complications per 1,000 births in the late 1930s to 223 per 1,000 births in 1960. Again, these abortion data suggest reproductive behaviour changes starting in the pre-World War II period, lending support to the hypothesis of a much earlier phase of the fertility transition. Studies in other countries, conducted later, corroborated the existence of similar trends.

Armijo and Monreal estimated that in one year, 1960, Chile spent 184,000 hospital bed-days to service abortion complications, or a total expenditure of US$1 million (in 1990s US dollars, the figure would be at least ten times higher). To improve on hospital statistics Armijo and Monreal (1965: 264–5), utilizing censal data, drew a representative random sample of 2,464 dwellings for greater Santiago in 1961. Later, in 1963–4, samples were obtained for two provinces:

Concepción in the south, and Antofagasta in the north of Chile. For these three areas, information was obtained for 3,776 women aged 20–45. Of these women, 41.3 per cent voluntarily admitted a history of abortion, which made a total of 3,989 abortions of all kinds, and 23 per cent (885 women) admitted to having had an induced abortion. The majority of women with a record of induced abortion admitted having had between one and three (74.6 per cent for Santiago; 87.5 for Concepción; and 63.4 for Antofagasta). This startling information raised the total number of induced abortions to 2,415. Equally startling was the fact that 8.4 per cent of the women who admitted having had an induced abortion had more than seven. It is difficult to underestimate the impact of these findings.

An important question relating to the nature of the first phases of the fertility transition, at a time when methods of contraception were largely of poor efficacy, is: what were the characteristics of women who resorted to induced abortion when an unwanted pregnancy occurred? Were they mostly single, young, working in office or industrial jobs? The answer is no. They were almost universally married, and as Armijo and Monreal (1965: 267) concluded: 'it was found that middle-class women actually had more abortions than the dependants of workmen'. The greatest abortion rate was among women who had had 4 to 6 previous pregnancies, which meant that most abortions occurred among women who had at least three living children. It must be remembered that while induced abortion was being used to control fertility, it was (and still is) illegal in Chile.

The Chilean studies were followed in 1967 with a programme of comparative research on induced abortion and family planning, known as PEAL and conducted by CELADE. This new series of studies was conducted in a number of locations: Bogotá (1968), Panama City (1969), Buenos Aires (1969), and Lima (1970). Later Bolivia, Nicaragua, and Paraguay applied the CELADE methodology and conducted studies on induced abortion, mostly in urban locations (Gaslonde 1975).

The evidence obtained from these urban studies indicated that abortion prevalence was high, particularly so where birth rates were lower, and that there were not only important urban–rural differences but also important differences by education and socio-economic status. As in the Chilean case, this new evidence indicated that abortion was most common among urban, older, married women who already had three or four children. Gaslonde (1975: 18) noted that abortion rates had risen in all cities, except Buenos Aires, in the five years preceding the surveys and that the rise had been particularly important in Bogotá, Lima, Panama City, and Asunción. In Lima the rise was particularly sharp with yearly increases of 24 per cent. Abortion rates, based on number of abortions per 100 women of reproductive age for the twelve-month period preceding the survey, were similar to those found earlier for Santiago (26.2 per cent) by Armijo and Monreal (1965: 265). The corresponding rate for Bogotá was 18 per cent, for Lima 32, for Panama 27, for Asunción 33, and for Buenos Aires 19 (for Buenos Aires only, the rate is for the four years preceding the survey). These rates universally tended to rise with parity as well as with age, with older women having experienced the highest rise in abortion rates over the five years preceding the survey. A drop in the abortion rate was noted for most cities among the younger women who, presumably, were now using more efficient birth control methods (Gaslonde 1975).

In Mexico, where the situation concerning abortion was not known, two studies were conducted by the Mexican Social Security Institute (IMSS), the first in 1967–8 and the second over the period 1967–71. The objectives of these studies being to ascertain the socio-economic and demographic characteristics of women with abortion complications and to identify high-risk women in order to prevent unnecessary induced abortions. The first study was an epidemiological investigation based on a representative sample of 2,000 women aged 16 to 49, identified from a systematic random sample of the total population covered by the IMSS. The second was a study carried out in three large IMSS Mexico City maternity hospitals (Ordoñez 1975). The latter study collected information on 61,964 patients over a period of five years, who had been admitted into the three hospitals for treatment of complications following an abortion. Of the 1,753 women actually interviewed in the first study, 468 admitted having had one or more induced abortions (26.7 per cent). While these figures are not representative of the entire population of Mexico City, they are indicative of the magnitude of the problem. Using these two studies, Ordoñez (1975: 28) calculated that in 1971 in Mexico City there were approximately 700,000 illegal induced abortions.

The Mexican studies were particularly useful in determining the characteristics of women who had abortions. As in other countries, the data revealed that women reporting abortion were more likely to have repeated abortions. For example, of 3,714 women admitted into a special contraceptive programme to reduce induced abortion, the average number of abortions per woman was three. In Mexico, as in other Latin American countries, the majority of women having abortions were housewives, with working women having the highest rates. Ordoñez (1975: 29) concludes: 'as noted in other Latin American countries, abortion is considerably more frequent among women living in stable unions than among single women . . . The problem of abortion among single women is minimal.' The main reasons among these women to resort to induced abortion is economic (insufficient income to feed the existing family) and too many children already; the two amounting to 65 per cent of all reasons given (42.3 per cent economic and 22.5 per cent large family size).

Another conclusion was the difference in the condition under which induced abortions were performed: the wealthier classes obtained safe services from private medical practitioners and the poorer groups from clandestine abortion clinics that do not meet even minimum sanitary standards. There are, of course, exceptions and private physicians in several countries have tried to provide services to low-income women under safe and healthy conditions. Many hospitals in Latin America, where laws concerning abortion are restrictive, face the demand from women with incomplete abortions on a day-to-day basis. The problem is often compounded in countries where the hospital must report to the police cases of induced abortion, adding to the woman's emotional problems. One solution is to report induced as spontaneous abortions, thus making it very difficult to ascertain the magnitude of the problem, yet from a humane viewpoint it is the only option open to providers (Viel: 1988).

As Latin American governments accepted the reality that emerged from fertility and abortion research, they recognized the rights of couples, and particularly of women, to effective contraception, either by allowing private-sector family planning programmes to expand or by integrating these services into existing maternal and child care programmes. The question, often tantalizing, as to what other actors are involved in the support of the fertility transition in Latin America arises. In fact, little is known about the dynamics of contraceptive use: do most women learn about and start using contraception as a result of coming into contact with services offered by family planning programmes and then continue using independently from these organized services? Do they rely more on private medical practitioners or are they sufficiently independent so that contraceptive supplies from pharmacies and distribution posts are all they need?

Public versus Private Sector

Most Latin American countries today have public-sector family planning programmes—either functioning independently within health ministries or integrated as part of maternal and child care programmes—but what makes the region quite unique is the continuing mix, with varying degrees of service capacity, of both private- and public-sector programmes. In addition, these are backed by important commercial or social marketing activities. To a certain extent the tradition of clinic-based, specialized services, independent from public health services has continued and influenced the way women seek these services, even today. Table 10.2 clearly shows that private sector programmes still play an important role in contraceptive supply. Public services offering contraception came much later, in part as a result of the legitimization of family planning in the late 1960s. Many Latin American governments, following the 1974 Bucharest Population Conference, began to incorporate family planning into their public health services, often as part of maternal and child care programmes. In countries such as Brazil, where the government has traditionally opposed or taken a 'let's wait and see' attitude towards the provision of family planning services, the private sector is particularly strong with 47 per cent of those using a method declaring that it was obtained from private sector services in 1986. In Colombia, which had both public and private services from almost the start, the public sector after gaining some advantage in the late 1970s is now substantially behind private services, the corresponding prevalence being 24.4 per cent and 38.7 per cent in 1986. The strength of private programmes is also clear in Costa Rica, El Salvador, and Guatemala, and they have gained strength also in the Dominican Republic. The main exception to this rule is Mexico where public-sector programmes are

Table 10.2. *Latin America: contraceptive prevalence by public- and private-sector programmes, available countries*

<table>
<tr><th>Country</th><th>Year</th><th>Public sector</th><th>Private sector</th></tr>
<tr><td>Brazil</td><td>1977</td><td>n.a.</td><td>11.0[a]</td></tr>
<tr><td></td><td>1986</td><td>17.5</td><td>47.0</td></tr>
<tr><td>Colombia</td><td>1974</td><td>14.0</td><td>17.0</td></tr>
<tr><td></td><td>1977</td><td>26.1</td><td>22.5</td></tr>
<tr><td></td><td>1984</td><td>23.9</td><td>31.2</td></tr>
<tr><td></td><td>1986</td><td>24.4</td><td>38.7</td></tr>
<tr><td>Costa Rica</td><td>1978</td><td>26.0</td><td>38.0</td></tr>
<tr><td></td><td>1981</td><td>25.0</td><td>41.0</td></tr>
<tr><td></td><td>1984</td><td>26.4</td><td>38.5</td></tr>
<tr><td>Dominican Republic</td><td>1976</td><td>12.8</td><td>11.2</td></tr>
<tr><td></td><td>1977</td><td>10.0</td><td>21.0</td></tr>
<tr><td></td><td>1986</td><td colspan="2">50.0[b]</td></tr>
<tr><td>Ecuador</td><td>1974</td><td>2.0</td><td>1.0</td></tr>
<tr><td></td><td>1982</td><td colspan="2">39.9[b]</td></tr>
<tr><td></td><td>1987</td><td colspan="2">44.3[b]</td></tr>
<tr><td>El Salvador</td><td>1976</td><td>7.3</td><td>14.5</td></tr>
<tr><td>Guatemala</td><td>1972</td><td>2.1</td><td>5.0</td></tr>
<tr><td></td><td>1973</td><td>2.7</td><td>1.0</td></tr>
<tr><td></td><td>1974</td><td>3.0</td><td>1.4</td></tr>
<tr><td></td><td>1977</td><td>7.0</td><td>n.a.</td></tr>
<tr><td></td><td>1987</td><td>8.4</td><td>14.3</td></tr>
<tr><td>Mexico</td><td>1973</td><td>1.0</td><td>12.2</td></tr>
<tr><td></td><td>1975</td><td>9.0</td><td>5.0</td></tr>
<tr><td></td><td>1976</td><td>12.0</td><td>9.0</td></tr>
<tr><td></td><td>1978</td><td>19.0</td><td>21.0</td></tr>
<tr><td></td><td>1979</td><td>19.5</td><td>18.3</td></tr>
<tr><td></td><td>1982</td><td>20.6</td><td>17.4</td></tr>
</table>

Sources: Dominican Republic (1987: 39); Ecuador (1988: 58); for all other countries, Ross *et al*. (1988: 208–9).

Note: Prevalence rates are for all methods for currently married women.

[a] Oral contraceptives only.
[b] No separate breakdown available.

stronger, the result of a clear policy, government support, and a vast network of public health services through both the Ministry of Public Health and Mexican Social Security Institute clinics and their outreach programmes.

In the twenty-year period between the mid-1960s and the mid-1980s, the Latin American countries with both the highest level of development and of programme effort have shown considerable fertility declines: Colombia and Mexico, which rank high on both counts, experienced reductions of 2.8 and 2.6 children per woman, while those with the lowest ranking for both indicators, such as Guatemala, Honduras, and Haiti, have experienced very small fertility reductions (Table 10.3). The importance of development on fertility change is evidenced in the cases of Chile and Panama, both of which have declines of 2.5 children per woman despite ranking weak and moderate respectively on programme effort. Even countries with weak programme effort, such as Brazil and Venezuela, have experienced substantial fertility declines.

Table 10.3. ***Latin America: fertility decline 1960/5–1980/5, development level 1980, and programme effort 1982***

Development index	Programme effort							
	Strong		Moderate		Weak		Very weak	
High	Colombia	2.8	Jamaica	2.1	Brazil	2.3		
	Mexico	2.6	Panama	2.5	Chile	2.5		
			Trinidad	2.1	Guyana	2.8		
					Venezuela	2.4		
Upper-middle			Dominican Republic	3.1	Ecuador	1.9	Bolivia	0.4
					Peru	1.9	Nicaragua	1.4
			El Salvador	1.6			Paraguay	2.0
Lower-middle					Guatemala	0.7		
					Honduras	1.2		
Low					Haiti	1.1		

Source: Bongaarts *et al.* 1990.

Note: Fertility decline = average decrease in births per woman between 1960–5 and 1980–5.

Countries with strong or moderate programme effort, such as Colombia, Dominican Republic, Trinidad—all with fertility reductions averaging 2 children or more since the 1960s—reflect another important change in contraceptive behaviour, an indication of yet another phase in the region's fertility transition. This change is the determination of women (and a few men) to voluntarily end reproduction by surgical means. Fig. 10.1 shows clearly that sterilization has risen rapidly in the twenty-year period. The contraceptive profile of the countries with the highest prevalence increases show the important role that sterilization is now playing, exceeding 30 per cent in the case of the Dominican Republic and almost touching 20 per cent in Colombia, Ecuador, and Mexico.

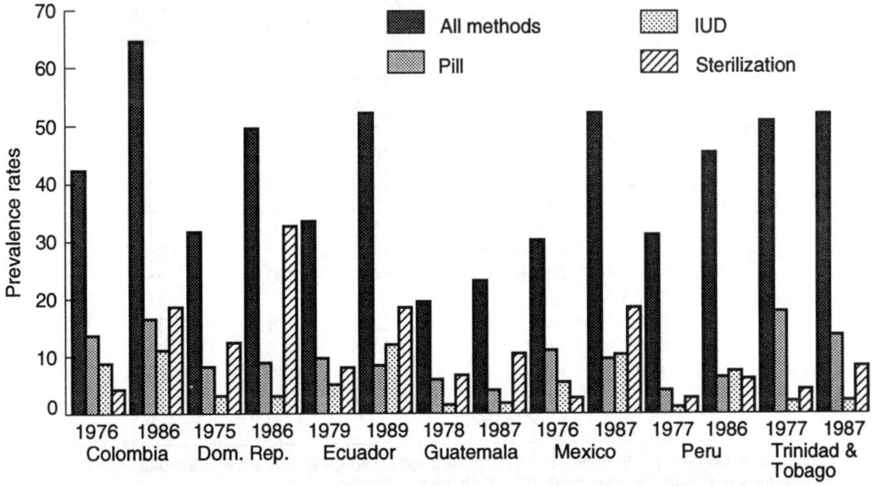

Fig.10.1. ***Latin America: prevalence rates 1975–1985, selected countries***

Source: Chapter 8

But the high total prevalence in many Latin American countries revealed in Fig. 10.1 for the 1980s is not fully explained by programme supplies or the strength of their programmes. There are countries with very weak programme effort, such as Peru, but with high prevalence of use. In effect, there is another key actor in the supply-side of contraception: the pharmacies, and the role they play in supplying over-the-counter methods. Table 10.4 provides startling evidence of the importance of pharmacies in the provision of contraceptive supplies in Latin America. For example, in Colombia of all women using pills in 1986, 75 per cent obtained them from pharmacies, 10 per cent from public, and 9 per cent from private programmes (in fact PROFAMILIA, the large private-sector programme, assisted in this process by launching a social marketing programme with over-the-counter sales in the late 1970s, while concentrating clinic services on provider-dependent contraception, including male and female sterilization); and injectable methods are also predominantly distributed by pharmacies, as are condoms and other barrier methods. In the Dominican Republic, Ecuador, and Guatemala, pharmacies also appear as strong providers of pills, condoms, and injectables although proportionately they play a lesser role than organized programmes. In Mexico, despite the strength of the national family planning programme, 30 per cent of all methods in the late 1970s were obtained from

Table 10.4. ***Latin America: contraceptive utilization[a] by method and source of service, available countries***

Country	Year	Method	Sector		Pharmacy
			Public	Private	
Colombia	1986	Pill	10.0	8.9	75.3
		Injectables	10.7	13.5	73.4
		Condoms	3.3	18.7	65.0
		Other barrier	0.0	5.8	88.9
Dominican Republic	1986	Pill	40.9	13.1	16.7
		IUD	70.9	29.1	0.0
		Condoms	32.5	8.2	42.2
Ecuador	1987	Pill	31.0	15.0	20.0
		Injectables	10.0	5.0	15.0
		Other barrier	29.0	16.0	21.0
Guatemala	1987	Pill	29.2	40.0	12.1
		Injectables	5.9	70.6	11.8
		Condoms	12.9	12.8	69.2
		Other barrier	14.2	50.0	35.7
Mexico	1979	All	51.1	17.6	31.3
	1982	All	53.2	15.3	31.3
	1987	All	61.8	16.2	21.9
Peru	1986	Pill	57.2	36.5	0.0
		IUD	34.9	46.5	9.3
		Injectables[b]	9.1	30.2	9.1

Sources: Colombia (1988: 60); Dominican Republic (1987: 44); Ecuador (1988: 62); Guatemala (1989: 56); Mexico (1989: 48–9); Peru (1988: 68).

[a] % of users of a particular contraceptive method, by source.
[b] Includes a large proportion of 'other sources' (51.6%).

pharmacies; and, as recently as 1987, one fifth of all methods were obtained from this source. The data presented confirm the importance of pharmacies as direct suppliers of family planning in Latin America. How or why do women turn to pharmacies, what role do pharmacists play in advising on the choice of methods, what are the advantages of going to a pharmacy *vis-à-vis* a regular clinic? These are questions that need further research. It also appears that Latin American women like injectable contraceptives, which are not always available through organized programmes (DMPA is not approved by the US Food and Drug Administration, therefore programmes that receive supplies through US international assistance programmes cannot distribute this method). Injectable contraceptives can easily be provided by pharmacists who are licensed to give injections. One of the few studies that have looked into the role of pharmacists in contraceptive distribution concluded that for Buenos Aires the pharmacist, who is in a situation of particular advantage to articulate the demand for contraceptives, is in fact handicapped by his work environment to assume a counselling role in the selection of methods 'and his chances to intervene, offering professional advise to assist in order that the decisions made consider efficacy and safety, are nil' (Balán and Ramos 1989: 29). It is possible that the Argentinian population, with its long history of low fertility, may be much more sophisticated and better informed on matters relating to contraception than that of other countries. It is also possible that family planning programmes have a particularly important role as facilitators during the period when fertility decline accelerates. However, as countries enter a more advanced phase in their fertility transition, organized services become more focused, e.g. on the under-served, and contraception becomes the responsibility of a variety of commercial distributors, primarily pharmacies.

Conclusion

This chapter traces the origins of fertility changes and of lower family-size values in Latin America, including the adoption of favourable attitudes toward contraception, drawing primarily on information collected during the 1960s and 1970s on abortion, and more recently on fertility and contraceptive prevalence. It concludes that Latin American fertility has undergone a complex transition with several different phases, two of which are discussed in some detail: an earlier one, more restricted to middle and upper socio-economic groups, going back in some countries to the 1940s; and a later or more generalized mass transition starting toward the end of the 1960s, propelled by new demographic and economic conditions. It explores the role played by family planning programmes in moulding these phases and suggests that they played an instrumental role as facilitators of the mass transition rather than as the agents responsible for these changes. In fact, the available evidence suggests that by the late 1960s, in most countries of the region, 'excess fertility' was the norm and that a real unmet demand for fertility regulation existed everywhere. When the organized programmes started, the profile of their first clientele was that of an urban woman, in her late twenties or older, whose family size exceeded her family ideals, and whose fertility was completed. The medical profession had a leading role in the study of issues surrounding reproduction—particularly the incidence and reasons for induced abortion in societies where the practice is illegal—and, on the basis of this research, it advocated the need for contraceptive services. At first, they were often small scale, urban-based, and semi-experimental in nature, serving a population where the latent demand for contraception was high. Their initial success, the subsequent support received from external funding sources, and the general world atmosphere of crisis surrounding the population issue provided an environment propitious for their rapid expansion.

What emerges in the 1980s is a situation where family planning services are widely available through a mix of private and public service programmes as well as through commercial channels, particularly pharmacies, which supply contraceptives to a large proportion of users. Most Latin American countries have, by 1990, completed the main phases of their fertility transitions and achieved substantial birth-rate reductions. Contraception is nearly universally accepted and widely practised by couples everywhere. The main differences are in the mix of supply sources, the relative effect of private v. public programme performance, and, generally, the degree of articulation between family planning programmes and public policy.

References

Armijo, R., and Monreal, T. (1965), 'The Problem of Induced Abortion in Chile', in C. V. Kiser (ed.), 'Components of Population Change in Latin America', *Milbank Memorial Fund Quarterly*, 43/4(2): 263–72.

Balán, J., and Ramos, S. (1989), 'La Medicalización del Comportamiento Reproductivo: Un Estudio Exploratorio sobre la Demanda de Anticonceptivos en los Sectores Populares', Buenos Aires: Centro de Estudios de Estado y Sociedad, CEDES (Unpublished).

Bongaarts, J., Mauldin, W. P., and Phillips, J. F. (1990), 'The Demographic Impact of Family Planning Programs', *Studies in Family Planning*, 21/6: 299–310.

Caldwell, J. C. (1982), *Theory of Fertility Decline* (London: Academic Press).

Coale, A., and Hoover, E. M. (1958), *Population Growth and Economic Development in Low Income Countries* (Princeton: Princeton University Press).

Colombia, Corporación Centro Regional de Población (1988), *Segunda Encuesta Nacional de Prevalencia del Uso de Anticoncepción, 1980* (Bogotá).

Delgado-García, R. (1966), 'Perspectives of Family Planning Programs' in J. M. Stycos and J. Arias (eds.), *Population Dilemma in Latin America* (Washington: Potomac Books).

Dominican Republic, Consejo Nacional de Población y Familia (1987), *Encuesta Demográfica de Salud: DHS-86* (Santo Domingo: Alfa & Omega).

Ecuador, Centro de Estudios de Población y Paternidad Responsable (1988), *Encuesta Demográfica y de Salud Familiar 1987* (Quito: Ediciones Culturales UNP, SA).

García, M. L., and Carvajal, J. (1979), 'Efectos de los Programas de Planificación de la

Familia en el Desarrollo de los Países de Centro América y Panamá', in V. Urquidi, and J. B. Morelos (eds.), *Población y Desarrollo en América Latina* (Mexico: El Colegio de México).

Gaslonde, S. (1975), 'Studies on Fertility and Abortion in Asunción, Bogotá, Buenos Aires, Lima and Panama City', in *The Epidemiology of Abortion and Practices of Fertility Regulation in Latin America: Selected Reports* (PAHO, Scientific Publication, 306; Washington).

Guatemala, Ministerio de Salud Pública y Asistencia Social (1989), *Encuesta Nacional de Salud Materno Infantil 1987* (Guatemala: Instituto de Nutrición de Centro America y Panamá).

Jelin, E., and Feijoo, M. (1980), 'Trabajo y Familia en el Ciclo de Vida Femenino: el Caso de los Sectores Populares de Buenos Aires', *Estudios CEDES*, 3/8–9.

Kahl, J. (1967), 'Modern Values and Fertility Ideals in Brazil and Mexico', *Journal of Social Issues*, **23**/4: 99–114.

Loyo, G. (1963), from article in *Public and International Affairs*, **11**: 131, cited in Stycos (1968).

—— (1974), 'The Demographic Problems of Mexico and Latin America', in T. McCoy (ed.), *The Dynamics of Population Policy in Latin America* (Ballinger Publishing Co., Cambridge, Mass.).

Mexico, Secretaría de Salud (1989), *Encuesta Nacional sobre Fecundidad y Salud 1987* (Mexico City: Dirección General de Planificación Familiar).

Miró, C., and Rath, F. (1965), 'Preliminary Findings of Comparative Fertility Surveys in Three Latin American Cities', in 'Components of Population Change in Latin America', C. V. Kiser (ed.), *Milbank Memorial Fund Quarterly*, 43/4(2): 36–62.

Ordoñez, B. R. (1975), 'Induced Abortion in Mexico City: Summary Conclusions From two Studies Conducted by the Mexican Social Security Institute' in *The Epidemiology of Abortion and Practices of Fertility Regulation in Latin America: Selected Reports* (PAHO Scientific Publication, 306; Washington).

Peru, Dirección General de Demografía (1988), *Encuesta Demográfica y de Salud Familiar (ENDES 1986): Informe General* (Lima: Instituto Nacional de Estadistica).

Requena, M. (1965), 'Studies of Family Planning in the Quinta Normal District of Santiago: The Use of Contraceptives', in C. V. Kiser (ed.), 'Components of Population Change in Latin America', *Milbank Memorial Fund Quarterly*, **43**/4(2): 69–94.

Ross, J., Rich, M., Molzan, J. P., and Pensak, M. (1988), *Family Planning and Child Survival, 100 Developing Countries* (New York: Columbia University).

Schmink, M. (1984), 'Household Economic Strategies: Review and Research Agenda', *Latin American Research Review*, **19**/3: 87–101.

Simon, J. (1981), *The Ultimate Resource* (Princeton: Princeton University Press).

Soto, G. Z. (1976), *América Latina: Actividades Desarrolladas por los Programas de Planificación de la Familia, 1974* (Santiago: CELADE), Serie A, 144.

Stycos, J. M. (1968), *Human Fertility in Latin America* (Ithaca, NY: Cornell University Press).

Taucher, E. (1979), 'Efectos Demográficos y Socioeconómicos de los Programas de la Planificación de la Familia en la América Latina', in V. Urquidi and J. B. Morelos, (eds.), *Población y Desarrollo en América Latina* (Mexico: El Colegio de México).

Unión Panamericana, Secretaría General, Organización de Los Estados Americanos, (1967), 'Reunión sobre políticas de población en relación al desarrollo en América Latina', *Revista Interamericana de Ciencias Sociales*, **4**/2, whole issue, 72 pp.

United Nations, Department of International Economic and Social Affairs, (1989), *Levels and Trends of Contraceptive Use as Assessed in 1988* (ST/ESA/SER.A/110; New York: UN).

Viel, B. (1988), 'Latin America', in P. Sachdev (ed.), *International Handbook on Abortion* (New York: Greenwood Press).

Part III

Social Determinants, Reproductive Intentions, and Fertility Change

11 Theoretical Views of Fertility Transitions in Latin America: What is the Relevance of a Diffusionist Approach?

JORGE H. BRAVO

Introduction

Transition theory has pervaded demographic thinking since early in this century, and in spite of some limitations as an explanatory model of observed demographic trends, continues to provide a basis for broad generalizations about fertility change. Some of its well-known main elements—such as the emphasis on the global process of modernization, the consequent improvements in survival, female employment opportunities, and other changes leading to the increase in the relative cost of children—are also incorporated, more formally, in modern micro-economic models.[1] Critical assessments of transition theory, based on evidence from some recent empirical studies of fertility declines (much of it coming from the findings of the Princeton European Fertility and the WFS projects), have expressed doubts about the usefulness of this approach. The absence of clear, consistent associations between fertility declines, mortality and other 'modernization' variables, the verification of multiple exceptions and apparent asynchronies between the changes in socio-economic variables and fertility, constitute some of the evidence cited for this line of argument.[2] Ideational changes, having more to do with the social diffusion of low fertility norms and behaviour, are given centrality over individual economic calculus.

To be sure, this alternative type of approach to interpreting fertility transitions is not completely novel. According to Gösta Carlsson (1966: 149) transition theory had, by the 1960s, lost its dominant role to the 'innovation' approach, which (according to the same author) can be characterized by the following three elements: (1) the consideration of fertility control as a recent invention in human culture; (2) the emphasis on the importance of the spread of knowledge about contraception; and (3) the assumption of lags and gradients in the spread of skills

[1] Given stable preferences, in these models the changes in fertility are attributed ultimately to variations in the exogenous socio-economic variables that have an effect on supply, demand and regulation costs. Versions more flexible in this regard are found, e.g. in Easterlin *et al.* (1980), Becker and Lewis (1973), and Becker (1981), and others which allow for the possibility of changing preferences and quality–quantity trade-offs.

[2] The evaluation of the validity and significance of these deficiencies differs among authors; compare, e.g. Chesnais (1986) with Cleland and Wilson (1987).

and attitudes among groups defined by criteria related to socio-economic status or place of residence. When Carlsson examined the case of Sweden these ideas were so central in the literature—and the conclusion that certain groups led the decline to be followed later by others, so common—that 'it would be tedious to give quotations' (Carlsson 1966: 151). More recently, Knodel and Van de Walle (1979) and Cleland and Wilson (1987) among others have argued, in the face of both historical and contemporary evidence, in favour of ideational change as a main cause of fertility change. Others (e.g. Retherford and Palmore 1983; Dyson 1984; Watkins 1987) think that emphasis on ideational and diffusion processes would be useful in future research.

It is generally recognized that many of the elements of these two broad views need not be logically contradictory: modernization and socio-economic change may facilitate, or even induce, the spread of ideas about contraception and ideal family sizes; and cultural diffusion may affect individuals differently according to their position in society. In fact, much of the theoretical elaboration that has been the basis of previous fertility research in Latin America, has implicitly incorporated elements of both (e.g. CLACSO 1974, 1985; Demografía y Economía, 1981: various contributors; González *et al.* 1980, 1982), although in general only socio-economic factors are explicitly discussed and evaluated. Lacking a broadly accepted synthetic view, a basic tension remains between the different approaches, expressed in terms of socio-economic v. ideational change, the emphasis on demand v. supply factors,[3] or—to use Carlsson's terminology—of innovation v. adjustment processes.

This chapter will be dedicated to reviewing and discussing some general aspects of the diffusion hypothesis—in the sense to be discussed below—through a preliminary assessment of its usefulness for the interpretation of fertility declines in Latin America.

The Diffusionist Approach: Problems and Possibilities

Broad societal and institutional factors (McNicoll 1980; Greenhalgh 1988) are considered by many to be no less important for understanding fertility trends than purely economic ones, and few would dismiss them altogether. But the view that emphasizes ideational change is far from a well-established theory, and diffusion, in the view of many researchers, 'remains largely a postulated rather than a demonstrated mechanism, and it raises troubling issues' (Watkins 1987: 666). Given the present interest in Latin America, we will reflect upon the possibilities and limitations of this approach in the context of real transitions within the region. The analysis will consider some stylized facts about Latin American fertility transitions and, in that light, discuss the following questions: What would be the advantages of this approach with respect to others? What is meant by

[3] 'supply' being broadly understood to include the access to contraceptive knowledge and supply of contraception; this is different from the more precise concept of supply in modern economic models.

'diffusion': processes different and independent from 'economic' changes?, or perhaps complementary ones? What is it that diffuses: contraceptive knowledge, motivation, or socio-economic change itself? What type of diffusion is the most relevant, inter- or intra-generational, between or among population subgroups? Are the initiation lags between groups or classes, as Carlsson affirms, necessary to the theory? Lastly, problems with some types of evidence that may be considered supportive of such an approach are discussed. The conclusions will point to the consideration of the diffusion approach as useful for the description of fertility declines in the region, to the relevance of intra-generational, inter-class modes of spread of both attitudes and actual reproductive behaviour, and to the difficulties of discriminating among basic causes in previous studies, i.e. empirically ascribing the observed trends to socio-economic or to other types of 'ideational' change.

Why a Diffusionist Approach?

One possible reason for choosing to consider a theoretical approach different from classical transition theory, is that the alternative might provide an explanation of some aspects of fertility change that the reference approach cannot explain, or can explain only to a limited extent. In Latin America, there appear to be some broad facts consistent with transition theory. One of them is the precedence of mortality declines with respect to fertility declines, at least during 1950–90, a period of time within which a fair number of transitions have unfolded. In order to examine this question, two different criteria are used here to determine the timing of a decline in these variables: a reduction of 10 per cent or more with respect to its 1950 value, and the reduction to a level below some pre-specified 'threshold'.[4] By any one of these criteria (see Fig. 11.1), infant mortality declines have preceded fertility declines (by an average of about three quinquennia) in the eighteen countries considered, the conclusion being robust with respect to small changes in the specification of the percentage change or the chosen threshold levels: one would have to set the infant mortality threshold below 90 per 1,000 (while holding the TFR threshold at 5) to find some exceptions to the general conclusion, and below 70 per 1,000 to seriously challenge it. It should also be noted that mortality started to fall substantially in most Latin American countries well before 1950 (Arriaga 1970), so this conclusion seems to be a fairly solid one.[5]

There are other facts which are only partially supportive of the standard transition theory. For example, the association between selected socio-economic variables and fertility, as illustrated in Fig. 11.2. Although of the right overall sign, the relationships with fertility have shifted downwards and become less steep between 1960 and 1990. Particularly suggestive in this regard are the regression

[4] The specification of thresholds necessarily involves some degree of arbitrariness. The values adopted for this exercise correspond approximately to the midpoint between the lowest and highest observed value during 1950–90 for each variable of interest in all eighteen countries considered; this yields a threshold TFR of 5, and a threshold IMR of 100 per 1,000.

[5] Cutright and Hargens (1984), who study threshold effects in a multivariate context, reach similar conclusions as well.

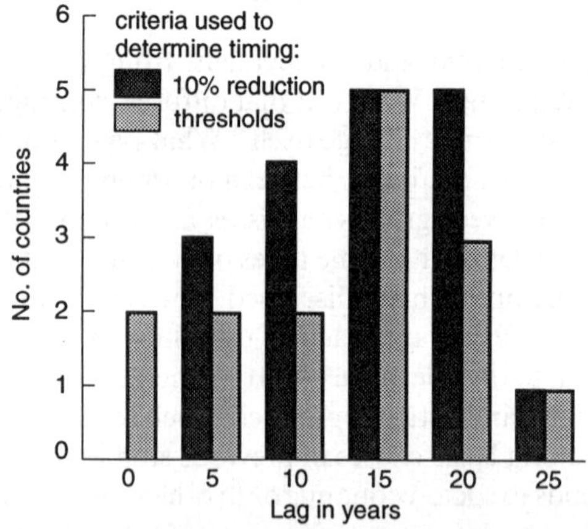

Fig. 11.1. ***Latin America: lag with which fertility declines follow mortality declines***

Source: For TFRs, CELADE (1988: 37–8, table 4d); for infant mortality rate, CELADE (1989: 35–6, table 5); for urbanization rate, UN (1991: 108–11, table A1); for adult illiteracy rates, UNESCO (1965: 38–41, table 4; 1991: 47–50, table 2); for per capita GDP, CEPAL (unpublished data, elaborated on the basis of official statistics)

Note: This figure excludes Argentina and Uruguay, which are countries that had reached low fertility and mortality levels by the beginning of this century.

curves showing fertility rates as a function of per capita GDP, illiteracy rates, infant mortality rates, and urbanization rates (all curves are polynomials fitted by ordinary least squares). If the fitted multiple regression equation of 1960 (including all four socio-economic variables) is used to predict 1990 TFRs,[6] in all cases but the Southern Cone countries[7] the fertility declines are underestimated, on average by about 35 per cent. None the less, it is noteworthy that the four socio-economic variables, taken together, account for two-thirds to three-fourths of the cross-sectional fertility differences.

A much weaker relation is observed between the changes in the TFR and these variables: multiple regression estimates (not shown here) suggest that the changes in socio-economic variables account for less than half of the variance in fertility declines, no single coefficient is statistically significant and some even have the wrong sign. In the 1980s, real per capita income and some other development indicators have actually worsened in many Latin America countries (CEPAL 1990) while, as documented in the next section, both desired and actual fertility showed a persistent declining trend in most of them. These recently observed positive associations between fertility and development indicators (both declining) are in part a reflection of short-term reactions rather than long-run relationships, but it would be much more difficult to argue that there are confounding short-term effects when analysing the thirty-year trends mentioned above. In any case, I do not place too much weight on these observations in themselves, since the data

[6] The estimated regression equation is $TFR_{1960} = 8.9 - 0.002 \cdot GDP - 0.0418 \cdot ILL + 0.0155 \cdot IMR - 0.021 \cdot URB$; $R^2 = 0.75$, Adjusted $R^2 = 0.67$. All coefficients except that of IMR are statistically significant at the 5% level. GDP = per capita GDP in 1980 US$, ILL = adult illiteracy rate, IMR = infant mortality rate, and URB = urbanization rate. The sources of data appear in Fig. 11.1.

[7] In Argentina, Chile, and Uruguay the fertility change is overestimated by 0.4 to 0.9 children.

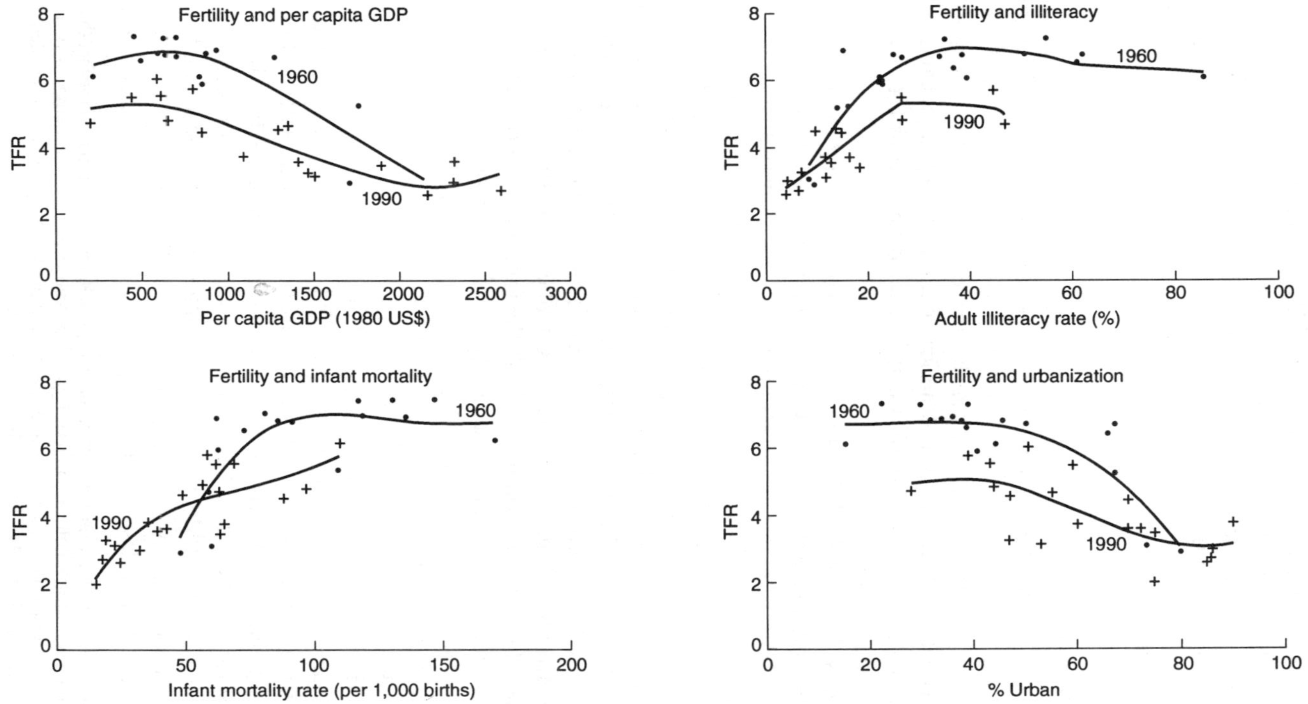

Fig.11.2. ***Latin America: fertility and selected socio-economic indicators in twenty countries 1960 and 1990***

Source: See Fig. 11.1.

Notes: The analysis is based on twenty countries: Argentina, Bolivia, Brazil, Colombia, Costa Rica, Cuba, Chile, Ecuador, El Salvador, Guatemala, Haiti, Honduras, Mexico, Nicaragua, Panama, Paraguay, Peru, Dominican Republic, Uruguay, and Venezuela. The graph of fertility by per capita GDP excludes Cuba, which has a different national accounting system, and Venezuela, because it is a very extreme outlier. The graph of fertility by illiteracy excludes Cuba and Nicaragua because of lack of data for 1960.

contained in Fig. 11.2, also used in the regression analyses, are reasonable but rough estimates of the variables represented in the plots.

Recapitulating, it is clear that fertility declines have in general been preceded by mortality declines, and that the more developed Latin American countries are more likely to have lower fertility and to have started their transition earlier, but the discriminating power of the development indicators has declined during the last three decades, and currently the changes in these variables are not strong predictors of fertility declines. These stylized facts will be considered in the following discussion about diffusion.

The Object of Diffusion

In principle, diffusion may refer to the desire for a reduced number of children, to the perception of a real possibility of controlling fertility, to the availability of effective control methods (so that desires may be met, or met more closely), or to some combination of these. In the Latin American countries, only actual and, to a much more limited extent, desired fertility can be studied empirically for a significant number of countries.[8]

Data from the WFS and the DHS projects carried out during the last two decades (see for example Chapter 12) show that, although differences continue to exist among educational and residential groups in the Latin American countries, almost all subgroups have reduced their levels of desired fertility (an indicator of the demand for children, in the context of economic models of fertility), the tendency being toward a certain degree of homogenization of family size desires both across strata and among countries. The same is true of *actual* fertility estimated from survey data in Brazil, Colombia, Dominican Republic, Ecuador, Paraguay, and Peru (Brizuela 1988; Colombia 1988; Daly 1985; Dominican Republic 1987; Ortíz and Alcántara 1988; Ramírez *et al.* 1988; Rutenberg *et al.* 1987; Weinberger *et al.* 1989). These findings are confirmed, with the exceptions noted below, by direct and indirect fertility estimates based on census data in Costa Rica, Cuba, Chile, Honduras, Mexico, Panama, and Paraguay (Cuba 1981; INE–CELADE 1989; Honduras 1986; Martínez 1980; Panama 1984; Paraguay 1988). Some of these trends are also shown in the graphs in Chapters 1 and 22).

The estimates from both types of sources show the existence of countries where fertility declines have occurred across the board, with little or no lag between subpopulations (e.g. Cuba, after the revolution); countries where, after a perceptible time lag, all groups have ultimately followed the first pattern (e.g. Chile, Brazil, and Paraguay, since the 1960s); and also countries where some socio-economic groups have reduced their fertility, but others have maintained high levels and do not show signs of decline as yet (e.g. contemporary Honduras and Peru).

In sum, both actual and desired fertility appear to be sensible objects of the

[8] It is more problematic to evaluate the changes in contraceptive knowledge, in spite of the fact that this type of information is routinely collected in fertility surveys: knowledge of some method is virtually universal in most countries, but the accuracy and relevance of this knowledge is difficult to determine and compare over time (Fort 1989; Maynard-Tucker 1989).

study of diffusion; and declines in both variables have crossed the boundaries of almost all educational and residence strata within the Latin American countries once fertility declines have become noticeable at the national level.

The Relationship between Diffusion and Economic Change

Some researchers have stressed the importance of cultural, ideational, institutional or other types of societal changes that may affect the process of fertility decision-making or the terms under which decisions are made (for related ideas see, for example, McNicoll 1980; Handwerker 1986; Greenhalgh 1988). In the context of analyses of diffusion, it is frequently acknowledged that these factors do not necessarily exclude economic determinants, but the interrelations between these sets of factors are rarely articulated with clarity, and the discussion often ends up trying to support one approach vs. another. It seems more reasonable to place the independence assumption in a relative context: even those who are very critical of the transition or 'demand' theories, and their associated socio-economic determinants, recognize that 'this [diffusion] does not preclude *broad* economic factors, but strongly suggests the influence of new knowledge, ideas and aspirations that can spread independently of *individual* economic circumstances' (Cleland and Wilson 1987: 24, 25; my emphasis).

Along these lines, it might be argued that there is a set of economic changes that pervades all socio-economic strata (e.g. improved internal and international communications), that may be linked to the diffusion of ideas about fertility, and another set of changes at the individual level (increases in income, educational level, or changes in the place of residence), which although important in the analysis of fertility differentials, turn out to be much less crucial in explaining the temporal change in behaviour. Both types of changes surely deserve some weight in the explanation of the regional fertility trends, but it appears that at least in the recent past, the first set has been particularly important, since most of the decrease in measured fertility seems to be due to reductions within groups: Rodríguez (Chapter 2) estimates compositional effects to account for a small proportion of recent fertility changes, while Weinberger *et al.* (1989: table 4) find that in three out of four countries (Colombia, Dominican Republic, Ecuador), most of the fertility change is due to changes in rates, and little due to compositional shifts in education, the exception being Peru, where the reverse is true. Our regression estimates suggest that fertility changes at the national level tend to be underestimated by cross-sectional relationships, but that these can account for approximately 60 per cent of observed changes, a significant proportion in the context of these types of analyses. Needless to say, these are only a couple of initial bits of evidence, that must be corroborated (or contradicted) by further research.

What Type of Diffusion?

Geneticists and other social scientists (e.g. Cavalli-Sforza and Feldman 1981) generally distinguish three diffusion modes: (1) vertical, where a given feature is transmitted across generations, from parents to children, (2) horizontal, where transmission occurs among members of the same generation, and (3) oblique, where transmission occurs from parents of a given group to the children of another one. Some authors, such as Anderton *et al.* (1987), emphasize or assume (e.g. Demetrius 1989) the inter-generational mode of transmission, in different analytical contexts. In applications to the process of fertility transition as a whole, the vertical mode of transmission cannot but play a marginal role, because its predominance would lead in the long run to a process just opposite to the transition (unless one was willing to accept very extreme mortality differentials): the low-fertility group would progressively lose representation in the population, and total fertility would not decline, but rather tend to stabilize around the mean level of the high-fertility group.

Instead, the existence of horizontal (or oblique) diffusion in Latin America is suggested by the fact that in general, once the trend of fertility decline becomes manifest at the national level, most or all of the major population subgroups reduce their fertility in a roughly synchronous manner, and do so over a relatively short period of time. This means that, in looking for the channels through which diffusion may occur, intra-generational, inter-group modes of transmission appear to be relevant. Evidently, high-fertility parents will not necessarily transmit high-fertility values to their children, so that inter-generational transmission of values different from own behaviour could take place, but this is just another way of saying that the horizontal diffusion of behaviour is dominant.

Lags and the Channels of Spread

Are the initiation lags—as Carlsson argued—really necessary for a diffusion hypothesis? They certainly are if one insists on specifying the process as one of innovation-diffusion, but in general this need not be the case. Low fertility of one group compared to another does not necessarily establish the first as a true leader, unless this behaviour induces the precipitation of the transition; i.e. declines in other groups as well. Indeed, available data indicate that pre-transitional fertility levels differ among and within Latin American countries, but there is no general evidence showing that these differentials change significantly during the pre-transitional period. The few pieces of direct and indirect evidence that do exist for Cuba, Chile, Colombia, Costa Rica, Honduras, Mexico, and Peru (Guzmán and Rodríguez 1992; Bravo 1990) suggest the contrary: sustained pre-decline fertility differentials and sizeable proportions of women with low completed parity during the pre-transition period. The relative stability of pre-transitional fertility differentials and the contemporaneous decline across groups indicate that it is not necessary that a specific socio-economic group lead the transition, albeit this can happen in some countries: it may have been the case in Costa Rica (Rosero 1984), and with more certainty during the early stages of the decline in Brazil (González *et al.* 1982: ch. 2).

Thus, it is not reasonable to assume, in general, that fertility control is an absolutely new behaviour at the onset of the transition; it is doubtful that this was the case in nineteenth-century Europe, and is even more doubtful that this holds for twentieth-century Latin America: diffusion has occurred many times long after the innovation of low fertility behaviour existed in certain subpopulations; or to state it more directly, diffusion has not followed automatically the introduction of fertility control by some population subgroups. This shifts attention to the question of what makes a given behaviour generalizable, i.e. what are the variables and/or channels through which the process is precipitated and continued. Post-war modernization in many Latin American societies, including the gradual consolidation of a middle class within economic systems that experienced significant structural change (Syrquin 1986) and the greater internal and international integration made possible by improved communications, are factors that, in all likelihood, facilitated this process. The extension of health care and other social services may also play an important role (González *et al.* 1982; Potter *et al.* 1987). On the other hand, 'structural' (i.e. economic, spatial, and social) heterogeneity, unless compensated by redistributive actions of the state (González 1980), can pose serious obstacles to the onset of the transitions and can help explain the persistence of the significant socio-economic fertility differentials observed before and after the initiation of the transitions. Thus, social, political, and economic factors emerge again as important potential contributors to the onset of fertility decline and to the persistence of differentials, even in cases when little weight may be assigned to these factors in the explanation of the subsequent diffusion processes.

Another possible vehicle for diffusion is the national family planning programmes, which have certainly played a role in the improved provision of and information about contraceptives, and have therefore helped to legitimize and to facilitate access to fertility control (CELADE 1992). However, they do not appear to have determined changes in basic motivations or attitudes (as measured by survey questions on desired fertility at the national scale), since these have evolved similarly in countries that differ in the strength of their family planning programmes and official population policy (e.g. see Chapter 12, Table 12.3).

Types of Evidence of Diffusion

One of the few global predictions of the diffusion approach that is not immediately deduced from transition theory or other such models, is that fertility change should permeate socio-economic categorizations. That fertility has declined within groups during the transition, i.e. that the transitions are not due solely or even mainly to compositional changes, is a fact generally supported by the evidence cited previously. A somewhat more direct approach has been to discard an economic motivation behind the effect produced by a variable conventionally called 'socio-economic'. An example is the analysis of Cleland and Rodríguez (1988) who, using individual level data from the WFS programme, show that a woman's occupation has a very reduced effect on fertility once her education is controlled, suggesting that the effect of education on fertility does not act through its economic consequences, but does so 'through less tangible, cognitive channels' (Cleland and Rodríguez 1988: 438). In general, this second approach involves adding variables that either constitute controls for the conventional socio-economic effects, or more directly reflect effects of variables closely related to diffusion mechanisms. The nature and role of local or personal networks (Goldberg 1976; Retherford and Palmore 1983; Watkins 1991) can also provide useful insights on how diffusion takes place.

The problems with these kinds of evidence, on the other hand, are not difficult to pinpoint: the residual type is only suggestive, and the diffusion 'effect' is hardly measurable in that context, unless one is willing to define diffusion as the within-group changes, a very indirect approximation at best. The more direct approach is problematic in that in general, there are very few variables that reflect diffusion effects exclusively, and most of them can be interpreted to reflect also some aspect of socio-economic development or modernization, broadly understood. Moreover, few studies have directly addressed interactions with socio-economic or policy 'filters' that facilitate or obstruct the diffusion process. Interactions between diffusion elements and socio-economic change appear to be relevant and their incorporation seems to be necessary to be able to explain (1) the persistence of substantial pre-decline differentials for extended periods of time, as well as (2) the timing of the onset of sustained overall fertility reductions. Different types and intensities of inter-group social interaction have been recently studied by Rosero and Casterline (1992) in the context of theoretical diffusion models; empirical analysis on the basis of such models could open the way for better understanding of the processes involved. Diffusion effects expressed as autoregressive, endogenous feedback fertility behaviour (Montgomery 1992) appears to be another promising and more satisfactory statistical approach.

Summary and Conclusion

International and within-group dynamics of fertility trends in Latin America have been examined in a comparative perspective, in order to assess the relevance of broad theoretical approaches to fertility changes; the analyses of differentials at a point in time, useful as they may be, tell only a limited portion of the story of the fertility transitions in the region. The analysis suggests that interesting processes, though still poorly understood, seem to take place across countries and population subgroups over time.

This chapter has reviewed some of the principal aspects of a diffusionist approach based on an examination of the available evidence about the changes in fertility, which is used to delineate some general characteristics of the transition processes within the region. These may be summarized as follows: at the international level, mortality and development indicators—such as per capita income, literacy, and urbanization—correlate with fertility in the direction predicted by standard transition theory, but these relations have shifted and become less pronounced over the last three decades, suggesting that substantial 'structural change' has occurred which is not accounted for by changes in these variables. In spite of the fact that there are persistent socio-economic differentials, once the trend of fertility decline has become manifest at the national level during the same time period, most of the major population subgroups have reduced their fertility, and have done so over a relatively short period of time. Ideal family size has also declined across the board since the mid-1970s, and these trends have apparently been little affected by the economic stagnation or retrogression of the 1980s.

In this context, a diffusionist perspective seems to be helpful in the description of a process of change in both desired and actual fertility, where the intra-generational, inter-group modes of spread appear to be relevant. Its relevance as a truly explanatory model is less certain, given the difficulties of distinguishing diffusion effects from other underlying causes in previous empirical studies. Socio-economic factors and social interaction could play an important role in attempting to explain pre-transitional fertility differentials over extended periods of time and the timing of the onset of national declines.

References

Anderton, D. *et al.* (1987), 'Intergenerational Transmission of Relative Fertility and Life Course Patterns', *Demography*, 24/4: 467–80.

Arriaga, E. (1970), *Mortality Decline and its Demographic Effects in Latin America* (Population Monograph Series, No. 6; (Berkeley and Los Angeles: University of California).

Becker, G., and Lewis, H. (1973), 'On the Interaction between the Quantity and Quality of Children'. *Journal of Political Economy*, 81/2 (2): S279–S288.

Becker, G. (1981), *A Treatise on the Family* (Cambridge, Mass.: Harvard University Press).

Bravo, J. (1990), 'Cambios en la Paridez Completa y la Difusión de la Reducción de la Fecundidad en Latinoamérica en el Siglo XX: Un Análisis Basado en Datos Censales', *História e Populaçao: Estudos sobre a América Latina* (São Paulo, Brazil: ABEP–IUSSP–CELADE).

Brizuela, F. (1988), *Paraguay: Diferenciales Geográficos y Socio-económicos de la Fecundidad, 1960–1979* (Asunción, Paraguay: Dirección de Estadística y Censos).

Carlsson, G. (1966), 'Decline of Fertility: Innovation or Adjustment Process', *Population Studies*, 20/2: 149–74.

Cavalli-Sforza, L., and Feldman, M. (1981), *Cultural Transmission and Evolution: A Quantitative Approach* (Princeton: Princeton University Press).

CELADE (1988), *Demographic Bulletin*, 41 (Year 21) (Santiago, Chile).

—— (1989), *Demographic Bulletin*, 44 (Year 21) (Santiago: Chile).

—— (1992), 'Population Policy: A Perspective from Latin America and the Caribbean' (CELADE Serie A, No. 262, LC/DEM/R.111; Santiago, Chile).

CEPAL (1990), *Productive Transformation with Equity* (Economic Commission for Latin America and the Caribbean, UN LC/G. 1601–P; New York).

Chesnais, J. C. (1986), *La Transition démographique: Étapes, formes et implications économiques—Étude des séries temporelles (1720–1984) Relative à 67 Pays* (Travaux et Documents, Cahier No. 113; Paris: INED).

CLACSO (1974), *Reproducción de la Población y Desarrollo, i. Revisión Crítica de los Estudios de Fecundidad en América Latina* (Buenos Aires: Consejo Latinoamericano de Ciencias Sociales).

—— (1985), *Reproducción de Población y Desarrollo*, 5. *Transiçao de Fecundidade; Analise e Perspectivas*, comp. Neide Patarra (São Paulo, Brazil: Consejo Latinoamericano de Ciencias Sociales, Comisión de Población y Desarrollo).

Cleland, J., and Wilson, C. (1987), 'Demand Theories of the Fertility Transition: an Iconoclastic View', *Population Studies*, 41/1: 5–30.

—— and Rodríguez, G. (1988), 'The Effect of Parental Education on Marital Fertility in Developing Countries', *Population Studies*, 42: 419–42.

Colombia (1988), *Encuesta de Prevalencia, Demografía y Salud* (Bogotá, Colombia: Ministerio de Salud de Colombia, CCRP, IRD).

Cuba (1981), *Cuba: El Descenso de la Fecundidad 1964–1978* (Havana: Comité Estatal de Estadística and CELADE).

Cutright, P., and Hargens, L. (1984), 'The Threshold Hypothesis: Evidence from Less Developed Latin American Countries', *Demography* 21/4: 459–73.

Daly, H. E. (1985), 'Marx and Malthus in North-east Brazil: A Note on the World's Largest Class Differential in Fertility and its Recent Trends', *Population Studies*, 39/2: 329–38.

Demetrius, L. (1989), 'The Demographic Evolution of Human Populations: the Role of Selection and Environmental Factors', *Demography* 26/3: 353–72.

Demografía y Economía (1981), *Demografía y Economía*, 15/2 (46).

Dominican Republic (1987), *Encuesta Demográfica y de Salud DHS-1986* (Santo Domingo: CONAPOFA).

Dyson, T. (1984), 'Future LDC Demographic Research: Some Thoughts on Data, Methods, Theory', in Université Catholique de Louvain, Département de démographie, *La Démographie en Perspective: Visages Futures des Sciences de la Population et de leur Enseignement* (Chaire Quételet), 45–75.

Easterlin, R., Pollack, R., and Wachter, M. (1980), 'Toward a More General Economic Model of Fertility Determination: Endogenous Preferences and Natural Fertility', in Easterlin (ed.), *Population and Economic Change in Developing Countries* (Chicago: University of Chicago Press).

Fort, A. (1989), 'Investigating the Social Context of Fertility and Family Planning: a Qualitative Study in Perú'. *International Family Planning Perspectives*, 15/3: 88–95.

Goldberg, D. (1976), 'Residential Location and Fertility', in R. Ridker (ed.), *Population and Development: The Search for Selective Interventions* (Baltimore, Md.: Johns Hopkins University Press), ch. 12.

González, G. (1980), 'Styles of Development and Fertility Decline', in Hahn and Mackensen (eds.), *Determinants of Fertility Trends: Theories Reexamined* (Liège, Belgium: IUSSP).

—— (1982), *Estrategias de Desarrollo y Transición Demográfica: Los Casos de Brasil, Costa Rica, Cuba y Chile* (Santiago: CELADE).

Greenhalgh, S. (1988), 'Fertility as Mobility: Sinic Transitions', *Population and Development Review*, 14/4: 629–74.

Guzmán, J. M., and Rodríguez, J. (1992), La Fecundidad Pre-Transicional en América Latina: Un Capítulo Olvidado', *Proceedings, Conference on the Peopling of the Americas*, Veracruz, México, 18–23 May.

Handwerker, P. (1986), *Culture and Reproduction: An Anthropological Critique of Demographic Transition Theory* (Boulder Colo.: Westview Press).
Honduras (1986), *Fecundidad: Diferenciales Socioeconómicos de la Fecundidad 1960–1983* (Dirección General de Estadísticas y Censos, Consejo Superior de Planificación Económica, CELADE and ACDI, Serie A, No. 1047; San José).
INE–CELADE (1989), *La Transición de la Fecundidad en Chile 1950–1985* (Fascículo F/CHI. 7; Santiago, Chile).
Knodel, J. (1977), 'Family Limitation and the Fertility Transition: Evidence from the Age Patterns of Fertility in Europe and Asia', *Population Studies*, 31/2: 219–49.
Knodel, J., and Van de Walle, E. (1979), 'Lessons From the Past: Policy Implications of Historical Fertility Studies', *Population and Development Review*, 5/2: 217–45.
McNicoll, G. (1980), 'Institutional Determinants of Fertility Change', *Population and Development Review*, 6/3: 441–62.
Martínez, J. (1980) (ed.), *The Demographic Revolution in Mexico, 1970–1980* (Mexico: Manantou).
Maynard-Tucker, G. (1989), 'Knowledge of Reproductive Physiology and Modern Contraceptives in Rural Perú', *Studies in Family Planning*, 20/4: 215–24.
Montgomery, M. (1992), 'The Diffusion of Fertility in Taiwan: Estimates from Pooled Cross-Section, Time-Series Models', paper presented at the 1992 Population Association of America Meeting, 30 Apr.–2 May, Denver, Colo.
Ortíz, J., and Alcántara, E. (1988), 'Contribución de las Variables Intermedias en los Cambios de la Fecundidad Peruana en el Período 1969–1978', in J. Ortíz and E. Alcántara (eds), *Cambios en la Fecundidad Peruana* (Cusco, Peru: Centro de Investigación en Población).
Panama (1984), *Panamá: el Descenso de la Fecundidad Según Variables Socio-económicas y Geográficas, 1965–1977* (Ministerio de Planificación y Política Económica and CELADE, Serie A, No. 1046; San José).
Paraguay (1988), *Paraguay: Diferenciales Geográficos y Socio-económicos de la Fecundidad 1960–1979* (Dirección General de Estadísticas y Censo, CELADE, and ACDI, Serie A, No. 1047; San José).
Potter, J., Mojarro, O., and Núñez, L. (1987), 'The Influence of Health Care on Contraceptive Acceptance in Rural Mexico', Unpublished monograph, Feb.
Ramírez, N., Santara, I., De Moya Espinal, F., and Tactuk, P., (1988), 'Los Cambios en la Fecundidad Dominicana', in *República Dominicana: Población y Desarrollo* (San José, Costa Rica: CELADE).
Retherford, R., and Palmore, J. (1983), 'Diffusion Processes affecting Fertility Regulation', in R. Bulatao, and R. D. Lee (eds.), *Determinants of Fertility in Developing Countries* (New York: Academic Press).
Rosero, L. (1984), 'El Descenso de la Natalidad en Costa Rica', in *Mortalidad y Fecundidad en Costa Rica* (San José: Asociación Demográfica Costarricense).
—— and Casterline, J. (1992), 'Modeling Diffusion Effects in Fertility Transitions', forthcoming in *Population Studies*; draft version available as a PSTC Working Paper Series 92–01, Population Studies and Training Center, Brown University, Jan. 1992.
Rutenberg, N., Ochoa, L., and Arruda, J. (1987), 'The Proximate Determinants of Low Fertility in Brazil', *International Family Planning Perspectives*, 13/3: 75–80.
Syrquin, M. (1986), 'Growth and Structural Change in Latin America since 1960: A Comparative Analysis', *Economic Development and Cultural Change*, 34/3: 433–54.
United Nations (1991), World Urbanization Prospects 1990 (New York: UN).

UNESCO (1965) *Statistical Yearbook* (Paris: UNESCO).
—— (1991) *Rapport mondial sur l'éducation 1991* (Paris: UNESCO).
Watkins, S. (1987), 'The Fertility Transition: Europe and the Third World Compared', *Sociological Forum* 2/4: 645–73.
Watkins, S. (1991), 'More Lessons from the Past: Women's Informal Networks and Fertility Decline', IUSSP Seminar on the Course of Fertility Transition in Sub-Saharan Africa, Harare, Zimbabwe, 19–22 Nov.
Weinberger, M., Lloyd, C., and Blanc, A. (1989), 'Women's Education and Fertility: A Decade of Change in Four Latin American Countries', *International Family Planning Perspectives*, 15/1: 4–14.

12 Wanted Fertility in Latin America: Trends and Differentials in Seven Countries*

JOHN BONGAARTS and ROBERT LIGHTBOURNE

Introduction

Over the past three decades fertility has declined rapidly in Latin America. According to the most recent United Nations estimates, the TFR of the continent fell from over 6 births per woman in the 1950s to 3.6 in the late 1980s. The rate of change in fertility since the mid-1970s has been more rapid than in any other major region of the developing world (United Nations 1989).

To obtain further insight into the determinants of recent fertility declines in Latin American countries, this chapter examines variation in wanted fertility, both within countries and between countries, and also over time. Specifically, we compare actual fertility as measured by the total fertility rate with preferred fertility as measured by a new wanted total fertility rate developed by Bongaarts (1990) which reflects the fertility level that would prevail if women were to fully implement their preferences for terminating childbearing. Through examining these two indicators, we analyse trends in actual and preferred fertility at the aggregate national level and also by level of education and rural–urban residence.

The data for our analysis are taken from fertility surveys undertaken in the period 1975–89. The seven countries included are Colombia, Costa Rica, Dominican Republic, Ecuador, Jamaica, Peru, and Trinidad and Tobago. For each country, two surveys are available, the first invariably being a WFS, and the second usually being a DHS, except for Costa Rica and Jamaica. Since the first wave of surveys took place between 1975 and 1980 and the second wave between 1986 and 1989, the time elapsed between the first and second survey rounds is on average a decade (see Table 12.1). All these surveys measure fertility, reproductive preferences, education, and place of residence. With only minor exceptions these variables are measured in the same way in all the surveys. The results are therefore reasonably comparable across both time and space.

This chapter contains four main sections. First, an outline of the methodology is presented. This is followed by a summary of trends and differentials in actual fertility. The third section describes trends and differentials in wanted fertility. The fourth section provides conclusions.

* Financial support for this study was provided by NIH Grant R01-HD-23138.

Methodology for Estimating Wanted Fertility

In recent years a considerable amount of technical improvement has occurred in the measurement of the quantum of children desired. The various developments are briefly reviewed here.

Self-reported Desired Family Size

The earliest method for estimating the desired number of children, dating back to the Indianapolis Fertility Study of the 1940s, was to ask respondents to tell the interviewer how many children they wanted. This method has long been under attack, on a variety of grounds. In particular, women who surpass their desired stopping-point may 'rationalize' additional births by revising upward the number desired, and women who are just starting out childbearing may have no real idea of how many children they want. Additionally, in some societies women may have given little thought to the number of children they wish to have.

The wording of questions on desired family size has varied greatly between different surveys. In the WFS, respondents were asked 'If you could choose exactly the number of children to have in your whole life, how many would that be?' Subsequent analysis showed strong variation by parity in answering this question, implying rationalization of undesired births. The DHS employed a new question intended to reduce rationalization by anchoring the time referent to the beginning of childbearing, and asked respondents 'If you could go back to the time you did not have any children and could choose exactly the number of children to have in your whole life, how many would that be?'

Unfolding Theory

Using a fairly complex sequence of questions, Coombs, Coombs, and McClelland (1975) proposed a methodology for estimating the total number of children desired. These questions have not been asked in the surveys considered in this chapter, and so the resulting estimates are not discussed here. An application of the Coombs method to Korean data has been reported by Kim and Choi (1981).

Parity-progression Estimates of Desired Family Size

A variety of authors have proposed methods for estimating the number of births desired through making use of information on current parity and whether more children are wanted, including Udry, Bauman, and Chase (1973), Lightbourne (1977, 1985), Pullum (1981), Rodríguez and Trussell (1981), and Nour (1983). When uncorrected for fecundity impairments, natural fertility, infant mortality, and non-marriage, the least biased of these estimators come fairly close to replicating the self-reported mean desired family size (Lightbourne 1985). When corrected for these factors, (Lightbourne 1981) the parity progression estimates are significantly lower and in principle can be fine tuned so that they come close to the wanted TFR estimates described below. This convergence is important in cross validating other methods. On the other hand, the fine tuning is extremely laborious and requires estimation of many factors that often have to be indirectly inferred, such as the natural fertility schedule, the infecundity schedule, and so forth. For this reason, some researchers abandoned synthetic cohort estimation in favour of wanted total fertility rates, because of the greater inherent simplicity and fewer data requirements of the latter approach.

Wanted TFRs

The notion of a wanted TFR as a policy relevant measure seems to have been first explicitly used by Blake and das Gupta (1972) and has subsequently been used by Westoff (1981), Blanc (1982), Lightbourne (1985, 1987), and Bongaarts (1990).

The emergence of the wanted TFR as a measure of the desired number of births is significant for several reasons. First, because it is conceptually and computationally simple, and is methodologically a much more credible indicator of the desired quanta of births than is self-reported desired family size. A second reason the wanted TFR is an important development is that it often estimates a substantially lower number of wanted births than self-reported desired family size, and has led to the now increasingly accepted finding that the wanted number of births is in many countries substantially lower than the mean self-reported desired family size (Lightbourne 1985; Bongaarts 1990).

Based on the birth histories provided by the WFS, a very simple method emerged for direct calculations of the wanted total fertility rate, first proposed by Westoff (1981). The wanted TFR is identical to an ordinary TFR except that unwanted births are suppressed from the numerators. In other words, the numerators consist of wanted births at each age 15–19 ,..., 45–49 while the denominators consist of person-years lived by all women at each age 15–19 ,..., 45–49. The great advantage to the wanted TFR is its straightforward interpretation as the number of wanted births that women would have if unwanted childbearing were to be avoided.

Several different methods have emerged for suppressing unwanted births from the numerator. The first, used by Westoff (1981), Blanc (1982), and Lightbourne (1985), employed several alternative criteria in determining whether a birth was unwanted or not, as outlined in variants 1 and 2 below.

Wanted Total Fertility Rate, Variant 1: Under one variant, which we will denote WTFR1 (for Wanted Total Fertility Rate No. 1), a birth is counted as unwanted and is excluded from the numerator if it is in excess of the individual respondent's self-reported desired family size.

Wanted Total Fertility Rate, Variant 2: Under a second variant, which we will denote WTFR2 (for Wanted Total Fertility Rate No. 2), a birth is counted as unwanted and excluded from the numerator if the respondent reported it as unwanted in response to a direct question. Ascertainment of unwantedness was achieved in the WFS by asking 'Thinking back to the time before you became pregnant with your last child, had you wanted to have any more children?' The subsequent round of the DHS used an improved question that distinguished births that were permanently unwanted from births that were mistimed, which was worded: 'Just before you became pregnant with (NAME), did you want to have that child then, did you want to wait until later, or did you want no more children at all?'

New Wanted TFR: Under a third variant of the wanted TFR, proposed by Bongaarts (1990), which we will denote NWTFR (for New Wanted Total Fertility Rate), a totally different approach to excluding unwanted births from the numerator was put forward, that has the advantage of relying on a less biased source of information.

Variant 1 depends on the accuracy of reports of desired family size, which is widely known to be upwardly biased by *ex post facto* rationalization of undesired last births. Variant 2 depends on the adequacy of the reporting of the wantedness status of recent births, which also appears to be subject to systematic bias in the direction of reporting unwanted births as wanted (Goldman *et al.* 1989). The NWTFR, on the other hand, depends on the accuracy of reporting whether an additional birth is wanted, which is held to have no systematic bias. The NWTFR, in our view, is an unbiased estimator of the fertility level that would prevail if women were to fully implement their preferences for terminating childbearing, unlike the prior two variants.

Computing the NWTFR

The first step in computing the NWTFR is to calculate what might be called the 'want-more' TFR, preferably using a reference period framed on the two years prior to the survey. The denominators for this variant are calculated as for any other standard survey TFR, namely as the person-years lived at each age by all women in the population. The numerators, however, include only births in the reference period to that subset of women who at time of interview say they wish to have additional children, suitably subdivided by age of mother at time of birth.

The second step in the NWTFR is then to add to this special 'want more' TFR an adjustment for wanted last births. This adjustment is needed because women who completed their childbearing by having their last wanted birth during the two years prior to survey will at time of survey report to the interviewer that they do not want to bear more children, so that their wanted last births are wrongly excluded from the special want-more TFR calculated in step 1. By adding a correction for these wanted last births, the NWTFR is obtained.[1]

[1] NWTFR is estimated with the following equation: NWTFR = WMTFR + 1 – C + 0.086 where WMTFR is the want-more TFR which includes only births to women who at the time of the survey want to continue childbearing. The correction factor C is set equal to the proportion of married women wanting more children at the end of the reproductive years. (This is normally age group 40–44, but to reduce sampling errors we have used here the average for age groups 35–39, 40–44, and 45–49.) The factor 0.086 is needed if the NWTFR is calculated for a two-year period before the survey date;

It is emphasized here that given correct data, all three methods are unbiased estimators of the desired number of births, with the very desirable properties of automatic correction for gender preference, child mortality, non-marriage, and physical and behavioural obstacles to childbearing, in particular fecundity impairments and lowered frequency of coitus as couples age. The data for the NWTFR, however, is argued to have much less bias and therefore greater credibility than the data for WTFR1 and WTFR2.

Variation in Estimates of Wanted Fertility

It can be seen in Fig. 12.1 that the different methods provide substantially different estimates of the number of children wanted. It can be seen that self-reported desired family size almost invariably provides a substantially higher estimate of the mean number of children wanted than does any of the three types of wanted TFR. The results in Fig. 12.1—presented both for the total population and for education and residence subpopulations—confirm prior findings that when estimated using the wanted TFR approach, the number of wanted births is almost always substantially below the number of children wanted estimated by self-reported desired family size.

It is important to stress that wanted fertility rates are automatically adjusted for gender preference and child mortality, and to note that these findings thus

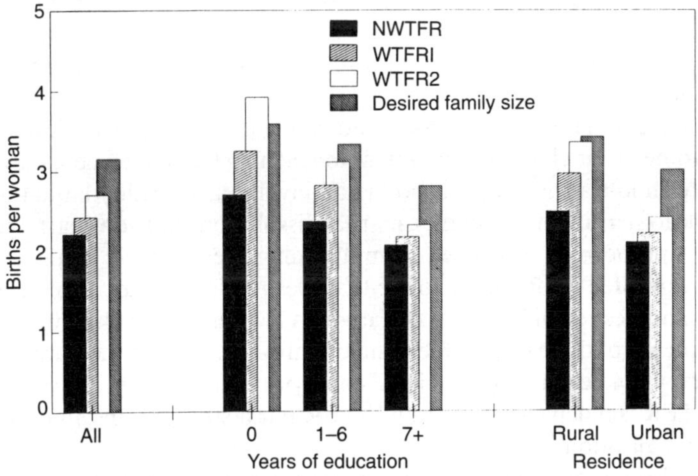

Fig. 12.1. ***New wanted TFR, desired TFR, reported wanted TFR, and desired family size, by level of education and place of residence***

Source: **Averages for five DHS surveys**

it adjusts for the fact that a few women who want no more children at the time of the survey had more than one wanted birth in the past two years. See Bongaarts (1990) for further details. Since in the WFS infecund women were not asked if they wanted more children, the results for WFS and DHS are not strictly comparable. In application of the above procedure women identified as infecund in the WFS were assumed to want no more children.

contradict the speculations of a number of authors who in the past have surmised that the number of wanted births must be substantially higher than desired family size, when appropriate adjustments are made to compensate for the deaths of desired children and for gender preference.

Another important finding is that for DHS surveys, the average number of births wanted estimated using NWTFR is lower than the number estimated by either WTFR1 or WTFR2. This finding is of significance because it indicates somewhat better prospects for further fertility decline than was hitherto thought. These results also hold at the individual country level (detail omitted) as well as for the cross-country aggregations shown.

WFS results are omitted from Fig. 12.1 because variant 2 cannot be comparably calculated, since, unlike the DHS, the WFS questionnaire provided no basis for discriminating between permanently unwanted births and mistimed births. As a result of this, when WFS data are used, WTFR2 estimates a lower number of births wanted than does the NWTFR.

The causes of the differences between these alternative measures of preferred fertility have been discussed in some detail in Bongaarts (1990). Briefly, the main reason why WTFR2 and NWTFR differ is an upward bias in WTFR2, which is the consequence of an apparent reluctance of mothers to report recently born children as unwanted. The size of this bias varies widely among subgroups from a high of 1.2 births per woman in the least educated groups to only 0.2 among women with seven or more years of education (see Fig. 12.1). The difference between self-reported desired family size and the NWTFR is due to a number of factors of which rationalization and involuntary family limitation are the most important.

Rationalization refers to an upward adjustment in the reported desired family size as women bear children subsequent to reaching the point where they wish to terminate childbearing. The second factor, involuntary fertility limitation, is attributable to sterility, subfecundity, marital dissolution, and non-marriage, which prevent a proportion of women from attaining their desired family size, thus yielding a wanted TFR that is lower than desired family size. Prolonged postponement of desired births may contribute to involuntary fertility limitation. As a consequence of these factors the desired family size exceeds the wanted TFR in both surveys and each subgroup in all countries examined here. Variant 1 of the wanted TFR is much closer to the NWTFR but it still contains an upward bias from rationalization.

Before closing this section, it is useful to comment briefly on the precise interpretation to be placed upon the estimates of the NWTFR on which our analysis is based. First, it has been argued elsewhere (Lightbourne 1985, 1987) that full implementation of both terminating and postponing preferences can imply a significantly lower number of wanted births than full implementation solely of preferences for terminating childbearing. The results presented below, in our view properly account for the time-of-survey structure of terminating preferences, and they take account of postponing preferences in so far as these are currently being implemented (i.e. by effective contraceptive use among women who say they want more children but who in the present wish to postpone having their next birth). However, to the extent that women who wish to postpone are not fully implementing this preference, the NWTFR will overestimate the TFR that would come into being under full implementation of both terminating and postponing preferences. If women postpone sufficiently long, they may postpone some births all the way to menopause. Although in Latin America the large majority of women stop childbearing well before menopause, the impact of further postponing behaviour in this continent may be non-trivial as is suggested by Lightbourne (1987). Second, it should be noted that period fertility and its wanted and unwanted components may be affected not only by the preferred number of births, but also by changes in postponing behaviour. For example, during a period of economic hardship couples may want to delay their births more than is usual, as apparently was the case in many of the developed countries during the severe economic depression and the widespread unemployment of the 1930s. Such a delay in childbearing can cause reductions in the wanted TFR without a change in desired family size. The NWTFR correctly captures these changes in the true wanted TFR.

Trends and Differentials in Actual TFR

Estimates of the TFRs for the two surveys in each of the seven countries included in this analysis are presented in Table 12.1. On average, fertility declined from 4.5 to 3.5 births per woman between the first round of surveys in the late 1970s and the second round in the late 1980s. This decline is comparable to that for Latin America as a whole, and, although the seven countries are not randomly selected, they appear to be fairly representative of reproductive trends in the region.

Table 12.1. *Latin America and the Caribbean: trends in TFRs, selected countries*

Country	First survey (WFS)	Second survey (DHS)	Fertility change	First survey date	Second survey date	Years elapsed
Colombia	4.6	3.1[a]	−1.5	1976	1986	10.3
Costa Rica	3.5	3.6	0.1	1976	1986	9.6
Dominican Republic	5.2	3.6	−1.6	1975	1986	11.3
Ecuador	5.2	4.3	−0.9	1979	1987	7.8
Jamaica	4.4	2.8[b]	−1.6	1975	1988	12.8
Peru	5.3	4.0	−1.3	1977	1986	9.1
Trinidad and Tobago	3.2	3.0	−0.2	1977	1987	10.0
AVERAGE	4.5	3.5	−1.0			10.1

[a] Survey by Asociación Demográfica Costarricense.
[b] Survey by Jamaica National Family Planning Board with technical assistance from Centers for Disease Control, Atlanta.

Fertility trends vary widely among countries. The fertility reductions observed in Colombia, Dominican Republic, Ecuador, Jamaica, and Peru occurred at rates greater than 1.0 birth per woman per decade. This extremely rapid pace of change has been rivalled by few other countries in the developing world. In contrast, fertility levels changed little in Costa Rica and Trinidad and Tobago, countries where fertility was already low in the mid-1970s. In both these countries, fertility declined rapidly during the 1960s, but it has stalled at well above the replacement level since the mid-1970s. This is an interesting and unusual phenomenon that is not found to the same extent outside Latin America. Several other Latin American countries, including Argentina, Chile, and Uruguay have experienced a similar leveling off in fertility with TFRs near 3 (United Nations 1989). On the other hand, several island countries such as Cuba and Barbados have experienced sustained fertility declines reaching the replacement level.

Previous studies of Latin American fertility have documented large differentials by level of education and between urban and rural women. In fact, these differences are larger in Latin America than has been observed in any other major region of the developing world (United Nations 1987; Weinberger *et al.* 1989). Table 12.2 presents estimates of the TFR by education[2] and residence in each of the seven countries. In every country and in each survey fertility is negatively associated with the level of education and urban residence (the only exception is Trinidad and Tobago where no significant fertility difference between rural and urban areas was found in the DHS). To facilitate the examination of differentials and trends, Table 12.2 and Fig. 12.2 present the average TFRs of the seven countries for each social group. In the WFS round of surveys, women with no education had, on average, 6.1 births compared with 2.8 for women with seven or more years of education, a gap of 3.3 births; in the second round of surveys, this gap between least and most educated women had narrowed to 2.7 births, suggesting a pattern of convergence. Similarly, the fertility of rural women exceeded that of urban women in the WFS (5.7 v. 3.6 births per woman) as well as in the DHS (4.5 v. 3.0 births per woman), with a similar narrowing in the differential. Several conclusions similar to those reached by Weinberger *et al.* (1989) can be drawn from the data in Table 12.2 and Figure 12.2:

- Fertility differentials by level of education and urban/rural residence are large and in the expected direction, i.e. the more modern groups have lower fertility.

[2] The zero education category had fewer than 500 woman-years in Costa Rica 1985, Jamaica 1989, and both surveys in Trinidad and Tobago. The observed TFRs in these cases were discarded because of the large sampling errors. For the purpose of calculating averages for each round of surveys the TFR for each of the affected cells is estimated by multiplying the survey's TFR for all women by the ratio A/B; A is the sum of TFRs of women with zero education excluding Costa Rica 1985, Jamaica 1989, and Trinidad and Tobago both dates; B is the sum of total fertility rates of all education groups, excluding Costa Rica 1985, Jamaica 1989, and Trinidad and Tobago for 1977 and 1987. For example, the TFR for all women for Costa Rica 1987 was 3.6, and the ratio A/B for the second round of surveys was formed using (4.81 + 5.41 + 6.71 + 6.5) / (3.11 + 3.63 + 4.34 + 4.01). The estimated TFR for Costa Rica 1987 for the zero education group thus becomes 5.59.

Table 12.2. *Latin America and the Caribbean: TFRs in period 0–24 months before survey by level of education and place of residence*

Country and survey	Education			Residence		All
	0[a]	1–6	7+	Rural	Urban	
Colombia						
WFS-76	7.4	4.9	2.8	6.7	3.6	4.6
DHS-86	4.8	3.9	2.3	4.6	2.6	3.1
Costa Rica						
WFS-76	4.7	3.8	2.7	4.3	2.9	3.5
ADC-85	*	4.4	2.8	4.4	3.0	3.6
Dominican Republic						
WFS-75	6.9	5.9	2.7	7.0	3.6	5.2
DHS-86	5.4	4.1	2.8	4.8	3.0	3.6
Ecuador						
WFS-79/80	7.5	6.1	2.7	6.5	3.9	5.2
DHS-87	6.7	5.1	3.0	5.4	3.6	4.3
Jamaica						
WFS-75/6	4.7	4.9	2.9	4.9	3.8	4.4
NFPB-89	*	3.4	2.5	3.0	2.6	2.8
Peru						
WFS-77/8	6.9	4.9	3.0	7.1	4.4	5.3
DHS-86	6.5	5.0	2.7	6.3	2.9	4.0
Trinidad and Tobago						
WFS-77	*	3.7	2.8	3.5	3.0	3.2
DHS-87	*	3.5	2.9	3.0	3.1	3.0
MEAN						
Survey 1	6.1	4.9	2.8	5.7	3.6	4.5
Survey 2	5.4	4.2	2.7	4.5	3.0	3.5

Notes: ADC = Asociación Demográfica Costarricense; NFPB = Jamaica National Family Planning Board and Centers for Disease Control, Atlanta; * = fewer than 250 respondents.

[a] See text, n. 2.

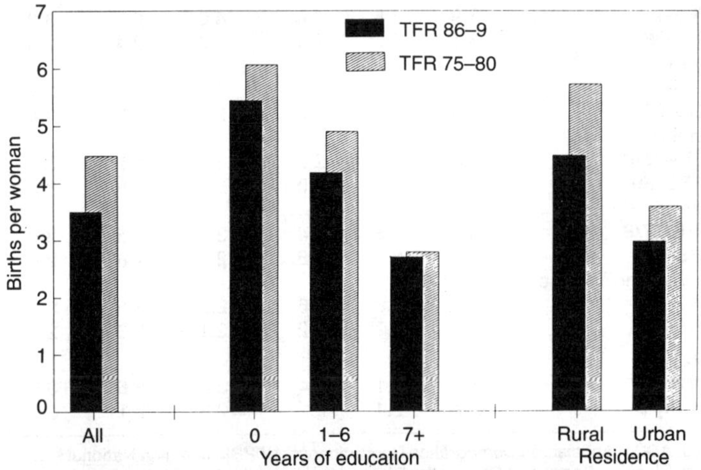

Fig. 12.2. *TFRs by level of education and place of residence*

Source: Averages for five DHS surveys.

- Fertility differentials between subgroups have diminished over time.
- The fertility of the most highly educated women has remained remarkably constant over time, while the other education groups experienced significant fertility declines.

These generalizations apply with minor exceptions to the individual countries included in Table 12.2. (In examining this table it should be noted that sampling and other errors are far from negligible and differences between TFRs of 0.2 or 0.3 are typically not statistically significant.)

Trends and Differentials in Wanted Fertility

Estimates of the new wanted TFR are presented in Table 12.3 by level of education and place of residence. The initial level of the NWTFR (i.e. observed between 1975 and 1980 in WFS inquiries) varied surprisingly little among countries, with

Table 12.3. ***Latin America and the Caribbean: NWTFR 0–24 months before survey by level of education and place of residence, selected countries***

Country and year	Education			Residence		All
	0[a]	1–6	7+	Rural	Urban	
Colombia						
WFS-76	3.9	2.7	2.2	3.3	2.4	2.7
DHS-86	2.0	2.2	1.8	2.3	1.8	2.0
Costa Rica						
WFS-76	3.3	3.2	2.6	3.2	2.7	3.0
ADC-85		3.0	2.3	3.1	2.3	2.7
Dominican Republic						
WFS-75	3.9	3.6	2.4	4.0	2.7	3.3
DHS-86	3.1	2.7	2.4	2.8	2.4	2.5
Ecuador						
WFS-79/80	4.4	3.8	2.4	3.9	2.8	3.4
DHS-87	2.9	2.5	2.2	2.8	2.2	2.4
Jamaica						
WFS-75/6	2.8	3.3	2.5	3.3	2.7	3.0
NFPB-89		1.9	2.0	2.0	1.9	1.9
Peru						
WFS-77/8	3.6	2.6	2.4	3.8	2.5	3.0
DHS-86	2.9	2.2	1.8	2.6	1.8	2.0
Trinidad and Tobago						
WFS-77	*	2.8	2.6	2.7	2.5	2.6
DHS-87	*	2.2	2.2	2.1	2.3	2.2
MEAN						
Survey 1	3.6	3.1	2.4	3.4	2.6	3.0
Survey 2	2.7	2.4	2.1	2.5	2.1	2.3

Notes: ADC = Asociación Demográfica Costarricense; NFPB = Jamaica National Family Planning Board and Centers for Disease Control, Atlanta; * = fewer than 250 respondents.

[a] See text, n. 2.

a range of only 0.7 births. The minimum of this range was 2.6 births (Trinidad and Tobago) and the maximum was 3.3 (Dominican Republic). However, while the wanted number of births varied comparatively little, the actual number of births in the seven WFS inquiries at hand varied much more substantially, ranging from 3.2 births in Trinidad and Tobago to 5.3 in Peru. When countries are ranked by level of TFR in the WFS wave of surveys, as shown in Table 12.4, it can be seen that the NWTFR and the actual TFR are only weakly correlated.

Table 12.4. *Latin America and the Caribbean: TFRs and NWTFRs, selected countries*

Country	TFR	NWTFR
Peru	5.3	3.0
Dominican Republic	5.2	3.3
Ecuador	5.2	3.4
Colombia	4.6	2.7
Jamaica	4.4	3.0
Costa Rica	3.5	3.0
Trinidad and Tobago	3.2	2.6

Source: WFS surveys 1975–78.

The implication of this finding is that much of the between-country variation in actual fertility is due to variation in unwanted fertility rather than to variation in number preference. A similar conclusion is reached if one examines the results for the second round of surveys.

In the decade between the first and second surveys, the overall trend in the NWTFR across all countries was downward, from an average of 3.0 wanted births in the first round to 2.3 wanted births in the second, a decline of 0.7. On average the proportion of fertility that was wanted decreased slightly between the two survey rounds, indicating a continuation of a trend first documented by Blanc (1982). All the individual countries experienced a reduction in the NWTFR, ranging from a comparatively small drop in Costa Rica (0.3 births) to a much larger fall of 1.0 birth in Jamaica.

A ranking of countries by the decline in the total fertility rate between the first and second surveys in Table 12.5 shows that this decline is correlated with the trend in the wanted TFR. Costa Rica and Trinidad and Tobago stand out as unusual cases. These countries have experienced little change in fertility since the mid-1970s and they had the smallest change in wanted fertility. One possible explanation of this stalling of fertility at levels above three births per woman is that it is largely due to a stabilization of fertility preferences well above the replacement level, which would raise the question of why preferences have stabilized at such a high level in these two countries. Further research into this important issue is highly desirable because it could well be that other countries with rapid past fertility declines will experience stalling fertility in the near future.

Table 12.5. ***Latin America and the Caribbean: trends in TFRs and NWTFRs, selected countries***

Country	Trend in	
	TFR	NWTFR
Jamaica	–1.6	–1.0
Dominican Republic	–1.6	–0.8
Colombia	–1.5	–0.7
Peru	–1.3	–1.0
Ecuador	–0.9	–0.6
Trinidad and Tobago	–0.1	–0.4
Costa Rica	+0.1	–0.3

Sources: Calculations based on Tables 12.2 and 12.3.

We now turn to examining socio-economic differentials in wanted fertility levels. The averages in Table 12.3 and Fig. 12.3 show that at the time of the WFS the least educated women wanted 3.6 births compared to 2.4 births among the most educated women, a differential of 1.2 births. Eight to ten years later this differential had narrowed, with the least educated women wanting 2.7 births, as compared with 2.1 births among the most educated women, a differential of only 0.6 wanted births. A similar narrowing in differentials in wanted fertility can be observed in the comparison between rural and urban women. At the time of the WFS, the NWTFR for urban women was 2.6 births compared with 3.4 for rural women, a difference of 0.8 births. By the time of the DHS, however, the differential in wanted fertility had declined to 0.4 births. A similar reduction in differentials in the reported desired family size also occurred (data not shown). These findings indicate that in the countries examined here, women of different social strata are converging toward a narrow range of fertility preferences.

Perhaps the most striking result in Fig. 12.3 is the steep gradient in unwanted fertility according to socio-economic group. The unwanted TFR of women with no education exceeded by more than two births the rate among women with more than primary education in both survey rounds. Similarly, rural women had more than twice the unwanted fertility of urban women. Clearly, women in the higher social strata have much better control over their fertility and are more successful at implementing their fertility preferences than rural women or women with low levels of education.

Conclusion

A general conclusion to be drawn from this analysis is that most of the variation in actual fertility at the time of both WFS and DHS is not due to variation in the number of children wanted but instead due to differential success in controlling fertility to desired levels, which is consistent with prior findings by Lightbourne

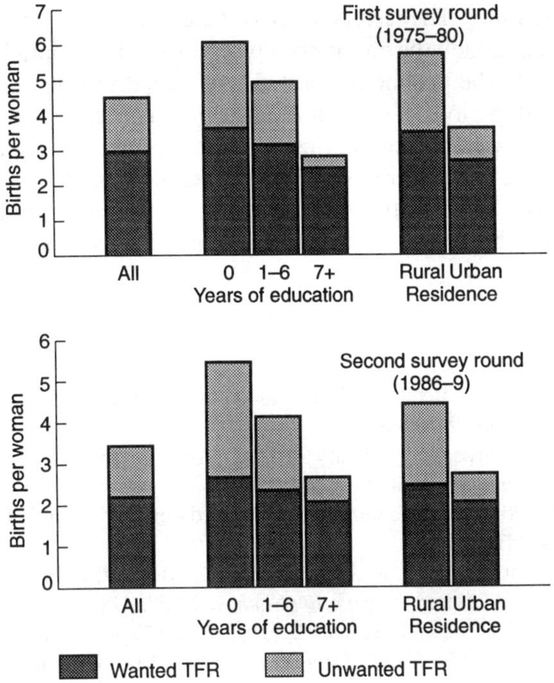

Fig. 12.3. ***Actual and wanted TFR by level of education and place of residence***
Source: Averages for five DHS surveys

(1984) for three Caribbean countries surveyed by WFS. Another way of expressing this is to note that the variation in actual fertility was due mostly to variation in unwanted fertility. If unwanted fertility were to be successfully avoided, the fertility differentials between socio-economic groups would be very much smaller than was observed. Similarly, if unwanted fertility had been avoided, the fertility differentials among countries would have been very much smaller, both at the time of the WFS, in the mid- to late 1970s, and at the time of the DHS, in the mid- to late 1980s.

Another important conclusion—perhaps the most significant from a policy standpoint—is that in both the WFS and the DHS, unwanted fertility was highly prevalent in all of the countries, and in particular among the low socio-economic strata. Presumably this is in large part caused by a lack of ready access to contraceptives and the inadequacy of available contraceptive methods.

In closing, we should note that we have limited our analysis to describing trends and differentials in actual and wanted fertility, and have not made an attempt to explain our findings in terms of the rapid social and economic changes that have occurred throughout Latin America in recent decades. It is likely that actual and wanted fertility have declined largely as part of the normal process of economic and social development. However, an important partial explanation for the very rapid decline in fertility in several countries could be the economic crisis of the early 1980s. The results reported here are for only two points in time for each country and lack the continuous monitoring that would have permitted one to say whether the decline in wanted and actual fertility was closely correlated in time with periods of economic hardship. In order to test this hypothesis one would need to assemble reliable time series of economic statistics such as consumer price indices, inflation rates and real per capita income, as well as corresponding indicators of fertility and wanted fertility. This would be a worthy endeavour, but was beyond the resources of the present writers at this time.

References

Blake, J., and das Gupta, P. (1972), 'The Fallacy of the Five Million Women: A Re-estimate', *Demography*, **9**: 569–88.

Blanc, Ann (1982), 'Unwanted Fertility in Latin America and the Caribbean', *International Family Planning Perspectives*, **8/4**: 156–62.

Bongaarts, John (1990), 'The Measurement of Wanted Fertility', *Population and Development Review*, **16**: 487–506.

Coombs, C. H., Coombs, C. L., and McClelland, G. H. (1975), 'Preference Scales for Number and Sex of Children', *Population Studies*, **29**: 273–98.

Goldman, N., Westoff, C. F., and Moreno, L. (1989), *Peru Experimental Study: An Evaluation of Fertility and Child Health Information* (DHS, Maryland and Office of Population Research, Princeton University).

Kim, N. I., and Choi, B. M. (1981), *Preferences for Number and Sex of Children and Contraceptive Use in Korea* (WFS Scientific Reports, No. 22; Voorburg: International Statistical Institute).

Lightbourne, R. E. (1977), 'Family Size Desires and the Birth Rates they Imply', PhD thesis, University of California.

—— (1981), 'Some Improved Measures of Desired Family Size: An Application to 14 Developing Countries', Paper presented at Population Association of America Annual Meeting, Washington, DC.

—— (1984), '*Fertility Preferences in Guyana, Jamaica and Trinidad and Tobago, from World Fertility Survey, 1975–77: A Multiple Indicator Approach*' (WFS Scientific Reports, No. 68; Voorburg: International Statistical Institute).

—— (1985), 'Individual Preferences and Fertility Behavior', in J. Hobcraft, and J. Cleland (eds.), *Demography of Developing Countries: Insights from the World Fertility Survey* (Oxford: Oxford University Press).

—— (1987), 'New Approaches to Estimating the Demand for Children', *United Nations Population Bulletin*, 23–4: 21–43.

Nour, S. el (1983), 'On the Estimation of the Distribution of Desired Family Size for a Synthetic Cohort', *Population Studies*, **37/2**: 315–22.

Pullum, T. W. (1981) 'Adjusting Stated Fertility Preferences for the Effect of Actual Family Size, with Applications to World Fertility Survey Data', in G. E. Hendershot and P. J. Placek (eds.), *Predicting Fertility: Demographic Studies of Birth Expectations* (Lexington, Mass.: Lexington Books).

Rodríguez, G., and Trussell, T. J. (1981), 'A Note on Synthetic Cohort Estimates of Desired Family Size', *Population Studies*, **35/2**: 321–8.

Udry, J. R., Bauman, K. E., and Chase, C. L. (1973), 'Population Growth in Perfect Contraceptive Populations', *Population Studies*, **27/2**: 365–71.

United Nations (1987), 'Fertility Preferences', ch. 2 in *Fertility Behavior in the Context of Development: Evidence from the World Fertility Survey* (Department of International Economic and Social Affairs, Population Studies, No. 100; New York: UN).

United Nations (1989), *World Population Prospects, 1988* (Department of International and Social Affairs, Population Studies, No. 106; New York: UN).

Weinberger, M. B., Lloyd, C., and Blanc, A. (1989), 'Women's Education and Fertility: A Decade of Change in Four Latin American Countries', *International Family Planning Perspectives*, **15**: 4–14.

Westoff, C. F. (1981), 'Unwanted Fertility in Six Developing Countries', *International Family Planning Perspectives*, **7**: 43–52.

13 Reproductive Intentions and Fertility in Latin America

CHARLES F. WESTOFF and LORENZO MORENO

Recent research has substantiated the importance of reproductive preferences in the determination of fertility (Westoff 1990). In this chapter we analyse reproductive preferences at three levels. The first objective is to examine family-size norms and to determine whether there has been any change in the number of children considered ideal in various Latin American populations. We then focus on the extent of unwanted fertility, from which we can deduce the level of fertility that would prevail if all births were wanted. Finally, we turn our attention to the reproductive intentions of the women of these populations, offer some fertility forecasts based on these intentions, and review trends and differentials in these preferences over recent years. This analysis is supported (in Appendix 13.1) with a summary of a methodological evaluation of the validity of survey data on intentions, since some demographers are sceptical of their predictive utility.

All the estimates in these analyses are based on data collected in the DHS and WFS projects. Data for the eight Latin American countries in the first phase of the DHS are included along with five WFS countries for time trend comparisons.

Family Size Norms

A question was included in both survey projects on what has been labelled 'desired number of children' in WFS or 'ideal number of children' in the DHS. The basic formulation of this question is: 'If you could choose exactly the number of children to have in your whole life, how many would that be?' The purpose of this question is to assess the fertility norms in different populations rather than reproductive intentions. The differences in the countries are revealing (Table 13.1). The two countries with the lowest level of ideal family size are Bolivia and Peru. Bolivia, in particular, is an anomaly in that it has, next to Guatemala, the highest actual fertility of any of these countries. Guatemala, on the other hand, shows the highest ideal, quite consistent with the highest observed fertility. Brazil and Colombia have low values on this measure of fertility norms; they are virtually indistinguishable at every parity. Ecuador and Mexico also show very similar patterns but at a slightly higher level than Brazil and Colombia, while the Dominican Republic shows a higher level of ideal family size than any country in the group except Guatemala.

Table 13.1. *Latin America: mean ideal number of children by number of living children (ever-married women), selected countries*

Country	Year	No. of living children (including current pregnancy)							
		0	1	2	3	4	5	6+	Total
Bolivia	1989	2.2	2.3	2.4	2.8	3.0	3.1	3.5	2.8
Brazil	1986	2.4	2.4	2.6	3.2	3.5	3.5	4.0	3.0
Colombia	1986	2.3	2.3	2.6	3.0	3.4	3.6	4.1	3.0
Dominican Republic	1986	3.1	2.9	3.2	3.6	4.0	4.1	4.5	3.6
Ecuador	1987	2.5	2.5	2.8	3.2	3.4	3.9	4.8	3.3
Guatemala	1987	3.5	3.2	3.4	3.8	4.2	5.0	5.9	4.1
Mexico	1987	2.4	2.5	2.7	3.2	3.5	4.1	4.4	3.3
Peru	1986	2.1	2.2	2.5	3.0	2.9	3.3	3.6	2.9

There has been a significant decline in the mean ideal number of children over the past decade (Table 13.2). In the five countries for which we can assess trends, the decline has been in the approximate range of 20 to 33 per cent. The basic conclusion that fertility norms are shifting downward seems clear.

Table 13.2. *Latin America: mean ideal number of children (for ever-married women) and changes over the decade, selected countries*

Country	Year	Mean ideal no.	% decline
Bolivia	1989	2.8	
Brazil	1986	3.0	
Colombia	1976	4.1	
	1986	3.0	27
Dominican	1975	4.6	
Republic	1986	3.6	22
Ecuador	1979	4.1	
	1987	3.3	19
Guatemala	1987	4.1	
Mexico	1976–7	4.4	
	1987	3.3	32
Peru	1977–8	3.8	
	1986	2.9	24

In a sense, the ideal number of children is the upper limit of the number that women personally want, given the realities of their lives. In order to focus more realistically on what the fertility of a population might be if women were to have the number they actually want, we next estimate the prevalence of unwanted births.

Wanted and Unwanted Fertility

The level of wanted fertility in a population is defined as the fertility that would prevail if no unwanted births occurred. Unwanted births are those reported by the mother that would never have occurred if her preference had prevailed. This 'excess' fertility is the fertility occurring after the last wanted birth and is not to be confused with births that were wanted but which occurred sooner than preferred. Although such timing failures can influence the lengths of birth intervals, which, in turn, can affect the age at maternity and thus the length of the generation and the rate of growth, their demographic importance is secondary to that of the magnitude of births that would never occur. The more important demographic potential of longer birth intervals lies in the 'later means fewer' effect, which reduces the amount of exposure to the risk of unwanted births.

The level of wanted or desired fertility has been measured in different ways in various studies. In this analysis as well as in the DHS Comparative Report on Reproductive Preferences (Westoff 1991), we have relied on the procedure developed by Lightbourne for WFS (Lightbourne 1985, 1987) that deletes births in the past year that exceed the desired number. This procedure was selected both because of our interest in comparing trends in countries that participated in both WFS and DHS and because there is some evidence (Bongaarts 1990) that relying on the women's report of unwanted births underestimates unwanted fertility.

The rates in Table 13.3 indicate that total fertility is still quite high in some of these countries, especially in Guatemala and Bolivia. The rates have declined significantly during the past decade in the countries for which we show data from two points in time. The level of wanted fertility is lower in Peru (2.3) than in its neighbour Ecuador (2.9). For all countries but Colombia, wanted fertility remains at a level that exceeds replacement. Except for Guatemala where wanted fertility is considerably higher (4.5) than replacement, the countries included here fall in the range from 2.1 to 2.9. In all countries, wanted fertility has declined substantially.

Table 13.3. *Latin America: TFRs with estimated desired and unwanted components for 12 months preceding the WFS and DHS inquiries, selected countries*

Country	Year	TFR	Total desired fertility rate	Total unwanted fertility rate	% unwanted
Bolivia	1987	5.0	2.8	2.2	44
Brazil	1986	3.4	2.2	1.2	35
Colombia	1978	4.5	3.4	1.1	24
	1987	2.9	2.1	0.8	28
Dominican	1975	5.1	3.8	1.3	25
Republic	1986	3.5	2.6	0.9	26
Ecuador	1979	5.2	4.1	1.1	21
	1987	4.4	2.9	1.5	34
Guatemala	1987	5.5	4.5	1.0	18
Mexico	1976	5.6	4.5	1.1	20
	1987	4.1	2.9	1.2	29
Peru	1977–8	5.1	3.5	1.6	31
	1986	4.0	2.3	1.7	42

Since wanted births comprise the major part of fertility, the results all point to the importance of studying reproductive intentions.

Reproductive Intentions

A recent analysis of the predictive validity of reproductive intentions (summarized in Appendix 13.1) has indicated that the proportion of women in the population that report they want no more children is a reasonably good predictor of the TFR several years (typically five years) later. It operates mainly through the intermediate variable of contraceptive practice. This evidence greatly increases confidence in the utility of such measures and makes intentions an important dependent variable in its own right.

The basic question on reproductive intentions asked in the DHS is: 'Would you like to have a (another) child or would you prefer not to have any (more) children?' This question was asked only of currently married women. In the WFS, the comparable questions on intentions were asked only of women who reported that it was physically possible to have a child whereas in the DHS all married women were asked the question. In order to achieve comparability, women classified as infecund in the DHS[1] are excluded from these tabulations (an average of 15 per cent). In fact, there is little difference between all married women and all married fecund women in the proportion who want no more children.[2]

The proportion of women who want no more children (Table 13.4) ranges across these countries from 47 to 75 per cent. These percentages would imply TFRs in the short-term future between 4.3 and 2.2, according to the regression equation connecting these two variables observed for eighty-seven populations (Westoff 1990). Such a forecast seems highly questionable especially for Bolivia and for Peru where recent surveys have estimated TFRs of 5.0 and 4.0 respectively for the mid-1980s. In the case of Bolivia, there would seem to be a considerable amount of unmet need if one believes the high proportion of women who report not wanting any more children. In Peru, there is also an extremely high proportion of women who wish to terminate childbearing, which would imply a contraceptive prevalence rate higher than the 46 per cent observed. This gap between intentions, contraceptive practice, and fertility in Bolivia and Peru is consistent with the high rate of unwanted fertility in these countries but a more realistic forecast is provided by combining both intentions and contraceptive practice. This equation predicts a TFR of 4.2 for Bolivia and 3.2 for Peru.

[1] A behavioural criterion of fecundity was developed for use in the DHS which classified as infecund those women who had had at least five years of exposure to the risk of pregnancy without any contraceptive use and who had not had a live birth during that period.

[2] The magnitude of the difference is typically a rate 1–2% higher when infecund women are excluded. The difference is greater at the older ages and higher marriage durations where the infecund would be concentrated.

Table 13.4. *Latin America: fertility rates predicted from the % who want no more childen and contraceptive prevalence rates selected countries*

Country	Year	%age who want no more[a]	Contra-ceptive prevalence	Current[b] TFR	Future TFR[c] predicted from	
					% want no more[a]	% want no more and contra-ceptive prevalence[e]
Bolivia	1989	68	30	5.0	2.7	4.2
Brazil	1986	64	66	3.4	3.0	2.4
Colombia	1986	69	63	2.9	2.7	2.4
Dominican Republic	1986	63	50	3.5	3.1	3.2
Ecuador	1987	65	44	4.4	3.0	3.5
Guatemala	1987	47	23	5.5	4.3	5.0
Mexico	1987	65	53	4.1	3.0	3.1
Peru	1986	75	46	4.0	2.2	3.2

a Based on denominator of all currently married, fecund women.
b Based on exposure in the 12 months preceding the survey.
c For the period approximately five years after the survey.
d TFR = 7.69 – 0.073 (WNM).
e TFR = 7.22 – 0.21 (WNM) – 0.053 (PREV).

A similar picture prevails in Ecuador and Guatemala where intentions have not yet been translated fully into contraceptive behaviour. In both countries, the fertility rate predicted from taking both intentions and contraceptive prevalence into account indicates a value about a half a child higher than that from intentions alone. On the other hand, the TFRs in Colombia, the Dominican Republic, and Mexico are similar whether predicted from intentions alone or from both intentions and contraceptive prevalence.

Brazil shows the reverse picture. The TFR predicted from intentions alone is 3.0; if the high prevalence rate in that country (66 per cent) is also included in the equation, the predicted TFR is 2.4.

The predictive validity of the equation including both intention and prevalence can be evaluated by examining how well it would have forecast the TFRs in these countries over the recent past. This exercise was conducted for six Latin American countries with the requisite data for eleven tests. The average difference between the predicted and the observed TFR (estimated five years later) is 8 per cent; all but one show a predicted value either the same or lower than that observed. The most deviant case is Peru with its gap between the high proportion of women wishing to terminate fertility and its contraceptive prevalence.

The proportions of women who want no more children are depicted in Fig. 13.1 by age and by number of living children. As would be expected, the proportion who wish to terminate childbearing increases with age and with parity. The high proportions who want no more in Peru and Bolivia are dramatically reflected in the teenage years and among women with no children. In both countries, the proportion exceeds 40 per cent among teenagers and is over 12 per cent among childless women. In all countries, the proportion who want no more children increases at each successive age (with only few exceptions) and with parity. In every country except Guatemala, the majority of women with two children now express a preference to terminate fertility, a change that, for the most part, has occurred in the past decade.

The effects of urban–rural residence and of education on reproductive intentions are illustrated in Fig. 13.2. In fact, residence shows hardly any effect except in Guatemala where women in the cities are significantly more likely to want no more children than women in rural areas.

There is some irregular tendency for the proportion intending to terminate fertility to decline with increasing education but the clearest finding is (again with the exception of Guatemala) that the highest proportion intending to avoid any further childbearing is in the category with little or no schooling and the lowest proportion is in the most highly educated group. This negative relationship between level of education and reproductive intention is consistent with the higher incidence of unwanted fertility in rural areas.[3]

For five of the countries, the same relationships are superimposed on the bar graphs (in Figs. 13.1 and 13.2) for data collected in the WFS. This permits examination of trends in the proportion who want no more births for different age-groups and parities, and by residential and educational groupings. There appears to be no concentration of the overall increase in the proportion who want no more children at any particular age or parity, although little change is evident among teenagers or childless women (except in Peru which does show an increase within the teenage population). Both rural and urban areas and all educational levels participated in the increase in the proportion wanting to terminate childbearing.

Summary and Conclusion

In this chapter we have reviewed reproductive preferences in eight Latin American countries based on DHS-I data and also on WFS data for five of the countries. Fertility norms in the form of the ideal number of children show values approximately between three and four children and reveal significant declines over the past decade. Declines in the TFR over the decade have been caused mainly by declines in the desired component, although unwanted births still account for 20 to 40 per cent of the TFR. About two-thirds of married women in these countries (lower in Guatemala and higher in Peru) say they want no more children. This information on reproductive intentions is combined with contraceptive prevalence to forecast the TFR for the period five years after the last

[3] See rates in the standard DHS First Country Reports.

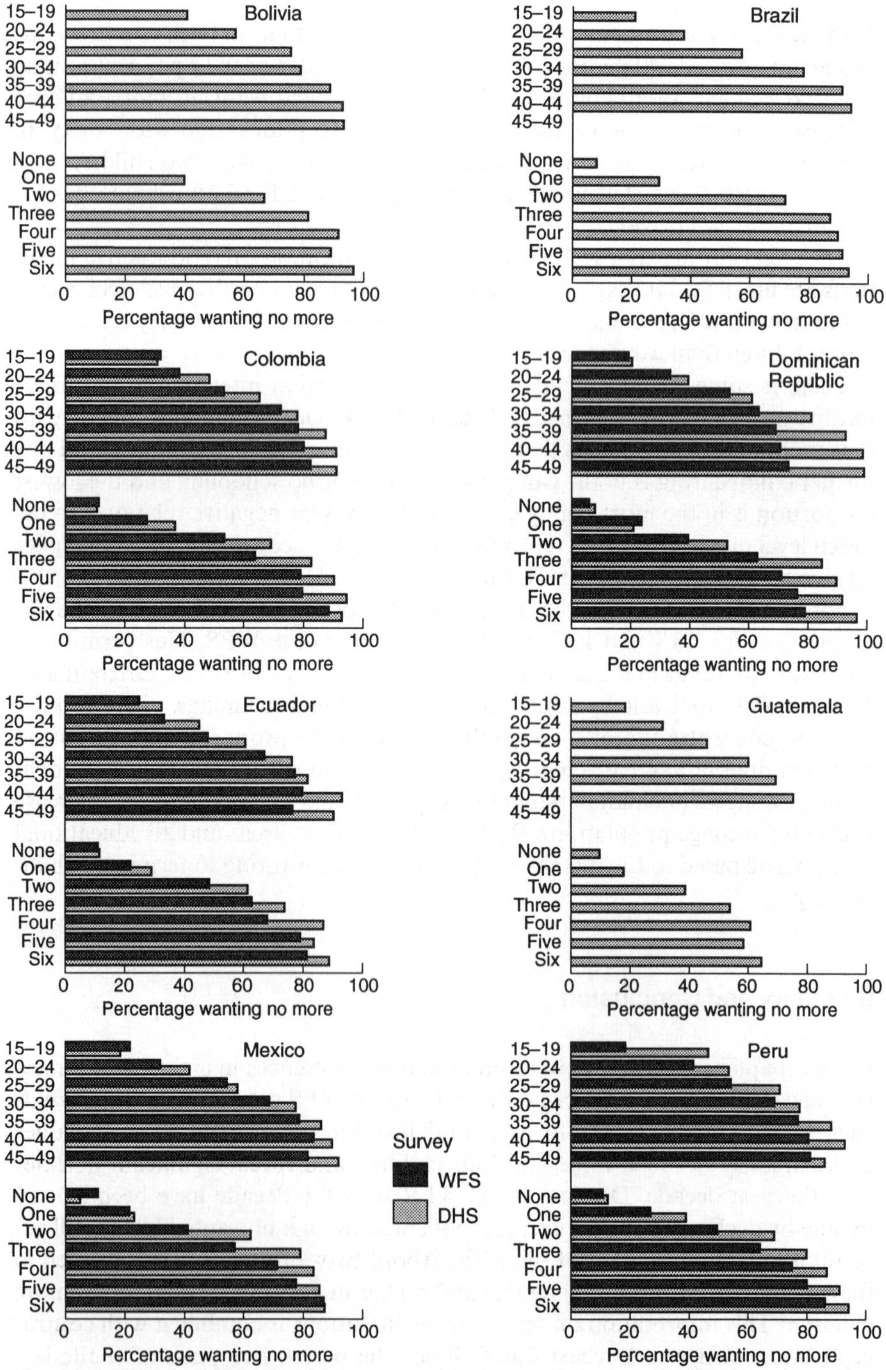

Fig. 13.1. ***Latin America: % among currently married women (excluding infecund) wanting no more children by age and parity***

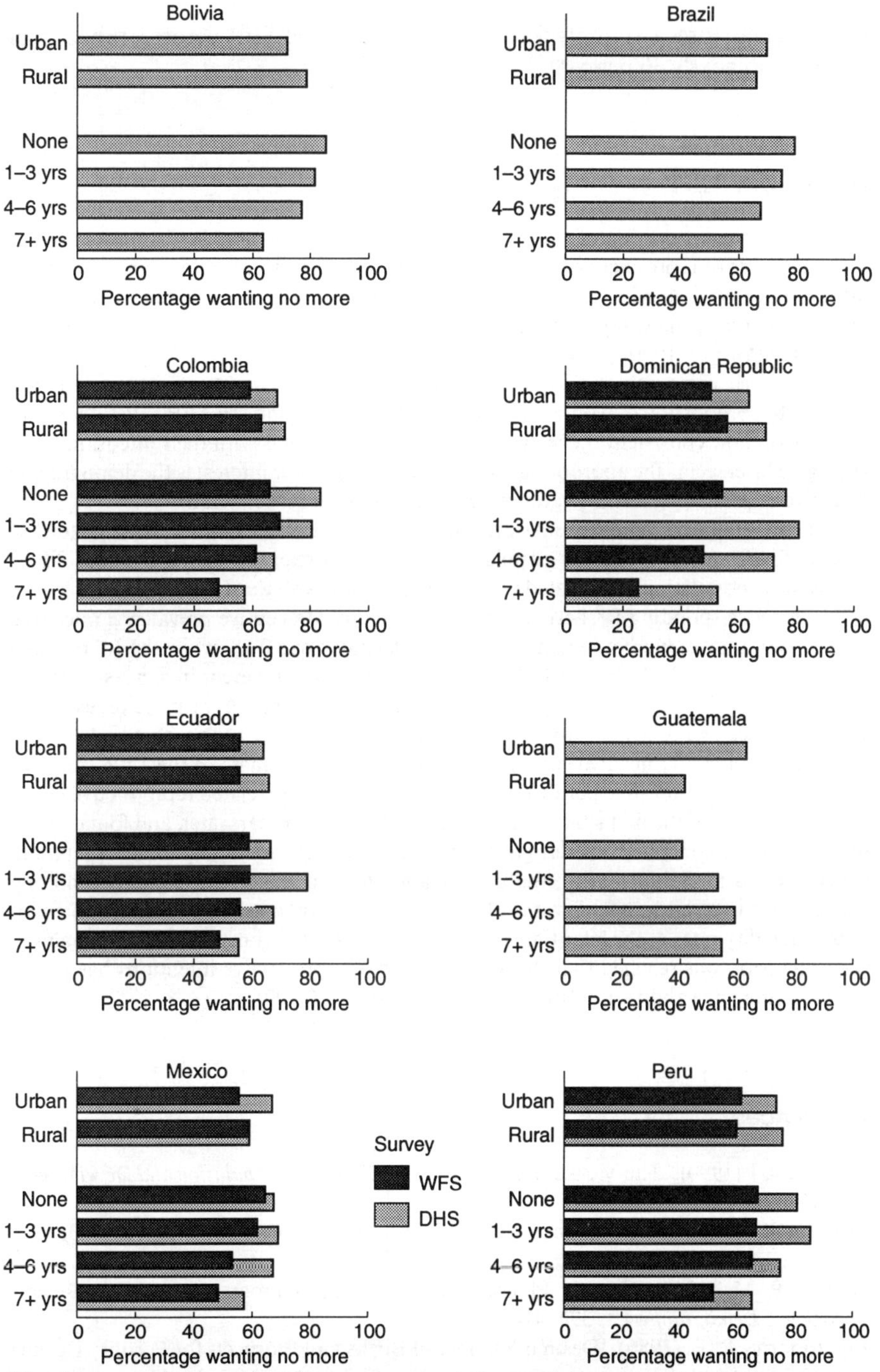

Fig. 13.2. ***Latin America: % among currently married women (excluding infecund) wanting no more children by residence and education***

survey. These forecasts imply further reductions in the TFR across a range from nearly 10 to nearly 30 per cent.

Appendix 13.1

Reliance on the proportion of women who report wanting no more births presumes that such measures of reproductive preference are valid predictors of fertility. Not all demographers have been convinced of this (Demeny 1988; Hauser 1967). It therefore seemed timely to evaluate the validity of reproductive intentions, a study that has recently been completed (Westoff 1990). We review the general results here.

Unlike earlier research on this topic, the basic strategy was to estimate the association between the proportion of women who want no more births and the TFR rate rather than focusing on how consistent the fertility of individual women is with their intentions. The aggregate level seems the appropriate one considering that our interest is the demographic objective of predicting fertility rates rather than in individual behaviour.

Data on intentions, contraceptive prevalence, and fertility rates were assembled for 134 surveys for 87 mostly national populations. The proportion of the variance of TFRs across these populations associated with the proportion who want no more children was 0.76. The corresponding R^2 between intentions and contraceptive prevalence rates (the mechanism intervening between intentions and fertility) was 0.78, while the R^2 between prevalence and the TFR was 0.91. To reduce the ambiguity inherent in a cross-sectional analysis, where fertility may be determining intentions (rather than the more plausible reverse sequence), we followed two strategies using the subset of countries that had data for two points in time (either two surveys or a survey and an estimate of the TFR from another source for a later time period). In the first analysis we correlated reproductive intentions at the time of the first survey with fertility rates 2.5 to 5 years later, and found an R^2 of 0.71. In the second analysis, designed to further reduce the ambiguity of interpretation, we controlled for initial parity; the proportion who wanted no more children among women with two children at the time of the first survey explained 80 per cent of the variance in fertility rates at the later time period. From these and from other similar analyses, the conclusion was reached that the measurement of reproductive intentions has a high level of aggregate validity. For further details see Westoff (1990).

References

Bongaarts, J. (1990), 'The Measurement of Wanted Fertility', *Population and Development Review* 16/3: 487–506.

Demeny, P. (1988), 'Social Science and Population Policy', *Population and Development Review* 14/3: 451–79.

Hauser, P. M. (1967), 'Family Planning and Population Programs: A Book Review Article', *Demography* 4/1: 397–414.

Lightbourne, R. E. (1985), 'Desired Number of Births and Prospects for Fertility Decline in 40 Countries', *International Family Planning Perspectives*, 11/2: 34–47.

—— (1987), 'Reproductive Preferences and Behavior', in J. Cleland, J. C. Scott (eds.), *The*

World Fertility Survey: An Assessment (Oxford: Oxford University Press), pp. 836–61.

Westoff, Charles F. (1990), 'Reproductive Intentions and Fertility Rates', *International Family Planning Perspectives*, 16/5: 84–9.

—— (1991), *Reproductive Preferences: A Comparative View* (DHS Comparative Studies, 3; Columbia: Macro International).

14 Social Change and Transitions in the Life Histories of Colombian Women

CARMEN ELISA FLÓREZ

Introduction

Modernization can be defined as a basic transformation in a country's economic and social organization. Economic aspects of this transformation include a sustained increase in real per capita income, and significant changes in the industrial, occupational, and geographic distribution of productive resources, as well as in the degree to which the economy is monetarized. Modernization also implies dramatic social changes, principally in education, public health services, and levels of urbanization. The economic and social changes generate changes in human behaviour, for example greater freedom from paternal authority, higher ambitions for individual advancement and for the advancement of one's children, as well as changes in demographic behaviour, including fertility, mortality, and migration, and, as a result, family structure.

The best-known change in demographic behaviour associated with modernization is the movement from high to low levels of mortality and fertility, a process known as the 'demographic transition'. A decline in mortality usually precedes a decline in fertility. The drop in fertility is usually accompanied by conscious limitation of family size and has been formally conceptualized as an evolution from a 'natural fertility regime' to one of deliberate fertility control (Easterlin 1983). Although this 'fertility transition' has accompanied the modernization process in all societies, the connection between the two processes is not very clear. As various authors have pointed out, fertility transitions have occurred under a wide range of conditions, in societies at different levels of modernization, and they have occurred at widely differing rates of change (Coale 1973; Knodel and van de Walle 1979).

The most common approaches to identifying the relationship between the modernization process and fertility transition are: (1) multivariate regression analyses between fertility and measures that reflect various aspects of social and economic modernization (education, urbanization, etc.), along with other possible determinants such as cultural conditions (race, religion, etc.) (Richards 1983); (2) analysis of the 'proximate determinants', in which modernization affects fertility only indirectly, through three groups of intermediate factors or variables: exposure to the risk of pregnancy, to conception, and to birth (Davis and

Blake 1956; Bongaarts 1978); and (3) an expansion of the proximate determinants approach, the 'synthesis framework', in which the modernization variables directly affect the demand for and supply of children and the costs of fertility regulation (Easterlin 1983). These three factors, in turn, determine the use of birth control. This last factor, along with the other proximate determinants, determines the level of fertility. All three methods may be used to analyse fertility at the individual level, as measured by the total number of live-born children, or at the social level, by the TFR.

In recent years, fertility analysis has increasingly emphasized the importance of a dynamic analysis of sequential decision-making. Accordingly, each birth is influenced by a different set of motivations and cultural and family circumstances. Among these changing conditions are the births themselves: each birth changes the family's circumstances so as to affect the probability and the timing of subsequent births (Namboodiri 1983). Although the framework for the analysis of proximate determinants is not appropriate for a dynamic analysis of the complex interactions between the individual life cycle and the process of social change, it does provide a comprehensive examination of how modernization and cultural variables can affect fertility decisions. However, although the focus on sequential decision-making for fertility is appealing, it requires longitudinal information on not only fertility but also socio-economic, demographic, and cultural variables.

This chapter will attempt to contribute to a dynamic analysis of Colombian fertility. Based on a life-history perspective, the relationships between fertility behaviour and certain modernization factors are conceptualized as being the result of a sequential process of decision-making. To this end, the life-histories of women are studied over a period of time that captures the changes that occur with demographic modernization. Specifically, this study has two basic aims. First, it attempts to document changes and differentials in how the early stages of the life history of Colombian women are organized, as a consequence of the demographic and structural changes associated with modernization. Secondly, it aims to document the association between the modernization variables and parity progression ratios, using basic elements of multivariate regression and life-table analysis.

Reference Framework: Demographic and Structural Changes in Colombia

Over the past five decades, Colombia has experienced the process widely known as the demographic transition. The proccss began towards the end of the 1930s, when mortality conditions began to improve. Life expectancy at birth rose from 44 years in 1938 to 61 years in 1978. Later, towards the beginning of the 1960s, fertility began to decline. The total fertility rate declined from 7.04 in 1960–4 to 4.6 in 1972–3, and to 3.2 in 1985, a reduction of somewhat more than 50 per cent in a little over twenty years. The declines in mortality and fertility occurred first in urban areas, followed about a dozen years later by reductions in rural areas (Ochoa 1980). According to the 1985 census, the TFR was 2.7 for urban areas and 4.6 for rural areas, but both these figures show a modern pattern of age-specific fertility typical of a population whose fertility is no longer 'natural' (Flórez *et al.* 1987). Furthermore, while this demographic process was initiated first in urban areas, it also began among the more advantaged socio-economic groups (Banguero 1983; Flórez 1990).

Both cross-sectional and longitudinal studies demonstrate the relationship between the fertility transition and the structural, social, and economic changes associated with modernization. Among the changes in the social structure are: increased levels of education, rapid urbanization, increased coverage by health services, women's increased participation in the labour force, and greater access to and use of family planning methods. Between 1938 and 1985, the illiteracy rate in Colombia dropped from 48 per cent to 18 per cent, while the primary school attendance rate[1] rose from 56 per cent in 1951 to 81 per cent in 1985. The proportion of the population living in urban centres went from 31 per cent in 1938 to 62 per cent in 1973 and to 67 per cent in 1985; that is, it doubled in a period of 35 years. The increased coverage by health services contributed to a decline in the infant mortality rate; from 200 deaths per 1,000 live births in 1938 to 61 per 1,000 in 1978, and to 40 per 1,000 in 1985. The female labour-force participation rate in rural areas[2] went from 16 per cent in 1971 to 27 per cent in 1980 and to 36 per cent in 1985. The use of contraceptive methods also increased significantly. The proportion of women in union using contraceptive methods rose from less than 15 per cent in 1969 to 63 per cent in 1986. This increase was made possible because of family planning programmes and services offered in public health centres and by private institutions. Since these two sectors began operations in the middle of the 1960s, they have succeeded in reaching high levels of coverage for prenatal services, contraceptive delivery, and medical care.

The demographic transition in Colombia has been subject to a wide range of studies of a cross-sectional nature that have made it possible to describe and measure the process. Similarly, recent longitudinal studies, developed by the Centro de Estudios sobre Desarrollo Económico (CEDE) (Centre for the Study of Economic Development) (Flórez 1989), provide evidence that demographic modernization has occurred through a variety of changes in the process of family-building, in both urban and rural parts of the country and across all socio-economic groups (Flórez 1989). These studies make clear that in Bogotá, a metropolitan urban centre, there have been substantial changes in the formation and expansion phases of family formation,[3] with large differences among

[1] The primary school attendance rate measures the ratio between the population that attends primary school and the total population that potentially should attend, that is the population 7–11 years of age.

[2] The rate of labour-force participation is defined as the ratio between the economically active population and the population of working age.

[3] The family is formed with union or marriage, and is expanded by the birth of children.

socio-economic groups. However, in rural areas, there has been considerable change in the expansion, but not in the formation, phase, with little difference across socio-economic groups. For urban women in the highest socio-economic classes, changes in nuptiality have contributed to a decline in their fertility. For urban women in the middle and lower socio-economic groups, and for all rural women, nuptiality has not played an important role in fertility decline. Women in union, whether urban or rural and in all socio-economic classes, have reduced the size of their families by means of a significant increase in their use of contraceptive methods (Flórez 1989).

Data Source and Methodology

The Data

This analysis uses information from both the longitudinal urban survey of Bogotá in 1984 and the rural survey of 1986, both carried out by the CEDE of the University of Los Andes. These surveys were designed to collect life-histories, based on demographic and socio-demographic variables, for two cohorts of women considered to represent behaviour before and after the demographic transition. The urban study was based on a sample of women born between 1935 and 1939 (older cohort), and 1955 and 1959 (younger cohort). A two-stage, pre-stratified probability sample was employed,[4] yielding 1,074 completed interviews (496 from the older cohort and 578 from the younger). The rural study was designed to represent the rural population of the highlands of the Andean region (Altiplano of Cundinaboyaca), an area of the country in which cultural and geographical patterns are similar to those of Bogotá, having better socio-economic conditions than the national rural average.[5] The rural study selected women born between 1937–46 (older cohort) and 1955–61 (younger cohort). A two-stage probability sample was used and yielded 1,111 completed interviews (578 from the older cohort and 533 from the younger). The selected dwellings were post-stratified by household conditions, state of tenancy, source of economic support, isolation, and access to public and community services. Cluster analysis and factorial analysis were used to constitute two socio-economic classes, high and low.[6]

The rural and urban surveys used similar questionnaires to obtain information on women and their households at the time of interview and to collect life-history

[4] The stratification of dwellings prepared by the National Administrative Statistics Department (DANE) in 1981 was used; this stratification was done by type of construction, quality of the dwelling unit, availability of services, location and other related information. The six groups identified by DANE were separated into two: a lower stratum, including groups 1 and 2, and an upper stratum, made up of groups 3 to 6.

[5] This area has easy access to urban centres, better water and electric services, and higher educational levels than the average for Colombia.

[6] The initial analysis defined three social classes: high, middle, and low. However, the large differences between the upper and lower classes, and the relative similarity between the behaviour of the high and middle groups, led to a subsequent redefinition of only two classes: high and low.

information with respect to residence, education, paid work, unpaid work (household work and production for home consumption in rural areas), nuptiality, fertility, and family planning. The life-history matrix of women is the principal source of information for this article. The availability of complete life histories with respect to residence, education, paid work, cohabitation, fertility, and use of family planning not only allows the reconstruction of each woman's activities for every age from 12 to 25 years,[7] it also permits an analysis of the likelihood of certain demographic events (transitions) that influence reproduction (parity progression ratios), as well as their relationship in the course of a woman's life to certain modernization factors.

Methodology

This study has two basic objectives. First, it attempts to document changes and differentials in how the early stages of Colombian women's life history are organized to respond to demographic and structural changes associated with modernization. Secondly, it aims to document the relationship between the modernization variables and parity progression ratios, using basic elements of multivariate regression and life tables (proportional hazard life-table models).

The first objective is, therefore, to describe differences in the experiences of the two cohorts of women in terms of various private and socio-economic activities undertaken in the course of their lives. Given that the selected cohorts represent behaviour before and after the demographic transition, these differentials provide an indicator of the effect of demographic and socio-economic modernization on the organization of the early stages of the life histories of Colombian women. With the information, it is possible to reconstruct women's activities between the ages of 12 and 25 in four major areas: participation in the educational system, in paid work, in nuptiality (living with a husband), and in motherhood (having children). The differentials also make it possible to study combinations of those activities. In order to describe the experiences of each cohort, the number of women active in each of these four areas was calculated for each age from 12 to 25. From this information, the proportion of person-years in each activity, and in combinations of them, were calculated for women aged 12–25.[8] This information indicates levels of each activity by women's age. Hence, the mixture of activities characterizes the nature of the life history. For this analysis, sixteen possible combinations of education, paid work, marriage, and motherhood were identified.

The second major objective of the study is a dynamic analysis of fertility. For this purpose, marriage (cohabitation) and the individual reproductive behaviour

[7] The upper age limit is 25 years since the experience of the younger cohorts is incomplete.

[8] For each age, the survey looks at the activity of the woman in each of the life areas. Since any activity in one area during part of the year is treated as a person-year of activity, this analysis overestimates the number of person-years spent in each area and in the combinations of areas. This is particularly true for the more discontinuous activities, such as work.

(fertility) of women were considered to be the dependent variables. Based on the life-history perspective that is the framework for the information, the relationships between these dependent variables and the independent variables (represented by the modernization variables) are conceptualized as the result of a sequential decision-making process. Specifically, life-table models based on proportional hazards were used. The hazard is the probability that an event (transition) will occur at a particular moment (or age) to a particular individual, given that the individual is exposed to the risk at that moment. The hazard determines the occurrence and the time of occurrence of the events, and is, therefore, the fundamental unit of analysis in a model of the history of events (Allison, 1984). The dependent variable of interest is whether an event (marriage, or a birth of order n) occurs to a person exposed to the risk of experiencing that event (a single woman, or a woman of parity n-1 respectively) during the year (age) of exposure to the risk (during the first, second, third, and so forth, year of exposure to the risk of the event). Included as independent variables are female education, participation in the labour force (experience and occupational status), origin (place of birth), place of residence, use of family planning methods, and other demographic control variables.

Results

Activities during the Initial Stages of Women's Life Histories

Attending School The opportunity to enrol in a country's educational system has historically always been greater in urban areas than in rural areas, and when education is neither free nor compulsory, a child's chance of receiving a school education also depends on the family's income level. These differences are reflected in age-specific patterns of school attendance in Colombia (Table 14.A1). School attendance is substantially lower among rural women, and increases in school attendance from one cohort to another are also smaller in the rural sector. For example, among young rural women of the high socio-economic group, fewer than one-third stayed in school after the age of 13, which corresponds to the beginning of secondary school. In contrast, there were notable increases in school attendance among urban women, with half of the young urban cohort of the high socio-economic group staying in school until the age of 17. Furthermore, almost one-third—a high proportion—of young urban women from the high socio-economic group were still in school at around the age of 20.

In summary, young rural women from the low socio-economic group spend less than 10 per cent of this period of their lives in school, compared with nearly 50 per cent for young urban women in the high group (Table 14.1). Thus, involvement in the educational system has become an increasingly important activity for the more recent cohorts of women, an aspect of their lives that is closely linked to changes in the country's socio-economic structure.

Table 14.1. *Colombia: % of person-years between the ages of 12 and 25 spent in certain activities, by socio-economic group, cohort, and area of residence*

Cohort and area	Both strata			Lower stratum						Upper stratum			
	In school	Working		In union	With children	In school	In labour force	In union	With children	In school	In labour force	In union	With children
		Labour force	Paid work										
Total:													
Younger	34.2	35.8	25.8	32.5	27.6	20.8	39.3	36.2	31.8	41.5	34.0	30.5	25.4
Older	15.6	31.5	18.5	37.3	28.8	7.4	38.1	39.1	32.0	18.8	28.9	37.0	27.6
Urban:													
Younger	37.7	31.1	28.0	31.9	26.6	23.2	33.7	35.5	30.7	45.3	29.8	30.0	24.4
Older	17.4	24.0	20.1	37.0	28.2	8.3	26.6	37.4	31.4	20.4	23.1	36.9	27.1
Rural:													
Younger	13.7	63.3	13.5	36.4	33.9	9.5	66.0	39.6	36.8	16.6	61.3	34.2	31.8
Older	7.3	66.1	11.1	38.6	31.8	5.1	69.6	40.1	33.4	8.9	63.5	37.5	30.6

Joining and Being in the Female Labour Force Fewer than one-quarter of women are involved in productive work[9] at the age of 12 or 13. Among young urban women in the high socio-economic class, the percentage engaged in productive work increases substantially up to the age of 22, reaching somewhat more than half the cohort, but remaining almost constant at later ages (Table 14.A2). Thus, it is clear that productive work has become much more common among recent urban cohorts. Among rural women in the low group, the proportion engaged in productive work rises to almost 70 per cent by the age of 15, and changes only slightly at higher ages. Hence, rural women, in both the younger and the older cohorts, spend a larger part of their early adult years in productive work; more than 60 per cent of time between the ages of 12 and 25 years (Table 14.1).

However, the pattern of labour-force participation is quite different in rural areas, if we consider solely paid work (Table 14.A2).[10] The young rural cohort dedicates only 13 per cent of this period to paid work, while the young urban cohort dedicates 28 per cent. In both rural and urban areas, the proportion of time spent in paid activities increases between cohorts, thus providing evidence of some kind of a shift towards paid work on the part of the more recent cohorts.

Marital Experience The proportion of women in union (whether legal or consensual) in each cohort follows a typical pattern. Union starts at the age of 15, and rises to 75 per cent by the age of 25 (Table 14.A3). Rural women enter union at earlier ages than do urban women. Nuptial experiences by socio-economic class indicate that the women in the higher groups marry somewhat later, and by age 25, a slightly lower proportion is in a marital relationship. In urban areas, among young women in the low socio-economic group, close to 36 per cent of time between the ages of 12 and 25 was spent in marital union, compared to 30 per cent among their contemporaries in the high socio-economic group (Table 14.1).

Initial Stages of the Reproductive Experience The fertility transition generally manifests itself through a drop in fertility rates after the age of 25 years, and especially among women of high parity, as a consequence of increased use of contraceptive methods. This is evident from the proportion of women who have had at least one child by age 12–25, since this finding reveals behaviour patterns that are much less differentiated between the two cohorts (Table 14.A4). In practice, somewhat more than one-quarter of the person-years of urban women, and one-third of those of rural women were spent with at least one child. None the less, the proportion of women with at least one child is closely related to the findings on nuptiality, that is, there are substantial residential differences by socio-economic class. The younger urban women of both the upper and the lower socio-economic group initiated their reproductive roles later than did older women. Among the lower classes living in rural areas, younger women started their reproductive lives

[9] All productive activities, paid or not, are included. In rural areas, farm work, work in market gardens, and work in a family business are all included, whether the work is done to create produce for home consumption, for sale, or for barter.

[10] In urban areas, productive work and paid work are considered the same thing.

earlier than did older women, while in the upper socio-economic group, there was no difference. For example, by age 18, 30 per cent of younger rural women in the lower socio-economic class had already had at least one child, whereas only 20 per cent of the older cohort had done so.

The complexity and differentials in early life histories for the two cohorts of women are shown in Tables 14.A1–4, by area of residence. There were large increases in school attendance among the more recent cohorts, this being higher among urban women. Labour-market participation became more common among the urban cohorts, but changed less among rural women. At the same time, labour-force entry occurs at later ages among urban women, because they are staying in school longer. The time spent in marital union is shorter for urban woman than for rural women, declining between cohorts only in the upper socio-economic group. Fertility experiences at early ages indicate that urban women start their reproductive role somewhat later, while rural women in the lower socio-economic groups do so earlier. This behaviour is closely linked to nuptiality patterns.

In addition to differences in the amount of time spent in each of these life areas, the early stages of women's life histories are influenced by the way in which these different activities are combined at each age. The combinations of these 'demographic' activities are what determine, for example, a woman's classification in one of the groups commonly recognized as 'student', 'working mother', or 'traditional wife and mother'. To identify these patterns, the activities are cross-classified (yes/no) in each of the four life areas for every year of age from 12 to 25, by cohort and by area of residence (Table 14.2).

One of the most common combinations of activities is illustrated by women who remain in the educational system while single, childless and not engaged in productive activity, that is 'students'. This role is most predominant among higher-class urban women of the more recent birth cohort. Other common combinations are 'working woman' (not in school, working, single, and childless) and 'working mother' (not in school, working, in union, and with children). Two quite common classifications in both cohorts are the 'traditional wife' (not in school, not working, in union, and with children), and 'waiting' (a transitional state in which a woman is not attending school, has no productive work, and is still single and childless). Notwithstanding, the changes between cohorts have reduced the importance of these two last roles, especially among urban women. The more recent cohorts have had the advantage of better opportunities for investment in human capital and have received returns on these investments through productive work. This is particularly true for younger urban women of the upper stratum, who are the group that possesses the resources and opportunities for this type of life.

Modernization and Reproductive Behaviour

We shall restrict ourselves here to an analysis of the relationship between the modernization variables and parity progression ratios at second- and third-order

Table 14.2. *Colombia: % of person-years between the ages of 12 and 25 spent by women in combinations of activities, by cohort, origin, and area of residence*

Activity				Total		Rural		Urban	
Education	Employment	Marital Status	Children	Younger	Older	Younger	Older	Younger	Older
In school	Working	In union	Children	0.5	0.0	0.2	0.1	0.6	0.0
In school	Working	In union	No children	0.6	0.1	0.2	0.1	0.6	0.1
In school	Working	Not in union	Children	0.1	0.0	0.0	0.1	0.1	0.0
In school	Working	Not in union	No children	4.8	1.7	5.3	2.7	4.7	1.4
In school	Not working	In union	Children	1.2	0.2	0.0	0.0	1.4	0.3
In school	Not working	In union	No children	0.8	0.4	0.0	0.0	0.9	0.5
In school	Not working	Not in union	Children	0.2	0.0	0.1	0.0	0.2	0.1
In school	Not working	Not in union	No children	25.9	13.2	7.8	4.4	29.1	15.0
Not in school	Working	In union	Children	8.6	8.5	19.8	21.8	6.6	5.6
Not in school	Working	In union	No children	2.8	3.4	4.8	7.2	2.5	2.6
Not in school	Working	Not in union	Children	1.8	1.2	3.2	2.1	1.6	1.0
Not in school	Working	Not in union	No children	16.7	16.6	29.8	32.1	14.4	13.2
Not in school	Not working	In union	Children	14.4	17.7	9.6	6.9	15.2	20.1
Not in school	Not working	In union	No children	3.7	6.9	1.9	2.5	4.0	7.9
Not in school	Not working	Not in union	Children	0.8	1.1	1.2	0.8	0.8	1.2
Not in school	Not working	Not in union	No children	17.1	28.9	16.2	19.3	17.3	31.0

Table 14.3. *Colombia: proportional hazards model of the risk of having a second child by age, among married women*

Variable and category	Urban	Rural
Education level		
None	1.172	1.076
Incomplete primary	1.024	1.120
Complete primary	1.000	1.000
Incomplete secondary	0.722**	0.802[a]
Complete secondary +	0.558**	
Occupational experience		
None	1.000**	1.000
Industry	0.737**	1.014
Services	0.651**	0.690**
Household work	0.592**	0.718**
Agriculture	n.a.	0.749**
Occupational status		
Does not work	1.000	1.000
Unpaid work	1.193	1.089
Paid work	1.144	1.094
Type of place of origin		
Urban	1.000	0.944
Rural	0.907	1.000
Type of place of residence		
Urban	1.000	0.847
Rural	304.0**	1.000
Use of contraception		
None	1.000	1.000
Modern methods	0.836*	0.588**
Traditional methods	0.808*	0.938
Age at first union		
Before age 20	203.7**	3.561**
20–23	1.000	1.000
After age 23	0.252**	0.279**
Log likelihood	–2772.59	–3304.23
Model Chi Square Statistic	674.89	663.27
degrees of freedom	15	15
N	833	909
Wilcoxon Chi Square Statistic	27.64	14.66
Savage Chi Square Statistic	28.93	19.02
degrees of freedom	5	5

Notes: * = p-value < 0.05; ** = p-value < 0.01 (both two-tailed)

[a] In the rural models the two highest educational categories were combined into one.

parities. Proportional hazards life-table models were estimated, and were grouped ('stratified') by cohort and by socio-economic class (Tables 14.3 and 14.4). All variables were considered to be categorical and refer to the time the event occurred or to the time of the survey, if the information for the woman is incomplete with respect to the event in question.

Relationships between the modernization variables and fertility are similar for second- and third-order parity. The probability of having a second (or third) child

Table 14.4. *Colombia: proportional hazards model of the risk of having a third child by age, among married women*

Variable and category	Urban	Rural
Education level		
None	0.974	1.060
Incomplete primary	0.864	1.188*
Complete primary	1.000	1.000
Incomplete secondary	0.698**	1.092*[a]
Complete secondary +	0.570**	
Occupational experience		
None	1.000	1.000
Industry	0.951	1.082
Services	0.807*	0.834
Household work	0.683**	1.056
Agriculture	n.a.	0.821*
Occupational status		
Does not work	1.000	1.000
Unpaid work	1.187	1.170*
Paid work	0.964	1.693**
Type of place of origin		
Urban	1.000	0.892
Rural	1.024	1.000
Type of place of residence		
Urban	1.000	0.748**
Rural	1.213**	1.000
Use of contraception		
None	1.000	1.000
Modern methods	0.745**	0.295**
Traditional methods	0.771*	0.841
Age at first union		
Before age 20	222.9**	4.552**
20–23	1.000	1.000
After age 23	250.4**	0.200**
Log likelihood	–2025.1	–2876.82
Model Chi Square Statistic	552.06	731.52
degrees of freedom	15	15
N	724	867
Wilcoxon Chi Square Statistic	26.50	5.21
Savage Chi Square Statistic	29.58	7.67
degrees of freedom	5	5

Notes: * = p-value < 0.05; ** = p-value < 0.01 (both two-tailed)

[a] In the rural models the two highest educational categories were combined into one.

is strongly affected by women's educational level and their work experience. The urban and rural results consistently show that educational level exerts an effect that takes the form of an inverted J: completion of primary school is the point beyond which education begins to have a depressive effect on the probability that the demographic events will occur. If this is related to the life histories of urban and rural women discussed in the preceding section, it is clear that the high degree to which young urban women stay in school has been largely responsible for their greater change in fertility. In spite of the increased educational participation of rural women, they do not remain in the system long enough, and frequently do not even complete their primary schooling. On the other hand, urban women, and especially those in the upper socio-economic classes, attain secondary and higher levels of education (Flórez 1989).

Labour-force experience exerts a negative effect on fertility, independently of the type of working activity, while occupational status (whether the work is paid or not) does not show either consistent or significant effects. It appears that the relationship between working and the likelihood of any of the demographic events is determined not only by the type of activity, but also by contact with the labour-market. Experience in modern or traditional activities, as compared with the experience of non-working women, reduces the likelihood of these events. However, the effects of work experience are stronger in urban than in rural areas, suggesting, as might be expected, a greater opportunity cost of the woman's time in urban areas. The non-significance of occupational status suggests that decisions about fertility are a cumulative process throughout life, and are not affected by labour-force status once the decision has been made. The fact that the effect shows up through work experience and not through occupational status would suggest that the effect of work activity on fertility is a long-term, and not a short-term, effect.

The results by residence indicate that even though origin (place of birth) does not have an important effect on these demographic probabilities, place of residence at the time of the event has a stronger effect. This is evidence of the influence of greater access to educational, health, and contraceptive services; improvements in the infrastructure in general; the rising costs of raising children; and the opportunity cost of time for women living in urban areas.

In urban and rural areas, the practice of family planning showed significant and depressive effects on the probability of attaining second- or third-order parity, the effect being stronger for higher parity. The significance of this variable demonstrates the important role that family planning has had in Colombia's fertility transition.

General Conclusions

The changes in Colombia's social structure that have occurred over the past several decades involved changes in many interrelated aspects of life, such as health, education, labour-force participation, rural–urban migration, and human behaviour, especially on the part of women (who demonstrated greater independence and more ambition to improve their status). All these changes, in turn, affected fertility levels and how Colombian women organized the early stages of their life histories, these effects being sharply differentiated according to women's socio-economic class and area of residence.

Among the younger cohort of urban women, especially the upper socio-economic groups, attendance at secondary school and university became fairly common. Remaining in the educational system for a longer period is associated with some delay in family formation. Previously, the lives of adolescent women were not structured through contact with educational establishments or the labour-market. Perhaps the main impact of the increased importance of school attendance is the structure that this lends to young women's lives. The increasing importance of women's participation in economic activity led to a positive return on the investment in education, thus providing even more structure to young women's lives. This is especially noticeable in urban areas, where opportunities for paid work are more common.

In most circumstances, higher levels of education and greater participation in paid work reduce fertility. The connection between fertility, education, and work (both labour-force experience and occupational status)—the modernization variables—is conceptualized as the result of a sequential decision-making process. The results provide evidence that the depressive effect of education does not appear until certain levels of education have been reached. It appears from the findings that completed primary education is the level at which education begins to have a negative effect on the probability of high parity levels. The effect of working seems to be a long-term, rather than a short-term, one.

Place of residence plays an important role in determining the likelihood that the demographic events related to fertility will occur. Women living in urban areas generally have access to better education, a broader range of job opportunities—especially access to paid work—a more favourable public health setting, better access to contraceptive methods, and improved chances for social mobility, while they face greater financial and opportunity costs in raising children. The practice of family planning methods has a significant effect, and the effect is even more pronounced for births of higher order. This demonstrates the important role played by the availability and acceptance of contraceptive methods in Colombia's fertility transition.

Appendices

Table 14.A1. *Colombia: % of women studying by age, and % of person-years spent studying (PYSS) between ages 12 and 25, by cohort, socio-economic status, and area of residence*

Cohort and age	All			Urban			Rural		
	All	Low	High	All	Low	High	All	Low	High
Younger cohort									
12	76.9	66.0	82.9	80.8	69.4	86.7	54.4	49.6	57.9
13	64.3	48.1	73.2	69.2	52.3	78.1	35.3	28.1	40.5
14	56.4	38.8	66.1	62.0	44.0	71.4	24.0	14.3	31.1
15	52.6	31.7	64.1	58.5	36.2	70.2	17.8	10.3	23.3
16	46.3	27.1	56.9	51.9	31.1	62.9	13.7	8.0	17.8
17	37.0	22.7	44.9	41.4	26.5	49.2	11.3	4.5	16.2
18	30.3	18.0	37.0	33.8	20.8	40.6	9.8	4.9	13.3
19	23.4	11.2	30.1	26.3	12.9	33.3	6.6	3.1	9.1
20	21.4	8.0	28.8	24.3	9.1	32.3	4.5	3.1	5.5
21	18.2	3.7	26.2	20.6	3.9	29.4	3.9	2.7	4.9
22	16.4	4.6	22.8	18.6	5.1	25.6	3.6	2.2	4.5
23	13.9	4.7	19.0	15.8	5.4	21.2	3.0	1.8	3.9
24	12.2	4.4	16.6	14.0	5.2	18.7	1.9	0.4	2.9
25	8.9	2.8	12.3	10.2	3.3	13.9	1.3	0.4	1.9
PYSS (12–25)	34.2	20.8	41.5	37.7	23.2	45.3	13.7	9.5	16.6
Older cohort									
12	53.0	35.0	59.9	56.9	37.2	63.3	34.9	28.9	39.3
13	41.5	25.2	47.8	45.2	27.8	51.0	24.2	18.2	28.6
14	34.4	17.4	41.0	38.7	20.3	44.8	14.7	9.5	18.5
15	28.1	11.4	34.5	32.3	14.1	38.2	8.8	4.1	12.2
16	18.3	5.9	23.1	21.1	7.0	25.8	5.2	2.9	6.8
17	15.3	2.9	20.1	17.8	3.5	22.5	3.8	1.2	5.7
18	9.6	1.7	12.6	11.0	1.9	14.0	3.3	1.2	4.8
19	5.8	1.2	7.6	6.7	1.3	8.4	2.1	0.8	3.0
20	4.1	1.3	5.2	4.7	1.3	5.8	1.7	1.2	2.1
21	3.1	1.2	3.8	3.5	1.1	4.3	1.2	1.7	0.9
22	2.1	0.7	2.6	2.3	0.5	2.9	0.9	1.2	0.6
23	1.6	0.1	2.1	1.8	0.0	2.4	0.5	0.4	0.6
24	1.1	0.1	1.4	1.2	0.0	1.6	0.5	0.4	0.6
25	0.7	0.1	1.0	0.8	0.0	1.0	0.5	0.4	0.6
26	0.6	0.3	0.7	0.6	0.3	0.8	0.3	0.4	0.3
27	0.5	0.1	0.6	0.6	0.0	0.8	0.2	0.4	0.0
28	0.5	0.1	0.6	0.6	0.0	0.8	0.2	0.4	0.0
29	0.6	0.1	0.7	0.6	0.0	0.8	0.2	0.4	0.0
30	0.6	0.1	0.8	0.7	0.0	0.9	0.3	0.4	0.3
31	0.5	0.1	0.7	0.6	0.0	0.8	0.3	0.4	0.3
32	0.5	0.1	0.6	0.6	0.0	0.8	0.2	0.4	0.0
33	0.4	0.1	0.6	0.5	0.0	0.7	0.2	0.4	0.0
34	0.5	0.3	0.6	0.6	0.3	0.7	0.2	0.4	0.0
35	0.5	0.3	0.6	0.6	0.3	0.7	0.2	0.4	0.0
36	0.9	0.5	1.0	1.0	0.5	1.2	0.2	0.4	0.0
37	0.7	0.1	0.9	0.8	0.0	1.1	0.2	0.4	0.0
38	0.7	0.1	0.9	0.8	0.0	1.1	0.2	0.4	0.0
39	0.7	0.3	0.8	0.8	0.3	1.0	0.2	0.4	0.0
40	0.4	0.3	0.5	0.5	0.3	0.6	0.2	0.4	0.0
PYSS (12–25)	15.6	7.4	18.8	17.4	8.3	20.4	7.3	5.1	8.9

Table 14.A2. *Colombia: % of women working by age, and % of person-years spent working (PYSW) between ages 12 and 25, by cohort, socio-economic status, and area of residence*

Cohort and age	All			Urban			Rural		
	All	Low	High	All	Low	High	All	Low	High
Younger cohort									
12	11.0	16.3	8.1	5.5	10.1	3.1	43.3	46.0	41.4
13	12.8	19.7	9.0	7.0	13.4	3.7	46.7	50.0	44.3
14	16.3	24.6	11.7	10.4	18.5	6.2	50.3	53.6	47.9
15	23.5	31.6	19.0	17.4	24.9	13.4	59.1	63.4	56.0
16	28.9	37.9	23.9	23.1	31.8	18.5	62.9	67.0	59.9
17	34.5	44.1	29.2	29.2	38.7	24.3	64.9	69.6	61.5
18	39.4	48.2	34.6	34.6	42.7	30.3	67.4	74.1	62.5
19	40.7	46.4	37.6	36.1	41.1	33.5	67.7	71.9	64.7
20	44.1	48.0	42.0	39.5	42.7	37.9	71.1	73.2	69.6
21	46.8	47.8	46.2	42.8	42.6	42.9	69.8	72.8	67.6
22	50.7	46.2	53.1	47.3	41.0	50.6	70.2	71.0	69.6
23	51.6	46.9	54.2	48.2	41.9	51.5	71.3	70.5	71.8
24	50.3	46.2	52.5	46.7	41.2	49.5	71.1	70.1	71.8
25	51.2	45.9	54.1	47.9	40.7	51.7	70.4	71.0	69.9
PYSW (12–25)	35.8	39.3	34.0	31.1	33.7	29.8	63.3	66.0	61.3
Older cohort									
12	13.9	21.8	10.8	7.6	13.0	5.8	42.9	45.9	40.8
13	16.1	25.2	12.6	9.5	15.7	7.5	46.5	51.2	43.2
14	18.8	28.3	15.2	11.9	18.4	9.8	50.7	55.4	47.3
15	24.2	35.9	19.7	16.3	24.3	13.6	60.9	67.8	56.0
16	27.2	39.2	22.5	19.2	27.8	16.3	64.0	70.2	59.5
17	32.5	41.6	28.9	24.8	30.1	23.1	67.6	73.1	63.7
18	36.8	43.3	34.4	29.6	31.7	28.9	70.2	74.8	67.0
19	37.0	41.0	35.5	29.6	28.6	30.0	71.1	74.8	68.5
20	39.6	43.4	38.1	31.8	31.3	32.0	75.3	76.4	74.4
21	37.9	41.7	36.5	30.1	28.9	30.5	74.0	76.9	72.0
22	39.5	42.2	38.5	31.9	29.7	32.6	74.9	76.4	73.8
23	39.4	43.1	37.9	31.6	30.8	31.9	75.1	76.9	73.8
24	38.0	42.5	36.3	29.8	29.7	29.9	75.8	77.3	74.7
25	39.8	44.7	37.9	32.0	32.8	31.7	75.8	77.3	74.7
26	39.7	44.1	38.1	31.9	32.2	31.8	75.8	76.4	75.3
27	39.5	45.5	37.2	31.8	34.1	31.1	75.1	76.4	74.1
28	38.8	44.9	36.5	31.1	33.3	30.4	74.6	76.4	73.2
29	37.7	43.1	35.6	30.0	31.2	29.6	73.2	75.6	71.4
30	38.1	44.2	35.7	30.4	32.8	29.6	73.5	75.2	72.3
31	37.7	42.8	35.7	30.3	31.7	29.9	71.6	73.1	70.5
32	38.1	43.6	35.9	30.8	32.8	30.2	71.5	73.1	70.2
33	39.0	43.0	37.4	31.9	31.4	32.0	71.8	74.4	69.9
34	40.9	44.2	39.6	34.2	33.3	34.5	71.5	74.0	69.6
35	43.8	47.4	42.4	37.7	37.8	37.6	72.0	73.6	70.8
36	44.8	46.5	44.2	38.9	36.7	39.7	72.0	73.1	71.1
37	44.7	47.1	43.8	38.6	37.2	39.1	72.7	74.0	71.7
38	44.9	49.5	43.2	38.8	40.6	38.2	73.4	74.0	72.9
39	44.8	50.7	42.5	38.6	42.1	37.5	73.4	74.4	72.6
40	45.1	50.7	43.0	38.9	42.1	37.9	73.7	74.4	73.2
PYSW (12–25)	31.5	38.1	28.9	24.0	26.6	23.1	66.1	69.6	63.5

Table 14.A3. *Colombia: % of women in union by age, and % of person-years spent in union (PYSU) between ages 12 and 25, by cohort, socio-economic status, and area of residence*

Cohort and age	All			Urban			Rural		
	All	Low	High	All	Low	High	All	Low	High
Younger cohort									
12	0.1	0.3	0.0	0.1	0.3	0.0	0.0	0.0	0.0
13	0.3	0.9	0.0	0.4	1.0	0.0	0.2	0.0	0.3
14	1.8	3.2	1.0	1.9	3.4	1.1	1.1	1.8	0.6
15	4.8	7.1	3.6	4.9	7.2	3.7	4.3	6.3	2.9
16	10.1	12.0	9.0	9.8	11.7	8.8	11.6	13.4	10.4
17	17.1	18.9	16.1	16.6	17.9	15.8	20.5	23.7	18.1
18	25.5	29.5	23.2	24.1	27.9	22.1	33.4	37.1	30.7
19	36.4	41.6	33.5	35.2	40.2	32.5	43.5	48.2	40.1
20	45.0	54.1	40.0	43.8	53.6	38.6	52.2	56.3	49.2
21	53.1	60.0	49.3	52.1	59.2	48.4	58.7	63.8	55.0
22	58.5	64.6	55.2	57.4	63.3	54.3	65.3	71.0	61.2
23	63.4	68.2	60.8	62.4	66.7	60.1	69.2	75.0	65.0
24	68.6	71.8	66.8	67.6	70.5	66.1	74.1	78.1	71.2
25	70.9	75.1	68.6	70.0	74.2	67.8	76.0	79.5	73.5
PYSU (12–25)	32.5	36.2	30.5	31.9	35.5	30.0	36.4	39.6	34.2
Older Cohort									
12	0.2	0.0	0.3	0.3	0.0	0.4	0.0	0.0	0.0
13	0.8	0.4	0.9	0.7	0.0	0.9	1.0	1.7	0.6
14	3.9	4.4	3.7	3.9	3.8	3.9	3.8	6.2	2.1
15	10.7	10.5	10.8	11.3	10.7	11.5	8.1	9.9	6.8
16	16.0	16.6	15.7	16.0	16.4	15.8	16.1	17.4	15.2
17	23.7	25.8	22.9	22.7	25.2	21.9	28.0	27.3	28.6
18	33.3	32.6	33.6	32.7	31.9	32.9	36.2	34.3	37.5
19	40.9	41.9	40.6	39.9	40.6	39.7	45.7	45.5	45.8
20	50.1	53.7	48.7	48.8	52.3	47.7	55.9	57.4	54.8
21	57.2	60.1	56.1	56.4	58.5	55.7	60.9	64.5	58.3
22	65.4	66.3	65.1	65.2	64.4	65.5	66.6	71.5	63.1
23	68.6	71.1	67.7	68.4	70.2	67.8	69.7	73.6	67.0
24	73.3	73.4	73.3	73.6	72.8	73.9	72.0	74.8	69.9
25	77.9	76.8	78.4	78.4	76.7	78.9	76.0	76.9	75.3
26	80.3	78.3	81.1	81.1	79.4	81.7	76.5	75.2	77.4
27	81.7	79.0	82.7	83.0	81.0	83.6	75.6	73.6	77.1
28	83.3	80.5	84.4	84.8	82.9	85.4	76.5	74.0	78.3
29	83.8	81.6	84.6	85.3	84.0	85.8	76.6	75.2	77.7
30	84.8	83.6	85.3	86.0	85.0	86.3	79.2	79.8	78.9
31	85.0	83.2	85.6	86.1	84.5	86.7	79.6	79.8	79.5
32	85.5	84.2	86.0	86.8	85.8	87.0	79.9	79.8	80.1
33	84.9	83.8	85.3	85.9	85.3	86.1	80.1	79.8	80.4
34	85.1	84.2	85.5	86.1	85.3	86.3	80.6	81.0	80.4
35	84.8	84.0	85.1	85.8	85.3	85.9	80.1	80.6	79.8
36	84.4	82.8	84.9	85.4	84.0	85.9	79.6	79.8	79.5
37	83.9	83.5	84.0	84.9	85.0	84.8	79.4	79.3	79.5
38	83.9	83.5	84.1	84.8	84.5	84.9	79.8	80.6	79.2
39	82.7	80.8	83.5	83.5	80.9	84.3	79.4	80.6	78.6
40	82.3	79.6	83.3	83.0	79.4	84.2	78.7	80.2	77.7
PYSU (12–25)	37.3	38.1	37.0	37.0	37.4	36.9	38.6	40.1	37.5

Table 14.A4. ***Colombia: % of women with children by age, and % of person-years spent with children (PYSC) between ages 12 and 25 by cohort, socio-economic status, and area of residence***

Cohort and age	All			Urban			Rural		
	All	Low	High	All	Low	High	All	Low	High
Younger cohort									
12	0.0	0.0	0.0	0.0	0.0	0.0	0.0	0.0	0.0
13	0.1	0.3	0.0	0.1	0.3	0.0	0.0	0.0	0.0
14	0.5	1.4	0.0	0.5	1.4	0.0	0.6	1.3	0.0
15	1.2	3.1	0.2	1.1	3.1	0.0	2.1	3.1	1.3
16	4.5	6.2	3.6	4.3	5.9	3.5	5.6	7.6	4.2
17	9.6	10.8	9.0	9.0	9.9	8.5	13.3	14.7	12.3
18	15.6	18.4	14.0	14.0	16.1	12.9	24.8	29.5	21.4
19	24.2	27.8	22.3	22.5	25.8	20.8	34.1	37.5	31.7
20	35.2	40.2	32.5	33.2	37.7	30.8	47.1	52.2	43.4
21	46.0	53.4	41.8	44.3	52.1	40.2	55.7	59.8	52.8
22	53.2	61.5	48.6	51.4	60.2	46.8	63.2	67.4	60.2
23	58.8	68.5	53.4	56.8	67.1	51.5	70.0	75.0	66.3
24	66.4	74.1	62.2	64.6	72.6	60.4	76.9	81.3	73.8
25	71.5	79.1	67.4	69.9	77.8	65.8	81.1	85.3	78.0
PYSC (12–25)	27.6	31.8	25.4	26.6	30.7	24.4	33.9	36.8	31.8
Older cohort									
12	0.0	0.0	0.0	0.0	0.0	0.0	0.0	0.0	0.0
13	0.0	0.0	0.0	0.0	0.0	0.0	0.0	0.0	0.0
14	0.9	1.7	0.6	0.8	1.6	0.6	1.4	2.1	0.9
15	4.0	3.3	4.3	4.4	3.5	4.7	2.4	2.9	2.1
16	7.5	8.1	7.3	8.0	8.6	7.8	5.5	6.6	4.8
17	12.4	13.5	12.0	12.3	13.4	11.9	12.8	13.6	12.2
18	18.4	22.7	16.7	17.5	22.5	15.9	22.3	23.1	21.7
19	26.3	32.1	24.1	25.0	31.4	22.9	32.2	33.9	31.0
20	36.1	40.6	34.3	34.5	39.2	33.0	43.1	44.6	42.0
21	45.8	49.9	44.2	44.5	47.9	43.3	52.1	55.4	49.7
22	54.6	60.5	52.3	53.5	59.8	51.4	59.7	62.4	57.7
23	59.9	68.0	56.8	58.5	67.6	55.5	66.3	69.0	64.3
24	66.3	71.6	64.3	65.2	70.6	63.4	71.5	74.4	69.3
25	71.3	75.6	69.7	70.4	74.1	69.1	75.8	79.8	72.9
26	77.5	80.0	76.5	76.9	78.9	76.3	79.9	83.1	77.7
27	80.1	83.8	78.7	79.7	83.5	78.4	82.4	84.7	80.7
28	83.3	87.0	81.9	83.0	87.2	81.6	84.8	86.4	83.6
29	86.3	88.9	85.2	86.4	89.1	85.5	85.6	88.4	83.6
30	87.2	89.2	86.4	87.3	89.1	86.7	86.9	89.7	84.8
31	88.4	90.6	87.6	88.5	90.2	87.9	88.2	91.7	85.7
32	89.3	90.7	88.8	89.3	90.2	89.0	89.6	92.1	87.8
33	90.2	91.8	89.6	90.0	91.2	89.6	91.0	93.4	89.3
34	91.0	92.8	90.2	90.8	92.3	90.3	91.7	94.2	89.9
35	91.5	93.4	90.7	91.3	92.8	90.8	92.2	95.0	90.2
36	92.7	94.0	92.2	92.7	93.4	92.4	93.1	95.9	91.1
37	92.8	94.2	92.3	92.7	93.4	92.5	93.4	96.3	91.4
38	93.0	94.7	92.3	92.9	93.9	92.5	93.6	96.7	91.4
39	93.0	94.7	92.4	92.9	93.9	92.6	93.6	96.7	91.4
40	93.0	94.7	92.4	92.9	93.9	92.6	93.6	96.7	91.4
PYSC (12–25)	28.8	32.0	27.6	28.2	31.4	27.1	31.8	33.4	30.6

Table 14.A5. *Colombia: % of women in different occupations by age, and % of person-years spent in those occupations (PYSO) between ages 12 and 25 by cohort, socio-economic status, and area of residence*

Cohort and age	All					Urban					Rural				
	Asal	Mod	Tran	Mix	Trad	Asal	Mod	Tran	Mix	Trad	Asal	Mod	Tran	Mix	Trad
Younger cohort															
12	5.0	0.2	4.4	1.0	5.5	4.9	0.2	4.3	0.9	0.1	5.8	0.0	5.3	1.5	36.6
13	6.6	0.2	5.5	1.5	5.6	6.4	0.2	5.2	1.5	0.1	8.1	0.0	7.3	1.7	37.7
14	9.8	0.3	7.9	2.2	5.9	9.5	0.3	7.6	2.3	0.2	11.1	0.0	9.8	1.9	38.6
15	15.9	1.2	11.6	4.2	6.5	16.2	1.5	11.4	4.3	0.1	14.6	0.0	12.6	3.2	43.3
16	20.4	1.1	13.5	7.7	6.6	20.9	1.2	13.4	8.2	0.2	17.4	0.2	13.9	4.9	43.9
17	24.5	3.7	14.4	9.2	7.2	25.8	4.3	14.6	9.8	0.6	17.3	0.4	13.1	5.6	45.8
18	28.8	7.8	15.3	8.8	7.5	30.8	8.9	15.9	9.2	0.6	17.1	1.1	11.8	6.4	48.0
19	30.6	10.6	13.2	9.3	7.6	32.8	12.1	13.5	9.8	0.7	17.3	2.1	10.9	6.6	48.2
20	32.6	13.3	12.9	9.8	8.1	35.3	15.1	13.5	10.4	0.6	17.4	3.4	9.8	6.6	51.4
21	35.1	16.0	13.3	9.5	8.0	38.6	18.2	14.2	10.2	0.3	14.8	3.2	7.9	5.6	53.1
22	39.0	20.0	12.9	9.3	8.5	43.4	22.8	14.0	9.9	0.6	13.3	3.8	6.4	5.6	54.4
23	39.3	20.1	13.0	10.1	8.4	43.7	22.8	14.2	10.8	0.4	13.3	4.3	5.8	6.4	54.8
24	36.9	19.0	12.2	10.4	8.7	41.3	21.5	13.6	11.1	0.5	11.4	4.1	4.5	6.4	56.1
25	37.3	19.7	12.3	10.8	8.4	42.0	22.4	13.8	11.6	0.1	9.9	3.9	3.9	5.8	56.7
PYSO (12–25)	25.8	9.5	11.6	7.4	7.3	28.0	10.8	12.1	7.9	0.4	13.5	1.9	8.8	4.9	47.8
Older cohort															
12	6.4	0.4	4.9	1.1	7.4	6.5	0.5	5.0	1.1	1.0	6.1	0.2	4.7	1.0	37.0
13	8.1	0.7	5.6	1.9	7.8	8.3	0.9	5.5	2.1	1.0	7.6	0.2	6.2	1.2	38.9
14	10.5	1.4	6.9	2.2	8.3	10.7	1.7	6.7	2.4	1.2	9.5	0.0	8.0	1.4	41.3
15	14.0	1.6	9.1	3.9	9.6	14.3	1.9	9.0	4.2	1.2	12.5	0.0	9.7	2.4	48.8
16	16.3	2.1	10.3	4.6	10.2	17.0	2.5	10.4	5.0	1.2	12.6	0.0	9.9	2.4	51.7

17	20.7	3.9	12.1	6.0	10.5	22.1	4.7	12.3	6.8	1.1	14.2	0.5	11.2	2.1	53.8
18	23.1	5.3	12.9	8.2	10.4	25.1	6.2	13.4	9.5	0.5	14.0	1.0	10.7	2.4	56.1
19	22.9	6.2	11.1	9.3	10.4	25.0	7.3	11.3	10.7	0.3	13.3	1.2	10.4	2.6	56.9
20	24.9	7.6	11.7	9.3	11.0	27.3	8.9	12.1	10.6	0.3	13.8	1.6	10.2	3.5	60.0
21	23.1	7.4	11.5	7.9	11.1	25.5	8.8	12.1	9.0	0.3	11.8	1.4	8.3	3.3	61.1
22	24.2	8.0	11.6	8.6	11.4	27.0	9.3	12.5	9.8	0.3	11.1	1.9	7.4	2.9	62.6
23	22.7	7.9	11.9	7.9	11.6	25.5	9.2	13.1	9.0	0.3	9.9	2.1	6.4	2.9	63.7
24	20.9	7.3	11.6	7.4	11.7	23.3	8.5	12.7	8.3	0.3	10.0	2.1	6.6	3.1	64.0
25	21.5	7.2	11.6	9.0	12.0	24.2	8.4	12.9	10.4	0.3	9.0	1.9	5.5	2.6	65.7
26	21.5	7.6	11.5	8.7	12.0	24.3	8.8	12.8	10.0	0.3	8.8	2.1	5.2	2.6	65.9
27	21.0	7.4	11.1	9.1	11.9	23.7	8.6	12.4	10.5	0.3	8.5	2.1	4.8	2.6	65.6
28	20.2	6.9	10.8	9.3	11.8	22.7	8.0	12.1	10.7	0.3	8.5	2.1	4.8	2.8	64.9
29	19.1	6.5	10.7	8.9	11.7	21.4	7.4	12.0	10.3	0.3	8.3	2.1	4.7	2.4	64.0
30	19.0	6.4	11.1	8.8	11.7	21.4	7.4	12.6	10.1	0.3	8.3	2.1	4.3	2.8	64.4
31	18.5	6.5	10.9	8.8	11.5	20.9	7.5	12.5	10.1	0.3	7.4	1.9	3.8	2.8	63.1
32	18.7	6.4	10.6	9.6	11.5	21.1	7.4	12.1	11.1	0.3	7.4	1.9	3.5	3.1	63.0
33	18.3	6.5	10.8	10.2	11.4	20.7	7.6	12.4	11.7	0.2	7.4	1.9	3.6	3.3	63.0
34	19.3	6.4	11.7	11.4	11.4	21.9	7.4	13.5	13.2	0.2	7.3	1.7	3.5	3.1	63.1
35	19.8	6.3	13.0	12.9	11.5	22.6	7.3	15.1	15.0	0.2	6.6	1.7	3.1	3.3	63.8
36	19.9	6.7	13.6	13.0	11.6	22.8	7.8	15.9	15.1	0.2	6.2	1.7	2.9	3.3	64.0
37	19.0	6.7	13.4	12.7	11.8	21.8	7.8	15.7	14.8	0.3	6.2	1.9	2.9	3.1	64.7
38	19.2	7.0	13.0	13.1	11.8	21.9	8.1	15.1	15.3	0.3	6.7	2.1	3.1	3.3	64.9
39	18.9	6.9	13.1	12.9	11.9	21.6	8.1	15.3	15.0	0.3	6.4	1.6	2.9	3.3	65.6
40	19.9	6.8	13.2	13.2	11.9	22.8	8.0	15.4	15.2	0.3	6.2	1.6	2.8	3.8	65.6
PYSO (12–25)	18.5	4.8	10.2	6.2	10.2	20.1	5.6	10.6	7.1	0.7	11.1	1.0	8.2	2.4	54.4

References

Allison, P. D. (1984), *Event History Analysis* (Sage Series, 07–046, Beverly Hills).

Banguero, H. (1983), 'Desarrollo Socioeconómico y Cambio Poblacional en Colombia', Final Report to National Department of Planning (DNP) CEDE, University of Los Andes, Bogotá.

Bongaarts, J. (1978), 'A Framework for Analyzing the Proximate Determinants of Fertility', *Population and Development Review*, 4: 105–32.

Coale, A. J. (1973), 'The Demographic Transition', in IUSSP, *International Population Conference 1973*, i (Liège: IUSSP), 53–72.

Cochrane, S. H. (1983), 'Effects of Education and Urbanization on Fertility', in R. A. Bulatao and R. E. Lee (eds.), *Determinants of Fertility in Developing Countries* (New York: Academic Press), ii. 587–626.

Davis, K., and Blake, J. (1956), 'Social Structure and Fertility: An Analytic Framework', *Economic Development and Cultural Change*, 4: 211–35.

Easterlin, R. (1983), 'Modernization and Fertility: A Critical Essay', in R. A. Bulatao and R. D. Lee (eds.), *Determinants of Fertility in Developing Countries* (New York: Academic Press), ii. 562–86.

Flórez, C. E. (1989), 'El Proceso de Formación de la Familia', Document presented at the Seminar on Family and Politics in Latin America, May 1989, Mexico City, Mexico.

—— (1990), *The Demographic Transition and Women's Life Course in Colombia* (Tokyo: United Nations University Press).

—— Echeverri, R., and Méndez, R. (1987), 'Análisis Demográfico del Censo de 1985: Fecundidad', Departamento Administrativo Nacional de Estadística and CEDE, Universidad de Los Andes, Bogotá.

—— and Hogan, D. (1990), 'La Transición Demográfica y el Cambio en las Historias de Vida en Colombia', *Desarrollo y Sociedad*, 25: 125–55.

Knodel, J., and van de Walle, E. (1979), 'Lessons From the Past: Policy Implications of Historical Fertility', *Population and Development Review*, 5: 217–45.

Namboodiri, N. K. (1983), 'Sequential Fertility Decision Making and the Life Course', in R. A. Bulatao and R. D. Lee (eds.), *Determinants of Fertility in Developing Countries* (New York: Academic Press), ii. 444–72.

Ochoa, L. H. (1982), 'El Descenso de la Fecundidad en Colombia y sus Implicaciones Demográficas', in L. H. Ochoa (ed.), *Implicaciones Demográficas del Descenso de Fecundidad en Colombia* (Monografías de la Corporación Centro Regional de Población, 18 (Apr.)).

Richards, T. (1983), 'Statistical Studies of Aggregate Fertility Change: Time Series or Cross Sections', in R. A. Bulatao and R. D. Lee (eds.), *Determinants of Fertility in Developing Countries* (New York: Academic Press), ii. 737–56.

Part IV

Consequences of Fertility Decline

15 The Social Consequences of Rapid Fertility Decline during a Period of Economic Crisis

JOSEPH E. POTTER

Introduction

It is difficult, if not impossible, to consider the consequences of demographic change in isolation from the impact of other changes that are taking place in a society. That is particularly true in the face of the drastic deterioration of living standards that has taken place in Latin America since 1980, and what seem to be radical attempts by governments to either restructure or replace now bankrupt 'styles of development'. There is a very real possibility that the influence of fertility decline has been swamped by the more general effects of 'the crisis', and the structural adjustment policies that have accompanied it. Moreover, in these circumstances, the pertinent question concerns whether and how falling birth rates may have moderated or accentuated the effects of the crisis, rather than any direct effect that they might have had on welfare.

In this context, as in others, an inevitably daunting aspect of the examination of the consequences of rapid fertility decline (or any other demographic change) is to choose the relevant aspects of individual or collective welfare on which to focus. The literature is, of course, a source of guidance for selecting appropriate areas of focus. Although, by some accounts, 'the subject of the consequences of population growth . . . receives much less than its due' (McNicoll 1984), a great deal has been written on the effects of rapid population growth on economic development in poor countries, as well as on the effects of below replacement fertility in industrial societies. Yet among the various questions that have been raised in these discussions some questions seem far more pertinent than others to the contemporary situation in Latin America.

It is at this point that the crisis looms large, and directs our focus away from some topics and toward others. For example, it would seem grotesque in the present circumstances to ask what influence fertility decline had on savings and investment. Whatever the effect might have been, it would surely be imperceptible in the tidal wave of economic disarray and decapitalization that has swept over the region. Additionally, the gravity of the circumstances commands us to concentrate on the impact of rapid fertility decline in the recent past and immediate future, rather than in the more distant future. It is true that, twenty or thirty years from now, dependency ratios will worsen and there will be major questions about how the elderly are to be supported. But those problems, while real enough, are contingent on the success or failure of current efforts to overcome the burden of international debt, and to elude the stagnation that besets the vast majority of Latin American economies in the 1980s.

If we are to focus on the most immediate impacts of the rapid decline in fertility that has taken place in the 1970s and 1980s, and leave the question of the macro-economic impact of this change to one side, then the questions we are left with refer to the welfare of women and children. In particular, how has the health and education of the children born during these two decades been affected by their having had fewer siblings, and belonging to smaller generations than they would have had, had fertility not declined? And, how has the decline in the number of live births, and increased control over the reproductive process, affected the situation of women in Latin America? It is on these questions that I will attempt to reach some preliminary conclusions.

Primary Education and its Priority as a Social Policy in an Era of Austerity and Shrinking Enrolments

One sector that has been identified as being strongly affected by rapid population growth and high fertility is education. In Gavin Jones's authoritative study (1975), for example, it was demonstrated that fertility decline would make it easier and less costly to improve the coverage and enhance the quality of education. Fewer teachers would have to be recruited, fewer buildings constructed, etc. And the effects would be felt soon after the fact, long before there would be any repercussions on the growth of the labour force. There was an apparently unambiguous dividend to be obtained from fertility decline.

The literature on less developed countries contrasts sharply with recent analyses of the implications for education of below-replacement fertility in industrialized societies (Coale 1986; McNicoll 1986). Strong connections have been identified between demographic trends and education, but the relations identified are perverse. Preston's (1984) forceful analysis of the US situation seems to have convinced most observers that a declining school-age population was responsible, at least in part, for a marked worsening in the quality of primary and secondary schooling since the 1960s. One mechanism involved the market for teachers. As the demand for new teachers fell, in line with matriculation, so did teachers' salaries. One result was that the 'quality' of teachers declined—increasingly less able people chose teaching as a career. The other complementary change was a decline in the political clout of the parents of school-age children as they became an increasingly small and less vocal part of the electorate.

The reports on what has happened to education in Latin America in the last decade at first sight adhere more closely to the Preston script than to that of Jones. The dividend from reduced fertility has clearly not materialized. Quality seems to have fallen, coverage is not much improved, and drop-out rates are high, even at the primary level.[1] Teachers' salaries have fallen drastically, and there is increasing polarization between public and private education (World Bank 1986). Should these trends be interpreted as the result of the general contraction in government spending on social policies, and highlighted as one of the more poignant side effects of the debt crisis? Or are there some structural elements that carry over from the Preston analysis?

My inclination is to worry that even in a less austere budgetary environment, education, and particularly public primary education, may not fare well. The demographic obstacles to progress identified by Preston are, of course, only a part of the problem. The pertinent bureaucracies are massive, often inefficient and inequitable, and sometimes corrupt. Radical administrative reforms and energetic leadership could do much to improve the situation. But what of other priorities, and the inability of governments and politicians to focus on and finance a wide range of social programmes?

Education's principal rival for social spending in the USA was health care for the elderly. As a result of the growth in the numbers of people over the age of 65, and the political support their claims mobilized, the health care industry in the USA enjoyed rapid growth in size and sophistication throughout the 1960s and 1970s. In marked contrast to education, the medical profession was able to recruit the brightest undergraduates and to provide doctors with spiralling real incomes. This same sort of trade-off can be seen in budgetary allocations in Brazil where, as a percentage of the total central government budget, expenditures on education declined from 8.3 to 6.6 per cent, and expenditures on health increased from 6.7 to 8.5 per cent. An even more extreme shift seems to have taken place in Mexico, where central government expenditure on education fell from 17.8 per cent of total central government spending in 1978 to 10.2 per cent in 1985 and 6.5 per cent in 1987 (World Bank 1988). Here, the share of central government spending devoted to health also declined, but not as rapidly, with the result that expenditures on health as a percentage of expenditures on education increased from 75 per cent in 1978 to 120 per cent in 1987 (BANAMEX 1989).

What are the prospects that such a one-sided competition between education and health will persist in Latin America? According to a recent study of adult health in Brazil (World Bank 1989), they are excellent. Partly as a product of the demographic and epidemiologic transitions taking place in the population, and partly as a result of political and administrative change, demand for curative care of degenerative diseases and injuries can be expected to sky-rocket. The first and foremost source of this demand is dramatic growth in the elderly population as a result of the past history of high fertility coupled with significant mortality

[1] In Mexico e.g. the coverage of primary education increased from 94% in 1982–3 to 98% in 1987–8. The %age of children entering primary school who would eventually graduate from primary school (based on current drop-out rates) also rose slightly over this period, but remains unacceptably low at only 55%. Of children graduating from primary school, the fraction proceeding to secondary school has remained virtually constant at about 84% (BANAMEX 1989).

decline. Second are rates of morbidity and mortality from cardiovascular disease and cancers, which, in the absence of major efforts at prevention, are more likely to rise than fall. (So far, attempts to reduce spiralling risk factors such as smoking and exposure to pollution have received minimal financial support.) The final factor is increased demand for medical treatment of these 'new' diseases, based on expanded entitlement to health care (the Constitution of 1988 stipulates that there be just one publicly financed health care system and that access to this system be the universal right of all Brazilians) and the general medicalization of the society.

The Brazilian case, while certainly dramatic, may not be exceptional in this regard. The spectre of burgeoning demands for social spending on hospital-based curative medicine is probably real enough for most other countries in the region. Mexico, for example, recently added health care to the rights declared in the Constitution, and has greatly increased coverage of the major social security institutions. It is hard to imagine that even in countries where there is already much greater access to health care and more emphasis on prevention, there will not be a serious imbalance between the demand for curative care and the services that public health institutions will be in a position to supply.

Pointing to the recent experience of children and the elderly in the USA, and then to the prognosis for adult health in Brazil, does, I would submit, serve two purposes. First it raises a question about the conventional expectation that rapid fertility decline leads to an improvement in the coverage and quality of primary education. Second, it serves to warn us that the disappointing experience of the last decade may not be just the result of a transitory, crisis-induced austerity. The implication is not that school age children would be better off had there been more of them, but rather that fertility decline, even in the absence of a radical curtailment of spending on social programmes, would not have ensured an improvement in the schools those children would be able to attend.

The Links between Rapid Fertility Decline and Falling Infant Mortality Rates in a Period of Economic Crisis

While children in Latin America may not be receiving a better education now than they were a decade ago, their chances of surviving infancy and childhood are greatly improved. Since social expenditures and personal incomes were falling in most countries during the decade of the 1980s, the seemingly inescapable interpretation is that fertility decline was responsible for offsetting the impact of deteriorating incomes and services. This surprising result is more than even ardent proponents of family planning might have hoped for or dared to predict. And it is only reluctantly acknowledged by those who are making an effort to document the social impact of the crisis (UNICEF 1987).

In the past decade, there has been a considerable amount of analysis and discussion devoted to the question of how fertility patterns or family-building strategies affect infant and child mortality. The principal questions have concerned what might be called the 'bio-demographic' determinants of risk, and the degree to which the prevalence of high-risk pregnancies changes during the course of a decline in fertility. Interest in these questions, more often than not, has hinged on building a case for family planning programmes, or for focused efforts to reduce mortality by way of averting high-risk pregnancies.

Initially, the two principal fertility-related determinants of infant mortality were considered to be the mother's age and parity (Nortman 1974). The observed variation in risk according to these variables was thought to be related to the mother's reproductive fitness or capacity. The latter concept, although vague, was more 'biological' than 'social'. By the early 1980s, however, the influence of these variables on mortality was judged to be less important and consistent than that of spacing birth. The hypothesis that a child's survival prospects were inversely related to the closeness of preceding and following pregnancies received strong support from the mass of pregnancy history data collected by the WFS (Hobcraft *et al.* 1983 and 1985).

These relationships, as well as the use that may be made of them to estimate the change in infant and child mortality that can be attributed to change in the proportions of births falling into different risk categories during the course of fertility decline, are well reviewed by Erica Taucher (Chapter 16). The conclusion of studies conducted in Costa Rica (1960–77) and Chile (1972–87) is that the change in the distribution of births by order and maternal age accounts for about 20 per cent of the observed decline in infant mortality. Although none of the studies cited deals exclusively with the post-1980 period, my impression is that such a decomposition would account for a similar proportion of the infant mortality decline observed during this time frame.

While there do not seem to be studies of the evolution of the distribution of birth-interval lengths (and, particularly, frequency of births occurring after intervals of less than twenty-four months) during the period of fertility decline, it is not likely that change in this dimension would account for a significant proportion of the change in mortality. In the cross-section of national populations, lower levels of fertility are not generally associated with longer birth intervals, in part because higher contraceptive prevalence is associated with shorter durations of breast-feeding (Bongaarts 1987*a*).[2]

We are thus left with the difficult task of accounting for over three-quarters of a substantial decline in infant and child mortality that took place during years when the economic situation of most Latin American households was rapidly deteriorating. The contexts in which this sort of phenomenon occurred are as varied as those of Chile, Brazil, and Mexico. What sort of explanations have been offered?

The Chilean case is well documented and has drawn the most comment. The infant mortality rate declined monotonically from 82.2 per 1,000 in 1970 to 19.5

[2] What happened to the duration of breast-feeding in the course of the fertility declines that have taken place in Latin America is not well documented. It seems to have increased in Brazil and declined in Mexico.

per 1,000 in 1985. In their review of the Chilean experience, Hakkert and Goza (1989) point out that the last seven years of the 1970s was a period when free market economics was institutionalized, 'with concomitant exacerbation of social inequality, declining consumption levels of the poorest population segments, and even a 14.4 per cent drop in the GDP in 1975'. The experience in the early 1980s included a major decline in the GDP and periods of extremely high unemployment (Foxley and Raczynski 1984). The reasons for the persistent downward trend in mortality offered by Haignere (1983) and by Raczynski and Oyarzo (1981) centre on the increases in expenditures on mother and child health and nutrition programmes, as well as on the change in the composition of births. The latter included a decline in the proportion of infants born into the poorest households as well as the change in the distribution by age of mother and parity.[3]

The Brazilian case is less well documented, and has given rise to more confusion, since estimates based on vital registration have occasionally been at odds with those based on censuses and surveys (Hakkert and Goza 1989). An additional anomaly is the probable increase in mortality in certain urban areas of the country during the boom years of the late 1960s. Explanations for the decline in infant and child mortality that seems to have taken place in the two decades since 1970 include investments in sanitation programmes and water supplies, immunization campaigns and the promotion of oral rehydration, state programmes to provide nutritional supplements, as well as change in the composition of births by age of mother, parity, and social class (Oya Sawyer 1988; Hakkert and Goza 1989).

In addition to identifying various changes that could have contributed to child survival, most authors have usually mentioned reasons why mortality might not have responded directly and immediately to the economic deterioration experienced in these countries. Hakkert and Goza (1989) refer to various social control mechanisms that are not immediately affected by cutbacks on social spending, while Taucher (Chapter 16) notes that couples appear to be able to postpone childbearing beyond the most severe cuts in wages. There is also the likelihood that determinants such as the mother's nutritional status and the environmental sanitation are 'stocks' which have been built up over a considerable period of time, and are not quickly eroded.[4]

These various explanations do not, in my view, add up to a compelling interpretation of recent experience in Latin America. I would suggest that the observed phenomena can only be accounted for by attributing to fertility decline a more powerful and direct influence on child survival, or by postulating that both fertility and mortality change are driven by transformations in values, knowledge, and behaviour that are only loosely tied to material conditions. These are not mutually exclusive or clearly separable alternatives, and each deserves serious consideration.

[3] In Taucher's analysis (Chapter 16), controlling for mother's education increases the proportion of the Chilean decline explained by change in the structure of births from 20 to 30%.

[4] This is an idea that Lincoln Chen has advanced on a number of occasions.

One way that fertility decline could have a greater influence on mortality would be for it to lead to a pronounced reduction in the proportion of children born to mothers whose reproductive health status is poor or impaired. I have argued elsewhere that age, parity, and spacing status are not the only indications of pregnancy risk that may be taken into account by either mothers or those who counsel them on reproductive decisions (Potter 1988). Other potentially recognizable indicators of excess maternal and foetal risk are a history of difficulties with pregnancy or labour, previous complications of delivery, diabetes, hypertension, jaundice, malaria, chronic infections, iron-deficiency anaemia, and malnutrition (Haaga 1987).

Have women who have terminated their reproductive careers by surgical sterilization been selected on the basis of an assessment of risk based on more than age and parity? Are women who perceive themselves to be at high risk of either losing their next pregnancy or jeopardizing their own health status by carrying a pregnancy to term, more likely than others to want to practise family planning effectively? The answer to such questions seems to be yes. In Brazil, doctors were prohibited by the code of medical ethics from performing female sterilizations except when the patient is at high risk. In Cuba and Mexico, the prevention of high-risk pregnancies was a high priority of the medical authorities in charge of maternal and child health. Moreover, health risks are frequently explicitly mentioned by respondents in the small number of fertility surveys that have explored the reasons for using contraception with open-ended questions, such as those carried out by BEMFAM in the north-east region of Brazil.

Selection of this sort is consistent with emerging views that knowledge of health risks and what can be done about them has been a major determinant of infant and child mortality (Preston and Haines 1991; Preston 1985). So is the fact that the downward trend in mortality in most Latin American countries has shown little or no responsiveness to sharp declines in real wages. A further possibility is that the world is indeed as Caldwell has described it, and that what we are witnessing is a transformation in values and ideas concerning children and family life (Caldwell 1986; Caldwell *et al.* 1983). Reduced fertility has enabled mothers (and relevant others) to make greater emotional investments in their children, and these bonds—together with the behaviour that they induced—have had a dramatic influence on survival.[5]

Fertility Decline, Labour-Force Participation, and the Status of Women

Few sets of relationships raise as many questions about the direction of causality as those between economic conditions, fertility, labour-force participation, and the status of women. The pertinent developments have been analysed repeatedly

[5] Of course, other factors are also behind the change in the parent–child relationship, and greater emotional investment in children, in turn, leads to reduced fertility.

and in great depth for industrialized countries such as Great Britain, Norway, and the United States, and there is still considerable disagreement over the extent to which the decline in fertility and the increase in labour-force participation constituted responses to changing economic conditions, the extent to which they were driven by the changing status of women in these societies, and the extent to which fertility and labour-force participation rates each influenced the other, independently of trends in values or economic conditions. The same sort of debate could be held about Latin America, where a seemingly steady increase in women's labour-force participation has accompanied rapid fertility decline, and has persisted in the face of the sudden economic deterioration that occurred in the 1980s. But the much greater incidence of severe poverty and the highly problematic position of many women in these societies lend urgency to the discussion.

In this brief overview, I will avoid tackling the quantitative information that pertains to the influence of fertility on labour force participation, which Marta Mier y Teran has taken up in considerable detail for the case of Mexico. Rather, the focus will be on three quite specific issues that pertain to the impact of fertility decline on the status of women in the region. The first is the straightforward, quantitative impact of fertility decline on the amount of time that women spend in different family statuses. The second question concerns the impact that the substantial increase in contraceptive practice and the fertility decline it has led to may have had in the realm of sexuality. The third and final issue to be raised is the 'psychological costs' of increased labour-force participation and reduced fertility. The first of these questions is concrete, and has lent itself to empirical exploration with existing data. The second and third questions, however important they might be, are far less accessible. I raise them with a view towards stimulating future research rather than summarizing present knowledge.

Family Demography

Fortunately, the influence of fertility decline on family demography has just been explored in some depth for Brazil by Goldani (1989). This study used the family status life-table methodology developed by Bongaarts (1987*b*) and applied to the USA by Watkins *et al.* (1987), and retrospective data on the life courses of Brazilian women collected in the 1984 National Household Sample Survey (Pesquisa Nacional Amostra de Domicilios or PNAD). It includes comparisons of 'transitional' and 'post-transitional' stages, where the former refers to the experience of real cohorts whose reproductive experience was complete, and the latter to the experience of the synthetic cohort in the years that immediately preceded the survey.

Perhaps the main conclusion to be drawn from Goldani's analysis is that the substantial difference in fertility between these two stages did *not* lead to an appreciable change in the time that Brazilian women could expect to spend as the mothers of small children. What the fertility decline did do was offset the very strong positive influence of mortality decline on the time spent in motherhood.

Thus, the number of adult years spent as a mother of children under 18 years increased from 18 to 20 between the transitional and post-transitional stages, and the number of adult years spent as a mother of children under 5 fell slightly from 9.6 to 9.1. In the absence of fertility decline, the decrease in mortality alone would have led mothers to spend 22 and 11 years, in these respective states.

An initial reaction to these simulations might be increased willingness to think about fertility decline as a response to changes in mortality, along the lines long ago suggested by Davis (1963). The simulations might also lead to scepticism about the potential of the rapid fertility decline observed in Latin America to have caused the large increases in labour force participation that have occurred in the region.[6]

Sexuality

The question concerning the impact that access to modern contraception and the control it affords over reproduction may have had on sexuality is an issue on which opinions are likely to differ, in large part due to the lack of research on sexuality in Latin America in the last decade. At the most general level, Loyola (1992) has pointed to the historical importance that the gradual separation of sex from reproduction has had, over time, on the forms of unions between the sexes in Western society. Here, the advent of modern contraception is seen as a critical part of a larger transformation of the 'mode of reproduction' in which female sexuality passes from being the subject of rigid control to being esteemed in its own right, emotions are given greater reign, and there is a shift in the terms of exchange between the sexes.

As evidence of change in the system of human reproduction in Latin America and in Brazil in particular, Loyola points first to the decline in fertility, and then to the increase in: divorces involving consensual unions; the number of single persons, single mothers, and single-parent families; and sexual freedom and homosexuality. In her assessment, these changes have had substantial and swift repercussions, 'at least among the better-educated middle and upper classes in large urban centers, where the "individualist–egalitarian" ideological model of love relationships is quite widespread'.

At a more immediate level, Balán and Ramos (1989) have addressed the question of whether the adoption of contraception has enabled women to obtain greater enjoyment from sex by removing or limiting anxiety concerning an unwanted pregnancy. The results of their focus groups conducted among lower-class women in Buenos Aires was that while contraception was sometimes valued positively on this account, that was not the usual case. On the one hand, fear of pregnancy was often replaced by fear of a method's side effects, or, in the case of barrier methods, with inconvenience and inhibition. Moreover, they found

6 Weinberger *et al.* (1989) have made a comparison of the WFS and the DHS surveys in Colombia, the Dominican Republic, Ecuador, and Peru that shows the decline in the % of respondents with a living child under 6 was much less than the decline in the TFR between the two surveys.

that many women viewed sex as an obligation rather than as something to be enjoyed.

It is, of course, highly unlikely that anyone will ever be in a position to draw empirically based conclusions concerning trends in such aspects of sexuality and the nature of sexual unions in Latin America or anywhere else. Even less likely is a firm assessment of contraceptive practice in promoting that change. Yet, twenty or thirty years ago, it was often alleged that men in Latin America resisted contraception on the grounds that it would undermine their ability to subordinate women as their sexual property. The fact that this resistance has dissipated or been overcome has to have been important to women in the region.

Women's Experience of Maternity and Work

The final question concerns women's experience of maternity and work during the crisis, as fertility declined and female labour-force participation increased. As Oliveira (1989) has observed, we do not know what the expanding presence of women in the workforce will mean for the organization of daily life and household maintenance, and whether it will change traditional patterns of relationships between the sexes. It has often been suggested that work outside the home helps to break down the isolation that women in different sectors have been subjected to, and that the power of women varies in accordance with the importance of their earnings to the household budget. On the other hand, being 'forced' by economic necessity to find paid employment and to have fewer children may not necessarily lead to an improvement in a woman's welfare, and may entail the sacrifice of highly valued activities and pleasures, as well as deterioration in a marital relationship.

The window on internal household dynamics and personal experience in the workforce that I will rely on for these remarks consists of a series of in-depth interviews on maternity and work conducted in Tijuana, Merida, and Mexico City (Oliveira 1992; García and Oliveira 1992*a* and 1992*b*). The picture that emerges in the draft reports that they have prepared to date is an intricate mosaic. Nevertheless, several important themes emerge. The first is, simply, the enduring importance of motherhood and children as a source of identity and satisfaction. Even middle-class women who have a career orientation toward their work, or poor women who find their work useful and satisfying, consider childbearing to be the most important experience and part of their lives. Moreover, among women who have successfully limited their fertility to 2 or 3 live births, there is a longing to have had more children and to have been able to spend more time with them. On the other hand, the costs of children, in terms of expenditures and the time and work that looking after them entails, are keenly felt. Successful birth control, which seems to be far from being the norm among these respondents, is, thus, both a sacrifice and a blessing.

Paid employment, while valued by some, is simply viewed as something necessary to guarantee a minimum living standard for the family, and the children in particular. Moreover, most employed respondents firmly maintain that their children would be better taken care of if that responsibility did not have to be entrusted to others. Among these respondents who work only out of necessity, some recognize positive aspects of their employment, such as a sense of achievement, independence, and the opportunity it affords them to break out of the isolation of their homes. The effects of paid employment on gender relations within the household, however, do not appear to be uniformly positive. In the extreme situation when the respondent becomes the sole support of the household, the treatment she receives or puts up with seems to be worse than it otherwise might be.

Conclusion

As the various chapters included in this volume indicate, the pace and scope of the rise in contraceptive practice and the ensuing decline in fertility have been massive in the last two decades in most of Latin America. Child mortality, domestic arrangements, and female labour-force participation have also undergone quite dramatic transformation in many countries of the region. Yet, fully aware of the poor economic performance of the last decade in Latin America, most observers would be unwilling to believe that women and children in the region are better off now than they were ten years ago. It is a daunting setting in which to attempt an evaluation of the consequences of fertility decline, even having circumscribed the task as I did at the outset.

Although the review that I have undertaken could only be described as cursory and impressionistic, several conclusions have emerged that may stand up to further scrutiny. It is not without interest that several of these conclusions are at odds with the earlier literature on the consequences of fertility decline. While Jones's studies of sectoral effects showed that fertility decline would facilitate attaining educational goals, the quality of education in Latin America, particularly of primary and secondary education, seems to have improved little in recent years, in spite of the decline in the size of birth cohorts. Rather, whatever dividend was generated by lessening demand for school teachers and classrooms seems to have been appropriated by other social sectors, particularly the health sector, where demand was expanding rapidly due both to growth of the adult population, and to increased coverage of social security and public health systems.

If education fared badly in the austere environment of the 1980s, child survival seems to have fared remarkably well. Here, the gains seem to have outstripped whatever improvements might have resulted from changes in the distribution of births by mothers' age and parity, or from improvements in the quantity and quality of medical services. The lesson that I have drawn from this experience is that child survival is more closely tied to fertility than was previously thought, and that the connections are as much social as bio-demographic. Nevertheless, the result is surprising and problematic for those attempting to delineate the social impact of structural adjustment (e.g. Lustig 1991).

In its venture into the more qualitative aspects of women's experience of controlled fertility and increased labour-force participation, this review also yielded a few preliminary conclusions. The very limited information that is available on sexuality and gender relations suggests that increased contraceptive practice and labour-force participation do not automatically lead to improvements in these realms. Moreover, it is clear that maternity and child-rearing still occupy a very central place in women's lives, and that having fewer children than their mothers did is seen by many women less as an opportunity than as an inevitable and painful fact of life in the harsh circumstances of the moment.

There is a danger that this review has been too negative. Perhaps, in a few years time, living standards will be on the rise in the region, and reforms in social policies will accompany the reforms in economic policy. Then, it may be easier for social scientists to point to improvements in the condition of women and children, and to relate those changes to the transformation in reproductive patterns that took place in the 1980s. Moreover, I may well not have done justice to the possibility that without fertility decline and the rapid adoption of modern contraception, the situation would have been even worse than it is. Yet, I suspect that when more is known about the social effects of fertility decline in Latin America and in other regions of the world, there will be ample grounds for revising the expected relationships. Furthermore, as these populations age in the next three decades, we will most certainly gain an increased appreciation of the costs of the high fertility that preceded the rapidly declining fertility that is the focus of this volume.

References

Balán, Jorge, and Ramos, Silvina (1989), *La Medicalización del Comportamiento Reproductivo: Un Estudio Exploratorio sobre la Demanda de Anticonceptivos en los Sectores Populares* (CEDES/29; Buenos Aires: CEDES).

BANAMEX (1989), *México Social 1988–1989, Indicadores Seleccionados* (Mexico City: Departamento de Estudios Sociales).

Bongaarts, John (1987*a*), 'Does Family Planning Reduce Infant Mortality Rates?' *Population and Development Review*, **13/2** (June), 323–34.

—— (1987*b*), 'The Projection of Family Composition over the Life Course with Family Status Life Tables', in J. Bongaarts *et al.* (eds.), *Family Demography* (Oxford: Clarendon Press).

Caldwell, John C. (1986), 'Routes to Low Mortality in Poor Countries', *Population and Development Review*, **12/2** (June), 171–220.

—— Reddy, P. H., and Caldwell, Pat (1983), 'The Social Component of Mortality Decline: An Investigation in South India Employing Alternative Methodologies', *Population Studies*, **37/2** (July), 185–205.

Coale, Ansley J. (1986), 'Demographic Effects of Below-Replacement Fertility and their Social Implications', *Population and Development Review*, 12 (suppl.): 203–16.

Davis, Kingsley (1963), 'The Theory of Change and Response in Modern Demographic History', *Population Index*, **29**: 345–66.

Foxley, A., and Raczynski, D. (1984), 'Vulnerable Groups in Recessionary Situations: The Case of Children and the Young in Chile', *World Development*, 12/3: 233–46.

García, Brigida, and Oliveira, Orlandina (1992*a*), 'Maternidad y trabajo en México: Una aproximación microsocial', Mimeo.

—— —— (1992*b*), 'El significado del trabajo femenino en los sectores populares urbanos', Mimeo.

Goldani, Ana Maria (1989), 'Women's Transitions: The Intersection of Female Life Course, Family and Demographic Transition in Twentieth Century Brazil', Doct. Diss. University of Texas at Austin.

Haaga, John G. (1987), 'Mechanisms for the Association of Maternal Age, Parity, and Birthspacing with Infant Health', unpublished background paper prepared for the NAS Working Group on the Health Consequences of Contraceptive Use and Controlled Fertility.

Haignere, Clara S. (1983), 'The Application of the Free-Market Economic Model in Chile and the Effects on the Population's Health Status', *International Journal of Health Services*, **13/3**: 389–405.

Hakkert, Ralph, and Goza, F. W. (1989), 'The Demographic Consequences of Austerity in Latin America', in W. L. Carate (ed.), *Lost Promises: Debt, Austerity, and Development in Latin America* (Boulder, Colo.: Westview Press).

Hobcraft, J., McDonald, J. W., and Rutstein, S. (1983), 'Child-Spacing Effects on Infant and Early Child Mortality', *Population Index*, **49**: 585–618.

—— —— —— (1985), 'Demographic Determinants of Infant and Early Child Mortality: A Comparative Analysis', *Population Studies*, **39**: 363–85.

Jones, Gavin W. (1975), *Population Growth and Educational Planning in Developing Nations* (New York: Irvington Press).

Loyola, Maria Andrea (1992), 'Sexuality and Forms of Union between the Sexes', in *El Poblamiento de las Américas, Veracruz 1992, Actas* (Liège: IUSSP).

Lustig, Nora (1991), 'Mexico: The Social Impact of Adjustment', Mimeo.

McNicoll, Geoffrey H. (1984), 'Consequences of Rapid Population Growth: Overview and Assessment', *Population and Development Review*, 10/2: 177–240.

—— (1986), 'Economic Growth with Below-Replacement Fertility', *Population and Development Review*, 12 (suppl.), 217–38.

Nortman, Dorothy (1974), *Parental Age as a Factor in Pregnancy Outcome and Child Development* (Reports on Population/Family Planning, No. 16, New York: The Population Council).

Oliveira, Orlandina (1989), 'Empleo femenino en México en tiempos de recesión económica: Tendencias recientes', in *Fuerza de Trabajo Femenina en México: Características y Tendencias* (Mexico City: UNAM).

—— (1992), 'Jefas de hogar y violencia doméstica', Mimeo.

Oya Sawyer, Diana (1988), 'As mortes no Brasil: Mais o menos?', Paper presented at the Conference on the Demography of Inequality in Contemporary Latin America, Gainesville, Fla.

Potter, Joseph E. (1988), 'Does Family Planning Reduce Infant Mortality?', *Population and Development Review*, 14/1: 179–87.

Preston, Samuel H. (1984), 'Children and the Elderly: Divergent Paths for America's Dependents', *Demography* 21/4: 435–57.

—— (1985), 'Resources, Knowledge and Child Mortality: A Comparison of the US in the late Nineteenth Century and Developing Countries Today', in IUSSP, *International Population Conference, 1985* (Liège: IUSSP), iv. 373–86.

—— and Haines, M. R. (1991), *Fatal Years: Child Mortality in Late Nineteenth Century America* (Princeton: Princeton University Press).

Raczynski, D., and Oyarzo, C. (1981), '¿Por qué cae la tasa de mortalidad infantil en Chile?', *Colección Estudios CIEPLAN*, 6: 45–83.

UNICEF (1987), *Ajuste com Dimensão Humana* (Brasilia: Ideal).

Watkins, Susan, Menken, Jane A., and Bongaarts, John (1987), 'Demographic Foundations of Family Change', *American Sociological Review*, 52/3: 346–58.

Weinberger, Mary Beth, Lloyd, C., and Blanc, A. K. (1989), 'Women's Education and Fertility: A Decade of Change in Four Latin American Countries', *International Family Planning Perspectives*, **15/1**: 4–14, 28.

World Bank (1989), *Adult Health in Brazil: Adjusting to New Challenges* (Report No. 7807-BR; Washington).

—— (1986), *Brazil: Finance of Primary Education* (Washington).

—— (1988), *Brazil: Public Spending on Social Programs; Issues and Options* (Report No. 7086-BR; Washington).

16 The Impact of Fertility Decline on Levels of Infant Mortality

ERICA TAUCHER

Introduction

The beneficial effects of fertility decline on infant mortality were postulated as early as the beginning of the twentieth century by Newsholme and Newman, although at that time, no data were available for the investigation of the authors' hypothesis (Woods *et al.* 1988, 1989). In his analysis of the decline in infant mortality in England and Wales, Woods concludes that declining fertility—both marital and illegitimate—since 1870 helped to reduce infant mortality by reducing parity and by increasing spacing between pregnancies.

The impact of fertility decline on infant mortality is of particular interest in the Latin American and Caribbean region. All the family planning programmes that have been developed in the region since the 1960s have as one of their objectives the improvement of maternal and child health (Taucher 1979*a*). In terms of maternal health, the principal effect hoped for is a reduction in the frequency of induced abortion, as a result of its replacement by contraception. At the same time it is hoped that the health of both mothers and their children will be favourably affected by the fertility decline resulting from these programmes, through modifications in the distribution of births in terms of the parity and age of the mother and the length of the birth-spacing interval.

In Chile, for example, the principal reason for officially incorporating fertility regulation services into the maternal and child health care programme in 1965 was the high level of maternal morbidity–mortality due to abortion found in that country. In fact, the fertility decline that occurred after 1965 was accompanied by a large drop in the number of hospitalizations related to abortion, and in maternal mortality from this cause (Taucher 1986).

The literature reviews of Buchanan (1976) and Rinehart *et al.* (1985) present numerous examples of the relationship between parity and maternal morbidity–mortality. In the studies that were reviewed, ante-partum and post-partum haemorrhages, hypertension, prolapses, rupture of the uterus, and pregnancy-related toxaemia were some of the complications most often found among high-parity women. On the other hand, some complications occur most commonly among first-time mothers, especially the very young. Maternal mortality increases steadily with parity. Nevertheless, in some studies it has been observed that mortality at the birth of the first child is higher than in the case of the second child, leading to a J-shaped relationship. The relationship of maternal mortality to age, parity, and birth interval has also been studied by Nortman (1974), and in the research cited in the review by Rinehart (1985). It may be seen then that patterns of maternal morbidity–mortality in relation to these factors are similar to those of infant mortality. Hence, any discussion of the changes that fertility decline causes in the distribution of births, or of the effects of fertility decline on infant mortality, will also be pertinent to maternal health. For this reason, and because there are few studies in this area being carried out in developing countries, because of problems in obtaining adequate data, the present chapter will focus only on infant mortality.

The fact that the analysis focuses on the effects of fertility decline on infant mortality does not imply that other determinants of infant mortality, such as socio-economic status, health programmes directed at mothers and children, general health conditions, and many more, should be ignored. Moreover, it should be kept in mind that the effects of such factors may be confounded with the effect of factors specific to the level of fertility. On the other hand, there may be common determinants of both health and fertility.

In this chapter, the mechanisms through which a reduction in fertility may act on infant mortality are summarized. Then the differentials in infant mortality—in terms of birth order, age of mother, and birth interval—are analysed. Along with discussion of possible confounding variables, reference will be made to the difficulty of obtaining adequate data to separate out the true relationships from those that may be spurious. Finally, an attempt will be made to give an overall view of the state of fertility and infant mortality in the region.

The Mechanism through which Fertility Decline Acts on Infant Mortality

Many studies of countries or geographical regions within countries show a direct relationship between levels of fertility and various health indicators, such as infant and early childhood mortality, maternal mortality, etc. Both types of variable are associated, in turn, with indicators of social and economic development that might explain the observed relationships. However, it is supposed that in addition to these common determinants, there are direct relationships between fertility and infant health. In order to clarify these relationships, it is necessary to analyse the mechanisms through which fertility decline might have an impact on health indicators.

Certain mechanisms appear obvious at the individual or family level. Jones (1969), for example, discusses the advantages to households with modest incomes of having fewer children, adequately spaced, since this practice increases the available income per capita, making possible a reduction in levels of malnutrition and overcrowding, thereby permitting better care of the children, their improved health, and improved access to education.

At the macro-level, it is also evident that a stabilization in, or reduction of, the number of births could benefit developing countries by improving the ratio of health resources to the demand for prenatal care, maternity care, and child care (Taucher 1982). There is no consensus, however, as to the benefits that fertility decline might imply for a country's development (Taucher 1979*a*).

Nevertheless, when improved child health is cited as an objective of family planning programmes, what is hoped for is that fertility decline will bring about a change in patterns of birth distribution with respect to risk factors for children, since these patterns are related to levels of fertility. Among these factors are premature and late maternal age, high birth orders, and excessively short birth intervals. Births in these unfavourable categories are likely to be frequent when fertility is high.

In addition, it is hoped that fertility will be reduced among the lowest socio-economic groups, which are made up of people having higher levels of morbidity–mortality and fertility, and with scarce or non-existent access to contraception (unless government family planning programmes have been introduced). All these structural changes would lead to a birth distribution more favourable to lower infant morbidity and mortality.

Risk Factors associated with Fertility

There is an extensive literature on the risks to infant health associated with different categories of birth order, age of mother and birth interval. Among the literature reviews on the subject, those of Buchanan (1976) and Rinehart *et al.* (1985) deserve special mention. The Inter-American Investigation of Childhood Mortality, carried out in fifteen separate country projects between 1968 and 1970 (Puffer and Serrano 1975), made it possible to study neonatal mortality and deaths of children below 1 year of age in relation to maternal age and parity, and to examine infant mortality due to immaturity, nutritional deficiency, and low birth weight in relation to those variables.

At the beginning of the 1970s, the interest aroused by this topic led the World Health Organization to sponsor a collaborative transnational study of family formation patterns and their impact on health (World Health Organization 1976). The WFS programme, conducted during the second half of the 1970s, provided an important source of data for the study of infant mortality in relation to birth order, age of the mother, and birth intervals, since these surveys included pregnancy histories and questions on the survival of live-born children (Taucher 1982 and 1985; Rutstein 1984; Acsadi Associates 1985; Acsadi and Johnson-Acsadi 1986; Hobcraft *et al.* 1985; etc.). In the Americas, there are also at least two countries in which it has been possible to conduct studies based on data from vital statistics to investigate the relation between infant mortality and birth order and the age of the mother: Chile (Taucher 1979*b*, 1979*c*, 1980, 1988) and Costa Rica (Sosa 1984).

Birth Order or Parity

In general, studies of the relationship between infant mortality and birth order all reach similar findings: the greatest risk of death occurs at high birth orders (Omran 1971, 1985; Puffer and Serrano 1975). On the other hand, there is no consensus on the risk of infant mortality associated with the first live-born child. For example, using data from the WFS, Acsadi Associates (1985) identifies nine countries in which the mortality of the first-born child is consistently lower than that of children of subsequent orders, and nine other countries in which the mortality of the first child exceeds that of the second and third orders, only to increase substantially for those of order seven or higher.

In a study based on data from the WFS conducted in Costa Rica, Mexico, Paraguay, and Peru, only in Mexico did first-born children have higher infant mortality than those of orders two and three (Taucher 1985). In analyses of the vital statistics of Chile, where 200,000 births occur annually, data covering 1972 to the present reveals that the infant mortality of the first child is always lower than that of higher birth orders. On the other hand, in Chile, as in other countries, causes of mortality analysed by birth order show that, with the exception of birth trauma as a cause of neonatal mortality, and accidents as a cause of post-neonatal mortality, mortality for all other causes increases regularly with birth order, both for the 1972 birth cohort and for that of 1978 (Taucher 1985).

Age of the Mother

In a large number of studies it has been established that there is a greater risk of infant mortality when the mother is too young, or when she is near the end of her fertile years. In 1974 Nortman carried out an exhaustive review of existing studies and data. She analysed maternal and foetal mortality; stillbirths; perinatal, infant, and neonatal mortality; maternal mortality by cause; and morbidity associated with pregnancy, childbirth, and the post-partum period. The majority of the relationships with maternal age are J- or U-shaped, showing the greatest risk to health, both for mothers and their children, when children are born near the extremes of the fertile period. Similar findings are shown by Rinehart *et al.* (1985), Omran (1985), and Acsadi and Johnson-Acsadi (1986).

Birth Interval

The relationship between the length of the preceding birth interval and infant mortality has also been studied in numerous research papers cited in the literature reviews carried out by Omran (1985), Rinehart *et al.* (1985), and others who have investigated the topic. In all cases it emerges that the risks diminish as the interval increases, and that intervals of less than two years are associated with the highest rates of infant mortality. Hobcraft *et al.* (1983) and Acsadi Associates (1985), using data from the WFS, confirm these enormous differences in infant mortality with respect to the length of the birth interval. Acsadi and Johnson-Acsadi (1986) find that the effect is at a maximum in countries with high infant mortality. They also show that the risk increases again when the interval is prolonged beyond four years. Wolfers and Scrimshaw (1975) showed the relationship between birth order and infant, neonatal, and post-neonatal mortality in Guayaquil, Ecuador. It has also been possible in other countries of the Americas to analyse infant mortality using data from the WFS (Acsadi Associates 1985; and Acsadi and Johnson-Acsadi 1986).

Relationships among Birth Order, Maternal Age, and Birth Interval

The associations described above are univariate relationships, and thus may be influenced by the distribution of the births with respect to other risk factors. One of the important interactions is between parity and the mother's age at birth. It was this interaction that motivated Nortman (1974) to carry out most of her analysis in terms of the age of the mother within birth-order groups. This interaction also provides one of the explanations for the discrepancies among various researchers concerning the relative risk of infant mortality to children of order 1 as compared with the risk to those of orders 2 or 3, or to those of orders 2–6.

In the Chilean vital statistics data for 1987, as can be seen in Fig. 16.1, for mothers up to 29 years of age, births of order 1 have consistently lower infant mortality than those of subsequent orders. From age 30 onwards, in contrast, the mortality of the first child is greater than that of the second, as was observed by Puffer and Serrano in 1975. None the less, the infant mortality rate of the first child born to mothers under 20 years of age is higher than that found among older age-groups, with the exception of first births to women 40 years and over. For this reason, if first-order births have a high proportion of very young mothers and/or a high proportion of older mothers, this will tend to make the overall mortality rate for the first child higher than for the second. In 1987, the situation of first births in Chile was favourable: 63 per cent were to mothers aged 20–29, among whom the infant mortality rate was 13.2 per 1,000, one of the lowest of the various subgroups. In addition, first births to mothers in this group accounted for 26 per cent of total births in the country.

Variations in infant mortality by age of mother (for Chile in 1987), within categories of birth order, illustrated in Fig. 16.2, show that the relationship is U-shaped or in the form of a backwards J. It is remarkable how regularly the rates for the successive birth orders rise from order 2 upwards. It is also clear that first births have lower mortality than those of the following orders only for mothers younger than 30. However, there are not only interactions between age of mother and birth order. The very sharp increase in infant mortality with birth order among young mothers shown in Fig. 16.1 must be influenced in large part by short birth intervals, if these women are to have several children at such a young age. The birth interval is a datum that cannot be obtained from the vital statistics analysed here.

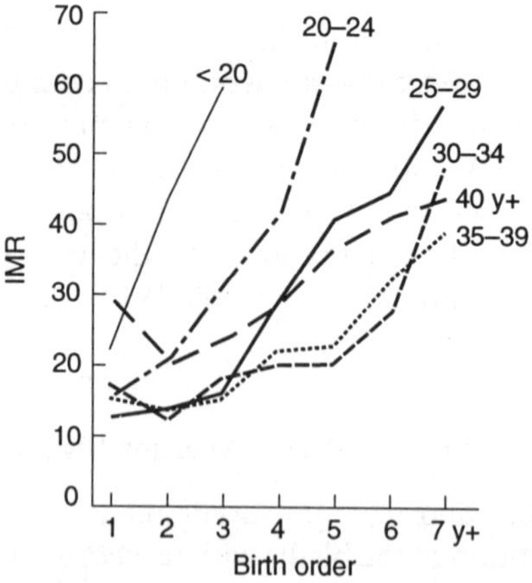

Fig. 16.1. ***Chile, 1987: infant mortality rates by birth order within maternal age groups***

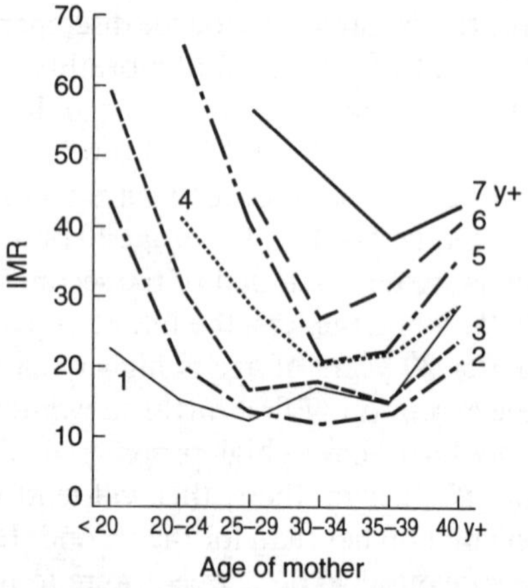

Fig. 16.2. ***Chile, 1987: infant mortality rates by maternal age within birth order groups***

In a study based on data from the WFSs of Costa Rica, Mexico, Paraguay, and Peru, the authors were able to analyse the relationship between infant mortality and the three variables simultaneously (Taucher 1982). They found that the rising trend with birth order, the J- or U-shape with age of mother, and the decrease in infant mortality as the preceding birth interval becomes longer, persist within the categories of the other two variables.

Intermediate Variables

The causal interpretation of differences in infant mortality by birth order, age of mother, and birth interval, which is the basis for assuming that there will be beneficial effects for the health of the child as a result of fertility decline, has been discussed by several authors. For example, Bongaarts (1987) believes that higher infant mortality at advanced maternal ages is due to the effects of other confounding variables, in particular socio-economic ones. He illustrates his hypothesis by showing that the relative infant mortality of children born to older mothers, as compared with that of mothers aged 20–29, is more pronounced in countries with low infant mortality than in countries with high rates. His findings coincide with observations for Chile in 1950 and 1972. In the first of those years, infant mortality was 133 per 1,000, whereas in 1972 it was 73 per 1,000. The mortality differentials, both by birth order and by age of mother, were less pronounced in 1950 than in the year of lower mortality. In turn, in 1972, the differentials were more pronounced for the children of mothers with a high level of education than for those with less schooling (Taucher 1979*b*). This observation gave rise to the hypothesis of the predominantly biological origin of those differentials, which was explored in later work (Taucher 1982).

Just as mortality differentials between the sexes have been increasing with declining mortality, it was thought that it would be easier for a differential of biological origin to manifest itself more clearly when it is not dominated by an excess of adverse environmental factors. In an attempt to discover whether infant mortality differentials by birth order, age of mother, and length of preceding birth interval could be due to a predominance of births occurring to women in low socio-economic groups, who have the highest risk factors, the percentage of births to mothers with low levels of education was analysed for each category of birth order, age of the mother, and birth interval in four countries, using data from the WFS (Taucher 1982 and 1985). The analysis revealed that there was a clear increase in infant mortality with birth order, and a U-shaped curve with respect to the age of the mother. Both of these findings underline the importance of the relationship between the specific rates and these two variables. On the other hand, no similar pattern was found with respect to birth interval. For the first two variables, the distribution by level of education, which was used as a proxy for socio-economic level, seemed to confirm that the differentials were not due to birth order or to age, but, rather, that they were a consequence of the social class to which the births belonged. However, when the rates for each category were standardized according to the birth distribution by mother's level of education, it was found that the standardized rates coincided closely with the observed rates. This is explained by the fact that within each level of maternal education, infant mortality rates by birth order and by age of the mother had a similar pattern to that found for all births.

Although this result does not exclude a possible role for other variables, it does support the medical reasoning that it is more favourable to the health of the mother and the child if she has a small family size, when she is neither too young nor too old, and with a spacing of at least 18 months between births.

In 1985, using data from the WFSs of thirty-nine countries, Hobcraft carried out an analysis of the effect of the three variables in question on neonatal and post-neonatal mortality and on the mortality of children aged 1 year and aged 2–4 years. Working with the births that occurred between five and fifteen years before the interview, he controlled for the sex of the child, the number of children and their survival rates in earlier years, and the mother's education, using a log-linear analysis with no interaction terms. He concluded that the higher infant mortality at advanced maternal ages is due to the socio-economic variables that are confounded with age. In addition, he found a greater risk among first births and among those of order seven or higher, with no gradient from order 2–6.

In 1987 Bongaarts developed a model using the relative risks with respect to age of mother, birth order and birth interval, worked out by Hobcraft in 1987. With it he predicted that fertility decline would have an adverse effect on infant mortality, because it would increase the proportion of first-born children, who would run a higher relative risk of infant mortality (a risk of 1.62 when compared to children of order 2–6). The model gave rise to an interesting debate among Trussell, Potter, and Bongaarts himself (Trussell *et al.* 1988).

Providing new data for the discussion, Table 16.1 presents infant mortality rates for Chile in 1978, by birth order, and by the mother's age and level of education. Given that the major area of doubt centres around the relative risk of the first child with respect to that of subsequent birth orders, it is not necessary to control for the length of the preceding birth interval or for the survival of previously born children. It has to be assumed, however, that there is no interaction of the results with the sex of the child, a factor that Hobcraft controlled for in 1985, and for which the data are not shown in the cross-tabulation.

The largest relative risk for first-born children, compared with those of order two, is 1.23, and corresponds to the children of mothers with low levels of education aged 35–39 years. Such births constitute 0.5 per cent of the total of 218,581 births on which these figures are based. The analysis also shows that the pattern of increase in infant mortality with birth order is maintained within the mother's educational group. According to these data, there is no need to fear that a decline in fertility might increase infant mortality by increasing the proportion of first births, unless the vast majority of births were postponed until age 35 or later.

One possible explanation for discrepancies between the results obtained from vital statistics and the results based on fertility surveys is that in the latter, interviews are conducted only with women of childbearing age. The analysis covers periods of fifteen to twenty years before the survey, in order to obtain a sufficient number of births and deaths, and this means that first-order births and births to mothers younger than 30–35 years include a high proportion of births that occurred at a time when infant mortality was much higher than in more recent periods. For the latter periods, registered births are of higher orders, and are concentrated among mothers of more advanced age. This would tend to reduce the size of the differentials by increasing mortality at low birth orders and reducing it at higher orders. A similar effect would be produced with respect to low and high maternal ages.

Table 16.1. *Chile: infant mortality rates by birth order, age, and level of education of the mother, 1978*

Age	Birth order							
	Total	1	2	3	4	5	6	7+
Low level of education								
< 20	59.5	51.8	79.3	104.4	—	—	—	—
20–24	45.0	33.5	45.7	57.5	68.2	78.4	—	—
25–29	40.5	30.9	36.9	15.7	48.7	55.6	68.7	83.0
30–34	40.2	28.7	27.4	34.1	43.8	43.5	58.5	71.7
35–39	46.2	38.7	31.4	37.3	46.3	66.7	45.9	61.6
40+	53.4	—	—	35.6	—	—	—	—
All ages	47.8	40.7	46.8	46.2	52.8	58.6	62.0	70.3
High level of education								
< 20	42.3	35.2	69.9	—	—	—	—	—
20–24	30.2	20.9	38.1	57.1	—	—	—	—
25–29	22.5	15.7	19.3	31.5	46.2	—	—	—
30–34	23.6	16.1	17.5	20.6	39.9	47.2	—	—
35–39	37.9	29.9	28.9	32.0	44.2	—	—	—
40+	—	—	—	—	—	—	—	—
All ages	28.9	22.6	28.8	34.8	52.5	46.0	80.7	126.5
All levels of education								
< 20	55.4	46.9	77.6	116.4	163.7	—	—	—
20–24	39.4	27.1	42.9	57.4	74.9	84.1	142.1	150.4
25–29	33.3	22.2	27.8	34.1	48.2	53.7	74.9	84.6
30–34	35.0	22.3	22.4	28.0	42.7	44.2	56.8	75.2
35–39	45.8	34.9	30.4	35.0	45.6	58.6	46.2	66.1
40+	55.7	—	41.8	31.7	46.6	71.3	58.2	70.5
All ages	40.9	32.7	39.4	42.3	56.2	56.6	64.1	73.0

Notes: — = fewer than 500 births in the cell. Low education includes none and basic (3.8 and 59.7% of total births respectively). High education combines secondary and higher (36.5% of total births).

One thing that clearly cannot be analysed using vital statistics data is the influence of completed family size and its determinants on the lower mortality of children of low birth order. In an attempt to do this using data from the WFS, the following women were defined as having completed their families: those who had been sterilized; those who were using efficient contraceptive methods and said that they did not want more children; and those who had been in a stable union for more than five years, were not pregnant, and had not given birth within the preceding five years. However, the number of births to such women was so small that no valid estimates could be obtained (Taucher 1982).

Another topic that has been much debated recently is that of birth interval. Hobcraft *et al.* (1983) found that, controlling for maternal age, birth order, education of the mother and sex of the child, infant mortality is always higher after short birth intervals. On the other hand, Potter (1988*a*) developed a theory related to the use of contraceptives, morbidity, and the utilization of health services to explain the greater apparent health risk for short birth intervals, a relationship that could also be partly explained by deficiencies in the data collected in the surveys.

Those who accept that there is a relationship between infant mortality and length of the preceding birth interval have tried to find its cause. The most acceptable explanation appears to be the maternal depletion syndrome described by Jelliffe in 1966. Other possibilities include competition with the previous child, the greater frequency of infections (Pebley and Elo 1989), and prematurity, which could be more frequent with short preceding birth intervals and is a known risk factor (Retherford *et al.* 1989).

Estimating the Effect of Fertility Decline

There are several possible techniques for measuring the mechanisms by which fertility decline acts on maternal and child health. The greatest barrier to the estimation of this measure is the lack or scarcity of adequate data. The other major problem is the difficulty of separating the effects of the fertility decline *per se* from the effect of other variables.

There are several possible methods of estimation: (1) Simple correlations between health and fertility indicators in countries or geographic units, or ratios between health trends and fertility indicators over time; (2) multivariate analysis, using data from countries or geographical subdivisions of countries in which the health indicator is the dependent variable, and fertility is included among the independent or predictor variables, or, in the case of surveys in which the unit of observation is the child, the dependent variable is survival, and the explanatory variables are the characteristics of the child or of its mother; (3) the application of models derived from multivariate analyses, using the independent variables that are found or, in the absence of direct observations, that have been estimated, for a country or region, to predict what will happen to its level of infant mortality; and (4) standardization of rates to estimate the effect of changes in the distribution of births that can be linked to the decline in fertility.

The Availability, Advantages, and Disadvantages of the Data

The system of vital statistics, which constitute the optimal source of data for the study of fertility and infant mortality, is problematic because the registration of these statistics is still underdeveloped in many countries of the region (UNFPA 1982). Nevertheless, many of these countries have estimates of fertility and infant mortality levels, thus permitting the study of trends in fertility and infant mortality over time.

To be able to estimate the effect that changes in the distribution of births due to the decline in fertility has on infant mortality, it is necessary to obtain data on birth order, age of the mother, interval since the preceding birth and some socio-economic variables, at least for the births. In the *Demographic Yearbook*, for example (United Nations 1970, 1987), data may be found on live births by birth order and age of mother. However, there are no data on intervals between births. In 1979 Van Houte-Minet reported on an inventory of the fertility and stillbirth data that are gathered on vital statistics and census forms, and on the data on these vital events that are published in the various countries of the world.

Age-specific mortality rates can be calculated when the same data appear in both the birth statistics and the statistics bearing on deaths of children under one year of age, that is when deaths can be matched with births. However, given that such data are available for only a few countries, most studies use survey data to calculate infant mortality differentials with respect to those variables.

The WFS, which was conducted during the second half of the 1970s, collected data on pregnancy histories and on child survival. It therefore appeared to be a valuable source of data for calculating infant mortality differentials with respect to different variables. However, the study of infant mortality was not an intended objective of the survey. Its principal advantage is that the data for the mother and the child come from the same informant. Its principal drawback is that the number of vital events captured is very small. This makes it necessary to use information for dates long before the survey. For example, taking births that occurred one to twenty-one years before the survey, it was possible to gather data on 22,000 births for Mexico and 20,000 for Peru. Hobcraft *et al.* (1985) analysed births occurring five to fifteen years before the survey, which reduced the number of births available for analysis by half. On the other hand, the vital statistics for Chile, which has a population of about 12 million, provide information on over 200,000 births each year.

One consequence of this, in combination with the fact that interviews were held with women of reproductive age, is, as has already been mentioned, that more births of low orders and among young mothers are available for analysis, and that these occurred in large proportion fifteen to twenty years earlier, when fertility and infant mortality were higher. In contrast, births of higher order and births to older women tended to occur more recently, when infant mortality had already declined. This may reduce the intensity of the differentials observed for these variables.

Another disadvantage of the surveys is that it is very difficult to locate fertility levels in time and thereby determine their trend. Nor are the units of observation sufficiently numerous to allow detection of changes in the distribution of births over time.

Some Different Estimation Techniques

Analysis of Correlations or Trend Ratios However strong the correlation between infant mortality and fertility, or the relationship between the trends in these variables, no inference can be made from them about causality; nor is it possible to detect, even if a causal relation actually exists, whether infant mortality is reduced by the decline in fertility, or vice versa. In spite of this limitation, because the relationships are easy to understand, they are frequently presented in chart form, in documents that have widespread circulation, aimed at a public that has little familiarity with complex statistical methods.

Multivariate Analysis This technique—by means of the selection and hierarchical structuring of the influence on infant mortality of the different independent variables, among them the relationships with fertility—permits the elimination of some of the disadvantages associated with the study of simple correlations. One real problem is the difficulty of finding indicators of equal quality for the different units of observation, if several countries or geographical subdivisions are analysed. It also frequently happens that one tries to measure the influence of a large number of variables with very few units of observation, which is incorrect from a statistical point of view. These problems are less important when it is possible to work with the child—its characteristics and those of its mother—as the unit of observation, as happens with fertility surveys. Nevertheless, it is difficult to estimate the effect of the correlation among the independent variables when all the possible observations are included in the model. The models sometimes succeeded in explaining only a small proportion of the total variation, and yet the coefficients of the different variables are accepted uncritically.

Application of Models To be able to use models for the prediction of the effects of fertility decline, a series of conditions must be fulfilled, and it is usually difficult to discover whether this has been done. The most basic condition is that the relationships between the predictor variables and the dependent variable must be valid for the new unit of observation to which the model is to be applied. In most cases, this is difficult or impossible to verify. The countries whose data are used to construct the models are often different from those for which data do not exist. In the case of multivariate models, the lack of data for some of the independent variables with which the model was constructed makes the estimated parameter values inapplicable. When the model implies assumptions on changes in birth distribution, based on the reduction in fertility, it is possible that the experience of countries in which the data exist is not necessarily valid for other countries to which researchers wish to apply the model.

The Effect of Changes in the Distribution of Births This is the simplest and most direct way of measuring or predicting the effect under investigation. The major problem is, again, the availability of data.

Fertility decline is always accompanied by a reduction in the proportion of high-order births, and the proportion of births to older mothers also declines. The proportion of births to very young mothers varies, however. In the initial phase of the fertility decline, these births usually increase in relative importance because the reduction begins among women of intermediate and more advanced age. Only when improved education and access to contraception have reached younger women, does the importance of births to very young women decline as a proportion of all births (United Nations 1970 and 1987).

Little is known about the impact of fertility decline on the length of the birth interval. Using data from French fertility surveys, Desplanques (1986) found that the average length of the interval increased from 3.2 years in 1962 to 3.9 years in 1981. The mean age of mothers between births of successive orders, as derived from vital statistics, has the limitation that we do not know which children of a given order will have another sibling. In Chile, there was a large increase between 1972 and 1987 in maternal age differentials between successive birth orders up to order three, as may be seen in Table 16.2. The data in this table, as noted above, suffer from problems of interpretation.

Table 16.2. *Chile: difference in mean maternal ages between births of successive orders, 1972 and 1987*

Between orders	1972	1987
2 and 1	1.96	3.24
3 and 2	1.86	2.85
4 and 3	1.64	1.74
5 and 4	1.41	1.38

Sources: INE 1972 and 1987.

In terms of socio-economic factors, it is possible that when fertility began to decline, the reduction occurred more markedly among women of higher socio-economic status. If that were so, general levels of infant mortality could rise, because of the decline in the proportion of births with the most favourable conditions for survival. The reverse situation would occur at a later stage of the decline, when the fertility reduction is concentrated among the lowest socio-economic groups.

The literature reveals a wide range of different calculations of reductions in infant mortality, and all the studies attribute the results to longer spacing between births, smaller family size, and more appropriate maternal ages. Some studies calculate, through standardization, the level of infant mortality that would have resulted simply from a change in the distribution of the births (Morris *et al.* 1975; Trussell and Pebley 1984; Omran 1985; Taucher 1979*b*, 1985). Some authors include in their discussion some mention of the influence of socio-economic factors, or they calculate the effect of structural changes on levels of infant mortality (Potter 1988*b*; Taucher 1985, 1989). In 1982 Ochoa studied changes in the structure of mortality and morbidity by age and cause resulting from the demographic changes brought about by the decline in fertility.

As already mentioned, it is extremely difficult to measure structural changes using survey data. The two Latin American countries in which it has been possible to estimate the influence of changes in the distribution of births on infant mortality, using vital statistics data, are Costa Rica and Chile. In Costa Rica, the method used was to calculate the ratio of the regression coefficient of the trend in infant mortality rates (standardized by the structure of births) to the coefficient of the trend in the observed rates, as described by Morris *et al.* (1975). In 1984 Sosa found that the combined changes in the structure by birth order and age of the mother explained 21 per cent of the decline in infant mortality observed between 1960 and 1977. The changes in composition by birth order alone explain 24 per cent of the decline, and changes by maternal age explain 5 per cent. This means that the effects are not additive.

This finding is corroborated by data from Chile for the years 1972 and 1987. Changes in the structure by birth order explain 8.7 per cent of the total decline, and changes by age of the mother, 3 per cent, while both variables together explain 20.3 per cent. This means that the interaction effect in Costa Rica was negative −8 percentage points—whereas in Chile, the effect of the combined changes was favourable and positive, exceeding the sum of the two separate changes by 8.7 percentage points; that is, it increased the sum of the individual changes by 74 per cent. For this reason, it is impossible to interpret adequately the contribution of structural changes with respect to a single variable, nor can the contributions of several variables be added together without taking their interaction into account.

To show the changes in the distribution of births that result from the decline in fertility, high-risk births were defined on the basis of the actual rates found in Chile. In the case of birth order and age of mother, these were: second-order births or higher to women under 20 years of age; births of order four or higher to women aged 20–24; births of order five or higher to women 25–29; and births of order seven or higher to women in the remaining age-groups. The proportion of births in those categories as a percentage of all births (excluding births of unknown, classification), is shown in Table 16.3, along with the TFRs for various years.

Table 16.3. *TFRs and % of high-risk births in four countries, various years*

Country	Year	TFR	% at high risk	Year	TFR	% at high risk
Costa Rica	1965	6.6	48.9	1984	3.5	15.4
Chile	1972	3.4	22.0	1987	2.5	5.8
El Salvador	1966	6.6	36.2	1984	5.6	25.7
Panama	1966	5.6	42.4	1984	3.5	23.6

Sources: United Nations (1970, 1987); Ross *et al*. (1988).

The table indicates that when fertility declines, a lower percentage of births are high-risk. When comparisons are made between countries, there is no strict relationship between the two measures. Countries with the same total fertility rates have very different percentages of high-risk births, which means that one should be cautious in extrapolating possible effects to countries or settings different from those for which information is available.

Between 1972 and 1982, changes in the distribution of births by birth order, age of mother and level of education of the mother explain 29.5 per cent of the total decline in the infant mortality rate in Chile (Taucher 1986). In this calculation, 1972 age-specific mortality rates in terms of these variables were applied to births occurring in 1982. The rate, which was obtained by dividing the sum of the expected deaths by the total number of births, is the infant mortality rate that would have been observed in 1982 as a result only of change in the distribution of births. The ratio of the difference between that rate and the 1972 rate to the difference observed between the 1972 and 1982 rates is the percentage of the total decline attributable to the distributional change.

An attempt was also made to explore the birth-distribution hypothesis to explain why infant mortality continued to fall in Chile, despite wide swings in the country's economic situation between 1967 and 1984. The theory was that couples partly avoided having children because of the unfavourable economic situation (Taucher 1984, 1989). The analysis did, indeed, find a close relationship between cumulative fertility at birth orders 1–3 and the economic situation, as measured by per capita GNP (Fig. 16.3).

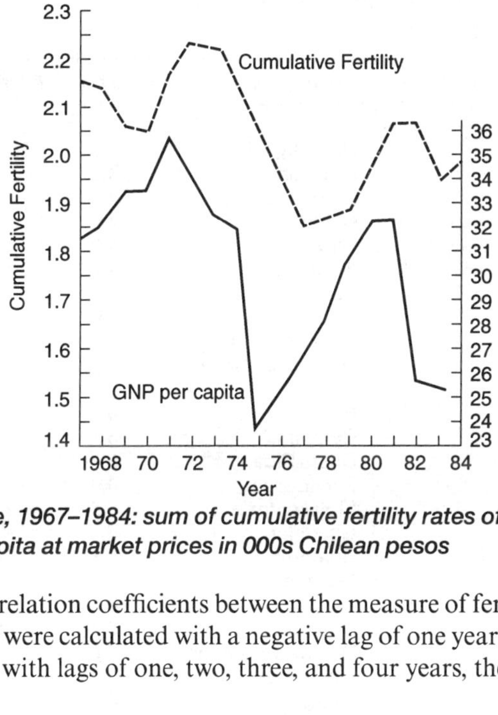

Fig. 16.3. ***Chile, 1967–1984: sum of cumulative fertility rates of birth orders 1–3 and GNP per capita at market prices in 000s Chilean pesos***

When the correlation coefficients between the measure of fertility and the economic indicator were calculated with a negative lag of one year (–1), for the same year (lag 0) and with lags of one, two, three, and four years, the following values were found:

r(–1) = 0.18
r(0) = 0.55
r(1) = 0.84
r(2) = 0.83
r(3) = 0.60
r(4) = 0.26

If causality could be attributed to these correlations, they would show that the response of fertility to the economic situation is strongest one and two years later, and that it has positive sign.

Fertility and Infant Mortality Levels in Latin America and the Caribbean

To complete this study, the fertility and infant mortality situations of various Latin American and Caribbean countries is summarized for the periods 1950–5 and 1985–90 (Table 16.4). Clearly, no causal inferences can be made from these data, but it is interesting to note the tremendous changes in both measures that occurred during the period in question.

Table 16.4. *Latin America and the Caribbean: Classification of countries by level of the TFR in 1950–1955 and 1985–1990, and average infant mortality rates for different population groups*

Period and TFR level	Country	TFR	Average IMR
1950–5			
Low	Uruguay	2.7	57
Moderate	Argentina	3.2	64
High	Barbados	4.7	
	Chile	4.9	
	Cuba	4.0	
	Jamaica	4.2	92.5
	Panama	5.7	
	Puerto Rico	5.0	
	Trinidad & Tobago	5.3	
	Other Caribbean	4.9	
Very high	Bolivia	6.7	
	Brazil	6.1	
	Colombia	6.7	
	Costa Rica	6.7	
	Ecuador	6.9	
	El Salvador	6.5	
	Guadeloupe	5.6	
	Guatemala	7.1	
	Guyana	6.6	
	Haiti	6.1	
	Honduras	7.1	129.8
	Windward Islands	6.6	
	Martinique	5.7	
	Mexico	6.7	
	Nicaragua	7.3	
	Dominican Republic	7.5	
	Paraguay	6.6	
	Peru	6.9	
	Surinam	6.6	
	Venezuela	6.5	
1985–90			
Low	Barbados	2.0	
	Chile	2.5	
	Cuba	2.0	
	Guadeloupe	2.2	
	Guyana	2.7	

	Windward Islands	2.9	
	Jamaica	2.9	
	Martinique	2.1	
	Puerto Rico	2.4	
	Trinidad & Tobago	2.7	18.9
	Uruguay	2.6	
	Other Caribbean	2.5	
Moderate	Argentina	3.3	
	Brazil	3.5	
	Colombia	3.6	
	Costa Rica	3.3	
	Dominican Republic	3.6	36.0
	Panama	3.1	
	Surinam	3.0	
	Venezuela	3.8	
High	Ecuador	4.6	
	El Salvador	5.1	
	Guatemala	5.8	
	Haiti	5.6	
	Honduras	5.6	
	Mexico	4.0	
	Nicaragua	5.5	
	Paraguay	4.5	
	Peru	4.5	
Very high	Bolivia	6.1	110.0

Sources: United Nations 1988.

Notes: IMR = Infant Mortality Rate; low = <2.9; moderate = 3.0–3.9; high = 4.0–5.9; very high = 6.0+.

Discussion and Conclusions

All the international literature reviewed by this author shows greater risk to maternal and child health for births of high order, births to women at the extremes of their reproductive years, and births occurring after short intervals. In the high-risk categories of birth order and maternal age, a greater proportion of births are to women in the lower socio-economic groups. However, this fact is not sufficient to explain the differentials, because the pattern of the rates persists even within those socio-economic groups. And with the exception of birth trauma and accidents, the differentials in infant mortality by birth order and age of mother also hold for the different groups of causes of neonatal and post-neonatal death.

The main problems in estimating the effect of fertility decline on infant health stem from the lack of data and the complexity of the relationships and interactions among multiple explanatory and intervening variables. Since there are few countries for which vital statistics data can be used for estimation, it has been necessary to make use of survey data, especially data from the WFS. Part of the explanation for the discrepancies among the findings of various researchers who have examined the risk of infant mortality of first-born children compared with that of subsequent birth orders might be the different distributions of first-order births by age of mother found in the different socio-economic groups, as well as the differences in the various data sources. Another important factor might be that, when women of reproductive age are interviewed, first-born children and those of young mothers belong preferentially to periods in which infant mortality was higher.

Among the various methods available for measuring the impact of fertility decline on infant mortality, those that are based on changes in birth distribution (in terms of birth order, age of mother and spacing) seem to be the most appropriate. These techniques also make it possible to measure the interaction among the different factors, which has been quite considerable in studies based on vital statistics. It is also important to take into account the effect that fertility decline exerts on birth distributions among different socio-economic groups.

The proportion of the decline in infant mortality that can be attributed to a reduction in fertility varies in different studies, but it seldom exceeds 30 per cent. While this may well be due to the fact that insufficient information is available to measure the entire effect of fertility decline, it should also be interpreted as suggesting that a number of other factors have an impact on levels and trends of infant mortality. Primary health care programmes, improved levels of education, urbanization, the availability of safe drinking water, and the more equitable distribution of income, among other factors, all strongly influence a population's health conditions and the probabilities of survival. This does not detract however from the importance of the beneficial effects that fertility decline appears to have on maternal and child health.

References

Acsadi Associates (1985), *Family Planning and the Well-being of Women and Children* (London: International Planned Parenthood Federation).

Acsadi, G. T. F., and Johnson-Acsadi, G. (1986), *Optimum Conditions for Childbearing* (London: International Planned Parenthood Federation).

Bongaarts, J. (1987), 'Does Family Planning Reduce Infant Mortality Rates?', *Population and Development Review*, 13/2: 323–34.

Buchanan, R. (1976), *Efecto de la Paridad en la Salud Materna* (Informes Médicos Serie J, No. 8; Washington: George Washington University).

Desplanques, G. (1986), '50 ans de fécondité en France: Rangs et intervalles entre naissances', *Population*, 41/2: 233–58.

Hobcraft, J. N. (1987), 'Does Family Planning Save Children's Lives?', Technical background paper prepared for the International Conference on Better Health for Women and Children through Family Planning, Nairobi, Kenya, 5–9 Oct., cited in Bongaarts (1987).

—— MacDonald, J. W., and Rutstein, S. O. (1983), 'Child-Spacing Effects on Infant and Early Childhood Mortality', *Population Index* 49/4: 585–618.

—— MacDonald, J. W., and Rutstein, S. O. (1985), 'Demographic Determinants of Infant and Early Childhood Mortality', *Population Studies*, 39/3: 363–85.

Instituto Nacional de Estadísticas, Servicio de Registro Civil e Identificación, Ministerio de Salud (1972), *Anuario de Demografía 1972* (Santiago: INE).

—— (1987), *Anuario de Demografía 1987* (Santiago: INE).

Jones, G. W. (1969), *The Economic Effect of Declining Fertility in Less Developed Countries* (Population Council, occasional paper; New York).

Jelliffe, D. B. (1966), *The Assessment of Nutritional Status of the Community* (WHO Monograph Series, *53*; Geneva: WHO).

Morris, N., Udry, R., and Chase, C. (1975), 'Shifting Age-parity Distribution of Births and the Decrease in Infant Mortality', *American Journal of Public Health*, 65 (Apr.): 359–62.

Nortman, D. (1974), 'Parental Age as a Factor in the Outcome of Pregnancy and in Child Development', *Consejo de Población*, 16, pub. in Spanish as *Edad de los Padres como Factor en el Resultado del Embarazo y del Desarrollo del Niño* (Bogotá: Asociación Colombiana para el Estudio de la Población).

Ochoa, L. H. (1982) (ed.), 'Implicaciones Socioeconómicas y Demográficas del Descenso de la Fecundidad en Colombia', *Monografías de la Corporación Centro Regional de Población*, 18 (Apr.).

Omran, A. R. (1971), 'Beneficios para la Salud de la Planificación Familiar.' (MCH/71.7; Geneva: WHO).

—— (1985). 'Fecundidad y Salud: La Experiencia Latinoamericana', PAHO, Pan-american Health Office, Regional Office of the WHO, Washington.

Pebley, A. R., and Elo, I. T. (1989), 'The Relationship of Birth Spacing and Child Health', IUSSP, *International Population Conference*, 1989, (Liège: IUSSP).

Potter, J. E. (1988*a*), 'Birth Spacing and Child Survival: A Cautionary Note Regarding the Evidence from WFS', *Population Studies*, 42/3: 443–50.

—— (1988*b*), 'Does Family Planning Reduce Infant Mortality?', *Population Development Review*, 14/1: 179–87.

Puffer, R. R., and Serrano, C. V. (1975); 'Birth-weight, Maternal Age and Birth Order: Three Important Determinants of Infant Mortality,' (Scientific Publication, No. 294; Washington: PAHO/WHO).

Retherford, R. D., Kim Choe, M., Thapa, S., and Gubhaju, B. B. (1989), 'To What Extent does Breastfeeding Explain Birth Interval Effects on Early Childhood Mortality?', *Demography*, 26/3: 439–50.

Rinehart, W., Kols, A., and Moore, S. (1985), *Madres y Niños Más Sanos Mediante la Planificación Familiar* (Population Reports. Series J, 27 (May–June): Baltimore, Md.: Population Information Program, Johns Hopkins University).

Ross, J. A., Rich, M., Molzan, J. P., and Pensak, M. (1988), *Family Planning and Child Survival. 100 Developing Countries* (Columbia University, New York: Center for Population and Family Health).

Rutstein, S. O. (1984), *Infant and Child Mortality: Levels, Trends and Demographic Differentials* (WFS Comparative Studies, No. 43); Voorburg: International Statistical Institute).

Sosa, D. (1984), *Interrelación Entre la Fecundidad y la Mortalidad Infantil en Costa Rica, 1960–1977: Mortalidad y Fecundidad en Costa Rica* (San José: Asociación Demográfica Costarricense).

Taucher, E. (1979*a*), 'Efectos Demográficos y Socio-económicos de los Programas de Planificación de la Familia en la América Latina', in V. L. Urquidi and J. B. Mordos (eds.), *Población y Desarrollo en América Latina* (Mexico City: El Colegio de México).

—— (1979*b*), *Mortalidad Infantil en Chile: Tendencias, Diferenciales y Causas*. Mimeo, CELADE, Santiago.

—— (1979*c*), 'La Mortalidad Infantil en Chile.' *Notas de Población*, 7/2: 35–72.

—— (1980), 'Measuring the Health Effects of Family Planning Programs: The Role of Surveys in the Analysis of Family Planning Programs', in A. Hermalin and B. Enturisle (eds.), *Proceedings of Seminar held in Bogotá, Colombia, 28–31 October 1980* (Liège: Ordina Editions), 441–50.

—— (1982), 'Effects of the Decline of Fertility on Levels of Infant Mortality: A Study based on Data from Five Latin American Countries', Unpublished report to the Ford and Rockefeller Foundations.

—— (1984), 'Adaptación de la Conducta Reproductiva a las Contingencias Económicas', Report to UNICEF, Santiago.

—— (1985), *The Influence of Family Planning Programmes on Infant Mortality Levels: Studies to Enhance the Evaluation of Family Planning Programmes* (*Population Studies*, No. 87, ST/ESA/SER.A/87; New York: UN Department of International Economic and Social Affairs), 79–94.

—— (1986), 'Fecundidad y Salud Materno-infantil', *Boletín Asociación Chilena de Protección a la Familia*, 22 (July–Dec.), 26–46.

—— (1988), *The Effect of Fertility Decline on Infant Mortality* (Technical Study 57s; Ottawa: International Development Research Centre). (Also available in Spanish and French.)

—— (1989), 'Behavioural Factors in Demographic Responses to Economic Crisis', Presented to the Informal Session: Demographic Responses to the Economic Crisis, of the XXI International Population Conference of the International Union for the Scientific Study of Population, New Delhi, India, 20–7 Sept. 1989.

Trussell, J., and Pebley, A. R. (1984), *The Potential Impact of Changes in Fertility on Infant, Child and Maternal Mortality* (World Bank Staff Working Papers, No. 698; Population and Development Series, No. 23; Washington).

—— Potter, J., and Bongaarts, J. (1988), 'Does Family Planning Reduce Infant Mortality?', *Population and Development Review*, 14/1: 171–90.

United Nations (1970), *Demographic Yearbook 1969* (New York: UN Department of International Economic and Social Affairs).

—— (1987), *Demographic Yearbook 1986* (New York: UN Department of International Economic and Social Affairs).

—— (1988), *World Demographic Estimates and Projections 1950–2025* (ST/ESA/SER.R/79; New York: UN Department of International Economic and Social Affairs).

UNFPA (United Nations Fund for Population Activities) (1982), *Diagnóstico del Registro Civil Latinoamericano* (Montevideo: Instituto Interamericano del Niño).

Van Houte-Minet, M. (1979), *Inventaire des données collectées et publiées dans le domaine de la fécondité et de la mortinatalité* (Documents of the Union, No. 15; Liège: IUSSP).

Wolfers, D., and Scrimshaw, S. (1975), 'Child Survival and Intervals between Pregnancies in Guayaquil, Ecuador', *Population Studies*, 29/3: 479–96.

Woods, R. I., Watterson, P. A., and Woodward, J. H. (1988), 'The Causes of Rapid Infant Mortality Decline in England and Wales, 1861–1921. Part I', *Population Studies*, 42/3: 343–66.

——— ——— ——— (1989), 'The Causes of Rapid Infant Mortality Decline in England and Wales, 1861–1921. Part II', *Population Studies*, 43/1: 113–32.

World Health Organization (1976), 'Family Formation Patterns and Health', in A. R. Omran and C. C. Standley (co-ordinators and eds.), An international collaborative study in India, Iran, Lebanon, Philippines, and Turkey (Geneva: WHO).

17 The Fertility Transition and Adolescent Childbearing: The Case of Colombia

ELENA PRADA-SALAS

Introduction

Since the early 1980s, there has been growing concern about the issue of adolescent pregnancy and early childbearing, not only in developed but also in developing countries. The concern arises out of the possible adverse demographic, social, and economic effects that accompany early conjugal union and the subsequent beginning of childbearing at very early ages.

In Colombia, in spite of the dramatic decline in total fertility that occurred during the period 1969–86, fertility among teenagers did not decline as rapidly as it did among older age-groups. Similarly, the pace of family formation, defined as the age at which reproductive activity begins, has not undergone the type of major change that might have been expected in light of Colombia's overall decline in fertility and its rate of economic development. And although the present ASFR of 78 births per 1,000 women aged 15–19 years is one of the lowest in tropical South America, it is still high compared to levels in developed countries.

It is difficult to predict future patterns of adolescent fertility in Colombia, because the society is passing through a process of such profound social, economic and cultural change. Nevertheless, for a developing society like Colombia, which is becoming increasingly urbanized and industrialized, and in which better and higher levels of education and training are becoming increasingly important, the postponement of childbearing until after the age of 20 is an important policy goal. An abundant literature on the subject has shown that early childbearing is associated with such adverse demographic effects as larger family size, and that it contributes to shortening the average time between generations, thereby leading to a more rapid rate of population growth. In addition to these adverse demographic effects, early childbearing also has negative social and economic consequences for the mother, for her child, and for society in general. The adolescent mother may leave school early, thus reducing her likelihood of completing her education and becoming better equipped to compete in the labour-market, both of which are factors that might enable her to achieve an adequate enough income level to support herself and her child. Without such a capability, the adolescent mother and her child run the risk of becoming a burden on society.

The level of adolescent childbearing is dependent on both the size and the rate of change in the fertility rates of women 15–19 relative to the overall fertility of the country, as well as to the size of the female population in the 15–19 age-group. It is necessary, therefore, to estimate the actual number of births that are occurring among adolescents, since this number may be rising even where their fertility rates may be on the decline.

What are trends in adolescent fertility in Colombia likely to be in the coming years, given the behaviour patterns that existed between 1969 and 1986 and in the light of current levels of childbearing among this age-group? Speculating a little, one might anticipate that adolescent fertility could follow one of three possible paths. It might decline even more quickly than has been the case up to the present, if one or several of the following factors are present: a large rise in age at entry into conjugal union; a more widespread use of effective contraceptive methods; and/or a greater resort to abortion (even illegal abortion) by women aged 15–19. It is possible, on the other hand, that the decline in adolescent fertility will continue at the same pace as it did between 1969–76 and 1976–86—at almost 2.5 percentage points yearly—if the same patterns of reproductive behaviour continue to operate in the same manner. At the other extreme, the adolescent fertility rate, particularly extra-marital fertility, might even increase as a result of a large rise in age at marriage because of improved educational levels among young women. In fact this tendency is already visible in Colombia.

The aim of this study is to examine the recent fertility behaviour of adolescents during the years of Colombia's demographic transition, especially in terms of educational levels; the consequences of early childbearing; the country's present situation compared with that of others in the Latin American region; and a possible future course of action for the coming years.

The Demographic Transition in Colombia

One of the most widely examined aspects of Colombia's demographic history, documented by a number of researchers, has been the huge decline in fertility that occurred between the end of the 1960s and the end of the 1980s. The first evidence of the beginning of a fertility transition in Colombia was noted in an analysis of data from the National Fertility Survey of 1969 (Elkins 1973). Later, the results of the 1973 census made it possible to confirm the continuation of this decline (Potter *et al.* 1976). The finding was then definitively corroborated by an analysis of the results of the 1976 WFS (Prada and Bailey 1977). Subsequent national surveys carried out in 1978 and 1980 (Ochoa *et al.* 1983) and in 1986 (Prada and Ojeda 1987) continued to substantiate a decline in fertility, although this was occurring at a slower rate than during the period between 1969 and 1976.

As Table 17.1 indicates, the TFR in Colombia declined from 6.7 in 1969 to 3.8 in 1978, that is, a decline of 43 per cent, compared with one of only 8 per cent between 1980 and 1986, when the average number of children per woman went from 3.6 to 3.3. In other words, there has been a tendency toward stabilization, or a deceleration of the fertility decline.

Table 17.1. *Colombia: TFRs among women in union aged 15 to 49 years, by area of residence and year*

Area of residence	1969	1973	1976	1978	1980	1986
TOTAL	6.7	4.6	4.4	3.8	3.6	3.3
Urban	5.2	3.5	3.5	3.1	3.0	2.8
Rural	9.2	6.7	6.3	5.4	5.1	4.9

Both urban and rural fertility have fallen at a similar pace, although the urban trend seems to have decelerated during the last few years, while rural fertility continues its same rate of decline. Similarly, by 1986 levels of fertility in both areas of the country had been reduced to almost half the levels found at the end of the 1960s. As a result, the differential between urban and rural women of 4 live births by the end of a woman's fertile period had narrowed to only 2 by the mid-1980s.

Another important aspect of Colombia's fertility decline has to do with its structure: the highest peak of fertility has shifted to earlier ages. The ASFRs shown in Table 17.2 indicate that in 1969 the highest level was found among women 25–29 years, while by 1986 it was occurring among women aged 20–24. It

Table 17.2. *Colombia: ASFRs and % change, by area of residence and year*

Residence and age-group	Year			% Change		
	1969	1976	1986	1969–76	1976–86	1969–86
TOTAL						
15–19	118	96	78	19	19	34
20–24	270	215	181	20	16	33
25–29	300	211	17	130	19	43
30–34	272	163	121	40	26	56
35–39	195	124	79	36	36	59
40–44	90	52	30	42	42	67
45–49	25	22	9	12	59	64
TFR	6.4	4.4	3.3	31	25	48
Urban						
15–19	96	76	64	21	16	33
20–24	226	190	158	16	17	30
25–29	242	178	146	26	18	40
30–34	204	134	99	34	26	51
35–39	134	84	57	37	32	57
40–44	71	45	21	37	53	70
45–49	13	11	5	15	54	61
TFR	4.9	3.6	2.8	27	22	43
Rural						
15–19	143	160	117	−12	21	18
20–24	323	313	247	3	21	24
25–29	361	310	248	14	20	31
30–34	323	250	175	23	30	23
35–39	257	221	129	14	42	50
40–44	109	90	45	17	50	59
45–49	35	46	16	−31	65	54
TFR	7.8	6.9	4.9	12	29	37

should also be noted that all age-groups participated in Colombia's decline in fertility between 1969 and 1986, and there is evidence that the most significant declines occurred among older women. The decline was of the order of 34 and 67 per cent for young women 15–19 and 40–44 years respectively. Among adolescents, the proportional decline was similar in both periods under consideration (19 per cent).

The same patterns persist if the data are examined separately for urban and rural populations. Nevertheless, the declines in fertility from 1969 to 1986 were smaller for rural women (ranging from 18 to 59 per cent) than for urban women (between 30 and 70 per cent). Similarly, the decline among rural women occurred later, with the largest drop occurring between 1976 and 1986. In that later year, ASFRs among rural women aged 25–29 were as high as those among women aged 20–24 years.

Along with the sharp change in fertility, the country has continued along a path of increasing socio-economic development, illustrated by higher levels of urbanization and industrialization, higher levels of schooling, and increases in the levels of higher education.

Up until the early 1960s Colombia was a predominantly rural country, with low educational levels, especially among women. Since that time, however, there have been significant changes. For example, in 1951 a little more than two-thirds of the population lived in the countryside. This proportion had fallen significantly by 1964 (to 48 per cent), and by 1985 it represented only 33 per cent of the total population. Women's low educational levels are reflected in the illiteracy rates of women older than 15. In 1951 40 per cent of those over 15 years of age did not know how to read or write; this proportion had dropped to 22 per cent by 1973, and at the present time it is around 14 per cent. Along with this change, the demand for intermediate and higher education has been increasing in recent years (DANE 1985).

The overall rate of female labour-force participation among rural women increased from 16 per cent in 1971 to 27 per cent in 1980. For city women aged 15 to 49 years, the participation rate for 1985 was 39 per cent (see Chapter 14). In addition to the processes of urbanization and modernization, improvements in education, and increased female participation in the labour-market, towards the end of the 1960s, the introduction of organized programmes of family planning also contributed to the decline in fertility, by increasing knowledge and use of contraceptive methods. In 1978 90 per cent of women of reproductive age knew of at least one contraceptive method. By 1986 this proportion had risen to 99 per cent. Furthermore, among women in union, contraceptive use showed a sustained increase between the first survey in 1969 and the DHS of 1986 (DHS-86). In 1969 28 per cent of women in union were using a contraceptive method, compared with 65 per cent by 1986. The most pronounced increases were among rural residents, for whom this proportion went from 15 per cent in 1969 to 53 per cent in 1986. Among urban women, the change was from 45 to 70 per cent for those same years. As a result, the urban–rural differential in contraceptive use declined from 30 to 17 percentage points during the years in question. The gains in contraceptive use were achieved in large measure through demand for the pill, female sterilization, and the IUD (Prada and Ojeda 1987).

While all the factors mentioned here created favourable conditions for fertility decline in Colombia, the mass communications media, which have developed widely since the 1970s, also influenced changes in the attitudes and reproductive behaviour of the general population. As well as promoting the use of consumer goods from more developed countries, the media transmitted new ideas about women's roles in society, the ideal family size best suited to the needs of the new society, certain aspects of sexuality, especially those pertaining to women, and the separation of procreation from sexual pleasure. The demands of a new and modern urban society created new pressures and imposed greater costs for the support of a large family. For this reason, in addition to a decline in the actual number of births, the ideal family size has also dropped, going from 4.5 in 1969 (Estrada *et al.* 1973) to 2.7 in 1986 (CCRP *et al.* 1986).

Adolescent Fertility in Colombia

In 1986, according to the DHS, the level of adolescent fertility, measured as the number of births per 1,000 women aged 15–19 years, was 78. As may be seen in Table 17.3, this rate represents a substantial decrease compared to 1969, when it was 118 per 1,000. The decline in adolescent fertility was much more pronounced among rural residents than among city-dwellers. For the former, the rate dropped from 160 births in 1973–6 to 117 per 1,000 in the 1981–6 period. In urban areas, the drop was from 76 to 64 per 1,000.

Table 17.3. ***Colombia: number of live births per 1,000 women aged 15–19, national total, by area of residence, and by year***

Area of residence	Year		
	1965–9	1973–6	1981–6
TOTAL	118	97	78
Urban	96	76	64
Rural	143	160	117

Besides place of residence, educational achievement has a strong influence on fertility: women with more schooling generally have much lower fertility by the end of their childbearing period than those with little or no schooling. Data from the DHS-86 show that the fertility of Colombian women aged 15–19 with no education was 174 per 1,000, a much higher rate than the overall rate for women 15–19 (78), or that of young women with a few years of secondary education or completed secondary schooling (48) (Prada *et al.* 1988).

In spite of a reduction in the adolescent fertility rate, a very young age structure could result in a larger number of births among women in this age-group. Table 17.4 provides estimates of births to women aged 15–19 in 1969 and 1986, and the proportion that these represented in relation to the total number of annual live births in the country. These estimates were made by applying the fertility rates found in the fertility surveys of the years 1969, 1976, and 1986 to the estimated population aged 15–19 in those same years. The estimated number of births to women aged 15–19 increased slightly, from 130,000 to 131,000 between 1969 and 1976, but declined to 125,000 in 1986, a drop of about 5 per cent as compared with 1976. However, as a proportion of total births, there has been no change, since births to young women aged 15–19 in 1986 continued to represent 15 per cent of all births. This finding seems to indicate that today's adolescents are less likely to give birth than in the past, but that the children of these young mothers represent the same proportion of total births as they did in the past. This may be due to the present population structure, which itself is a result of changes that have taken place in natality and mortality. That is, fertility declines among older women mean that the births occurring among the youngest age-group account for the same proportion of the total number of births occurring in the country.

Table 17.4. ***Colombia: estimated number of births to women aged 15–19 and % of total births***

Year	Total births to women aged 15–19	% of total births
1969	130,070	15
1976	130,988	17
1986	124,808	15

The proportion of all births that are adolescent births is very similar to the proportions found in Argentina, Costa Rica, the Dominican Republic, Guatemala, Mexico, Nicaragua, and Puerto Rico, but is higher than the proportions found in Bolivia, Canada, Martinique, and even the United States (Singh and Wulf 1990).

Trends in First Births

Examination of the fertility of women aged 15–19 does not reveal the complete experience of this group, since the majority of these young women have not lived through the full five years of this period (that is, through the ages of 15, 16, 17, 18, and 19). To obtain more complete data, the previous experience of women aged 20–24 should be observed, since these women have already concluded all their adolescent years. This measure is perhaps more accurate as a basis for examining trends in family formation behaviour over time.

Table 17.5 shows that early childbearing in Colombia has changed slightly in recent years, with a reduction in the proportion of women who bear their first child before the age of 20. Twenty-five years ago, four out of every ten women were mothers before the age of 20, but this proportion has declined to three out of ten among women currently aged 20 to 24.

Table 17.5. ***Colombia: proportion of women aged 20 to 24 who bore their first child before the age of 20 years, by current age, level of education, and area of residence***

No. of women	Current age					
	20–24	25–29	30–34	35–39	40–44	45–49
TOTAL	32.1	35.3	32.4	36.5	38.3	42.1
Residence:						
Urban	29.1	32.5	29.6	33.6	37.8	38.9
Rural	40.4	44.6	40.2	43.2	38.7	47.1
Education:						
Primary or less	49.6	47.3	41.5	45.2	40.8	45.1
Secondary or more	20.8	24.2	18.6	17.1	25.9	23.4

Source: DHS-86.

Rural women (40.4 per cent) and those who have primary education or less (49.6 per cent) are more likely to give birth during their adolescent years than women who live in urban areas (29.1 per cent) or those who have secondary or higher education (20.8 per cent). The educational differences are more striking than the residential ones, but among the most educated group, little change can be observed. Twenty-five years ago 23 per cent of women aged 20–4 had their first child before the age of 20, and this proportion is now 21 per cent. These data are surprising if one takes into account the fact that a longer stay in the educational system should lead to a postponement of both conjugal union and childbearing. Apparently this is not happening in the way that might have been expected, despite the educational advances that have been observed as a result of increased school enrolment in Colombia.

This rather inconsistent pattern of change in the timing of family formation is similar to that experienced in Peru and Mexico. A more regular and consistent change can be seen in the Dominican Republic, Canada, Trinidad and Tobago, and the United States (Singh and Wulf 1990).

Some Consequences of Early Childbearing

There is abundant evidence—especially from developed countries—as to the drawbacks of early childbearing. For example, higher rates of morbidity and mortality have been observed among both young mothers and their new-born babies, as well as lower levels of schooling, larger families and a higher probability of dissolution of union for adolescent mothers than for mothers over 20 years of age.

It has been shown that cephalo-pelvic disproportion often leads to more prolonged labour, and its consequences, and that complications such as toxaemia and eclampsia, are more common among very young mothers. Nevertheless, the results of research in developed countries have shown that it is before the age of 16 that the probability of these complications is highest, and that in the later years of adolescence (17–19), with adequate and timely prenatal care, the risks of birth complications, prematurity, low weight of the new-born, and higher mortality can be substantially reduced.

It has also been observed that children born to adolescent mothers are less likely to survive than those born to mothers aged 20–29. Some observers believe that because of the low educational level of many young mothers, they are poorly prepared to care properly for a new-born, and even if they are ready, they may not be economically able to provide their infants with the care they need. It is also argued that pregnant teenagers receive less prenatal care, or, because of a lack of knowledge, shame, or fear of reporting their condition, often seek medical help only at a late stage in the pregnancy. The complications or risks of complications faced by pregnant adolescents are probably due to a combination of biological and social factors (UN 1989). The available Colombian evidence attributes greater significance to social factors, given that early childbearing is more common among young women living in rural areas and with lower educational levels, for whom health resources are scarcer and more inaccessible (Singh and Wulf 1990).

While a lower level of schooling is associated with a higher probability of early childbearing, early pregnancy may also cause a young woman to abandon her studies, which means that she will complete fewer years of schooling than young women who postpone their childbearing until after the age of 20. The relationship is demonstrated quite strongly for Colombia in the data of the DHS-86. Table 17.6 indicates that higher proportions of women who postponed their fertility until after the age of 20 completed the five years of basic education or some secondary schooling.

The table shows that among women aged 20–29 who became mothers after the age of 20, 74 per cent completed their primary education. These proportions are higher for urban women (82 per cent) than for rural women (49 per cent). At higher levels of education, that is, ten years or more, the same relationship obtains. Only 9 per cent of urban residents and 1 per cent of those in rural areas who gave birth before they were 20 continued their secondary studies.

As well as receiving less education, women who begin their reproductive life during adolescence have, on average, larger families than those who postpone childbearing until after the age of 20. Table 17.7 shows that women who bore their first child when they were adolescents had 2–3 more children than those who put off childbearing until after they turned 20. For example, women aged 45–49 who had their first child in adolescence have nearly three more children than those who first gave birth after the age of 20.

Table 17.6. ***Colombia: % of women who completed 5+ or 10+ years of education, by age at first birth, residence, and present age***

Residence/ age	Years of education			
	5+		10+	
	Age <20	Age >20	Age <20	Age >20
TOTAL				
20–29	56	74	7	23
30–39	34	57	4	17
40–49	24	36	2	6
Urban				
20–29	67	82	9	29
30–39	45	66	6	20
40–49	35	47	2	8
Rural				
20–29	32	49	1	7
30–39	13	31	0	5
40–49	6	14	1	2

Table 17.7. ***Colombia: average number of live-born children of women aged 35–39, 40–44, and 45–49 according to the age at which they bore their first child, by residence and level of schooling achieved***

Residence/ education	Current age					
	35–39		40–44		45–49	
	<20	>20	<20	>20	<20	>20
TOTAL	5.4	3.3	6.4	4.4	7.8	5.2
Residence:						
Urban	4.9	2.9	5.7	3.9	6.8	4.4
Rural	6.5	4.4	8.0	5.4	9.2	6.7
Education:						
Primary or less	5.7	3.7	6.7	4.6	8.0	5.5
Secondary or more	3.7	2.6	4.8	3.3	5.3	3.6

Source: DHS-86.

The inverse relationship between the age of the mother at first birth and her completed family size is a little stronger among rural residents in Brazil and Guatemala, as well as in Colombia. In contrast, in the Dominican Republic, Ecuador, El Salvador, Mexico, and Peru, the inverse relationship is somewhat stronger among urban residents (Singh and Wulf 1990). Similarly, the inverse relationship obtains for every age-group. In fact, women aged 40 to 44 years who had postponed childbearing until after the age of 20 had on average one child less than women aged 35–39 who became mothers as adolescents (4.4 v. 5.4). And these younger women still have ten remaining fertile years, which means that they are at risk of increasing the size of their families even further.

Regardless of educational level, women who have their first child during adolescence have higher fertility than those who put off childbearing until later. In effect, among women aged 35–39 with six years or less of education, the difference between those who began their reproductive life early and those who waited until after the age of 20 is two children (5.7 v. 3.7, on average, respectively). However, among women with more than six years of education, the difference is only one child.

Finally, another consequence of forming a family at very early ages is that women who enter union during adolescence have a higher probability than their counterparts of experiencing marital (or union) dissolution. Table 17.8 demonstrates the instability of unions that begin when women are very young. In 1976, among women ever in union aged 30–39, one-third of the unions begun in adolescence had been dissolved, compared with only 18 per cent of those started after the age of 20. This relationship is more marked among urban residents and among women with lower levels of schooling.

Table 17.8. ***Colombia: % of first unions dissolved by age at first union (controlled for duration of union), present age, residence, and educational level***

Residence/ education	Present age					
	20–29		30–39		40–49	
	<20	>20	<20	>20	<20	>20
TOTAL	22	10	30	18	38	24
Residence						
Urban	25	12	33	19	41	26
Rural	15	5	26	15	33	20
Education						
Primary or less	21	12	30	18	39	25
Secondary or more	22	8	29	17	31	18

If we add to this finding the fact that many births to adolescents occur outside of legal or stable union, it is likely that both the new-born and the mother will live in adverse conditions. A 1986 study of Colombian adolescents found that 20 per cent of first births to adolescents were among single mothers, and another 12 per cent were among women who had formed their union when they were already at least two or three months pregnant (Prada *et al.* 1988). Beginning a family in this manner, on a rather fragile basis, in the absence of adequate education to face the challenge of raising a child, is likely to lead to another series of social problems for Colombian society, problems such as homeless children, covert infanticide, juvenile delinquency, and prostitution.

Conclusions and Discussion

Some of the principal findings of this study on adolescent fertility in Colombia are as follows:

1. Both adolescent and overall fertility in Colombia have declined. However, the decline has not been as pronounced among adolescents as among women in older age-groups. Among women 15–19 years of age, age-specific fertility decreased by 34 per cent between 1969 and 1986, while among women aged 40–44, it dropped by 67 per cent.
2. The ASFR among adolescents is about 78 per 1,000, similar to the rate observed in Brazil and Peru, but noticeably lower than that found in Mexico and Ecuador.
3. In spite of a decline in adolescent fertility in Colombia, rates continue to be high in rural areas and among women with little or no schooling (117, 127, and 174 per 1,000 respectively).
4. Women who begin childbearing during adolescence have less education as well. Among women 25–29 who began childbearing after the age of 20, three-quarters managed to complete the basic level of primary schooling. In contrast, among those who had their first child during adolescence, only half achieved this level and very few continued their studies at the secondary level.
5. Colombian women who start childbearing during adolescence have, on average, more children than those who postpone this step until a later age. Women aged 35–39 who bore their first child when they were adolescents have, on average, two more children than those who put off childbearing until after the age of 20.
6. Conjugal unions that are begun during adolescence have a greater chance of ending in divorce or separation. Among women aged 30–39 who entered a union before the age of 20, one-third had dissolved this union, compared with only 18 per cent of those whose union began after the age of 20.
7. It is young residents of rural areas and those with lower levels of education who experience the highest fertility, and who are most likely to begin their reproductive lives during adolescence.

The results of this analysis confirm in large measure many of the findings of previous studies carried out in other countries on the negative consequences associated with early childbearing. When the fertility trends of young Colombian women are compared with those of other Latin American countries, it can be seen that in Colombia, there has been a decline in fertility among all age-groups (including those aged 15–19), while in Brazil and Peru, adolescent fertility rates have risen, even though fertility has fallen among the overall population (Singh and Wulf 1990: 62).

The number of births to adolescent women in Colombia has also declined, but as a proportion of the total number, births among women 15–19 continue to account for 15 per cent. In contrast, in some other Latin American countries, particularly Cuba, this proportion has continued to rise. According to the 1990 study by Singh and Wulf, referred to several times in the present analysis, births to adolescents represented 10.4 per cent of all the births in Cuba in 1950–5, but rose to account for 25 per cent in the period 1985–90.

Despite some differences in the patterns of reproductive behaviour of young people in various Latin American countries, there is a common factor shared by all, and that is the striking similarity in the proportions of young women who begin childbearing during adolescence and the slow rate of change occurring in patterns of early childbearing. Between 30 and 35 per cent of women in Brazil, Colombia, the Dominican Republic, Ecuador, Mexico, Peru, and Trinidad and Tobago have their first child before they are 20 years old (Singh and Wulf 1990). And in all these countries, even though the overall TFR has fallen, and despite the progress made in education, the occurrence of first births at early ages continues without major change. It is possible, therefore, that early childbearing will continue to have a high value placed on it as an important form of self-realization for women, and that education will only affect reproductive behaviour once women have demonstrated their procreative capacity. Other social and cultural values, such as early age at marriage, may also be acting to slow the change in the pattern of early initiation into childbearing. In some regions of Colombia, even now, there is strong social pressure on young women not to reach the age of 20 without having established a formal conjugal relationship. And furthermore, during their first years of married life, social and family pressure is exerted on the couple to demonstrate their fecundity. These are the kinds of values that programmes for adolescents should attempt to influence, in order to offset the adverse consequences of adolescent childbearing. This is especially true in light of the fact that adolescents are now becoming sexually active earlier than ever, and are establishing more consensual than legal unions, which in general are more unstable. These patterns carry with them an increased risk that young women will conceive children out of wedlock, who will grow up without the presence of a father.

Formal educational curricula should, therefore, include concepts and subjects that offer women alternative roles and alternative sources of self-esteem. Such concepts would dissociate childbearing from sexual pleasure, would help women question the concept of machismo, and would encourage a delay in childbearing until women are physically, economically, and psychologically mature enough to bear and raise children.

References

CCRP (Corporación Centro Regional de Población), IRD (Institute for Resource Development, Westinghouse) and Ministry of Health of Colombia (1986), *Colombia: Prevalence, Demographic and Health Survey* (Bogotá: CCRP–IRD–Ministry of Health).

DANE (1985), *50 Años de Estadísticas Educativas* (Bogotá: DANE).

Elkins, H. (1973), 'Cambio de Fecundidad', in *La Fecundidad en Colombia* (Bogotá: Asociación Colombia de Facultades de Medicina).

Estrada, A., Heredia, R., Prada, E., Rivera, J., and Umaña, M. (1973), *Características Socio-demográficas de las Mujeres Colombianas*, National Fertility Survey: Rural Part (Bogotá: Asociación Colombiana de Facultades de Medicina, División de Medicina Social y Población).

Ochoa, L. H., Ordoñez, M., Bayona, A., Rico, J., and Rico, Ana (1983), 'Perfil Socio-económico y Demográfico de la Población Colombiana', mimeograph (Bogotá: Corporación Centro Regional de Población).

Potter, J., Ordoñez, M., and Measham, A. (1976), 'The Rapid Decline in Colombian Fertility', *Population and Development Review*, **2**: 509–28.

Prada, E., and Ojeda, G. (1987), 'Selected Findings from the Demographic and Health Survey in Colombia, 1986', *International Family Planning Perspectives*, **13**: 116–17.

—— and Bailey, J. (1977), 'Fertility Trends in Colombia: Something Important has Happened', paper presented at the Annual Meeting of the Population Association of America, St Louis.

—— Singh, S., and Wulf, D. (1988), *Adolescentes de Hoy, Padres de Mañana: Colombia* (New York: Alan Guttmacher Institute).

Singh, S., and Wulf, D. (1990), *Today's Adolescents, Tomorrow's Parents: A Portrait of the Americas* (New York: Alan Guttmacher Institute).

United Nations (1989), *Adolescent Reproductive Behaviour*, ii. *Evidence from Developing Countries* (ST/ESA/SER.A/109/Add. 1; New York: UN).

18 The Implications of Mexico's Fertility Decline for Women's Participation in the Labour Force*

MARTA MIER Y TERÁN

Introduction

Housework, which is an important activity in the lives of most women, is determined in large measure by the composition of the household, in particular, the number and ages of children and adults. In societies where fertility is in sharp decline, the domestic burden diminishes as the number of children is reduced, and women have greater opportunities to undertake other activities, such as participation in the labour force.

During the process of fertility transition, as the number of children drops, there are changes in the timing of the demographic events in women's lives that demarcate the stages related to their roles as mothers. Among these events are the birth of the first child, the birth of the last child, the beginning of the youngest child's attendance at school, the marriage or departure from the parental home of the youngest child, etc.

In one interesting study, the effects of the demographic transition on the family trajectories of US women were analysed for the period 1800 to 1980 (Watkins *et al.* 1987). During this period, life expectancy at birth rose from 40 to 78 years, and the TFR declined from eight to two live-born children. One of the principal changes was in the proportion of their adult lives (15 years and over) that married mothers spent with children under the age of 5; this fell from one-third in 1800 to merely one-tenth in 1980.

An analysis of the experience of several industrialized countries since the end of the last century shows a drastic reduction in the number of years that women devote to childbearing (UN 1988). Age at first birth has changed relatively little, whereas the age at which the last child is born has dropped sharply. In the case of Japan, for example, where the transition was relatively late and rapid, the median age of women at the birth of their first child rose from 23 to 26 years, and age at

* Brígida García and Orlandina de Oliveira made available to me unpublished documents from their project 'Fertility, Work, and Female Subordination in Mexico'. Patricia Martínez and Miguel Sánchez provided help in the preparation of the tabulations. Susheela Singh offered valuable comments and suggestions on the first draft of this chapter. My sincere thanks to them all.

the birth of the last child declined from 39 to 28 years, so that the interval between the birth of the first and the last child was reduced from sixteen to merely two years over the course of four decades. In the other countries, the figures are less remarkable, given that when the study began, these countries were already well advanced in their transition to low fertility. Nevertheless, as a result of a decline in their age at the birth of the last child there was still a reduction in the time that women spend having children.

The experience of women who had terminated their reproductive period (that is, women aged 40–9) was also analysed in the developing countries that took part in the WFS. Even though the majority of these women had spent their most concentrated childbearing years before the beginning of the fertility transition (their mean number of children in all cases being greater than 5), important differences were found in the duration of their childbearing period (from under fourteen to up to twenty years), as a result of differences in women's median age at the birth of the last child. These medians ranged from 33 to 40 years.

These analyses indicate the importance of reductions in that part of women's lives that is spent having children, and increases in the number of years they spend after that stage of family formation. What is more, the years that a woman no longer dedicates to childbearing occur during a stage of her life in which she is likely to be fully active, so she will probably have greater opportunities to join the labour-market.

This leads us to consider the relationship between fertility and female labour-force participation. Although it is generally accepted that the connection between these two factors is a negative one, there is no consensus on the nature or the direction of the causal link (Kupinsky 1977). However, recent analyses on the topic frequently mention the influence of fertility on labour-force participation and point to the effect of family size on the type of work that women carry out (García and Oliveira 1989).

The number of children, as well as their ages, lead to considerable differences in the burden of domestic chores borne by women. It has been found that the age of the youngest child is the principal determinant of how women spend their time (Mueler 1982). Where traditional female activities are concerned, tasks that can be done in the home or that permit the presence of children at the place of work, that do not require fixed hours, and part-time jobs are more accessible to women with children, particularly when the children are small and there are many of them.

In the case of Mexico, important economic and social changes have occurred since the 1940s. The population has become primarily urban, the size of the agricultural sector has decreased substantially, levels of education have risen considerably, mortality has declined dramatically, and female labour-force participation has increased, particularly during the past two decades.

Up until about 1970, all these changes coexisted with high fertility. The fertility transition only began at the end of the 1960s, very shortly before the sharp reversal of official policy on population matters, from one opposed, to one favourable to a reduction in demographic growth. It should be pointed out that the decline in fertility coincides with the increase in female participation in the labour-market.

The purpose of the present study is to analyse the relationship between the decline in fertility and female labour-force participation in Mexico. To achieve that objective, longitudinal analyses, which consider the history of labour-force participation as well as women's reproductive history, would be desirable; however, no information is available that would permit that type of study. The Mexican Fertility Survey (WFS-76), the National Demographic Survey (NDS-82) and the National Fertility and Health Survey (NFHS-87) provide data on the family formation process during the fertility transition. The information they provide on women's economic activity permits only limited comparison between surveys; in the case of labour-force participation at the time of interview, the data from the 1976 and the 1987 surveys are relatively comparable, and the same is true of the information on labour-force participation before first union and before the birth of the first child.[1] Further information on female economic activity in Mexico is scarce, and its relationship with fertility receives little attention.

The study uses data from the survey tapes as well as secondary information from those surveys and from other sources. The organization of the material is as follows: in the next section, the characteristics of Mexico's fertility decline are presented. Changes in female labour-force participation are discussed in the third section. In the fourth part of the chapter, the possible effect of fertility decline on women's participation in Mexico's labour force is analysed, and the last section contains some final considerations.

[1] Women frequently work in the home, part-time, or seasonally, without receiving any monetary reward. To capture employment with these characteristics is a complex task, and the results are extremely sensitive to the manner in which the questions are put and to the person who answers them. The information on women's economic activity in the three surveys comes from the individual questionnaire; that is, it is provided by the woman herself. However, the questions on current work differ among the three surveys. In 1976 if the respondent worked, she was asked whether she was paid in cash or in kind, or if she worked on the family's lands (farm) (garden). In the 1982 survey one question was asked on work during the previous week, and another on work during the preceding year. In 1987 the question concerned current work and work during the preceding twelve months. As may be seen, the information from the first and last surveys on current working is relatively comparable, whereas data from the 1982 survey is not. Additionally, the 1982 participation rates obtained from the question on work during the previous week are generally lower than those obtained in 1976, which is implausible, given that the trend in female activity shown by other sources is one of continuous increase since 1970. Oliveira and García (1990), in an attempt to obtain data on employment characteristics from the three surveys for 1976, 1982, and 1987, used information on 'principal work in the last year'. The trend obtained by these authors is plausible, and led to the decision to use their estimates of age-specific rates for 1982 in the present study. Finally, for this study, the data on current activity from the 1987 survey were obtained from several questions, according to the person on whom the interviewee depended economically. If she was self-sufficient, she was asked about her current work at the beginning of the section on socio-economic characteristics, in the part addressed to the economic head of household; if she depended economically on another person, she was asked about her current work at the end of the same section.

Fertility Decline in Mexico

With some minor variations, fertility in Mexico remained high up until just before 1970. Annual crude birth rates hovered around 44 births per 1,000, and the total fertility rate was above 6 live births per woman. Around 1970 a large and rapid decline in fertility began: the TFR dropped from 6.8 children in 1970 to 3.8 in 1986, a decline of 44 per cent in a period of sixteen years.

Retrospective surveys have made it possible to establish with a certain degree of precision characteristics of the country's fertility since 1950. During the first years of that period, there was an increase in fertility levels, followed by a reduction starting near the end of the 1960s (Quilodrán 1983).

Beginning in 1970, the TFRs show a drop of 11 per cent between 1970 and 1974, and the pace of this decline accelerated considerably in the following four years, reaching a reduction of 18 per cent; after 1978 the pace of decline tended to slow down, but remained rapid: 15 per cent between that year and 1982, and 10 per cent in the following four years (Table 18.1).

Table 18.1. *Mexico: ASFRs and TFRs, 1970–1986*

Age-group	Year					Change (%)
	1970	1974	1978	1982	1986	1970–82
15–19	126	105	132	105	84	33
20–24	308	290	242	229	202	34
25–29	326	302	229	194	203	38
30–34	280	256	189	155	143	49
35–39	196	178	140	116	97	51
40–44	110	83	64	45	34	69
TFR (15–44)	6.8	6.1	5.0	4.2	3.8	44
Change between periods (%)		11	18	15	10	

Sources: For 1970 and 1974, SSP (1979: 138); three-year averages; for the other years, SSA (1989: 36).

Between 1970 and 1986 there was a strong rejuvenation of ASFRs, and the decline in fertility was greater among older than among younger women: the rates for women aged 20–30 declined by 36 per cent, while among women 30–40, they dropped by 50 per cent; and the reduction among women 40–44 reached 69 per cent. Hence, women aged 20–29 increased their contribution to total fertility from 46 per cent to 53 per cent.

These levels and this trend are not homogeneous among the different sectors of the population; in particular, there are wide differences in reproductive patterns by place of residence. At the beginning of the 1970s (1972–6), women in rural areas had 8 children, on average, by the end of their reproductive lives, while women in metropolitan areas had 6; in 1984–6, as a result of differing rates at which fertility declined, the differentials in the TFR were even greater, since the mean number of children was 6 in rural areas and 3 in metropolitan areas. This happened because in the earlier period, the fertility calendar was already younger in the metropolitan areas, and during the period under observation the rejuvenation was also greater in these areas, so that the differences in the calendar by locality became even more pronounced (Zavala de Cosío 1990).

Urban women born in 1942–6 were the first to limit the size of their families and to rejuvenate their fertility calendar (Zavala de Cosío 1988, 1990). This downward trend is observed at the national level, but it should be mentioned that in urban areas, women in these same cohorts had higher fertility than that of their rural counterparts in previous cohorts.

In 1987, by the age of 20, one-half of all women had entered their first marital union and had borne their first child a year later. Both age at first union and age at the birth of the first child have changed only slightly, with no clearly defined trend during recent years. Entry into some type of marital union is a generalized fact, and almost all women become mothers: among women at the end of their reproductive period (those aged 40–49), only 5 per cent remained single, and 7 per cent had never had a live-born child.

Family formation patterns vary considerably among different groups, especially by place of residence and level of schooling. Half of women in rural localities marry for the first time before the age of 18 and have their first child before they are 20 years old, whereas among women in metropolitan areas, the median ages for these events are four and three years greater, respectively. Half of women with no schooling enter their first conjugal union before the age of 17 and bear their first child before they are 19; this occurs six and five years later respectively, for women who have at least a secondary education (Quilodrán 1983; SSA 1989).

The application of more refined techniques to the pregnancy history data of the WFS has made it possible to characterize changes in the process of family formation with greater precision (Juárez 1989). This research also points to changes in the intensity and the timing of childbearing, beginning with the interval between the third and fourth birth among women aged 30–34 (the generation born in 1942–6).

Since nuptiality and breast-feeding patterns do not appear to have had a decisive influence (Chapter 6) on fertility, it would appear that the most important mechanism to have made the decline possible has been the use of contraceptive methods. Little is known about abortion, although its practice has probably not risen significantly, in view of the greater access to contraception that has existed.

Among married women of reproductive age in 1976, 30 per cent were using some contraceptive method; by 1979 this proportion had risen to 38 per cent, then to 48 per cent in 1982 and 53 per cent in 1987. In that year, levels of use differed considerably among the various population groups; for example, in rural localities, 33 per cent of women in union reported that they were using some form of contraception, while in metropolitan areas, this proportion was twice as high (SSA 1989).

On the other hand, as the use of contraceptives rose, the methods employed also changed. In 1976 the most commonly used methods, in order of importance, were the pill, traditional methods—rhythm, withdrawal, or herbs—and the IUD, whereas ten years later they were tubal ligation, the IUD, and the pill. Sterilization, from being practically non-existent, has become the leading method in Mexico (SSA 1989). It is relevant to note that in 1987 36 per cent of women practising family planning had been sterilized, that is more than one in three, and in many of these cases (26 per cent) the sterilized women had no previous history of contraceptive use. This shows that in Mexico, contraception is used more to limit family size than for birth-spacing. These findings further substantiate the fact that family formation patterns have mostly changed with respect to the size of women's completed families and their age at last birth, since birth intervals at early orders have not changed significantly.

To illustrate these tendencies more clearly, the experience of four groups of women who have completed their families will be analysed. Two of the groups are made up of women who are near the end of their reproductive period (women aged 40–44), and the remaining two, of younger women (aged 30–34) who have been sterilized or whose last live-born child is at least 5 years old. Even though these last two groups are not representative of all the women in their birth cohort, this comparison provides some indication of the future behaviour of the cohorts that had not yet completed their reproductive period by the time of the most recent survey.

Women in the oldest cohort (born in 1932–7) lived through the years in which government activities in the area of family planning only started as their fertile years were ending, while women in the intermediate cohorts (born in 1942–7) were 25 and older when those activities were starting. The most recent cohorts (born in 1952–7) experienced the changed government policies and programmes right from the beginning of their reproductive lives. In addition, the women born between 1942 and 1947 have already been characterized in other studies as the initiators of the process of change in the reproductive patterns of the country (Zavala de Cosío 1988; Juárez 1989). Thus, we can compare the experience of women whose family formation patterns date from before the fertility decline with the experience of women who began the transition process, and that of women who are continuing it.

Among the older cohorts (1932–7), half the women were married for the first time by the age of 19, they had had their first child a year later and their last one by the age of 37, and their seven children were born within a space of sixteen years (see Table 18.2). Comparing this group with the following cohort (1942–7), one sees some delay in age at first union, a decline of 1.4 children in completed family size, and a reduction of three years in women's age at the birth of the last child.

As expected, age at the completion of the family depends in large measure on the number of children borne. Half of women with completed family sizes of one, two, or three children have already had them by the age of 30, while those who bear ten or more children complete their families ten years later. Age at the birth of the last child drops from one generation to the next, almost solely as a result of

Table 18.2. *Mexico: indicators of the family formation process for women who have ceased childbearing,[a] generations 1932–1937, 1942–1947, and 1952–1957*

	Age at observation			
	1932–1937	1942–1947		1952–1957
	40–44	40–44	30–34	30–34
women with completed families compared to total (%)	100	100	20	47
distribution of women by parity (%)[b]				
1 to 3 children	17	24	56	59
4 to 6 children	27	38	36	37
7 to 9 children	30	25	7	4
10 or more children	26	13	1	0
mean number of children per mother	7.2	5.8	3.5	3.0
median age at first union[c]	18.6	19.7	18.7	19.4
median age at birth of first child[c]	20.5	21.0	20.5	20.6
median age at birth of last child by parity[c]				
1 to 3 children	29.8	29.9	24.5	25.3
4 to 6 children	34.7	34.8	26.2	27.7
7 to 9 children	37.3	35.7	*	29.4
10 children or more	39.7	40.4	*	26.6
All	36.9	34.1	25.6	26.6

Sources: Tapes from WFS-76 and NFHS-87.

Note: * = fewer than 20 cases

[a] It was considered that all women aged 40 to 44 had completed childbearing; from the group aged 30–34, only women who had been sterilized and those whose last live-born child was at least 5 years old were included.

[b] The proportions of women without live-born children among the group aged 40–44 years was 89 and 6% respectively, for the generations of 1932–7 and 1942–7; among the group aged 30–34 years, these were 9 and 12% respectively, for the generations of 1942–7 and 1952–7.

[c] Calculated with respect to the total number of women who have undergone the event: women ever in union in the first case and women with at least one live-born child in the second. For the women aged 30 to 34 years, these median ages were calculated with respect to the total number of women of these ages who would have undergone the event.

change in the distribution of women by parity, since women's ages at the completion of their families, within a given completed family size, are practically the same (Table 18.2).

When the women who complete their families at an early age are considered, their relative importance increases substantially between the 1942–7 generation and the cohorts who are ten years younger. Among this group, close to one-half have completed childbearing by the age of 30. This points to a sharp reduction in age at the birth of the last child between the cohorts that began the fertility transition process and those born ten years later (1952–7).

Assuming that the last-born children survive until the beginning of pre-school (until they are 4 years old), half of the mothers in the oldest cohorts would have had the possibility of re-entering the labour force by age 41, while among the intermediate cohorts, this possibility would have started by age 38, and for the most recent group, it would have been at about the age of 34.

For the cohorts born after 1957, given the trends in age at first union and the birth of the first child, as well as increases in the use of sterilization, it may be expected that women's age at family completion will continue to fall.

Changes in Women's Economic Activity

As in many other countries, the labour-force participation of Mexican women has increased considerably in recent years. In 1950 13 per cent of women aged 12 and over reported that they were in the labour force; this proportion rose to 16 per cent in 1970, to 21 per cent in 1979, to 25 per cent in 1982, and to 32 per cent in 1988 (Oliveira and García 1989; INEGI 1989). The trend in male participation has not changed as dramatically, and consequently the proportion of the total labour force that is made up of women has increased significantly: it was 19 per cent in 1970, 25 per cent in 1979, and 32 per cent in 1988 (Pedrero 1990).

Oliveira and García (1989) have developed a useful analysis of the female labour force and of structural changes in the Mexican labour force since 1950. The authors claim that the first two decades were a period of economic growth, during which time possibilities increased for educated young women to get jobs as paid workers in the modern branches of the tertiary sector, connected with urbanization, industrialization, and the expansion of the state bureaucracy. In spite of that trend, domestic employment continued to be important: for example, in 1970 one out of every four female workers in Mexico City were domestics in private homes. The 1970s were characterized by a period of economic recession followed by a partial recovery in the last years of the decade; employment in the tertiary sector grew more rapidly than in the secondary sector; the proportion of women employed in the tertiary sector grew, as a result of an increase in paid labour; and changes in the organization of industrial labour, as well as the expansion of factories assembling products for export, made jobs available to women in the secondary sector. Finally, the 1980s were characterized by the severe economic crisis that began in 1982, and during which workers' real wages declined by more than a third between 1981 and 1986.

Although there is no information on the national labour force in those years, data are available on urban employment. Oliveira (1989) analysed changes in the labour force between 1983 and 1987. He found that the tertiary sector maintained its preponderant role in absorbing the female labour force; the increase in female activity in this period was due, in large part, to an increase in self-employed workers. Unpaid labour, according to this author, is likely to be associated with quite different processes and mechanisms. The economic recession prompted an increase in self-employment among the poorest sectors, who were obliged to diversify their sources of income; but as well, the reorganization of industrial activity stimulated both subcontracting by big businesses and work in the home, which led to an increase in non-wage labour.

Pedrero (1990) carried out an interesting study of female labour-force participation in the three largest metropolitan areas of the country (Mexico City, Monterrey, and Guadalajara) between 1978 and 1987. He found a considerable increase in female participation in the three cities (with annual growth rates of around 4 per cent). The employment sector with the highest proportion of women working, both in 1978 and in 1987, was the service sector; manufacturing industries, on the other hand, yielded second place to commerce. Changes were observed within both the manufacturing and the service sector. In manufacturing, the relative importance of the traditional clothing and footwear industries declined, while the food industry grew, along with other modern areas such as chemical, rubber and plastics industries, etc. In services, domestic labour declined significantly; in Guadalajara, for example, its importance dropped by almost half (going from 42 per cent to 23 per cent of all employed women).

In another study, Oliveira and García (1990) analysed data on female labour-force participation coming from surveys carried out in 1976, 1982, and 1987. For the period coinciding with the years of economic growth (1976–82), the authors found a strong increase in the labour-force participation of women aged 20–49 with a moderate level of education (complete secondary), whereas during the years of economic recession (1982–7), the largest increases occurred among women with no schooling or with only incomplete primary schooling.

There appear to have been important changes in the contribution made by women of different ages to levels of labour-force participation between 1976 and 1987 (Table 18.3). In 1976 participation rates did not vary much among the various age-groups;[2] only women aged 25–29 showed a somewhat lower level than average, while women aged 20–24 and those aged 35–39 had higher rates. These changes are certainly associated with the different stages of family formation that women pass through. Between 1976 and 1982 female labour-force participation rose considerably among young women (those less than 30 years) and, during the following five years, the largest increases occurred among women of intermediate age (30–44), whose rates increased by more than 40 per cent. In 1987 there are two striking facts about the participation rates of women aged 20–44: these rates are very high (four out of every ten women work); and they hardly vary by women's age. This suggests that, in the most recent year, the heavier domestic burden associated with the first stages of family formation does not prevent women working for pay.

In the study on metropolitan areas discussed earlier, labour-force participation rates are analysed beginning with women aged 12 (Pedrero 1990). In 1978 about one of every four adolescent women (under 20) worked, but between that year and 1987, their labour-force participation fell dramatically in both Mexico City and Monterrey. This decline is associated with a longer stay in the educational system on the part of young women in those two cities. In the case of older women (those 55 and older), there is a decline in labour-force participation in all three metropolitan areas. Among women of childbearing age (20–44 years),

[2] In 1976 the rate for the group aged 15–19 is not comparable, because young single women without children were not interviewed.

Table 18.3. *Mexico: age-specific labour-force participation rates of all women in 1976, 1982, and 1987*

Age-groups	Participation rates (%)		
	1976	1982	1987
15–19	10[a] (485)	[b]	26 (2,269)
20–24	29 (1,707)	39 (2,022)	39 (1,716)
25–29	24 (1,415)	34 (1,602)	39 (1,503)
30–34	26 (1,148)	29 (1,343)	39 (1,284)
35–39	29 (1,053)	28 (1,109)	40 (1,043)
40–44	27 (820)	26 (950)	37 (824)
45–49	27 (682)	26 (759)	32 (654)
TOTAL	26 (7,310)	32+ (7,786)	35 (9,293)

Sources: Tapes of WFS-76 and NFHS-87. For 1982, the information comes from Oliveira and García (1990).

Note: Figures in parentheses refer to numbers of women.

[a] In the 1976 survey, of women aged 15 to 19, only those ever in union or with at least one live-born child were interviewed.

[b] For 1982, it was not possible to obtain the value of this rate for women aged 15 to 19, so the rate for all women corresponds to those aged 20 to 49 years.

participation rates are higher than for the country as a whole, and they increased considerably between 1978 and 1987. Nevertheless, in both years, in contrast to what was found at the national level in 1976 and 1987, work activity in the three metropolitan areas declines with increasing age. This suggests that female labour-force participation is different in the cities than in rural areas, with the relative participation of young women being greater in the cities.

With respect to the labour pattern of the different generations of women, it is important to point out that the participation of a given cohort rises as its age increases, and that participation has risen among the more recent cohorts (Table 18.3). For example, women born between 1952 and 1957 (those who were 20–24 years in 1976) increased their participation from 29 per cent to 34 per cent by the time they were 25–30 in 1982, and to 39 per cent by the time they were 30–35 in 1987. Although at lower levels, the two previous cohorts (1947–52 and 1942–7) also showed a continuous increase in labour-force participation with increasing age. This suggests, similar to Pedrero's findings for metropolitan areas, that women in the youngest cohorts who become economically active do not later abandon paid employment, in spite of the responsibility for household work imposed on them by the role of wife and mother.

Fertility and Female Labour-Force Participation

As mentioned earlier, fertility in Mexico has declined considerably over the last two decades, while women's participation in the labour force has increased. The relationship between these two processes is analysed below.

When one considers the ages at which changes in women's reproductive patterns and labour-force participation occur, it turns out that these do not always coincide. From 1970 onward, the largest declines in fertility, as shown above, occurred among women aged 30 or older, while the largest increases in labour-force participation were among younger women. Only between 1982 and 1987 was there also an increase in the labour-force participation of women aged 30–44 years (Tables 18.1 and 18.3). However, it is important to point out that among the birth cohorts of women who initiated the demographic transition, the ages at which changes occurred in women's reproductive patterns did coincide with the ages at which their labour-force participation altered. Beginning with the 1942–7 cohorts, rates of economic activity increased steadily. In addition, it is precisely the women born between 1942 and 1947 who initiated change in the pattern of family formation.

When changes in the stages of women's lives are located in time, it turns out that the increase in labour-force participation of the 1942–7 generation occurred after they were 35, when more than half of the women had already had their last child. Women born in 1947–52 began to increase their labour-force participation at even earlier ages (30–34 years), but it rose even more in the following five-year period, when they were 35–39. At that age, the majority of the women had most probably completed their families. Finally, women born between 1952 and 1957 show a substantial increase in economic activity at 25–29 years of age, and above all, in the following five-year period, when more than half had probably completed their childbearing. Thus, with successively younger generations, participation in the labour-market is increasingly common, and within a given generation, as age increases, labour-force participation also rises. Women born between 1942 and 1957 have had lower fertility than their predecessors, but they have not postponed either matrimony or the birth of the first child to any significant degree. This finding suggests that among the more recent cohorts, women have increasingly been able to raise their families and remain in the labour force. At the same time, as they complete their families, which occurs at ever younger ages, some women return to the labour-market.

There are two factors related to women's life course that determine their labour-force participation: marital status and the current stage of family formation. The presence of a spouse makes a big difference.[3] In Mexico in 1976, among women aged 20–9, only 17 per cent of those in union were in the labour force, compared to 56 per cent of single women, and 60 per cent of widowed or separated women. In the following years, the women whose participation increased the

[3] Among Mexican women aged 20–49, 15% were single in 1976, compared with 18% in 1987. For both years, only 10% of the women ever in union were widowed, divorced, or separated.

most (by 62 per cent between 1976 and 1987) were women in union. However, even in this later year, the differentials are still large: the participation rates are 28 per cent among women in union, compared with 61 and 71 per cent respectively, among single women and among the separated or widowed (Oliveira and García 1990). In the three metropolitan areas of the country, there were also large differentials by marital status during the period 1978–87, but the largest increase in female labour-market activity again occurred among women who were married or in consensual union (Pedrero 1990).

In order to deepen our understanding of the influence of the different stages of family formation, two types of analysis were conducted. In one, continuity of employment was studied in relation to entry into first marriage and the birth of the first child; in the second, women's labour-force participation was examined in terms of the age of the youngest child.

Family Formation and Labour-Force Continuity

Continuity in employment was studied using information on work prior to first union, during the interval preceding the first birth and at the time of interview. The data, which come from the surveys of 1976 and 1987,[4] are deficient, especially among older women (40–49 years) and for work during the interval before the first birth in the 1976 survey. Despite these problems, they shed light on some important characteristics of women's life history (Table 18.4).

More than half of women ever in union with at least one live-born child worked before entering their first union (alternative A); in 1987 one in three women said that she had worked between the time of her first marriage and the birth of her first child (alternative B); at the time of interview, 21 per cent of women were working in 1976 and 31 per cent in 1987 (alternative C). Entry into first marriage caused half of the women who had worked while they were single to give up their jobs (complement of alternative D). Of the women in union who worked before the birth of the first child, almost two-thirds were in the labour force at the time of the interview (alternative E); among the younger groups (aged 20 to 29), this proportion offers a better approximation and shows that, of the women who have worked after entering their first union, fewer than half give up work because of the birth of the first child.

[4] These data only give an approximation of the extent of continuity in the labourforce, since there might be multiple interruptions of work that escape observation at two times in a woman's life, in addition to the time of interview. In particular, between the interval preceding the birth of the first child and the time of the survey there may have been multiple changes, especially among women whose first live birth was in the distant past. Thus, the discontinuity estimated here would be a lower limit to the discontinuity that really exists. The 1982 survey was not included in this part of the analysis because, as mentioned previously, the data on current labour-force activity are not totally comparable with those of the other two surveys. In addition, since retrospective information is included, it was considered convenient to limit the analysis to the first and last surveys. Furthermore, in the case of work before first union and during the interval preceding the birth of the first child, the data should be similar in the two surveys, since the majority of women aged 30–49 in 1987 were 20–39 in 1976. The fact that labour-force participation during the interval preceding the first birth in 1976 was so low indicates that the data in this survey suffer from underestimation.

Table 18.4. *Mexico: proportion of women ever in union and with at least one live-born child, according to various alternatives for previous labour-force participation, 1976 and 1987*

Age-groups	Labour-force participation alternatives										
	A	B	C	D	E	F	G	H	I	J	K
1976											
20–24	57	14	14	19	60	58	6	20	6	10	8
25–29	56	13	17	20	66	67	8	24	8	12	8
30–34	59	16	22	21	68	68	13	27	9	13	3
35–39	54	17	27	24	67	65	18	33	8	13	5
40–44	50	15	24	19	65	64	14	32	6	10	9
45–49	44	16	26	26	70	69	15	37	8	14	4
20–49	54	15	21	21	66	65	12	28	8	12	7
1987											
20–24	55	27	23	45	54	53	10	33	13	21	8
25–29	58	34	29	53	54	53	11	41	16	25	4
30–34	57	32	34	51	65	66	15	47	19	30	4
35–39	57	31	36	50	72	73	14	51	21	32	5
40–44	53	30	35	52	68	71	16	50	19	31	7
45–49	47	25	30	46	65	66	10	49	14	26	4
20–49	55	29	30	50	63	63	12	45	17	27	5

Sources: Tapes of WFS-76 and NFHS-87.

Notes: Labour-force alternatives = women who worked: (A) Before first union; (B) During the interval preceding the first birth; (C) At the time of interview; (D) During the interval preceding the first birth, having worked before first union; (E) At the time of interview, having worked during the interval preceding the first birth; (F) At the time of interview, having worked before first union and during the interval preceding the first birth; (G) At the time of interview, not having worked before first union, nor during the interval preceding the first birth; (H) At the time of interview, having worked previously; (I) At all three times; (J) At all three times, having worked at some time; (K) At none of the three times.

As expected, the women most likely to be in the labour-market are those who have worked in earlier stages of their lives (alternatives E, F, and H). Continuity in employment is low for all women; for example, in 1987 when the labour-force participation of women in union was high, only 17 per cent reported having worked at all three moments (alternative I); when only workers (those who said they had worked at one or more of the three observation points) are considered, 27 per cent had worked at all three points (alternative J).

It appears that the major employment paths of women who have started a family are of three types. First are women who never worked, who represent slightly more than one-third of the total. Although we do not know whether these women worked at some time between the birth of their first child and the time of interview, given that first entry into the labour-market during the latter stages of family formation is infrequent, it may be supposed that they have 'never' worked. Second are women who worked before starting a family (55 per cent). Among this group, approximately two out of every three stop working during the initial stages of the formation of their families, while the rest (nearly 30 per cent) do not interrupt paid activity, but combine it with raising their small children. It should be pointed out that re-entry is frequent, since among women who worked before the birth of the first child, one in two rejoined the labour force at a later stage. In contrast, the incorporation for the first time of women who have already begun having a family is not usual, even at ages at which it is to be expected that the youngest children would have begun to attend school (alternative G).

As might be expected, there were minimal changes between the two periods in levels of labour-force participation before entry into first marriage, in the likelihood of entering the labour-market for the first time at later stages, and in the proportion of women who never worked (alternatives A, G, and K respectively). The change occurs in present work (alternative C), as a result of greater labour-force continuity (alternative J) and more frequent re-entry of the women with a history of labour-force participation (alternative H).

Finally, among the most recent generations, labour-force experience is found more often; the older generations are less likely to have worked before first union and during the interval prior to the birth of the first child and, in contrast, more likely never to have worked. None the less, this generational effect is offset by the effect on current labour-force participation of the heavier domestic burden shouldered by women during the first stages of family formation.

Age of Youngest Child and Mother's Labour-Force Participation

In both 1982 and 1987 Christenson (1990) found significantly lower participation in the labour force among women who were married or in consensual union and who had children under the age of 6. Oliveira and García (1990) observed that in 1976 and in 1987 it was mothers with small children (0–3 years) who were least likely to be in the labour force, and that among this group, the number of children (1 and 2, or 3 or more) has very little impact on these levels.

The findings of these authors corroborate the suggestion made in the introduction that the age of the youngest child has a decisive effect on the mother's labour-force participation. We proceed, therefore, to analyse the degree of this influence among women in different cohorts and of differing ages. Given that children become more independent as they grow up, we thought it pertinent to separate children into three age-categories: those aged 0–2 years, who require constant care; those aged 3–5, who have acquired some degree of independence and indeed some of whom may attend school as pre-schoolers; and those aged 6 and older, most of whom are already attending primary school and are self-sufficient in terms of basic care. In addition, the age of the youngest children is also associated with stages in the life course of their mothers. The vast majority of women whose youngest child is more than 5 years old will have finished bearing children; in contrast, many of the women who have very small children (0–2 years) will have still more children in the future.

Both labour-force participation rates and age-trends in these measures differ widely by the age of the youngest surviving child in 1976 and 1987 (Fig. 18.1 and Table 18.5). The participation rates of mothers with very small children are considerably lower than those of mothers with older children: 45 per cent in 1976 and

31 per cent in 1987. In both survey years, the trend in participation rates by mother's age deserves special comment, since it is the reverse among mothers who have completed childbearing and those who have very small children: among the former, it is the youngest women who work most, whereas among women with very small children, older women are most likely to be in the labour force. Thus, the widest differentials in labour-force participation by age of the children are found among young women. These women belong to recent cohorts, and those who have completed their families no longer have the burden of caring for small children. They are mainly women of low fertility, which is associated with high levels of schooling and residence in cities. All these factors point to a higher rate of labour-force participation among young mothers who have completed their families. In contrast, among women of more advanced age, the majority of those with small children also have large families, who impose a greater economic burden. On the other hand, such women can usually count on help from their older children in taking care of the smaller ones.

Important changes occurred between 1976 and 1987. The decline in fertility gave rise to a decrease in the proportion of mothers with very small children and an increase in the proportion of mothers who had completed their families, resulting in higher participation rates in 1987 than in 1976. However, the marked increase in the labour-force participation rate of all women (48 per cent) is due above all to the increase in the participation of women having small children (56

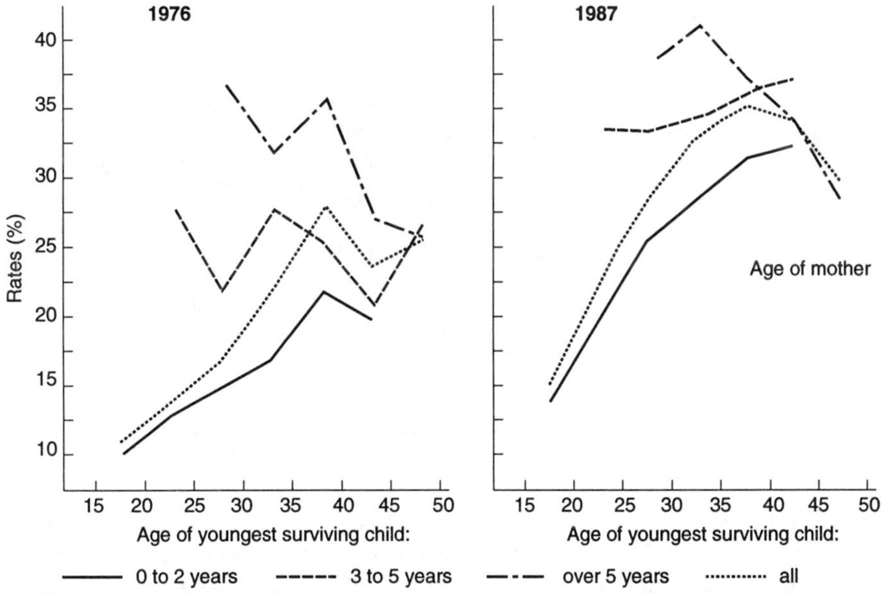

Fig. 18.1. ***Mexico: age-specific rates of labour-force participation of women ever in union and with at least one surviving child, by age of youngest child***

Source: Table 18.5

Table 18.5. *Mexico: age-specific labour-force participation rates of women ever in union and with at least one surviving child, by age of the youngest child in 1976 and 1987 (%)*

Age-groups of mothers	Age of the youngest child (years)			
	0–2	3–5	6 and over	all
1976				
15–19	10	*	*	11
	(293)	(11)	(16)	(320)
20–24	13	28	*	14
	(866)	(87)	(20)	(973)
25–29	15	22	37	17
	(843)	(230)	(54)	(1,127)
30–34	17	28	32	22
	(604)	(259)	(150)	(1,013)
35–39	22	26	36	27
	(453)	(258)	(261)	(972)
40–44	20	21	27	24
	(163)	(208)	(375)	(746)
45–49	*	27	26	26
	(43)	(85)	(493)	(621)
TOTAL	16	25	29	21
	(3,265)	(1,138)	(1,369)	(5,772)
1987				
15–19	14	*	*	15
	(228)	(5)	(0)	(233)
20–24	20	34	*	23
	(666)	(147)	(10)	(823)
25–29	26	34	39	29
	(748)	(277)	(111)	(1,136)
30–34	29	35	42	34
	(508)	(335)	(266)	(1,109)
35–39	32	37	38	36
	(251)	(248)	(432)	(931)
40–44	33	38	35	35
	(96)	(133)	(535)	(764)
45-49	*	*	29	30
	(11)	(49)	(535)	(595)
TOTAL	25	35	35	31
	(2,508)	(1,194)	(1,889)	(5,591)

Sources: Tapes of the WFS-76 and NFHS-87.

Notes: * = number of cases below 50, so rates not calculated. The numbers in parentheses correspond to the number of cases.

per cent for mothers with children younger than 3, and 40 per cent for mothers with children aged 3–5). In contrast, women who had completed their family formation showed moderate increases (around 20 per cent). As a consequence of the difference in these increases, by 1987 participation rates are more similar across different stages of women's lives. What is more, during this same period, labour-force participation increased among women of all ages who had small children. This finding appears to be due to higher levels of participation among both young women who are beginning their families, and older women who have large families.

There are large differences in the type of work that married women do, depending on the age and number of their children (García and Oliveira 1989). In 1976 women without children or with only a few children were frequently employed in non-manual labour; women with three or more children more often worked in agricultural activities or were self-employed. As has been seen, between 1976 and 1982 there was a considerable expansion of the types of employment that are least compatible with child-raising (non-manual and manual work for wages). Nevertheless, the participation of young women starting their families increased considerably. During the following five-year period, self-employment, which is easier to reconcile with child-raising, increased significantly for all women in union. Hence, in 1987, in spite of the greater homogeneity in levels of participation among women with families at differing stages of formation, the type of jobs women did were more heterogeneous. This is due above all to the fact that women with large families and small children have been able to enter the labour-market, but mainly by being self-employed (García and Oliveira 1989).

Final Considerations

Although we are still far from being able to evaluate the total impact of fertility decline on labour-force participation in Mexico, there are several elements that link changes in reproductive patterns to women's representation in the workforce. Women born between 1942 and 1947 began both the process of fertility transition and the trend toward greater participation in the labour force. Among these cohorts, changes in fertility, as well as in labour-force activity, occurred at relatively late ages and at a time when the economy of the country was in full recession. Everything suggests that these women, some of whom had finished having large families at earlier ages than previous generations, others of whom still had small children at home at an advanced age, when faced with the necessity of responding to a drop in real wages, either re-entered the labour-market, or became self-employed workers. The more recent cohorts (1947–57), as well as sharing the experience of their predecessors at late ages, lived through the first stages of family formation during times of economic growth, when it was possible for women with an intermediate level of schooling to join the labour force, even in jobs thought to be incompatible with child-raising. In addition, even though these women stopped working during certain stages of their reproductive lives, the fact of having acquired some work experience made it more likely that they would be able to re-enter the paid labour force at a later stage.

Among the most recent cohorts, it is expected that the rise in labour-force participation will continue, among other reasons because of increases in levels of schooling, declines in fertility, and the precarious economic situation that most of the population is facing. Additionally, the demand for employment is growing rapidly as a consequence both of the entry of large new cohorts, and the growing incorporation of women into the labour force. These factors, added to the difficulty faced by businesses in creating employment, make it probable that in the years to come, women will continue in the labour force largely as self-employed workers.

It is clear that current (and future) patterns of female labour-force participation in the country suggest serious problems for the development of children and for the health of their mothers. For women with small children, paid work implies reliance on somebody else to take care of the children during working hours. Given the scarce infrastructure for the care of small children, the vast majority of workers have to seek other options. In particular, women whose role in the labour force has increased most rapidly in recent years, and women with little or no schooling working for themselves, do not have access to day-care centres, or to any similar service. Frequently, the working mother must decide to leave her children in the care of a relative, take care of them herself while she works, or leave them at home by themselves.[5]

The structure of the family plays an important role in the labour-force participation of women who have begun to form their families. Christenson (1990) found that the presence of another adult woman in the household had a significant effect on the working activity of married women, both in 1982 and in 1987. When the working woman lacks institutional support or domestic help—another adult in the household, be it a relative or servant—she cannot provide the attention and care that her children need. As a result, many children run the risk of accidents and of contracting diseases associated with inappropriate workplace conditions. Furthermore, when she does not have this support, the working woman must do domestic chores as well as her paid activity, which entails an enormous burden of work, and probably has negative repercussions on her health.

This chapter has studied the effect of fertility decline on female labour-force participation without addressing the possible influence of women's work on reproductive patterns. However, there are elements which suggest that an inverse relationship also exists. For example, the work experience of young women before starting their families, the work experience of older women who have already begun childbearing, low wage patterns, which make it necessary for women to continue working even after marriage and child-rearing, and the lack of child-care resources, are among some of the factors that probably encourage working women to limit their births. Added to this is relatively easy access to contraceptive methods in Mexico, which makes it entirely plausible that female participation in the labour-market has an impact on reproductive patterns.

[5] The data from the 1982 survey corroborate this hypothesis: of the women who had children and were working, only 5% had institutional support for the care of their children, while 55% counted on help from a relative, 11% depended on their older children, 9% on another person who was paid, 18% cared for their children themselves, and 12% left their children at home by themselves.

In future studies, longitudinal analyses should be done that will permit a more in-depth study of the issues that have been presented here. It will be particularly important to make available information that illuminates the sequence of events related to nuptiality, fertility and paid work in the course of a woman's life. On the other hand, as has been shown, childbearing patterns, as well as those of female labour-force participation, differ considerably by women's level of schooling and place of residence, which means that it is also essential to investigate these types of behaviour among different population groups. Such an analysis would permit a better approach to the complex relationships that exist in Mexico between the fertility transition and women's increased labour-force participation.

References

Christenson, B. A. (1990), 'Family Structure of Households and Labour Force Participation of Married Women in Mexico', Paper presented at the IV Reunión Nacional Sobre la Investigación Demográfica en México, Mexico City, Sociedad Mexicana de Demografía.

García, B., and de Oliveira, O. (1984), 'Mujer y Dinámica Poblacional en México', *Encuentro*, No. 5, vol. 2/1, Jalisco (México), El Colegio de Jalisco, pp. 75–107.

—— and—— (1988), 'Participación Económica Femenina y Fecundidad: Aspectos Teóricos y Metodológicos', in *Memoria de la Reunión sobre Avances y Perspectivas de la Investigación Social en Planificación Familiar en México* (Mexico: Secretaría de Salud), 191–6.

—— and—— (1989), 'Cambios en la Presencia Femenina en el Mercado de Trabajo. ¿Quiénes Participan y Dónde?' (Unpublished).

García E. F. (1982), 'Algunos Diferenciales de Fecundidad en México', in *Lecturas en Materia de Seguridad social, Planificación Familiar y Cambio Demográfico*, (Mexico; IMSS), 489–504.

INEGI (Instituto Nacional de Estadística, Geografía e Informática) (1989), Preliminary data from the National Employment Survey, held in the second trimester of 1988, Aguascalientes (unpublished).

Juárez, F. (1989), 'Revisión de los Estudios Sobre la Estimación de la Fecundidad en México a Partir de Encuestas Retrospectivas' in Beatriz Figueroa (ed.), *La Fecundidad en México: Cambios y Perspectivas* (Mexico: El Colegio de México), 121–65.

—— and Quilodrán, J. (1990), 'Mujeres Pioneras del Cambio Reproductivo en México', *Revista Mexicana de Sociología*, 52/1: 33–49.

Kupinsky, S. (1977), 'The Fertility of Working Women in the United States: Historical Trends and Theoretical Perspectives' in Stanley Kupinsky (ed.), *The Fertility of Working Women: A Synthesis of International Research* (New York: Praeger), 188–249.

McDonald, P. (1984), *Nuptiality and Completed Fertility: A Study of Starting, Stopping and Spacing Behaviour* (WFS Comparative Studies, 35; Voorburg: International Statistical Institute).

Menken, J. L. (1985), 'Age and Fertility: How Late Can You Wait?', *Demography*, 22: 469–84.

Mueler, E. (1982), 'The Allocation of Women's Time and its Relation to Fertility' in

Richard Anker *et al.* (eds.), *Women's Roles and Population Trends in the Third World* (London: International Labour Office), 55–86.

Oliveira, O. (1989), 'Empleo Femenino en México en Tiempos de Recesión Económica: Tendencias Recientes', in Jenifer Cooper *et al.* (comp.), *Fuerza de Trabajo Femenina Urbana en México*, (Mexico: Coordinación de Humanidades, UNAM and M. A. Porrúa Eds.), 29–66.

—— García, B. (1989), 'Expansión del Trabajo Femenino y Transformación Social en México: 1950–1987' (Unpublished).

—— —— (1990), 'El Nuevo Perfil del Mercado de Trabajo Femenino: 1976–1987', paper presented to the IV Reunión Nacional sobre Investigación Demográfica en México, Sociedad Mexicana de Demografía, Mexico City.

Pedrero, M. (1990), 'Evolución de la Participación Económica Femenina en los Ochenta', *Revista Mexicana de Sociología*, **52**: 133–49.

Quilodrán, J. (1983), 'Niveles de Fecundidad y Patrones de Nupcialidad en México', (Unpublished).

SPP (Secretaría de Programación y Presupuesto) (1979), *Encuesta Mexicana de Fecundidad: Primer Informe Nacional* (Mexico: SPP Dirección General de Estadística).

SSA (Secretaría de Salud) (1989), *Encuesta Nacional sobre Fecundidad y Salud 1987* (Mexico: SSA, Dirección General de Planificación Familiar).

Standing, G. (1983), 'Women's Work Activity and Fertility' in R. Bulatao and R. D. Lee (eds.), *Determinants of Fertility in Developing Countries: A Summary of Knowledge* (Washington: National Academy Press), 416–38.

United Nations (1985), *Women's Employment and Fertility. A Comparative Analysis of World Fertility Survey Results for 38 Developing Countries* (Department of International Economic and Social Affairs, Population Studies, no. 96; New York: UN).

United Nations (1988), 'Fertility and Women's Life Cycle', *World Population Trends and Policies: 1987 Monitoring Report* (Department of International Economic and Social Affairs, Population Studies, no. 103; New York: UN), 301–22.

Watkins, S. C., Menten, J. A., and Bongaarts, J. (1987), 'Demographic Foundations of Family Change', *American Sociological Review*, **52**: 346–58.

Zavala de Cosío, M. E. (1988), *Cambios de la Fecundidad en México* (México: SSA, Dirección General de Planificación Familiar).

—— (1990), 'Niveles y Tendencias de la Fecundidad en México: 1900–1985', paper presented at the IV Reunión Nacional sobre Investigación Demográfica en México, Sociedad Mexicana de Demografía, Mexico City.

Part V

Patterns of Fertility Change: Case Studies

19 A Century and a Quarter of Fertility Change in Argentina: 1869 to the Present

EDITH A. PANTELIDES

Introduction

This chapter will review the course of fertility change in Argentina over the past century and a quarter. Our slice of history begins in 1869, the date of the first national population census, but we shall include some indicators from earlier dates. The story ends towards the present, in the first half of the 1980s, the most recent period for which data are available.

During this century and a quarter, we witness the drop in the country's levels of fertility, interrupted only by two brief 'baby boom' periods. In this chapter we will concentrate on analysing the early stages of the process of decline, up to the moment at which it is obvious that the fertility 'transition' has been completed. It is necessary to attempt to understand why fertility levels fell in Argentina so much earlier than in the rest of Latin America (except Uruguay). We believe that the available data do not allow us to definitively state what happened and why, but they do suggest plausible explanations. Of the two periods when fertility rose, the first (end of the 1940s) has not been studied and, once again, the data and resources available offer little hope that this may be done. The second period (the 1970s) is more accessible; there already exists one study that attempts to establish its characteristics (Pantelides 1989), and whose conclusions will be summarized here.

The work of a demographer who wishes to study Argentine fertility is very similar to that of a detective. The first hurdle is the very existence of the data. Both in the past and at present the data from the vital statistics system are fragmentary and provide little information beyond the age of the mother (sometimes) and the sex of the new-born child. In even earlier years, in some provinces, there is much more detailed information, but it is discontinuous, both over time and as regards the collection criteria used and the variables considered (see Pantelides 1984*b*: appendix tables). Even in the recent past there are frequent changes with respect to the time unit, that is, the definition of the *year* to which the data refer (including or not part of the vital events occurring in earlier or later years). An additional complication arises out of the registration amnesties, which the provinces decreed at various times, and which produce 'artificial' increases in the number of births.

The censuses are an interesting alternative source, even though their irregular spacing and the long periods without data collection that occurred towards the middle of this century diminish their usefulness. Since the early days, the census asked questions about fertility, but the tables produced from the responses tend to vary from one census to another, making comparisons difficult. The universe of women of whom the question is asked also varies (age limits and marital status), and in the past the unit does not necessarily seem to have been the live-born child.

The second obstacle is the quality of the data. An earlier work (Pantelides 1984*b*) evaluated the census data and included assessments by other authors. These may be summarized by saying that the problems of quality do not prevent the sketching of a general overview, but they do not permit subtleties in the measurements. The problems of data quality continue, with varying degrees of seriousness, up to the present.

Using what is found, estimating what is not available, and observing fragments, the demographer, in detective's guise, tries to decipher reality. That was our experience and the following paragraphs describe the results of that labour.

The Beginning of the Fertility Transition

As we have already stated, the case of the fertility transition in Argentina is interesting because it happened so early within the Latin American context. If, as Lesthaeghe (1977) proposes, we take the decade in which the CBR falls irreversibly below 30 per 1,000 (Table 19.1), Argentina reaches this milestone during the 1930s, 100 years after France, the first country to experience the fertility transition, but only ten years later than Italy and Spain, the two countries that have contributed most heavily to the present composition of the Argentine population. In Latin America, only Uruguay reached this level ten years before Argentina.

Table 19.1. ***Decade during which the CBR fell below 30 per 1,000, selected countries***

Decade	Country
1830	France
1840	Ireland
1890	Sweden, Denmark, England and Wales, Scotland, Australia, New Zealand
1900	Holland, Norway, Germany
1910	Canada, Austria, Hungary, Czechoslovakia, United States
1920	Italy, Spain, Portugal, Uruguay
1930	Poland, Bulgaria, Rumania, Argentina
1940	Soviet Union, Cuba
1950	Yugoslavia, Japan
1960	Chile

Sources: Lesthaeghe (1977: 14); Rothman (1970: 7); Gutiérrez (1975); US Bureau of the Census (1980); Cuba, Centro de Estudios Demográficos (n.d.).

However, it is important to determine not only when the level of fertility changed substantially, but also when the process of decline itself began. The problem lies in the fact that only very poor information exists before 1869 and for the period 1869–95, the two periods that should be examined most carefully. For fertility before 1869 we only have estimates made for two cities: Corrientes and Cordoba. The work of Mychaszula *et al.* (1989) estimates fertility in the city of Corrientes at the beginning of the nineteenth century, using the own-children method with data from a municipal census of 1820. Depending on the mortality level adopted, the TFR of the city of Corrientes would have been between 7 (with mortality equivalent to level 4 of the West model life-tables of Coale and Demeny) and 8.5 children per woman (with an even higher level of mortality, equivalent to level 1 of the same model tables). On the basis of comparisons with later estimates and an analysis of the age and sex structure of the population of Corrientes (where a very pronounced absence of adult males is observed), those authors favoured the lower TFR, on the order of 7 children. An I_f of 0.54 would be associated with this level of fertility, rising to 0.64 if the higher mortality were accepted.

The fertility estimates for the city of Cordoba begin much earlier. Ferreyra (1989), using Henry's family reconstruction model, estimates married fertility from the end of the sixteenth century. The completed family size of women married at the age of 20 (the mean age at first marriage, also estimated by this author, is over 20 years) is 7.7 children for the period 1573–1649 and 7.6 children for 1650–1725. Celton (1987) calculates this same measure for 1750–1800, obtaining a final family size of 8.1 for women married at the age of 20. All the estimates mentioned so far for the city of Cordoba are for fertility within marriage, and its level should, therefore, be higher than the fertility of all women. Finally, Duje (1989), using the own-children method, estimates a TFR of 4.7 for 1825–40. This level is too low, and inconsistent with all the other estimates. Its calculation was influenced by substantial under-enumeration of children below 5 years of age, and also by the mortality table used, which was level 7 of the Coale-Demeny West family.[1]

It may be seen that these fragmentary estimates point to a fertility level that could be expressed as a TFR of about 7 children. This is the magnitude that Arretx *et al.* (1977) calculated, on the basis of the 1895 census, for the whole country. It would seem that fertility did not undergo great changes until 1895. Nevertheless, anyone who approaches the study of Argentine fertility via an analysis of the CBR would not hesitate to affirm that the process of decline began towards the end of the nineteenth century (Table 19.2). In fact the TFR already showed a decline of about 10 per cent between the dates of the two first national population censuses: 1869 and 1895. Another measure of total fertility, the GFR

[1] Note the strong influence of the mortality level adopted in the estimates for the city of Corrientes as mentioned earlier. Duje (1989) estimated the TFR based on children aged 6 to 10 years, who are the least affected by underestimation and by homelessness, as over 6 children per woman.

Table 19.2. *Argentina: CBR, GFR, TFR, and total fertility index (I_f), Censuses of 1869–1980*

Date	CBR	GFR	I_f	TFR[a]
1869	49.1	252.1	0.58	6.8
1895	44.5	247.8	0.55	7.0
1914	36.5	166.4	0.42	6.2
1947	26.3	99.8	0.26	3.2
1960	23.6	92.5	0.25	3.1
1970	23.2	91.7	0.25	3.1
1980	24.8	102.8	0.28	3.3

Sources: Taken, with modifications, from Pantelides (1989). Measures originally calculated by Arretx *et al.* (1977), Camisa (1965), Lattes (1975), Torrado (1970).

[a] The TFRs for the first four dates correspond to the period 1870–4, 1895–9, 1915–19 and 1945–9 respectively.

shows the same trend. Coale's total fertility index (I_f) also shows some decline. However, as indicated above, the TFR shows no such change, and locates the time of the beginning of fertility decline later, between 1895 and 1914.

The reasons for the apparent disagreement among the various measures lie in their very nature: only the TFR's evolution is unaffected by changes in the volume and in the age–sex distribution of the population, although it, in turn, is a measure for a hypothetical cohort and requires the acceptance of certain assumptions. Between 1869 and 1895 the impact of the massive overseas immigration to Argentina may be clearly seen. The population's growth rate accelerates, and the age–sex distribution changes (the central part of the pyramid becomes wider, particularly for males). But while it is true that the majority of the immigrants were of reproductive age, their contribution to the birth rate is not automatic. This is seen from the fact that whereas the population grew by 128 per cent between 1869 and 1895, and the female population of reproductive age grew by 126 per cent, births increased by only 103 per cent. With these considerations we wish to indicate that the decline shown by some of the measures for this first period is not necessarily due to a real decline in fertility. On the contrary, we believe that the significant decline began after 1895. Support for this belief comes not only in evidence from the TFR but also in certain additional evidence, none of it definitive, but which forms a relatively consistent body.

Part of the evidence arises out of the examination of the mean number of children per non-single woman in the second through fourth national population censuses (Table 19.3). It is seen there that the mean number does not vary between 1895 and 1914. It is difficult to believe that this mean number would have declined before 1895 and then remained constant. However, given that this measure is affected by the age structure (even when, as here, it is relatively well controlled, since only non-single women are included), its study does not provide absolute certainty. But if we proceed to observe the distribution of non-single

Table 19.3. *Argentina: distribution of non-single women by parity and mean number of children per non-single woman, dates of available census data, 1895–1947*

Date	% of women at each parity								Mean no. of children
	Total	0	1	2	3	4	5	6+	
1895	100.0	9.7	11.8	12.3	11.5	10.7	9.2	34.8	4.7
1914	100.0	10.6	12.4	12.2	10.9	9.9	8.6	35.4	4.6
1947	100.0	13.1	18.6	19.3	12.7	8.7	6.3	21.3	3.4
1960	100.0	15.2	21.4	24.9	13.7	7.8	4.9	12.1	2.7

Source: Pantelides (1982).

Notes: The data for 1895 refer to married women and widows over the age of 12 years; for 1914, to married women and widows over the age of 14; for 1947, to women 15 years of age and over who were married, widowed, separated, and divorced; and for 1960 to all non-single women. In the censuses of 1895 and 1914 the categories of separated and divorced did not exist.

women by parity, between 1895 and 1914, there is not yet any indication that fertility has begun to decline: there is no reduction in the proportion of women at the highest parities, and only very small increases in that of women with no children or only one child. In addition, if the parity progression ratios are calculated for those cohorts aged between 45 and 49 years in 1885 and in 1895,[2] no changes are observed in the ten years separating these two dates (Pantelides 1983). In summary, on the basis of the estimates of the TFR and the distribution of parities (although made for non-single women only), we believe that fertility changed very little before 1895.

On the other hand, the index I_f tells us that fertility was below the level usually reached in the absence of voluntary control (the level represented by that of married Hutterite women). This indicates, then, that there would be some degree of fertility control but that that control would not have been increasing over time before 1895. It is practically impossible to verify this hypothesis, but a study of the existence of differential reproductive behaviour provides some data to support it.

Fertility Differences at the Beginning of the Transition

Given a level of fertility that is high and stable, but subject to a certain degree of control, and given the early decline of that fertility, the question arises whether we are in the presence of an entire population whose fertility is for some reason below the maximum (improbable), or whether it is the case that some segments of the society have lower fertility than others and, if this is so, which those segments

[2] These relations indicate the probability that a woman with a given number of children has at least one more child. They are generally used with longitudinal data, but here we have used cross-sectional data. It was not possible to extend the analysis because the oldest cohorts with completed fertility are very small (a sample from the census was used) and random variation appears in the averages.

Table 19.4 *Argentina: mean number of children per non-single woman for two cohorts with complete fertility in 1895, by urban or rural residence*

Age	Mean no. of children			Year in which cohort was aged 45–49 years
	Total	Urban[a]	Rural	
55–59	6.4	6.1	6.7	1885
45–49	6.3	5.7	6.8	1895

Source: Pantelides (1983).

[a] Concentrations of population of 2,000 or more inhabitants are considered to be urban.

are.[3] Note that, although small, there is a systematic difference between urban and rural fertility, the former being somewhat lower (Table 19.4).[4] This datum is important, since during the whole period of fertility transition there was a parallel process of rapid urbanization.

To confirm that residence establishes (for reasons that will not concern us here) differences in fertility level, another possible form of approximation with the available data is to observe fertility by jurisdiction. The selected jurisdictions represent a broad spectrum of fertility levels, the dominant forms of production and the proportion of immigrants in the population. It is clear that the Federal Capital has lower fertility levels than the remaining areas, even at the earliest dates, when its own fertility was not dropping (Table 19.5). The comparison between the Federal Capital and the provinces is equivalent to the comparison between a totally urban population and others that include both urban and rural areas, with the latter predominating. That is, further evidence is added in support of the existence of the rural–urban fertility difference, even at a time when fertility was high and, by our criteria, essentially stable.

It is also worth while studying the differential that may exist between the fertility of the native Argentine population and that of the immigrant population, mainly European. The reasons for this interest lie in the fact that the early decline in fertility is usually seen as yet another effect of the massive European immigration to Argentina between the middle of the nineteenth century and the first third of the twentieth. This immigration originated above all in Italy and Spain, countries which, though not at a very advanced stage of transition, did have lower fertility levels than those of Argentina (Pantelides 1984*b*).[5] As Table 19.6 shows, both in 1895 and in 1914 native-born women had somewhat higher fertility than

[3] A pioneering work in this area is that of Somoza (1968), who reached conclusions similar to ours with respect to urban–rural differences, and those by nationality, and also detected differences by degree of literacy among immigrants.

[4] The true differences are possibly greater than those registered, since the information on rural fertility may be of lower quality than for urban fertility.

[5] We have discussed in other documents (Pantelides 1984*b* and 1986) the conceptual and methodological problems involved in attempting to isolate the influence of immigration on fertility. To repeat those arguments here would unduly lengthen the present work.

Table 19.5. *Argentina: mean number of children ever born to non-single women and GFRs, in six jurisdictions, dates of available census data*

Year	Federal Capital	Buenos Aires	Santa Fe	Mendoza	Tucumán	Catamarca
GFR						
1869	187.1	252.3	259.8	186.1	252.3	213.9
1881	—	241.7	—	—	—	—
1887	204.8	—	288.7	—	—	—
1895	172.4	256.8	232.1	197.7	233.0	183.4
1904	138.1	—	—	—	—	—
1909	115.9	—	—	—	—	—
1914	104.8	188.5	194.4	209.5	205.4	183.4
1936	44.3	—	—	—	—	—
1947	47.0	78.5	82.1	119.3	169.2	156.2
1960	47.8	76.9	80.2	101.3	136.3	152.0
1970	59.6	83.4	76.2	97.1	121.4	132.3
1980	65.6	91.9	91.7	107.8	133.4	138.8
Mean number of children, standardized[a]						
1895	4.2	5.1	—	—	—	—
1904	4.1	—	—	—	—	—
1909	4.2	—	—	5.4	—	—
1914	4.0	4.9	5.0	5.0	5.1	4.9
1936	2.8	—	—	—	—	—
1947	2.4	3.1	3.4	4.1	4.8	5.1

Sources: Pantelides (1984*b*).

[a] The standard population adopted refers to non-single women of the Federal Capital in 1936, given the quality of the data and the fact that they were classified by age-group and duration of marriage.

Table 19.6. *Argentina: mean number of children[a] born to non-single women by national origin, in six jurisdictions, 1895 and 1914*

Jurisdiction	1895			1914		
	Total	Native	Immigrant	Total	Native	Immigrant
Federal Capital	4.2	4.5	4.2	4.0	4.2	3.9
Buenos Aires	5.1	5.5	4.7	4.9	5.4	4.7
Santa Fe	—	—	—	5.0	5.2	4.9
Mendoza	—	—	—	5.0	5.2	4.8
Tucumán	—	—	—	5.1	5.1	4.6
Catamarca	—	—	—	4.9	5.0	4.7

Source: Pantelides (1984*b*).

[a] Standardized by duration of marriage, using the non-single female population of the Federal Capital in 1936.

immigrants. The difference is small but systematic, and indicates that the presence of immigrants lowers the level of fertility.[6]

[6] The nationality is that of the women. The nationality of the husbands is unknown. Although several authors have pointed out the presence of high levels of endogamy (Baily 1980; Szuchman 1977), this fact obscures the relationships which might be postulated between fertility in the countries of origin and destination.

The problem of isolating the relative influences of residence and of national origin on fertility is complicated by the fact that the European immigrants mainly settled in urban areas. In 1869, for example, whereas 25.3 per cent of the native-born lived in urban areas, and 6.2 per cent in the Federal Capital, the corresponding percentages for immigrants were 51.9 and 43.8 respectively. The differences, although less marked, remain at later dates (Pantelides 1984*b*: 161). None the less, it is clear from the comparison of the native-born and immigrant populations among jurisdictions, and especially the Federal Capital versus the rest of the country, that there is a double influence. Note, for example, in Table 19.6, that while there is a difference in fertility between the native-born and immigrants, there is also a difference in fertility within the native population, and similarly within the immigrant population, according to their jurisdiction of residence (the argument could be extended to urban–rural differences).

Adding to the foregoing analysis, Table 19.7 shows that not only are there differences in reproductive behaviour between natives and immigrants, but also between immigrants of the various national origins. That is, there is a pattern peculiar to the French, the Italians, etc. It is difficult to attribute these differences to 'post-migratory' experiences. Evidently, the differences resulting from being of one or another nationality are not lost after migration, in particular those affecting reproductive behaviour.

Table 19.7. ***Argentina: distribution of non-single women by number of children born in four regions, cohorts of women married for 20–24 years in 1914, selected nationalities***

Region	% of women at indicated parities					
	0	1–3	4–6	7–9	10+	Total
Federal Capital						
Native-born	9.1	22.6	29.3	24.3	14.7	100.0
Italian	8.3	21.2	30.5	26.2	13.8	100.0
Spanish	9.7	25.2	29.6	22.8	12.7	100.0
French	14.7	36.8	30.0	13.4	5.1	100.0
Buenos Aires						
Native-born	6.0	13.1	20.1	29.8	31.0	100.0
Italian	6.2	13.7	25.8	31.4	22.9	100.0
Spanish	7.0	16.0	27.0	29.6	20.4	100.0
French	8.0	22.3	28.0	24.8	16.9	100.0
Santa Fe						
Native-born	5.7	14.6	21.6	28.8	29.3	100.0
Italian	4.6	11.4	23.8	31.1	29.1	100.0
Spanish	7.4	17.4	29.7	27.0	18.5	100.0
French	7.4	21.6	30.9	24.0	16.1	100.0
Mendoza						
Native-born	5.9	15.1	21.4	28.9	28.7	100.0
Italian	3.5	13.6	25.0	35.8	22.1	100.0
Spanish	6.1	14.9	26.3	32.8	19.9	100.0

Source: Pantelides (1984*b*).

To take the most obvious case, French women clearly tended to remain childless, or to have fewer than 3 children, to a greater degree than the other groups (recall that Table 19.7 includes only women who had already been married for 20 to 24 years, so that they were near the end of their reproductive lives). However, among the French women of the Federal Capital that behaviour was much more 'extreme' than among the French women of other provinces. Thus there is an effect due to nationality and another due to place of residence. The alternative interpretation, that there was selectivity by previous levels of fertility in the settlement patterns of the immigrants, is weakened by the fact that native-born women also show differential reproductive behaviour by area of residence, in the same direction as that of immigrants.

Mechanisms for Fertility Control during the Initial Stages of the Transition

A review—which we do not consider to be exhaustive—of sources of qualitative and quantitative information from the period in which the decline in fertility occurred did not provide information on the mechanisms the population might have used to control its fertility. It is obvious which contraceptive methods were not being used, since at that time none of the modern methods existed. Of the remaining intermediate variables (or proximate determinants), we only have data on nuptiality. Unfortunately, these data suffer from serious problems. First, when the vital statistics are considered as a source, only legal marriages are registered. These are only a fraction—of unknown magnitude—of the total of stable unions. To make things worse, the proportion of consensual unions varies according to social and economic characteristics. For example, for a few points in time data are available on births by legitimacy and nationality of the parents for the province of Buenos Aires. There it is discovered that while 32 per cent of the children of native-born mothers were illegitimate, only 3 per cent of the children of immigrant mothers were (Pantelides 1984*b*: 174). Although the proportion of illegitimate births is in no way identical to the proportion of consensual unions, the evidence given by these figures is striking. To continue with this example, depending on the proportion of immigrants in a particular population, the data on legal marriages would be more or less representative of the overall matrimonial situation.

It is clear from the census data that a high proportion of persons in consensual unions have been reported as single (see Pantelides 1984*a*). This means that measures such as the mean age at marriage calculated by the method of Hajnal, which is based on the proportion of single persons by age, are not meaningful. Other indicators, such as the percentage single at age 45–49 (a usual indicator of permanent celibacy) are also of doubtful interpretation. In 1895, for example, this percentage was 22 for men and 17 for women (Pantelides 1984*b*: 256), very high when compared with percentages ranging from 6 to 15 in France, Great Britain, Italy, and Spain for the same period. What part of this percentage is really permanent celibacy is difficult to say, but we believe that this indicator is less problematic, since by that age a large proportion of unions have been legalized.

With the appropriate caveats, Table 19.8 shows the mean age at legal marriage of the women who married before the age of 50 in the six jurisdictions we have been studying. This mean age is relatively high, in part due to the legalization of consensual unions through late marriage, and in part because second (or later) marriages are included. Concerning the points of interest in this study, only in the Federal Capital is a slight increase in the mean age at legal marriage noted during the period of fertility transition. We suggest cautiously that the increase in age at marriage does not seem to have been one of the mechanisms that contributed to the decline in fertility, nor does it seem to explain the lower fertility in the Federal Capital, even before the beginning of the transition.

Table 19.8. ***Argentina: mean age at marriage (including second marriages) of women legally married before the age of 50, in six jurisdictions, 1881–1947***

Year	Federal capital	Buenos Aires	Santa Fe	Mendoza	Tucumán	Catamarca
1881	—	22.8	—	—	23.4	—
1885	—	22.3	—	—	—	—
1890	23.1	22.8[a]	—	—	—	—
1895	23.0	22.6	—	—	23.4	—
1900	23.3	23.0	21.2[b]	—	22.6	—
1905	23.3	—	—	—	23.2	—
1910	25.0	—	—	—	22.7	25.2[c]
1915	24.5[d]	22.6	21.8	22.4	23.1	24.6
1920	—	—	—	—	23.4	—
1925	—	—	—	22.7	23.5	—
1930	—	—	—	22.3	22.3	—
1935	—	—	—	—	23.2	—
1940	—	23.6	—	—	—	—
1947	—	—	—	—	24.7	—

Source: Pantelides (1984*b*).

Note: Marriages of those under the age of 15 have been counted as at age 14; those 12–16 were supposed at age 15; under 20 was taken to be 17; 45 and over was counted as 47, and 46 and over as 48.

[a] 1888
[b] 1899
[c] 1911
[d] 1913

Information available for a few years and places suggests that differences in mean age at marriage also are not determinants of the lower fertility of immigrants. For 1895 we can calculate the mean age at marriage by Hajnal's methods, and it turns out that in the jurisdictions of interest, the age at marriage of native-born women exceeds that of immigrants by two to four years. The same occurs in the cities of La Plata in 1909, Santa Fe in 1907 and 1923, and Rosario in 1900 and 1906 (Pantelides 1984*b*: table 5.11). Nevertheless, we recall that the mean ages calculated by this method are also inflated by the late legalization of *de facto* unions, and that this effect is greater among native-born women since *de facto* unions are infrequent among immigrants.

The Transition Process and Recent Trends

Returning to the information contained in Tables 19.2, 19.3, and 19.5 we may observe at least four aspects of the fertility decline not discussed so far. The first is that the fertility decline, whatever the measure used, accelerates after 1914. The second is that after 1947 there is a stagnation or deceleration in that decline that continues, but at a slower pace and with interruptions. The third is that in 1980 a rise in fertility occurred. The fourth is that, although at the national level it may be considered that the transition was essentially completed, there are provinces in which the fertility decline has begun only recently. There is also a fifth phenomenon, which cannot be observed because the tables referred to show measures only for the dates of the censuses; this is an increase in the birth rate (and perhaps in fertility) towards the end of the 1940s and the beginning of the 1950s.

Of the points mentioned, we shall concern ourselves only with the baby boom of the 1970s, since the other phenomena are self-evident (to the degree of detail desired in this chapter) or cannot be studied more deeply with the data (and resources) available.

If the various fertility indicators are examined, it may be noted that after a period of gradual decline in fertility, there is an increase during the 1970s. Among the cross-sectional measures, the CBR reaches a minimum of 22.3 per 1,000 in 1965 and a maximum of 24.8 in 1980, and the GFR goes from 87.8 to 107.8 between the same dates. The TFR, on the other hand, which was 2.93 in the first of those years, reached 3.32 in the second (Pantelides 1989). The increments are not spectacular, but one must go back before 1950 or even 1940 to find similar values.

Although complete data are not available for all the cohorts involved, it is possible, by making a few assumptions, to estimate how this rise in fertility would really affect women's completed fertility. This has been done (Pantelides 1989) under two hypotheses. The first, called the maximum hypothesis, supposes that at the ages for which no information is available (always the extreme ages, of low weight in the calculations), fertility was equal to that of the women of the same age at the closest point in time for which there are data. The minimum hypothesis supposes that fertility at those ages was equal to the lowest level registered during the period 1955–80. Table 19.9 shows the results, under these two hypotheses, for the whole country and the Federal Capital, where this phenomenon was most noticeable.

If these hypotheses are correct, there will be a small increase—more noticeable in the Federal Capital—in the average completed family size of these cohorts. Table 19.9 only shows the maximum range of the increases expected under each hypothesis, but each of the cohorts that concludes its fertility after 1980 and until at least 1995 will have a larger number of children than the previous one.

Table 19.9. ***Argentina and the Federal Capital: ASFRs and completed fertility for selected cohorts***

Age	Year of commencement			
	Country		Federal Capital	
	1955	1965	1950	1965
Minimum hypothesis				
15–19	60	60	13(E)	22
20–24	164	156	82	96
25–29	158	181	117	162
30–34	122	129	78	103
35–39	69	69(E)	44	34(E)
40–44	25	24(E)	14	10(E)
45–49	4(E)	4(E)	2	1(E)
Total cohort fertility	3.01	3.12	1.75	2.14
Year of completion of reproductive period	1985	1995	1980	1995
Maximum hypothesis				
15–19	60	60	13(E)	22
20–24	164	156	82	96
25–29	158	181	117	162
30–34	122	129	78	103
35–39	69	73(E)	44	51(E)
40–44	25	25(E)	14	13(E)
45–49	4(E)	4(E)	2	2(E)
Total cohort fertility	3.01	3.14	1.75	2.25
Year of completion of reproductive period	1985	1995	1980	1995

Source: Pantelides (1989).

Note: (E) = estimate.

While the phenomenon is not overly impressive when observed year by year, its cumulative effect will be important. In the areas where the increase was greatest: Federal Capital, Mendoza, Buenos Aires, Cordoba, its effects will be all the more notable because these include almost all the areas that make up the lower part of the range of variation of fertility in the country. The case of the Capital, where the increase meant moving from a gross reproduction ratio below 1 to one above that value, is the most remarkable.

Conclusions

We have surveyed the process of fertility decline in Argentina, with the intention of providing a descriptive overview.

We have devoted some time to attempting to determine the moment at which the fertility decline began, finding this to be after 1895.

Always using information not completely adequate for our purposes, we have tried to show that the massive arrival of foreign immigrants from countries with fertility levels lower than Argentina's had a depressive effect on fertility levels, but that this was combined with local factors, such as the progressive concentration of the population in areas with lower fertility (specifically the urban areas).

We also suggest that age at marriage, the only indicator of an intermediate variable that we could calculate, does not seem to have been a decisive factor in the decline of Argentine fertility.

Finally, we also paid some attention to the 1970s, to observe more closely the latest period of 'baby boom', and reached the conclusion that there was a real increase in completed cohort fertility.

We believe that, overall, we have obtained a relatively complete, though not very deep, picture of a process which, until now, has not been dealt with in its entirety.

References

Arretx, C., Mellafe, R., and Somoza, J. (1977), 'Estimación de la Fecundidad Mediante el Método de los Hijos Propios: Aplicación a Datos de la Argentina de 1895', *Notas de Población*, 5/14: 83–107.

Baily, S. (1980), 'Marriage Patterns and Immigrant Assimilation to Buenos Aires, 1882–1923', *Hispanic American Historical Review*, 60/1: 32–48.

Camisa, Z. (1965), *Argentina: Proyección de la Población por Sexo y Edad, 1960–1980* (Santiago: CELADE).

Celton, D. (1987), 'La Población de la Provincia de Córdoba a Fines del Siglo XVIII', Doct. diss., Universidad Nacional de Córdoba, Argentina.

Cuba, Centro de Estudios Demográficos (n.d.), *La Población de Cuba* (CICRED Series; Havana).

Duje, N. E. (1989), 'Fecundidad e Ilegitimidad en Córdoba (Argentina), 1780–1840', paper given at ABEP, IUSSP, and CELADE, Congress on the History of the Population in Latin America, Ouro Preto, 2–6 July 1989.

Ferreyra, M. del C. (1989), 'Nupcialidad y Fecundidad en una Ciudad Americana Durante el Siglo XVII: El caso de Córdoba (Argentina)', paper given at ABEP, IUSSP, and CELADE, Congress on the History of the Population of Latin America, Ouro Preto, 2–6 July 1989.

Gutiérrez, R. H. (1975), *La Población de Chile* (CICRED Series; Paris).

Lattes, A. E. (1975), 'El Crecimiento de la Población y sus Componentes Demográficos Entre 1870 y 1970', in Z. Recchini de Lattes and A. Lattes (eds.), *La Población de Argentina* (CICRED Series; Buenos Aires).

Lesthaeghe, R. J. (1977), *The Decline of Belgian Fertility, 1800–1970* (Princeton: Princeton University Press).

Mychaszula, S., Pantelides, E. A., and Foschiatti, A. M. (1989), 'La Fecundidad en la Ciudad de Corrientes a Principios del Siglo XIX', Paper presented at ABEP, IUSSP, and CELADE, Congress on the History of the Population in Latin America, Ouro Preto, 2–6 July 1989.

Pantelides, E. A. (1982), *Las Mujeres de Alta Fecundidad en la Argentina: Pasado y Futuro* (Cuadernos del CENEP, No. 22; Buenos Aires).

—— (1983), 'La Transición Demográfica Argentina: Un Modelo No Ortodoxo', *Desarrollo Económico*, 88: 511–33.

—— (1984*a*), *Análisis y Propuesta de Corrección de la Información Sobre Estado Civil en los Cuatro Primeros Censos Nacionales Argentinos* (CENEP, Serie Estadísticas Sociodemográficas, 2; Buenos Aires).

—— (1984*b*), 'The Decline of Fertility in Argentina, 1869–1947', doct. diss., University of Texas at Austin (Ann Arbor: University Microfilms).

—— (1986), 'Notas Respecto a la Posible Influencia de la Inmigración Europea sobre la Fecundidad de la Argentina', *Estudios Migratorios Latinoamericanos*, 1/3.

—— (1989), *La Fecundidad Argentina desde Mediados del Siglo XX*, (Cuadernos del CENEP, No. 41; Buenos Aires).

Rothman, A. M. (1970), *Evolución de la Fecundidad en Argentina y Uruguay* (Centro de Investigaciones Sociales, Documento de Trabajo, No. 69, Instituto T. Di Tella; Buenos Aires).

Somoza, Jorge L. (1968), 'Nivel y Diferenciales de la Fecundidad en la Argentina en el Siglo XIX', *Milbank Memorial Fund Quarterly*, 46/3(2): 57–77.

Szuchman, M. D. (1977), 'The Limits of the Melting Pot in Urban Argentina: Marriage and Integration in Cordoba, 1869–1909', *Hispanic American Historical Review*, 57/1: 24–50.

Torrado, S. (1970), 'Natalidad y Fecundidad en Argentina desde Fines del Siglo XIX', paper presented at IUSSP, Regional Latin America Conference on Population, Mexico.

United States, Bureau of the Census (1980), *Statistical Abstract of the United States: 1980* (Washington).

20 Bolivia: The Social and Geographic Context of Trends in Fertility

HUGO TÓRREZ PINTO

Introduction

Within the context of Latin America, Bolivia's pattern of demographic change has been quite distinctive. While many countries in the region are experiencing the pressure of rapid demographic growth, Bolivia's territory is sparsely settled, even though its regional distribution is uneven. The country's patterns of fertility, mortality, and migration have created a rate of population growth that is by no means the highest in the region. The data indicate that Bolivia's population increased over the last thirty-five years by only 130 per cent, whereas in the Andean region as a whole (excluding Colombia and Chile), the corresponding increase was over 180 per cent.

It is well known that fertility is one of the fundamental components of population growth. In Bolivia this demographic variable has revealed quite distinct patterns, when compared with the experience of other countries. In fact, in the thirty to thirty-five years prior to 1950, levels of fertility remained high and unchanging. However, this did not lead to rapid population growth, as occurred in other countries, because the high level of fertility was, and still is, accompanied by high levels of mortality, especially infant mortality.

Fertility and mortality are usually studied in association with other background characteristics, in an attempt to understand population phenomena within the context of a country's socio-economic, political, and cultural setting. In fact, many analysts believe that the demographic factors reflect wider social conditions, and are closely related to a country's socio-economic and cultural characteristics. Other analysts consider demographic variables to be phenomena that operate at the level of the individual, being exclusively biological determinants.

There have been only two national population censuses in Bolivia in the last forty years, and these were carried out in 1950 and 1976. In addition, national demographic surveys were conducted in 1975 and 1980. More recently, the National Population and Housing Survey in 1988 (NPHS-88) and the National Demographic and Health Survey in 1989 (NDHS-89) have been carried out. The present document will analyse patterns of Bolivian fertility over the past fifteen or twenty years in the light of the results of the last national census and the most recent surveys.

A Look at the Past

In the course of Bolivia's integration into the international mercantile system, the country's productive base became only partially developed, and in a geographically uneven way, following trends of capitalist accumulation focused mainly on urban locations. This process was accompanied by the formation of a highly unequal social structure and by the creation of human settlements in specific regions of the country. As a result, population distribution has historically been determined by the location of the dominant economic activities, principally mining.

Before 1952,[1] capitalist development in Bolivia was limited to mining, and did not succeed in reaching the majority of the population, giving rise, instead, to large sectors of the indigenous population living under a closed, subsistence economy. This led to economic stagnation in the rural sector. According to the 1950 census, 88 per cent of the country's population lived in traditional areas (the Altiplano and the valleys), which cover 41 per cent of Bolivia's territory. Fertility and mortality were both extremely high; the TFR was close to 7 per woman,[2] while life expectancy at birth was only 41 years (Figs. 20.1 and 20.2).

Bolivia's social structure until the beginning of the 1950s was based on servile productive relationships, a very low level of technology in agriculture and a poverty-stricken proletariat, and, as such, it did not require an educated labour force; it only needed the intensive utilization of human labour. The need to incorporate individuals into the labour force at an early age made education an obstacle to the continued functioning of the system. The material living conditions imposed by this system kept the majority of the population in absolute ignorance. This was reflected in extremely high levels of illiteracy—68 per cent in 1950—while no more than 4 per cent of the population had more than nine years of schooling.

The low levels of education and the high level of illiteracy prevailing until 1952 reflect economic conditions at the time. Rudimentary agricultural and manufacturing technology did not require a highly educated labour force, and the population's low income did not permit access to adequate education, thus creating a large mass of poor people: peasants, artisans, service and retail trade workers, low-level salaried employees, and subgroups of the urban population who did not benefit from the prevailing model of development and distribution.

Within this framework, most Bolivians lacked housing with an even minimal level of comfort, and were denied even the most basic health services. At the time

[1] The National Revolution occurred in 1952. This event, and the succeeding reforms, are the most significant facts in the country's recent history, due to their impact on the transformation of Bolivia's economic structure. Among other things, economic exploitation, which had led to the extreme impoverishment of the numerically small proletariat (occupied in mining activities) and of the majority of the peasantry, was abolished; the main power groups (mine-owners and landholders) were eliminated from the political scene, and servile forms of agricultural labour were abolished, turning the peasant into a smallholder and participant in the market economy.

[2] Nevertheless, this rate was not so different from that of other Latin American countries, the great majority of which reported TFRs of 6.5 and 7.0 children per woman until the early 1960s.

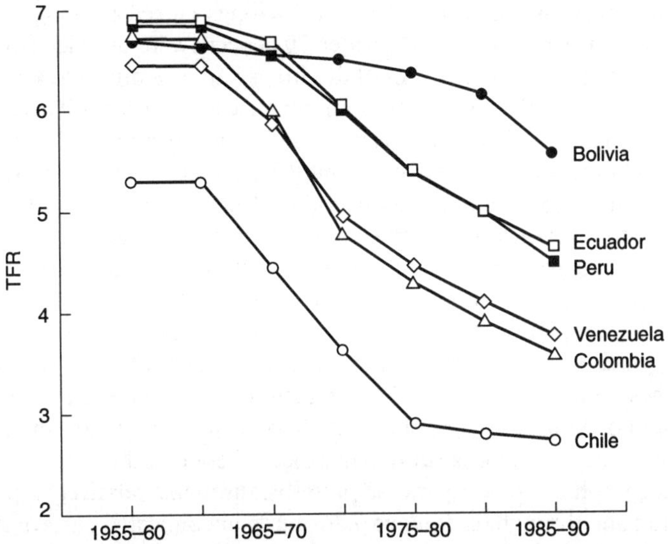

Fig. 20.1. ***Latin America: TFRs 1950–1990, selected countries***

Sources: CELADE, *Demographic Bulletin*, 41; estimates from NDHS (Bolivia) 1989

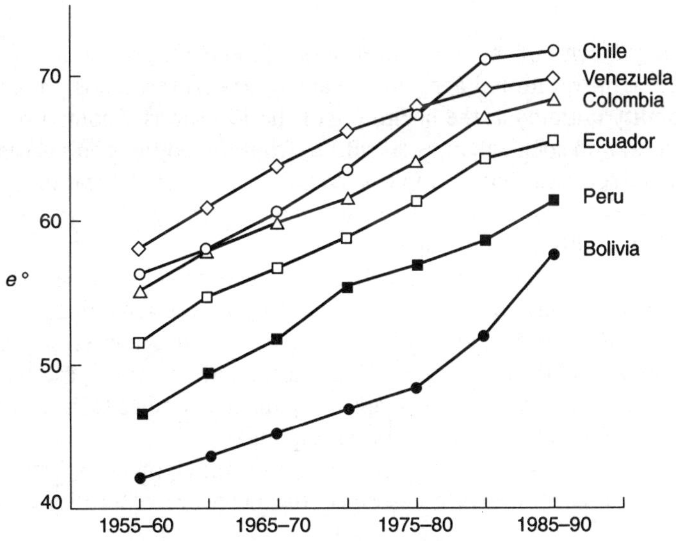

Fig. 20.2. ***Latin America: life expectancy at birth (e^0) 1955–1990, selected countries***

Sources: CELADE, *Demographic Bulletin*, 44; estimates from NDHS (Bolivia) 1989

of the 1950 census, 46 per cent of urban dwellings lacked running water, and among those with access to drinking water, 70 per cent were supplied from a central system; furthermore, 54 per cent of dwellings had no sanitary services, and if this service was available, it was for community use in most cases. This is the context surrounding the high levels of fertility and mortality already described.

From 1952 onwards, a development model characterized by predominantly capitalist forms of production was introduced into Bolivia. This led, among other things, to diversification of the country's economic and social structure, a more intensive integration of the economic system, both spatially and regionally, and increased population mobility. On the other hand, policies of colonization and territorial integration were established in order to diversify economic activity and, implicitly, reduce demographic pressures in the country's traditional regions. These changes contributed to a redefinition of the country's population structure and dynamics. Geographic and socio-occupational movement was encouraged in some cases and permitted in others; these had the effect of changing Bolivia's geographic and occupational patterns, through a relatively rapid rate of urbanization and through the linkage of formerly unconnected parts of the country, as well as through expanded population settlements in the eastern part of Bolivia.

The 1976 population and housing census showed that 80 per cent of the total population was still living in traditional areas, while Bolivia's eastern territories continued to be underpopulated; secondly, in spite of the social reforms undertaken since 1952, both fertility (TFR of 6.5) and mortality continued to be high, as reflected in a life expectancy at birth of somewhat over forty-six years (Figs. 20.1 and 20.2).

In 1976 the majority of the population was still made up of the lower social classes, working in traditional agricultural activities.[3] Nevertheless, the process of social mobility initiated at the beginning of the 1950s was accompanied by a series of cultural and social changes, resulting from the population's access to a number of social services. One example is the impulse given to education by campaigns aimed at reducing illiteracy to 32 per cent, which significantly increased school attendance, although only up to the age of 13.

As all schooling takes place in Spanish, use of the official language increased, as did the diffusion of urban, modernizing patterns. At the same time, migrants coming from rural areas brought with them their own language as they moved into squatter areas and the major cities. This interaction gave rise to the existence of a large mass of the population who speak Spanish as well as their native languages. That is, bilingualism began to be widespread.

These changes, however, did not result in significant changes in fertility and mortality. As has already been fully described, the mean level of fertility in Bolivia

[3] The stratification studies based on the 1976 census show that the great majority of the Bolivian population (80%) was made up of the socio-economic group categorized as the 'lower stratum', including the following specific subgroups: unpaid agriculture (peasants), paid agriculture, unpaid non-agriculture, and paid non-agriculture.

remained at almost constantly high levels throughout the twenty or twenty-five years prior to 1976, with TFRs ranging between 6.8 and 6.5. On the other hand, a decline in mortality merely led to an increase of just under seven years in life expectancy at birth.

It should be emphasized that Bolivia's economic history has been characterized in recent years by a period of strong growth, mainly between 1962 and 1978, followed by a period of sharp decline until 1985, only to be followed by renewed growth in 1987 (Bolivia, Ministerio de Planeamiento y Coordinación 19: 1). This pattern of development, however, has not created sufficient economic growth to improve the living conditions of the majority of Bolivians. Bolivia's moderately abundant and diverse natural resources, given the size of its population, have been inefficient and unequally distributed. At the same time, the country's workforce has not been able to find either sufficient employment or the necessary means for its full development. It must be added that long-standing neglect of education has produced an unqualified labour force, which in urban areas works mainly in the so-called 'informal sectors'. In this context, more urban women are in the labour-force activity than was so in the past.

There have recently been a number of surveys designed to examine the relationships between demographic and socio-economic variables. The largest of these studies have been the National Population and Housing Survey, held in 1988, and the National Demographic and Health Survey, conducted in 1989. Initial results from these surveys show that Bolivia's TFR declined by about 1.5 children in the ten to twelve years preceding the two surveys; similarly, infant mortality seems also to have declined during that period, going from 151 to 102 per 1,000 live births (Fig. 20.3).[4] Although the declines in these two variables were to be expected, where fertility is concerned, the socio-economic and cultural conditions, and the level of contraceptive practice do not seem to have changed sufficiently to account for this decline, unless the use of abortion, which is difficult to measure, is becoming a practice of major dimensions.[5]

Knowledge of Fertility Levels, Trends, and Differentials

As mentioned above, patterns of fertility in Bolivia have been quite distinctive, when compared to those of other countries. The literature on the subject shows that from 1950 until the beginning of the 1960s, fertility in Latin America remained high. The mean completed family size ranged between 6 and 7, except in the countries of the Southern Cone and Cuba. Since then, many countries have begun to experience declines in their fertility levels, with varying trends: some abruptly,

[4] Although several different sources were used to determine the demographic indicators (survey for the more recent estimates and census for the older ones), this does not invalidate the comparability of the results.

[5] On the other hand, the estimated infant mortality rate is close to that shown in population projections. For the period 1985–90, it was anticipated that the IMR would decline to a level of 109 per 1,000 live births.

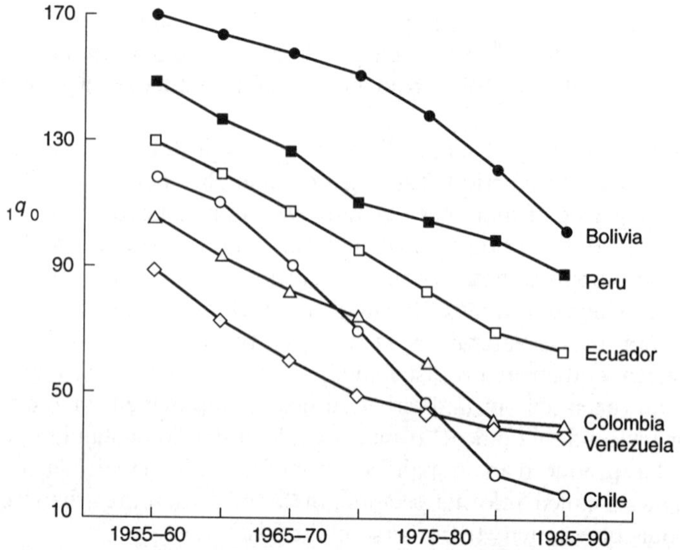

Fig. 20.3. ***Latin America: infant mortality rates ($_1q_0$) 1955–1990, selected countries***

Sources: CELADE, *Demographic Bulletin*, 44; estimates from NDHS (Bolivia) 1988

such as Colombia, Venezuela, and Costa Rica, and others more gradually, such as Peru, Paraguay, and Mexico (CONAPO–the Pathfinder Fund 1989: 79). Thus, fertility rates in Latin America are undergoing a clear process of overall decline at present (Fig. 20.1 shows fertility trends in countries of the Andean area).

In the case of Bolivia, while it is true that fertility seemed to decline, the reduction was not substantial; the TFR remained practically unchanged and at high levels, 6.8 children per woman for the period 1955–60 and 6.5 for the quinquennium 1970–5 (INE–CELADE 1985) (Fig. 20.1). To this must be added the fact that long-term official projections have estimated a rate of 6.3 for the period 1980–5. The stability prior to 1976 is the result of two opposing trends: a declining trend in urban areas and a rising trend in rural areas (Carafa *et al.* 1983: 99). None the less, the pace of change differs by urban–rural residence and by region. For example, Fig. 20.4 shows the change in fertility in the Altiplano region during the period 1964–74. In the principal city (La Paz), the seat of government and the main centre of economic activity, the decline in fertility has been quite pronounced. On the other hand, in the highly rural areas,[6] the trend was in the reverse direction.

To understand the special features of Bolivia's urban fertility more clearly it is necessary to examine experience in the country's three major cities: La Paz,

[6] In the context of the Project on Population Policy, the Bolivian population was divided into three major regions, Altiplano, Valleys, and Plains. Each region was in turn segmented according to a typology of urban concentration and manner of rural settlement, namely principal cities, secondary cities, other urban, rural populations with urban influence, and rural populations with no urban influence. This last group is referred to as the highly rural setting, or high rural.

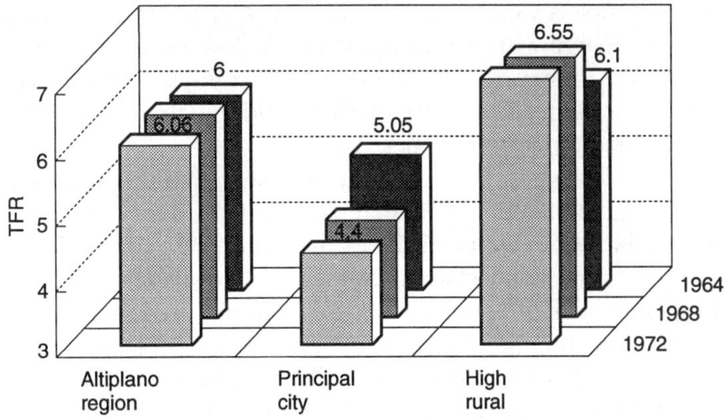

Fig. 20.4. ***Altiplano: trends in fertility in two widely differing regions 1964–1972***

Sources: Population policy project, special tabulations from 1976 census

Cochabamba, and Santa Cruz, which together account for somewhat more than 70 per cent of the total urban population. The TFR in 1970–5 was estimated at 4.6 children per woman for the three cities taken as a whole. This measure is almost two children lower than the national average, and masks fairly important variations among the cities. In fact, Santa Cruz and Cochabamba both show higher fertility than does La Paz, at 5.0, 4.8, and 4.4 children respectively (see Fig. 20.5). These differences are not of great magnitude; however, if the situation within each city is studied, paying special attention to women's social class, more substantive differences are detected. An analysis involving two social strata, middle–high and low, makes it clear that there are differences in urban fertility within a single class. And the differences are more pronounced in the case of the women belonging to the middle–high group (see Fig. 20.5). On the other hand,

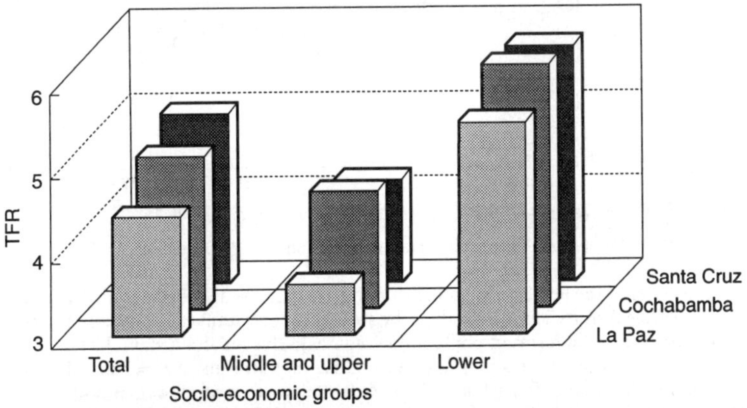

Fig. 20.5. ***Bolivia: fertility levels among upper-middle and lower class social groups in the major cities 1970–1975***

Sources: Project on Population Policy, special tabulations from the 1976 Census

the greatest contrast is seen when the fertility of women in the middle-high class in La Paz is compared with that of women in the lower class in Cochabamba, a difference of more than two children. These findings highlight the differences that are masked by the aggregate averages, which could lead to weak policy guidelines in social and population programmes.[7]

At this point it is appropriate to conduct a brief analysis of trends in fertility in each city during the period immediately prior to 1976. Figs. 20.6 and 20.7 illustrate the variations both within each city and among the social groups in question. Fig. 20.6 shows that between 1964 and 1976,[8] there was a considerable decline in fertility in all three cities. It should be emphasized that at the beginning of the period, women in Santa Cruz had had approximately 5.8 children by the end of their fertile life, that is almost one child more than at the end of the period. The fertility trend in Cochabamba was somewhat similar. In contrast, in La Paz, the 1964 TFR appears to have been somewhat lower than the values observed in the other cities, but the decline up to the end of the period seems to have been less

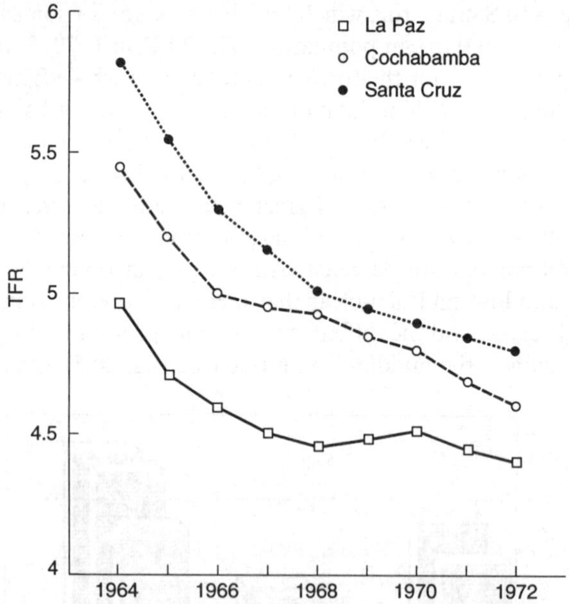

Fig. 20.6. ***Bolivia: trends in fertility in the major cities 1964–1972***

Sources: Project on Population Policy, special tabulations from the 1976 Census

[7] An explanation of the fertility differences among the cities under consideration requires both a determination of the fertility levels of each of the social groups within each city, and the relative importance of those groups in terms of population volume. In this respect it should be mentioned that in La Paz, 43% of the population belonged to the middle–high stratum; in Cochabamba this proportion was somewhat higher, at 45%, while in Santa Cruz the fraction was lower, only 40%.

[8] Fertility trends before 1976 have been estimated using the 'own children' technique. As is well known, this procedure makes it possible to estimate fertility by age for the 10 or 15 years prior to the moment of the census or other demographic data collection. That is why the period 1964–76 is considered in the present section.

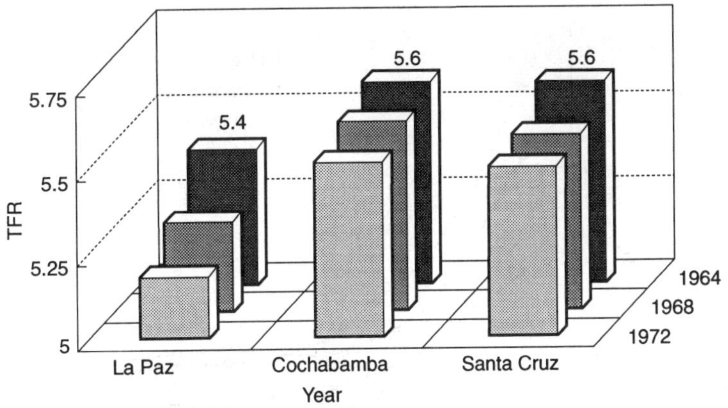

Fig. 20.7. ***Bolivia: fertility trends among the low-paid workers in the major cities 1964–1972***

***Sources*: Project on Population Policy, special tabulations from the 1976 Census**

intense and, in fact, the level seems to have remained fairly stable between 1968 and 1972.

The decline in fertility did not occur in all sectors, but rather in certain social groups. In particular, fertility among women in the lower groups did not decline at all (Fig. 20.7); specifically, the fertility of lower-stratum wage-earners remained almost stable, or changed only a little in some periods (Carafa *et al.* 1983: 104). In contrast, in the middle–high group, the decline in fertility was significant and of varying intensity. According to Fig. 20.8, the reduction was greater in Santa Cruz, being approximately 1.5 children; in the other cities, the decline was also fairly large, involving a reduction of somewhat more than one child.

The declining trend of fertility in urban areas was to be expected; in contrast, the pattern in rural areas, no matter which region of the country, was less predictable. Fig. 20.9 indicates the fact that rural fertility actually increased, mainly beginning in the second half of the 1960s, and by 1972 reaching increases of nearly one child in the Altiplano and Valleys regions. This finding raises several questions. Why, in the social groups in which we assume that births were not being regulated, was fertility only moderately high around 1964? Why did fertility increase in the period in question? According to Carafa *et al.* (1983: 126), the rise in fertility in Bolivia's rural areas may have been caused by the single or combined action of a variety of factors, among them, possible changes in nuptiality, a reduction in involuntary sterility resulting from certain venereal diseases, and an increase in the age of female widowhood, as a result of reductions in male adult mortality.

On the other hand, estimates of possible mortality trends have been calculated. Although these estimates are derived from indirect techniques, the results indicate that in rural areas, the risk of mortality among children under the age of one year had risen slightly in the ten to twelve years prior to 1976. In contrast, infant mortality in urban areas declined somewhat over the same period (see Fig. 20.10). In the light of these results it may be conjectured that fertility dynamics in the rural

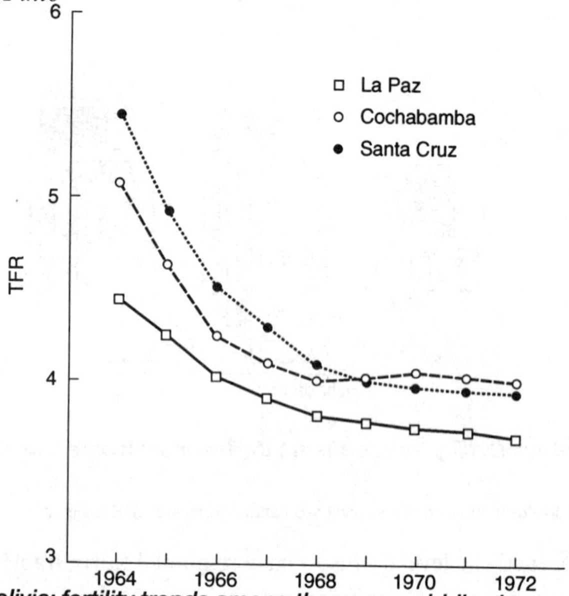

Fig. 20.8. ***Bolivia: fertility trends among the upper-middle classes of the major cities 1964–1972***

Sources: Project on Population Policy, special tabulations from the 1976 Census

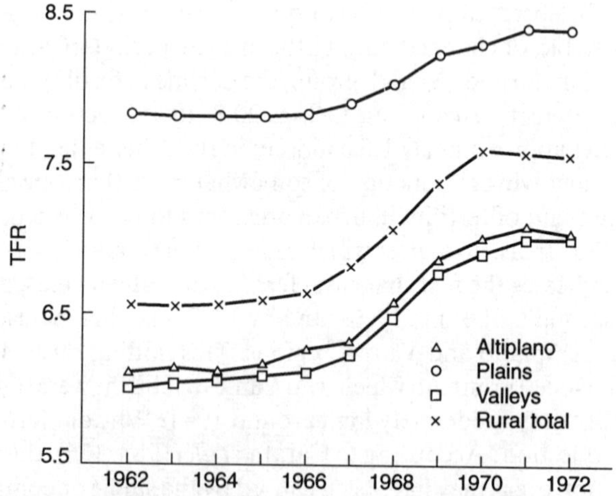

Fig. 20.9. ***Bolivia: fertility trends in rural areas 1964–1972***

Sources: Project on Population Policy, special tabulations from the 1976 Census

areas were to some extent a response to deteriorating living conditions in those areas, translated into exposure to a higher likelihood of death among the new-borns.

Finally, it should be emphasized that these trends have had the effect of increasing fertility differentials between the extreme urban and rural population groups as well as between social classes. Thus, it is estimated, at the mid-point of the period 1970–5, rural fertility in the Plains region was practically double that observed in the city of La Paz.

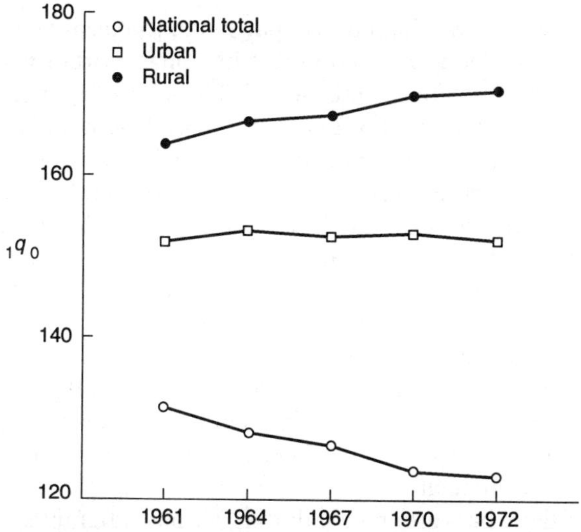

Fig. 20.10. ***Bolivia: trends in infant mortality ($_1q_0$) (per 1,000 live births)***
Source: Special tabulations of the 1976 Census

Recent Experience

Because there has not been a census in recent years, it is not possible to produce estimates or analyses similar to those presented in the preceding sections. However, the studies recently conducted by the INE, the NPHS, and the NDHS permit the calculation of fertility estimates and possible trends, although not in as great a detail as we would have liked.

The first estimates made by INE, using data from the NPHS, offer some indication that fertility in Bolivia has undergone a very sharp decline, from the 6.5 children per woman estimated for the period 1970–5, to 5.0 at a date close to the year of the survey (1988) (INE–FNUAP 1989: 47). Another estimate, based on the data from the NDHS, corroborates this result, and appears to confirm the fertility trend of recent years.[9] However, it should be stressed that certain factors believed to be associated with fertility change have themselves not undergone the changes necessary to account for this decline. Even though illiteracy levels continued to drop from 32 per cent of the population in 1976 to 19 per cent in 1988, the number of years of instruction completed by the population, particularly the female population, continues to be very low. Although the level of unemployment is not extremely high, there has been an increase in participation in the informal and service sectors of the labour force, where education and skills are not important. In the face of their need to increase household income, women have joined the labour force, but in part-time or occasional jobs, usually inside the

[9] A probable explanation for the agreement may lie in the fact that the documentation and material for the design of the NDHS sample were provided by the NPHS; that is, a subsample of the Primary Sampling Units of the NPHS was selected for the NDHS.

households.[10] Although vaccination campaigns and preventive actions to improve child health have led to an important reduction in mortality risks, access to basic services and health care is quite limited. The form of economic and social development established in recent years finds its correlates in these patterns.

On the other hand, while the proportion of women in union has increased since 1976,[11] the use of contraceptives and the practice of family planning among married women are still not well established. According to data from the NDHS, only 30 per cent of women in union are using a contraceptive method, of whom 12 per cent are using a modern method, and 18 per cent, a traditional method (INE–DHS 1990: 43). Forty per cent of women in cities and other urban centres use contraceptive methods, while only 20 per cent of those in the rural areas do so, and most rural women resort to traditional methods (almost 15 per cent). Only women with a high level of schooling (ten or more years) practise contraception in large proportions, close to 55 per cent; however, the size of this population group is relatively small.

In the light of these background conditions, we have attempted to correct the fertility estimates and trends over the past fifteen years, to make them consistent and plausible in the overall context of Bolivian life. In 1985–90 the overall TFR in Bolivia was 5.6 children per woman. This rate is a weighted average of an urban rate of 3.9 and a rural rate of 7.0 (Fig. 20.11). The decline by approximately one child that has occurred over the past twelve to fourteen years does not appear to be the result of a continuous, uniform process, nor is it a result of a combined decline in fertility in urban and rural areas. Rather, it seems that there has been a significant decline only in the last five years[12] and mainly in urban settings.[13] However, we cannot discount the possibility that fertility has begun to decline, even if only slightly, in rural areas.

Conclusion

Most socially and economically underdeveloped countries are characterized by high levels of both fertility and mortality, which explains why demographic

[10] Recent studies of the relationship between women's level of participation in economic activity and their fertility in major Bolivian cities have shown that women in unpaid activities had higher fertility than those not in the labour force, which would indicate that women experience little incompatibility between their reproductive and their productive roles. For further references see Tórrez *et al.* (1989).

[11] The results of the 1988 NPHS show that the proportion of non-single women by age-group, with the exception of those under the age of 25 years, increased to a not insignificant degree, in both urban and rural areas. Likewise, the ratio of women in union to those not in union has increased in similar fashion.

[12] Smoothing of the retrospectively estimated age-specific rates given in the NDHS report (table 4.2) confirms the finding that between 1973 and 1983 the TFR gradually declined.

[13] The final report of the NDHS, published in January 1990, demonstrates that levels of fertility in Bolivia remained relatively constant until the period 1980–1984. It also shows, allowing for the difference between the mean number of children born to women aged 40–49 years and the TFR in the five years preceding the survey, that the declining trend has been more pronounced in the urban areas than in other sectors of the country.

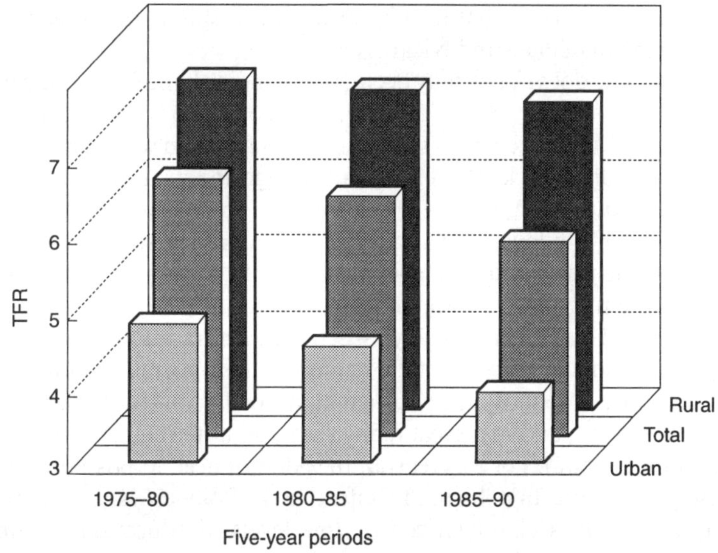

Fig. 20.11. ***Bolivia: estimated fertility trends in urban and rural areas 1975–1990***

Source: Estimates based on the results of NDHS (Bolivia) 1989

indicators, principally natality and mortality rates, are used to express a country's stage of development. And high birth and death rates are related to other indicators, such as education, health, the health infrastructure, the state of the labour force, etc.

When compared with other countries, fertility trends in Bolivia have revealed quite distinct patterns. Until the first years of the 1960s, with the exception of the countries of the Southern Cone and Cuba, fertility in Latin America remained at a high level and only slightly changing, with TFRs of about 6 to 7 children per woman. Since then, many countries have seen their rates decline, some abruptly and others more moderately. In Bolivia, by comparison, between 1955 and 1975, fertility remained high, with an average TFR of around 7 children by the end of a woman's reproductive life. However, this conduct reflected two clearly different trends: rising fertility in the rural context, and declining in the urban case.

The information shows that starting in the second half of the 1960s, and until the middle of the 1970s, rural fertility increased, reaching average levels of over 7 children per woman. During this same period, urban fertility declined considerably, reaching a level just over 5 children per woman. Although this trend was to be expected, the rural situation appears to have been a response to the poor chances of survival among new-borns. The most recent estimates indicate that fertility is now about four children per woman in urban areas, and seven in rural areas. This means that in the twelve to fifteen years before 1988, total fertility declined considerably, but only as a result of the decline in urban areas. This was also accompanied by a significant decline in mortality. In spite of this overall decline, there is no doubt that fertility in Bolivia is still high, exceeded only by levels found in Guatemala and Nicaragua.

Fertility decline does not usually occur simultaneously, or follow the same path of change, in all sectors. This is particularly true for Bolivian society, which is characterized by a high degree of social heterogeneity, and whose inhabitants are exposed to very different levels of social advantage and distribution of wealth. If one asked who, in Bolivia, has many children, the immediate response would be: the population in the lower social groups, who represent somewhat more than two-thirds of the total. It should also be asked why those groups have so many children. In the first place, reproductive behaviour in these groups begins with early nuptiality. This fact is probably associated with traditional cultural norms, but there are also social factors that reinforce those norms. Among the poor, young people leave school much earlier than do the youth of the middle and upper social groups, and in a great many cases, do not even have the opportunity of attending school. For this reason, they do not need to postpone marriage, or, consequently, the first birth. In effect, it is Bolivia's large impoverished population—which is characterized by low levels of education, an unskilled labour force, low levels of productivity and income, and exposure to higher risks of mortality—that has the highest level of fertility in the country.

References

Bolivia, Ministerio de Planeamiento y Coordinación (19 *Estrategia de Desarrollo Económico y Social 1989–2000* La Paz: Ministeris de Planeamiento y Coordinación.

Carafa, C., González, G., Ramírez, V., Pereira, R., and Tórrez, H. (1983), *Luz y Sombra de la Vida, Mortalidad y Fecundidad en Bolivia* (La Paz: Project on Population Policy).

CELADE (1988) *Demographic Bulletin*, 41 (Year 21) (Santiago: Chile).

—— (1989) *Demographic Bulletin*, 44 (Year 22) (Santiago: Chile).

CONAPO–the Pathfinder Fund (1989), *Mujer, Trabajo y Reproducción Humana en Tres Contextos de Bolivia* (La Paz: CONAPO–Pathfinder Fund).

INE–CELADE (1985), *Bolivia: Estimaciones y Proyecciones de Población, Total del País 1950–2025, Urbana y Rural 1970–2000* (Fascide F/Boll; La Paz: INE–CELADE).

INE–DHS (1990), *Bolivia: Encuesta Nacional de Demografía y Salud 1989* (La Paz: INE–DHS).

INE–FNUAP (1989), *Bolivia Encuesta Nacional de Población y Vivienda 1988, Resultados Finales* (La Paz: INE).

21 The Fertility Transition in Brazil: Causes and Consequences

JOSÉ ALBERTO MAGNO DE CARVALHO and
LAURA RODRÍGUEZ WONG

Introduction

Brazil has proceeded through the 1980s and is approaching the twenty-first century while undergoing one of the greatest transformations in its demographic history, led by an unprecedented, rapid, and universal decline in fertility. The objective of the present chapter is to discuss this change, some of its determinants, and its most important consequences. More than simply an analysis of new data or recent discoveries, this chapter is a summary of the discussions which this unexpected behaviour has stimulated among students of the current Brazilian situation.

For this purpose a brief overview is given of the historical and socio-economic context in which this transformation in fertility behaviour occurred. A description of the varied path followed by fertility during the period between 1940 and 1985 is presented, along with the reaction of fertility behaviour to the particular style of socio-economic development being experienced in the country. In addition, to clarify the fact that such changes are giving rise to structural transformations in the composition of the population, some attention is paid to the strength of their impact. Emphasis is placed both on the demographic consequences, for example, the destabilization of the age structure, as well as on the alterations required in policies aimed at children, the aged, the labour-market, etc.

Brazil's Fertility Transition in the Period 1940–1985

Given that all phenomena of demographic dynamics are embedded in a specific social and economic framework, general reference should be made here to the context within which the Brazilian population profile is drawn, to serve as background for the study of the evolution of fertility which follows. Also, since this is the variable which in large measure determines the demographic structure of a population, it is convenient to include in this section a description, however superficial, of the demographic behaviour of the country during the period in question.

The Historical and Economic Context

Brazil reached the end of the 1980s as the eighth largest economy in the world due, among other factors, to its diversified economic growth, which on several occasions during the preceding decade exceeded 10 per cent per annum.

In fact, since 1940 Brazil has been seen as a country which is entering the industrialized age on a large scale. During the 1950s, under a policy of import substitution, a powerful urban middle class became consolidated to the detriment of the agricultural sector; one consequence of this was an increase in the internal north-to-south migratory flow.

Some years later there arose what is known as the 'Brazilian economic miracle', occurring between about 1968 and 1974. During this period the emphasis was on external markets, causing yet further concentration of wealth and a reduction in the purchasing power of the working class in general and of the least-favoured in particular; in fact the real value of wages and salaries had been deteriorating since 1960/1.[1]

Around 1980, in spite of a certain degree of social progress, the rural exodus continued. For the first time there was a decrease in the size of the rural population and the country became predominantly urban as more than half of its inhabitants now live in cities. The external debt continued to rise at an alarming rate, reaching six or seven times the level of a decade earlier.

Due to its participation in the world economic system, the economic recession was felt in Brazil much more than in the other countries of Latin America, particularly because it is one of the most industrialized countries in the area. In fact, for several consecutive years during the first half of the 1980s, the indicators of economic growth were negative; informal employment grew by 6 per cent a year between 1981 and 1983 and infant mortality increased in large metropolitan areas such as São Paulo. On this occasion not only did the low-income sector suffer most from the recession, but the middle class in general was also severely affected.

At the level of the main regions of the country (see Table 21.1), the inequalities which have characterized the country since the colonial period have become more acute over the past few years, in spite of the growth and diversification of the national economy. In the southern part of the country, São Paulo has become one of the most advanced areas, standing out clearly ahead of the once prosperous north-eastern region. The socio-economic indicators shown in Tables 21.1 and 21.2, although they do show social progress in the sense that there has been an increase in literacy rates, dwellings with water, sewerage, and electricity, etc., also show this contrast quite clearly, and illustrate these sharp differences: poverty and backwardness in the north, and development, production, and progress in the south.

[1] In 1964 the external debt was estimated to be about US$ 3 billion; by 1974 it had become US$ 17 billion; in 1984 it had reached roughly US$ 100 billion (Wood and Carvalho 1988).

Table 21.1. *Brazil: % distribution of population and national income by region, 1949–1980*

Region	% of population			% of national income		
	1950	1970	1989	1949	1970	1980
Brazil[a]	100.0 (51.94)	100.0 (93.14)	100.0 (119.00)	100.0	100.0	100.0
North	3.6	3.9	4.9	1.7	2.3	3.2
North-East	34.6	30.3	29.3	14.1	12.0	12.2
South-East	43.4	42.7	43.5	66.5	65.0	62.2
South	15.1	17.7	16.0	15.9	17.0	17.3
Centre West	3.3	5.4	6.3	1.8	3.7	5.1

Sources: For 1950, 1970, and 1980: IBGE (1987); for 1949: BAER (1979).

Note: Figures in parentheses refer to absolute number (in millions of inhabitants).

Table 21.2. *Brazil: Measures of well-being for selected regions, 1970–1980*

Indicators	1970	1980	Ratio 1980/70
Literacy rate			
North-East	39.2	47.7	1.2
South-East	71.1	79.3	1.1
Ratio	(1.8)	(1.7)	—
Proportion of the population aged 15–19 with 9 to 12 years of schooling			
North-East	6.0	17.0	2.8
South-East	12.0	26.0	2.2
Ratio	(2.0)	(1.5)	—
Proportion of dwellings with drinking water			
North-East	12.4	30.1	2.4
South-East	44.2	65.9	1.5
Ratio	(3.6)	(2.2)	—
Proportion of dwellings with sewerage or septic tank			
North-East	8.0	16.4	2.1
South-East	37.2	56.2	1.5
Ratio	(4.7)	(3.4)	—
Proportion of dwellings with electricity			
North-East	23.3	42.0	1.8
South-East	61.6	81.3	1.3
Ratio	(2.6)	(2.0)	—

Source: 1970 and 1980: Wood and Carvalho (1988).

Population Behaviour

The impact of this long-standing inequality in living conditions across regions is reflected in the population dynamics of each area, whatever the variable considered. Thus, for example, since 1960—when census statistics began to be reliable at the regional level—life expectancy at birth has shown a difference in excess of fifteen years between the most and the least developed regions. When regional differences in income distribution are considered, even greater inequalities are found: during the 1970s, the richest groups in the most advanced regions were able to live a quarter of a century (24.1 years) longer than the poorest groups in the least developed regions (Wood and Carvalho 1988).

Considering Brazil as a whole, we find that its demographic history during the reference period was determined mainly by the birth rate and by mortality, since foreign immigration peaked around the 1930s. The country continued to have high rates of growth during the following decades because mortality, which had previously shown signs of a slight decrease, entered a period of rapid decline. Martine (1987) indicates a reduction of 35 per cent in the CDR during the 1940s, followed by a further 28 per cent in the 1950s. At the same time the birth rate remained relatively constant around 45 per 1,000, declining by a mere 3 per cent during the 1940s and by about 10 per cent during the 1950s and 1960s. All this meant the continuous growth of the population at a mean annual growth rate of approximately 3 per cent. During the following decades the fall in the birth rate caused the growth rate to diminish to about 2.5 per cent by 1980.

At present, everything seems to indicate that even before the beginning of the 1990s the growth rate will, for the first time in Brazil in the twentieth century, fall below 2 per cent. In fact, as will be seen below, if the declining trend in fertility continued during the quinquennium 1985–90, Brazil will have experienced an average annual growth of 1.8 per cent (see Table 21.7).

Fertility Trends (1940–1985)

With respect to the level of fertility, Fig. 21.1 and Table 21.3 show that from the beginning of the period under study until 1960, the TFR remained practically constant, or even rose slightly. This stability is due, among other factors, to the predominance of agriculture in the economy of the period and to positive attitudes towards extended families with many children, principally, as will be seen below, in the vast northern and north-eastern regions.

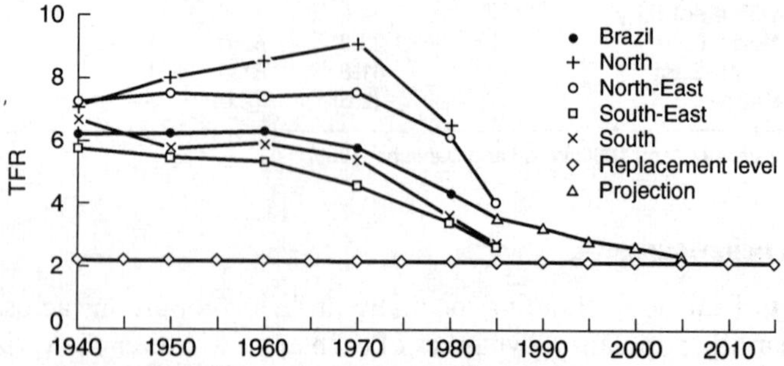

Fig. 21.1. *Brazil and main regions: TFR 1940–2010*

Table 21.3. *Brazil: TFRs* by region, 1940–1984*

Region	Period					
	1940	1950	1960	1970	1980	1984
Brazil	6.16	6.21	6.28	5.76	4.35	3.53
North	7.17	7.97	8.56	8.15	6.45	—
North-East	7.15	7.50	7.39	7.53	6.13	4.00
South-East	5.70	5.45	5.34	4.56	3.45	2.70
South	5.65	5.70	5.89	5.42	3.63	2.79
Centre West	6.36	6.86	6.74	6.42	4.51	3.06

Sources: For 1940 to 1980: Mendes *et al*. (1985); 1984: Oliveira and Silva (1986) and NHSS-84.

* Number of live-born children which a woman of a hypothetical cohort would have by the end of her reproductive period, if she were subject to the ASFRs of the reference period, and in the absence of mortality.

Thus, the trend to lower fertility began tentatively during the 1960s, but later showed a definite downward trend, with a velocity which could hardly have been forecast by the mathematical functions or sociological inferences in vogue fifteen years ago. This rapid decline was first seen among the more privileged urban social groups of the most developed regions, then during the 1970s and 1980s it was experienced by all social classes, both urban and rural, among the most diverse regions. Thus it is that the TFR was 5.8 in 1970, 4.3 in 1980, and very probably less than 3.5 around 1990.[2]

For the country as a whole, the decline in fertility throughout the 1960s was less than 10 per cent; during the 1970s it was 25 per cent, and during the 1980s the decline was approximately 20 per cent within the first five years alone.

It should also be emphasized that, although during the last fifty years the reduction at the national level was about 50 per cent, the intercensal statistics, the use of indirect methods, and the vital registers show two important peculiarities (Leite 1980; Wong 1985; Fernández and Carvalho 1986). On the one hand, the definitively accelerated decline started just before the beginning of the 1970s. On the other hand, a large part of the decline is located in two very specific periods: the first is concentrated in the first half of the 1970s, when the TFR went from 5.8 to 4.3 in 1976 (a reduction of 25 per cent) and then remained near that level until the end of the decade; the second occurred during the first five years of the 1980s when, again changing abruptly, the TFR dropped to 3.5 (a decline of nearly 18 per cent). A more detailed explanation of these two periods is given in the following section.

Turning to the regions, just as the socio-economic indicators revealed sharp differentials between the main regions of the country, fertility is also vastly different across the regions, as shown in Fig. 21.1. The TFRs of the northern and north-eastern regions are always clearly well above the national average; at the

[2] This is suggested by the data from the NHSS (National Household Sample Survey) of 1984 (see Table 21.3).

same time, in complementary fashion, the levels of the south and south-east are below average.

A detailed look at the regional data shows that the high-fertility regions had levels which were constant or even increasing from 1940 to 1960. Fertility continued to increase in the north-east until 1950, when it reached 7.5 children per woman, a level which remained constant for approximately twenty years; the north also showed rising levels, and its TFR peaked around 1960, ten years later than in the north-east; the highest level of fertility observed in the north region was close to 9 children per woman.[3] The causes of the increase—or stability at high levels—and the late decline in relation to the other regions of the country, are those mentioned in the commentary on the national behaviour; other factors that play an important role in this trend are the persistence of high levels of mortality in these areas and selective migration—first from the north-eastern region and then from the north—towards those regions which in 1950–60 were building their industrial infrastructure. That is, to the extent that the groups which migrate within the country are characterized by lower fertility levels, this selectivity may have postponed the beginning of the fertility decline in their regions of origin even longer than it would otherwise have been. The definitive decline in these two great regions occurred from 1970 onwards, with levels around 8 children per woman dropping, fifteen years later, to a TFR of about 4.5.

The regions with traditionally low fertility levels, mainly the south-eastern region, which contains almost half the population of the country, show a differentiated declining trend during the reference period. Until 1960 the decline was quite gradual, less than 10 per cent and the level was about 5.5 children per woman. Later the decline became much more pronounced, leading to a TFR of 3.5 by 1980, with increasing acceleration at the end of the first half of the 1980s, when the average TFR for the whole of the southern and south-eastern part of the country was clearly below 3 children per woman. In the state of São Paulo—fairly representative of those areas, as it includes slightly more than half their inhabitants—the TFR was approximately 2.7 in 1985, representing a reduction of 25 per cent since 1980.

In summary, observation of the period 1940–85 shows that, starting from distinct regional levels which were relatively constant until the beginning of the 1970s, a decline began which was differentiated in both time and space, and became generalized by the early 1980s. The decline continues, having reached unexpectedly low levels, and the trend is towards increasing uniformity across the regions.

[3] It is likely that the low quality of the data may be a strong argument for questioning the trends of the 1940s, 1950s, or even the 1960s, in regions where it is supposedly more difficult to collect good information, as in the present case. None the less, the use of different data and methods, based on the censuses of 1970 and 1980, shows consistent results, suggesting that the trends really were as described. The methods which show this behaviour are, mainly, the method of Brass—which uses responses on live-born children—and the 'own-children' method, which uses parenthood and age relationships.

Socio-Economic Transformations and Fertility Decline

The explanation of what is happening in Brazil in terms of reproduction is no doubt very complex, the more so as it covers such diverse situations, which, although affected differently by the socio-economic transformations, nevertheless give the same response: a transition of unprecedented rapidity to unexpectedly low levels of fertility. In this section we attempt to synthesize the debate which has arisen in recent years in search of an explanation, a search which has utilized propositions ranging from the so-called 'demographic transition' to the unjust distribution of wealth, and which has included factors such as the practically permanent economic crisis, diminishing libido, the impact of the mass communications media and the role of international family planning agencies, among others.[4]

For this purpose, emphasis is placed on two periods which are believed important to an understanding of the phenomenon; these, as already mentioned, are approximately the beginning of the 1970s and the beginning of the 1980s. These periods are described below, in terms of the first half of each decade, in an attempt to relate the socio-economic transformations to the evolution of fertility which may be seen as a reaction to them.

The First Great Drop: First Half of the 1970s

In reality, as has been emphasized, fertility began to decline a little before the beginning of the 1970s; however, during the five-year period 1970–5, it was the low-income rural and urban sectors which led the decline, in a clear response to the transformations of the period, since in the large cities and among the privileged sectors, fertility was already diminishing. Carvalho *et al.* (1981) associate this decline with structural and cyclical factors.

On the one hand, in accordance with the development which the country was undergoing, there was an intensification of the process of 'proletarianization', characterized not only by its consolidation in the urban areas but also because even in the countryside the peasants were also starting to work for wages,[5] and were thus subject to absolutely different rules of the market and of consumption from those that characterized tenant farming, sharecropping, subsistence economy, etc. This process undoubtedly modified the traditionally positive attitudes towards large families.

On the other hand, it was during this period that the first clear signals of the deterioration in living conditions appeared: the real minimum wage continued to decline, and infant mortality in São Paulo and Belo Horizonte (two of the three largest metropolitan areas responsible for the industrial growth) continued to rise

[4] In this regard, see Berquó 1980; Carvalho *et al.* 1981; Merrick and Berquó 1983; Paiva 1983; Martine 1987; Wood and Carvalho 1988.

[5] Even though data from different sources are used to compare the labour force (1970 Census and NHSSs), the data make it quite clear that the participation of paid agricultural labour grew much more rapidly during the first half of the 1970s than in the previous twenty years covered by the censuses (Carvalho *et al.* 1981).

until at least 1973. In both cities the graph of infant mortality looks like a mirror image of the graph of real wages (Carvalho *et al.* 1981), the former rising as the latter declines. Finally, the growth of the production of food for domestic consumption fell considerably during that period, causing prices to rise faster than the cost of living. The rise in prices was even greater because, in addition, the wage-earning population was also growing rapidly. Consequently, the cost of subsistence increased for agricultural workers, who during this period were becoming part of the proletariat, and therefore were much more subject to the market's laws of supply and demand.

Among the rural population converted into proletariat, the extended family no longer fulfils the functions it did in earlier epochs; that is, children no longer participate in the production of consumer goods, which in turn must be acquired at ever-increasing market prices, eliminating the economic advantage of forming and maintaining large families.

The urban middle class, growing in size and in its share of the national income and with increasing access to durable consumer goods thanks to the policy of direct consumer credit, continued its trend to small nuclear families. Among the families of unskilled urban workers, whose incomes are usually at the edge of subsistence, the prospect of the above-mentioned deterioration in living standards was a strong stimulus to the limitation of their offspring. At the same time, in the face of increases in the price of food, and given that a substantial proportion of income is used for the purchase of food, the solution was the entry of other family members into the labour-market, beginning with the wife. This strategy too had its effects on the pattern of reproduction, immediately limiting family sizes.

The fact that change in fertility was responsive both to a structural process and to a transient one explains why after 1975 fertility tended to remain constant—or even show slight increases—until approximately 1980. Both the information for 1977–8 and the results of the 1980 census show a small 'recovery' in fertility levels.[6] Analysis by cohort for the state of São Paulo also showed that the very sharp fall at the beginning of the decade was also the consequence of the postponement of births, as the same cohorts which underwent a sharp retraction in 1970–5 were those which five years later showed some degree of recovery (Wong 1985).

Coincidentally, during the second half of the 1970s, the purchasing power of wages tended to recover, and the amount of available dietary caloric and protein content also rose again (Paiva 1983).

The Second Great Drop: The First Half of the 1980s

The beginning of the 1980s once again brought evidence of a dramatic and generalized decline in fertility, varying between 15 and 25 per cent across all geographical and social groupings and supported by all data sources (Oliveira and

[6] The NHSS indicated an increase between 1976 and 1978, giving estimates of 4.26 and 4.40 respectively, with rises in practically all regions (Leite 1980). A comparison of the P/F ratios of Brass's method with the behaviour of age-specific parity from the 1980 census and the 1984 NHSS also shows an increase in fertility in the second half of the 1970s.

Simoes 1989; Wong 1986; Arruda, Rutenberg, *et al.* 1987). The reduction was so large that it also led to a substantial decline in the absolute number of births between 1982 and 1984, noted first in the capital cities and then extending to the entire country. Although the number of births stopped declining in 1985, it was still below the level registered in 1980.[7] Age-specific fertility rates indicate that the reduction was noticeably greater among older women, the first sign that this time a definitive reduction of completed family size was involved, and not only postponement of births. The proportional decline during 1980–4 increased with age throughout the entire range of childbearing ages, and was 30 per cent on average for women over the age of 35 (Wong 1986).

At the same time, after a period of relative stability which permitted certain advances, mainly in the areas of sanitation, health and education, representing a better distribution of wealth, the 1980s began in Brazil with a major crisis, not only in the economy but also political and institutional. This crisis was characterized, as already mentioned, by a deep recession, with employment levels at the end of the decade below those achieved at the beginning of the 1970s (Furtado 1982), and with negative growth of the GDP during the period 1981–4, mainly affecting the industrial sector and consequently the urban population.[8] At the same time the purchasing power of wages, which, after serious losses up to 1975, had begun to recover, fell once again beginning around 1982, and this time the drop was precipitous; according to the official statistics, wages in 1987 reached a level that was approximately 50 per cent of their value only five years earlier (See Table 21.8).

Finally, this time the inflationary spiral reached not only the poorest sectors, as had occurred during the 'economic miracle' of the 1970s, but also the middle class, whose purchasing power was seriously affected because a large fraction of their income was tied up in medium- and long-term credit instruments, so that they were obliged to include this factor in the cost-benefit calculation of the value of children (Faria 1988).

Once again, the coincidence of the drop in fertility with the structural transformations, and the cyclical turbulence which Brazilian society was passing through, are evidence that industrial development, modernization and above all urbanization have provoked—in different ways—a definitive change in values and attitudes related to number and survival of offspring, in absolutely all social strata. On the one hand, the population is responding with attitudes favourable to low fertility, in the same way as has occurred in the industrialized countries, where women have access to higher education and participate in the labour-market in more nearly equal conditions with men, and where the value of children is evaluated in terms of their monetary and psychological cost, etc. On the other hand, the unprecedented rapidity and universality of the process among

[7] According to the official statistics, the number of births occurring in 1980 and registered during that year was 2.77 million. In 1985 the number was 2.61 million.

[8] In 1981 the industrial sector had a growth rate of –9%, then –0.1% in 1982 and –6.6% in 1983 (IBGE 1988).

the poorest groups suggests another process of changing attitudes, that promoted by the penetration of the mass communications media, and by advances in the technology of fertility control (Martine 1987), the immediate availability of those methods, and the use of induced abortion.

A product of urbanization and of the need to expand domestic consumption of manufactured goods, the communications media are present in practically the entire country. The census has shown that in 1980, 75 per cent of dwellings had a radio and/or television set; by the beginning of 1990, the country's 4,500 municipalities will all receive at least one of the TV networks from the major urban centres. Given that the great mission of these media is to transform the spectator into an active consumer, television, largely disguised as a 'source of education, entertainment and relaxation for the family', winds up transmitting images of a modern, urban, desirable, upper middle-class Brazil. The soap operas and commercials portray social aspirations and behavioural norms derived from the most sophisticated sectors of the consumer market. The messages transmitted naturally affect the mass of the population, including not only the urban sector, which in any case has grown most rapidly, but also the small villages and isolated rural hamlets.[9] Such messages generally deal with young adults without children or with small families, who are rich and happy consumers. The relaxation of censorship, which during the 1970s circumscribed the freedom of communication, permitted, also as a means of promoting consumption, the fostering of the cult of the body and of sexuality, always shown without any connection to reproduction.[10] This relaxation now also permits diffusion of information on the continuing and generalized crisis through which Brazil is passing and the increasing violence and marginalization which it has caused. This type of message is mainly received by the middle class and by those who have some capacity for discrimination, provoking—or reinforcing—a feeling of insecurity about the future, in both the short and the long term. One of the consequences of that unstable future—widely documented in opinion polls[11]—is without doubt the limitation of offspring at any price.

Along with the role which the mass communications media may have played in changing attitudes about family size, access to contraceptive methods also helped promote the formation of these attitudes. The improvements in effectiveness and decline in the cost of contraception relative to the situation three or four decades ago were important contributory factors.

[9] Thus it is possible to find, even in populations which are apparently very little integrated into modern Western culture, such as the Indian reserves of the State of São Paulo, that a significant proportion are a captive audience of popular programmes such as the soap operas and long Sunday shows produced in the great metropolis of Rio de Janeiro and São Paulo. The proportion is even greater in these communities, given the practice of several families getting together for the sole purpose of watching a TV programme; in fact this custom is widely practised in the rest of the country as well, in the well-known 'tele-neighbour' phenomenon.

[10] Concerning the role of the mass communications media in Brazil during the 1980s, see Faria (1988).

[11] In this regard see e.g. the GALLUP/Brazil reports, 1984–5 and Listening Post do Brasil (Standard, Ogilvy & Mather), 1982–83–84, in Sherris and Moore (1985).

By the late 1980s, the prevalence of contraception in Brazil, according to both government and private statistics (Arruda, Rutenberg *et al.* 1987; Oliveira and Simoes 1989), was widespread, to such an extent that 99 per cent of women who had ever been married or in union had some knowledge of methods, and 60 per cent used contraception. However, two factors should be mentioned. First, there was no express implementation of any policy whatsoever for population control and/or family planning on the part of the government, even though the attitude was permissive from about 1970 onwards, when exhortations in support of population expansion fell into disuse. Secondly, the use of contraceptive methods is in practice limited to two methods: oral contraceptives and female sterilization, with the latter being slightly more common, reaching proportions noticeably higher than what might be expected in a country which, as we have noted, has no explicit population or family planning policy.[12] The dominance of these two methods is absolute in all regions of the country, with differences only as to which of the two is more common. In general, the two methods account for about 85 per cent of all cases; finally, it should be mentioned that rhythm, or the Ogino-Knauss method, is the third most commonly used, although it represents barely 6 per cent of users (see Table 21.4).

Given the greater presence of sterilization in the States with the lowest levels of socio-economic resources, such as Maranhao, Piauí, Alagoas, etc., situated in the north or north-east of the country (where in general more than 50 per cent of women who use any contraceptive method have been sterilized), it may be worth asking whether this method is resorted to especially by the poorest women, who are the least well informed and therefore more easily manipulated by antinatalist forces or unscrupulous health workers, who see in this method the simplest and surest way of dealing with low-income women, or those with closely spaced births, several Caesarean sections, etc. Alencar and Andrade (1989) asked this question, adding that, if this were true, sterilization would be a sort of 'inferior good', less utilized at the higher levels of the social scale. However, a study of the preliminary results of the Contraceptive Prevalence Survey by level of income and education, for the State of São Paulo, showed that the practice of sterilization increases with rising income, whereas oral contraceptives are more frequently used by less affluent women (Wong 1988). In the north-eastern region, Silva *et al.* (1988) found no differences with respect to per capita family income among sterilized women. Finally, Alencar and Andrade, in a study with national coverage, after controlling factors like age, which may be associated with income level, found a positive correlation between education and income, and sterilization. Thus they verified that the propensity to sterilization and social status are closely linked.

The use of oral contraceptives is especially high among young women. Ninety-two per cent of women purchase the pill in pharmacies (Arruda, Morris *et al.*

[12] At the national level, 40% of the married women who used some form of contraception were sterilized (Arruda, Rutenberg, *et al.* 1987). The statistics of industrialized countries show that the level of voluntary female sterilization is quite low in many countries; only two extreme cases stand out with approximately 25%: Switzerland and the USA (Sherris and Moore, 1985) although the situation is continually changing.

Table 21.4. ***Brazil: % distribution of married women between ages 15 and 54, by contraceptive use, by state, 1986***

Federative state	Total	Users					Non-Users
		Method used					
		Total	Steril-ization	Pill	Ogino-Knauss	Other	
Brazil	100.0	59.8	29.3	22.9	3.5	4.1	40.2
Northern region:							
Rondônia	100.0	62.1	32.0	23.6	5.0	1.4	37.9
Acre	100.0	59.6	31.9	23.4	4.3	—	40.4
Amazonas	100.0	60.9	37.7	18.8	3.4	1.0	39.1
Roraima	100.0	72.2	27.8	22.2	16.7	5.5	27.8
Pará	100.0	61.4	41.6	14.8	2.7	2.3	38.6
Amapá	100.0	75.0	28.6	42.8	3.6	—	25.0
Southern region:							
Maranhao	100.0	27.6	22.0	4.1	0.5	1.0	72.4
Piauí	100.0	38.5	24.1	10.8	1.0	2.6	66.5
Ceará	100.0	48.9	20.0	19.9	5.4	3.6	51.1
Rio Grande do Norte	100.0	57.5	29.5	17.8	2.5	7.7	42.5
Paraíba	100.0	47.7	22.8	16.7	4.7	3.5	52.3
Pernambuco	100.0	55.8	35.8	14.2	2.9	2.9	44.2
Alagoas	100.0	32.5	20.9	9.9	0.6	1.1	67.5
Sergipe	100.0	49.0	18.0	22.7	3.2	5.1	51.0
Bahia	100.0	52.9	24.9	18.9	3.6	5.5	47.1
South-Eastern region:							
Minas Gerais	100.0	61.3	25.9	25.1	4.9	5.4	38.7
Espírito Santo	100.0	68.5	29.5	35.3	2.4	1.3	31.5
Rio de Janeiro	100.0	72.1	33.4	30.0	4.4	4.3	27.9
Southern region:							
Paraná	100.0	67.3	31.7	29.5	2.4	3.7	32.7
Santa Catarina	100.0	71.3	22.1	36.4	5.4	5.4	28.7
Rio Grande do Sul	100.0	70.0	15.9	43.2	4.9	6.0	30.0
Centre-West region:							
Mato Grosso do Sul	100.0	70.2	43.0	22.9	1.8	2.5	29.6
Mato Grosso	100.0	42.8	23.8	16.8	1.2	1.0	57.2
Goias	100.0	68.1	50.9	12.8	2.2	2.2	31.9
Distrito Federal	100.0	76.0	42.2	26.6	3.2	4.0	24.0

Source: Oliveira and Simoes (1989).

1987), very often on the woman's own initiative, that is without any subsidy to the consumer, and without medical prescription. In this sense, as Martine (1987) points out, the pill, for better or for worse, is an extremely accessible method, so much so that people obtain it just as easily as a headache remedy.

Finally, reference should be made to the incidence of induced abortion. Although no reliable statistics are available, it is accepted that this is a common practice and equally accessible, in spite of the fact that there is a differential risk of morbidity and death among social classes due to the different degrees of cleanliness and medical qualification which money can purchase. The estimates vary between 1 and 3 million abortions per year, a number which is in any case very high in a country where there are 4 million live births annually. The high incidence of abortion is deduced from indirect evidence. During the 1960s, Bussamara *et al.* (1965) found that 60 per cent of the patients who had died of septicaemia in hospitals were victims of induced abortion; twenty-five years later, the PAHO (1985) commented that 70 per cent of the maternal deaths in Brazilian hospitals were from complications due to induced abortion, while an unknown number died from this cause outside the hospital system.

In summary, the fertility transition in Brazil seems to be a response both to the historical process of proletarization and urbanization peculiar to the Third World, and to the immediate conditions which the country is passing through at any given stage. The crisis of the 1980s accelerated the decline in fertility, as it brought home even more sharply the need for controlling family size and for access to effective contraception and abortion. This statement is in fact supported when the real value of the minimum wage—as a simple proxy for standard of living—and of the number of births for recent years are superimposed (see Fig. 21.2). The decline in the former is accompanied by the decline of the latter at the most severe point in the economic crisis, showing a clear response to current economic conditions. One would expect a displacement of at least a year (strictly, nine months) in the birth curve; however, the response is immediate, giving rise to the question of how much abortion is contributing to this behaviour. Finally, because of the age structure, a continuous decline in the number of births cannot be maintained; therefore, what is observed in the following years is a recovery, which none the less is very slow and far from the level reached before the crisis.

Consequences of the Fertility Transition

As may be seen from the foregoing, the great transformation of fertility is causing drastic changes in the population's structure, going well beyond its simple

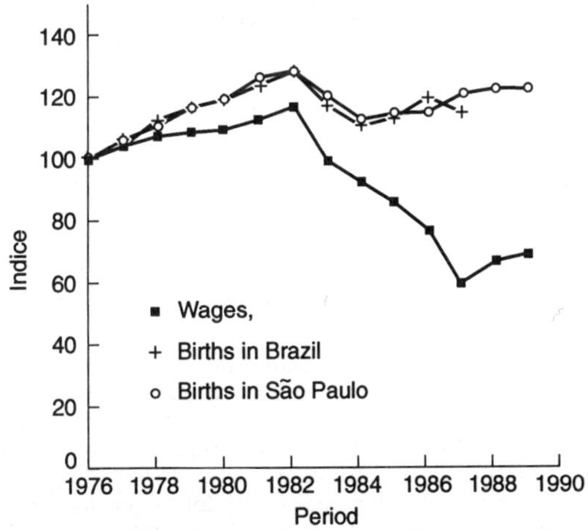

Fig. 21.2. ***Brazil and São Paulo: Births and the real value of the minimum wage***

demographic aspects. In the rest of this section, as well as a description of the demographic change, an overview will be given of its significance for fields such as education, employment, health, etc., in an effort to draw attention to the implications for planning and social policy in the short, medium and long term.

The Destabilization of the Age Structure

The most obvious and immediate consequence of the continuing decline in fertility over more than twenty years is the modification of the age structure of the population. Thus the generations born before the decline formed a structure with a broad base and high growth potential, which was not realized, due to the fact that the rapid decline in fertility resulted in a proportionately lower number of births. None the less, the growth rates remained high until the 1970s (2.4 per cent per annum), given that the contingent of women of reproductive age was also large because they belonged to generations born during a time of high or rising fertility.

Due to the decline in the level of fertility, the population has entered a continuous process of decreasing growth rates and of destabilization of its age structure. The older generations, born before the decline, form a broad-based pyramid. As the younger generations reach the reproductive ages, there will be a new reduction in the number of births even if there is no further decline in fertility rates. Thus the country's population, as it enters the last decade of this century, is far from having a stable age structure, since it includes generations born after the decline, which are increasing at varying rates, so that over certain periods some age-groups decrease in size. It is clear that, if the present trends in mortality and fertility continue, the total growth rate will fall rapidly, tending to a quasi-stable age structure by the middle of the twenty-first century.[13]

The Population's Composition in the Short Term

Knowing that the age structure will inevitably demonstrate oscillations for some time to come, it becomes extremely important to be able to visualize the population's behaviour over the next few decades, with respect to both its size and its rate of growth, especially now that relatively recent and reliable estimates of fertility are available. The projection prepared by Camarano *et al.* (1989), covering the period 1980–2010, incorporates the described fertility trends, with the additional assumption that the urban population will reach the replacement level of fertility

[13] On the basis of the projection made by Camarano *et al.* (1989) (see Tables 21.5 and 21.6), Carvalho (1988) projected the total population of Brazil from the year 2010 until 2100, maintaining mortality constant and using two hypotheses about fertility: Hypothesis 1, with a constant level of fertility (that of the period 2005–10 in Camarano *et al.* 1989) and Hypothesis 2 with the fertility function maintaining the same relative distribution as in 2005–2010, but with a level which produces a net reproduction ratio equal to 1.0. Under Hypothesis 1, the total population of Brazil in the year 2050 would be 258.883 million, with an annual growth rate of 0.4% (intrinsic growth rate of 0.3%). Under Hypothesis 2, these values would be 243.814 million and 0.2% (0.0%) respectively.

Table 21.5. *Brazil: projected TFRs and life expectancy, urban and rural populations, 1980–2010*

Period	Urban population		Rural population	
	TFR	Life expectancy	TFR	Life expectancy
1980–5	2.9	64.2	5.4	62.3
1985–90	2.5	65.8	4.6	63.5
1990–5	2.4	67.3	4.0	64.6
1995–2000	2.2	68.5	3.5	65.5
2000–5	2.2	69.6	3.2	66.3
2005–10	2.2	70.5	3.0	67.0

Source: Camarano *et al*. (1989).

Table 21.6. *Brazil: population projection by age-group (millions), 1980–2010*

Age	1980	1985	1990	1995	2000	2005	2010
TOTAL	120.194	133.358	145.895	158.228	170.265	182.426	194.399
0–4	17.264	16.923	16.597	16.712	16.825	17.463	17.613
5–9	15.160	16.943	16.642	16.351	16.490	16.622	17.271
10–14	14.279	15.031	16.813	16.525	16.245	16.391	16.530
15–19	13.591	14.197	14.952	16.733	16.453	16.181	16.331
20–24	11.525	13.473	14.085	14.846	16.625	16.355	16.091
25–29	9.452	11.389	13.329	13.947	14.712	16.487	16.230
30–34	7.694	9.308	11.231	13.161	13.785	14.555	16.324
35–39	6.360	7.547	9.147	1.053	12.969	13.599	14.372
40–44	5.730	6.205	7.381	8.962	10.849	12.746	13.381
45–49	4.658	5.550	6.027	7.187	8.746	10.607	12.480
50–54	4.114	4.465	5.339	5.817	6.955	8.485	10.309
55–59	3.144	3.885	4.238	5.087	5.561	6.669	8.158
60–64	2.448	2.905	3.613	3.961	4.774	5.241	6.307
65–69	2.031	2.185	2.614	3.271	3.607	4.369	4.818
70+	2.744	3.352	3.887	4.615	5.669	6.656	7.984
5–14	29.439	31.974	33.455	32.876	32.735	33.013	33.801
15–64	68.716	78.924	89.342	100.754	111.431	120.925	129.983
65+	4.775	5.537	6.501	7.886	9.275	11.025	12.802
Relative distribution (%)							
5–14	24.49	23.98	22.93	20.78	19.23	18.10	17.39
15–64	57.17	59.18	61.24	63.68	65.45	66.29	66.86
65+	3.97	4.15	4.46	4.98	5.45	6.04	5.59

Source: Camarano *et al*. (1989).

before the year 2000. The mortality and fertility trends implicit in the projection, as well as the resulting age distribution, are given in Tables 21.5 and 6.

By the year 2000 the country will have an estimated population of 170 million. The official projection of the Brazilian Institute of Geography and Statistics (IBGE), carried out at the beginning of the 1970s, and thus before the rapid decline in fertility was evident, estimated that at that date there would be a minimum of 201 million inhabitants, or a maximum of 213 million. Obviously, the difference of 43 or 31 million, if it arises, will be due entirely to the more or less intense decline in fertility since 1970.

The more than 30 million persons who would not be present in the year 2000 due to the post-1970 reduction in fertility would, logically, have been under 30 years of age, which undoubtedly means a corresponding change in the Brazilian age pyramid, not only at its base, but also in the relative distribution among the major age-groups shown at the end of Table 21.6 (5–14, 15–64, and 65+), which are more or less the target populations for educational, employment and social security policies, respectively.

In terms of growth rate, the aged population will grow by more than 3% annually until the year 2010. These high rates are independent of the fertility decline, since they involve persons born before 1950. Obviously, this very rapid growth, combined with the narrowing of the pyramid's base, will cause a significant increase in the proportion of the population over the age of 65 years (from 4.0 to 6.6 per cent between 1980 and 2010).

The population aged 15 to 64 will grow at an average annual rate of about 2.1 per cent until 2010, but this rate will gradually decline, from 2.8 per cent in 1980 to 1.5 per cent in 2010. This decline is due to the low growth rates among the younger working-age groups, which in certain periods may in fact have negative growth rates. In spite of the declining trend in this growth rate, this group's weight will increase from 57 per cent to 67 per cent during the period covered by the projection, once again due to the tremendous reduction in the weight of the population aged below 15 years. An additional consequence, which should be mentioned because of its importance to the economy, is the change in the dependency ratio, with the dependency of the under-15 group declining the most.

During this period, the population aged between 5 and 15 years will grow very slowly, at an average rate of about 0.5 per cent, a rate which will, however, reach negative values between 1990 and 2000.

The under-5 population, the object of policies directed to infants, will show a basically stationary pattern until the year 2010; after declining during the 1980s, it will begin to grow again slowly. In any case, this is the group whose relative size will change the most. It made up 14.4 per cent of the population in 1980 and will be only 9.2 per cent in 2010.

Some Implications for the Planning and Definition of Social Policy

The panorama presented for the period up to the year 2000 is not at all speculative, and is hypothetical only to a very minor extent. It represents a concrete reality, almost all of it already lived, given that twenty years have passed since the beginning of the process of rapid fertility decline, with less than ten years remaining until the year 2000.

Surprisingly, these very significant changes have until now gone practically unnoticed in the country's development plans and political and social projects. Generally speaking, national policies do not make any reference whatever to the new demographic dynamics, which are clearly creating new problems which must be faced, but which, at the same time, and fundamentally, are creating conditions favourable to the solution of some of Brazil's long-standing problems, particularly in the social area. There still remains, in the perception of many planners, and implicit in most projects, the vision, or belief in the existence of an extremely young population, whose age distribution is constant, with growth rates in the area of 3 per cent per annum, a population which is about to break the 200 million barrier before the end of the century in its inexorable rush towards a demographic explosion unless there is controlling intervention by the government.

The reality is clearly quite different. Until this is realized, government is losing a valuable opportunity to benefit the most needy part of the country's population by taking advantage of the favourable conditions created by the new Brazilian demographic pattern. At the same time, the chance to prepare to face problems which will of necessity arise in the medium and long term is also being lost.

To believe that the simple decline in fertility, with the consequent relative decrease in the number of persons, would automatically lead to the solution of social problems is pure neo-Malthusian *naïveté*. In spite of the tremendous decline of fertility throughout the whole country, the problems of needy children and of juvenile delinquency in the big cities have not been solved. On the contrary, these problems are continuously getting worse. The favourable conditions produced by the relative, and even absolute, reduction in the size of the target population which must be reached by social policy exist, and should be taken advantage of; the following paragraphs suggest some guidelines in this area.

1. Policies Oriented to Children In a country which has so many needs, and which is facing a serious economic crisis, it is necessary to be selective in choosing social policies, concentrating expenditures in those sectors which promise the greatest return in the medium and long term.

As seen above, the Brazilian population under the age of 5 years will probably be smaller in 2000 than it was in 1980, and will then increase slightly early in the next century. This is a highly favourable situation for massive investment and immediate returns among the youngest part of the population in the areas of health, nutrition and pre-school education. One example of this is the possibility of eradication of certain infectious diseases, such as poliomyelitis. If the accelerated decline in fertility continues in areas where the vaccination coverage against this disease is 75 per cent, as in the State of Pernambuco, it is probable that if the number of doses applied is maintained constant, coverage will reach 100 per cent towards the year 2000 (Albuquerque and Duarte 1988).

At the same time, the demand for pre-school education and day-care centres, which has been increasing noticeably (Rosemberg 1989), could be better attended to, since the number of children to be covered will remain approximately constant. In this way the youth and adult generations at the end of this century and the beginning of the next will be of 'higher quality', which in turn will guarantee the return on the investment made in them in formal education, health, training for the labour force, etc.

2. Educational Policy The projection which has been presented shows clearly that the growth rate of the school-age population to be served in the different levels of the educational system is diminishing, and will even turn negative during the 1990s, to recover slightly in the twenty-first century.

While up to 1970 the capacity of the Brazilian educational system had to expand at better than 3 per cent per annum to reduce the proportion of children not covered by the system, the rate of expansion can now be less intense. To refer again to the State of Pernambuco, the persistence of the fertility decline would signify a 20 per cent reduction in the pupil–classroom ratio if the present number of classrooms is maintained. Moreover, the present coverage of 71 per cent of the school-age population of this state could reach 100 per cent if the number of classrooms available today were increased by only 11 per cent (Albuquerque and Duarte 1988).

This favourable situation should not in any way become an argument for reducing, in relative terms, the scarce resources invested in the education of the young. Brazilian society is living through a singular opportunity to resolve once and for all the country's depressing educational situation, above all in primary and secondary schools. The present conditions, especially within the public sector, clearly show how this opportunity is being lost. The situation on the demand side is extremely favourable to the definition and implementation of an enlightened educational policy. It is time for teachers to be better trained, to become more professionalized, and make teaching a full-time occupation, etc. (Jones 1979).

3. The Labour-Market In contrast to the younger age-groups, the working-age population, between 15 and 64, is growing rapidly, about 2.5 per cent a year, and will continue to do so until the year 2000. It should nevertheless be pointed out that within this broad age interval, the subgroups which make it up will grow at quite different rates, varying from 1.0 per cent annually for youth aged 15 to 19 up to 3.4 per cent for those aged between 60 and 64 (Table 21.7). This change in the internal structure of the population of working age will cause an additional increase in the female population whose low fertility was already facilitating their access to the labour-market to fill the demand for young workers. On the other hand, to the extent that wages increase with age, there may be a tendency to improvements in the real value of the average wage.

The much less intense rhythm of increase in the young population, in addition to the obvious reduction in the pressure which they exert on the labour-market, offers more favourable conditions for improved technical training for this age-group before they begin to work, or even in the workplace. This, together with a significant improvement in the educational level of youth, could contribute decisively to a qualitative jump in Brazilian labour productivity.

4. Social Policies for the Aged The phenomenon, already present in Brazil, of old people abandoned both materially and in their family and affective relationships, will become a serious problem in the medium and long term. The projections

Table 21.7. ***Brazil: projected average annual growth rates, total population, and age-groups for selected periods, 1980–2010***

Age	1980–5	1985–90	1990–2000	2000–10	1980–2010
TOTAL	2.10	1.81	1.56	1.33	1.62
0–4	–0.40	–0.39	0.14	0.57	0.10
5–9	2.25	–0.36	–0.09	0.46	0.44
10–14	1.03	2.27	–0.34	0.17	0.49
15–19	0.88	1.04	0.96	–0.07	0.61
20–24	3.17	0.89	1.67	–0.33	1.12
25–29	3.80	3.20	0.99	0.99	1.82
30–34	3.88	3.83	2.07	1.70	2.54
35–39	3.48	3.92	3.55	1.03	2.76
40–44	2.10	3.53	3.93	2.12	2.87
45–49	3.56	1.66	3.79	3.62	3.34
50–54	1.66	3.64	2.68	4.01	3.11
55–59	4.33	1.75	2.75	3.91	3.23
60–64	3.48	4.46	2.83	2.82	3.20
65–69	1.47	3.65	3.27	2.94	2.92
70+	4.08	3.00	3.84	3.48	3.62
5–14	1.67	0.91	–0.22	0.32	0.46
15–64	2.81	2.51	2.23	1.55	2.15
65+	3.00	3.26	3.62	3.28	3.34

Source: Table 21.6.

show that it is the population over the age of 65 years which will grow the fastest until the end of the century, at extremely high rates, around 3.4 per cent annually. It is unlikely that this rate will change much, since in this case even more so than in the previous ones it is a question of projecting the survival of persons presently alive and effectively accounted for.

This trend to increasing relative importance of those aged 65 or more will accelerate at the beginning of the next century. This population will belong to ever-smaller families. Thus, the probability that the aged will have children or close relatives with whom to live is tending to diminish rapidly. This phenomenon is already quite well known in the developed countries, which in spite of all the resources at their command have not found an adequate and humane solution to this problem. With the decline of fertility at a much greater rhythm than these countries experienced during their demographic transition (and consequently with a much more rapid ageing of the population as well), Brazil will need to live with this problem without having resolved its other problems, more typical of underdevelopment. The country will thus face a paradoxical situation, all the more serious if the squalid social services provided by the state to old people in the Third World is taken into consideration.

The health system will have to prepare itself to attend adequately to this growing fraction of the population, whose morbidity is very distinct: respiratory and cardiovascular diseases, cancer and other degenerative diseases in general. On the other hand, the demand in other areas—such as pediatrics–gynaecology, etc.—will decrease.

The social security system will also have to serve a growing demand for payment of pensions, in a poor society which has legislation assuring retirement at extremely early ages. It will need to face a problem of equality with respect to the transfer of resources between the working-age generation, relatively smaller, and the retired generation, relatively larger.

5. Regional Planning In spite of the differentiated levels of economic performance, the various regions of Brazil have not experienced, at least in this century, a population decline in absolute terms. This has none the less occurred during the past decade in countless municipalities of economically stagnant areas and in the rural population as a whole.

There was a certain degree of population growth, even if it was below the natural growth rate, in the poorest regions, because the extremely high natural growth compensated for the losses due to emigration. On the other hand, the great migratory flows were sustained mainly by the rural populations. As the rural areas shrink in absolute terms, and their natural growth rate also declines, this source of population surplus will soon play an increasingly secondary role.

To the extent that the country's economic growth recommences, in the context of rapid decline in the population's natural growth rate, there will certainly be localized shortages of labour, giving internal migration a growing role as a balancing factor between the demand for and supply of labour. The 'attraction' component should become relatively more important than the 'expulsion'

Table 21.8. ***Brazil: Indexed evolution of the legal minimum wage (real values) and number of births, 1976–1989****

Period	Index nos.		
	Legal minimum wage	Birth	
		Brazil	São Paulo
1976	100.0	100.0	100.0
1977	104.2	103.6	105.8
1978	107.4	112.6	110.6
1979	108.4	116.4	116.3
1980	109.3	119.4	119.1
1981	112.6	123.8	126.2
1982	116.8	128.4	128.1
1983	99.2	117.1	120.2
1984	92.4	110.5	112.5
1985	85.8	113.1	114.3
1986	76.9	120.1	115.1
1987	59.6	114.9	121.1
1988	66.7	—	123.5
1989	69.4	—	122.9

Source: Fundaçao SEADE and IBGE (1976–87).

* Preliminary Data.

component. It should also be noted that while demographic growth differs across regions, the new technological base on which the economy will become developed also differs by region. Thus it is probable that the more advanced areas—such as the state of São Paulo—will attract proportionately more labour, reinforcing a migratory flow which seemed to have weakened in the 1970s (Giraldelli 1989). It is probable that the rate of outmigration from the stagnant areas, including their urban centres, will exceed any so far experienced in the country.

This trend may be seen as neutral—or even positive—to the extent to which the population becomes concentrated in the richer areas and possibly begins to benefit from a better standard of living. However, it should be kept in mind that throughout the whole history of the Third World, increasing concentration in the great urban centres has always meant reduced living standards for the least favoured sectors. As a result, it is clear that there are political costs which merit reflection, so that regional development strategies may be defined to achieve those goals which are considered desirable.

If the target populations of the various social policies are already reasonably well defined up to at least the year 2000 for the country as a whole, the same is not true when they are analysed from the regional and/or local point of view. Migration, combined with low natural growth, will make the margin of reliability of population estimates and projections increasingly variable as one descends from the national to the local level. This paradox demands long-range planning, combined with a flexible process at the regional or local level, which will require continuous evaluation of the situation and adjustment of the policies adopted.

Conclusions

The following conclusions may be drawn:

- Brazilian fertility, with a TFR ranging around 3.5, is undoubtedly situated at present at low levels, taking into account that the country is underdeveloped.
- The fertility decline has been associated with the social and economic transformations which the country has been undergoing. These transformations include industrialization and urbanization, which brought modernization to the country, in such a way that their development connotations took a 'perverse' path that is different from what was expected, in terms of the welfare and progress of the population. Thus, for example, while the growth of the secondary and tertiary sectors, a sign of accelerated urbanization, signified on the one hand an extended transportation and communications network, more technology, access to durable and semi-durable goods, access to education, etc., on the other hand it also lowered the quality of health services, and increased overcrowding, environmental pollution, peripheral and marginalized neighbourhoods, promiscuity, etc. in the urban population. The deterioration was so great that it went beyond the lower classes and reached the remaining sectors of

the society, discouraging the raising of large families. This was an unexpected byproduct, which was never set out as a conscious government goal, nor systematically sought.

- The undeniable reduction in fertility in this context appears today, not necessarily as a response to better living conditions, but as an adjustment strategy in the face of a new situation, of insecurity in the present and fear of the future.
- The decline in fertility is no longer a transient phenomenon. There is now an irreversible process of transition to definitely low levels, which fits well with the phenomenon known conventionally to demographers as the 'demographic transition'.
- The historical trend of fertility decline would certainly have continued whatever course development took; what however seems clear is that the extension in time, space and intensity of the socio-economic crisis, and the peculiar conditions of 'modernity' precipitated the declining trend, making the population wish to take short-cuts to arrive much more quickly at the replacement level.
- The consequences of the extremely sharp reduction in fertility, since it is a phenomenon which has been going on for two decades, are now concrete facts. There have been profound changes in the age structure of the population, which in turn will have a major impact on general broad areas of national life. These include alterations in the organization of resources for survival, which have always been scarce in the Brazilian context, and which, if they were now given their proper priorities through responsible planning, could mean a leap towards more humane development.

References

Albuquerque, S. P. de L., and Duarte, F. J. (1988), 'Pernambuco: A Queda da Fecundidade e as Demandas Sociais Básicas: 1980–2000', in *Encontro Nacional de Estudos Populacionais*, 6, iv (Belo Horizonte: ABEP), 177–98.

Alencar, A. de A., Andrade, E. C. de (1989), 'A Esterilização Feminina no Brasil', in *Encontro Nacional de Economia*, 17: 1051–79.

Arruda, J. M., Morris, L., Ferraz, E. A., Goldberg, H. (1987), 'Tendências Recentes da Fecundidade e do Planejamento Familiar no Nordeste: 1980–1986', in *Encontro Nacional de Estudos Populacionais*, 6 (São Paulo: ABEP), 111–36.

—— Rutenberg, N., Morris, L., Ferraz, E. A. (1987), *Pesquisa Nacional Sobre Saude Materno-infantil e Planejamento Familiar (PNSMIPF), Brasil, 1986* (Rio de Janeiro: BEMFAM).

Baer, W. (1979), *The Brazilian Economy: its Growth and Development* (Columbus: Grid Publishers).

Berquó, E. (1980), 'Algumas Indagações sobre a Recente Queda da Fecundidade no Brasil', Paper presented at Reunión del Grupo de Trabajo sobre el Proceso de Reproducción de la Población, Comisión de Población y Desarrollo, CLACSO, Teresópolis.

Bussamara, N., Lenir, M., and Leonor, P. (1965), 'Obituário Materno no Abortamento Criminoso', *Anais Brasileiros de Ginecologia*, **59**: 7–10.

Camarano, A. A., and Neupert, R. (1989), *Século XXI: A Quantas Andará a População Brasileira*? (Discussion Paper, 5; Rio de Janeiro: IPEA).

Carvalho, J. A. M. de (1988), 'O Tamanho da População Brasileira e Sua Distribuição Etária: Uma Visão Prospectiva', in *Encontro Nacional de Estudos Populacionais*, 6 (Belo Horizonte: ABEP), 37–66.

—— Paiva, P. de T. A., Sawyer, D. R. (1981), *A Recente Queda da Fecundidade no Brasil: Evidências e Interpretação* (CEDEPLAR Monograph, No. 12; Belo Horizonte: CEDEPLAR).

Faria, V. (1988), 'Politicas de Governo e Regulação da Fecundidade: Consequências Não Antecipadas e Efeitos Diversos' (unpublished).

Fernández, R. E., Carvalho, J. A. M. de (1986), 'A Evolução da Fecundidade no Brasil, Período 1957–1979', *Revista Brasileira de Estudos de População*, 3/2: 67–86.

Furtado, C. (1982), *A Nova Dependência: Dívida Externa e Monetarismo*, Rio de Janeiro: Paz e Terra.

Girardelli, B. W. (1989), 'O que Muda na Composição e no Volume da População Paulista Até o Final do Século XX?', *São Paulo em Perspectiva*, **3**: 7–14.

IBGE (1975–87), *Vital Statistics Registry* (Rio de Janeiro: IBGE).

—— (1987), *Estatísticas Históricas do Brasil: séries econômicas, demográficas e sociais de 1550–1985*, 3. *Séries Estatísticas Retrospectivas* (Rio de Janeiro: IBGE).

—— (1988), *Anuário Estatístico do Brasil 1987/1988* (Rio de Janeiro: IBGE).

Jones, G. W. (1979), 'La Planificación Educativa y el Crecimiento de la Población', in W. Robinson (ed.), *Planificación para la Población y el Desarrollo* (Bogotá: Consejo de Población).

Leite, V. da M. (1980), 'Níveis e Tendências da Mortalidade e da Fecundidade no Brasil a Partir de 1940', in *Encontro Nacional de Estudos Populacionais*, 2 (São Paulo: ABEP), 581–609.

Martine, G. (1987), 'A Recente Dinâmica Populacional e as Políticas Socio-demográficas', Paper presented to the Seminário Sobre Transição Demográfica: Como Ficam os Políticas Públicas, Centro de Treinamento para o Desenvolvimento Econômico, Brasília.

Mendes, M. M. S., Pereira, N. O. M., Dias, V. R. S. (1985), 'Avaliação dos Níveis e Tendências da Fecundidade, através de Alguns Modelos de Mensuração Indireta', *Revista Brasileira de Estatística*, **46**: 159–75.

Merrick, T., and Berquó, E. (1983), *The Determinants of Brazil's Recent Rapid Decline in Fertility* (National Academy of Sciences, Committee on Population and Demography, Report no. 23; Washington DC: National Academy Press).

Oliveira, L. A. P., and Simões, S. C. da S. (1989), *As Informações Sobre Fecundidade, Mortalidade e Anticoncepção nas PNADS* (Discussion paper, No. 15; Rio de Janeiro: IBGE).

Paiva, P. de T. A. (1983), 'Fecundidade e Padrão de Vida: a Experiência Recente', Paper presented to the Latin American Congress on Population and Development, 1983, Mexico.

PAHO (1985), *Health of Women in the Americas* (Washington DC: Scientific Publication, 488; PAHO).

Rosemberg, F. (1989) 'Ano 2000: Educação da Pequena Infância', *São Paulo em Perspectiva*, **3**: 32–5.

Santos, T. F. (1988), 'Tendências Recentes da Dinâmica Demográfica do Nordeste e Regiões Metropolitanas, Fortaleza, Recife e Salvador', in *Encontro Nacional de Estudos Populacionais*, 6, iv (Belo Horizonte: ABEP), 91–110.

Sherris, J., and Moore, S. H. (1985), *Recientes Adelantes en la Anticoncepción Vaginal* (Population Reports, Series H; Baltimore, MD: Johns Hopkins University).

Silva, N. L. P., Oliveira, L. A. P., Simões, C. C. S. (1988), 'Os Métodos Anticonceptivos Como um dos Fatores de Redução da Fecundidade Nordestina na Década de 80', in *Encontro Nacional de Estudos Populacionais*, 6, iv (Belo Horizonte: ABEP), 137–53.

Wong, L. R. (1985), 'Tendência Recente da Fecundidade no Estado de São Paulo', *Revista Brasileira de Estudos de População*, **2**: 75–103.

—— (1986), 'A Diminuição dos Nascimentos e a Queda de Fecundidade no Brasil dos Anos pós-80', in *Encontro Nacional de Estudos Populacionais*, 5, i (Belo Horizonte: ABEP).

—— (1988), 'A Prevalência de Métodos Anticoncepcionais no Estado de São Paulo', *Conjuntura Demográfica*, **3**: 11–22.

Wood, C. H., and de Carvalho, J. A. M. (1988), *The Demography of Inequality in Brazil* (Cambridge: Cambridge University Press).

22 The Fertility Transition in Cuba

SONIA CATASÚS CERVERA and
JUAN CARLOS ALFONSO FRAGA

Background

The evolution of the fertility of Cuban women has shown interesting and somewhat singular characteristics throughout the period of demographic transition in the Cuban population, and has obviously been a principal factor in this transition. In fact, Cuba's fertility transition within its process of demographic transition has been described by most demographers and other social science researchers as being early within the Latin American context (Hernández 1984); in addition, this process became more advanced and intense after the Revolution of 1959. For these reasons its study is of particular interest to researchers in Cuba as well as to those from other countries. This chapter summarizes the main aspects of this process, placing special emphasis on the socio-economic factors which condition it, as well as on the proximate determinants.

At the present time the population of Cuba is estimated to be approximately 10.6 million inhabitants, and its rate of growth during recent years is around 1 per cent per annum, undeniably one of the lowest in Latin America (SSC 1989). Fertility has a decisive influence on the dynamics of this behaviour. For the past ten years, Cuba's gross reproduction ratio (GRR) has been continuously below unity. In 1981 its estimated value reached a minimum of 0.78 daughters per woman, while by 1987 there had been a slight rise to 0.88. Mortality as well shows very low levels, as reflected in a life expectancy at birth for both sexes combined of 74.3 years for the period 1983–4 (over 76 years for women). The rate of infant mortality in 1989 was 11.1 deaths under the age of 1 year per 1,000 live births (SSC 1989).

Cuba is an urbanized country, with more than 72 per cent of its population residing in urban areas and with a population density of about 96 inhabitants per square kilometre. The population is ageing, with more than 12 per cent over the age of 60 years, and an average age which is rising: 27.0 and 29.5 in 1970 and 1981 respectively and 32 years by 1988.

Cuban demographic statistics are accepted internationally as solid and reliable, and numerous evaluations which have been carried out confirm this (SSC and CELADE 1978: 25). Nevertheless, even a good system of vital statistics cannot provide detailed information on demographic behaviour. For this reason it was decided, in 1987, to conduct the National Fertility Survey, interviewing 4,500 women of fertile age (15–49 years) throughout the country, as well as their immediate families. Technical and financial assistance for this task was provided by the United Nations Fund for Population Activities (UNFPA).

The design and execution of the survey were done by the State Statistical Committee. The National Fertility Survey inquired about the demographic and social background of the respondents, their union and pregnancy histories, fertility regulation, and other related topics. Data from this survey, plus that obtained from other research on fertility using census and survey data and vital statistics, are the sources for this analysis.

Levels and Trends in Fertility Since 1959

Catasús *et al.* (1975) have documented the early decline undergone by Cuban fertility in comparison with the remaining countries of Latin America, with relatively low values for the region even during the 1950s, when the birth rate was estimated at about 27 per 1,000. In 1955–60 the GRR was 1.83 in Cuba, whereas it varied between 3.15 and 3.38 in the countries of Central America, Mexico, and Venezuela; in Panama the rate was 2.64 and in Chile 2.44. Cuba was closer to countries such as Argentina (1.51) (Behm and Alfonso 1981) than to other countries in the region.

Between 1959 and 1979 two periods within the evolution of Cuban fertility may be clearly distinguished. The first, during which fertility rose until the GRR reached 2.30–2.28 (1963–4), lasted until approximately 1964; during the second, which began about that time, fertility declined until this trend was finally interrupted in 1979. This decline was sharpest during the second half of the 1970s.

The rise in fertility during the first years after the Revolution (up to 1964) is thought by various demographers (Behm and Alfonso 1981; Alvarez 1982; Catasús 1987) to be closely related to such factors as economic security, social stability, the development of social security, and the substantial increase in medical attention, all factors which might favour an increase in fertility, particularly after a long period during which those were not the characteristics which best described the socio-economic and political situation in Cuba.

Other factors, associated with proximate determinants such as the use of contraceptives and the interruption of pregnancy, also played an important part. In fact, between 1960 and 1964, the increase in fertility was intimately related to the limited use of contraception, due both to lack of knowledge and to the unavailability of contraceptives. As far as pregnancy termination is concerned, this was limited to those cases in which the presence of medical or social problems made it advisable; in addition, during the first years of this period there was massive emigration of medical personnel, among whom were the specialists who had concentrated on the practice of induced abortion.

Beginning in 1965, as indicated above, a decline in fertility was observed. By 1979 the GRR had reached the low level of 0.95 daughters per woman, a level very close to that of the economically developed countries; the determinants of this phenomenon are singular within Latin America. During this period of decline the relevant factors are different from those which previously prevailed: the conditioning factors must now be sought in the profound transformations generated by the Revolution in the society and in the family, which affect reproductive behaviour through several mechanisms. In particular, there was a revolutionary change in the woman's role, in her aspirations and in her possibility of satisfying them. Leaving behind a predominantly secondary role, women began to participate fully in the building of the new society, entering in growing numbers into paid work (27 per cent of the total were employed in 1975) and into cultural, political, and social activities. A higher level of education has become a desirable and achievable goal.

The health and survival of children were ensured by health programmes, in a country in which health services were free and rapidly reached universal coverage. On the other hand, the decline in infant mortality (a rate of 19.4 per 1,000 live births in 1979) meant that high fertility is no longer needed to replace children who die. Once family-based subsistence farming and any possibility of child labour had disappeared, children had much less economic value. All this contributed to making small families more desirable. Furthermore, family planning services became more widely available and abortion services became more accessible.

One characteristic of the process of fertility transition in Cuba should be emphasized: the revolutionary government never established an explicit population policy with the objective of reducing fertility. According to the Minister of Public Health, head of the Cuban delegation at the World Population Conference in Bucharest in 1974,

> Because of the rise in living standards resulting from our development policy, there has been an increasing decline in the birth rate . . . which made it possible to achieve a net growth rate which is still compatible with our development needs . . . To achieve this, it has been sufficient to respect the principle of the free decision to procreate, and to provide an adequate supply of contraceptive methods (Behm and Alfonso 1981: 64).

In other words, the structural changes produced by the Revolution have stimulated and extended the desire to limit family size, and these changes were particularly active during the period in question.

Along with the decline in levels of fertility during this period, there was also a change in the age structure of childbearing, which shows up markedly in the second half of the 1970s, although it began to be observed some years earlier. In 1975, out of a TFR of 2.74 children per woman, 55.1 per cent (1.51) was due to the fertility of women under the age of 25. In that very year the fertility rate of women aged 15–19 surpassed that of those aged 25–29 for the first time in the country's history (128.0 and 117.3 per 1,000 respectively). In 1979 the proportion of the TFR to women under age 25 was over 61 per cent. Fertility had not only declined substantially, but was also more concentrated among younger women.

Another aspect important to the analysis of this period is the relative homogenization of the fertility levels among geographic areas, and the attenuation of socio-economics differentials. The application of the own-children method to the Cuban National Demographic Survey of 1979 provided information which helps to define this process (Behm and Alfonso 1981).

The differences between urban and rural fertility have been analysed, as well as those among the six geographical regions, containing the fourteen provinces into which the country is divided. Fertility differentials have also been analysed according to the woman's educational level and her social group. Fig. 22.1 shows that in 1965, the urban and rural populations were in distinct phases of the fertility transition. In the urban sector, the TFR was only 4.1 children per woman, and was declining sharply. In the rural population, fertility was still 50 per cent higher than that of urban areas.

It is important to note that the decline in fertility was more intense among the rural than the urban population. The excess fertility of the rural area compared

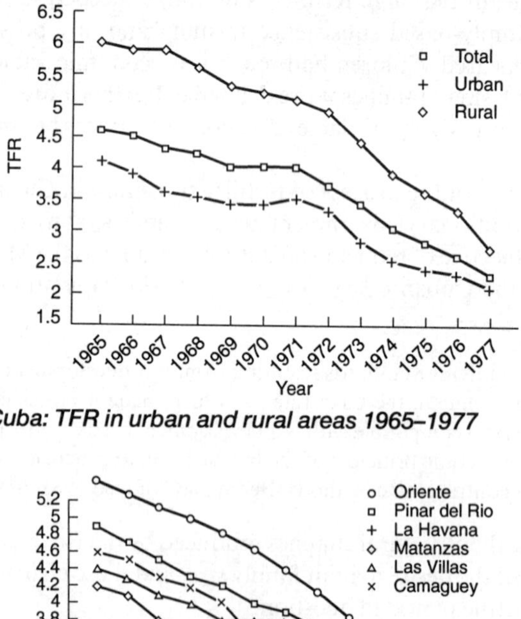

Fig. 22.1. ***Cuba: TFR in urban and rural areas 1965–1977***

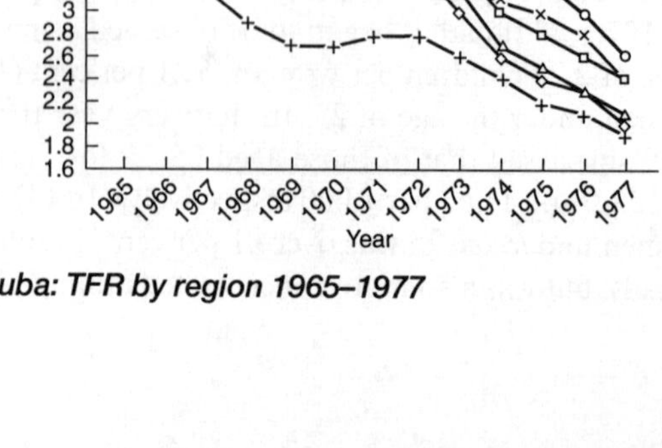

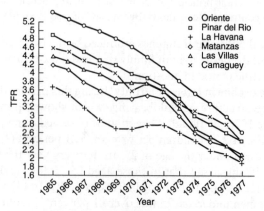

Fig. 22.1. ***Cuba: TFR by region 1965–1977***

with the urban, which was 2 children per woman in 1965, had been reduced to only 0.6 children by 1977.

The evolution of the TFR by geographic regions is shown in Fig. 22.2. In 1965 the TFR ranged from 3.7 children per woman in Havana to 5.4 in Oriente. Again it is clear that the regional contrasts tend to diminish: whereas the fertility level of the regions remains in the same order as before, the range of variation had diminished to 0.7 children per woman by 1977 (Havana 1.9; Oriente 2.6).

The inverse relation between a woman's educational level and her fertility has been analysed in countless documents. Fig. 22.3 shows clearly the postulated trend to uniformity, for various groups of women, by educational attainment. The process of reduction has been universal and has not simply occurred among the most highly educated women.

In turn, the study of fertility by social group (defined by the occupation of the household head) shows similar contrasts and evolution, which may be explained above all by differences in levels of schooling, and to a lesser degree by differences

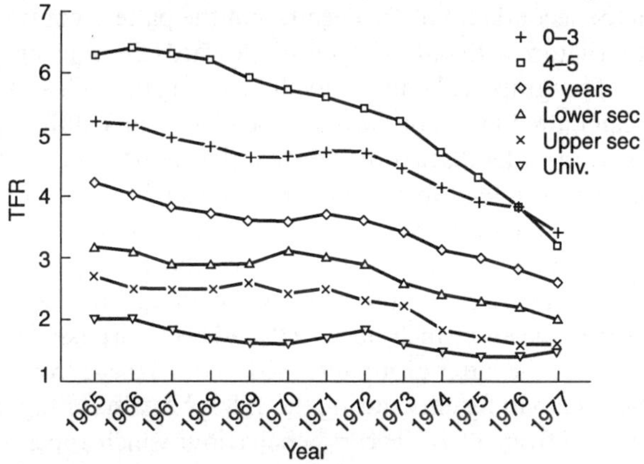

Fig. 22.3. ***Cuba: TFR by education 1965–1977***

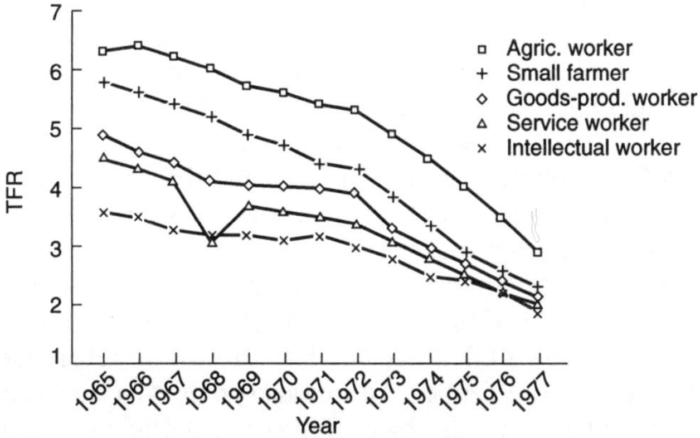

Fig. 22.4. ***Cuba: TFR by occupation 1965–1977***

in urban–rural residence. Again, there is a significant narrowing of the range of variation in fertility.

Cuban Fertility in the 1980s: The Current Situation

Evolution of Level, Structure by Age and Other Variables

Cuba entered the 1980s with a continuing decline in fertility levels, so that in 1981 the GRR was the lowest in the country's history at 0.78 daughters per woman, similar to the levels then current in countries such as Switzerland (0.74) and West Germany (0.70), and below those of others such as Japan (0.89), Sweden (0.82), and East Germany (0.88), all of which had a higher level of economic development than Cuba and were representative of the most advanced stages of the fertility transition on the international scene.

However, there was a modest recovery in fertility levels during the 1980s, particularly in the second half of the decade, but the pattern continued to be one of a young age structure with only a slight shift towards the older ages, and a more marked degree of geographical uniformity than during the 1970s, as well as showing an even greater attenuation of the main socio-economic differentials.

During the period under discussion it is clear that the level of fertility remained below the replacement rate (Table 22.1), for after a slight recovery in 1985, when the GRR reached 0.94, it declined once more. The behaviour by age is more interesting, as increases are observed in certain groups, the most important being that seen among women aged 25–29, traditionally the group with the second highest level of fertility in Cuba and which since 1975 had been surpassed in this position by those aged 15–19; the latter group returned to third place from 1984 on. This rearrangement of Cuban fertility during the 1980s has also brought higher rates among women aged from 30 to 39 years, a behaviour which appears to be related to the birth of children within second or third marriages, as will be discussed below.

The ratio of the TFR for those aged 15–24 to that for women 25–49 reflects the fact that during the first years of the 1980s, in general, the fertility of young women was around 1.5 times as great as that of the remaining women; this ratio began to descend slightly in 1983 and 1984, and continued to decrease during the following years, remaining however in excess of unity (Table 22.1).

Farnós (1985) has reflected on some important differential aspects of fertility, ratifying the growing tendency to homogenization of levels across various characteristics. First of all, using vital statistics data, he found that more than 70 per cent of municipalities (the smallest unit of the politico-administrative hierarchy in the country) are classified (in a typology designed by himself) in the category in which fertility is below a GRR of 0.90, that is, below the replacement level.

Along with this homogenization, Farnós also points to a clear decrease in the traditional differentials, among which a noticeable declining trend had already been observed during the 1970s.

Table 22.1. *Cuba: ASFRs, TFR, and GRR, 1980–1987*

Age-group	1980	1981	1982	1983	1984	1985	1986	1987
ASFRs								
15–19	86.3	83.5	90.7	90.6	83.8	92.9	80.9	81.5
20–24	116.8	113.8	129.9	125.2	120.3	126.8	110.0	116.9
25–29	70.9	67.8	82.8	86.7	88.3	95.7	85.8	92.5
30–34	37.4	36.3	41.4	43.9	44.1	46.5	45.1	49.9
35–39	16.2	14.6	18.2	17.0	16.6	18.5	17.8	18.3
40–44	4.6	4.1	3.6	3.5	3.4	3.9	3.2	3.3
45–49	1.8	2.4	2.8	1.1	0.7	1.2	1.6	1.1
TFR								
15–24	1.02	0.99	1.12	1.08	1.02	1.10	0.95	0.99
25–49	0.65	0.62	0.73	0.76	0.77	0.83	0.77	0.83
15–49	1.67	1.61	1.85	1.84	1.79	1.93	1.72	1.82
GRR	0.81	0.78	0.90	0.89	0.87	0.94	0.83	0.88
Ratio of TFR								
15–24/25–49	1.57	1.60	1.53	1.42	1.33	1.33	1.23	1.19

Source: SSC (1987: 69).

The inequalities in fertility levels between urban and rural areas, among educational groups and by economic activity in the different provinces have become less important. In fact, in many cases the fertility rates of women aged over 30 show no meaningful differences according to the above-mentioned characteristics (Farnós 1985: 6).

If we look at the situation about 1986, data available from ECLAC show that Cuba is one of the few countries in the Latin American region in which the cumulative change in the Gross Social Product per capita has been positive, and quite high (38.1 per cent) during the period 1981–6 (ECLAC 1987). To this must be added the greater diffusion and use of modern contraceptives, which allow couples to decide on the size of their family, the continuing availability of free abortion in hospitals, and the greater spread of sexual education, all factors which have had an impact on the evolution of the levels and structure of fertility in Cuba in the 1980s.

The Proximate Determinants of Fertility

As has been shown, the process of fertility transition in Cuba, as a component of the demographic process, has been closely related to the changes which have taken place on the island in the social and economic spheres, as a consequence of the politico-structural transformations which began in 1959. It is clear that these transformations have transcended the social area, and are reflected at both the family and the individual level. It is at the level of the family, and particularly of the couple, that decisions are made concerning the number of offspring and the spacing of births.

Various specialists (Alvarez 1982 and 1985; Alvarez and Farnós 1986; Farnós 1985; Hollerbach and Díaz-Briquets 1983; Mundigo and Landstreet 1983; Hernández 1984) have referred to the characteristics and peculiarities of Cuban fertility, in an attempt to establish the factors related to the changes described above. In this context, factors related to the growing participation of women—both from the quantitative and the qualitative points of view—in economic activity on one hand, and the attitudes and behaviour of youth to marriage and fertility (as they are the next childbearing cohorts) on the other, may be considered, among other things, as fundamental aspects that have had and will continue to have substantial impact on fertility trends (Catasús *et al.* 1987: chs. 2 and 3; González 1986).

The attitude of couples towards the number and spacing of their children, as a result of the new expectations of participation in socio-economic activities which the revolutionary process offers them, may be reflected in the changes undergone by the proximate determinants of fertility. In the case of Cuba, the chief proximate determinants are marriage, contraception, and induced abortion.

Marriage

During the period delimited by the last two population censuses (1970–81), the relative weight of those who are married or in union among the total population of women remained around 60 per cent; however, there were important variations within the group of women of fertile age. These changes manifested themselves first of all in a reduction of 8 per cent of those who declared that they had a partner, between 1970 and 1981. However, by 1987, a slight increase of 0.3 points is observed, and 63.1 per cent of fertile women are married or in union (SSC 1989).

In similar fashion, during the period 1970–87, among women of reproductive age, and specifically at the ages of highest fertility, it is seen that in 1970, 57 per cent of women who were married or in union were aged 15–24, while by 1987 this proportion had risen to 61.4 per cent.

In addition, the mean age at first marriage or union was 19.5 years in 1970, and had declined to 18.4 years by 1987. All of these measures suggest that a process of increase in marriage formation is occurring, and this may be related to similar behaviour observed in Cuban fertility in recent years.

Along with these phenomena, there is a change in the distribution by type of marital union among women aged 15–19, 20–24, and 25–29 (Catasús 1989). In 1970 more women were married than in non-marital unions in all these age-groups; however, since 1981 the proportion has been inverted for those under the age of 25. This situation may have an impact on the fertility of these age-groups, if the differential behaviour traditionally observed according to type of union is maintained.

These elements make it possible to conclude that the causes of the decline in Cuban fertility cannot be found in the postponement of marriage or union alone. Nevertheless, the high level of divorce and separation, as well as their increasing trend, are very important factors whose impact on fertility must be carefully evaluated.

During the period 1970–87, divorce in Cuba, measured via the gross divorce rate, increased by 10.3 per cent, rising from 2.9 to 3.2 divorces per 1,000 inhabitants per year (SSC 1987: 195). This rate, applied to population estimates, shows that 4.8 per cent of women of fertile age divorced in 1970, increasing to 7.3 per cent by 1981 and 6.6 per cent in 1987.

None the less, if women who were separated are added to the women designated as divorced in the 1980s, the situation could be seen as critical, since the previously mentioned increments would now reach 158 per cent and 252 per cent in 1981 and 1987 respectively. The category 'separated' was studied for the first time in Cuba in the National Demographic Survey of 1979, and includes 'those persons who, having formed part of a formal marriage or stable union, are separated and have not entered into any other conjugal union, that is who have not divorced and who are not living in union or with a partner' (SSC 1978: 10). Put another way, whereas in 1970 there were 11.2 divorced women of fertile age for every 100 who were married, this ratio reached 19.7 and 26.7 (now divorced or separated) per 100 women married or in union in 1981 and 1987 respectively. From the foregoing it may be deduced that the failure to consider separated women in 1970 may lead to an underestimation of the proportion whose union has been dissolved, since it must be kept in mind that from the methodological point of view in 1970 the separated women were included in the group of married or in-union women.

Thus, among those under the age of 30, the proportion of those who had terminated a union—whether legally or not—increased during the period 1970–87 by 6.7, 4, and 5 times for women aged 15–19, 20–24, and 25–29 respectively, due, basically, to the high percentages of women who in 1987 declared themselves to be separated.

In the specific case of divorced women, the variations are smaller, with a decline of 39 per cent among those aged 15–19 years, and an increase of 77 per cent and 51 per cent for the other two age-groups under consideration.

On the other hand, the 1987 fertility survey reveals that 35 per cent of women of childbearing age have had more than one union. If the situation of women aged 45–49 is considered, representing those women who for practical purposes have had all their possible unions, the percentage is quite similar; in the same way, 27 per cent of women under the age of 30 have already had more than one marriage or union.

From the preceding paragraphs, it may be deduced that a great deal of change in the marriage pattern is occurring, and that the process of marriage dissolution is increasing at a noticeable rate. If, along with these phenomena, the low level and the current increase in Cuban fertility are taken into account, it could be inferred, hypothetically, that Cuban women are motivated to have their second or third child largely by entering into a new union. On this point, the survey provides information indicating that within the universe under study, 42 per cent of children are first-borns and 28 per cent are second children; among women aged 45–49, an age-group in which the women have practically concluded childbearing, the two percentages are almost equal, at 27 per cent and 24 per cent respectively.

A more detailed analysis would be required to establish the degree of impact of the dissolution of unions on the present characteristics of Cuban fertility. However, in an attempt to obtain a preliminary indication, the proportions of women have been calculated by birth order and by union for those having 2 unions—who represent 35 per cent of the population—as shown in Table 22.2.

Table 22.2. ***Cuba: proportion of women with two unions by age-group, birth order, and order of union***

Age-group	Proportion of women with births of order:			
	One in		Two in	
	1st union	2nd union	1st union	2nd union
TOTAL	75.6	24.2	45.8	23.6
15–19	34.6	16.0	2.2	2.5
20–24	59.4	22.7	13.8	18.2
25–29	74.4	35.6	32.8	27.7
30–34	83.4	27.7	54.6	31.5
35–39	89.2	21.6	64.6	27.8
40–44	88.5	19.9	73.8	21.4
45–49	90.5	18.1	78.1	18.7

Source: SSC (1989).

Note: The total number of women with children within each order of union is taken to be 100%.

One notable feature of these results is its confirmation of the fact that the majority of the women with two unions have their first child during the first union (75.6 per cent). When the proportions of first births are compared by age of mother according to the number of the union, the change of direction in the trend from the group aged 25–29 onwards may be reflecting the fact that before the age of 30 high levels of marriage dissolution mentioned above, along with a relatively short duration of the first union, mean that a significant proportion of women have their first child during their second union.

On the other hand, even though the greatest percentage of women with two unions have had their second child during the first union (Table 22.2), those aged under 25 generally have it during their second union, which may indicate the beginning of a changing trend on the part of the youngest women. Although it still requires further analysis, this pattern would correspond to the hypothesis suggested above.

Fertility Regulation

The regulation of fertility by contraception and abortion are the principal determinants of the level of fertility in Cuba. The practice of abortion and the use of contraceptive methods are widespread in the country, as it is government policy to provide access to both these methods of fertility regulation without any restriction.

Abortion is a means of controlling births whose use, since before the triumph of the Revolution, has been more widespread in urbanized areas, particularly the national capital and the provincial capitals, than in rural areas. A brief analysis of the incidence of induced abortion, based on the relevant statistics, reveals that between 1980 and 1987 the number of abortions increased by 47 per cent, although during the last part of that seven-year period both increases and decreases are observed. Keeping in mind the caveat that the age structure may invalidate the comparison, the data in general reflect a mean number of abortions per 1,000 women which increases from 42.1 to 47.5 during the indicated period (MPH 1989*a*). The ratio of abortions to pregnancies has not changed significantly (by only 6 per cent) during the seven years under discussion, rising from 43.2 to 45.8 abortions per 100 pregnancies in 1980 and 1987 respectively.

More precise indicators show that whereas in 1981 it was estimated that by the end of her childbearing period the average woman had consciously terminated 1.51 pregnancies (Alvarez 1987: 448), at the present time this synthetic indicator varies between 1.64 for 1986 and 1.53 for 1988, which may signify a gradual increase from the levels of the beginning of the decade (estimates made on the basis of MPH 1989*b*).

Table 22.3, based on these rates, is presented with the aim of determining the distribution of abortions by age-group. From this table it is seen that abortion follows the characteristic pattern of Cuban fertility, in that the greatest proportion are found at ages below 30 years; women under the age of 20 have the second-highest proportion of abortions per woman, a phenomenon which becomes more striking by 1988. This suggests the need to continue orienting efforts towards this

Table 22.3. *Cuba: distribution of abortions and proportion of ever-in-union women who have had an induced abortion, by age-group, 1986–1988*

Age-group	Distribution of Abortions		Proportion of ever-in-union women who have had an abortion
	1986	1988	1987
Under 20	24.2	26.2	27.0
20–24	34.2	33.1	47.8
25–29	21.3	20.0	49.3
30–34	11.5	12.2	55.7
35–39	6.2	6.1	59.3
40–44	2.2	2.0	58.6
45–49	0.4[a]	0.4[a]	55.3
TOTAL	100.0	100.0	51.8

Sources: SSC 1987; MPH 1989*a*.

[a] Includes a few occurrences at older ages.

young population group—although a high percentage of young women report that they know of and use contraception (as will be seen below), it is likely that the contraceptive methods chosen are not used correctly or that contraceptive use begins only after the first unplanned and unwanted pregnancy has occurred.

The National Fertility Survey shows that more than 50 per cent of women who have ever been married or in union have had an abortion (Table 22.3), and the youngest women are no exception, as one in four of them have used this form of fertility regulation.

Concerning the knowledge and use of contraceptive methods, the 1987 survey investigated this topic by first asking an open-ended question about the methods which women of fertile age knew about, and later inquiring specifically about those methods which were not mentioned spontaneously by the respondent. The results show that 98.7 per cent of women spontaneously mentioned some method of avoiding pregnancy, and 99.5 per cent had heard of at least one method. These proportions once again show that there is widespread knowledge of the existence of methods of fertility regulation among the female population of childbearing age. This is confirmed by examining for comparative purposes the results obtained in a survey carried out in 1982 in three areas of the country with different degrees of socio-economic development (Catasús *et al.* 1988: 89). At that time, the inquiry about contraceptive knowledge yielded an estimate of 99.5 per cent for the urbanized area, 98.9 per cent for a partially urban area, and for a totally rural mountainous area 98.5 per cent of women who—without prompting—said that they had heard of some method of preventing pregnancy.

In particular, in 1987 the level of knowledge of the most effective methods (IUD, the pill, condoms, female sterilization, and the diaphragm, among others) varied between 99.8 per cent and 64 per cent, in the same order. Among the younger population, knowledge of condoms, a method whose use might be the most recommended since sexual relationships are not generally of long duration and/or with one partner, was the lowest.

This survey also revealed a high degree of ever-use of contraceptives (92.7 per cent) among women who have ever been married or in union. Analysis by age shows that it is the youngest women who declare the lowest level of ever-use, 84 per cent, as would be expected.

Taking for comparison the results of the 1982 study, an increase is seen in the use of contraceptives, since at that time the percentage of ever-in-union women who declared that they had ever used contraception varied, according to the area, between 66 per cent and 74 per cent (Catasús *et al.* 1988: 94).

In the 1987 study the IUD was the method ever-used by the highest proportion of users (70.1 per cent), followed by the pill (36 per cent). This pattern varied somewhat for the youngest women, among whom there is a small excess (of 1.5 percentage points) in the proportion of women who have ever used the pill, compared to those who have ever used the IUD. Within this group only a very small proportion—4 per cent—said that they had ever used condoms.

Results on current use by women who are married or in union, fertile and not pregnant at the time of the 1987 survey shows that a high proportion of women—88 per cent—was using some method of fertility control at the time of the survey. Among women under the age of 20 this percentage was close to 70 per cent, while for the rest it varied from 82 per cent to 94 per cent.

In summary, somewhat more than four of every five women studied protected themselves with one of the methods classified as efficient, and only 4 per cent of them used inefficient methods. The IUD, the most widely used method, is utilized by 40 per cent of exposed women, followed by female sterilization at 27 per cent.

The use of contraceptives as a means of spacing births is seen from the analysis of first birth intervals. The 1987 survey demonstrates that the greatest use of contraceptives occurs after the birth of the first child, and not to lengthen the time before the arrival of the first-born. In fact, 52 per cent of the women studied—with children born during the first five years of their union—declared a first-birth interval of 11 months or less from the moment of first union. Premarital conceptions are also relatively frequent: nearly 27 per cent said that their first child was born less than 9 months after the union began, and an additional 18 per cent before the beginning of the union. Studies carried out in several areas of the country for this purpose, using techniques such as the construction of life tables applied to first-birth intervals and inter-birth intervals, have similarly shown the presence of a relatively high rate of premarital conception (see e.g. Alvarez and Catasús 1984).

With the intention of evaluating the importance of some of the proximate determinants of Cuban fertility in recent years, and to compare this with the situation prior to 1981, when Cuba experienced its lowest level of fertility, Bongaarts's method was applied to the information from the 1981 and the 1987 surveys (Bongaarts 1982).

In the first place, a slight increase in total fertility is noted during the six-year period under examination (Table 22.4); this is slightly greater for marital fertility, both total and natural. On the other hand, for the country as a whole the use of contraceptives increased somewhat, although the level of use of the most effective methods remained stable.

Abortion, which is another form of fertility regulation, has shown a similar trend to that of contraceptive practice: survey estimates reveal a slight increase (of 5 per cent), very similar to that shown by the analysis of the vital statistics data on abortion.

In contrast, the specific indices of the model have remained practically unchanged; concerning the proportion of married women, the 4 per cent decrease in this index may reflect the increase in women who are neither married nor in union, which may in turn be related to the relative increase in the dissolution of unions mentioned earlier. The index of non-contraception, for its part, reflects the indicated small increase in the use of contraceptives, and its influence on fertility.

Although there was an increase in recourse to induced abortion, the effect of this factor on fertility actually diminished slightly. This may be related to interactions with the influence of contraceptive use.

Table 22.4. *Cuba: estimates of selected measures of fertility and indices of intermediate variables, 1981 and 1987*

	1981	1987	1987/1981
Measures			
TFR	1.52	1.82	1.20
Marital fertility rate	2.32	2.87	1.24
Natural Marital fertility rate	16.29	17.91	1.23
Contraceptive use	0.65	0.70	1.08
Contraceptive effectiveness	0.97	0.97	—
Total rate of induced abortion	1.51	1.59	1.05
Mean duration of infertility due to breast-feeding	3.79	3.79[a]	—
Indices			
Index of proportion married	0.655	0.632	0.96
Index of non-contraception	0.263	0.256	0.97
Index of induced abortion	0.604	0.628	1.04
Index of post-partum infertility	0.897	0.897[a]	—
Combined indices	0.089	0.091	0.98

Sources: For 1981, Alvarez (1987: 436–54); for 1987, SSC (1987: 69)

[a] As the mean duration of breast-feeding could not be estimated for 1987, the 1981 value, taken from the work of Hollerbach and Díaz-Briquets (1983: 121), was used for 1987.

From Bongaarts's indices it may be concluded that at present, among the proximate determinants considered, the use of contraceptive methods continues to play the predominant role in fertility regulation, followed by abortion and marriage, in that order.

Conclusions

As shown in this analysis, the Cuban fertility transition process has been early and rapid in the context of the evolution of fertility in Latin America. This transition has had the peculiarity that over the past thirty years it has been so intense that Cuba has attained a fertility level similar to that of the most socio-economically developed countries. In this process, the use of contraception and abortion have been increasingly important as the most significant proximate determinants; this may be explained as a response to the improvement in health conditions and in education, and to the increasing participation of women in the labour force and in social activities in general.

While Cuban fertility levels were already the lowest in Latin America at the beginning of the 1950s, the profound social change signified by the Revolution in 1959 caused fertility to descend to its present levels, which for more than a decade have been below replacement level, and are not expected to reach it again in the near term. It is noteworthy that this decline is present to the same degree in all social groups and administrative divisions. This trend to uniformity began in the 1960s, with a noticeable contraction in differentials according to these characteristics, which has become even stronger in the past few years.

Along with this trend to 'homogenization', there has been a shift of fertility towards the younger ages. The high rates among women aged 15–19 are particularly striking, and were only surpassed by the rates of women aged 20–24 for nearly a decade. Only during the last few years has there been a return to more traditional patterns, in which the highest rates are those of women aged 20–24 and 25–29 in that order.

We may conclude from this analysis that by the 1980s Cuban fertility transition was very advanced, ahead of the rest of Latin America. This development is related to the diffusion of values and the building of attitudes caused by the process of structural change and modernization which Cuban society has undergone in recent years, based on the profound economic and social transformations which have occurred. The socio-demographic characteristics of this transition are associated with and expressed through such aspects as marriage patterns, birth regulation, and others, some of which show behaviour unique in Latin America, making the study of the Cuban experience particularly interesting. In fact, the overall Cuban marriage pattern is undergoing important changes in its internal composition which favour consensual unions among the younger population, and an overall increase in the dissolution of unions and in remarriage.

On the other hand, the widespread availability and accessibility of effective modern methods for the regulation of fertility, have meant that a large proportion of women know and use the various methods of contraception, especially the effective ones. None the less, particularly among younger women there is need for more broadly based efforts which promote the timely use of contraception as an appropriate means of avoiding undesired pregnancies. Such efforts would help to reduce the use of abortion by this age-group.

In summary, it may be pointed out that during the 1980s, in the final phase of the Cuban fertility transition, contraception has played a leading role among the proximate determinants studied, followed by the use of induced abortion, and by marriage patterns in third place. This suggests that the increase in consensual unions and in remarriage which has recently occurred will not necessarily have the same repercussions on fertility as it had in the 1970s, when marriage patterns were the second most important of the intermediate variables studied.

References

Alfonso, J. C., and Tozo, S. (1985), *Evolución de la Mujer Cubana en 1984* (Havana: State Statistical Committee).

Alvarez, L. (1982), *La Tendencia de la Fecundidad en Cuba* (Havana: Institute for Health Development, Ministry of Public Health).

Alvarez, L. (1985), *Nivel, Estructura y Principales Características de la Fecundidad Cubana* (Havana: Institute for Health Development, Ministry of Public Health).

—— (1987), 'Determinantes Próximos de la Fecundidad en Cuba: Modelo de Bonngaarts', in *Revista Cubana de Administración de Salud*, 13/4 (Oct.–Dec.), 437–54.

—— and Catasús, C. (1984), *Estudios de los Intervalos Protogenésicos e Intergenésicos a Partir de Historia de Embarazos* (Centre for Demographic Studies, Monograph Series, 3; University of Havana).

—— and Farnós, A. (1986), *Factores Determinantes y Características de la Fecundidad Cubana* (Centre for Demographic Studies, Monograph Series No. 12; University of Havana).

Behm, H., and Alfonso, J. C. (1981), *Cuba: El Descenso de la Fecundidad 1964–1978* (San José, Costa Rica: State Statistical Committee and CELADE).

Bongaarts, J. (1982), 'Un Marco Para el Análisis de los Determinantes Próximos de la Fecundidad', in *Ensayos sobre Población y Desarrollo*, 3 (Bogotá: Population Council and Corporación Centro Regional de Población).

Catasús, S. (1989), *La Nupcialidad de los Jóvenes en Cuba: Su Comportamiento General* (Centre for Demographic Studies, Monograph Series, 24; University of Havana).

—— *et al.* (1975), *Evolución Estimada de la Fecundidad en Cuba, 1900–1950*, (Centre for Demographic Studies, Series 1, No. 5, Havana).

—— *et al.* (1987), 'La Reproducción de la Población y el Desarrollo Socioeconómico en Cuba', in Simposio Sobre Población y Desarrollo, V Conferencia de Ciencias Sociales, Centre for Demographic Studies, University of Havana.

—— *et al.* (1988), *Cuban Women: Changing Roles and Population Trends* (Women, Work and Development, No. 17; Geneva: International Labour Office).

ECLAC, Economic Commission for Latin America and the Caribbean (1987), *Balance Preliminar de la Economía Latinoamericana, 1986* (Santiago: ECLAC).

Farnós A. (1985), 'La Declinación de la Fecundidad y sus Perspectivas en el Contexto de los Procesos Demográficos en Cuba', scientific degree thesis, Centre for Demographic Studies, University of Havana.

—— and Catasús, S. (1976), 'La Fecundidad', in *La Población de Cuba* (Havana: Centre for Demographic Studies, University of Havana).

González, F. (1986), 'La Participación de la Mujer en la Fuerza de Trabajo y Fecundidad de Cuba. Un Estudio sobre Población y Desarrollo', Scientific degree thesis, Centre for Demographic Studies, University of Havana.

Hernández, R. (1984), *El Proceso de la Revolución Demográfica en Cuba* (Havana: Centre for Demographic Studies, University of Havana).

Hollerbach, P., and Díaz-Briquets, S. (1983), *Fertility Determinants in Cuba* (National Academy of Sciences, Committee on Population and Demography, Report No. 26; Washington: National Academy Press, Washington).

MPH (Ministry of Public Health), (1989*a*), 'Serie Cronológica de Obstetricia' (Havana; unpublished).

—— (1989*b*), 'Abortion Statistics' (Havana; unpublished).

Mundigo, A., and Landstreet, B. (1983), *Determinantes del Cambio de la Fecundidad en Cuba. Política y Tendencias Recientes* (Working Paper, The Population Council, Mexico City).

SSC (State Statistical Committee) (1978), *Encuesta Demográfica Nacional, Bases Metodológicas* (Havana: SSC).

—— (1987), *Anuario Demográfico, República de Cuba* (Havana: Institute for Statistical Research).

—— (1989), *National Fertility Survey, General Report* (Havana: Institute for Statistical Research).

SSC and CELADE, (1978), Proyección de la Población Cubana 1950–2000, Metodología y Resultados.

23 The Fertility Transition in Peru

DELICIA FERRANDO and CARLOS E. ARAMBURÚ

Introduction

The trend toward fertility decline in Latin America is well documented at the national level, as well as at the level of regional and administrative districts in many countries. This undoubtedly represents a great advance when comparing the present situation to that of a couple of decades ago, when practically nothing was known about what was occurring in subnational areas. However, explanations for the changes in fertility levels as well as for the present overall level of fertility are still inadequate. The indicators of fertility do summarize the reproductive behaviour of women of diverse socio-cultural sectors (Andean, coastal, jungle, the upper, middle, and lower strata, etc.), but they do not shed any light on the context of the decline.

In this chapter, specific aspects of fertility transition will be examined from the vantage point of the socio-cultural groups most relevant to Peruvian society, which is very heterogeneous economically and culturally. The aspects to be studied are:

- the changes in levels and structure of fertility on the coast, in the Andes and in the jungle, taking into account the type of area of residence (rural or urban).
- the level of nuptiality and contraception and variations in the pattern of use by method, given that these variables are considered to be the most powerful determinants of fertility decline. In order to understand the complexity of factors involved in contraceptive practice and in nuptiality, it is necessary to analyse generational changes and cultural differences in sexual behaviour and contraception. For this purpose, we will present the results of an earlier study on the cultural context of sexuality and attitudes to contraception of three age-cohorts of women in three cultural contexts. The three age-cohorts are: women under 25 years of age, women aged 25 to 34, and women aged 35 and over; the three cultural groups are: El Agustino, an urban zone on the fringe of the capital; Huaraz, a popular sector of an Andean city; and Pueblo Nuevo (Lambayeque), a small rural village on the country's northern coast.

The Process of Social Change: Modernization and Crisis

Between 1940 and 1980 Peru ceased to be a predominantly rural (65 per cent) and Andean society, with high levels of illiteracy (58 per cent), based on an agrarian economy (75 per cent of the economically active population). It took on a very different form with high levels of urbanization (more than 65 per cent), concentrated on the coast, with relatively low levels of illiteracy (16 per cent), and an urban economy characterized by the small contribution of the formal industrial sector and the dominance of the informal sector: street vendors, personal services and small businesses.

The demographic transition experienced in Peru from 1940 to 1980 was characterized by a rapid decline in mortality (42 per cent decline in infant mortality between 1940 and 1981), particularly between 1940 and 1960, and a lesser and later decline (36 per cent between 1960 and 1986) in fertility from the late 1960s onward. During this period the rapidly growing population almost tripled, rising from 6.2 million in 1940 to over 17.7 million in 1981 (Table 23.1).

Two factors must be taken into account in explaining the fertility transition in Peru. The first is the structural heterogeneity of Peruvian society, which is seen in contrasting living conditions among social groups, and also in differential processes of social, economic and demographic change. Thus, for example, in recent work based on census data from 1972 and 1981 (Arocena and Aramburú 1990), when the living conditions of the sixteen poorest provinces of the country were compared with the national average, it was found that inequalities in living standards have increased in terms of female illiteracy, stock of durable goods owned by household, child labour, and fertility indicators. Only in infant mortality was there a slight (10.5 per cent) reduction in the gap. In other words, in spite of the process of cultural and social modernization, the gaps in living conditions between rich and poor have increased.

The second factor which is central in influencing the decline in fertility is the profound and prolonged economic crisis suffered by Peru, which continues with variable intensity and has become more acute in the past two years. This crisis has given rise, between 1987 and 1989, to high inflation (30 per cent monthly and 2,700 per cent annually as of the end of that period), recession (the GDP fell by 12.2 per cent between January and December of 1989 with a negative trend since 1978, with the exception of 1985–6), and a deterioration of real wages, which in 1989 were 79 per cent of the real wage level of 1979, and only 43 per cent of the real wage level of the first half of 1988.

The central hypothesis of this chapter is that even though the process of economic and cultural modernization created favourable conditions for the beginning of the decline in fertility, it was the economic crisis that accelerated the process, causing it to extend to the lower classes in both urban and rural areas in the late 1970s. Modernization and crisis, then, are the two faces and two phases of the process of fertility transition in Peru. This chapter analyses the quantitative and qualitative dimensions of this phenomenon in the context of modernization.

Table 23.1. *Peru: selected demographic and socio-economic indicators, 1940–1981*

Indicators[a]	1940	1961	1972	1981	Annual % change		
					1940/61	1961/72	1972/80
1 Total population	6,207,967	9,906,746	13,538,203	17,762,231	2.2	2.9	2.6
2 Urban population (%)	35.4	47.4	59.5	65.0	3.7	5.1	3.6
3 Infant mortality rate	181.0	142.0	119.6	105.0	1.3	1.2	1.1
4 Illiteracy (%)	58.0	39.0	27.5	16.0	1.5	1.4	1.7
5 Active population in agriculture (%)	75.0	52.3	46.5	39.2	1.4	1.1	1.2
6 Rate of increase in GNP per capita	—	—	—	—	3.1	2.0	0.6
7 Rate of increase of labour productivity	—	—	—	—	40.6	22.6	2.9
8 Unemployment rate	—	—	—	—	4.2	6.8	10.1

Source: National censuses and National Accounts. Instituto Nacional de Estadística, Peru.

[a] In the case of indicators 1 and 2, the figures refer to the rate of population increase (total and urban). In the case of indicators 3 to 5, the figures represent the ratio between the value of the first year and the value of the second year.

Evolution and Trends in Fertility

The National Level

The evolution of fertility in Peru is examined through the TFR at two points during the period 1950–90 as selected for study by Peruvian demographers and those of CELADE. The first was in 1983 when the definitive results of the 1981 census became available, for population projections for the period 1950–2025. Then, in 1989, new calculations were made to revise the projections made in 1983, on the basis of findings by the NDHS that there had been a more pronounced decline in fertility since 1980 than had been assumed. Naturally, that revision was made only for 1980 and beyond.

The selection of values of the TFR by quinquennia was not an easy task, given the great amount of information from diverse sources of variable quality. In spite of the care taken in examining the different estimates, it is probable that the specialists involved were not in total agreement on the values and the periods selected for the TFR. The same can be said regarding ASFRs. Fig. 23.1 shows estimates of the TFR obtained by applying various techniques to all the sources of data available up to 1986 (see Appendix 23.1). The smoothed values adopted for quinquennia in the projection in current use are shown amongst the scattered points on the graph. The estimate for 1940 has also been added, both to Fig. 23.1 and to Table 23.2.

Historical information on the level of fertility in Peru is insufficient. However, certain studies (CEPD 1972, Lésevic 1984, Ferrando 1986, among others) verify that during the sixty-four years from 1876 to 1940, fertility seems to have remained unchanged, hovering around a TFR of 5.8 children per woman. From 1950 onwards, more precise information is available on the level of fertility. The estimated TFR for 1950 was 6.9, and it remained at this level until 1965. In fact, between 1940 and 1950, the national fertility level increased by 1.8 per cent annually, probably as a consequence of the substantial decline in mortality and morbidity, and improved fecundity, after 1940.

The decline in fertility began during the quinquennium 1965–70 and the evidence indicates that this was the result of socio-cultural and economic changes which Peruvian society had been experiencing since the early 1960s. The TFR, at 6.6 children per woman in the quinquennium 1965–70, rapidly declined to 4.7 in the quinquennium 1980–5 and is estimated to be 4.0 children per woman during the period 1985–90.

Between 1965 and 1970, the TFR fell by 0.8 per cent annually. This rate of decline doubled from 1970 to 1975, and reached 3.5 times the rate of 1965–70 in 1980 when the impact of the economic crisis, which had begun in 1975, worsened (Table 23.3). A fundamental element of the change was the use of contraceptives among younger and older women within the reproductive ages: the youngest age-group (15–19 years old) used contraception so that they could take better advantage of the extension of the educational system, and the older ones used it in order

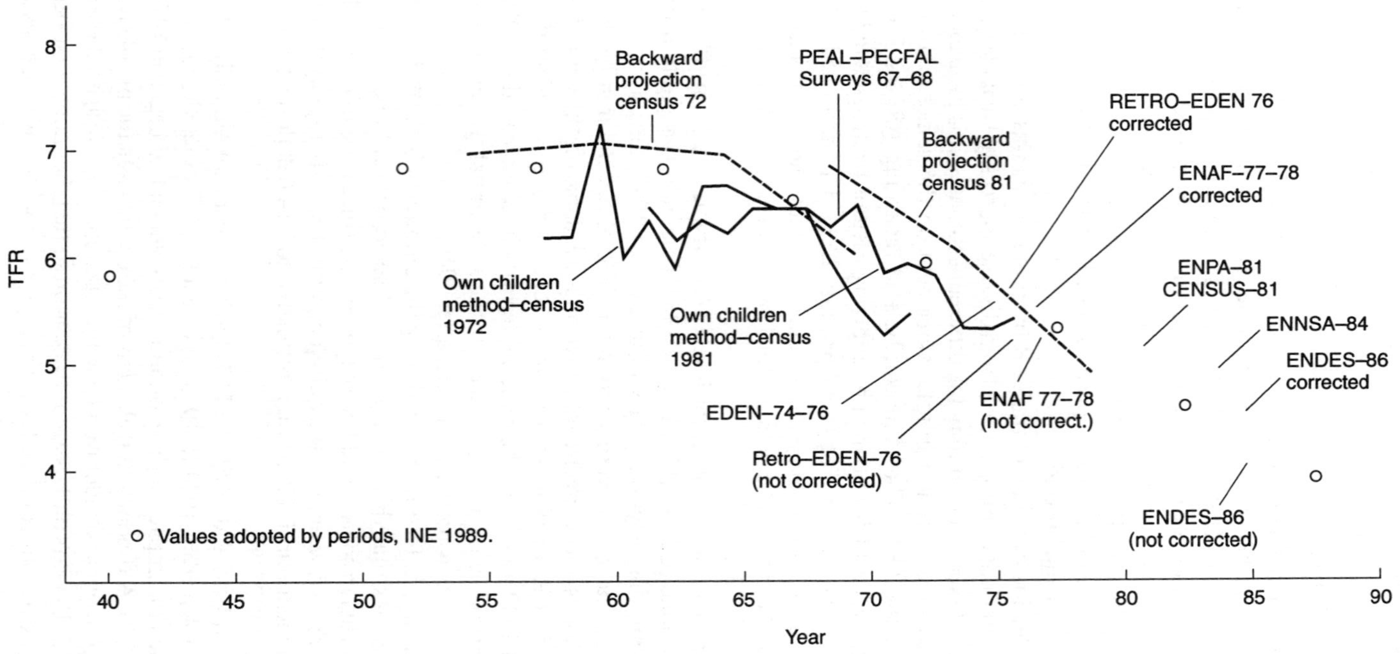

Fig. 23.1. ***Peru: fertility trends obtained by the estimation of TFR by different sources 1940–1986***

Source: INE 1983 and 1990

Table 23.2. *Peru: fertility trends 1940–1990*

Age-groups	Period								
	1940	1950–55	1955–60	1960–65	1965–70	1970–75	1975–80	1980–85	1985–90
ASFRs									
15–19	0.0821	0.1299	0.1299	0.1299	0.1023	0.0863	0.0925	0.0803	0.0719
20–24	0.2713	0.2929	0.2829	0.2829	0.2650	0.2467	0.2383	0.2054	0.1883
25–29	0.2833	0.3173	0.3173	0.3173	0.3031	0.2922	0.2652	0.2285	0.2030
30–34	0.2357	0.2755	0.2755	0.2755	0.2795	0.2658	0.2200	0.1900	0.1613
35–39	0.1758	0.2047	0.2047	0.2047	0.2152	0.2012	0.1738	0.1508	0.1207
40–44	0.0849	0.1130	0.1130	0.1130	0.1036	0.0886	0.0696	0.0607	0.0452
45–49	0.0280	0.0453	0.0453	0.0453	0.0433	0.0191	0.0162	0.0143	0.0096
TOTAL	1.1611	1.3686	1.3686	1.3686	1.3120	1.1999	1.0356	0.9300	0.8000
TFR	5.81	6.85	6.85	6.85	6.56	6.00	5.38	4.65	4.00
CRR	2.83	3.34	3.34	3.34	3.20	2.93	2.62	2.27	1.98
% distribution									
15–19	7.1	9.5	9.5	9.5	7.8	7.2	8.6	8.6	9.0
20–24	23.4	20.7	20.7	20.7	20.2	20.5	22.2	22.1	23.5
25–29	24.4	23.2	23.2	23.2	23.1	24.3	24.5	24.6	25.4
30–34	20.3	20.0	20.0	20.0	21.3	22.2	20.5	20.4	20.2
35–39	15.1	15.0	15.0	15.0	16.4	16.8	16.2	16.2	15.0
40–44	7.3	8.3	8.3	8.3	7.9	7.4	6.5	6.5	5.7
45–49	2.4	3.3	3.3	3.3	3.3	1.6	1.5	1.5	1.2
TOTAL	100.0	100.0	100.0	100.0	100.0	100.0	100.0	100.0	100.0

Sources: For 1940, Ferrando (1990); for 1950–80, INE and CELADE (1983); for 1980–90, INE (1990).

Note: CRR = Crude reproduction rate.

Table 23.3. *Peru: annual % change in the TFR and in ASFRs, 1940–1990*

Period	Annual % change in ASFRs and TFR							
	15–19	20–24	25–29	30–34	35–39	40–44	45–49	TFR
1940–50	+5.8	+0.4	+1.2	+1.7	+1.6	+3.3	+6.2	+1.8
1950–65	0.0	0.0	0.0	0.0	0.0	0.0	0.0	0.0
1965–70	–4.2	–1.3	–0.9	+0.3	+1.0	–1.7	–0.9	–0.8
1970–5	–3.1	–1.4	–0.7	–1.0	–1.3	–2.9	–11.2	–1.7
1975–80	+1.4	–0.7	–1.8	–3.4	–2.7	–4.3	–3.0	–2.1
1980–5	–2.6	–2.8	–2.8	–2.7	–2.6	–2.6	–2.3	–2.7
1985–90	–2.1	–1.7	–2.2	–3.0	–4.0	–5.1	–6.0	–2.8

Source: Table 23.2.

to limit the number of children. By 1980, the decline in fertility rates extended to all age-groups, becoming fairly homogeneous by the quinquennium 1985–90 (Table 23.3). During this period, younger women also increasingly began to use contraceptives for spacing births.

For the population as a whole, the period 1961–72 showed a slight decline in fertility (0.5 per cent annually), while between 1972 and 1981 the decline was four times as rapid (2.0 per cent annually, see Table 23.3). Between 1981 and 1986, the fertility decline was even sharper (3.3 per cent annually). Many studies on Peru (Lésevic and Ortiz 1987; Aramburú *et al.* 1987; Ferrando, 1986) present clear evidence of fertility decline among the high- and middle-income populations in the principal cities during the 1960s, as well as the beginning of a decline among the low-income urban populations. It was only in the late 1970s that the decline in fertility gradually expanded to the rest of the country to include the remaining women in rural areas. This period of fertility transition coincides with the years of deep recession and high inflation, that is, of economic crisis which, with some ups and downs, continues to this day.

Sub-national Areas

Type of Area of Residence: Urban areas have experienced a strong and sustained decline in fertility throughout the period under analysis. The TFR dropped by almost half in urban areas (from 6.0 to 3.8) between 1961 and 1986. In contrast, rural fertility still continued to rise until 1972. Its decline began about two decades ago, starting gradually during the period 1972–81 and increasing significantly during the quinquennium 1981–6 (Table 23.4).

Natural regions: The socio-cultural and economic differences among natural regions are appreciable and would explain contrasts in the evolution of fertility among these regions. The greatest changes occurred in Metropolitan Lima; fertility, which was already relatively low in 1961, declined more than in any other region (44 per cent) between 1961 and 1986 (from 5.6 to 3.1 children per woman). Meanwhile, in the rest of the coastal area, the decline was slightly less than 40 per cent; in the jungle (Selva region) it was almost 25 per cent and in the mountains it

Table 23.4. *Peru: fertility trends by area of residence, 1961–1981*

Age-groups	ASFRs				% distribution			
	Census 1961	Census 1972	Census 1981	DHS-86	Census 1961	Census 1972	Census 1981	DHS-86
Urban areas								
15–19	0.1007	0.0684	0.0763	0.0694	8.4	6.2	8.0	8.5
20–24	0.2809	0.2269	0.2526	0.2296	23.4	20.5	26.1	23.9
25–29	0.3018	0.2749	0.2443	0.2221	25.1	24.9	25.2	29.0
30–34	0.2667	0.2430	0.1921	0.1746	22.2	22.0	19.8	20.2
35–39	0.1723	0.1826	0.1318	0.1198	14.4	16.5	13.6	10.4
40–44	0.0655	0.0867	0.0581	0.0526	5.5	7.8	6.0	6.4
45–49	0.0122	0.0227	0.0126	0.0115	1.0	2.1	1.3	1.6
TOTAL	1.2001	1.1051	0.9678	0.8798	100.0	100.0	100.0	100.0
TFR	6.00	5.53	4.40	3.77				
CRR	2.93	2.70	2.15	1.84				
Rural areas								
15–19	0.1168	0.1420	0.1450	0.1514	7.5	8.7	9.5	11.4
20–24	0.3616	0.3411	0.3449	0.2639	23.2	21.0	22.6	19.8
25–29	0.3784	0.3557	0.3398	0.2743	24.3	21.9	22.3	20.6
30–34	0.2916	0.3280	0.2934	0.2998	18.7	20.2	19.3	22.5
35–39	0.2508	0.2707	0.2398	0.2192	16.1	16.7	15.7	16.5
40–44	0.1239	0.1427	0.1262	0.1044	7.9	8.8	8.3	8.0
45–49	0.0363	0.0440	0.0344	0.0166	2.3	2.7	2.3	1.2
TOTAL	1.5594	1.6242	1.5237	1.3299	100.0	100.0	100.0	100.0
TFR	7.80	8.12	7.62	6.65				
CRR	3.80	3.96	3.72	3.24				

Source: Elaborated by using data furnished by the INE.

Note: CRR = Crude reproduction rate.

was barely 14 per cent. It should be noted that in the mountains (Sierra region), fertility rose until 1972, beginning the process of decline only after 1972. On the other hand, the fertility level remained practically constant in the jungle region until 1972, declining, as in the mountain region, after 1972 (Tables 23.5 and 23.6).

Socio-ecological strata—Region and Place of Residence: This variable combines the natural region with the type of area, introducing modifications with respect to the census definition of both variables (Aramburú *et al.* 1987) and consequently, refining them. As was the case for regions and for type of area, during the first intercensal interval, 1962–72, fertility did not decline in all sectors. In the rural areas of the coast and the mountains, it rose. In contrast, in the last two periods, the decline became a generalized process, even though its intensity and subtleties were different among periods and among groups.

The upper and middle social strata in Lima already had relatively low fertility by 1961, the consequence of a decline which began early. The progress made in the education of both sexes and the diffusion of modern contraceptive methods explains this decline. The factors mentioned above produced changes in the patterns of nuptiality (raising the age at marriage) and of reproduction (delaying pregnancies and concentrating them within a relatively short period of the fertile age range). During the entire period analysed the TFR of Lima's upper and middle social strata was about half the national average TFR (Table 23.7).

The fertility of lower class women in Lima in 1961 was the same as that of women in the Andean mountains due to the great migratory flow of these peoples to the capital since 1950. The TFR of this group at that time was similar to the national average, but by 1981 their TFR was 20.5 per cent lower, due to a decline that was gradual and then accelerated. There are two features which characterize the trend of the TFR in the lower classes in Lima: its decline, which was substantially more rapid than that of the upper and middle classes, and its late incorporation into the process of fertility decline in Metropolitan Lima. It was only by 1972 that the difference in fertility levels between these social strata began to narrow. The contribution of each one of these classes to the fertility decline of Metropolitan Lima thus was distinct both in intensity and in timing (Table 23.7).

There are three social groups in the rest of the coastal region: people living in localities with 100,000 or more inhabitants, those living in urban localities with fewer than 100,000 inhabitants and those living on the rural coast. In the first, as in lower class Lima, the fertility decline was substantial and sustained over the whole period, although the decline was less pronounced than in Lima itself. It is important to note that at all three points in the period being analysed, the fertility level of the classes which include the large cities of the coast is lower than that which includes the lower classes of Lima. None the less, the difference in TFRs between the coastal areas and Lima-Popular increased until 1972 but almost disappeared by 1981 when the two reached similar levels. The decline in TFR in the coastal regions (including the three localities mentioned above) is steeper than that recorded for the TFR for Peru as a whole, and that of Lima's upper and middle class (Table 23.7).

Table 23.5. *Peru: fertility trends by regions, 1961–1981*

Age-groups	ASFRs				% distribution			
	Census 1961	Census 1972	Census 1981	DHS-86	Census 1961	Census 1972	Census 1981	DHS-86
Metropolitan Lima								
15–19	0.0962	0.0531	0.0487	0.0498	8.6	6.1	7.0	8.0
20–24	0.2823	0.1835	0.1639	0.1655	26.3	21.0	23.7	26.5
25–29	0.2957	0.2305	0.1869	0.1682	26.4	26.4	27.0	27.0
30–34	0.2259	0.1958	0.1530	0.0947	20.2	22.4	22.0	15.2
35–39	0.1472	0.1353	0.0968	0.0953	13.1	15.5	14.0	15.3
40–44	0.0553	0.0599	0.0360	0.0348	5.0	6.9	5.2	5.6
45–49	0.0170	0.0158	0.0073	0.0170	0.4	1.8	1.1	2.4
TOTAL	1.1196	0.8739	0.6926	0.6253	100.0	100.0	100.0	100.0
TFR	5.60	4.36	3.46	3.13				
CRR	2.26	2.13	1.67	1.52				
Rest of Coast								
15–19	0.1002	0.0819	0.0739	0.1001	7.3	6.0	7.0	12.0
20–24	0.3082	0.2719	0.2399	0.2024	22.6	20.0	22.7	24.5
25–29	0.3331	0.3187	0.2593	0.2059	24.4	23.5	24.5	24.9
30–34	0.2903	0.2937	0.2175	0.1915	21.2	21.6	20.6	23.2
35–39	0.2171	0.2380	0.1655	0.1032	15.9	17.5	15.6	12.5
40–44	0.0952	0.1225	0.0821	0.0237	7.0	9.0	7.8	2.9
45–49	0.0222	0.0324	0.0195	0.0000	1.6	2.4	1.8	0.0
TOTAL	1.3663	1.3591	1.0577	0.8260	100.0	100.0	100.0	100.0
TFR	6.83	6.80	5.29	4.13				
CRR	3.33	3.32	2.58	2.01				
Sierra								
15–19	0.0964	0.1008	0.0910	0.1045	7.3	6.7	7.0	8.1
20–24	0.3028	0.3034	0.2760	0.2624	22.8	20.2	21.3	20.3
25–29	0.3122	0.3420	0.3045	0.3109	23.5	22.8	23.6	24.1
30–34	0.2641	0.3182	0.2634	0.2433	19.9	21.2	20.4	18.9
35–39	0.2071	0.2574	0.2154	0.1982	15.6	17.2	16.7	15.4
40–44	0.1076	0.1349	0.1105	0.1469	8.1	9.0	8.6	11.4
45–49	0.0370	0.0429	0.0308	0.0230	2.8	2.9	2.4	1.8
TOTAL	1.3273	1.4996	1.2916	1.2892	100.0	100.0	100.0	100.0
TFR	6.64	7.50	6.46	6.45				
CRR	3.24	3.66	3.15	3.15				
Selva								
15–19	0.1566	0.1482	0.1426	0.1556	10.0	9.4	11.0	13.1
20–24	0.3682	0.3477	0.2962	0.2897	23.3	22.0	22.6	24.3
25–29	0.3792	0.3575	0.2891	0.3500	23.9	22.6	22.1	29.3
30–34	0.3106	0.3184	0.2953	0.2474	19.6	20.1	22.5	20.7
35–39	0.2508	0.2611	0.1804	0.1228	15.8	16.5	13.8	10.3
40–44	0.0940	0.1182	0.0893	0.0280	5.9	7.5	6.8	2.3
45–49	0.0242	0.0302	0.0160	0.0000	1.5	1.9	1.2	0.0
TOTAL	1.5835	1.5814	1.3089	1.1935	100.0	100.0	100.0	100.0
TFR	7.92	7.90	6.54	5.97				
CRR	3.86	3.86	3.19	2.91				

Source: Elaborated by using data furnished by the INE.

Note: CRR = Crude reproduction rate

Table 23.6. *Peru: annual % change in the TFR by area and region of residence, 1961–1986*

Period	Annual % change in the period						
	Peru	Regions				Area	
		Metropolitan Lima	Rest of Coast	Sierra	Selva	Urban	Rural
1961–72	–0.52	–2.03	–0.04	+1.19	–0.01	–0.72	+0.38
1972–81	–2.04	–2.26	–2.44	–1.52	–1.90	–2.24	–0.68
1981–6	–3.26	–1.96	–4.39	–0.03	–1.74	–4.42	–2.55

Sources: Tables 23.4 and 23.5.

The fertility of the urban coastal localities of fewer than 100,000 inhabitants declined slightly between 1961 and 1972 (9 per cent) and declined more rapidly (20 per cent) between 1972 and 1981. Note that the level of the TFR in this group is higher than that of the remainder of the coastal urban areas. Living on the coast and particularly in an urban area are not, then, sufficient conditions for homogeneous (low) fertility levels; it is also necessary for the population to be integrated into the modern world and to participate in the relative advantages which it offers.

The evolution in fertility of the rural coastal population reveals a totally different pattern from the urban one, which is similar to that of the rural mountain areas. Between 1961 and 1972, the fertility of rural coastal women increased by 10 per cent. This beginning of the process of change in fertility rates is attributable to a decline in morbidity and mortality. During the decade 1972–81, fertility fell by a little more than 12 per cent in rural coastal areas, but it was still 30.6 per cent above the national average in 1981. In only two decades the rural coastal zone changed rapidly from the initial stage of demographic transition (characterized by declining mortality and a slight increase in fertility) to the intermediate stage in which fertility begins to decline.

The Andean population was divided into two groups: mountain urban and mountain rural. The mountain urban area experienced a sustained though moderate decline in fertility since 1961. This is a change which began early and which was consistent throughout the past two decades. This pattern is similar to that of the urban coastal area, whose population is in localities of under 100,000 inhabitants, although the rate of decline is almost twice as slow. In the rural mountain area, fertility remained high and practically constant during the 1960s, and even tended to increase slightly between 1961 and 1972, undergoing only a slight decline during the decade 1972–81.

The two groups in the jungle area had the highest fertility levels in the country in 1961. Despite this fact, they experienced a rapid and sustained decline in TFR, experiencing the steepest decline of all the groups, during the period under study, including lower class Lima and all coastal areas with 100,000 or more inhabitants. It might be assumed that due to the extremely high initial level of the TFR

Table 23.7. *Peru: fertility trends by socio-ecological strata*

Socio-ecological strata	TFR			% change			Contribution of the strata to the observed change		
	1961	1972	1981	1961–72	1972–81	1961–81	1971–72	1972–81	1961–81
TOTAL	6.85	6.46	5.26	– 5.7	–18.6	–23.2	100.0	100.0	100.0
Urban areas									
Lima: middle/high	3.95	3.37	2.79	–14.7	–17.2	–29.4	18.9	10.7	19.6
Lima: popular	6.80	5.89	4.18	–13.4	–29.0	–38.5	17.3	18.2	17.5
Coast[a]	6.40	5.23	4.12	–18.3	–21.2	–35.6	23.6	13.3	16.1
Rest of Coast	6.82	6.20	4.95	–9.1	–20.2	–27.4	11.7	12.7	12.4
Sierra	7.10	6.30	5.53	–11.3	–12.2	–22.1	14.6	7.6	10.0
Selva	8.30	6.90	5.05	–16.9	–26.8	–39.2	21.8	16.8	17.9
Rural areas									
Coast	7.13	7.84	6.87	–10.0	–12.4	–3.6	–12.9	7.7	1.6
Sierra	7.58	8.00	7.09	5.5	–11.4	–6.5	–7.1	7.1	2.9
Selva	9.02	8.17	7.37	–9.4	–9.8	–18.3	12.1	5.9	8.3

Source: Aramburú *et al*. 1987

[a] Localities of 100,000 or more inhabitants.

in these jungle areas, the magnitude of the percentage decline would be relatively insignificant, but that is not the case. The TFR in 1961 (8.3) was 21 per cent higher than that for Peru as a whole while in 1981 (5.1) it was 4 per cent lower.

Finally, a slow and uninterrupted decline in the fertility of the rural population of the Selva region may be noted. However, since the fertility level in 1961 was extremely high, the fertility of this population in 1981 continued to be the highest of all groups, at 40 per cent above the national average (Table 23.7).

Changes in the Age Structure of Fertility

The percentage contribution of women of different age-groups to national fertility depends on many factors. Age at marriage is very important in populations which do not practise deliberate birth control, but in Peru this is not as important since a large proportion of women are in consensual or non-marital unions. Therefore, in Peru, the age at which non-marital unions are entered must also be considered. Other factors are the use of contraception; breast-feeding customs; post-partum abstinence; and the incidence of widowhood, divorce, and separation.

Obviously, the change in the TFR is due to variations in age-specific rates and in the distribution of women by age, which modify each age-group's contribution to total fertility. It is also obvious that the size of the decline was not homogeneous by age. The decline in the age-specific rates varied from a minimum of 33.4 per cent in the 20–24-year-old age-group, to a maximum of 79.0 and 60.0 per cent for women aged 45–49 and 40–44 years respectively. Given that the contribution of these last two groups to total fertility is very low, it follows that the fertility declines in women 15 to 19 years old and those 30 to 39 have the greatest impact on the TFR. Among the youngest (15 to 19 years), the decline appears to be due to a change in the patterns of nuptiality, namely an increase in the age at which they cease to be single. Although the average age at first union has risen by only one year since 1960 (21.7 years old in 1961 and 22.8 years old in 1981), there has been a considerable decrease in the number of very early marriages. Among the adolescents of the late 1950s, one in every twelve married before the age of 15, while among the adolescents of 1986 only one out of 40 did so (Ferrando *et al.* 1989). However, the proportion of 15–19-year-olds ever in a union is still moderately high (13 per cent, or about one in eight).

The proportion of fertility to older women has fallen slightly, as fertility declined (Table 23.2 and Fig. 23.2). While about 11–12 per cent of fertility occurred to women aged 35 or more through the mid- 1960s, this had fallen to about 7 per cent by the late 1980s. The proportion of fertility to women in the peak childbearing years, 20–29, rose from about 44 per cent to about 49 per cent by the late 1980s.

Fertility and Contraception

Numerous studies have demonstrated the close association between the rate of prevalence of contraceptive use and the TFR. For example, Bongaarts (1984)

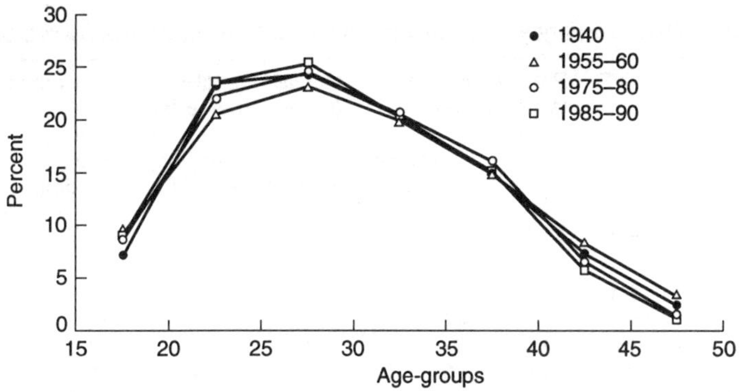

Fig. 23.2. ***Peru: relative distribution of ASFRs 1940–1990***
Source: Table 23.2.

showed, in a sample of eighty-three countries in and around 1980, that 85 per cent of the variance in the level of fertility was explained by the contraceptive prevalence rate. In a recent study (Aramburú 1990) of nineteen Latin American countries, it was found that there was a high and significant negative correlation (r = –0.694) between the TFR and the contraceptive prevalence rate during the period 1985–9.

Contraceptive prevalence and use of different methods will be examined briefly to explain regional variations in Peruvian fertility. Unfortunately, estimates over time by region and cultural zone are not available to permit a detailed analysis of the process of fertility decline and increase in the use of contraceptives.

Table 23.8 shows the level of fertility and contraceptive prevalence for regions of the country around 1986. Large differences in TFR may be noted among the various regions. For example, in the rural jungle and mountain areas the TFR is 7.3, whereas in Lima it is only 3.1. Although fertility has declined in all regions, the differentials have increased, as may be seen by a comparison with the data from Table 23.7 with earlier dates. Contraceptive prevalence ranges from only 10.6 per cent of women of fertile age in the northern mountains, to nearly 58 per cent in Lima in 1986. The correlation between fertility (TFR) and total contraceptive prevalence is high and negative (r = –0.80). When the correlation between TFR and prevalence of modern methods is examined, it is even more significant (r = –0.82). The same occurs if the same group of methods is considered, but only for women in consensual unions (r = –0.834). In contrast, the correlation between fertility and prevalence of traditional methods (rhythm, withdrawal, and folk methods) among women in consensual unions is low and altogether insignificant (r = –0.15). This leads to the conclusion that contraception, especially the use of modern contraceptive methods, is the intermediate variable which primarily explains regional variations in fertility. For this reason, attention should be drawn to the widespread use of traditional methods by women of various regions and different social classes, including Lima. Traditional methods (rhythm, withdrawal, and others) account for between 40 and 79 per cent of total

Table 23.8. ***Peru: fertility and contraceptive practice indicators by regions, 1986***

Region	TFR	Prevalence rate (all methods)		Prevalence rate (modern methods)		% women	
		All women	Currently in union	All women	Currently in union	still breast-feeding	still amenor-rhoeic
Peru	4.7	26.5	42.3	12.8	21.6	16.7	8.7
Metropolitan Lima	3.1	33.3	57.7	18.5	33.3	8.3	3.6
Coast	4.1	29.0	47.6	15.1	26.6	13.7	6.1
Coast–Urban	4.0	30.6	51.4	16.2	29.2	11.5	5.1
Coast–Rural	4.7	23.8	36.4	11.6	18.6	21.0	9.1
Coast–North	4.4	28.6	48.6	14.6	26.3	15.0	5.7
Coast–Centre	3.7	28.9	46.0	14.4	24.8	11.4	6.5
Coast–South	4.2	32.1	47.1	20.5	35.3	13.9	7.4
Sierra	6.5	19.0	28.6	5.8	9.5	25.4	14.0
Sierra–Urban	4.8	30.6	52.0	11.2	20.6	13.4	5.7
Sierra–Rural	7.3	12.3	17.2	2.6	4.1	32.7	18.9
Sierra–North	7.2	10.6	16.1	2.6	4.3	29.4	15.9
Sierra–Centre	6.5	23.4	33.7	8.0	14.1	27.8	16.3
Sierra–South	5.9	21.0	33.1	5.9	9.4	20.8	10.8
Selva	6.0	21.5	31.9	10.7	16.4	24.0	15.1
Selva–Urban	4.1	25.5	38.1	15.2	23.8	13.2	9.1
Selva–Rural	8.3	18.5	27.6	7.3	11.2	32.0	19.5
Selva–High	6.8	21.2	32.8	9.1	14.4	24.5	15.6
Selva–Low	5.2	21.8	30.9	12.2	18.2	23.6	14.7

Source: Special tabulations prepared by INANDEP using data from DHS-86, Basic and Experimental Surveys.

contraceptive prevalence in the various regions considered (see Table 23.9). Clearly, the lower the total prevalence, the greater the relative weight of traditional methods.

Abortion is clearly an important means of fertility control in Peru. While data are inadequate to measure the precise level of abortion, the available information shows that the level has increased from the late 1970s to the early 1980s. Indirect estimates of the level of abortion show that there were about 300 abortions for every 1000 births in 1981 (Singh and Wulf 1991).

These data suggest that Peruvian fertility still has ample room for decline, to the degree that not only total prevalence but especially the prevalence of modern methods can continue to increase. In other words, the decline in fertility would have been much greater if women's reproductive intentions had been achieved in response to the complex interaction of modernizing forces (in the cultural domain) with the economic crisis. This has not occurred in practice because of the high proportion of users of inefficient methods. The questions are, therefore, what are the barriers to greater use of modern contraceptives and, of course, to a sharper and less differentiated decline in fertility. The following section attempts to put forth several hypotheses and topics for further research which may contribute to answers to the above questions.

Table 23.9 *Peru: % distribution of women using contraceptive methods, 1986*

Region	Pill	IUD	Inject-able	Barrier methods	Condom	Steril-ization	Rhythm	Withdrawal and others	Prevalence rate
Peru	14.6	17.1	3.0	2.5	1.8	9.3	40.7	11.0	26.5
Metropolitan Lima	14.2	26.4	2.7	2.7	2.2	7.4	34.8	9.6	33.3
Coast	21.2	9.9	3.2	2.7	0.7	14.3	39.0	9.0	29.0
Coast–Urban	20.5	10.8	3.8	2.9	0.9	13.9	39.3	7.9	28.6
Coast–Rural	23.9	6.2	0.9	1.8	0.0	15.9	38.0	13.3	28.9
Coast–North	18.2	9.4	2.9	2.6	0.6	17.4	41.8	7.1	32.1
Coast–Centre	25.0	9.1	3.4	3.4	0.6	8.5	36.4	13.6	30.6
Coast–South	28.0	16.0	4.0	0.0	2.0	14.0	30.0	6.0	23.8
Sierra	6.4	10.2	2.6	2.4	2.6	6.0	55.8	14.0	19.0
Sierra–Urban	7.5	13.1	3.0	3.7	3.0	6.3	56.0	7.4	10.6
Sierra–Rural	4.9	5.9	2.2	0.5	2.2	5.4	55.7	23.2	23.4
Sierra–North	2.9	11.8	1.5	2.9	0.0	5.9	57.4	17.6	21.0
Sierra–Centre	9.8	7.6	6.0	2.2	1.1	7.6	53.8	11.9	30.6
Sierra–South	4.5	11.9	0.0	2.5	5.0	4.5	57.2	14.4	12.3
Selva	16.4	15.8	4.8	1.2	0.6	10.9	33.3	17.0	21.5
Selva–Urban	19.0	19.0	3.6	0.0	1.2	16.7	28.6	11.9	21.2
Selva–Rural	13.6	12.3	6.2	2.5	0.0	4.9	38.3	22.2	21.8
Selva–High	15.2	13.9	5.1	1.3	1.3	6.3	41.8	15.1	25.5
Selva–Low	17.4	17.4	4.7	1.2	0.0	15.1	25.6	18.6	18.6

Source: Special tabulations prepared by INANDEP using data from DHS-86, Basic and Experimental Surveys.

Contraception and Sexuality

The results of the three last national surveys of women of fertile age (ENAF-77–8 1977–8; ENNSA-84, and NDHS-86) as well as several surveys with more limited coverage (CNP-87; INANDEP-89) permit the following conclusions concerning reproductive intentions and the use of contraceptives:

- There is a generalized and growing desire among women in consensual unions to limit their fertility. According to the ENAF of 1977–8, more than 61 per cent of women of fertile age who were in consensual unions did not want any more children. According to the NDHS, this proportion had risen to 70 per cent in 1986. The most revealing point is that the desire to terminate reproduction is similar and even greater among women of the lower classes and in rural areas (76 per cent) than among women in Lima (73 per cent), according to the ENPA of 1981.
- Knowledge of modern contraceptive methods is apparently high and widespread. It was 81 per cent among women of fertile age in 1981 (ENPA) and 88 per cent in 1986 (NDHS). However, real knowledge, that is, knowledge sufficient to allow the woman to describe the correct use of the method, dropped to only half the apparent knowledge level in almost all the cases analysed in the 1989 INANDEP survey of the five largest cities not including Lima (Aramburú and Lí 1989). Furthermore, many of those who use a method use it incorrectly, particularly when using the pill (10–20 per cent) and the rhythm method (20–40 per cent).
- The principal barriers to use of modern contraceptive methods (based on non-users who do not want to become pregnant) are neither their accessibility (5 per cent) nor their cost (5 per cent), nor the husband's opposition (9 per cent) (NDHS-86). The main barriers are, fears of women of the damage that modern contraceptives may cause to their health (21 per cent) and lack of knowledge of a source or a method (31 per cent) (NDHS-86: tables 5–15, p. 73).
- In spite of the low usage of modern methods, there is growing acceptance of female sterilization among women living on the coast, both in urban and rural areas, especially on the northern coast and the urban areas of the jungle (Table 23.9). This is one of the methods that cause the least fears in women who are non-users of contraceptives.

To interpret these results adequately, it is necessary to investigate further the decision-making process of women of the lower classes regarding their sexuality and their reproduction. For example, the cultural factors related to woman's status, the immediate context which determines value judgements (family of origin and family of procreation) and the surrounding social context (community, reference group, and impact of the media) all have a decisive influence on their reproductive behaviour. Given the limitations on the length of the present work, only some of the most relevant findings of an in-depth study of sixty women in consensual unions from various generations and cultural contexts (Aramburú, *et al.* 1989), will be commented on here.

A characteristic feature of the reproductive life of older women from traditional contexts (rural coastal villages and poor neighbourhoods of the Andean cities) is their lack of control over key situations affecting their sexual lives. The woman's low status in the rural and Andean areas means that during the distinct phases of her life cycle it is her parents, boyfriend, and later her husband who decide all important aspects of her reproductive behaviour. Even if she is consulted, the decisions which directly affect her are almost always made by others. For example, her hopes for higher education or a job out of the home are frustrated by early pregnancy resulting from the wish to 'please her lover' or 'not to lose him'. The persistence of the identity of a woman with motherhood means that her children are born almost as soon as her conjugal life has begun, due to pressures not only from her husband, but also from both their families. To marry, become pregnant (almost always before formalizing the union) and assume the role of mother is the common pattern in these cultural contexts. Therefore, there is little use of contraception at the beginning of the union and little spacing between births. It is only when the woman has surpassed the desired number of children that she seeks to stop reproducing. For that purpose she frequently has to resort to abortion or to permanent methods such as sterilization. As shown in Table 23.5, the greatest relative decline in the ASFRs corresponds to women over 40 years of age.

Another central feature of lower-class culture is the temporal difference between knowledge of sexuality and sexual experience. Given the repressive context in which the adolescent is socialized, misinformation about her sexual and reproductive life is rampant. Because of this, experiences related to her biological development and sexuality occur, in the majority of cases, before the young woman is informed about their significance and consequences. This temporal difference between knowledge and direct experience includes menstruation. The majority of those interviewed, even the youngest ones from traditional backgrounds, consider menstruation an illness, the consequence of an internal wound, or a biological disorder, and therefore face it with fear and shame. This is also the case with the first sexual encounter. A large proportion of those who had pre-nuptial sexual relations (42 women of the 60 interviewed, particularly those from coastal areas, Lima and Pueblo Nuevo, which are more permissive in this regard) did not know, or knew only vaguely, the probable consequences of coitus. Additionally, in many cases the experience was unpleasant since it was accompanied by violence and abuse. In general, woman's sexual pleasure is devalued and only a few declared that they have a satisfying sex life, even within a conjugal union.

The interaction of male domination and female submission in key life decisions, sexual misinformation, and the devaluation of her sexuality make her incapable of planning her reproductive life ahead of time. For this reason, contraception is not considered until a woman has given birth to more children than she desires.

In addition, fears of supposed risks to health from modern contraceptives are partly the consequence of misinformation surrounding anything having to do with sexuality. These fears also arise from the central economic role which women play in the lower classes, the cost of regaining one's health in a context of high inflation, as well as the tremendous deterioration of buying power of the poorest groups. In this context, in order to ensure more egalitarian, better informed, and more effective access to contraception, it will be necessary to achieve profound changes in values and patterns that shape the sexuality of women in the lower classes.

Conclusions

- Fertility in Peru declined at various rates among socio-cultural groups beginning in the late 1960s. Between this time and 1986, fertility declined by 36 per cent dropping from a TFR of 6.8 children per woman in 1960–5 to a TFR of 4.5 in 1986.
- The process of fertility transition began in the upper and middle classes of the national capital of Lima during the 1950s, while in the lower-class urban sectors of the three natural regions it began during the 1960s; rural fertility, on the other hand, increased until the early 1970s and only then began to decline.
- Fertility decline, especially in the lower classes, responded first to the process of cultural modernization which in little more than two decades profoundly transformed Peru from a rural, Andean, illiterate, and agrarian society to an urban, coastal, literate, and commercial one. During the second phase (1972 onward), the fertility decline was extended to the rural areas and intensified as a result of families' responses to the deep economic crisis which has been afflicting Peru since 1975.
- No significant changes have occurred in nuptiality patterns and other results show that breast-feeding, while still an important determinant of fertility levels in Peru, probably has not increased in importance as the decline in fertility took place (chapter 6). It appears that the increase in contraception is the intermediate variable which has the greatest power to explain the drop in fertility. Total prevalence of contraceptives rose from 31 per cent in 1977–8 to 46 per cent in 1986, and prevalence of modern method use among women in consensual unions doubled from 11 to 23 per cent for the same time period. Abortion is also most likely to be an important contributor to fertility decline, but exact measures of its contribution are unavailable.
- Regional differences in fertility levels are strongly associated with contraceptive prevalence, especially prevalence of modern methods. Given the major presence of traditional methods and their low effectiveness, fertility would have declined more rapidly and more equally if there had been a greater acceptance of modern contraceptives.
- The low acceptance of contraceptive methods is due to cultural factors,

especially to the fear of their supposed side effects and to the lack of true knowledge. The persistence of cultural barriers to the use of these methods stems from the socio-cultural patterns of female sexuality in the lower classes. These patterns include misinformation about and devaluation of woman's sexuality, woman's submission to her father and spouse, the impossibility of woman's control of her own reproductive life, and the inability to foresee the consequences of having a large family.

Appendix 23.1: Sources of Data

Population Censuses

During this century Peru has held four population censuses, in 1940, 1961, 1972, and 1981. For the female population aged 12 years and over, the first two censuses gathered only past information about fertility: children ever born. To estimate the TFR, this information had to be combined with the births recorded in the vital register (an average of those births occurring in 1939, 1940, and 1941 for 1940, and in 1960, 1961, and 1962 for 1961). The two latter censuses compiled, in addition to the total number of children born, those born in the preceding year, making it possible to estimate the TFR indirectly (utilizing Brass's P/F method) on the basis of the census data only. In spite of their obvious limitations, the censuses are the fundamental basis for knowledge of fertility's evolution in Peru during the period 1940–60, for which no other sources are available. The combination of data from diverse sources completes the picture for more recent dates, and also allows the projection of the evolution's future behaviour.

Birth Registration

The Peruvian register of births is affected by, among others, two limitations: (1) a considerable, but variable, percentage of omission, and (2) a delay in the publication of the reports. These defects and others, like the quality of data, determine that registered births, classified by the age of the mother, cannot be used to calculate direct estimates of fertility.

Sample Surveys

Sample surveys are an indispensable complement to the demographic information gathered in Peruvian censuses and registers. These have been carried out quite frequently since the end of the 1960s and have made it possible to clear up doubts, fill gaps and explain certain aspects of the demographic patterns at the national and regional level. Between 1966 and 1968, the Rural Urban Fertility Survey (PEAL-PECFAL) took place, with a sample of 4,676 women of fertile age, for which (as far as fertility data are concerned) a full pregnancy history was recorded. Between 1974 and 1976, the National Demographic Survey (NDS) was held; using a prospective format or repeated visits, in which a representative sample of 48,000 persons of whom 10,672 were women of fertile age were surveyed. During the last round of visits (1976), a Retrospective Survey (RETRO) was applied, gathering information on live-born children and children born in the preceding year from all the women of fertile age registered in the NDS. Between 1977 and 1978, the National Fertility Survey (NFS) was held, with a sample of 5,640 ever-in-union women aged 15 to 49 years whose pregnancy history was recorded. The National Survey of Contraceptive

Table 23.A1 *Peru: sources of demographic data*

Source	Year	Coverage	Executing Agency	Components of Sample (women aged 15–49)	Geographic Disaggregation Possible	Information Used to Calculate TFR
Census	1940	National	Min. of Finance-Nat. Statistical Office (NSO)	1.5 million	District	Women of Fertile Age (WFA)
Birth Register	1939–41	National	Min. of Finance-NSO		District	Births by Age of Mother
Census	1961	National	Nat. Planning Institute (NPI)-NSO	2.2 million	District	Women of Fertile Age (WFA)
Birth Register	1960–62	National	NPI-NSO		District	Births by Age of Mother
PEAL-PECFAL	1969–70	National	Min. of Labour	4,676	PSU	Pregnancy History
Census	1972	National	National Bureau of Statistics & Censuses (NBSC)	2.2 million	District	Women of Fertile Age, Live-born Children, Children Born Last Year
NDS	1974–76	National	National Bureau of Statistics & Censuses (NBSC)	10,672	PSU	Women of Fertile Age, Live-born Children, Children Born Last Year

Retro-NDS	1976	National	National Bureau of Statistics & Censuses (NBSC)	10,672	PSU	Women of Fertile Age, Live-born Children, Children Born Last Year
NFS	1977–78	National	National Statistical Institute (NSI)	5,640	PSU	Pregnancy History
Census	1981	National	National Statistical Institute (NSI)	3.2 million	District	Women of Fertile Age, Live-born Children, Children Born Last Year
NSCP	1981	National	National Statistical Institute (NSI) & Min. of Health	6,437	PSU	Women of Fertile Age, Live-born Children, Children Born Last Year
NNHS	1984	National	NSI–Min. of Health–Westinghouse Health Systems	30,000 women aged 12–49	PSU	Women of Fertile Age, Live-born Children, Children Born Last Year
NDFHS (DHS)	1986	National	NSI–Nat. Pop. Council (NPC)–Westinghouse Health Systems	4,999	PSU	Pregnancy History

PSU: Primary Sampling Unit

Prevalence (NSCP) was held in 1981, with a sample of 6,437 women of fertile age. In 1984, the National Nutrition and Health Survey (NNHS) was carried out; this was not precisely a demographic survey, but had a section which collected information on children ever born and births during the preceding year, from a sample of 30,000 women of fertile age. Finally, in 1986, the Demographic and Family Health Survey (NDFHS) was held, compiling pregnancy histories from a sample of 4,999 women aged 15 to 49 years (Table 23.1).

The above-mentioned sources have made it possible to calculate indirect estimates of fertility both at the national level and for administrative divisions. All of them, in spite of their limitations and the fact that they are not at all congruent, have made it possible to establish a reasonably clear picture of the evolution and the structure of fertility from 1940 onward.

References

Aramburú, C. E. (1990), 'Is Population Policy Necessary? The Case of Latin America and the Andean Countries', Paper presented at the Symposium on the Politics of Induced Fertility Change, Bellagio, Italy, Feb. 1990.

—— Arias, R., and Fortunic, P. (1989), *De la Cintura para Arriba: Aspectos de la Sexualidad en Tres Contextos Culturales* (Lima: INANDEP).

—— Ferrando, D., Lésevic, D., and Mostajo, D. (1987), 'Estudio Diferenciado de la Fecundidad a Nivel Distrital' (Unpublished).

Aramburú, C. E., and Lí, D. (1989), 'La Anticoncepción en Cinco Ciudades del Perú: Mito y Realidad', in *Lugar de Encuentro*, 3/1–2 (Jan.–Apr.).

Arocena, V., and Aramburú, C. E. (1990), 'Las Provincias más Pobres del Perú', in 'Análisis Comparativo' (UNFPA-INANDEP) (unpublished).

Bongaarts, J. (1984), *Implications of Future Fertility Trends for Contraceptive Practice* (New York: Population Council).

CEPD (Centro de Estudios de Población y Desarrollo) (1972), *Informe Demográfico del Perú 1970* (Lima: CEPD).

Ferrando, D. (1990), 'La Población del Perú en el Período 1940–2000', in *La Población del Perú: Balance y Perspectivas* (Lima: Varillas y Mostajo).

—— (1986), 'Tendencias Regionales de la Fecundidad: 1969–1977' (Unpublished).

—— Singh, S., and Wulf, D. (1989), *Adolescentes de Hoy, Padres del Mañana: Perú* (Bogotá: Alan Guttmacher Institute).

INE (Instituto Nacional de Estadística) and CELADE (1983), 'Estimaciones y proyecciones de población. Total del país: 1950–2025. Urbana y rural: 1970–1995', *Boletín de Análisis Demográfico*, 25.

—— (1990), *Perú: Proyecciones revisadas de población 1980–2025* (Lima: INE).

INP (1986), *Encuesta de Fecundidad Comparativa* (Lima: INP).

Lésevic, B. (1984), *Hipótesis y evidencias sobre el proceso de recuperación demográfica de la población peruana durante el siglo XIX* (Lima: INANDEP).

—— and Ortiz, J. (1987), *Dos Estudios de Fecundidad* (Lima: CISEPA).

Singh, S., and Wulf, D. (1991), 'Cálculo de los Niveles de Aborto en el Brasil, Colombia, y el Perú, a Base de Datos Hospitalarios y de Encuestas de Fecundidad', *International Family Planning Perspectives* (Special Issue 1991), 14–19.

Index